SUNDAY MISSAL

A NEW EDITION

Sunday Masses for the Entire Three-year Cycle
Complete in One Volume
together with extracts from
the Sacramental Rites
and from The Divine Office

Introductions by Harold Winstone
Illustrations by Mark and Anne Primavesi

Texts approved for use in
England and Wales, Ireland, Scotland

Collins

Collins, a division of HarperCollins*Publishers*
77–85 Fulham Palace Road, London W6 8JB

First published in 1984
This edition 2005

ISBN
Standard Blue 0 00 720914 2
Standard Red 0 00 720911 8

Soft touch White 0 00 720912 6
Two tone Green/Tan 0 00 720913 4

© copyright compilation and editorial matter 1975, 1976, 1977, 1982 and 1984 HarperCollins*Publishers*

Concordat cum originali: John P. Dewis
Nihil obstat: Anton Cowan, *censor*
Imprimatur: Ralph Brown VG
    Westminster 20 March 1984

Acknowledgements
Excerpts from the English translation of the *Rite of Marriage* © 1969, International Committee on English in the Liturgy, Inc. (ICEL); the English translation of the *Rite of Holy Week* © 1970, excerpts from the English translation of *The Roman Missal* © 1973, ICEL; excerpts from the English translation of the *Rite of Confirmation*, Second Edition © 1975, ICEL; excerpts from the English translation of *Pastoral Care for the Sick: Rites of Anointing and Viaticum* © 1982, ICEL; excerpts from the English translation of *Christian Initiation of Adults* © 1982, ICEL. All rights reserved.

Extracts from scripture (excepting Psalm texts) from the *Jerusalem Bible* version of scripture, © 1966, 1967 and 1968, Darton, Longman and Todd and Doubleday & Company Inc.

Psalm texts from *The Grail Psalms* © 1963 The Grail (England), published by Collins.

The hymn 'Sing my tongue, the glorious battle', verses 1–4, translated by Percy Dearmer (1867–1936), is from the *English Hymnal* by permission of Oxford University Press.

The notes on Preparation for Baptism during Lent, and the editing of the Scrutinies and the Sacraments Section, is taken from *Glenstal Bible Missal*. A further treatment of these rites will be found in that missal.

Typographical design by Colin Reed
Data capture and manipulation by
Morton Word Processing Ltd, Scarborough, England
Printed and bound in China by Amity – FT 3555

CONTENTS

FEASTS OF THE LORD AND SOLEMNITIES

FROM THE DIVINE OFFICE

PRAYERS

PREFACE

Those who wish to prepare for Sunday Mass and to take an active part in its celebration need a Missal.

The Sunday Missal has proved extremely popular for this purpose since its publication in 1975, but with the revision of the Lectionary in 1980, a few changes have been made necessary.

This new edition has been revised to take into account these changes. It also includes an extended section of the Sacraments and new illustrations.

I am very happy to recommend this new edition.

✢ Basil J. Hume
Archbishop of Westminster

INTRODUCTION

Christ promised: 'Where two or three are gathered in my name, there am I in their midst.' This is particularly true when the people of God gather to celebrate the eucharist. Christ's Spirit is then present and active in the community, and is the source of their prayer and praise and the proclamation of God's wonderful works. Christ speaks to his people in his word and gives himself under the eucharistic signs of bread and wine to be the life and food of the community. When the priest greets the people with the words 'The Lord be with you', he is stating a fact – the Lord is with his people as they gather to celebrate the eucharist.

The Mass is a sacrifice of praise and thanksgiving. We obey the command of Christ, given to his apostles at the Last Supper, to do this in his memory. In the Mass, Christ offers himself to the Father as the sacrificial lamb of God, who takes away the sins of the world. And with himself, Christ offers us in his sacrifice, who by the Holy Spirit are made into the one body of Christ, a living sacrifice of praise.

The Mass is an act of worship, in which all present acknowledge and praise God. During the liturgy of the word, when the scriptures are read to the people it is God himself who is speaking. That is why the renewed liturgy gives such a principal place to the readings – they are an essential element in the act of worship that is the Mass. When we listen to the Gospel, we meet Christ himself.

The worshipping community is the people of God, won by Christ with his blood, called together by the Lord, and nourished by his word. This people is called to offer God the prayers of the entire human family; it is brought together and strengthened in unity by sharing in the body and blood of Christ. The more the people enter into the mystery of the eucharist by conscious, active and fruitful participation, the more they grow in holiness.

As we listen to the word of God, join in the prayers and song, offer the sacrifice and share the Lord's table together, so we become one body, which is Christ the Lord.

Table I

ORDER FOR GOSPEL READING
FOR SUNDAYS IN ORDINARY TIME

In order to do justice to the intention of the Lectionary, the five great 'sermons' in Matthew's Gospel will of necessity be the focal points of preaching and instruction. The narrative sections, which are placed in between the sermons, are composed in such a way that there is a unity and coherence in the whole work.

Unit I	**The figure of Jesus the Messiah**	Sundays 1-2
SUNDAY 1	The Baptism of Jesus	Mt 3:13-17
SUNDAY 2	The witness of John the Baptist	Jn 1:29-34
Unit II	**Christ's design for life in God's Kingdom**	Sundays 3-9
	Narrative:	
SUNDAY 3	The call of the first disciples	Mt 4:12-23
	Discourse:	
SUNDAY 4	The Sermon on the Mount (1)	Mt 5:1-12
SUNDAY 5	The Sermon on the Mount (2)	Mt 5:13-16
SUNDAY 6	The Sermon on the Mount (3)	Mt 5:17-37
SUNDAY 7	The Sermon on the Mount (4)	Mt 5:38-48
SUNDAY 8	The Sermon on the Mount (5)	Mt 6:24-34
SUNDAY 9	The Sermon on the Mount (6)	Mt 7:21-27
Unit III	**The spread of God's Kingdom**	Sundays 10-13
	Narrative:	
SUNDAY 10	The call of Levi	Mt 9:9-13
	Discourse:	
SUNDAY 11	The mission sermon (1)	Mt 9:36 10:8
SUNDAY 12	The mission sermon (2)	Mt 10:26-33
SUNDAY 13	The mission sermon (3)	Mt 10:37-42
Unit IV	**The mystery of God's Kingdom**	Sundays 14-17
	Narrative:	
SUNDAY 14	The revelation to the simple	Mt 11:25-30
	Discourse:	
SUNDAY 15	The parable sermon (1)	Mt 13:1-23
SUNDAY 16	The parable sermon (2)	Mt 13:24-43
SUNDAY 17	The parable sermon (3)	Mt 13:44-52

YEAR A: YEAR OF MATTHEW

Discourse and narrative stand side by side, so that the narrative chapters prepare the way for what follows in the discourses. Recognising the way in which the Lectionary has reflected the structure of Matthew's Gospel, will enable preachers and readers to see the context of the readings from one week to the next.

Unit V	**God's kingdom on earth The Church of Christ**	Sundays 18-24
	Narrative:	
SUNDAY 18	The feeding of five thousand	Mt 14:31-21
SUNDAY 19	Jesus walks on the waters	Mt 14:22-33
SUNDAY 20	The Canaanite woman	Mt 15:21-28
SUNDAY 21	Peter's confession: the primacy conferred	Mt 16:13-20
SUNDAY 22	The passion prophesied: discipleship	Mt 16:21-27
	Discourse:	
SUNDAY 23	The community sermon (1)	Mt 18:15-20
SUNDAY 24	The community sermon (2)	Mt 18:21-35
Unit VI	**Authority and invitation the ministry ends**	Sundays 25-33
	Narrative:	
SUNDAY 25	The parable of the labourers	Mt 20:1-16
SUNDAY 26	The parable of the two sons	Mt 21:28-32
SUNDAY 27	The parable of the wicked vinedressers	Mt 21:33-43
SUNDAY 28	The parable of the marriage feast	Mt 22:1-14
SUNDAY 29	Paying tribute to Caesar	Mt 22:15-21
SUNDAY 30	The greatest commandment	Mt 22:34-40
SUNDAY 31	Hypocrisy and ambition	Mt 23:1-12
	Discourse:	
SUNDAY 32	The final sermon (1)	Mt 25:1-13
SUNDAY 33	The final sermon (2)	Mt 25:14-30
Unit VII	**God's Kingdom fulfilled**	Sunday 34
SUNDAY 34	Christ the King	Mt 25:31-46

Table II
ORDER FOR GOSPEL READING
FOR SUNDAYS IN ORDINARY TIME

Mark's main interest is the person of Jesus himself. He follows Jesus through his public ministry in Galilee, outside Galilee and finally in Jerusalem itself immediately before the passion. The crisis is reached when the fundamental question is posed to the disciples: 'Who do you say I am?' Peter's confession of faith is, therefore, at the heart of Mark's Gospel. In the year of Mark the

Unit I	**The figure of Jesus the Messiah**	Sundays 1-2
SUNDAY 1	The baptism of Jesus	Mk 1:6b-11
SUNDAY 2	The call of Andrew and his friend	Jn 1:35-42
Unit II	**The Mystery progressively revealed**	Sundays 3-23
Stage I	*Jesus with the Jewish crowds*	*Sundays 3-9*
SUNDAY 3	The call of the first apostles	Mk 1:14-20
SUNDAY 4	A day in Capernaum (1)	Mk 1:21-28
SUNDAY 5	A day in Capernaum (1)	Mk 1:29-39
SUNDAY 6	The cure of a leper	Mk 1:40-45
SUNDAY 7	The cure of a paralytic	Mk 2:1-12
SUNDAY 8	The question of fasting	Mk 2:18-22
SUNDAY 9	Violation of the Sabbath	Mk 2:23–3:6
Stage II	*Jesus with his disciples*	*Sundays 10-14*
SUNDAY 10	Serious criticism of Jesus	Mk 3:20-35
SUNDAY 11	The parables of the Kingdom	Mk 4:26-34
SUNDAY 12	The calming of the storm	Mk 4:35-41
SUNDAY 13	Jairus' daughter; the woman in the crowd	Mk 5:21-43
SUNDAY 14	Jesus rejected at Nazareth	Mk 6:1-6
Stage III	*Jesus manifests himself*	*Sundays 15-23*
SUNDAY 15	The mission of the twelve	Mk 6:7-13
SUNDAY 16	Compassion for the crowds	Mk 6:30-34
SUNDAY 17	The feeding of five thousand	Jn 6:1-15
SUNDAY 18	The bread of life (1)	Jn 6:24-35
SUNDAY 19	The bread of life (2)	Jn 6:41-52
SUNDAY 20	The eucharist	Jn 6:51-58
SUNDAY 21	*Incredulity and faith*	Jn 6:61-70
SUNDAY 22	Jewish customs	Mk 7:1-8. 14-15. 21
SUNDAY 23	The cure of a deaf-mute	Mk 7:31-37

YEAR B: YEAR OF MARK

Lectionary observes faithfully the structure and message of the Gospel itself. One important peculiarity is that the Lectionary includes a major insert from the Gospel of John (Sundays 17-21: John 6 – the sermon on the 'Bread of Life'). This fits well into this part of Mark's Gospel, which is concerned with Jesus' revelation of himself, and is known as 'the Bread section'.

Unit III	**The Mystery of the Son of Man**	Sundays 24-34
Stage I	*The 'Way' of the Son of Man*	*Sundays 24-30*
SUNDAY 24	Peter's confession of faith	Mk 8:27-35
SUNDAY 25	Passion and resurrection prophesied	Mk 9:29-36
SUNDAY 26	Instructions for disciples	Mk 9:37-42. 44. 46-47
SUNDAY 27	Marriage and divorce	Mk 10:2-16
SUNDAY 28	The problem of wealth	Mk 10:17-30
SUNDAY 29	The sons of Zebedee	Mk 10:35-46
SUNDAY 30	The cure of Bartimaeus	Mk 10:46-52
Stage II	*Final revelation in Jerusalem*	*Sundays 31-33*
SUNDAY 31	The first commandment	Mk 12:28b-34
SUNDAY 32	The widow's mite	Mk 12:38-44
SUNDAY 33	The last things	Mk 13:24-32
Stage III	*The fulfilment of the mystery*	*Sunday 34*
SUNDAY 34	The solemnity of Christ the King	Jn 18:33b-37

Table III
ORDER FOR GOSPEL READING
FOR SUNDAYS IN ORDINARY TIME

Luke's Gospel represents Jesus' journey from Galilee to Jerusalem – a journey which is completed in the Acts of the Apostles by the journey of the Church from Jerusalem 'to the ends of the earth'. The Lectionary in the year of Luke represents faithfully his 'Travel Narrative' (chapters 9-19) – Jesus' journey to death, to resurrection and his return to the Father (see

Unit I	**The figure of Jesus the Messiah**	Sundays 1-2
SUNDAY 1	The baptism of Jesus	Lk 3:15-16. 21-22
SUNDAY 2	The marriage feast at Cana	Jn 2:1-12
Unit II	**Luke's programme for Jesus' ministry**	Sundays 3-4
SUNDAY 3	Prologue. The visit to Nazareth (1)	Lk 1:1-4; 4:14-21
SUNDAY 4	The visit to Nazareth (2)	Lk 4:21-30
Unit III	**The Galilean Ministry**	Sundays 5-12
SUNDAY 5	*The call of the first apostles	Lk 5:1-11
SUNDAY 6	The sermon on the plain (1)	Lk 6:17. 20-26
SUNDAY 7	The sermon on the plain (2)	Lk 6:27-38
SUNDAY 8	The sermon on the plain (3)	Lk 6:39-45
SUNDAY 9	The cure of the centurion's servant	Lk 7:1-10
SUNDAY 10	*The Widow of Naim	Lk 7:11-17
SUNDAY 11	*Jesus' feet anointed: the sinful woman	Lk 7:36-8:3
SUNDAY 12	Peter's confession of faith	Lk 9:18-24
Unit IV	**The first part of the 'Travel Narrative':**	Sundays 13-23
	The qualities Jesus demands of those who	
	follow him	
SUNDAY 13	*The journey to Jerusalem begins	Lk 9:51-62
SUNDAY 14	*The mission of the seventy-two	Lk 10:1-12. 17-20
SUNDAY 15	*The Good Samaritan	Lk 10:25-37
SUNDAY 16	*Martha and Mary	Lk 10:38-42
SUNDAY 17	*The importunate friend	Lk 11:1-13
SUNDAY 18	*The parable of the rich fool	Lk 12:13-21
SUNDAY 19	The need for vigilance	Lk 12:32-48
SUNDAY 20	'Not peace but division'	Lk 12:49-53
SUNDAY 21	Few will be saved	Lk 13:22-30
SUNDAY 22	True humility	Lk 14:1. 7-14
SUNDAY 23	The cost of discipleship	Lk 14:25-33

YEAR C: YEAR OF LUKE

Sundays 13-31). Luke's vision of the journey is not geographical or chronological. Rather it is seen as a journey for the whole Church and for the individual christian, a journey towards suffering and glory. Each Gospel passage should mean a great deal more to preacher and reader when it is seen in the context of the whole programme of readings for Year C.

Unit V	**The 'Gospel within the Gospel':**	Sunday 24
	the message of pardon and reconciliation	
	– the parables of God's mercy	
SUNDAY 24	*The lost coin, the lost sheep, and the	
	prodigal son	Lk 15:1-32
Unit VI	**The second part of the 'Travel Narrative':**	Sundays 25-31
	the obstacles facing those who follow Jesus	
SUNDAY 25	*The unjust steward	Lk 16:1-13
SUNDAY 26	*The rich man and Lazarus	Lk 16:19-31
SUNDAY 27	*A lesson on faith and dedication	Lk 17:5-10
SUNDAY 28	*The ten lepers	Lk 17:11-19
SUNDAY 29	*The unjust judge	Lk 18:1-8
SUNDAY 30	*The Pharisee and the tax collector	Lk 18:9-14
SUNDAY 31	*Zacchaeus	Lk 19:1-10
Unit VII	**The ministry in Jerusalem**	Sundays 32-33
SUNDAY 32	The resurrection debated	Lk 20:27-38
SUNDAY 33	The signs announcing the end	Lk 21:5-19
Unit VIII	**Christ the King: reconciliation**	Sunday 34
SUNDAY 34	*The repentant thief	Lk 23:35-43

Note: Passages marked with an asterisk are found only in the Gospel of Luke.

Table IV

ARRANGEMENT OF THE SECOND READING
FOR THE SUNDAYS IN ORDINARY TIME

Sunday	Year A	Year B	Year C
2	1 Corinthians 1-4	1 Corinthians 6-11	1 Corinthians 12-15
3	"	"	"
4	"	"	"
5	"	"	"
6	"	"	"
7	"	2 Corinthians	"
8	"	"	"
9	Romans	"	Galatians
10	"	"	"
11	"	"	"
12	"	"	"
13	"	"	"
14	"	"	"
15	"	Ephesians	Colossians
16	"	"	"
17	"	"	"
18	"	"	"
19	"	"	Hebrews 11-12
20	"	"	"
21	"	"	"
22	"	James	"
23	"	"	Philemon
24	"	"	1 Timothy
25	Philippians	"	"
26	"	"	"
27	"	Hebrews 2-10	2 Timothy
28	"	"	"
29	1 Thessalonians	"	"
30	"	"	"
31	"	"	2 Thessalonians
32	"	"	"
33	"	"	"

PRINCIPAL CELEBRATIONS OF THE LITURGICAL YEAR

Table V

Year	Sunday Cycle	Weekday Cycle	Ash Wednesday	Easter	Ascension	Pentecost	Corpus Christi	Ordinary Weeks of the Year				First Sunday of Advent	Year
								Before Lent		After Easter			
								Until	Week	From	Week		
2005	A	I	9 Feb	27 Mar	5 May	15 May	26 May	8 Feb	5	16 May	7	27 Nov	2005
2006	B	II	1 Mar	16 Apr	25 May	4 June	15 June	28 Feb	8	5 June	10	3 Dec	2006
2007	C	I	21 Feb	8 Apr	17 May	27 May	7 June	20 Feb	7	28 May	8	2 Dec	2007
2008	A	II	6 Feb	23 Mar	1 May	11 May	22 May	5 Feb	4	12 May	7	30 Nov	2008
2009	B	I	25 Feb	12 Apr	21 May	31 May	11 June	24 Feb	7	1 June	9	29 Nov	2009
2010	C	II	17 Feb	4 Apr	13 May	23 May	3 June	16 Feb	6	24 May	8	28 Nov	2010
2011	A	I	9 Mar	24 Apr	2 June	12 June	23 June	8 Mar	9	13 June	11	27 Nov	2011
2012	B	II	22 Feb	8 Apr	17 May	27 May	7 June	21 Feb	7	28 May	8	2 Dec	2012
2013	C	I	13 Feb	31 Mar	9 May	19 May	30 May	12 Feb	5	20 May	7	1 Dec	2013
2014	A	II	5 Mar	20 Apr	29 May	8 June	19 June	4 Mar	8	9 June	10	30 Nov	2014
2015	B	I	18 Feb	5 Apr	14 May	24 May	4 June	17 Feb	6	25 May	8	29 Nov	2015
2016	C	II	10 Feb	27 Mar	5 May	15 May	26 May	9 Feb	5	16 May	7	27 Nov	2016
2017	A	I	1 Mar	16 Apr	25 May	4 June	15 June	28 Feb	8	5 June	9	3 Dec	2017
2018	B	II	14 Feb	1 Apr	10 May	20 May	31 May	13 Feb	5	21 May	7	2 Dec	2018
2019	C	I	6 Mar	21 Apr	30 May	9 June	20 June	5 Mar	8	10 June	10	1 Dec	2019
2020	A	II	26 Feb	12 Apr	21 May	31 May	11 June	25 Feb	7	1 June	9	29 Nov	2020
2021	B	I	17 Feb	4 Apr	13 May	23 May	3 June	16 Feb	6	24 May	8	28 Nov	2021
2022	C	II	2 Mar	17 Apr	26 May	5 June	16 June	1 Mar	8	6 June	10	27 Nov	2022
2023	A	I	22 Feb	9 Apr	18 May	28 May	8 June	21 Feb	7	29 May	8	3 Dec	2023
2024	B	II	14 Feb	31 Mar	9 May	19 May	30 May	13 Feb	6	20 May	7	1 Dec	2024
2025	C	I	5 Mar	20 Apr	29 May	8 June	19 June	4 Mar	8	9 June	10	30 Nov	2025
2026	A	II	18 Feb	5 Apr	14 May	24 May	4 June	17 Feb	6	25 May	8	29 Nov	2026
2027	B	I	10 Feb	28 Mar	6 May	16 May	27 May	9 Feb	5	17 May	7	28 Nov	2027
2028	C	II	1 Mar	16 Apr	25 May	4 June	15 June	29 Feb	8	5 June	9	3 Dec	2028
2029	A	I	14 Feb	1 Apr	10 May	20 May	31 May	13 Feb	6	21 May	7	2 Dec	2029
2030	B	II	6 Mar	21 Apr	30 May	9 June	20 June	5 Mar	8	10 June	10	1 Dec	2030
2031	C	I	26 Feb	13 Apr	22 May	1 June	12 June	25 Feb	7	2 June	9	30 Nov	2031
2032	A	II	11 Feb	28 Mar	6 May	16 May	27 May	10 Feb	5	17 May	7	28 Nov	2032
2033	B	I	2 Mar	17 Apr	26 May	5 June	16 June	1 Mar	8	6 June	10	27 Nov	2033
2034	C	II	22 Feb	9 Apr	18 May	28 May	8 June	21 Feb	7	29 May	8	3 Dec	2034
2035	A	I	7 Feb	25 Mar	3 May	13 May	24 May	6 Feb	4	14 May	6	2 Dec	2035
2036	B	II	27 Feb	13 Apr	22 May	1 June	12 June	26 Feb	7	2 June	9	30 Nov	2036
2037	C	I	18 Feb	5 Apr	14 May	24 May	4 June	17 Feb	6	25 May	8	29 Nov	2037
2038	A	II	10 Mar	25 Apr	3 June	13 June	24 June	9 Mar	9	14 June	11	28 Nov	2038
2039	B	I	23 Feb	10 Apr	19 May	29 May	9 June	22 Feb	7	30 May	8	27 Nov	2039
2040	C	II	15 Feb	1 Apr	10 May	20 May	31 May	14 Feb	6	21 May	7	2 Dec	2040

PRAYERS
PREPARATION FOR MASS

I am the living bread which has come down from heaven.
Anyone who eats this bread will live forever;
and that bread that I shall give
is my flesh, for the life of the world.   *John 6:51*

This is what I received from the Lord and passed on to you: that
on the same night he was betrayed, the Lord Jesus took some
bread, and thanked God for it and broke it, and he said, 'This is
my body, which is for you; do this as a memorial of me.' In the
same way he took the cup after supper, and said, 'This cup is the
new covenant in my blood. Whenever you drink it, do this as a
memorial of me.' Until the Lord comes, therefore, every time you
eat this bread and drink this cup you are proclaiming his death.
Everyone is to recollect himself before eating this bread and
drinking this cup.   *1 Corinthians 11:23–26. 28*

The cup that we bless is a communion with the blood of Christ,
and the bread that we break is a communion with the body of
Christ.   *1 Corinthians 10:16*

Worship God in a way that is worthy of thinking beings, by
offering your living bodies as a holy sacrifice, truly pleasing to
God.   *Romans 12:1*

Examination of Conscience
If anyone should sin, we have our Advocate with the Father,
Jesus Christ, who is Just; he is the sacrifice that takes our sins
away.   *1 John 2:1*

You shall love the Lord your God with your whole heart.
Do I really love God, my heavenly Father, with my whole heart,
and try to obey his commandments?
    Do I hold the teaching of the Church?
    Do I profess my faith in God and in the Church publicly when
necessary, and act as a Christian in public and in private?
    Do I put my trust in money, wordly goods, wordly influence?
Have I always said my morning and evening prayers?
    Do I keep Sundays and the feasts of the Church? Have I
obeyed the precept of yearly confession and Easter communion?

You shall love your neighbour as yourself.
Do I truly love other people, or do I use them for selfish ends?
Have I given scandal in word or action?

Consider my family life. Remember that children owe their parents love, obedience and respect, and should help them in spiritual or material need.
Parents should help their children by giving good example, exercising proper parental authority and giving them a Christian education.
Married people should love each other in thought, word and deed.
Single people should respect the integrity of others and of themselves, and live chastely.

Have I been a source of peace and happiness to those with whom I live or work?
Have I shared enough of what I have with those who need it – my money, my time, my concern?
Have I despised, or given offence to, the poor, the sick, the aged, foreigners, people of different race or habits from myself?

Am I just, conscientious, honest, in my work?
Do I pay a just wage to those who work for me? Have I squandered my employer's time or defrauded him in any way?
Do I tell the truth?
Have I violated the rights of other people to life, physical integrity, reputation, honour or property?
Have I stolen what is not mine? If so, have I made restitution?
If anyone has offended me or done me harm, have I been ready to make peace and to forgive, for the love of Christ?

Be perfect as your heavenly Father is perfect.
Do I really believe in eternal life, and live as if I believed in it?
Do I try to grow in the spirit, by reading and meditating the word of God, by sharing the life of Christ through the sacraments, by denying myself?
Do I make an effort to overcome my faults and sinful habits?
Do I use my time and talents as a good servant of the Lord God?
Do I bear the sorrows and difficulties of life with patience and faith?
Do I always try to live according to the law of the Holy Spirit, in the true freedom of the children of God, or am I in fact the slave of any passion?

Prayer of St Ambrose

Lord Jesus Christ,
I approach your banquet table
in fear and trembling,
for I am a sinner,
and dare not rely on my own worth,
but only on your goodness and mercy.
I am defiled by many sins in body and soul,
and by my unguarded thoughts and words.

Gracious God of majesty and awe,
I seek your protection,
I look for your healing.
Poor troubled sinner that I am,
I appeal to you, the fountain of all mercy.
I cannot bear your judgement,
but I trust in your salvation.
Lord, I show my wounds to you
and uncover my shame before you.
I know my sins are many and great,
and they fill me with fear,
but I hope in your mercies,
for they cannot be numbered.

Lord Jesus Christ, eternal king, divine and human,
crucified for humanity,
look upon me with mercy and hear my prayer,
for I trust in you.
Have mercy on me,
full of sorrow and sin,
for the depth of your compassion never ends.
Praise to you, saving sacrifice,
offered on the wood of the cross for me and for all.
Praise to the noble and precious blood,
flowing from the wounds of my crucified Lord Jesus Christ
and washing away the sins of the whole world.

Remember, Lord, your creature,
whom you have redeemed with your blood.
I repent my sins,
and I long to put right what I have done.

Merciful Father, take away all my offences and sins;
purify me in body and soul,
and make me worthy to taste the holy of holies.

May your body and blood,
which I intend to receive, although I am unworthy,
be for me the remission of my sins,
the washing away of my guilt,
the end of my evil thoughts,
and the rebirth of my better instincts.
May it spur me on to works pleasing to you
and profitable to my health in body and soul,
and a firm defence
against the wiles of my enemies.
Amen.

(Tr. ICEL)

Prayer of St Thomas Aquinas before Holy Communion

Almighty, everlasting God,
I draw near to the sacrament of your only-begotten Son,
our Lord Jesus Christ.
I who am sick approach the physician of life.
I who am unclean come to the fountain of mercy;
blind, to the light of eternal brightness;
poor and needy, to the Lord of heaven and earth.
Therefore, I implore you, in your boundless mercy,
to heal my sickness, cleanse my defilement,
enlighten my blindness, enrich my poverty,
and clothe my nakedness.
Then shall I dare to receive the bread of angels,
the King of kings and Lord of lords,
with reverence and humility,
contrition and love,
purity and faith,
with the purpose and intention necessary
for the good of my soul.
Grant, I beseech you, that I may receive
not only the Body and Blood of the Lord,
but also the grace and power of the sacrament.
Most merciful God,
enable me so to receive the Body of your only-begotten Son,
our Lord Jesus Christ, which he took from the Virgin Mary,
that I may be found worthy to be incorporated
into his mystical Body, and counted among his members.
Most loving Father,
grant that I may one day see face to face

your beloved Son, whom I now intend to receive
under the veil of the sacrament,
and who with you and the Holy Spirit,
lives and reigns for ever,
one God, world without end. Amen.

(Tr. Stanbrook)

Invocation to the Holy Spirit
Lord Almighty,
send down upon this sacrifice your Holy Spirit.
May he declare this bread that we shall eat
to be the body of Christ,
and this cup that we shall drink
to be the blood of Christ.
May he strengthen and sanctify us
who eat this bread and drink this cup,
grant forgiveness of our sins
and deliver us from the wiles of the devil.
May he fill us with his presence
to make us worthy of Christ, your Son,
and obtain for us eternal life.

Adapted from *The Apostolic Constitutions*
4th century

For prayers of thanksgiving after Mass, turn to pp.105ff.
For other prayers, turn to pp.1069ff.

THE ORDER OF MASS

INTRODUCTORY RITES

The Mass begins with the Entrance Song. Then the celebrant greets the people. The Penitential Rite, the Glory to God, and the Opening Prayer follow. The purpose of these preliminary rites is to help the people, gathered for the celebration of Mass, to join with each other as a worshipping community, and to prepare them to listen to the Word of God and to celebrate the eucharist.

Entrance Procession
The celebrant and ministers go to the altar, while the Entrance Antiphon or Song is sung.

> **Entrance Antiphon:** turn to the Proper of the Mass of the Day *or* a hymn is sung

Greeting
All make the sign of the cross. The celebrant then greets all present and gives a brief introduction to the Mass of the Day.

Celebrant In the name of the Father, and of the Son, ✠ and of the Holy Spirit.
People **Amen.**
C The grace of our Lord Jesus Christ and the love of God and the fellowship of the Holy Spirit be with you all.
P **And also with you.**
or 2
C The grace and peace of God our Father and the Lord Jesus Christ be with you.
P **Blessed be God, the Father of our Lord Jesus Christ.**
or **And also with you.**
or 3
C The Lord be with you.
P **And also with you.**
The celebrant may briefly introduce the Mass of the Day.

Rite of Blessing and Sprinkling Holy Water

This rite may be used instead of the penitential rite at the beginning of Mass. If it is used, the Kyrie is not said.

The priest greets the people. A vessel containing the water to be blessed is placed before him.

Dear friends,
this water will be used
to remind us of our baptism.
Let us ask God to bless it
and to keep us faithful
to the Spirit he has given us.

1: God our Father,
your gift of water
brings life and freshness to the earth;
it washes away our sins
and brings us eternal life.

We ask you now
to bless ✠ this water,
and to give us your protection on this day
which you have made your own.
Renew the living spring of your life within us
and protect us in spirit and body,
that we may be free from sin
and come into your presence
to receive your gift of salvation.

or 2: Lord God almighty,
creator of all life,
of body and soul,
we ask you to bless ✠ this water:
as we use it in faith
forgive our sins
and save us from all illness
and the power of evil.

Lord,
in your mercy
give us living water,
always springing up as a fountain of salvation:
free us, body and soul, from every danger,
and admit us to your presence
in purity of heart.

or 3: During the Easter season
Lord God almighty,
hear the prayers of your people:
we celebrate our creation and redemption.
Hear our prayers and bless ✠ this water
which gives fruitfulness to the fields,
and refreshment and cleansing to man.
You chose water to show your goodness
when you led your people to freedom
through the Red Sea
and satisfied their thirst in the desert
with water from the rock.
Water was the symbol used by the prophets
to foretell your new covenant with man.
You made the water of baptism holy
by Christ's baptism in the Jordan:
by it you give us a new birth
and renew us in holiness.
May this water remind us of our baptism
and let us share the joy
of all who have been baptised at Easter.

Where it is customary, salt may be mixed with the holy water.
The priest blesses the salt, saying:
Almighty God,
we ask you to bless ✠ this salt
as once you blessed the salt scattered over the water
by the prophet Elisha.
Wherever this salt and water are sprinkled,
drive away the power of evil,
and protect us always
by the presence of your Holy Spirit.

The priest sprinkles himself, his ministers, and the people.
Meanwhile an appropriate song is sung.
When he returns to his place, the priest says:
May almighty God cleanse us of our sins,
and through the eucharist we celebrate
make us worthy to sit at his table
in his heavenly kingdom.   ℟ **Amen.**
When it is prescribed, the *Glory to God* is then sung or said, and
the Mass continues. Turn to p.32.

Penitential Rite

Invitation

The celebrant invites the people to call their sins to mind, and to repent of them. He may use the following, or similar words:

C   My brothers and sisters*,
     to prepare ourselves to celebrate the sacred mysteries,
     let us call to mind our sins.

or

     As we prepare to celebrate the mystery of Christ's love,
     let us acknowledge our failures
     and ask the Lord for pardon and strength.

or

     Coming together as God's family,
     with confidence let us ask the Father's forgiveness,
     for he is full of gentleness and compassion.

A pause for silent reflection follows. After the silence, one of the following three forms of the penitential rite is chosen:

A

All   **I confess to almighty God,**
        and to you, my brothers and sisters,
        that I have sinned through my own fault
        (All strike their breast)
        in my thoughts and in my words,
        in what I have done,
        and in what I have failed to do;
        and I ask blessed Mary, ever virgin,
        all the angels and saints,
        and you, my brothers and sisters,
        to pray for me to the Lord our God.

C   May almighty God have mercy on us,
     forgive us our sins,
     and bring us to everlasting life.

P   **Amen.**

*Other words such as 'my dear people, friends, dearly beloved, brethren,' may be used here and in similar places in the liturgy.

or C

C   Lord, we have sinned against you:
      Lord, have mercy.
P   **Lord, have mercy.**
C   Lord, show us your mercy and love.
P   **And grant us your salvation.**
C   May almighty God have mercy on us,
      forgive us our sins,
      and bring us to everlasting life.
P   **Amen.**

or C

C   You were sent to heal the contrite:
      Lord, have mercy.
P   **Lord, have mercy.**

C   You came to call sinners:
      Christ, have mercy.
P   **Christ, have mercy.**

C   You plead for us at the right hand of the Father:
      Lord, have mercy.
P   **Lord, have mercy.**

C   May almighty God have mercy on us,
      forgive us our sins,
      and bring us to everlasting life.
P   **Amen.**

The Kyrie

A plea for mercy. It is not said here if it has already been incorporated in the penitential rite.

C   Lord, have mercy.
P   **Lord, have mercy.**
C   Christ, have mercy.
P   **Christ, have mercy.**
C   Lord, have mercy.
P   **Lord, have mercy.**

Glory to God

A hymn of praise. It may be said or sung.
It is not used on the Sundays of Advent or Lent.

All **Glory to God in the highest,
and peace to his people on earth.**

**Lord God, heavenly King,
almighty God and Father,
we worship you, we give you thanks,
we praise you for your glory.**

**Lord Jesus Christ, only Son of the Father,
Lord God, Lamb of God,
you take away the sin of the world:
have mercy on us;
you are seated at the right hand of the Father:
receive our prayer.**

**For you alone are the Holy One,
you alone are the Lord,
you alone are the Most High,
Jesus Christ,
with the Holy Spirit,
in the glory of God the Father.   Amen.**

Opening Prayer

C Let us pray.
Celebrant and people pray silently for a while.
Then the celebrant says the opening prayer, which expresses
the theme of the day's celebration.

Opening Prayer:
turn to the Proper of the Mass of the Day

At the end of the prayer, the people make it their own by
responding:

P **Amen.**

LITURGY OF THE WORD

The Liturgy of the Word consists of *readings* from the scriptures; a *homily*, in which the minister explains the readings; the *Profession of Faith*, the creed of God's people; and the *Prayer of the Faithful* or *General Intercessions* in which the people intercede for all mankind.

> **Readings, Responsorial Psalm, Gospel Acclamation:**
> turn to the Proper of the Mass of the Day

First Reading
This is from the Old Testament or, during Eastertide, from the Acts of the Apostles. At the end of the reading:
Reader This is the word of the Lord.   *All* **Thanks be to God.**

Responsorial Psalm
The Psalm is a reflection on the First Reading. The Cantor sings or recites the psalm, and the people respond.

Second Reading
The New Testament Reading is generally from the letters of the apostles. It may be taken from the Acts of the Apostles, or from the book of the Apocalypse. At the end:
Reader This is the word of the Lord.   *All* **Thanks be to God.**

Gospel Acclamation and Gospel Reading
The Gospel Book may be carried in procession to the lectern. To acknowledge Christ in his word, all stand. A verse of welcome is sung or said. After the Gospel:
Reader   This is the Gospel of the Lord.
All   **Praise to you, Lord Jesus Christ.**

Homily
Through the readings, God has spoken to his people of redemption and salvation, and nourished their spirit with his word. The homily helps those present understand and reflect upon what they have heard.

Profession of Faith (Creed)

This is said on all Sundays of the Year.

We believe in one God,
  the Father, the Almighty,
  maker of heaven and earth,
  of all that is, seen and unseen.

We believe in one Lord, Jesus Christ,
  the only Son of God,
  eternally begotten of the Father,
  God from God, Light from Light,
  true God from true God,
  begotten, not made,
  of one Being with the Father.
  Through him all things were made.
  For us men and for our salvation
    he came down from heaven: All bow
  by the power of the Holy Spirit
    he became incarnate from the Virgin Mary,
    and was made man.

For our sake he was crucified under Pontius Pilate;
  he suffered death and was buried.
  On the third day he rose again
    in accordance with the Scriptures;
  he ascended into heaven
    and is seated at the right hand of the Father.
He will come again in glory to judge the living and the
      dead,
    and his kingdom will have no end.

We believe in the Holy Spirit, the Lord, the giver of life,
  who proceeds from the Father and the Son.
  With the Father and the Son he is worshipped and
    glorified.
  He has spoken through the Prophets.
  We believe in one holy catholic and apostolic Church.
  We acknowledge one baptism for the forgiveness of sins.
  We look for the resurrection of the dead,
    and the life of the world to come.   Amen.

Prayer of the Faithful

This opens with the celebrant's *Invitation*. There follow the *Biddings*, to which the people reply according to custom. The celebrant says the concluding prayer.   *P*   **Amen.**

LITURGY OF THE EUCHARIST

Preparation of the Altar and the Gifts

Procession with the Gifts and Taking of the Gifts

At the beginning of the liturgy of the eucharist, the gifts which will become the Lord's body and blood are brought to the altar. The offerings of the people may also be brought to the altar. During the procession of gifts, an offertory song may be sung. The gifts are received by the celebrant standing at a suitable place. Gifts other than bread and wine are not placed on the altar.

If no song is sung, then the people may make the responses to the prayer of offering given here.

C   Blessed are you, Lord, God of all creation.
Through your goodness we have this bread to offer,
which earth has given and human hands have made.
It will become for us the bread of life.

P   **Blessed be God for ever.**

C (quietly)   By the mystery of this water and wine
may we come to share in the divinity of Christ,
who humbled himself to share in our humanity.

Blessed are you, Lord, God of all creation.
Through your goodness we have this wine to offer,
fruit of the vine and work of human hands.
It will become our spiritual drink.

P   **Blessed be God for ever.**

C (quietly)   Lord God, we ask you to receive us
and be pleased with the sacrifice we offer you
with humble and contrite hearts.

The celebrant washes his hands, saying:

C   Lord, wash away my iniquity; cleanse me from my sin.

LORD

ACCEPT OUR SACRIFICE AS A HOLY EXCHANGE OF GIFTS

Invitation to Prayer

Pray, brethren, that our sacrifice*
may be acceptable to God, the almighty Father.

P **May the Lord accept the sacrifice at your hands
for the praise and glory of his name,
for our good, and the good of all his Church.**

Prayer over the Gifts
turn to the Proper of the Mass of the Day

People **Amen.**

EUCHARISTIC PRAYER

The whole congregation joins Christ in acknowledging the
works of God, and in offering the sacrifice.

Introductory Dialogue

C The Lord be with you.
P **And also with you.**
C Lift up your hearts.
P **We lift them up to the Lord.**
C Let us give thanks to the Lord our God.
P **It is right to give him thanks and praise.**

The celebrant continues alone.

Preface: turn to pp.62ff.

At the end of the Preface all sing or say the Acclamation:

All **Holy, holy, holy Lord, God of power and might,
heaven and earth are full of your glory.
Hosanna in the highest.**

**Blessed is he who comes in the name of the Lord.
Hosanna in the highest.**

The Eucharistic Prayer follows, pp.38ff.

*In England and Wales: 'my sacrifice and yours'

Eucharistic Prayer I

The passages within the brackets may be omitted if the
celebrant wishes.

We come to you, Father,
with praise and thanksgiving,
through Jesus Christ your Son.
Through him we ask you to accept and bless
these gifts we offer you in sacrifice.

We pray for the Church

We offer them for your holy catholic Church,
watch over it, Lord, and guide it;
grant it peace and unity throughout the world.
We offer them for N. our Pope,
for N. our bishop,
and for all who hold and teach the catholic faith
that comes to us from the apostles.

For the living

Remember, Lord, your people,
especially those for whom we now pray, N. and N.
Remember all of us gathered here before you.
You know how firmly we believe in you
and dedicate ourselves to you.
We offer you this sacrifice of praise
for ourselves and those who are dear to us.
We pray to you, our living and true God,
for our well-being and redemption.

To honour the saints

In union with the whole Church
we honour Mary,
*the ever-virgin mother of Jesus Christ our Lord and God.
We honour Joseph, her husband,
the apostles and martyrs

Special form of **In union with the whole Church**
Christmas and during the octave
**In union with the whole Church
we celebrate that day [night]
when Mary without loss of her virginity
gave the world its Saviour.
We honour her,***

Epiphany
**In union with the whole Church
we celebrate that day
when your only Son,
sharing your eternal glory,
showed himself in a human body.
We honour Mary,***

Holy Thursday
**In union with the whole Church
we celebrate that day
when Jesus Christ, our Lord,
was betrayed for us.
We honour Mary,***

From the Easter Vigil to the Second Sunday of Easter inclusive
**In union with the whole Church
we celebrate that day [night]
when Jesus Christ, our Lord,
rose from the dead in his human body.
We honour Mary,***

Ascension
**In union with the whole Church
we celebrate that day
when your only Son, our Lord,
took his place with you
and raised our frail human nature to glory.
We honour Mary,***

Pentecost
**In union with the whole Church
we celebrate the day of Pentecost
when the Holy Spirit appeared to the apostles
in the form of countless tongues.
We honour Mary,***

Peter and Paul, Andrew,
(James, John, Thomas,
James, Philip,
Bartholomew, Matthew, Simon and Jude;
we honour Linus, Cletus, Clement, Sixtus,
Cornelius, Cyprian, Lawrence, Chrysogonus,
John and Paul, Cosmas and Damian)
and all the saints.
May their merits and prayers
gain us your constant help and protection.
(Through Christ our Lord. Amen.)

For acceptance of this offering*

Father, accept this offering
from your whole family.
Grant us your peace in this life,
save us from final damnation,
and count us among those you have chosen.
(Through Christ our Lord. Amen.)

---

*From the Easter Vigil to the Second Sunday of Easter
Father, accept this offering
from your whole family
and from those born into the new life
of water and the Holy Spirit,
with all their sins forgiven.
Grant us your peace in this life,
save us from final damnation,
and count us among those you have chosen.
(Through Christ our Lord. Amen.)

Bless and approve our offering;
make it acceptable to you,
an offering in spirit and in truth.
Let it become for us
the body and blood of Jesus Christ,
your only Son, our Lord.
(Through Christ our Lord. Amen.)

The Lord's supper: the consecration

The day before he suffered
he took bread in his sacred hands
and looking up to heaven,
to you, his almighty Father,
he gave you thanks and praise.
He broke the bread,
gave it to his disciples, and said:
Take this, all of you, and eat it:
this is my body which will be given up for you.

When supper was ended,
he took the cup.
Again he gave you thanks and praise,
gave the cup to his disciples, and said:
Take this, all of you, and drink from it:
this is the cup of my blood,
the blood of the new and everlasting covenant.
It will be shed for you and for all men
so that sins may be forgiven.
Do this in memory of me.

Let us proclaim the mystery of faith:

Memorial acclamation of the people

1   **Christ has died,**
    Christ is risen,
    Christ will come again.

2   **Dying you destroyed our death,**
    rising you restored our life.
    Lord Jesus, come in glory.

3   **When we eat this bread and drink this cup,**
    we proclaim your death, Lord Jesus,
    until you come in glory.

4   **Lord, by your cross and resurrection**
    you have set us free.
    You are the Saviour of the world.

Memorial of the paschal mystery and offering

Father, we celebrate the memory of Christ, your Son.
We, your people and your ministers,
recall his passion,
his resurrection from the dead,
and his ascension into glory;
and from the many gifts you have given us
we offer to you, God of glory and majesty,
this holy and perfect sacrifice:
the bread of life
and the cup of eternal salvation.

Look with favour on these offerings
and accept them as once you accepted
the gifts of your servant Abel,
the sacrifice of Abraham, our father in faith,
and the bread and wine offered by your priest Melchisedech.
Almighty God,
we pray that your angel may take this sacrifice
to your altar in heaven.
Then, as we receive from this altar
the sacred body and blood of your Son,
let us be filled with every grace and blessing.
(Through Christ our Lord. Amen.)

For the dead

Remember, Lord, those who **have died**
and have gone before us marked with the sign of faith,
especially those for whom we **now pray**, N. and N.
May these, and all who sleep in **Christ**,
find in your presence
light, happiness, and peace.
(Through Christ our Lord. Amen.)

For us sinners

For ourselves, too, we ask
some share in the fellowship of your apostles and martyrs,
with John the Baptist, Stephen, Matthias, Barnabas,

(Ignatius, Alexander, Marcellinus, Peter,
Felicity, Perpetua, Agatha, Lucy,
Agnes, Cecilia, Anastasia)
and all the saints.
Though we are sinners,
we trust in your mercy and love.
Do not consider what we truly deserve,
but grant us your forgiveness.

Through Christ our Lord
you give us all these gifts.
You fill them with life and goodness,
you bless them and make them holy.

Final doxology: in praise of God
Through him,
with him,
in him,
in the unity of the Holy Spirit,
all glory and honour is yours,
almighty Father,
for ever and ever.
P **Amen.**

Turn to p.57.

FATHER YOU ARE HOLY · FOUNT OF HOLINESS · LET YOUR SPIRIT COME UPON THESE GIFTS TO MAKE THEM HOLY

THAT THEY MAY BECOME FOR US
THE BODY & BLOOD OF YOUR SON
OUR LORD
JESUS CHRIST

Eucharistic Prayer II

Preface

This may be replaced by another preface.

Father, it is our duty and our salvation,
always and everywhere
to give you thanks
through your beloved Son, Jesus Christ.

He is the Word through whom you made the universe,
the Saviour you sent to redeem us.
By the power of the Holy Spirit
he took flesh and was born of the Virgin Mary.

For our sake he opened his arms on the cross;
he put an end to death
and revealed the resurrection.
In this he fulfilled your will
and won for you a holy people.

And so we join the angels and the saints
in proclaiming your glory
as we sing (say):

Holy, holy, holy Lord, God of power and might,
heaven and earth are full of your glory.
Hosanna in the highest.
Blessed is he who comes in the name of the Lord.
Hosanna in the highest.

Invocation of the Holy Spirit

Lord, you are holy indeed,
the fountain of all holiness.
Let your Spirit come upon these gifts to make them holy,
so that they may become for us
the body and blood of our Lord, Jesus Christ.

The Lord's Supper

Before he was given up to death,
a death he freely accepted,
he took bread and gave you thanks.
He broke the bread,

gave it to his disciples, and said:

Take this, all of you, and eat it:
this is my body which will be given up for you.

When supper was ended, he took the cup.
Again he gave you thanks and praise,
gave the cup to his disciples, and said:

Take this, all of you, and drink from it:
this is the cup of my blood,
the blood of the new and everlasting covenant.
It will be shed for you and for all men
so that sins may be forgiven.
Do this in memory of me.
Let us proclaim the mystery of faith:

Memorial acclamation of the people

1 **Christ has died,**
   Christ is risen,
   Christ will come again.

2 **Dying you destroyed our death,**
   rising you restored our life.
   Lord Jesus, come in glory.

3 **When we eat this bread and drink this cup,**
   we proclaim your death, Lord Jesus,
   until you come in glory.

4 **Lord, by your cross and resurrection**
   you have set us free.
   You are the Saviour of the world.

The memorial prayer

In memory of his death and resurrection,
we offer you, Father, this life-giving bread,
this saving cup.
We thank you for counting us worthy
to stand in your presence and serve you.
May all of us who share in the body and blood of Christ
be brought together in unity by the Holy Spirit.

Intercessions for the Church
Lord, remember your Church throughout the world;
make us grow in love,
together with N. our Pope,
N. our bishop, and all the clergy.

(In Masses for the Dead the following may be added:
Remember N., whom you have called from this life.
In baptism he [she] died with Christ:
may he [she] also share his resurrection.)
Remember our brothers and sisters
who have gone to their rest
in the hope of rising again;
bring them and all the departed
into the light of your presence.

In communion with the saints
Have mercy on us all;
make us worthy to share eternal life
with Mary, the virgin mother of God,
with the apostles, and with all the saints
who have done your will throughout the ages.
May we praise you in union with them,
and give you glory
through your Son, Jesus Christ.

Final doxology: in praise of God

Through him,
with him,
in him,
in the unity of the Holy Spirit,
all glory and honour is yours,
almighty Father,
for ever and ever.   *P* **Amen.**

Turn to p.57.

Eucharistic Prayer III

Praise to the Father

Father, you are holy indeed,
and all creation rightly gives you praise.
All life, all holiness comes from you
through your Son, Jesus Christ our Lord,
by the working of the Holy Spirit.
From age to age you gather a people to yourself,
so that from east to west
a perfect offering may be made
to the glory of your name.

Invocation of the Holy Spirit

And so, Father, we bring you these gifts.
We ask you to make them holy by the power of your Spirit,
that they may become the body and blood
of your Son, our Lord Jesus Christ,
at whose command we celebrate this eucharist.

The Lord's Supper

On the night he was betrayed,
he took bread and gave you thanks and praise.
He broke the bread, gave it to his disciples, and said:

Take this, all of you, and eat it:
this is my body which will be given up for you.

When supper was ended, he took the cup.
Again he gave you thanks and praise,
gave the cup to his disciples, and said:

Take this, all of you, and drink from it:
this is the cup of my blood,
the blood of the new and everlasting covenant.
It will be shed for you and for all men
so that sins may be forgiven.
Do this in memory of me.

Let us proclaim the mystery of faith:
Memorial acclamation of the people
1 **Christ has died,
   Christ is risen,
   Christ will come again.**

2 **Dying you destroyed our death,
   rising you restored our life.
   Lord Jesus, come in glory.**

3 **When we eat this bread and drink this cup,
   we proclaim your death, Lord Jesus,
   until you come in glory.**

4 **Lord, by your cross and resurrection
   you have set us free.
   You are the Saviour of the world.**

The memorial prayer
Father, calling to mind the death your Son endured for our
    salvation,
his glorious resurrection and ascension into heaven,
and ready to greet him when he comes again,
we offer you in thanksgiving this holy and living sacrifice.

Look with favour on your Church's offering,
and see the Victim whose death has reconciled us to yourself.
Grant that we, who are nourished by his body and blood,
may be filled with his Holy Spirit,
and become one body, one spirit in Christ.

May he make us an everlasting gift to you
and enable us to share in the inheritance of your saints,
with Mary, the virgin Mother of God;
with the apostles, the martyrs,
(Saint N. – the saint of the day or patron saint) and all your saints,
on whose constant intercession we rely for help.

Lord, may this sacrifice,
which has made our peace with you,
advance the peace and salvation of all the world.

Strengthen in faith and love your pilgrim Church on earth;
your servant, Pope N., our bishop N.,
and all the bishops,
with the clergy and the entire people your Son has gained for
    you.
Father, hear the prayers of the family you have gathered here
    before you.
In mercy and love unite all your children wherever they may
    be.*
Welcome into your kingdom our departed brothers and
    sisters,
and all who have left this world in your friendship.
We hope to enjoy for ever the vision of your glory,
through Christ our Lord, from whom all good things come.

---

*In Masses for the dead, the following may be said:
Remember N.
In baptism he (she) died with Christ:
may he (she) also share his resurrection,
when Christ will raise our mortal bodies
and make them like his own in glory.
Welcome into your kingdom our departed brothers and
    sisters,
and all who have left this world in your friendship.
There we hope to share in your glory
when every tear will be wiped away.
On that day we shall see you, our God, as you are.
We shall become like you
and praise you for ever through Christ our Lord,
from whom all good things come.

Final doxology: in praise of God
Through him,
with him,
in him,
in the unity of the Holy Spirit,
all glory and honour is yours,
almighty Father,
for ever and ever.   *P* **Amen.**   Turn to p.57.

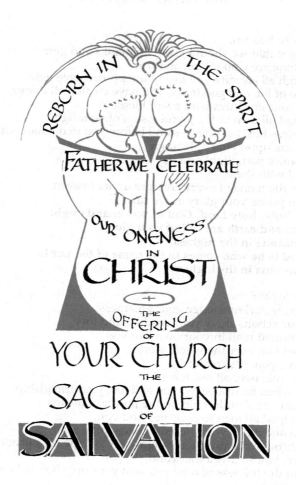

REBORN IN THE SPIRIT

FATHER WE CELEBRATE

OUR ONENESS

IN

CHRIST

✝

THE OFFERING OF

YOUR CHURCH

THE

SACRAMENT

OF

SALVATION

Eucharistic Prayer IV

Preface

Father in heaven,
it is right that we should give you thanks and glory:
you alone are God, living and true.
Through all eternity you live in unapproachable light.
Source of life and goodness, you have created all things,
to fill your creatures with every blessing
and lead all men to the joyful vision of your light.
Countless hosts of angels stand before you to do your will;
they look upon your splendour
and praise you, night and day.
United with them,
and in the name of every creature under heaven,
we too praise your glory as we say:

Holy, holy, holy Lord, God of power and might,
heaven and earth are full of your glory.
> **Hosanna in the highest.**
Blessed is he who comes in the name of the Lord.
> **Hosanna in the highest.**

Praise to the Father

Father, we acknowledge your greatness:
all your actions show your wisdom and love.
You formed man in your own likeness
and set him over the whole world
to serve you, his creator,
and to rule over all creatures.
Even when he disobeyed you and lost your friendship
you did not abandon him to the power of death,
but helped all men to seek and find you.
Again and again you offered a covenant to man,
and through the prophets taught him to hope for salvation.
Father, you so loved the world
that in the fullness of time you sent your only Son to be our
    Saviour.
He was conceived through the power of the Holy Spirit,
and born of the Virgin Mary,

a man like us in all things but sin.
To the poor he proclaimed the good news of salvation,
to prisoners, freedom,
and to those in sorrow, joy.
In fulfilment of your will
he gave himself up to death;
but by rising from the dead,
he destroyed death and restored life.
And that we might live no longer for ourselves but for him,
he sent the Holy Spirit from you, Father,
as his first gift to those who believe,
to complete his work on earth
and bring us the fullness of grace.

Invocation of the Holy Spirit

Father, may this Holy Spirit sanctify these offerings.
Let them become the body and blood of Jesus Christ our Lord
as we celebrate the great mystery
which he left us as an everlasting covenant.

The Lord's Supper

He always loved those who were his own in the world.
When the time came for him to be glorified by you, his
    heavenly Father,
he showed the depth of his love.

While they were at supper,
he took bread, said the blessing, broke the bread,
and gave it to his disciples, saying:
Take this, all of you, and eat it:
this is my body which will be given up for you.

In the same way, he took the cup, filled with wine.
He gave you thanks, and giving the cup to his disciples, said:
Take this, all of you, and drink from it:
this is the cup of my blood,
the blood of the new and everlasting covenant.
It will be shed for you and for all men
so that sins may be forgiven.
Do this in memory of me.

Let us proclaim the mystery of faith:

Memorial acclamation of the people

1 **Christ has died,**
  Christ is risen,
  Christ will come again.

2 **Dying you destroyed our death,**
  rising you restored our life.
  Lord Jesus, come in glory.

3 **When we eat this bread and drink this cup,**
  we proclaim your death, Lord Jesus,
  until you come in glory.

4 **Lord, by your cross and resurrection**
  you have set us free.
  You are the Saviour of the world.

The memorial prayer

Father, we now celebrate this memorial of our redemption.
We recall Christ's death, his descent among the dead,
his resurrection, and his ascension to your right hand;
and, looking forward to his coming in glory,
we offer you his body and blood,
the acceptable sacrifice
which brings salvation to the whole world.

Intercessions: for the Church

Lord, look upon this sacrifice which you have given to your
    Church;
and by your Holy Spirit, gather all who share* this one
    bread and one cup
into the one body of Christ, a living sacrifice of praise.

*ICEL translation: 'who share this bread and wine'.

Lord, remember those for whom we offer this sacrifice,
especially N. our Pope,
N. our bishop, and bishops and clergy everywhere.
Remember those who take part in this offering,
those here present and all your people,
and all who seek you with a sincere heart.

For the dead

Remember those who have died in the peace of Christ
and all the dead whose faith is known to you alone.

In communion with the saints

Father, in your mercy grant also to us, your children,
to enter into our heavenly inheritance
in the company of the Virgin Mary, the Mother of God,
and your apostles and saints.
Then, in your kingdom, freed from the corruption of sin and
    death,
we shall sing your glory with every creature through Christ
    our Lord,
through whom you give us everything that is good.

Final doxology: in praise of God

Through him,
with him,
in him,
in the unity of the Holy Spirit,
all glory and honour is yours,
almighty Father,
for ever and ever.
P **Amen.**

LET us PRAY AS JESUS TAUGHT US

ABBA FATHER

kingdom of heaven + hallowed be thy name + thy kingdom come + thy will be done on earth as it is in heaven + give us today our daily bread + forgive us our trespasses as we forgive those who trespass against us + and lead us not into temptation + but deliver us from evil + for thine is the kingdom, the power and the glory, for ever and ever. AMEN

COMMUNION RITE

Lord's Prayer
In accordance with the Lord's command, the faithful receive his body and blood as their spiritual food.

In the Our Father, all pray for daily food, and for forgiveness.

C Let us pray with confidence to the Father
in the words our Saviour gave us:

or 2

Jesus taught us to call God our Father,
and so we have the courage to say:

or 3

Let us ask our Father to forgive our sins
and to bring us to forgive those who sin against us:

or 4

Let us pray for the coming of the kingdom
as Jesus taught us:

All **Our Father, who art in heaven,**
hallowed be thy name;
thy kingdom come;
thy will be done on earth as it is in heaven.
Give us this day our daily bread;
and forgive us our trespasses
as we forgive those who trespass against us;
and lead us not into temptation,
but deliver us from evil.

C Deliver us, Lord, from every evil,
and grant us peace in our day.
In your mercy keep us free from sin
and protect us from all anxiety
as we wait in joyful hope
for the coming of our Saviour, Jesus Christ.

All **For the kingdom, the power, and the glory are yours,**
now and forever.

Sign of Peace

Before they share in the same bread, the people express their
love for one another, and pray for peace and unity.

C   Lord Jesus Christ, you said to your apostles:
     I leave you peace, my peace I give you.
     Look not on our sins, but on the faith of your Church,
     and grant us the peace and unity of your kingdom
     where you live for ever and ever.

P   **Amen.**

C   The peace of the Lord be with you always.

P   **And also with you.**

Then the deacon, or the celebrant, may add:

C   Let us offer each other the sign of peace.

All make a sign of peace according to local custom.

Breaking of the Bread

All **Lamb of God, you take away the sins of the world:
     have mercy on us.
     Lamb of God, you take away the sins of the world:
     have mercy on us.
     Lamb of God, you take away the sins of the world:
     grant us peace.**

While this is sung or said, the celebrant takes the host and
breaks it over the paten, saying quietly:

C   May this mingling of the body and blood of our Lord
        Jesus Christ.
     bring eternal life to us who receive it.

The celebrant quietly says one of the following prayers.

C   Lord Jesus Christ, Son of the living God,
     by the will of the Father and the work of the Holy Spirit
     your death brought life to the world.
     By your holy body and blood
     free me from all my sins and from every evil.
     Keep me faithful to your teaching,
     and never let me be parted from you.

or

Lord Jesus Christ,
with faith in your love and mercy
I eat your body and drink your blood.
Let it not bring me condemnation,
but health in mind and body.

C   This is the Lamb of God
who takes away the sins of the world.
Happy are those who are called to his supper.

All **Lord, I am not worthy to receive you,
but only say the word and I shall be healed.**

While the celebrant is receiving the body of Christ, the
communion antiphon or song is begun.

Communion Antiphon:
turn to the Proper of the Mass of the Day
or a hymn is sung

The People's Communion
The communicant is offered the host:
C   The body of Christ.   *P* **Amen.**

When the communicant is offered the chalice:
C   The blood of Christ.   *P* **Amen.**

After the communion of the people, a period of silence, a
psalm or song may follow. Then:
C   Let us pray.
Celebrant and people pray in silence for a while, unless the
silence has already been observed. Then the celebrant sings
or says the prayer after communion.

Prayer after Communion: turn to the Proper of
the Mass of the Day

The people respond: *P* **Amen.**

CONCLUDING RITE

(Omitted if a liturgical ceremony follows the Mass.)

If there are any brief announcements, they are made at this time.

C The Lord be with you.
P **And also with you.**

Blessing
1 Simple Form
C May almighty God bless you,
   the Father, and the Son, ✠ and the Holy Spirit.
P **Amen.**

or 2 Solemn Blessing
On certain days, a more solemn form of blessing may be used. It always ends with the blessing as above, 1.

Solemn Blessing
Blessings proper to certain days are given at the end of the Mass texts for those days.
Blessings which may be used on various days are given on pp. 90ff.

---

or 3 Prayer over the People
The celebrant may say a special prayer over the people. It always ends with the blessing as above, 1.

Prayer over the People: see pp. 95ff. below.

Dismissal

All are sent out into the world, to do good works, blessing and praising the Lord.

C   Go in the peace of Christ.

or

C   The Mass is ended, go in peace.

or

C   Go in peace to love and serve the Lord.
P   **Thanks be to God.**

At the Easter Vigil, on Easter Sunday, throughout the Easter Octave, and at Pentecost, 'Alleluia, alleluia!' is added to the dismissal formula and response.

The celebrant kisses and salutes the altar, then returns to the sacristy with his ministers.

PREFACES

These Prefaces may be used throughout the appropriate season.

ADVENT

P1   PREFACE OF ADVENT I
From the First Sunday of Advent until 16 December

Father, all-powerful and ever-living God,
we do well always and everywhere to give you thanks
through Jesus Christ our Lord.

When he humbled himself to come among us as a man,
he fulfilled the plan you formed long ago
and opened for us the way to salvation.

Now we watch for the day,
hoping that the salvation promised us will be ours
when Christ our Lord will come again in his glory.

And so, with all the choirs of angels in heaven
we proclaim your glory
and join in their unending hymn of praise:
Holy, holy, holy . . .

P2   PREFACE OF ADVENT II
17 December–24 December

Father, all-powerful and ever-living God,
we do well always and everywhere to give you thanks
through Jesus Christ our Lord.

His future coming was proclaimed by all the prophets.
The virgin mother bore him in her womb with love beyond all
    telling.
John the Baptist was his herald
and made him known when at last he came.
In his love Christ has filled us with joy
as we prepare to celebrate his birth,
so that when he comes he may find us watching in prayer,
our hearts filled with wonder and praise.

And so, with all the choirs of angels in heaven
we proclaim your glory
and join in their unending hymn of praise: **Holy, holy, holy . . .**

CHRISTMAS

P3   PREFACE OF CHRISTMAS I

Father, all-powerful and ever-living God,
we do well always and everywhere to give you thanks
through Jesus Christ our Lord.

In the wonder of the incarnation
your eternal Word has brought to the eyes of faith
a new and radiant vision of your glory.
In him we see our God made visible
and so are caught up in love of the God we cannot see.

And so, with all the choirs of angels in heaven
we proclaim your glory
and join in their unending hymn of praise: **Holy, holy, holy . . .**

P4   PREFACE OF CHRISTMAS II

Father, all-powerful and ever-living God,
we do well always and everywhere to give you thanks
through Jesus Christ our Lord.

Today you fill our hearts with joy
as we recognise in Christ the revelation of your love.
No eye can see his glory as our God,
yet now he is seen as one like us.

Christ is your Son before all ages,
yet now he is born in time.
He has come to lift up all things to himself,
to restore unity to creation,
and to lead mankind from exile into your heavenly kingdom.

With all the angels of heaven
we sing our joyful hymn of praise: **Holy, holy, holy . . .**

P5   PREFACE OF CHRISTMAS III

Father, all-powerful and ever-living God,
we do well always and everywhere to give you thanks
through Jesus Christ our Lord.

Today in him a new light has dawned upon the world:
God has become one with man,
and man has become one again with God.

Your eternal Word has taken upon himself our human weakness,
giving our mortal nature immortal value.
So marvellous is this oneness between God and man
that in Christ man restores to man the gift of everlasting life.

In our joy we sing to your glory
with all the choirs of angels: **Holy, holy, holy . . .**

P6   PREFACE OF EPIPHANY

Father, all-powerful and ever-living God,
we do well always and everywhere to give you thanks.

Today you revealed in Christ your eternal plan of salvation
and showed him as the light of all peoples.
Now that his glory has shone among us
you have renewed humanity in his immortal image.

Now, with angels and archangels,
and the whole company of heaven,
we sing the unending hymn of your praise: **Holy, holy, holy . . .**

P7   PREFACE OF THE BAPTISM OF THE LORD

Father, all-powerful and ever-living God,
we do well always and everywhere to give you thanks.

You celebrated your new gift of baptism
by signs and wonders at the Jordan.
Your voice was heard from heaven
to awaken faith in the presence among us
of the Word made man.

Your Spirit was seen as a dove,
revealing Jesus as your servant,
and anointing him with joy as the Christ,
sent to bring to the poor
the good news of salvation.

In our unending joy we echo on earth
the song of the angels in heaven
as they praise your glory for ever: **Holy, holy, holy . . .**

LENT

P8   PREFACE OF LENT 1

Father, all-powerful and ever-living God,
we do well always and everywhere to give you thanks
through Jesus Christ our Lord.
Each year you give us this joyful season
when we prepare to celebrate the paschal mystery
with mind and heart renewed.
You give us a spirit of loving reverence for you, our Father,
and of willing service to our neighbour.

As we recall the great events that gave us a new life in Christ,
you bring the image of your Son to perfection within us.

Now, with angels and archangels,
and the whole company of heaven,
we sing the unending hymn of your praise: **Holy, holy, holy . . .**

P9   PREFACE OF LENT II

Father, all-powerful and ever-living God,
we do well always and everywhere to give you thanks.

This great season of grace is your gift to your family
to renew us in spirit.
You give us strength to purify our hearts,
to control our desires,
and so to serve you in freedom.
You teach us how to live in this passing world,
with our heart set on the world that will never end.

Now, with all the saints and angels,
we praise you for ever: **Holy, holy, holy . . .**

P11   PREFACE OF LENT IV

Father, all-powerful and ever-living God,
we do well always and everywhere to give you thanks.
Through our observance of Lent
you correct our faults and raise our minds to you,
you help us grow in holiness,
and offer us the reward of everlasting life
through Jesus Christ our Lord.

Through him the angels and all the choirs of heaven
worship in awe before your presence.
May our voices be one with theirs
as they sing with joy the hymn of your glory: **Holy, holy, holy**

P12   PREFACE OF FIRST SUNDAY OF LENT

Father, all-powerful and ever-living God,
we do well always and everywhere to give you thanks
through Jesus Christ our Lord.

His fast of forty days
makes this a holy season of self-denial.
By rejecting the devil's temptations
he has taught us
to rid ourselves of the hidden corruption of evil,
and so to share his paschal meal in purity of heart,
until we come to its fulfilment
in the promised land of heaven.

Now we join the angels and the saints
as they sing their unending hymn of praise: **Holy, holy, holy . . .**

P13   PREFACE OF SECOND SUNDAY OF LENT

Father, all-powerful and ever-living God,
we do well always and everywhere to give you thanks
through Jesus Christ our Lord.

On your holy mountain he revealed himself in glory
in the presence of his disciples.
He had already prepared them for his approaching death.
He wanted to teach them through the Law and the Prophets
that the promised Christ had first to suffer
and so come to the glory of his resurrection.

In our unending joy we echo on earth
the song of the angels in heaven
as they praise your glory for ever: **Holy, holy, holy . . .**

Prefaces 14, 15, 16, are used only when the gospel texts to which they refer are read at Mass.

P14 PREFACE OF THIRD SUNDAY OF LENT

Father, all-powerful and ever-living God,
we do well always and everywhere to give you thanks
through Jesus Christ our Lord.

When he asked the woman of Samaria for water to drink
Christ had already prepared for her the gift of faith.
In his thirst to receive her faith
he awakened in her heart the fire of your love.

With thankful praise,
in company with the angels,
we glorify the wonders of your power: **Holy, holy, holy . . .**

P15 PREFACE OF FOURTH SUNDAY OF LENT

Father, all-powerful and ever-living God,
we do well always and everywhere to give you thanks,
through Jesus Christ our Lord.

He came among us as a man,
to lead mankind from darkness
into the light of faith

Through Adam's fall we were born as slaves of sin,
but now through baptism in Christ
we are reborn as your adopted children.

Earth unites with heaven
to sing the new song of creation,
as we adore and praise you for ever: **Holy, holy, holy . . .**

P16 PREFACE OF FIFTH SUNDAY OF LENT

Father, all-powerful and ever-living God,
we do well always and everywhere to give you thanks
through Jesus Christ our Lord.

As a man like us, Jesus wept for Lazarus his friend.
As the eternal God, he raised Lazarus from the dead.
In his love for us all,
Christ gives us the sacraments

to lift us up to everlasting life.
Through him the angels of heaven offer their prayer of adoration
as they rejoice in your presence for ever.
May our voices be one with theirs
in their triumphant hymn of praise: **Holy, holy, holy . . .**

P17   PREFACE OF THE PASSION OF THE LORD I

Father, all-powerful and ever-living God,
we do well always and everywhere to give you thanks.

The suffering and death of your Son
brought life to the whole world,
moving our hearts to praise your glory.
The power of the cross reveals your judgement on this world
and the kingship of Christ crucified.

We praise you, Lord,
with all the angels and saints in their song of joy:
Holy, holy, holy . . .

P19   PREFACE OF PASSION SUNDAY

Father, all-powerful and ever-living God,
we do well always and everywhere to give you thanks
through Jesus Christ our Lord.

Though he was sinless, he suffered willingly for sinners.
Though innocent, he accepted death to save the guilty.
By his dying, he has destroyed our sins.
By his rising, he has raised us up to holiness of life.

We praise you, Lord, with all the angels and saints
in their song of joy: **Holy, holy, holy . . .**

P20   PREFACE OF PRIESTHOOD (CHRISM MASS)

Father, all-powerful and ever-living God,
we do well always and everywhere to give you thanks.

By your Holy Spirit
you anointed your only Son
High Priest of the new and eternal covenant.
With wisdom and love you have planned
that this one priesthood should continue in the Church.

Christ gives the dignity of a royal priesthood
to the people he has made his own.
From these, with a brother's love,
he chooses men to share his sacred ministry
by the laying on of hands.

He appoints them to renew in his name
the sacrifice of our redemption
as they set before your family his paschal meal.
He calls them to lead your holy people in love,
nourish them by your word,
and strengthen them through the sacraments.

Father, they are to give their lives in your service
and for the salvation of your people
as they strive to grow in the likeness of Christ
and honour you by their courageous witness of faith and love.

We praise you, Lord, with all the angels and saints
in their song of joy: **Holy, holy, holy . . .**

EASTER

P21   PREFACE OF EASTER I

This Preface is said in the Masses of the Easter Vigil and Easter
Sunday and during the octave.

Father, all-powerful and ever-living God,
we do well always and everywhere to give you thanks
through Jesus Christ our Lord.

We praise you with greater joy than ever
on this Easter night [day],
when Christ became our paschal sacrifice.

He is the true Lamb who took away the sins of the world.
By dying he destroyed our death;
by rising he restored our life.

And so, with all the choirs of angels in heaven
we proclaim your glory
and join in their unending hymn of praise:
Holy, holy, holy . . .

P22   PREFACE OF EASTER II

Father, all-powerful and ever-living God,
we do well always and everywhere to give you thanks
through Jesus Christ our Lord.
We praise you with greater joy than ever in this Easter season,
when Christ became our paschal sacrifice.

He has made us children of the light,
rising to new and everlasting life.
He has opened the gates of heaven.
to receive his faithful people.
His death is our ransom from death:
his resurrection is our rising to life.

The joy of the resurrection renews the whole world,
while the choirs of heaven sing for ever to your glory:
Holy, holy, holy . . .

P23   PREFACE OF EASTER III

Father, all-powerful and ever-living God,
we do well always and everywhere to give you thanks
through Jesus Christ our Lord.

We praise you with greater joy than ever in this Easter season,
when Christ became our paschal sacrifice.

He is still our priest,
our advocate who always pleads our cause.
Christ is the victim who dies no more,
the Lamb, once slain, who lives for ever.

The joy of the resurrection renews the whole world,
while the choirs of heaven sing for ever to your glory:
Holy, holy, holy . . .

P24   PREFACE OF EASTER IV

Father, all-powerful and ever-living God,
we do well always and everywhere to give you thanks
through Jesus Christ our Lord.

We praise you with greater joy than ever in this Easter season,
when Christ became our paschal sacrifice.

In him a new age has dawned,

the long reign of sin is ended,
a broken world has been renewed,
and man is once again made whole.

The joy of the resurrection renews the whole world,
while the choirs of heaven sing for ever to your glory:
Holy, holy, holy . . .

P25   PREFACE OF EASTER V

Father, all-powerful and ever-living God,
we do well always and everywhere to give you thanks
through Jesus Christ our Lord.

We praise you with greater joy than ever in this Easter season,
when Christ became our paschal sacrifice.

As he offered his body on the cross,
his perfect sacrifice fulfilled all others.
As he gave himself into your hands for our salvation,
he showed himself to be the priest, the altar, and the lamb of
    sacrifice.

The joy of the resurrection renews the whole world,
while the choirs of heaven sing for ever to your glory:
Holy, holy, holy . . .

P26   PREFACE OF THE ASCENSION I

Father, all-powerful and ever-living God,
we do well always and everywhere to give you thanks.

(Today) the Lord Jesus, the king of glory,
the conqueror of sin and death,
ascended to heaven while the angels sang his praises.

Christ, the mediator between God and man,
judge of the world and Lord of all,
has passed beyond our sight,
not to abandon us but to be our hope.
Christ is the beginning, the head of the Church;
where he has gone, we hope to follow.

The joy of the resurrection and ascension renews the whole
    world.
while the choirs of heaven sing for ever to your glory:
Holy, holy, holy . . .

P27   PREFACE OF THE ASCENSION II

Father, all-powerful and ever-living God,
we do well always and everywhere to give you thanks
through Jesus Christ our Lord.

In his risen body he plainly showed himself to his disciples
and was taken up to heaven in their sight
to claim for us a share in his divine life.
And so, with all the choirs of angels in heaven
we proclaim your glory
and join in their unending hymn of praise: **Holy, holy, holy . . .**

P28   PREFACE OF PENTECOST

Father, all-powerful and ever-living God,
we do well always and everywhere to give you thanks.

Today you sent the Holy Spirit
on those marked out to be your children
by sharing the life of your only Son,
and so you brought the paschal mystery to its completion.

Today we celebrate the great beginning of your Church
when the Holy Spirit made known to all peoples the one true
    God,
and created from the many languages of man
one voice to profess one faith.

The joy of the resurrection renews the whole world,
while the choirs of heaven sing for ever to your glory:
Holy, holy, holy . . .

SUNDAYS IN ORDINARY TIME

P29   PREFACE OF SUNDAYS IN ORDINARY TIME I

Father, all-powerful and ever-living God,
we do well always and everywhere to give you thanks
through Jesus Christ our Lord.

Through his cross and resurrection
he freed us from sin and death
and called us to the glory that has made us
a chosen race, a royal priesthood,
a holy nation, a people set apart.

Everywhere we proclaim your mighty works
for you have called us out of darkness
into your own wonderful light.

And so, with all the choirs of angels in heaven
we proclaim your glory
and join in their unending hymn of praise:
Holy, holy, holy . . .

P30 PREFACE OF SUNDAYS IN ORDINARY TIME II

Father, all-powerful and ever-living God,
we do well always and everywhere to give you thanks
through Jesus Christ our Lord.

Out of love for sinful man,
he humbled himself to be born of the Virgin.

By suffering on the cross
he freed us from unending death,
and by rising from the dead
he gave us eternal life.

And so, with all the choirs of angels in heaven
we proclaim your glory
and join in their unending hymn of praise:
Holy, holy, holy . . .

P31 PREFACE OF SUNDAYS IN ORDINARY TIME III

Father, all-powerful and ever-living God,
we do well always and everywhere to give you thanks.

We see your infinite power
in your loving plan of salvation.
You came to our rescue by your power as God,
but you wanted us to be saved by one like us.
Man refused your friendship,
but man himself was to restore it
through Jesus Christ our Lord.

Through him the angels of heaven offer their prayer of adoration
as they rejoice in your presence for ever.
May our voices be one with theirs
in their triumphant hymn of praise: **Holy, holy, holy . . .**

P32   PREFACE OF SUNDAYS IN ORDINARY TIME IV

Father, all-powerful and ever-living God,
we do well always and everywhere to give you thanks
through Jesus Christ our Lord.

By his birth we are reborn.
In his suffering we are freed from sin.
By his rising from the dead we rise to everlasting life.
In his return to you in glory
we enter into your heavenly kingdom.

And so, we join the angels and the saints
as they sing their unending hymn of praise: **Holy, holy, holy . . .**

P33   PREFACE OF SUNDAYS IN ORDINARY TIME V

Father, all-powerful and ever-living God,
we do well always and everywhere to give you thanks.

All things are of your making,
all times and seasons obey your laws,
but you chose to create man in your own image,
setting him over the whole world in all its wonder.
You made man the steward of creation,
to praise you day by day for the marvels of your wisdom and
      power,
through Jesus Christ our Lord.

We praise you, Lord, with all the angels
in their song of joy: **Holy, holy, holy . . .**

P34   PREFACE OF SUNDAYS IN ORDINARY TIME VI

Father, all-powerful and ever-living God,
we do well always and everywhere to give you thanks.

In you we live and move and have our being.
Each day you show us a Father's love;
your Holy Spirit, dwelling within us,
gives us on earth the hope of unending joy.

Your gift of the Spirit,
who raised Jesus from the dead,
is the foretaste and promise
of the paschal feast of heaven.

With thankful praise,
in company with the angels,
we glorify the wonders of your power: **Holy, holy, holy . . .**

P35   PREFACE OF SUNDAYS IN ORDINARY TIME VII

Father, all-powerful and ever-living God,
we do well always and everywhere to give you thanks.

So great was your love
that you gave us your Son as our redeemer.
You sent him as one like ourselves,
though free from sin,
that you might see and love in us
what you see and love in Christ.
Your gifts of grace, lost by disobedience,
are now restored by the obedience of your Son.

We praise you, Lord, with all the angels and saints
in their songs of joy: **Holy, holy, holy . . .**

P36   PREFACE OF SUNDAYS IN ORDINARY TIME VIII

Father, all-powerful and ever-living God,
we do well always and everywhere to give you thanks.

When your children sinned
and wandered far from your friendship,
you reunited them with yourself
through the blood of your Son
and the power of the Holy Spirit.

You gather them into your Church,
to be one as you, Father, are one
with your Son and the Holy Spirit.
You call them to be your people,
to praise your wisdom in all your works.
You make them the body of Christ
and the dwelling-place of the Holy Spirit.

In our joy we sing to your glory
with all the choirs of angels: **Holy, holy, holy . . .**

P43   PREFACE OF THE HOLY TRINITY

Father, all-powerful and ever-living God,
we do well always and everywhere to give you thanks.

We joyfully proclaim our faith
in the mystery of your Godhead.
You have revealed your glory
as the glory also of your Son
and of the Holy Spirit:
three Persons equal in majesty,
undivided in splendour,
yet one Lord, one God,
ever to be adored in your everlasting glory.

And so, with all the choirs of angels in heaven
we proclaim your glory
and join in their unending hymn of praise:
Holy, holy, holy . . .

P44   PREFACE OF THE ANNUNCIATION
                        25 March

Father, all-powerful and ever-living God,
we do well always and everywhere to give you thanks
through Jesus Christ our Lord.

He came to save mankind by becoming a man himself.
The Virgin Mary, receiving the angel's message in faith,
conceived by the power of the Spirit
and bore your Son in purest love.

In Christ, the eternal truth,
your promise to Israel came true.
In Christ, the hope of all peoples,
man's hope was realised beyond all expectation.

Through Christ the angels of heaven
offer their prayer of adoration
as they rejoice in your presence for ever.
May our voices be one with theirs
in their triumphant hymn of praise: **Holy, holy, holy . . .**

P45   PREFACE OF THE SACRED HEART

Father, all-powerful and ever-living God,
we do well always and everywhere to give you thanks
through Jesus Christ our Lord.

Lifted high on the cross,
Christ gave his life for us,
so much did he love us.
From his wounded side flowed blood and water,
the fountain of sacramental life in the Church.
To his open heart the Saviour invites all men.
to draw water in joy from the springs of salvation.

Now, with all the saints and angels,
we praise you for ever: **Holy, holy, holy . . .**

P46   PREFACE OF THE TRIUMPH OF THE CROSS

Father, all-powerful and ever-living God,
we do well always and everywhere to give you thanks.

You decreed that man should be saved through the wood of the
    cross.
The tree of man's defeat became his tree of victory;
where life was lost, there life has been restored
through Christ our Lord.

Through him the choirs of angels
and all the powers of heaven
praise and worship your glory.
May our voices blend with theirs
as we join in their unending hymn:
Holy, holy, holy . . .

P47   PREFACE OF THE HOLY EUCHARIST I

This Preface is said in the Mass of the Lord's Supper on Holy
Thursday. It may be said on Corpus Christi and in votive Masses
of the Holy Eucharist.

Father, all-powerful and ever-living God,
we do well always and everywhere to give you thanks
through Jesus Christ our Lord.

He is the true and eternal priest
who established this unending sacrifice.
He offered himself as a victim for our deliverance

and taught us to make this offering in his memory.
As we eat his body which he gave for us,
we grow in strength.
As we drink his blood which he poured out for us,
we are washed clean.

Now, with angels and archangels,
and the whole company of heaven,
we sing the unending hymn of your praise:
Holy, holy, holy . . .

P48   PREFACE OF THE HOLY EUCHARIST II

This Preface is said on Corpus Christi and in votive Masses of the
Holy Eucharist.

Father, all-powerful and every living God,
we do well always and everywhere to give you thanks
through Jesus Christ our Lord.

At the last supper,
as he sat at table with his apostles,
he offered himself to you as the spotless lamb,
the acceptable gift that gives you perfect praise.

Christ has given us this memorial of his passion
to bring us its saving power until the end of time.

In this great sacrament you feed your people
and strengthen them in holiness,
so that the family of mankind
may come to walk in the light of one faith,
in one communion of love.
We come then to this wonderful sacrament
to be fed at your table
and grow into the likeness of the risen Christ.

Earth unites with heaven
to sing the new song of creation
as we adore and praise you for ever:
Holy, holy, holy . . .

P49   PREFACE OF THE PRESENTATION
                      OF THE LORD
                       2 February

Father, all-powerful and ever-living God,
we do well always and everywhere to give you thanks
through Jesus Christ our Lord.

Today your Son,
who shares your eternal splendour,
was presented in the temple,
and revealed by the Spirit
as the glory of Israel
and the light of all peoples.
Our hearts are joyful,
for we have seen your salvation,
and now with the angels and saints
we praise you for ever: **Holy, holy, holy . . .**

P50   PREFACE OF THE TRANSFIGURATION
                        6 August

Father, all-powerful and ever-living God,
we do well always and everywhere to give you thanks
through Jesus Christ our Lord.

He revealed his glory to the disciples
to strengthen them for the scandal of the cross.
His glory shone from a body like our own,
to show that the Church,
which is the body of Christ,
would one day share his glory.

In our unending joy we echo on earth
the song of the angels in heaven
as they praise your glory for ever: **Holy, holy, holy . . .**

P51   PREFACE OF CHRIST THE KING

Father, all-powerful and ever-living God,
we do well always and everywhere to give you thanks.

You anointed Jesus Christ, your only Son, with the oil of
     gladness,
as the eternal priest and universal king.

As priest he offered his life on the altar of the cross
and redeemed the human race

by this one perfect sacrifice of peace.

As King he claims dominion over all creation,
that he may present to you, his almighty Father,
an eternal and universal kingdom:
a kingdom of truth and life,
a kingdom of holiness and grace,
a kingdom of justice, love, and peace.

And so, with all the choirs of angels in heaven
we proclaim your glory
and join in their unending hymn of praise: **Holy, holy, holy . . .**

P52   THE DEDICATION OF A CHURCH I
In the dedicated church

Father, all-powerful and ever-living God,
we do well always and everywhere to give you thanks.
We thank you now for this house of prayer
in which you bless your family
as we come to you on pilgrimage.

Here you reveal your presence
by sacramental signs,
and make us one with you
through the unseen bond of grace.
Here you build your temple of living stones,
and bring the Church to its full stature
as the body of Christ throughout the world,
to reach its perfection at last
in the heavenly city of Jerusalem,
which is the vision of your peace.

In communion with all the angels and saints
we bless and praise your greatness
in the temple of your glory: **Holy, holy, holy . . .**

P53   THE DEDICATION OF A CHURCH II
Outside the dedicated church

Father, all-powerful and ever-living God,
we do well always and everywhere to give you thanks.

Your house is a house of prayer,
and your presence makes it a place of blessing.

You give us grace upon grace
to build the temple of your Spirit,
creating its beauty from the holiness of our lives.

Your house of prayer
is also the promise of the Church in heaven.
Here your love is always at work,
preparing the Church on earth
for its heavenly glory
as the sinless bride of Christ,
the joyful mother of a great company of saints.

Now, with the saints and all the angels
we praise you for ever: **Holy, holy, holy . . .**

P56   PREFACE OF THE BLESSED VIRGIN MARY I
                        Motherhood of Mary

Father, all-powerful and ever-living God,
we do well always and everywhere to give you thanks
as we celebrate the . . . . . of the Blessed Virgin Mary.

Through the power of the Holy Spirit,
she became the virgin mother of your only Son,
our Lord Jesus Christ,
who is for ever the light of the world.

Through him the choirs of angels
and all the powers of heaven
praise and worship your glory.
May our voices blend with theirs
as we join in their unending hymn:
Holy, holy, holy . . .

P57   PREFACE OF THE BLESSED VIRGIN MARY II

Father, all-powerful and ever-living God,
we do well always and everywhere to give you thanks,
and to praise you for your gifts
as we contemplate your saints in glory.

In celebrating the memory of the Blessed Virgin Mary,
it is our special joy to echo her song of thanksgiving.
What wonders you have worked throughout the world.
All generations have shared the greatness of your love.

When you looked on Mary your lowly servant,
you raised her to be the mother of Jesus Christ, your Son,
     ourLord,
the saviour of all mankind.

Through him the angels of heaven
offer their prayer of adoration
as they rejoice in your presence for ever.
May our voices be one with theirs
in their triumphant hymn of praise:
Holy, holy, holy . . .

P58   PREFACE OF THE IMMACULATE CONCEPTION
                    8 December

Father, all-powerful and ever-living God,
we do well always and everywhere to give you thanks.

You allowed no stain of Adam's sin
to touch the Virgin Mary.
Full of grace, she was to be a worthy mother of your Son,
your sign of favour to the Church at its beginning,
and the promise of its perfection as the bride of Christ, radiant in
     beauty.

Purest of virgins, she was to bring forth your Son,
the innocent lamb who takes away our sins.
You chose her from all women to be our advocate with you
and our pattern of holiness.

In our joy we sing to your glory
with all the choirs of angels: **Holy, holy, holy . . .**

P59   PREFACE OF THE ASSUMPTION
                    15 August

Father, all-powerful and ever-living God,
we do well always and everywhere to give you thanks,
through Jesus Christ our Lord.

Today the virgin Mother of God was taken up into heaven
to be the beginning and the pattern of the Church in its
     perfection,
and a sign of hope and comfort for your people on their pilgrim
     way.
You would not allow decay to touch her body,

for she had given birth to your Son, the Lord of all life,
in the glory of the incarnation.

In our joy we sing to your glory
with all the choirs of angels:
Holy, holy, holy . . .

P61   PREFACE OF SAINT JOHN THE BAPTIST

Father, all-powerful and ever-living God,
we do well always and everywhere to give you thanks
through Jesus Christ our Lord.

We praise your greatness
as we honour the prophet
who prepared the way before your Son.
You set John the Baptist apart from other men,
marking him out with special favour.
His birth brought great rejoicing:
even in the womb he leapt for joy,
so near was man's salvation.

You chose John the Baptist from all the prophets
to show the world its redeemer,
the lamb of sacrifice.
He baptised Christ, the giver of baptism,
in waters made holy by the one who was baptised.
You found John worthy of a martyr's death,
his last and greatest act of witness to your Son.

In our unending joy we echo on earth
the song of the angels in heaven
as they praise your glory for ever: **Holy, holy, holy . . .**

P62   PREFACE OF SAINT JOSEPH,
         HUSBAND OF MARY

Father, all-powerful and ever-living God,
we do well always and everywhere to give you thanks
as we honour Saint Joseph.

He is that just man,
that wise and loyal servant,
whom you placed at the head of your family.
With a husband's love he cherished Mary,

the virgin Mother of God.
With fatherly care he watched over Jesus Christ your Son,
conceived by the power of the Holy Spirit.

Through Christ the choirs of angels
and all the powers of heaven
praise and worship your glory.
May our voices blend with theirs
as we join in their unending hymn: **Holy, holy, holy . . .**

P63   PREFACE OF SAINTS PETER AND PAUL,
                           APOSTLES

Father, all-powerful and ever-living God,
we do well always and everywhere to give you thanks.
You fill our hearts with joy
as we honour your great apostles:
Peter, our leader in the faith,
and Paul, its fearless preacher.

Peter raised up the Church
from the faithful flock of Israel.
Paul brought your call to the nations,
and became the teacher of the world.
Each in his chosen way gathered into unity
the one family of Christ.
Both shared a martyr's death
and are praised throughout the world.

Now, with the apostles and all the angels and saints,
we praise you for ever: **Holy, holy, holy . . .**

P69   PREFACE OF HOLY MEN AND WOMEN I

Father, all-powerful and ever-living God,
we do well always and everywhere to give you thanks.

You are glorified in your saints,
for their glory is the crowning of your gifts.
In their lives on earth
you give us an example.
In our communion with them,
you give us their friendship.
In their prayer for the Church
you give us strength and protection.

This great company of witnesses spurs us on to victory,
to share their prize of everlasting glory,
through Jesus Christ our Lord.

With angels and archangels
and the whole company of saints
we sing our unending hymn of praise: **Holy, holy, holy . . .**

P70   PREFACE OF HOLY MEN AND WOMEN II

Father, all-powerful and ever-living God,
we do well always and everywhere to give you thanks.
You renew the Church in every age
by raising up men and women outstanding in holiness,
living witnesses of your unchanging love.
They inspire us by their heroic lives,
and help us by their constant prayers,
to be the living sign of your saving power.

We praise you, Lord, with all the angels and saints
in their song of joy: **Holy, holy, holy . . .**

P71   PREFACE OF ALL SAINTS
1 November

Father, all-powerful and ever-living God,
we do well always and everywhere to give you thanks.

Today we keep the festival of your holy city,
the heavenly Jerusalem, our mother.
Around your throne
the saints, our brothers and sisters,
sing your praise for ever.
Their glory fills us with joy,
and their communion with us in your Church
gives us inspiration and strength
as we hasten on our pilgrimage of faith,
eager to meet them.

With their great company and all the angels
we praise your glory
as we cry out with one voice: **Holy, holy, holy . . .**

P72   PREFACE OF MARRIAGE I

Father, all-powerful and ever-living God,
we do well always and everywhere to give you thanks.

By this sacrament your grace unites man and woman
in an unbreakable bond of love and peace.
You have designed the chaste love of husband and wife
for the increase both of the human family
and of your own family born in baptism.

You are the loving Father of the world of nature;
you are the loving Father of the new creation of grace.
In Christian marriage you bring together the two orders of
    creation:
nature's gift of children enriches the world
and your grace enriches also your Church.

Through Christ the choirs of angels
and all the saints
praise and worship your glory.
May our voices blend with theirs
as we join in their unending hymn: **Holy, holy, holy . . .**

P73   PREFACE OF MARRIAGE II

Father, all-powerful and ever-living God,
we do well always and everywhere to give you thanks
through Jesus Christ our Lord.

Through him you entered into a new covenant with your people.
You restored man to grace in the saving mystery of redemption.
You gave him a share in the divine life
through his union with Christ.
You made him an heir of Christ's eternal glory.

This outpouring of love in the new covenant of grace
is symbolized in the marriage covenant
that seals the love of husband and wife
and reflects your divine plan of love.

And so, with the angels and all the saints in heaven
we proclaim your glory
and join in their unending hymn of praise: **Holy, holy, holy . . .**

P74 PREFACE OF MARRIAGE III

Father, all-powerful and ever-living God,
we do well always and everywhere to give you thanks.

You created man in love to share your divine life.
We see his high destiny in the love of husband and wife,
which bears the imprint of your own divine love.

Love is man's origin,
love is his constant calling,
love is his fulfilment in heaven.
The love of man and woman
is made holy in the sacrament of marriage,
and becomes the mirror of your everlasting love.

Through Christ the choirs of angels
and all the saints
praise and worship your glory.
May our voices blend with theirs
as we join in their unending hymn: **Holy, holy, holy . . .**

P77 PREFACE OF CHRISTIAN DEATH I

Father, all-powerful and ever-living God,
we do well always and everywhere to give you thanks
through Jesus Christ our Lord.

In him, who rose from the dead,
our hope of resurrection dawned.
The sadness of death gives way
to the bright promise of immortality.

Lord, for your faithful people life is changed, not ended.
When the body of our earthly dwelling lies in death
we gain an everlasting dwelling place in heaven.

And so, with all the choirs of angels in heaven
we proclaim your glory
and join in their unending hymn of praise: **Holy, holy, holy . . .**

P78 PREFACE OF CHRISTIAN DEATH II

Father, all-powerful and ever-living God,
we do well always and everywhere to give you thanks
through Jesus Christ our Lord.

He chose to die
that he might free all men from dying.
He gave his life
that we might live to you alone for ever.

In our joy we sing to your glory
with all the choirs of angels: **Holy, holy, holy . . .**

P79   PREFACE OF CHRISTIAN DEATH III

Father, all-powerful and ever-living God,
we do well always and everywhere to give you thanks
through Jesus Christ our Lord.

In him the world is saved,
man is reborn,
and the dead rise again to life.
Through Christ the angels of heaven
offer their prayer of adoration
as they rejoice in your presence for ever.
May our voices be one with theirs
in their triumphant hymn of praise: **Holy, holy, holy . . .**

P80   PREFACE OF CHRISTIAN DEATH IV

Father, all-powerful and ever-living God,
we do well always and everywhere to give you thanks.

By your power you bring us to birth.
By your providence you rule our lives.
By your command you free us at last from sin
as we return to the dust from which we came.
Through the saving death of your Son
we rise at your word to the glory of the resurrection.

Now we join the angels and the saints
as they sing their unending hymn of praise: **Holy, holy, holy . . .**

P81   PREFACE OF CHRISTIAN DEATH V

Father, all-powerful and ever-living God,
we do well always and everywhere to give you thanks
through Jesus Christ our Lord.

Death is the just reward for our sins,
yet, when at last we die,

your loving kindness calls us back to life
in company with Christ,
whose victory is our redemption.

Our hearts are joyful,
for we have seen your salvation,
and now with the angels and saints
we praise you for ever: **Holy, holy, holy . . .**

SOLEMN BLESSINGS

The blessings which are given here may be used at the end of
Mass, or after the liturgy of the word, the office, and the
celebration of the sacraments.

The blessings confined to certain Solemnities are given after
the principal Mass of such days.

Advent
You believe that the Son of God once came to us;
you look for him to come again.
May his coming bring you the light of his holiness
and free you with his blessing. ℟ **Amen.**

May God make you steadfast in faith,
joyful in hope, and untiring in love
all the days of your life. ℟ **Amen.**

You rejoice that our Redeemer came to live with us as man.
When he comes again in glory,
may he reward you with endless life. ℟ **Amen.**

May almighty God bless you,
the Father, and the Son, ✛ and the Holy Spirit. ℟ **Amen.**

Easter Season
Through the resurrection of his Son
God has redeemed you and made you his children.
May he bless you with joy. ℟ **Amen.**

The Redeemer has given you lasting freedom.
May you inherit his everlasting life. ℟ **Amen.**

By faith you rose with him in baptism.
May your lives be holy,
so that you will be united with him for ever. ℟ **Amen.**

May almighty God bless you,
the Father, and the Son, ✛ and the Holy Spirit. ℟ **Amen.**

Beginning of the New Year
Every good gift comes from the Father of light.
May he grant you his grace and every blessing,
and keep you safe throughout the coming year. **Amen.**
May he grant you unwavering faith,
constant hope, and love that endures to the end. **Amen.**

May he order your days and work in his peace,
hear your every prayer,
and lead you to everlasting life and joy. **Amen.**

May almighty God bless you,
the Father, and the Son, ✟ and the Holy Spirit. **Amen.**

The Holy Spirit
[This day] the Father of light
has enlightened the minds of the disciples
by the outpouring of the Holy Spirit.
May he bless you
and give you the gifts of the Spirit for ever. ℟ **Amen.**

May that fire which hovered over the disciples
as tongues of flame
burn out all evil from your hearts
and make them glow with pure light. ℟ **Amen.**

God inspired speech in different tongues
to proclaim one faith.
May he strengthen your faith
and fulfil your hope of seeing him face to face. ℟ **Amen.**

May almighty God bless you,
the Father, and the Son, ✟ and the Holy Spirit. ℟ **Amen.**

Ordinary Time I: Blessing of Aaron (Numbers 6:24-26)
May the Lord bless you and keep you.
℟ **Amen.**

May his face shine upon you,
and be gracious to you. ℟ **Amen.**

May he look upon you with kindness,
and give you his peace. ℟ **Amen.**

May almighty God bless you,
the Father, and the Son, ✟ and the Holy Spirit. ℟ **Amen.**

Ordinary Time II (Philippians 4:7)
May the peace of God
which is beyond all understanding
keep your hearts and minds
in the knowledge and love of God
and of his Son, our Lord Jesus Christ. ℟ **Amen.**

May almighty God bless you,
the Father, and the Son, ✟ and the Holy Spirit. ℟ **Amen.**

Ordinary Time III
May almighty God bless you in his mercy,
and make you always aware of his saving wisdom. ℞ **Amen.**

May he strengthen your faith with proofs of his love,
so that you will persevere in good works. ℞ **Amen.**

May he direct your steps to himself,
and show you how to walk in charity and peace. ℞ **Amen.**

May almighty God bless you,
the Father, and the Son, ✠ and the Holy Spirit. ℞ **Amen.**

Ordinary Time IV
May the God of all consolation
bless you in every way
and grant you peace all the days of your life. ℞ **Amen.**

May he free you from all anxiety
and strengthen your hearts in his love. ℞ **Amen.**

May he enrich you with his gifts of faith, hope, and love,
so that what you do in this life
will bring you to the happiness of everlasting life. ℞ **Amen.**

May almighty God bless you,
the Father, and the Son, ✠ and the Holy Spirit. ℞ **Amen.**

Ordinary Time V
May almighty God keep you from all harm
and bless you with every good gift. ℞ **Amen.**
May he set his Word in your heart
and fill you with lasting joy. ℞ **Amen.**

May you walk in his ways,
always knowing what is right and good,
until you enter your heavenly inheritance. ℞ **Amen.**

May almighty God bless you,
the Father, and the Son, ✠ and the Holy Spirit. ℞ **Amen.**

The Blessed Virgin Mary
Born of the Blessed Virgin Mary,
the Son of God redeemed mankind.
May he enrich you with his blessings. ℞ **Amen.**

You received the author of life through Mary.
May you always rejoice in her loving care.   R/   **Amen.**

You have come to rejoice at Mary's feast.
May you be filled with the joys of the Spirit
and the gifts of your eternal home.   R/   **Amen.**

May almighty God bless you,
the Father, and the Son, ✠ and the Holy Spirit.   R/   **Amen.**

Apostles

May God who founded his Church upon the apostles
bless you through the prayers of Saint N.   R/   **Amen.**

May God inspire you to follow the example of the apostles,
and give witness to the truth before all men.   R/   **Amen.**

The teaching of the apostles has strengthened your faith.
May their prayers lead you
to your true and eternal home.   R/   **Amen.**

May almighty God bless you,
the Father, and the Son, ✠ and the Holy Spirit.   R/   **Amen.**

Dedication of a Church

The Lord of earth and heaven
has assembled you before him this day
to dedicate this house of prayer
[to recall the dedication of this church].
May he fill you with the blessings of heaven.   R/   **Amen.**

God the Father wills that all his children
scattered throughout the world
become one family in his Son.
May he make you his temple,
the dwelling-place of his Holy Spirit.   R/   **Amen.**

May God free you from every bond of sin,
dwell within you and give you joy.
May you live with him for ever
in the company of all his saints.   R/   **Amen.**

May almighty God bless you,
the Father, and the Son, ✠ and the Holy Spirit.   R/   **Amen.**

The Dead

In his great love,
the God of all consolation gave man the gift of life.
May he bless you with faith
in the resurrection of his Son,
and with the hope of rising to new life.   ℟   **Amen.**

To us who are alive
may he grant forgiveness,
and to all who have died
a place of light and peace.   ℟   **Amen.**

As you believe that Jesus rose from the dead,
so may you live with him for ever in joy.   ℟   **Amen.**

May almighty God bless you,
the Father, and the Son, ✠ and the Holy Spirit.   ℟   **Amen.**

PRAYERS OVER THE PEOPLE

These always conclude with the blessing:

May almighty God bless you,
the Father, and the Son, ✝ and the Holy Spirit. ℟ **Amen.**

---

1 Lord,
   have mercy on your people.
   Grant us in this life the good things
   that lead to the everlasting life you prepare for us.
   We ask this through Christ our Lord. ℟ **Amen.**

2 Lord,
   grant your people your protection and grace.
   Give them health of mind and body,
   perfect love for one another,
   and make them always faithful to you.
   Grant this through Christ our Lord. ℟ **Amen.**

3 Lord,
   may all Christian people both know and cherish
   the heavenly gifts they have received.
   We ask this in the name of Jesus the Lord. ℟ **Amen.**

4 Lord,
   bless your people and make them holy
   so that avoiding evil,
   they may find you the fulfilment of their longing.
   We ask this through Christ our Lord. ℟ **Amen.**

5 Lord,
   bless and strengthen your people.
   May they remain faithful to you
   and always rejoice in your mercy.
   We ask this in the name of Jesus the Lord. ℟ **Amen.**

6 Lord,
   you care for your people even when they stray.
   Grant us a complete change of heart,
   so that we may follow you with greater fidelity.
   Grant this through Christ our Lord. ℟ **Amen.**

7   Lord,
    send your light upon your family.
    May they continue to enjoy your favour
    and devote themselves to doing good.
    We ask this through Christ our Lord.   R⁄ **Amen.**

8   Lord,
    we rejoice that you are our creator and ruler.
    As we call upon your generosity,
    renew and keep us in your love.
    Grant this through Christ our Lord.   R⁄ **Amen.**

9   Lord,
    we pray for your people who believe in you.
    May they enjoy the gift of your love,
    share it with others,
    and spread it everywhere.
    We ask this in the name of Jesus the Lord.   R⁄ **Amen.**

10 Lord,
    bless your people who hope for your mercy.
    Grant that they may receive
    the things they ask for at your prompting.
    Grant this through Christ our Lord.   R⁄ **Amen.**

11 Lord,
    bless us with your heavenly gifts,
    and in your mercy make us ready to do your will.
    We ask this through Christ our Lord.   R⁄ **Amen.**

12 Lord,
    protect your people always,
    that they may be free from every evil
    and serve you with all their hearts.
    We ask this through Christ our Lord.   R⁄ **Amen.**

13 Lord,
    help your people to seek you with all their hearts
    and to deserve what you promise.
    Grant this through Christ our Lord.   R⁄ **Amen.**

14 Father,
    help your people to rejoice in the mystery of redemption
    and to win its reward.
    We ask this in the name of Jesus the Lord.   R⁄ **Amen.**

15 Lord,
    have pity on your people;
    help them each day to avoid what displeases you
    and grant that they may serve you with joy.
    We ask this through Christ our Lord.   ℟ **Amen.**

16 Lord,
    care for your people and purify them.
    Console them in this life
    and bring them to the life to come.
    We ask this in the name of Jesus the Lord.   ℟ **Amen.**

17 Father,
    look with love upon your people,
    the love which our Lord Jesus Christ showed us
    when he delivered himself to evil men
    and suffered the agony of the cross,
    for he is Lord for ever.   ℟ **Amen.**

18 Lord,
    grant that your faithful people
    may continually desire to relive the mystery of the eucharist
    and so be reborn to lead a new life.
    We ask this through Christ our Lord.   ℟ **Amen.**

19 Lord God,
    in your great mercy,
    enrich your people with your grace
    and strengthen them by your blessing
    so that they may praise you always.
    Grant this through Christ our Lord.   ℟ **Amen.**

20 May God bless you with every good gift from on high.
    May he keep you pure and holy in his sight at all times.
    May he bestow the riches of his grace upon you,
    bring you the good news of salvation,
    and always fill you with love for all men.
    We ask this through Christ our Lord.   ℟ **Amen.**

21 Lord,
    make us pure in mind and body,
    that we will avoid all evil pleasures
    and always delight in you.
    We ask this in the name of Jesus the Lord.   ℟ **Amen.**

22 Lord,
bless your people and fill them with zeal.
Strengthen them by your love to do your will.
We ask this through Christ our Lord. ℟ **Amen.**

23 Lord,
come, live in your people
and strengthen them by your grace.
Help them to remain close to you in prayer
and give them a true love for one another.
Grant this through Christ our Lord. ℟ **Amen.**

24 Father,
look kindly on your children who put their trust in you;
bless them and keep them from all harm,
strengthen them against the attacks of the devil.
May they never offend you
but seek to love you in all they do.
We ask this through Christ our Lord. ℟ **Amen.**

Feasts of saints

25 God our Father,
may all Christian people rejoice in the glory of your saints.
Give us fellowship with them
and unending joy in your kingdom.
We ask this in the name of Jesus the Lord. ℟ **Amen.**

26 Lord,
you have given us many friends in heaven.
Through their prayers we are confident
that you will watch over us always
and fill our hearts with your love.
Grant this through Christ our Lord. ℟ **Amen.**

LATIN TEXTS
for the People's parts of the Ordinary of the Mass

Introductory Rites

In nómine Patris, et Fílii, et Spíritus Sancti.
Amen.
<or

Dóminus vobíscum
(or another greeting)
Et cum spíritu tuo.

Confiteor

**Confíteor Deo omnipoténti et vobis, fratres,
quia peccávi nimis
cogitatióne, verbo, ópere et omissióne:
mea culpa, mea culpa, mea máxima culpa.
Ideo precor beátam Maríam semper Vírginem,
omnes Angelos et Sanctos,
et vos, fratres, oráre pro me
ad Dóminum Deum nostrum.**

Kyrie

C Kyrie, eléison.   P **Kyrie, eléison.**
C Christe, eléison.   P **Christe, eléison.**
C Kyrie, eléison.   P **Kyrie, eléison.**

Gloria

**Glória in excélsis Deo
  et in terra pax homínibus bonæ voluntátis.
Laudámus te,
  benedícimus te,
  adorámus te,
  glorificámus te,
  grátias ágimus tibi propter magnam glóriam tuam,
Dómine Deus, Rex cæléstis,
  Deus Pater omnípotens.
Dómine Fili unigénite, Iesu Christe,
Dómine Deus, Agnus Dei, Fílius Patris,
qui tollis peccáta mundi, miserére nobis;
qui tollis peccáta mundi,
súscipe deprecatiónem nostram.
Qui sedes ad déxteram Patris, miserére nobis.
Quóniam tu solus Sanctus, tu solus Dóminus,
  tu solus Altíssimus,
Iesu Christe, cum Sancto Spíritu: in glória Dei Patris.
Amen.**

After the first and second readings
Deo grátias.

Before the Gospel
C Dóminus vobíscum.   P **Et cum spíritu tuo.**
C Léctio sancti Evangélii secúndum N.   P **Glória tibi, Dómine.**

At the end of the Gospel
C Verbum Dómini.   P **Laus tibi, Christe.**

Creed
Credo in unum Deum,
Patrem omnipoténtem, factórem cæli et terræ,
    visibílium ómnium et invisibílium.
Et in unum Dóminum Iesum Christum,
Fílium Dei unigénitum,
    et ex Patre natum ante ómnia sæcula.
Deum de Deo, lumen de lúmine,
    Deum verum de Deo vero,
    génitum, non factum, consubstantiálem Patrí:
    per quem ómnia facta sunt.
Qui propter nos hómines
    et propter nostram salútem
    descéndit de cælis.
Et incarnátus est de Spíritu Sancto
    ex María Vírgine, et homo factus est.
Crucifíxus étiam pro nobis sub Póntio Piláto;
    passus et sepúltus est,
    et resurréxit tértia die, secúndum Scriptúras,
    et ascéndit in cælum, sedet ad déxteram Patris.
Et íterum ventúrus est cum glória,
    iudicáre vivos et mórtuos,
    cuius regni non erit finis.
Et in Spíritum Sanctum, Dóminum et vivificántem:
    qui ex Patre Filióque procédit.
Qui cum Patre et Fílio simul adorátur
    et conglorificátur:
    qui locútus est per prophétas.
Et unam, sanctam,
    cathólicam et apostólicam Ecclésiam.
Confíteor unum baptísma in remissiónem peccatórum.
Et exspécto resurrectiónem mortuórum,
    et vítam ventúri sæculi. Amen.

Response to offertory prayers
Benedíctus Deus in sǽcula.

Response to the Orate Fratres
**Suscípiat Dóminus sacrifícum de mánibus tuis
ad laudem et glóriam nóminis sui,
ad utilitátem quoque nostram
totiúsque Ecclésiæ suæ sanctæ.**

Dialogue before the Preface
C Dóminus vobíscum.
P **Et cum spíritu tuo.**
C Sursum corda.
P **Habémus ad Dóminum.**
C Grátias agámus Dómino Deo nostro.
P **Dignum et iustum est.**

Holy, holy, holy . . .
Sanctus, Sanctus, Sanctus Dóminus Deus Sabaoth.
　Pleni sunt cæli et terra glória tua.
　Hosánna in excélsis.
Benedíctus qui venit in nómine Dómini.

Acclamation after the Consecration
<1 **Mortem tuam annuntiámus, Dómine,
et tuam resurrectiónem confitémur, donec vénias.**

<2 **Quotiescúmque manducámus panem hunc
et cálicem bíbimus,
mortem tuam annuntiámus, Dómine, donec vénias.**

<3 **Salvátor mundi, salva nos,
qui per crucem et resurrectiónem tuam liberásti nos.**

Our Father
C 　Præcéptis salutáribus móniti,
　　　et divína institutióne formáti,
　　audémus dicere:
All **Pater noster, qui es in cælis:
　sanctificétur nomen tuum;
　　advéniat regnum tuum;
　fiat volúntas tua, sicut in cælo, et in terra.
　Panem nostrum cotidiánum da nobis hódie;
　et dimítte nobis débita nostra,
　　sicut et nos dimíttimus debitóribus nostris;
　et ne nos indúcas in tentatiónem;
　　sed líbera nos a malo.**

Acclamation after the Our Father

Quia tuum est regnum,
et potéstas, et glória
in sǽcula.

At the Pax
C Pax Dómini sit semper vobíscum.
P **Et cum spíritu tuo.**

Lamb of God
Agnus Dei, qui tollis peccáta mundi:
   miserére nobis.
Agnus Dei, qui tollis peccáta mundi:
   miserére nobis.
Agnus Dei, qui tollis peccáta mundi:
   dona nobis pacem.

Lord, I am not worthy
Domine, non sum dignus ut intres sub tectum meum; sed
tantum dic verbo, et sanabitur anima mea.

At the Prayer after Communion
C Dóminus vobíscum.
P **Et cum spíritu tuo.**
   Oremus.
At the conclusion of the Prayer:
P **Amen.**

At the Conclusion
C Dóminus vobíscum.
P **Et cum spíritu tuo.**
C Benedícat vos omnípotens Deus,
Pater, et Fílius, ✠ et Spíritus Sanctus.
P **Amen.**
C Ite, missa est.
P **Deo grátias.**

PRAYERS
THANKSGIVING AFTER MASS

With gratitude in your hearts sing psalms and hymns and inspired songs to God. *Colossians 3:16*

Go on singing and chanting to the Lord in your hearts, so that always and everywhere you are giving thanks to God who is our Father in the name of our Lord Jesus Christ. *Ephesians 5:19–20*

Pray constantly, and for all things give thanks to God, because this is what God expects you to do in Christ Jesus.

1 Thessalonians 5:18

From the Didache
As regards the Eucharist, give thanks first, for the cup:
We thank you, Father,
for the holy vine of David, your servant,
which you have made known to us
through your servant, Jesus.
To you be glory for ever!

And for the broken bread:
We thank you, Father,
for the life and knowledge
which you have made known to us
through your servant, Jesus.
To you be glory for ever!

In the same way that this bread which is now broken
was scattered upon the mountains,
and was gathered up again, to become one,
so may your Church be gathered together
from the ends of the earth into your kingdom,
for yours is the glory and the power
through Jesus Christ for ever.

And, after you are filled, give thanks in this manner:
We thank you, Holy Father, for your holy name,
which you have made to dwell in our hearts,
and for the knowledge, faith and immortality
which you have made known to us
through your servant, Jesus.
To you be glory for ever!

1st or 2nd century

Prayer of St Thomas Aquinas

I give you thanks,
Lord, holy Father, everlasting God.
In your great mercy,
you have fed me, a sinner and your unworthy servant,
with the precious Body and Blood of your Son,
our Lord Jesus Christ.
I pray that this holy communion
may not serve as my judgement and condemnation,
but as my forgiveness and salvation.
May it be my armour of faith
and shield of good purpose.
May it root out in me all vice and evil desires,
increase my love and patience,
humility and obedience,
and every virtue.
Make it a firm defence
against the wiles of all my enemies, seen and unseen,
while restraining all evil impulses of flesh and spirit.
May it help me to cleave to you, the one true God,
and bring me a blessed death when you call.
I beseech you to bring me, a sinner,
to that great feast where,
with your Son and the Holy Spirit,
you are the true light of your holy ones,
their flawless blessedness,
everlasting joy,
and perfect happiness.
Through Christ our Lord. Amen.

Anima Christi

Soul of Christ, sanctify me,
Body of Christ, save me,
Blood of Christ, inebriate me,
Water from the side of Christ, wash me,
Passion of Christ, strengthen me.
O good Jesus, hear me.
Within your wounds hide me.
Let me not be separated from you,
From the malicious enemy defend me,
In the hour of my death call me
And bid me come to you,

That with your saints I may praise you
For ever and ever. Amen.

O Sacrum Convivium
At this sacred banquet in which Christ is received,
the memory of his passion is renewed,
our lives are filled with grace
and a promise of future glory is given to us.

Adoro Te
Godhead here in hiding, whom I do adore
Masked by these bare shadows, shape and nothing more,
See, Lord, at thy service low lies here a heart
Lost, all lost in wonder at the God thou art.

Seeing, touching, tasting are in thee deceived;
How says trusty hearing? That shall be believed;
What God's Son has told me, take for truth I do;
Truth himself speaks truly or there's nothing true.

On the cross thy godhead made no sign to men;
Here thy very manhood steals from human ken:
Both are my confession, both are my belief,
And I pray the prayer of the dying thief.

O thou our reminder of Christ cruficied,
Living Bread, the life of us for whom he died,
Lend this life to me then: feed and feast my mind,
There be thou the sweetness man was meant to find.

Jesus whom I look at shrouded here below,
I beseech thee send me what I thirst for so,
Some day to gaze on thee face to face in light
And be blest for ever with thy glory's sight.

Tr Gerard Manley Hopkins

For prayers of preparation for Mass, turn to pp.21ff.
For other prayers, turn to pp.1069.

O KEY OF DAVID OPEN GATES OF LIFE

THE SEASON OF ADVENT

FIRST SUNDAY OF ADVENT   A

The Day Of The Lord

Today we rejoice that the night of our long pilgrimage to God's eternal city, the new Jerusalem, will soon be over. The Lord's unending Day is dawning. Already, in the words of Isaiah, we see 'the mountain of the Temple of the Lord' etched against the eastern sky. Let us wake up and stand ready.

Entrance Antiphon: To you, my God, I lift my soul, I trust in you; let me never come to shame. Do not let my enemies laugh at me. No one who waits for you is ever put to shame.

The Gloria is omitted.

Opening Prayer
Let us pray
  [that we may take Christ's coming seriously]

All-powerful God,
increase our strength of will for doing good
that Christ may find an eager welcome at his coming
and call us to his side in the kingdom of heaven
where he lives and reigns with you and the Holy Spirit,
one God, for ever and ever.

or

Let us pray
  [in Advent time
  with longing and waiting
  for the coming of the Lord]

Father in heaven,
our hearts desire the warmth of your love
and our minds are searching for the light of your Word.

Increase our longing for Christ our Saviour
and give us the strength to grow in love,
that the dawn of his coming
may find us rejoicing in his presence
and welcoming the light of his truth.

FIRST READING

A reading from the prophet Isaiah   2:1-5

*The Lord gathers all nations together into the eternal peace of God's
kingdom.*

The vision of Isaiah son of Amoz, concerning Judah and
Jerusalem.

In the days to come
the mountain of the Temple of the Lord
shall tower above the mountains
and be lifted higher than the hills.
All the nations will stream to it,
peoples without number will come to it; and they will say:

  'Come, let us go up to the mountain of the Lord,
  to the Temple of the God of Jacob
  that he may teach us his ways
  so that we may walk in his paths;
  since the Law will go out from Zion,
  and the oracle of the Lord from Jerusalem.'

He will wield authority over the nations
and adjudicate between many peoples;
these will hammer their swords into ploughshares,
their spears into sickles.
Nation will not lift sword against nation,
there will be no more training for war.

O House of Jacob, come,
let us walk in the light of the Lord.

This is the word of the Lord.

Responsorial Psalm   Ps 121:1-2.4-5. 6-9. ℟ cf. v.1
℟   **I rejoiced when I heard them say:**
'Let us go to God's house.'

1   I rejoiced when I heard them say:
'Let us go to God's house.'
And now our feet are standing
within your gates, O Jerusalem.   ℟

2   It is there that the tribes go up,
the tribes of the Lord.
For Israel's law it is,
there to praise the Lord's name.
There were set the thrones of judgement
of the house of David.   ℟

3   For the peace of Jerusalem pray:
'Peace be to your homes!
May peace reign in your walls,
in your palaces, peace!'   ℟

4   For love of my brethren and friends
I say: 'Peace upon you!'
For love of the house of the Lord
I will ask for your good.   ℟

SECOND READING
A reading from the letter of St Paul to the Romans   13:11-14
Our salvation is near.

You know 'the time' has come: you must wake up now: our
salvation is even nearer than it was when we were converted.
The night is almost over, it will be daylight soon – let us give up
all the things we prefer to do under cover of the dark; let us arm
ourselves and appear in the light. Let us live decently as people
do in the daytime: no drunken orgies, no promiscuity or licent-
iousness, and no wrangling or jealousy. Let your armour be the
Lord Jesus Christ.

This is the word of the Lord.

Gospel Acclamation Ps 84:8
Alleluia, alleluia!
Let us see, O Lord, your mercy
and give us your saving help.
Alleluia!

GOSPEL

A reading from the holy Gospel according to Matthew 24:37-44
Stay awake so that you may be ready.

Jesus said to his disciples: 'As it was in Noah's day, so will it be
when the Son of Man comes. For in those days before the Flood
people were eating, drinking, taking wives, taking husbands,
right up to the day Noah went into the ark, and they suspected
nothing till the Flood came and swept all away. It will be like this
when the Son of Man comes. Then of two men in the fields one is
taken, one left; of two women at the millstone grinding, one is
taken, one left.

'So stay awake, because you do not know the day when your
master is coming. You may be quite sure of this that if the
householder had known at what time of the night the burglar
would come, he would have stayed awake and would not have
allowed anyone to break through the wall of his house. Therefore, you too must stand ready because the Son of Man is
coming at an hour you do not expect.'

This is the Gospel of the Lord.

Prayer over the Gifts
Father,
from all you give us
we present this bread and wine.
As we serve you now,
accept our offering
and sustain us with your promise of eternal life.

Preface of Advent I, P1

Communion Antiphon: The Lord will shower his gifts, and our land
will yield its fruit.

Prayer after Communion
Father,
may our communion
teach us to love heaven.
May its promise and hope
guide our way on earth.

An appropriate Solemn Blessing or Prayer over the People may be used. See pp.90ff.

SECOND SUNDAY OF ADVENT   A

Our Baptism With The Holy Spirit And Fire

May the Lord who gave us this baptism purify us in our celebration today; for he can brook nothing that lacks integrity and truth. Then, through the Spirit of our baptism, united in heart and voice, we will be able to give glory to the God and Father of our Lord Jesus Christ.

Entrance Antiphon: People of Zion, the Lord will come to save all nations, and your hearts will exult to hear his majestic voice.

The Gloria is omitted.

Opening Prayer
Let us pray
   [that nothing may hinder us
   from receiving Christ with joy]

God of power and mercy,
open our hearts in welcome.
Remove the things that hinder us from receiving Christ with joy,
so that we may share his wisdom
and become one with him
when he comes in glory,
for he lives and reigns with you and the Holy Spirit,
one God, for ever and ever.

or

Let us pray
   [in Advent time
   for the coming Saviour to teach us wisdom]

Father in heaven,
the day draws near when the glory of your Son
will make radiant the night of the waiting world.

May the lure of greed not impede us from the joy
which moves the hearts of those who seek him.
May the darkness not blind us
to the vision of wisdom
which fills the minds of those who find him.

FIRST READING

A reading from the prophet Isaiah
He judges the wretched with integrity.   11:1-10

A shoot springs from the stock of Jesse,
a scion thrusts from his roots:
on him the spirit of the Lord rests,
a spirit of wisdom and insight,
a spirit of counsel and power,
a spirit of knowledge and of the fear of the Lord.
(The fear of the Lord is his breath.)
He does not judge by appearances,
he gives no verdict on hearsay,
but judges the wretched with integrity,
and with equity gives a verdict for the poor of the land.
His word is a rod that strikes the ruthless;
his sentences bring death to the wicked.

Integrity is the loincloth round his waist,
faithfulness the belt about his hips.

The wolf lives with the lamb,
the panther lies down with the kid,
calf and lion cub feed together
with a little boy to lead them.
The cow and the bear make friends,
their young lie down together.
The lion eats straw like the ox.
The infant plays over the cobra's hole;
into the viper's lair
the young child puts his hand.
They do no hurt, no harm,
on all my holy mountain,
for the country is filled with the knowledge of the Lord
as the waters swell the sea.
That day, the root of Jesse
shall stand as a signal to the peoples.
It will be sought out by the nations
and its home will be glorious.

This is the word of the Lord.

Responsorial Psalm   Ps 71:1-2. 7-8. 12-13. 17. ℟ cf.v.7

℟ **In his days justice shall flourish
and peace till the moon fails.**

1 O God, give your judgement to the king,
    to a king's son your justice,
    that he may judge your people in justice
    and your poor in right judgement. ℟

2 In his days justice shall flourish
    and peace till the moon fails.
    He shall rule from sea to sea,
    from the Great River to earth's bounds. ℟

3 For he shall save the poor when they cry
    and the needy who are helpless.
    He will have pity on the weak
    and save the lives of the poor. ℟

4 May his name be blessed for ever
    and endure like the sun.
    Every tribe shall be blessed in him,
    all nations bless his name. ℟

SECOND READING

A reading from the letter of St Paul to the Romans   15:4-9
Christ is the saviour of all men.

Everything that was written long ago in the scriptures was meant
to teach us something about hope from the examples scripture
gives of how people who did not give up were helped by God.
And may he who helps us when we refuse to give up, help you
all to be tolerant with each other, following the example of Christ
Jesus, so that united in mind and voice you may give glory to the
God and Father of our Lord Jesus Christ.

   It can only be to God's glory, then, for you to treat each other
in the same friendly way as Christ treated you. The reason Christ
became the servant of circumcised Jews was not only so that God
could faithfully carry out the promises made to the patriarchs, it
was also to get the pagans to give glory to God for his mercy, as
scripture says in one place: For this I shall praise you among the
pagans and sing your name.

   This is the word of the Lord.

Gospel Acclamation Lk 3:4. 6
Alleluia, alleluia!
Prepare a way for the Lord,
make his paths straight,
and all mankind shall see the salvation of God.
Alleluia!

GOSPEL

A reading from the holy Gospel according to Matthew 3:1-12
Repent, for the kingdom of heaven is close at hand.

In due course John the Baptist appeared; he preached in the wilderness of Judaea and this was his message: 'Repent, for the kingdom of heaven is close at hand.' This was the man the prophet Isaiah spoke of when he said:

A voice cries in the wilderness:
Prepare a way for the Lord,
make his paths straight.

This man John wore a garment made of camel-hair with a leather belt round his waist, and his food was locusts and wild honey. Then Jerusalem and all Judaea and the whole Jordan district made their way to him, and as they were baptised by him in the river Jordan they confessed their sins. But when he saw a number of Pharisees and Sadducees coming for baptism he said to them, 'Brood of vipers, who warned you to fly from the retribution that is coming? But if you are repentant, produce the appropriate fruit, and do not presume to tell yourselves, "We have Abraham for our father," because, I tell you, God can raise children for Abraham from these stones. Even now the axe is laid to the roots of the trees, so that any tree which fails to produce good fruit will be cut down and thrown on the fire. I baptise you in water for repentance, but the one who follows me is more powerful than I am, and I am not fit to carry his sandals; he will baptise you with the Holy Spirit and fire. His winnowing-fan is in his hand; he will clear his threshing-floor and gather his wheat into the barn; but the chaff he will burn in a fire that will never go out.'

This is the Gospel of the Lord.

Prayer over the Gifts
Lord,
we are nothing without you.

As you sustain us with your mercy,
receive our prayers and offerings.

Preface of Advent I, P1

Communion Antiphon: Rise up, Jerusalem, stand on the heights,
and see the joy that is coming to you from God.

Prayer after Communion
Father,
you give us food from heaven.
By our sharing in this mystery,
teach us to judge wisely the things of earth
and to love the things of heaven.

An appropriate Solemn Blessing or Prayer over the People may
be used. See pp.90ff.

THIRD SUNDAY OF ADVENT   A

The Joy Of Expectancy

*At his coming Christ fulfilled the expectations of the prophets. He made
the blind see again, the lame walk, and the lepers clean. We must not lose
heart in face of all the evils of the world, for we too have a glorious
expectation.*
Come, Lord Jesus, and save us.

Entrance Antiphon: Rejoice in the Lord always; again I say, rejoice!
The Lord is near.

The Gloria is omitted.

Opening Prayer
Let us pray
    [that God will fill us with joy
    at the coming of Christ]

Lord God,
may we, your people,
who look forward to the birthday of Christ
experience the joy of salvation
and celebrate that feast with love and thanksgiving.

or
Let us pray
     [this Advent
     for joy and hope in the coming Lord]

Father of our Lord Jesus Christ,
ever faithful to your promises
and ever close to your Church:
the earth rejoices in hope of the Saviour's coming
and looks forward with longing
to his return at the end of time.

Prepare our hearts and remove the sadness
that hinders us from feeling the joy and hope
which his presence will bestow,
for he is Lord for ever and ever.

FIRST READING

A reading from the prophet Isaiah   35:1-6. 10
God himself is coming to save you.

Let the wilderness and the dry-lands exult,
let the wasteland rejoice and bloom,
let it bring forth flowers like the jonquil,
let it rejoice and sing for joy.

The glory of Lebanon is bestowed on it,
the splendour of Carmel and Sharon;
they shall see the glory of the Lord,
the splendour of our God.

Strengthen all weary hands,
steady all trembling knees
and say to all faint hearts,
'Courage! Do not be afraid.

'Look your God is coming,
vengeance is coming,
the retribution of God;
he is coming to save you.'

Then the eyes of the blind shall be opened,
the ears of the deaf unsealed,
then the lame shall leap like a deer
and the tongues of the dumb sing for joy,
for those the Lord has ransomed shall return.

They will come to Zion shouting for joy,
everlasting joy on their faces;
joy and gladness will go with them
and sorrow and lament be ended.

This is the word of the Lord.

Responsorial Psalm   Ps 145:6-10. R̸ cf. Is 35:4
   R̸ **Come, Lord, and save us.**

or

   R̸ **Alleluia!**

1   It is the Lord who keeps faith for ever,
     who is just to those who are oppressed.
     It is he who gives bread to the hungry,
     the Lord, who sets prisoners free.   R̸

2   It is the Lord who gives sight to the blind,
     who raises up those who are bowed down,
     the Lord, who protects the stranger
     and upholds the widow and orphan.   R̸

3   It is the Lord who loves the just
     but thwarts the path of the wicked.
     The Lord will reign for ever,
     Zion's God, from age to age.   R̸

SECOND READING
A reading from the letter of St James   5:7-10
Do not lose heart, because the Lord's coming will be soon.

Be patient, brothers, until the Lord's coming. Think of a farmer:
how patiently he waits for the precious fruit of the ground until it
has had the autumn rains and the spring rains! You too have to
be patient; do not lose heart, because the Lord's coming will be
soon. Do not make complaints against one another, brothers, so
as not to be brought to judgement yourselves; the Judge is
already to be seen waiting at the gates. For your example,
brothers, in submitting with patience, take the prophets who
spoke in the name of the Lord.

This is the word of the Lord.

Gospel Acclamation   Is 61:1 (Lk 4:18)
  Alleluia, alleluia!
  The spirit of the Lord has been given to me.
  He has sent me to bring good news to the poor.
  Alleluia!

GOSPEL

A reading from the holy Gospel according to Matthew   11:2-11
Are you the one who is to come, or have we got to wait for someone else?

John in his prison had heard what Christ was doing and he sent
his disciples to ask him, 'Are you the one who is to come, or have
we got to wait for someone else?' Jesus answered, 'Go back and
tell John what you hear and see; the blind see again, and the lame
walk, lepers are cleansed, and the deaf hear, and the dead are
raised to life and the Good News is proclaimed to the poor; and
happy is the man who does not lose faith in me.'

As the messengers were leaving, Jesus began to talk to the
people about John: 'What did you go out into the wilderness to
see? A reed swaying in the breeze? No? Then what did you go
out to see? A man wearing fine clothes? Oh no, those who wear
fine clothes are to be found in palaces. Then what did you go out
for? To see a prophet? Yes, I tell you, and much more than a
prophet: he is the one of whom scripture says: Look, I am going
to send my messenger before you; he will prepare your way
before you. I tell you solemnly, of all the children born of
women, a greater than John the Baptist has never been seen; yet
the least in the kingdom of heaven is greater than he is.'

This is the Gospel of the Lord.

Prayer over the Gifts
Lord,
may the gift we offer in faith and love
be a continual sacrifice in your honour
and truly become our eucharist and our salvation.

Preface of Advent I or II, P1 or P2

Communion Antiphon: Say to the anxious: be strong and fear not,
our God will come to save us.

Prayer after Communion
God of mercy,
may this eucharist bring us your divine help,

free us from our sins,
and prepare us for the birthday of our Saviour,
who is Lord for ever and ever.

An appropriate Solemn Blessing or Prayer over the People may
be used. See pp.90ff.

FOURTH SUNDAY OF ADVENT   A
Mary's Child: The Emmanuel

*God's choice rested on the House of David which was to bring forth the
Emmanuel, the God-with-us. But Mary's Child was to belong to all the
nations. We are one of those nations who, by God's call, belong to Jesus
Christ.*

Entrance Antiphon: Let the clouds rain down the Just One, and the
earth bring forth a Saviour.

The Gloria is omitted.

Opening Prayer
Let us pray
 [as Advent draws to a close,
  that Christ will truly come into our hearts]

Lord,
fill our hearts with your love,
and as you revealed to us by an angel
the coming of your Son as man,
so lead us through his suffering and death
to the glory of his resurrection,
for he lives and reigns with you and the Holy Spirit,
one God, for ever and ever.

 or

Let us pray
 [as Advent draws to a close
  for the faith that opens our lives
  to the Spirit of God]

Father, all-powerful God,
your eternal Word took flesh on our earth
when the Virgin Mary placed her life
at the service of your plan.

Lift our minds in watchful hope
to hear the voice which announces his glory
and open our minds to receive the Spirit
who prepares us for his coming.

FIRST READING

A reading from the prophet Isaiah   7:10-14
The maiden is with child.

The Lord spoke to Ahaz and said, 'Ask the Lord your God for a
sign for yourself coming either from the depths of Sheol or from
the heights above.' 'No,' Ahaz answered 'I will not put the Lord
to the test.'

Then Isaiah said:

'Listen now, House of David:
are you not satisfied with trying the patience of men
without trying the patience of my God, too?
The Lord himself, therefore,
will give you a sign.
It is this: the maiden is with child
and will soon give birth to a son
whom she will call Emmanuel,
a name which means "God-is-with-us".'

This is the word of the Lord.

Responsorial Psalm   Ps 23:1-6. R̷ cf. vv.7. 10
    R̷ **Let the Lord enter!**
       He is the king of glory.

1 The Lord's is the earth and its fullness,
   the world and all its peoples.
   It is he who set it on the seas;
   on the waters he made it firm.   R̷

2 Who shall climb the mountain of the Lord?
   Who shall stand in his holy place?
   The man with clean hands and pure heart,
   who desires not worthless things.   R̷

3 He shall receive blessings from the Lord
   and reward from the God who saves him.
   Such are the men who seek him,
   seek the face of the God of Jacob.   R̷

SECOND READING

A reading from the letter of St Paul to the Romans 1:1-7

Jesus Christ, descendant of David, Son of God.

From Paul, a servant of Christ Jesus who has been called to be an apostle, and specially chosen to preach the Good News that God promised long ago through his prophets in the scriptures.

This news is about the Son of God, who, according to the human nature he took, was a descendant of David: it is about Jesus Christ our Lord who, in the order of the spirit, the spirit of holiness that was in him, was proclaimed Son of God in all his power through his resurrection from the dead. Through him we received grace and our apostolic mission to preach the obedience of faith to all pagan nations in honour of his name. You are one of these nations, and by his call belong to Jesus Christ. To you all, then, who are God's beloved in Rome, called to be saints, may God our Father and the Lord Jesus Christ send grace and peace.

This is the word of the Lord.

Gospel Acclamation Mt 1:23
    Alleluia, alleluia!
    The virgin will conceive and give birth to a son
    and they will call him Emmanuel,
    a name which means 'God-is-with-us'.
    Alleluia!

GOSPEL

A reading from the holy Gospel according to Matthew 1:18-24

Jesus is born of Mary who was betrothed to Joseph, son of David.

This is how Jesus Christ came to be born. His mother Mary was betrothed to Joseph; but before they came to live together she was found to be with child through the Holy Spirit. Her husband Joseph, being a man of honour and wanting to spare her publicity, decided to divorce her informally. He had made up his mind to do this when the angel of the Lord appeared to him in a dream, and said 'Joseph son of David, do not be afraid to take Mary home as your wife, because she has conceived what is in her by the Holy Spirit. She will give birth to a son and you must name him Jesus, because he is the one who is to save his people from their sins.' Now all this took place to fulfil the words spoken by the Lord through the prophet:

The virgin will conceive and give birth to a son
and they will call him Emmanuel,

a name which means 'God-is-with-us'. When Joseph woke up he
did what the angel of the Lord had told him to do: he took his
wife to his home.

This is the Gospel of the Lord.

Prayer over the Gifts
Lord,
may the power of the Spirit,
which sanctified Mary the mother of your Son,
make holy the gifts we place upon this altar.
Preface of Advent II, P2

Communion Antiphon: The Virgin is with child and shall bear a
son, and she will call him Emmanuel.

Prayer after Communion
Lord,
in this sacrament
we receive the promise of salvation;
as Christmas draws near
make us grow in faith and love
to celebrate the coming of Christ our Saviour,
who is Lord for ever and ever.

An appropriate Solemn Blessing or Prayer over the People may
be used. See pp.90ff.

THE SEASON OF CHRISTMAS

25 December

NATIVITY OF OUR LORD **A,B,C**

Solemnity

Vigil Mass

This Mass is celebrated during the afternoon of 24 December, before or after Evening Prayer I of Christmas.

Jesus, Son of David

God prepared the people of Israel to receive his Son. May we too be ready to welcome him.

Entrance Antiphon: Today you will know that the Lord is coming to save us, and in the morning you will see his glory.

Opening Prayer
Let us pray
   [that Christmas morning will find us at peace]

God our Father,
every year we rejoice
as we look forward to this feast of our salvation.
May we welcome Christ as our Redeemer,
and meet him with confidence when he comes to be our judge,
who lives and reigns . . .

   or

Let us pray
   [and be ready to welcome the Lord]

God of endless ages, Father of all goodness,
we keep vigil for the dawn of salvation
and the birth of your Son.

With gratitude we recall his humanity,
the life he shared with the sons of men.
May the power of his divinity
help us answer his call to forgiveness and life.

FIRST READING

A reading from the prophet Isaiah   62:1-5
The Lord takes delight in you.

About Zion I will not be silent,
about Jerusalem I will not grow weary,
until her integrity shines out like the dawn
and her salvation flames like a torch.
The nations then will see your integrity,
all the kings your glory,
and you will be called by a new name,
one which the mouth of the Lord will confer.
You are to be a crown of splendour in the hand of the Lord,
a princely diadem in the hand of your God;
no longer are you to be named 'Forsaken',
nor your land 'Abandoned',
but you shall be called 'My Delight'
and your land 'The Wedded';
for the Lord takes delight in you
and your land will have its wedding.
Like a young man marrying a virgin,
so will the one who built you wed you,
and as the bridegroom rejoices in his bride,
so will your God rejoice in you.

This is the word of the Lord.

Responsorial Psalm   Ps 88:4-5. 16-17. 27. 29. R℣ cf. v.2
   R℣ **I will sing for ever of your love, O Lord.**

1 'I have made a covenant with my chosen one;
   I have sworn to David my servant:
   I will establish your dynasty for ever
   and set up your throne through all ages.'   R℣

2 Happy the people who acclaim such a king,
   who walk, O Lord, in the light of your face,
   who find their joy every day in your name,
   who make your justice the source of their bliss.   R℣

3　'He will say to me: "You are my father,
　　my God, the rock who saves me."
　　I will keep my love for him always;
　　for him my covenant shall endure.'　℟

SECOND READING

A reading from the Acts of the Apostles　　　13:16-17. 22-25
Paul's witness to Christ, the son of David.

When Paul reached Antioch in Pisidia, he stood up in the
synagogue, held up a hand for silence and began to speak:

'Men of Israel, and fearers of God, listen! The God of our
nation Israel chose our ancestors, and made our people great
when they were living as foreigners in Egypt; then by divine
power he led them out.

'Then he made David their king, of whom he approved in
these words, "I have selected David son of Jesse, a man after my
own heart, who will carry out my whole purpose". To keep his
promise, God has raised up for Israel one of David's descendants, Jesus, as Saviour, whose coming was heralded by John
when he proclaimed a baptism of repentance for the whole
people of Israel. Before John ended his career he said, "I am not
the one you imagine me to be; that one is coming after me and I
am not fit to undo his sandal".'

　　This is the word of the Lord.

Gospel Acclamation
　　Alleluia, alleluia!
　　Tomorrow there will be an end to the sin of the world
　　and the saviour of the world will be our king.
　　Alleluia!

GOSPEL

A reading from the holy Gospel according to Matthew　　1:1-25
The ancestry of Jesus Christ, the son of David.

A genealogy of Jesus Christ, son of David, son of Abraham:
Abraham was the father of Isaac,
Isaac the father of Jacob,
Jacob was the father of Judah and his brothers,
Judah was the father of Perez and Zerah, Tamar being their
　　mother,
Perez was the father of Hezron,

Hezron the father of Ram,
Ram was the father of Amminadab,
Amminadab the father of Nahshon,
Nahshon the father of Salmon,
Salmon was the father of Boaz, Rahab being his mother,
Boaz was the father of Obed, Ruth being his mother,
Obed was the father of Jesse;
and Jesse was the father of King David.

David was the father of Solomon, whose mother had been
Uriah's wife,
Solomon was the father of Rehoboam,
Rehoboam the father of Abijah,
Abijah the father of Asa,
Asa was the father of Jehoshaphat,
Jehoshaphat the father of Joram,
Joram the father of Azariah,
Azariah was the father of Jotham,
Jotham the father of Ahaz,
Ahaz the father of Hezekiah,
Hezekiah was the father of Manasseh,
Manasseh the father of Amon,
Amon the father of Josiah;
and Josiah was the father of Jechoniah and his brothers.
Then the deportation to Babylon took place.

After the deportation to Babylon:
Jechoniah was the father to Shealtiel,
Shealtiel the father of Zerubbabel,
Zerubbabel was the father of Abiud,
Abiud the father of Eliakim,
Eliakim the father of Azor,
Azor was the father of Zadok,
Zadok the father of Achim,
Achim the father of Eliud,
Eliud was the father of Eleazar,
Eleazar the father of Matthan,
Matthan the father of Jacob;
and Jacob was the father of Joseph the husband of Mary; of her
was born Jesus who is called Christ.

   The sum of generations is therefore: fourteen from Abraham
to David; fourteen from David to the Babylonian deportation;
and fourteen from the Babylonian deportation to Christ.

* This is how Jesus Christ came to be born. His mother Mary was betrothed to Joseph; but before they came to live together she was found to be with child through the Holy Spirit. Her husband Joseph, being a man of honour and wanting to spare her publicity, decided to divorce her informally. He had made up his mind to do this when the angel of the Lord appeared to him in a dream and said, 'Joseph son of David, do not be afraid to take Mary home as your wife, because she has conceived what is in her by the Holy Spirit. She will give birth to a son and you must name him Jesus, because he is the one who is to save his people from their sins.' Now all this took place to fulfil the words spoken by the Lord through the prophet:

The Virgin will conceive and give birth to a son
and they will call him Emmanuel,

a name which means 'God-is-with-us'. When Joseph woke up he did what the angel of the Lord had told him to do: he took his wife to his home and, though he had not had intercourse with her, she gave birth to a son; and he named him Jesus.*

This is the Gospel of the Lord.*

*Shorter form, verses 18-25. Read between * *

In the Profession of Faith, all genuflect at *and was made man*.

Prayer over the Gifts

Lord,
as we keep tonight the vigil of Christmas,
may we celebrate this eucharist
with greater joy than ever
since it marks the beginning of our redemption.

Preface of Christmas I-III, P3-P5

Communion Antiphon: The glory of the Lord will be revealed, and all mankind will see the saving power of God.

Prayer after Communion

Father,
we ask you to give us a new birth
as we celebrate the beginning
of your Son's life on earth.
Strengthen us in spirit
as we take your food and drink.

The Christmas Solemn Blessing (see p.135 below), or an appropriate Prayer over the People may be used (see pp.95ff.).

Mass at Midnight

A Saviour Is Born For Us

Tonight we celebrate the birth of a Child who was to bring the joy of God's saving love to the whole world. And we make our own the jubilant cry of the angels: 'Glory to God in the highest.'

Entrance Antiphon: The Lord said to me: You are my Son; this day have I begotten you.

or

Let us all rejoice in the Lord, for our Saviour is born to the world. True peace has descended from heaven.

Opening Prayer

Let us pray
  [in the peace of Christmas midnight
  that our joy in the birth of Christ
  will last for ever]

Father,
you make this holy night radiant
with the splendour of Jesus Christ our light.
We welcome him as Lord, the true light of the world.
Bring us to eternal joy in the kingdom of heaven,
where he lives and reigns with you and the Holy Spirit,
one God, for ever and ever.

or

Let us pray
  [with joy and hope
  as we await the dawning of the Father's Word]

Lord our God,
with the birth of your Son,
your glory breaks on the world.

Through the night hours of the darkened earth
we your people watch for the coming of your promised Son.
As we wait, give us a foretaste of the joy that you will grant us
when the fullness of his glory has filled the earth.
who lives and reigns with you for ever and ever.

FIRST READING

A reading from the prophet Isaiah

9:1-7

A Son is given to us.

The people that walked in darkness
has seen a great light;
on those who live in a land of deep shadow
a light has shone.
You have made their gladness greater,
you have made their joy increase;
they rejoice in your presence
as men rejoice at harvest time,
as men are happy when they are dividing the spoils.
For the yoke that was weighing on him,
the bar across his shoulders,
the rod of his oppressor,
these you break as on the day of Midian.
For all the footgear of battle,
every cloak rolled in blood,
is burnt
and consumed by fire.
For there is a child born for us,
a son given to us
and dominion is laid on his shoulders;
and this is the name they give him:
Wonder-Counsellor, Mighty-God,
Eternal-Father, Prince-of-Peace.
Wide is his dominion
in a peace that has no end,
for the throne of David
and for his royal power,
which he establishes and makes secure
in justice and integrity.
From this time onwards and for ever,
the jealous love of the Lord of hosts will do this.

This is the word of the Lord.

Responsorial Psalm Ps 95:1-3. 11-13. ℟ Lk 2:11

℟ **Today a saviour has been born to us;
he is Christ the Lord.**

1 O sing a new song to the Lord,
sing to the Lord all the earth.
O sing to the Lord, bless his name. ℟

2 Proclaim his help day by day,
   tell among the nations his glory
   and his wonders among all the peoples.   ℟

3 Let the heavens rejoice and earth be glad,
   let the sea and all within it thunder praise,
   let the land and all it bears rejoice,
   all the trees of the wood shout for joy
   at the presence of the Lord for he comes,
   he comes to rule the earth.   ℟

4 With justice he will rule the world,
   he will judge the peoples with his truth.   ℟

SECOND READING

A reading from the letter of St Paul to Titus   2:11-14
God's grace has been revealed to the whole human race.

God's grace has been revealed, and it has made salvation possible for the whole human race and taught us that what we have to do is to give up everything that does not lead to God, and all our worldly ambitions; we must be self-restrained and live good and religious lives here in this present world, while we are waiting in hope for the blessing which will come with the Appearing of the glory of our great God and saviour Christ Jesus. He sacrificed himself for us in order to set us free from all wickedness and to purify a people so that it could be his very own and would have no ambition except to do good.

This is the word of the Lord.

Gospel Acclamation   Lk 2:10-11
   Alleluia, alleluia!
   I bring you news of great joy:
   today a saviour has been born to us, Christ the Lord.
   Alleluia!

GOSPEL

A reading from the holy Gospel according to Luke   2:1-14
Today a saviour has been born to you.

Caesar Augustus issued a decree for a census of the whole world to be taken. This census – the first – took place while Quirinius was governor of Syria, and everyone went to his own town to be

registered. So Joseph set out from the town of Nazareth in Galilee
and travelled up to Judaea, to the town of David called Bethlehem, since he was of David's House and line, in order to be
registered together with Mary, his betrothed, who was with
child. While they were there the time came for her to have her
child, and she gave birth to a son, her first-born. She wrapped
him in swaddling clothes, and laid him in a manger because there
was no room for them at the inn. In the countryside close by
there were shepherds who lived in the fields and took it in turns
to watch their flocks during the night. The angel of the Lord
appeared to them and the glory of the Lord shone round them.
They were terrified, but the angel said, 'Do not be afraid. Listen, I
bring you news of great joy, a joy to be shared by the whole
people. Today in the town of David a saviour has been born to
you; he is Christ the Lord. And here is a sign for you: you will
find a baby wrapped in swaddling clothes and lying in a manger.'
And suddenly with the angel there was a great throng of the
heavenly host, praising God and singing:

> 'Glory to God in the highest heaven,
> and peace to men who enjoy his favour'.

This is the Gospel of the Lord.

In the Profession of Faith, all genuflect at the words, *and was made
man.*

Prayer over the Gifts
Lord,
accept our gifts on this joyful feast of our salvation.
By our communion with God made man,
may we become more like him
who joins our lives to yours,
for he is Lord for ever and ever.

Preface of Christmas, I-III, P3-P5

Communion Antiphon: The Word of God became man; we have
seen his glory.

Prayer after Communion
God our Father,
we rejoice in the birth of our Saviour.
May we share his life completely
by living as he has taught.

Solemn Blessing
Bow your heads and pray for God's blessing.

When he came to us as man,
the Son of God scattered the darkness of this world,
and filled this holy night (day) with his glory.
May the God of infinite goodness
scatter the darkness of sin
and brighten your hearts with holiness.   ℞   **Amen.**

God sent his angels to shepherds
to herald the great joy of our Saviour's birth.
May he fill you with joy
and make you heralds of his gospel.   ℞   **Amen.**

When the Word became man,
earth was joined to heaven.
May he give you his peace and good will,
and fellowship with all the heavenly host.   ℞   **Amen.**

May almighty God bless you,
the Father, and the Son, ✚ and the Holy Spirit.   ℞   **Amen.**

Mass at Dawn

The First Dawn Of A New Age

*We celebrate the marvellous events of the first morning of a new world,
when the kindness and love of God our Saviour made us his holy people,
the Lord's Redeemed, his 'sought-after', and his 'city-not-forsaken'.*

Entrance Antiphon: A light will shine on us this day, the Lord is
born for us: he shall be called Wonderful God, Prince of peace,
Father of the world to come; and his kingship will never end.

Opening Prayer
Let us pray
    [that the love of Christ
    will be a light to the world]

Father,
we are filled with the new light
by the coming of your Word among us.
May the light of faith
shine in our words and actions.

or

Let us pray
　　[for the peace
　　　that comes from the Prince of Peace]

Almighty God and Father of light,
a child is born for us and a son is given to us.

Your eternal Word leaped down from heaven
in the silent watches of the night,
and now your Church is filled with wonder
at the nearness of her God.

Open our hearts to receive his life
and increase our vision with the rising of dawn,
that our lives may be filled with his glory and his peace,
who lives and reigns for ever and ever.

FIRST READING

A reading from the prophet Isaiah　　　62:11-12
Look, your saviour comes.

This the Lord proclaims
to the ends of the earth:

　　Say to the daughter of Zion, 'Look,
　　your saviour comes,
　　the prize of his victory with him,
　　his trophies before him'.
　　They shall be called 'The Holy People',
　　'The Lord's Redeemed'.
　　And you shall be called 'The-sought-after',
　　'City-not-forsaken'.

　　This is the word of the Lord.

Responsorial Psalm　　　　　　　Ps 96:1. 6. 11-12
　　℟　**This day new light will shine upon the earth:**
　　　the Lord is born for us.

1　The Lord is king, let earth rejoice,
　　the many coastlands be glad.
　　The skies proclaim his justice;
　　all peoples see his glory.　℟

2   Light shines forth for the just
     and joy for the upright of heart.
     Rejoice, you just, in the Lord;
     give glory to his holy name. ℟

SECOND READING

A reading from the letter of St Paul to Titus   3:4-7
It was for no reason except his own compassion that he saved us.

When the kindness and love of God our saviour for mankind were revealed, it was not because he was concerned with any righteous actions we might have done ourselves; it was for no reason except his own compassion that he saved us, by means of the cleansing water of rebirth and by renewing us with the Holy Spirit which he has so generously poured over us through Jesus Christ our saviour. He did this so that we should be justified by his grace, to become heirs looking forward to inheriting eternal life.

    This is the word of the Lord.

Gospel Acclamation   Lk 2:14
     Alleluia, alleluia!
     Glory to God in the highest heaven,
     and peace to men who enjoy his favour.
     Alleluia!

GOSPEL

A reading from the holy Gospel according to Luke   2:15-20
The shepherds found Mary and Joseph and the baby.

Now when the angels had gone from them into heaven, the shepherds said to one another, 'Let us go to Bethlehem and see this thing that has happened which the Lord has made known to us.' So they hurried away and found Mary and Joseph, and the baby lying in the manger. When they saw the child they repeated what they had been told about him, and everyone who heard it was astonished at what the shepherds had to say. As for Mary, she treasured all these things and pondered them in her heart. And the shepherds went back glorifying and praising God for all they had heard and seen; it was exactly as they had been told.

    This is the Gospel of the Lord.

In the Profession of Faith, all genuflect at *and was made man.*

Prayer over the Gifts

Father,
may we follow the example of your Son
who became man and lived among us.
May we receive the gift of divine life
through these offerings here on earth.

Preface of Christmas I-III, P3-P5

Communion Antiphon: **Daughter of Zion, exult; shout aloud, daughter of Jerusalem! Your King is coming, the Holy One, the Saviour of the world.**

Prayer after Communion

Lord,
with faith and joy
we celebrate the birthday of your Son.
Increase our understanding and our love
of the riches you have revealed in him,
who is Lord for ever and ever.

Solemn Blessing as at Mass at Midnight, p.135, or an appropriate Prayer over the People, pp.95ff., may be used.

Mass During the Day

The Word Made Flesh

For us the Word of God is no longer the message spoken by prophets, but the messenger of God in person, the eternal Word begotten of the Father before time began.

Entrance Antiphon: **A child is born for us, a son given to us; dominion is laid on his shoulder, and he shall be called Wonderful-Counsellor.**

Opening Prayer

Let us pray
    [for the glory promised by the birth of Christ]

Lord God,
we praise you for creating man,
and still more for restoring him in Christ.
Your Son shared our weakness:

may we share his glory,
for he lives and reigns with you and the Holy Spirit,
one God, for ever and ever.

or

Let us pray
[in the joy of Christmas
because the Son of God lives among us]

God of love, Father of all,
the darkness that covered the earth
has given way to the bright dawn of your Word made flesh.

Make us a people of this light.
Make us faithful to your Word,
that we may bring your life to the waiting world.

FIRST READING
A reading from the prophet Isaiah
All the ends of the earth shall see the salvation of our God.
52:7-10

How beautiful on the mountains,
are the feet of one who brings good news,
who heralds peace, brings happiness,
proclaims salvation,
and tells Zion,
'Your God is king!'
Listen! Your watchmen raise their voices,
they shout for joy together,
for they see the Lord face to face,
as he returns to Zion.
Break into shouts of joy together,
you ruins of Jerusalem;
for the Lord is consoling his people,
redeeming Jerusalem.
The Lord bares his holy arm
in the sight of all the nations,
and all the ends of the earth shall see
the salvation of our God.

This is the word of the Lord.

Responsial Psalm   Ps 97:1-6. ℟ v.3

℟   **All the ends of the earth have seen
      the salvation of our God.**

1   Sing a new song to the Lord
     for he has worked wonders.
     His right hand and his holy arm
     have brought salvation. ℟

2   The Lord has made known his salvation;
     has shown his justice to the nations.
     He has remembered his truth and love
     for the house of Israel. ℟

3   All the ends of the earth have seen
     the salvation of our God.
     Shout to the Lord all the earth,
     ring out your joy. ℟

4   Sing psalms to the Lord with the harp,
     with the sound of music.
     With trumpets and the sound of the horn
     acclaim the King, the Lord. ℟

SECOND READING

A reading from the letter to the Hebrews   1:1-6
God has spoken to us through his Son.

At various times in the past and in various different ways, God
spoke to our ancestors through the prophets; but in our own
time, the last days, he has spoken to us through his Son, the Son
that he has appointed to inherit everything and through whom
he made everything there is. He is the radiant light of God's glory
and the perfect copy of his nature, sustaining the universe by his
powerful command; and now that he has destroyed the defilement of sin, he has gone to take his place in heaven at the right
hand of divine Majesty. So he is now as far above the angels as
the title which he has inherited is higher than their own name.

God has never said to any angel: You are my Son, today I
have become your father, or: I will be a father to him and he a son
to me. Again, when he brings the First-born into the world, he
says: Let all the angels of God worship him.

This is the word of the Lord.

Gospel Acclamation
Alleluia, alleluia!
A hallowed day has dawned upon us.
Come, you nations, worship the Lord,
for today a great light has shone down upon the earth.
Alleluia!

GOSPEL

A reading from the holy Gospel according to John   1:1-18
The Word was made flesh, and lived among us.

*In the beginning was the Word:
the Word was with God
and the Word was God.
He was with God in the beginning.
Through him all things came to be,
not one thing had its being but through him.
All that came to be had life in him
and that life was the light of men,
a light that shines in the dark,
a light that darkness could not overpower.*

A man came, sent by God.
His name was John.
He came as a witness,
as a witness to speak for the light,
so that everyone might believe through him.
He was not the light,
only a witness to speak for the light.

*The Word was the true light
that enlightens all men;
and he was coming into the world.
He was in the world
that had its being through him,
and the world did not know him.
He came to his own domain
and his own people did not accept him.
But to all who did accept him
he gave power to become children of God,
to all who believe in the name of him
who was born not out of human stock
or urge of the flesh
or will of man

but of God himself.
The Word was made flesh,
he lived among us,
and we saw his glory,
the glory that is his as the only Son of the Father,
full of grace and truth*.

John appears as his witness. He proclaims:
'This is the one of whom I said:
He who comes after me
ranks before me
because he existed before me.'

Indeed, from his fullness we have, all of us, received–
yes, grace in return for grace,
since, though the Law was given through Moses,
grace and truth have come through Jesus Christ.
No one has ever seen God;
it is the only Son, who is nearest to the Father's heart,
who has made him known.

> * This is the Gospel of the Lord*.

* Shorter Form, verses 1-5. 9-14. Read between*
In the Profession of Faith, all genuflect at *and was made man*.

Prayer over the Gifts
Almighty God,
the saving work of Christ
made our peace with you.
May our offering today
renew that peace within us
and give you perfect praise.

Preface of Christmas I-III, P3-P5

Communion Antiphon: All the ends of the earth have seen the
saving power of God.

Prayer after Communion
Father,
the child born today is the Saviour of the world.
He made us your children.
May he welcome us into your kingdom
where he lives and reigns with you for ever and ever.

Solemn Blessing as at Mass at Midnight, p.135, or an appropriate
Prayer over the People may be said. See pp.95ff.

Sunday in the Octave of Christmas

THE HOLY FAMILY OF
JESUS, MARY AND JOSEPH   A

Where there is no Sunday occurring between 25 December and
1 January, this feast is celebrated on 30 December, with one
reading only before the Gospel.

The Holy Family

*We celebrate that Holy Family of Nazareth which is the model for all who
fear the Lord and walk in his ways.*

Entrance Antiphon: The shepherds hastened to Bethlehem, where
they found Mary and Joseph, and the baby lying in a manger.

Opening Prayer
Let us pray
  [for peace in our families]

Father,
help us to live as the holy family,
united in respect and love.
Bring us to the joy and peace of your eternal home.
  or
Let us pray
  [as the family of God,
  who share in his life]

Father in heaven, creator of all,
you ordered the earth to bring forth life
and crowned its goodness by creating the family of man.
In history's moment when all was ready,
you sent your Son to dwell in time,
obedient to the laws of life in our world.

Teach us the sanctity of human love,
show us the value of family life,
and help us to live in peace with all men
that we may share in your life for ever.

FIRST READING
A reading from the Book of Ecclesiasticus   3:2-6. 12-14
He who fears the Lord respects his parents.

The Lord honours the father in his children,

and upholds the rights of a mother over her sons.
Whoever respects his father is atoning for his sins,
he who honours his mother is like someone amassing a fortune.
Whoever respects his father will be happy with children of his
   own,
he shall be heard on the day when he prays.
Long life comes to him who honours his father,
he who sets his mother at ease is showing obedience to the Lord.
My son, support your father in his old age,
do not grieve him during his life.
Even if his mind should fail, show him sympathy,
do not despise him in your health and strength;
for kindness to a father shall not be forgotten
but will serve as reparation for your sins.

   This is the word of the Lord.

Responsorial Psalm   Ps 127:1-5. ℟ cf. v.1
   ℟   **O blessed are those who fear the Lord**
         and walk in his ways!

1   O blessed are those who fear the Lord
      and walk in his ways!
      By the labour of your hands you shall eat.
      You will be happy and prosper.   ℟

2   Your wife like a fruitful vine
      in the heart of your house;
      your children like shoots of the olive,
      around your table.   ℟

3   Indeed thus shall be blessed
      the man who fears the Lord.
      May the Lord bless you from Zion
      all the days of your life!   ℟

SECOND READING

A reading from the letter of St Paul to the Colossians   3:12-21
Family life in the Lord.

You are God's chosen race, his saints; he loves you and you
should be clothed in sincere compassion, in kindness and
humility, gentleness and patience. Bear with one another; forgive
each other as soon as a quarrel begins. The Lord has forgiven
you; now you must do the same. Over all these clothes, to keep
them together and complete them, put on love. And may the

peace of Christ reign in your hearts, because it is for this that you were called together as parts of one body. Always be thankful.

Let the message of Christ, in all its richness, find a home with you. Teach each other, and advise each other, in all wisdom. With gratitude in your hearts sing psalms and hymns and inspired songs to God; and never say or do anything except in the name of the Lord Jesus, giving thanks to God the Father through him.

Wives, give way to your husbands, as you should in the Lord. Husbands, love your wives and treat them with gentleness. Children, be obedient to your parents always, because that is what will please the Lord. Parents, never drive your children to resentment or you will make them feel frustrated.

This is the word of the Lord.

Gospel Acclamation Col. 3:15. 16
Alleluia, alleluia!
May the peace of Christ reign in your hearts;
let the message of Christ find a home with you.
Alleluia!

GOSPEL

A reading from the holy Gospel according to Matthew
Take the child and his mother and escape into Egypt. 2:13-15. 19-23

After the wise men had left, the angel of the Lord appeared to Joseph in a dream and said, 'Get up, take the child and his mother with you, and escape into Egypt, and stay there until I tell you, because Herod intends to search for the child and do away with him.' So Joseph got up and, taking the child and his mother with him, left that night for Egypt, where he stayed until Herod was dead. This was to fulfil what the Lord had spoken through the prophet:

I called my son out of Egypt.

After Herod's death, the angel of the Lord appeared in a dream to Joseph in Egypt and said, 'Get up, take the child and his mother with you and go back to the land of Israel, for those who wanted to kill the child are dead'. So Joseph got up and, taking the child and his mother with him, went back to the land of Israel. But when he learnt that Archelaus had succeeded his father Herod as ruler of Judaea he was afraid to go there, and being warned in a dream he left for the region of Galilee. There he settled in a town called Nazareth. In this way the words spoken through the prophets were to be fulfilled:

He will be called a Nazarene.

This is the Gospel of the Lord.

Prayer over the Gifts
Lord,
accept this sacrifice
and through the prayers of Mary, the virgin Mother of God,
and of her husband, Joseph,
unite our families in peace and love.

Preface of Christmas I-III, P3-P5

Communion Antiphon: Our God has appeared on earth, and lived among men.

Prayer after Communion
Eternal Father,
we want to live as Jesus, Mary, and Joseph,
in peace with you and one another.
May this communion strengthen us
to face the troubles of life.

An appropriate Solemn Blessing or Prayer over the People may be used. See pp.90ff.

1 January: Octave of Christmas

SOLEMNITY OF MARY, MOTHER OF GOD
A,B,C

Mary, Through Whom The World Would Be Blessed

We too bless God for Mary, who bore for us the Child she named Jesus, the Saviour.

Entrance Antiphon: A light will shine on us this day, the Lord is born for us: he shall be called Wonderful God, Prince of peace, Father of the world to come; and his kingship will never end.
or
Hail, holy Mother! The child to whom you gave birth is the King of heaven and earth for ever.

Opening Prayer
Let us pray
[that Mary, the mother of the Lord,
will help us by her prayers]

God our Father,
may we always profit by the prayers
of the Virgin Mother Mary,
for you bring us life and salvation
through Jesus Christ her Son
who lives and reigns with you and the Holy Spirit,
one God, for ever and ever.

or

Let us pray
    [in the name of Jesus,
    born of a virgin and Son of God]

Father,
source of light in every age,
the virgin conceived and bore your Son
who is called Wonderful God, Prince of peace.

May her prayer, the gift of a mother's love,
be your people's joy through all ages.
May her response, born of a humble heart,
draw your Spirit to rest on your people.

FIRST READING

A reading from the book of Numbers   6:22-27

They are to call down my name on the sons of Israel, and I will bless them.

The Lord spoke to Moses and said, 'Say this to Aaron and his sons: "This is how you are to bless the sons of Israel. You shall say to them:

    May the Lord bless you and keep you.
    May the Lord let his face shine on you and be gracious to you.
    May the Lord uncover his face to you and bring you peace."

This is how they are to call down my name on the sons of Israel, and I will bless them.'

This is the word of the Lord.

Responsorial Psalm   Ps 66:2-3. 5. 6. 8. ℟ v.2
    ℟   **O God, be gracious and bless us.**

1   God, be gracious and bless us
    and let your face shed its light upon us.
    So will your ways be known upon earth
    and all nations learn your saving help. ℟   (continued)

2 Let the nations be glad and exult
   for you rule the world with justice.
   With fairness you rule the peoples.
   you guide the nations on earth.

   ℟ **O God, be gracious and bless us.**

3 Let the peoples praise you, O God;
   let all the peoples praise you.
   May God still give us his blessing
   till the ends of the earth revere him.   ℟

SECOND READING

A reading from the letter of St Paul to the Galatians   4:4-7
God sent his Son, born of a woman.

When the appointed time came, God sent his Son, born of a
woman, born a subject of the Law, to redeem the subjects of the
Law and to enable us to be adopted as sons. The proof that you
are sons is that God has sent the Spirit of his Son into our hearts:
the Spirit that cries, 'Abba, Father', and it is this that makes you a
son, you are not a slave any more; and if God has made you son,
then he has made you heir.

   This is the word of the Lord.

Gospel Acclamation   Heb 1:1-2
   Alleluia, alleluia!
   At various times in the past
   and in various different ways,
   God spoke to our ancestors through the prophets;
   but in our own time, the last days,
   he has spoken to us through his Son.
   Alleluia!

GOSPEL

A reading from the holy Gospel according to Luke   2:16-21
*They found Mary and Joseph and the babe . . . When the eighth day
came, they gave him the name Jesus.*

The shepherds hurried away to Bethlehem and found Mary and
Joseph, and the baby lying in the manger. When they saw the
child they repeated what they had been told about him, and
everyone who heard it was astonished at what the shepherds
had to say. As for Mary, she treasured all these things and

pondered them in her heart. And the shepherds went back
glorifying and praising God for all they had heard and seen; it
was exactly as they had been told.

When the eighth day came and the child was to be circumcised, they gave him the name Jesus, the name the angel had
given him before his conception.

This is the Gospel of the Lord.

Prayer over the Gifts
God our Father,
we celebrate at this season
the beginning of our salvation.
On this feast of Mary, the Mother of God,
we ask that our salvation
will be brought to its fulfilment.

Preface of the Blessed Virgin Mary I or II, P56 or P57

Communion Antiphon: Jesus Christ is the same yesterday, today,
and for ever.

Prayer after Communion
Father,
as we proclaim the Virgin Mary
to be the mother of Christ and the mother of the Church,
may our communion with her Son
bring us to salvation.

An appropriate Solemn Blessing or Prayer over the People may
be used. See pp.90ff.

SECOND SUNDAY AFTER CHRISTMAS A,B,C

Christ, The Wisdom of God

*We celebrate Christ, the incarnate wisdom of God who has come to dwell
in our midst.*

Entrance Antiphon: When peaceful silence lay over all, and night
had run half of her swift course, your all-powerful word, O Lord,
leaped down from heaven, from the royal throne.

Opening Prayer
Let us pray
[that all mankind may be enlightened by the gospel]

God of power and life,
glory of all who believe in you,
fill the world with your splendour
and show the nations the light of your truth.

or

Let us pray
[aware of the dignity to which we are called
by the love of Christ]

Father of our Lord Jesus Christ,
our glory is to stand before the world
as your own sons and daughters.

May the simple beauty of Jesus' birth
summon us always to love what is most deeply human,
and to see your Word made flesh
reflected in those whose lives we touch.

FIRST READING

A reading from the book of Ecclesiasticus   24:1-2. 8-12
The wisdom of God has pitched her tent among the chosen people.

Wisdom speaks her own praises,
in the midst of her people she glories in herself.
She opens her mouth in the assembly of the Most High,
she glories in herself in the presence of the Mighty One;

'Then the creator of all things instructed me,
and he who created me fixed a place for my tent.
He said, "Pitch your tent in Jacob,
make Israel your inheritance.'
From eternity, in the beginning, he created me,
and for eternity I shall remain.
I ministered before him in the holy tabernacle,
and thus was I established on Zion.
In the beloved city he has given me rest,
and in Jerusalem I wield my authority.
I have taken root in a privileged people
in the Lord's property, in his inheritance.'

This is the word of the Lord.

Responsorial Psalm   Ps 147:12-15. 19-20. R̥ Jn 1:14

R̥ **The Word was made flesh,
and lived among us.**

or

R̥ **Alleluia!**

1   O praise the Lord, Jerusalem!
Zion, praise your God!
He has strengthened the bars of your gates,
he has blessed the children within you.   R̥

2   He established peace on your borders,
he feeds you with finest wheat.
He sends out his word to the earth
and swiftly runs his command.   R̥

3   He makes his word known to Jacob,
to Israel his laws and decrees.
He has not dealt thus with other nations;
he has not taught them his decrees.   R̥

SECOND READING

A reading from the letter of St Paul to the Ephesians 1:3-6. 15-18
He determined that we should become his adopted sons through Jesus.

Blessed be God the Father of our Lord Jesus Christ, who has blessed us with all the spiritual blessings of heaven in Christ. Before the world was made, he chose us, chose us in Christ, to be holy and spotless, and to live through love in his presence, determining that we should become his adopted sons, through Jesus Christ, for his own kind purposes, to make us praise the glory of his grace, his free gift to us in the Beloved.

That will explain why I, having once heard about your faith in the Lord Jesus, and the love that you show towards all the saints, have never failed to remember you in my prayers and to thank God for you. May the God of our Lord Jesus Christ, the Father of glory, give you a spirit of wisdom and perception of what is revealed, to bring you to full knowledge of him. May he enlighten the eyes of your mind so that you can see what hope his call holds for you, what rich glories he has promised the saints will inherit.

This is the word of the Lord.

Gospel Acclamation   cf. 1 Tim 3:16
　　Alleluia, alleluia!
　　Glory be to you, O Christ, proclaimed to the pagans;
　　Glory be to you, O Christ, believed in by the world.
　　Alleluia!

GOSPEL
A reading from the holy Gospel according to John   1:1-18
The Word was made flesh, and lived among us.

* In the beginning was the Word:
the Word was with God
and the Word was God.
He was with God in the beginning.
Through him all things came to be,
not one thing had its being but through him.
All that came to be had life in him
and that life was the light of men,
a light that shines in the dark,
a light that darkness could not overpower.*

A man came, sent by God.
His name was John.
He came as a witness,
as a witness to speak for the light,
so that everyone might believe through him.
He was not the light,
only a witness to speak for the light.

* The Word was the true light
that enlightens all men;
and he was coming into the world.
He was in the world
that had its being through him,
and the world did not know him.
He came to his own domain
and his own people did not accept him.
But to all who did accept him
he gave power to become children of God,
to all who believe in the name of him
who was born not out of human stock
or urge of the flesh
or will of man
but of God himself.

The Word was made flesh,
he lived among us,
and we saw his glory,
the glory that is his as the only Son of the Father,
full of grace and truth.*

John appears as his witness. He proclaims:
'This is the one of whom I said:
He who comes after me
ranks before me
because he existed before me.'

Indeed, from his fullness we have, all of us, received –
yes, grace in return for grace,
since though the Law was given through Moses,
grace and truth have come through Jesus Christ.
No one has ever seen God;
it is the only Son, who is nearest to the Father's heart,
who has made him known.

   This is the Gospel of the Lord.

*Shorter Form, verses 1-5. 9-14. Read between *

Prayer over the Gifts
Lord,
make holy these gifts
through the coming of your Son,
who shows us the way of truth
and promises the life of your kingdom.

Preface of Christmas I-III, P3-P5

Communion Antiphon: He gave to all who accepted him the power
to become children of God.

Prayer after Communion
Lord,
hear our prayers.
By this eucharist free us from sin
and keep us faithful to your word.

An appropriate Solemn Blessing or Prayer over the People may
be used. See pp.95ff.

6 January
or the Sunday between 2 January and 8 January

THE EPIPHANY OF THE LORD   A,B,C
Solemnity

The Revelation Of Christ To The World

We join all the people of the world in worshipping the infant King of the Jews.

Entrance Antiphon: The Lord and ruler is coming; kingship is his, and government and power.

Opening Prayer
Let us pray
    [that we will be guided by the light of faith]

Father,
you revealed your Son to the nations
by the guidance of a star.
Lead us to your glory in heaven
by the light of faith.

or

Let us pray
    [grateful for the glory revealed today
    through God made man]

Father of light, unchanging God,
today you reveal to men of faith
the resplendent fact of the Word made flesh.

Your light is strong,
your love is near;
draw us beyond the limits which this world imposes,
to the life where your Spirit makes all life complete.

FIRST READING

A reading from the prophet Isaiah   60:1-6
Above you the glory of the Lord appears.

Arise, shine out Jerusalem, for your light has come,
the glory of the Lord is rising on you,
though night still covers the earth
and darkness the peoples.

Above you the Lord now rises
and above you his glory appears.
The nations come to your light
and kings to your dawning brightness.

Lift up your eyes and look round:
all are assembling and coming towards you,
your sons from far away
and daughters being tenderly carried.

At this sight you will grow radiant,
your heart throbbing and full;
since the riches of the sea will flow to you;
the wealth of the nations come to you;

camels in throngs will cover you,
and dromedaries of Midian and Ephah;
everyone in Sheba will come,
bringing gold and incense
and singing the praise of the Lord.

This is the word of the Lord.

Responsorial Psalm   Ps 71:1-2. 7-8. 10-13. ℟ cf. v.11
℟ **All nations shall fall prostrate before you, O Lord.**

1 O God, give your judgement to the king,
to a king's son your justice,
that he may judge your people in justice
and your poor in right judgement. ℟

2 In his days justice shall flourish
and peace till the moon fails.
He shall rule from sea to sea,
from the Great River to earth's bounds. ℟

3 The kings of Tarshish and the sea coasts
shall pay him tribute.
The kings of Sheba and Seba
shall bring him gifts.
Before him all kings shall fall prostrate,
all nations shall serve him. ℟

4 For he shall save the poor when they cry
and the needy who are helpless.
He will have pity on the weak
and save the lives of the poor. ℟

SECOND READING

A reading from the letter of St Paul to the Ephesians   3:2-3. 5-6
It has now been revealed that pagans share the same inheritance.

You have probably heard how I have been entrusted by God with
the grace he meant for you, and that it was by a revelation that I
was given the knowledge of the mystery. This mystery that has
now been revealed through the Spirit to his holy apostles and
prophets was unknown to any men in past generations; it means
that pagans now share the same inheritance, that they are parts
of the same body, and that the same promise has been made to
them, in Christ Jesus, through the gospel.

This is the word of the Lord.

Gospel Acclamation   Mt 2:2
    Alleluia, alleluia!
    We saw his star as it rose
    and have come to do the Lord homage.
    Alleluia!

GOSPEL

A reading from the holy Gospel according to Matthew   2:1-12
We saw his star and have come to do the king homage.

After Jesus had been born at Bethlehem in Judaea during the
reign of King Herod, some wise men came to Jerusalem from the
east. 'Where is the infant king of the Jews?' they asked. 'We saw
his star as it rose and have come to do him homage.' When King
Herod heard this he was perturbed, and so was the whole of
Jerusalem. He called together all the chief priests and the scribes
of the people, and enquired of them where the Christ was to be
born. 'At Bethlehem in Judaea,' they told him 'for this is what the
prophet wrote:

    And you, Bethlehem, in the land of Judah
    you are by no means least among the leaders of Judah,
    for out of you will come a leader
    who will shepherd my people Israel.'

Then Herod summoned the wise men to see him privately. He
asked them the exact date on which the star had appeared, and
sent them on to Bethlehem. 'Go and find out all about the child,'

he said 'and when you have found him, let me know, so that I too may go and do him homage .' Having listened to what the king had to say, they set out. And there in front of them was the star they had seen rising; it went forward and halted over the place where the child was. The sight of the star filled them with delight, and going into the house they saw the child with his mother Mary, and falling to their knees they did him homage. Then, opening their treasures, they offered him gifts of gold and frankincense and myrrh. But they were warned in a dream not to go back to Herod, and returned to their own country by a different way.

This is the Gospel of the Lord.

Prayer over the Gifts
Lord,
accept the offerings of your Church,
not gold, frankincense and myrrh,
but the sacrifice and food they symbolise:
Jesus Christ, who is Lord for ever and ever.

Preface of Epiphany, P6

Communion Antiphon: We have seen his star in the east and have come with gifts to adore the Lord.

Prayer after Communion
Father,
guide us with your light.
Help us to recognise Christ in this eucharist
and welcome him with love,
for he is Lord for ever and ever.

Solemn Blessing
Bow your heads and pray for God's blessing.

God has called you out of darkness,
into his wonderful light.
May you experience his kindness and blessings,
and be strong in faith, in hope, and in love. ℟ **Amen.**

Because you are followers of Christ,
who appeared on this day as a light shining in darkness,
may he make you a light to all your sisters and brothers.
℟ **Amen.**

The wise men followed the star,
and found Christ who is light from light.
May you too find the Lord
when your pilgrimage is ended.   ℟ **Amen.**

May almighty God bless you,
the Father, and the Son, ✠ and the Holy Spirit.   ℟ **Amen.**

Sunday after 6 January

THE BAPTISM OF THE LORD   A

First Sunday in Ordinary Time
Feast

This feast is omitted when the Epiphany is celebrated on this
Sunday.

The Baptism Of The Lord

*The Father anointed his beloved son, Jesus, with the Holy Spirit and with
power, to bring healing and peace to all the nations.*

Entrance Antiphon: When the Lord had been baptised, the
heavens opened, and the Spirit came down like a dove to rest on
him. Then the voice of the Father thundered: This is my beloved
Son, with him I am well pleased.

Opening Prayer
Let us pray
    [that we will be faithful to our baptism]

Almighty, eternal God,
when the Spirit descended upon Jesus
at his baptism in the Jordan,
you revealed him as your own beloved Son.
Keep us, your children born of water and the Spirit,
faithful to our calling.

    or

Father,
your only Son revealed himself to us by becoming man.
May we who share his humanity
come to share his divinity,
for he lives and reigns with you and the Holy Spirit,
one God, for ever and ever.

or

Let us pray
[as we listen to the voice of God's Spirit]

Father in heaven,
you revealed Christ as your Son
by the voice that spoke over the waters of the Jordan.

May all who share in the sonship of Christ
follow in his path of service to man,
and reflect the glory of his kingdom
even to the ends of the earth,
for he is Lord for ever and ever.

FIRST READING

A reading from the prophet Isaiah
Here is my servant in whom my soul delights.

42:1-4. 6-7

Thus says the Lord:

> Here is my servant whom I uphold,
> my chosen one in whom my soul delights.
> I have endowed him with my spirit
> that he may bring true justice to the nations.
>
> He does not cry out or shout aloud,
> or make his voice heard in the streets.
> He does not break the crushed reed,
> nor quench the wavering flame.
>
> Faithfully he brings true justice;
> he will neither waver, nor be crushed
> until true justice is established on earth,
> for the islands are awaiting his law.
>
> I, the Lord, have called you to serve the cause of right;
> I have taken you by the hand and formed you;
> I have appointed you as covenant of the people and light of
> the nations,
>
> to open the eyes of the blind,
> to free captives from prison,
> and those who live in darkness from the dungeon.

This is the word of the Lord.

Responsorial Psalm   Ps 28:1-4. 9-10. ℟ v.11

℟ **The Lord will bless his people with peace.**

1   O give the Lord you sons of God,
    give the Lord glory and power;
    give the Lord the glory of his name.
    Adore the Lord in his holy court. ℟

2   The Lord's voice resounding on the waters,
    the Lord on the immensity of waters;
    the voice of the Lord, full of power,
    the voice of the Lord, full of splendour. ℟

3   The God of glory thunders.
    In his temple they all cry: 'Glory!'
    The Lord sat enthroned over the flood;
    the Lord sits as king for ever. ℟

SECOND READING

A reading from the Acts of the Apostles   10:34-38
God had anointed him with the Holy Spirit.

Peter addressed Cornelius and his household: 'The truth I have
now come to realise' he said 'is that God does not have favourites, but that anybody of any nationality who fears God and does
what is right is acceptable to him.

   'It is true, God sent his word to the people of Israel, and it was
to them that the good news of peace was brought by Jesus Christ
– but Jesus Christ is Lord of all men. You must have heard about
the recent happenings in Judaea; about Jesus of Nazareth and
how he began in Galilee, after John had been preaching baptism.
God had anointed him with the Holy Spirit and with power, and
because God was with him, Jesus went about doing good and
curing all who had fallen into the power of the devil.'

   This is the word of the Lord.

Gospel Acclamation   cf. Mk 9:8
    Alleluia, alleluia!
    The heavens opened and the Father's voice resounded:
    'This is my Son, the Beloved. Listen to him.'
    Alleluia!

GOSPEL

A reading from the holy Gospel according to Matthew 3:13-17

As soon as Jesus was baptised he saw the Spirit of God coming down on him.

Jesus came from Galilee to the Jordan to be baptised by John. John tried to dissuade him. 'It is I who need baptism from you,' he said 'and yet you come to me!' But Jesus replied, 'Leave it like this for the time being; it is fitting that we should, in this way, do all that righteousness demands.' At this, John gave in to him.

As soon as Jesus was baptised he came up from the water, and suddenly the heavens opened and he saw the Spirit of God descending like a dove and coming down on him. And a voice spoke from heaven, 'This is my Son, the Beloved; my favour rests on him.'

This is the Gospel of the Lord.

Prayer over the Gifts
Lord,
we celebrate the revelation of Christ your Son
who takes away the sins of the world.
Accept our gifts
and let them become one with his sacrifice,
for he is Lord for ever and ever.

Preface of the Baptism of the Lord, P7

Communion Antiphon: This is he of whom John said: I have seen and have given witness that this is the Son of God.

Prayer after Communion
Lord,
you feed us with bread from heaven.
May we hear your Son with faith
and become your children in name and in fact.

An appropriate Solemn Blessing or Prayer over the People may be used. See pp.90ff.

After the Baptism of the Lord, until Lent, the cycle of Sundays in Ordinary Time begins. The number of Sundays between the Baptism of the Lord and the First Sunday of Lent varies: see the Table of Principal Celebrations.

For Masses of the Sundays in Ordinary Time, Cycle A, see below, pp.373ff.

WHAT DOTH THE LORD REQUIRE?
MICAH
DO JUSTICE
WALK WISELY
LOVE MERCY
WITH YOUR GOD

THE SEASON OF LENT

PREPARATION FOR BAPTISM

Lent is a period of purification and enlightenment or illumination, the final stage of preparation for those catechumens who are to be baptised during the Easter Vigil.

The stages in the final process of becoming a christian are:

1) *Election*, that is the choice and admission of those judged worthy to receive the sacraments of christian initiation. This takes place, properly, during Mass of the First Sunday of Lent.

2) *Scrutinies*, the intention of which is to free the newly 'elect' from sin and the devil, and to give them strength in Christ. These take place during Mass on the Third, Fourth and Fifth Sundays of Lent.

3) *Presentation of the creed and the Lord's Prayer* – usually on a weekday.

The election and the scrutinies take place after the homily at Sunday Mass. When these rites take place, the readings at the Mass are always taken from *cycle A*. The elect should be dismissed before the offertory rite of the Mass begins. When the elect have gone out the General Intercessions and the Profession of Faith are said. For pastoral reasons both of these may be omitted.

If these rites are celebrated on weekdays there are special Mass formulae.

*In this missal the rites are given at the end of the particular Sundays of Year A. As a general rule only one formula for a particular prayer or section is given.

ASH WEDNESDAY A,B,C

Penitence is an essential part of the Christian life, for none of us can measure up to the tremendous vocation that is ours as Christians. We are in constant need of the mercy and forgiveness of God. Today we express this by taking part in an impressive corporate act of penitence and reconciliation, beseeching God for the grace to use with profit the 'favourable time' of preparation for the celebration of Christ's Passover feast.

The ashes used today come from the branches blessed the preceding year for Passion Sunday.

Entrance Antiphon: Lord, you are merciful to all, and hate nothing you have created. You overlook the sins of men to bring them to repentance. You are the Lord our God.

The penitential rite and the Gloria are omitted.

Opening Prayer

Let us pray
  [for the grace to keep Lent faithfully]

Lord,
protect us in our struggle against evil.
As we begin the discipline of Lent,
make this season holy by our self-denial.

or

Let us pray
  [in quiet remembrance of our need for redemption]

Father in heaven,
the light of your truth bestows sight
to the darkness of sinful eyes.
May this season of repentance
bring us the blessing of your forgiveness
and the gift of your light.

FIRST READING

A reading from the prophet Joel 2:12-18
Let your hearts be broken, not your garments torn.

'Now, now – it is the Lord who speaks –
come back to me with all your heart,

fasting, weeping, mourning.'
Let your hearts be broken not your garments torn,
turn to the Lord your God again,
for he is all tenderness and compassion,
slow to anger, rich in graciousness,
and ready to relent.
Who knows if he will not turn again, will not relent,
will not leave a blessing as he passes,
oblation and libation
for the Lord your God?
Sound the trumpet in Zion!
Order a fast,
proclaim a solemn assembly,
call the people together,
summon the community,
assemble the elders,
gather the children,
even the infants at the breast.
Let the bridegroom leave his bedroom
and the bride her alcove.
Between vestibule and altar let the priests,
the ministers of the Lord, lament.
Let them say,
'Spare your people, Lord!
Do not make your heritage a thing of shame,
a byword for the nations.
Why should it be said among the nations,
"Where is their God?"'
Then the Lord, jealous on behalf of his land,
took pity on his people.

This is the word of the Lord.

Responsorial Psalm   Ps 50:3-6. 12-14. 17. Ry v.3
  Ry **Have mercy on us, O Lord, for we have sinned.**

1 Have mercy on me, God, in your kindness.
   In your compassion blot out my offence.
   O wash me more and more from my guilt
   and cleanse me from my sin.   Ry

2 My offences truly I know them;
   my sin is always before me.
   Against you, you alone, have I sinned:
   what is evil in your sight I have done. ℟

3 A pure heart create for me, O God,
   put a steadfast spirit within me.
   Do not cast me away from your presence,
   nor deprive me of your holy spirit. ℟

4 Give me again the joy of your help;
   with a spirit of fervour sustain me.
   O Lord, open my lips
   and my mouth shall declare your praise. ℟

SECOND READING

A reading from the second letter of St Paul   5:20 – 6:2
to the Corinthians
Be reconciled to God . . . now is the favourable time.

We are ambassadors for Christ; it is as though God were
appealing through us, and the appeal that we make in Christ's
name is: be reconciled to God. For our sake God made the sinless
one into sin, so that in him we might become the goodness of
God. As his fellow workers, we beg you once again not to neglect
the grace of God that you have received. For he says: At the
favourable time, I have listened to you; on the day of salvation I
came to your help. Well, now is the favourable time; this is the
day of salvation.

This is the word of the Lord.

Gospel Acclamation   Ps 50:12. 14
   Praise to you, O Christ, king of eternal glory!
   A pure heart create for me, O God,
   and give me again the joy of your help.
   Praise to you, O Christ, king of eternal glory!
or   cf. Ps 94:8

   Praise to you, O Christ, king of eternal glory!
   Harden not your hearts today,
   but listen to the voice of the Lord.
   Praise to you, O Christ, king of eternal glory!

GOSPEL

A reading from the holy Gospel according to Matthew

6:1-6. 16-18

Your Father who sees all that is done in secret will reward you.

Jesus said to his disciples:

'Be careful not to parade your good deeds before men to attract their notice; by doing this you will lose all reward from your Father in heaven. So when you give alms, do not have it trumpeted before you; this is what the hypocrites do in the synagogues and in the streets to win men's admiration. I tell you solemnly, they have had their reward. But when you give alms, your left hand must not know what your right is doing; your almsgiving must be secret, and your Father who sees all that is done in secret will reward you.

'And when you pray, do not imitate the hypocrites: they love to say their prayers standing up in the synagogues and at the street corners for people to see them. I tell you solemnly, they have had their reward. But when you pray go to your private room and, when you have shut your door, pray to your Father who is in that secret place, and your Father who sees all that is done in secret will reward you.

'When you fast do not put on a gloomy look as the hypocrites do: they pull long faces to let men know they are fasting. I tell you solemnly, they have had their reward. But when you fast, put oil on your head and wash your face, so that no one will know you are fasting except your Father who sees all that is done in secret; and your Father who sees all that is done in secret will reward you.'

    This is the Gospel of the Lord.

Blessing and Giving of Ashes

After the homily the priest joins his hands and says:

Dear friends in Christ,
let us ask our Father
to bless these ashes
which we will use
as the mark of our repentance.

Silent prayer

Lord,
bless the sinner who asks for your forgiveness

and bless ✛ all those who receive these ashes.
May they keep this lenten season
in preparation for the joy of Easter.

or

Lord,
bless these ashes ✛
by which we show that we are dust.
Pardon our sins
and keep us faithful to the discipline of Lent,
for you do not want sinners to die
but to live with the risen Christ,
who reigns with you for ever and ever.

He sprinkles the ashes with holy water in silence.
The priest then places ashes on those who come forward, saying to each:

Turn away from sin and be faithful to the gospel.

or

Remember, man, you are dust
and to dust you will return.

Meanwhile some of the following antiphons or other appropriate songs are sung.

1 Come back to the Lord with all your heart;
   leave the past in ashes,
   and turn to God with tears and fasting,
   for he is slow to anger and ready to forgive.

2 Let the priests and ministers of the Lord
   lament before his altar, and say:
   Spare us, Lord; spare your people!
   Do not let us die for we are crying out to you.

3 Lord, take away our wickedness.

These may be repeated after each verse of Psalm 50, Have mercy on me, God, see above, p.164.

Responsory

Direct our hearts to better things, O Lord;
heal our sin and ignorance.
Lord, do not face us suddenly with death,
but give us time to repent.

℟ **Turn to us with mercy, Lord; we have sinned against you.**
℣ Help us, God our saviour, rescue us for the honour of
         your name.
℟ **Turn to us with mercy, Lord; we have sinned against you.**

After the giving of ashes the priest washes his hands; the rite
concludes with the prayer of the faithful.
The Profession of Faith is not said.

Prayer over the Gifts
Lord,
help us to resist temptation
by our lenten works of charity and penance.
By this sacrifice
may we be prepared to celebrate
the death and resurrection of Christ our Saviour
and be cleansed from sin and renewed in spirit.

Preface of Lent IV, P11

Communion Antiphon: The man who meditates day and night on
the law of the Lord will yield fruit in due season.

Prayer after Communion
Lord,
through this communion
may our lenten penance give you glory
and bring us your protection.

FIRST SUNDAY OF LENT   A

Christ, The Second Adam

*Today we celebrate Christ, the Second Adam, who overcame temptation
and sin, and by his obedience won back the world to God.*

Entrance Antiphon: When he calls to me, I will answer; I will
rescue him and give him honour. Long life and contentment will
be his.

The Gloria is omitted.

Opening Prayer
Let us pray
     [that this Lent will help us reproduce in our lives

the self-sacrificing love of Christ]

Father,
through our observance of Lent,
help us to understand the meaning
of your Son's death and resurrection,
and teach us to reflect it in our lives.

or

Let us pray
  [at the beginning of Lent
  for the spirit of repentance]

Lord our God,
you formed man from the clay of the earth
and breathed into him the spirit of life,
but he turned from your face and sinned.

In this time of repentance
we call out for your mercy.
Bring us back to you
and to the life your Son won for us
by his death on the cross,
for he lives and reigns for ever and ever.

FIRST READING

A reading from the book of Genesis   2:7-9. 3:1-7
The creation and sin of our first parents.

The Lord God fashioned man of dust from the soil. Then he
breathed into his nostrils a breath of life, and thus man became a
living being.

The Lord God planted a garden in Eden which is in the east,
and there he put the man he had fashioned. The Lord God
caused to spring up from the soil every kind of tree, enticing to
look at and good to eat, with the tree of life and the tree of the
knowledge of good and evil in the middle of the garden.

The serpent was the most subtle of all the wild beasts that the
Lord God had made. It asked the woman, 'Did God really say
you were not to eat from any of the trees in the garden?' The
woman answered the serpent, 'We may eat the fruit of the trees
in the garden. But of the fruit of the tree in the middle of the
garden God said, "You must not eat it, nor touch it, under pain
of death".' Then the serpent said to the woman, 'No! You will
not die! God knows in fact that on the day you eat it your eyes

will be opened and you will be like gods, knowing good and
evil.' The woman saw that the tree was good to eat and pleasing
to the eye, and that it was desirable for the knowledge that it
could give. So she took some of its fruit and ate it. She gave some
also to her husband who was with her, and he ate it. Then the
eyes of both of them were opened and they realised that they
were naked. So they sewed fig-leaves together to make themselves loin-cloths.

This is the word of the Lord.

Responsorial Psalm   Ps 50:3-6. 12-14. 17. R̷ cf. v.3
   R̷ **Have mercy on us, O Lord, for we have sinned.**

1 Have mercy on me, God, in your kindness.
    In your compassion blot out my offence.
    O wash me more and more from my guilt
    and cleanse me from my sin.   R̷

2 My offences truly I know them;
    my sin is always before me.
    Against you, you alone, have I sinned;
    what is evil in your sight I have done.   R̷

3 A pure heart create for me, O God,
    put a steadfast spirit within me.
    Do not cast me away from your presence,
    nor deprive me of your holy spirit.   R̷

4 Give me again the joy of your help;
    with a spirit of fervour sustain me.
    O Lord, open my lips
    and my mouth shall declare your praise.   R̷

SECOND READING

A reading from the letter of St Paul to the Romans   5:12-19
However great the number of sins committed, grace was even greater.

*Sin entered the world through one man, and through sin death,
and thus death has spread through the whole human race
because everyone has sinned.* Sin existed in the world long
before the Law was given. There was no law and so no one could
be accused of the sin of 'law-breaking', yet death reigned over all
from Adam to Moses, even though their sin, unlike that of
Adam, was not a matter of breaking a law.

Adam prefigured the One to come, but the gift itself considerably outweighed the fall. If it is certain that through one man's fall so many died, it is even more certain that divine grace, coming through the one man, Jesus Christ, came to so many as an abundant free gift. The results of the gift also outweigh the results of one man's sin: for after one single fall came judgement with a verdict of condemnation, now after many falls comes grace with its verdict of acquittal. *If it is certain that death reigned over everyone as the consequence of one man's fall, it is even more certain that one man, Jesus Christ, will cause everyone to reign in life who receives the free gift that he does not deserve, of being made righteous. Again, as one man's fall brought condemnation on everyone, so the good act of one man brings everyone life and makes them justified. As by one man's disobedience many were made sinners, so by one man's obedience many will be made righteous.

This is the word of the Lord.*

*Shorter Form, verses 12. 17-19. Read between *

Gospel Acclamation   Mt 4:4
Praise to you, O Christ, king of eternal glory!
Man does not live on bread alone
but on every word that comes from the mouth of God.
Praise to you, O Christ, king of eternal glory!

GOSPEL
A reading from the holy Gospel according to Matthew   4:1-11
Jesus fasted for forty days and the tempter came.

Jesus was led by the Spirit out into the wilderness to be tempted by the devil. He fasted for forty days and forty nights, after which he was very hungry, and the tempter came and said to him, 'If you are the Son of God, tell these stones to turn into loaves.' But he replied, 'Scripture says:

Man does not live on bread alone
but on every word that comes from the mouth of God.'

The devil then took him to the holy city and made him stand on the parapet of the Temple. 'If you are the Son of God' he said 'throw yourself down; for scripture says:

He will put you in his angels' charge,

and they will support you on their hands
in case you hurt your foot against a stone.'

Jesus said to him, 'Scripture also says:

You must not put the Lord your God to the test.'

Next, taking him to a very high mountain, the devil showed him
all the kingdoms of the world and their splendour. 'I will give
you all these' he said, 'if you fall at my feet and worship me.'
Then Jesus replied, 'Be off, Satan! For scripture says:

You must worship the Lord your God,
and serve him alone.'

Then the devil left him, and angels appeared and looked after
him.

This is the Gospel of the Lord.

After the homily, the Election or Enrolment of candidates for
baptism may follow. See below, pp.173ff.

Prayer over the Gifts
Lord,
make us worthy to bring you these gifts.
May this sacrifice
help to change our lives.

Preface of First Sunday of Lent, P12 or of Lent I or II, P8 or P9

Communion Antiphon: Man does not live on bread alone, but on
every word that comes from the mouth of God.

or

The Lord will overshadow you, and you will find refuge under
his wings.

Prayer after Communion
Father,
you increase our faith and hope,
you deepen our love in this communion.
Help us to live by your words
and to seek Christ, our bread of life,
who is Lord for ever and ever.

An appropriate Solemn Blessing or Prayer over the People may
be used. See pp.90ff.

RITE OF ELECTION OR
ENROLMENT OF CANDIDATES FOR BAPTISM

Presentation of the Candidates

The candidates are summoned by name. Each comes forward accompanied by his godparent. The celebrant enquires if they are ready for the sacraments: have they listened to the word of God, sought to follow it in their lives, associated with their brothers and sisters in prayer? The godparents, before God, reply in the affirmative.

The celebrant then asks the candidates if they wish to receive the sacraments. On their replying in the affirmative, they are asked to give their names for enrolment. While this process is being gone through, Ps 15, for example, may be sung.

Admission or election

The celebrant explains briefly what has been done, and then informs the candidates that they have been chosen for initiation. They reply:

Thanks be to God.

The celebrant then continues as follows:

Now it is your duty and ours to ask the help of God. He is always faithful to those he calls. Be faithful to him in return and strive courageously to reach the goal your calling opens up to you.

Then the celebrant turns to the godparents and reminds them in these or similar words:

These catechumens have been entrusted to you in the Lord, and you have given us a favourable report. By your loving care and example continue to help them until they receive the sacraments of God's life.

He invites them to place their hand on the shoulder of the candidate whom they are presenting, or to make some other gesture to indicate this.

Prayer for the Elect

This is made as follows, or in similar words:

Celebrant: My brothers and sisters: Today we begin Lent and look forward to our celebration of the life-giving mysteries of our Lord's suffering, death, and resurrection. These chosen men (and women), whom we lead with us to the Easter sacraments, look to us for an example of Christian life. Let us pray to the

Lord for them and for ourselves that we may be strengthened by each other's mutual efforts, and so come to share the joys of Easter.

Reader: For our catechumens that they may always remember this day when they were chosen and be thankful for the blessing they have received from heaven, let us pray to the Lord:

℞   **Lord, hear our prayer.**

Reader: That they may use this lenten season to undertake with us the burden of self-denial and perform works of holiness, let us pray to the Lord:

℞   **Lord, hear our prayer.**

Reader: For their teachers, that they may always offer the sweetness of God's word to those who are searching for it, let us pray to the Lord:

℞   **Lord, hear our prayer.**

Reader: For their godparents, that they may give these catechumens a good example by their consistent living of the Gospel, both in their personal actions and in their duties to society, let us pray to the Lord:

℞   **Lord, hear our prayer.**

Reader: For their families, that, far from placing any obstacles in the way of these catechumens, they may assist them to follow the urging of the Holy Spirit, let us pray to the Lord:

℞   **Lord, hear our prayer.**

Reader: For our community, that during this Lent we may excel in fidelity to prayer and in charity, let us pray to the Lord:

℞   **Lord, hear our prayer.**

Reader: For all who have not yet overcome their hesitation, that they may trust in Christ and one day join our community as brothers and sisters, let us pray to the Lord:

℞   **Lord, hear our prayer.**

In the above prayer, the usual petition for the needs of the Church and the whole world is added if the catechumens are to be dismissed and the general intercessions will be omitted during the Mass.

The celebrant extends his hands over the elect and concludes with this prayer:

God our Father,
you created the human race

that you might also be the One who makes it ever new.
Count these adopted children
as sons (and daughters) reborn to your new covenant.
Make them children of the promise.
Although they cannot reach eternal life by their own nature,
may they come to share it by the power of your love.
We ask this through Christ our Lord.   ℟   **Amen.**

Dismissal of the Elect
The celebrant dismisses the elect with these or similar words:

You have been chosen by God and have entered with us on the
way of Lent. May Christ himself be your way, your truth, and
your life, especially during the approaching scrutinies when we
shall meet with you again. For the present, go in peace.

Elect: **Amen.**

SECOND SUNDAY OF LENT   A

Our Transfigured Lord

*Our natural inclination is to stay where we are, to make a tent and settle
comfortably. But God is continually urging us on to a land he will show
us. We follow our transfigured Lord in faith, putting our trust in him
and bearing his hardships for the sake of the good news he has brought us.*

Entrance Antiphon: Remember your mercies, Lord, your tenderness from ages past. Do not let our enemies triumph over us; O
God, deliver Israel from all her distress.

or

My heart has prompted me to seek your face; I seek it, Lord; do
not hide from me.

The Gloria is omitted.

Opening Prayer
Let us pray
    [for the grace to respond
    to the Word of God]

God our Father,
help us to hear your Son.
Enlighten us with your word,
that we may find the way to your glory.

or

Let us pray
    [in this season of Lent
    for the gift of integrity]

Father of light,
in you is found no shadow of change
but only the fullness of life and limitless truth.

Open our hearts to the voice of your Word
and free us from the original darkness that shadows our vision.
Restore our sight that we may look upon your Son
who calls us to repentance and a change of heart,
for he lives and reigns with you for ever and ever.

FIRST READING

A reading from the book of Genesis   12:1-4
The call of Abraham, the father of God's people.

The Lord said to Abram, 'Leave your country, your family and
your father's house, for the land I will show you. I will make you
a great nation; I will bless you and make your name so famous
that it will be used as a blessing.

    'I will bless those who bless you:
    I will curse those who slight you.
    All the tribes of the earth
    shall bless themselves by you.'

So Abram went as the Lord told him.

    This is the word of the Lord.

Responsorial Psalm   Ps 32:4-5. 18-20. 22. ℟ v.22
    ℟   **May your love be upon us, O Lord,
        as we place all our hope in you.**

1   The word of the Lord is faithful
    and all his works to be trusted.
    The Lord loves justice and right
    and fills the earth with his love.   ℟

2   The Lord looks on those who revere him,
    on those who hope in his love,
    to rescue their souls from death,
    to keep them alive in famine.   ℟

3   Our soul is waiting for the Lord.
    The Lord is our help and our shield.
    May your love be upon us, O Lord,
    as we place all our hope in you.   ℟

SECOND READING

A reading from the second letter of St Paul to Timothy   1:8-10
God calls and enlightens us.

With me, bear the hardships for the sake of the Good News,
relying on the power of God who has saved us and called us to be
holy – not because of anything we ourselves have done but for
his own purpose and by his own grace. This grace had already
been granted to us, in Christ Jesus, before the beginning of time,
but it has only been revealed by the Appearing of our saviour
Christ Jesus. He abolished death, and he has proclaimed life and
immortality through the Good News.

This is the word of the Lord.

Gospel Acclamation   Mt 17:5
    Glory and praise to you, O Christ!
    From the bright cloud the Father's voice was heard:
    'This is my Son, the Beloved. Listen to him.'
    Glory and praise to you, O Christ!

GOSPEL

A reading from the holy Gospel according to Matthew   17:1-9

His face shone like the sun.

Jesus took with him Peter and James and his brother John and led
them up a high mountain where they could be alone. There in
their presence he was transfigured; his face shone like the sun
and his clothes became as white as the light. Suddenly Moses
and Elijah appeared to them; they were talking with him. Then
Peter spoke to Jesus. 'Lord,' he said 'it is wonderful for us to be
here; if you wish, I will make three tents here, one for you, one
for Moses and one for Elijah.' He was still speaking when
suddenly a bright cloud covered them with shadow, and from
the cloud there came a voice which said, 'This is my Son, the
Beloved; he enjoys my favour. Listen to him'. When they heard
this, the disciples fell on their faces, overcome with fear. But
Jesus came up and touched them. 'Stand up,' he said 'do not be
afraid.' And when they raised their eyes they saw no one

but only Jesus.

As they came down from the mountain Jesus gave them this order. 'Tell no one about the vision until the Son of Man has risen from the dead.'

This is the Gospel of the Lord.

Prayer over the Gifts
Lord,
make us holy.
May this eucharist take away our sins
that we may be prepared
to celebrate the resurrection.

Preface of Second Sunday of Lent, P13 or of Lent I or II, P8 or P9

Communion Antiphon: This is my Son, my beloved, in whom is all my delight: listen to him.

Prayer after Communion
Lord,
we give thanks for these holy mysteries
which bring to us here on earth
a share in the life to come,
through Christ our Lord.

An appropriate Solemn Blessing or Prayer over the People may be used. See pp.90ff.

THIRD SUNDAY OF LENT   A

The Living Water

Christ quenches our spiritual thirst with the living water: the love of God which is poured into our hearts by the Holy Spirit. We pray for those who are prepared for this baptism.

Entrance Antiphon: My eyes are ever fixed on the Lord, for he releases my feet from the snare. O look at me and be merciful, for I am wretched and alone.

or

I will prove my holiness through you. I will gather you from the ends of the earth; I will pour clean water on you and wash away all your sins. I will give you a new spirit within you, says the Lord.

The Gloria is omitted.

Opening Prayer

Let us pray
> [for confidence in the love of God
> and the strength to overcome all our weakness]

Father, you have taught us to overcome our sins
by prayer, fasting and works of mercy.
When we are discouraged by our weakness,
give us confidence in your love.

or

Let us pray
> [to the Father and ask him
> to form a new heart within us]

God of all compassion, Father of all goodness,
to heal the wounds our sins and selfishness bring upon us
you bid us turn to fasting, prayer, and sharing with our brothers.
We acknowledge our sinfulness, our guilt is ever before us:
when our weakness causes discouragement,
let your compassion fill us with hope
and lead us through a Lent of repentance to the beauty of Easter
    joy.

FIRST READING

A reading from the book of Exodus   17:3-7
Give us water to drink.

Tormented by thirst, the people complained against Moses.
'Why did you bring us out of Egypt?' they said. 'Was it so that I
should die of thirst, my children too, and my cattle?' Moses
appealed to the Lord. 'How am I to deal with this people?' he
said. 'A little more and they will stone me!' The Lord said to
Moses, 'Take with you some of the elders of Israel and move on
to the forefront of the people; take in your hand the staff with
which you struck the river, and go. I shall be standing before you
there on the rock, at Horeb. You must strike the rock, and water
will flow from it for the people to drink.' This is what Moses did,
in the sight of the elders of Israel. The place was named Massah
and Meribah because of the grumbling of the sons of Israel and
because they put the Lord to the test by saying, 'Is the Lord with
us, or not?'

    This is the word of the Lord.

Responsorial Psalm   Ps 94:1-2. 6-9. R℣ v.8

R℣   **O that today you would listen to his voice:**
      'Harden not your hearts.'

1   Come, ring out our joy to the Lord;
     hail the rock who saves us.
     Let us come before him, giving thanks,
     with songs let us hail the Lord.   R℣

2   Come in; let us bow and bend low;
     let us kneel before the God who made us
     for he is our God and we
     the people who belong to his pasture,
     the flock that is led by his hand.   R℣

3   O that today you would listen to his voice!
     'Harden not your hearts as at Meribah,
     as on that day at Massah in the desert
     when your fathers put me to the test;
     when they tried me, though they saw my work.'   R℣

SECOND READING

A reading from the letter of St Paul to the Romans   5:1-2. 5-8

The love of God has been poured into our hearts by the Holy Spirit which has been given us.

Through our Lord Jesus Christ by faith we are judged righteous and at peace with God, since it is by faith and through Jesus that we have entered this state of grace in which we can boast about looking forward to God's glory. This hope is not deceptive, because the love of God has been poured into our hearts by the Holy Spirit which has been given us. We were still helpless when at his appointed moment Christ died for sinful men. It is not easy to die even for a good man – though of course for someone really worthy, a man might be prepared to die – but what proves that God loves us is that Christ died for us while we were still sinners.

     This is the word of the Lord.

Gospel Acclamation   cf. Jn 4:42.15
     Glory to you, O Christ, you are the Word of God!
     Lord, you are really the saviour of the world;
     give me the living water, so that I may never get thirsty.
     Glory to you, O Christ, you are the Word of God!

GOSPEL

A reading from the holy Gospel according to John   4:5-42
A spring welling up to eternal life.

*Jesus came to the Samaritan town called Sychar, near the land that Jacob gave to his son Joseph. Jacob's well is there and Jesus, tired by the journey, sat straight down by the well. It was about the sixth hour. When a Samaritan woman came to draw water, Jesus said to her, 'Give me a drink.' His disciples had gone into the town to buy food. The Samaritan woman said to him, 'What? You are a Jew and you ask me, a Samaritan, for a drink?' – Jews, in fact, do not associate with Samaritans. Jesus replied:

'If you only knew what God is offering
and who it is that is saying to you:
Give me a drink,
you would have been the one to ask,
and he would have given you living water.'

'You have no bucket, sir,' she answered 'and the well is deep: how could you get this living water? Are you a greater man than our father Jacob who gave us this well and drank from it himself with his sons and his cattle?' Jesus replied:

'Whoever drinks this water
will get thirsty again;
but anyone who drinks the water that I shall give
will never be thirsty again:
the water that I shall give
will turn into a spring inside him, welling up to eternal life.'

'Sir,' said the woman 'give me some of that water, so that I may never get thirsty and never have to come here again to draw water.'* 'Go and call your husband' said Jesus to her 'and come back here.' The woman answered, 'I have no husband.' He said to her, 'You are right to say, "I have no husband"; for although you have had five, the one you have now is not your husband. You spoke the truth there.' *'I see you are a prophet, sir' said the woman. 'Our fathers worshipped on this mountain, while you say that Jerusalem is the place where one ought to worship.' Jesus said:

'Believe me, woman, the hour is coming
when you will worship the Father
neither on this mountain nor in Jerusalem.

You worship what you do not know;
we worship what we do know;
for salvation comes from the Jews.
But the hour will come – in fact it is here already –
when true worshippers will worship the Father in spirit and
      truth:
that is the kind of worshipper
the Father wants.
God is spirit,
and those who worship
must worship in spirit and truth.'

The woman said to him, 'I know that Messiah – that is, Christ
– is coming; and when he comes he will tell us everything.' 'I
who am speaking to you,' said Jesus 'I am he.'*

At this point his disciples returned, and were surprised to
find him speaking to a woman, though none of them asked,
'What do you want from her?' or, 'Why are you talking to her?'
The woman put down her water jar and hurried back to the town
to tell the people, 'Come and see a man who has told me
everything I ever did; I wonder if he is the Christ?' This brought
people out of the town and they started walking towards him.

Meanwhile, the disciples were urging him, 'Rabbi, do have
something to eat;' but he said, 'I have food to eat that you do not
know about.' So the disciples asked one another, 'Has someone
been bringing him food?' But Jesus said:

'My food
is to do the will of the one who sent me,
and to complete his work.
Have you not got a saying:
Four months and then the harvest?
Well, I tell you:
Look around you, look at the fields;
already they are white, ready for harvest!
Already the reaper is being paid his wages,
already he is bringing in the grain for eternal life,
and thus sower and reaper rejoice together.
For here the proverb holds good:
one sows, another reaps;
I sent you to reap
a harvest you had not worked for.
Others worked for it;
and you have come into the rewards of their trouble.'

* Many Samaritans of that town had believed in him on the strength of the woman's testimony when she said, 'He told me all I have ever done,' so, when the Samaritans came up to him, they begged him to stay with them. He stayed for two days, and when he spoke to them many more came to believe; and they said to the woman, 'Now we no longer believe because of what you told us; we have heard him ourselves and we know that he really is the saviour of the world.'

This is the Gospel of the Lord.*

*Shorter Form, verses 5-16. 19-26. 39-42. Read between *

After the homily the First Scrutiny of the candidates for baptism may take place. The texts are given below, p.184.

Prayer over the Gifts
Lord,
by the grace of this sacrifice
may we who ask forgiveness
be ready to forgive one another.

Preface of Third Sunday of Lent, P14

If there have been Scrutinies and when Eucharistic Prayer I is used, the special forms of *Remember, Lord, your people,* and *Father, accept this offering,* are said:

Remember, Lord, these godparents
who will present your chosen men and women for baptism
(the names of the godparents are mentioned).
Lord, remember all of us . . .

Father,
accept this offering
from your whole family.
We offer it especially for the men and women
you call to share your life
through the living waters of baptism.
(Through Christ our Lord. Amen.)

Communion Antiphon: Whoever drinks the water that I shall give him, says the Lord, will have a spring inside him, welling up for eternal life.

Prayer after Communion
Lord,
in sharing this sacrament
may we receive your forgiveness
and be brought together in unity and peace.

An appropriate Solemn Blessing or Prayer over the People may be used. See pp.90ff.

FIRST SCRUTINY

After the Homily the elect and their godparents come before the celebrant. He invites all to pray in silence, and the elect to show their spirit of repentance by bowing or kneeling.

A solemn intercessory *Prayer for the Elect* follows. While this prayer is being said for the elect, the godparents place their right hand on the shoulder of the one they are sponsoring.

Celebrant: The Church has confidently chosen these men and women whose long preparation will be over at Easter. Let us pray that they will be ready and will find Christ in his sacraments.

Reader: That they may keep the word of God in their hearts and learn to understand it more deeply, let us pray to the Lord:

R⁀　　**Lord, hear our prayer.**

Reader: That they may learn to know Christ who came to save what had been lost, let us pray to the Lord:

R⁀　　**Lord, hear our prayer.**

Reader: That they may humbly acknowledge their sinfulness, let us pray to the Lord:

R⁀　　**Lord, hear our prayer.**

Reader: That they may sincerely reject anything in their lives which is displeasing to Christ or opposed to him, let us pray to the Lord:

R⁀　　**Lord, hear our prayer.**

Reader: That the Holy Spirit, who searches the hearts of all men, may strengthen their weakness with his power, let us pray to the Lord:

R⁀　　**Lord, hear our prayer.**

Reader: That the same Holy Spirit may teach them to know the things of God and how to please him, let us pray to the Lord:

R⁀　　**Lord, hear our prayer.**

Reader: That they and their families may put their hope in Christ and receive peace and holiness from him, let us pray to the Lord:
℟ **Lord, hear our prayer.**

Reader: That we ourselves in preparation for the feast of Christ's resurrection may amend our hearts and be loving to all men, let us pray to the Lord:
℟ **Lord, hear our prayer.**

Reader: That throughout the whole world the sick may be restored to health, the broken may be made whole again, the lost be found, and the found be saved, let us pray to the Lord:
℟ **Lord, hear our prayer.**

The celebrant may adapt the introduction and invocations according to various circumstances. The usual petition for the needs of the Church and the whole world is added if the catechumens are to be dismissed and the general intercessions will be omitted in the Mass.

Exorcism

After the prayer, the celebrant turns to the elect and with hands joined says:

Let us pray.

God our Father,
you sent your Son to be our Saviour:
these men (and women) preparing for baptism
thirst for living water as did the Samaritan woman.
May the word of the Lord change their lives too,
and help them to acknowledge the sins and weaknesses that
    burden them.
Keep them from relying too much on themselves
and never let the powers of evil deceive them.
Free them from the spirit of falsehood
and help them recognise any evil within themselves,
that with hearts cleansed from sin
they may advance on the way to salvation.
We ask this through Christ our Lord.   ℟ **Amen.**

The celebrant then lays his hand in silence on each one of the elect, if this can be done conveniently.

Then he extends his hands over the elect and continues:

Lord Jesus,
you are the fountain we thirst for;
you are the teacher we seek;
you alone are the Holy One.
These chosen ones open their hearts honestly
to confess their failures
and be forgiven.
In your love, free them from evil,
restore their health, satisfy their thirst, and give them peace.
By the power of your name,
which we call upon in faith,
stay with them and save them.
Command the spirit of evil to leave them,
for you have conquered that spirit by rising to life.
Show your chosen people the way of life in the Holy Spirit
 that they may grow closer to the Father and worship him,
for you are Lord for ever and ever.   R/   **Amen.**

An appropriate song may be sung, for example, Psalms 6, 25, 31,
37, 38, 39, 50, 114, 129, 138, or 141.

Dismissal of the Elect
Then the celebrant dismisses the elect:

Go in peace until we meet at the next scrutiny.
May the Lord be with you always.

Elect: **Amen.**

FOURTH SUNDAY OF LENT   A

Our Shepherd-King In This Valley Of Darkness

*We walk in the darkness of this world, often assailed by fear and
misgiving. But Christ, the Shepherd-King, the second David, lights up
our way for us and cures our congenital blindness as he leads us to his
kingdom.*

Entrance Antiphon: Rejoice, Jerusalem! Be glad for her, you who
love her; rejoice with her, you who mourned for her, and you
will find contentment at her consoling breasts.

The Gloria is omitted.

Opening Prayer
Let us pray
   [for a greater faith and love]

Father of peace,
we are joyful in your Word,
your Son Jesus Christ,
who reconciles us to you.
Let us hasten toward Easter
with the eagerness of faith and love.

or

Let us pray
   [that by growing in love this lenten season
   we may bring the peace of Christ to our world]

God our Father,
your Word, Jesus Christ, spoke peace to a sinful world
and brought mankind the gift of reconciliation
by the suffering and death he endured.

Teach us, the people who bear his name,
to follow the example he gave us:
may our faith, hope, and charity
turn hatred to love, conflict to peace, death to eternal life.

FIRST READING

A reading from the first book of Samuel   16:1. 6-7. 10-13
David is anointed king of Israel.

The Lord said to Samuel, 'Fill your horn with oil and go. I am
sending you to Jesse of Bethlehem, for I have chosen myself a
king among his sons.' When Samuel arrived, he caught sight of
Eliab and thought, 'Surely the Lord's anointed one stands there
before him,' but the Lord said to Samuel, 'Take no notice of his
appearance or his height for I have rejected him; God does not
see as man sees; man looks at appearances but the Lord looks at
the heart.' Jesse presented his seven sons to Samuel, but Samuel
said to Jesse, 'The Lord has not chosen these.' He then asked
Jesse, 'Are these all the sons you have?' He answered, 'There is
still one left, the youngest; he is out looking after the sheep.'
Then Samuel said to Jesse, 'Send for him; we will not sit down to
eat until he comes.' Jesse had him sent for, a boy of fresh
complexion, with fine eyes and pleasant bearing. The Lord said,
'Come, anoint him, for this is the one.' At this, Samuel took the

horn of oil and anointed him where he stood with his brothers; and the spirit of the Lord seized on David and stayed with him from that day on.

This is the word of the Lord.

Responsial Psalm   Ps 22. ℟ v.1
  ℟   **The Lord is my shepherd;**
        there is nothing I shall want.

1   The Lord is my shepherd;
    there is nothing I shall want.
    Fresh and green are the pastures
    where he gives me repose.
    Near restful waters he leads me,
    to revive my drooping spirit.   ℟

2   He guides me along the right path;
    he is true to his name.
    If I should walk in the valley of darkness
    no evil would I fear.
    You are there with your crook and your staff;
    with these you give me comfort.   ℟

3   You have prepared a banquet for me
    in the sight of my foes.
    My head you have anointed with oil;
    my cup is overflowing.   ℟

4   Surely goodness and kindness shall follow me
    all the days of my life.
    In the Lord's own house shall I dwell
    for ever and ever.   ℟

SECOND READING

A reading from the letter of St Paul to the Ephesians   5:8-14
Rise from the dead and Christ will shine on you.

You were darkness once, but now you are light in the Lord; be like children of light, for the effects of the light are seen in complete goodness and right living and truth. Try to discover what the Lord wants of you, having nothing to do with the futile works of darkness but exposing them by contrast. The things which are done in secret are things that people are ashamed even to speak of; but anything exposed by the light will be illuminated and anything illuminated turns into light. That is why it is said:

Wake up from your sleep,
rise from the dead,
and Christ will shine on you.

This is the word of the Lord.

Gospel Acclamation   Jn 8:12
   Glory to you, O Christ, you are the Word of God!
   I am the light of the world, says the Lord;
   anyone who follows me will have the light of life.
   Glory to you, O Christ, you are the Word of God!

GOSPEL

A reading from the holy Gospel according to John   9:1-41
*The blind man went off and washed himself, and came away with his
sight restored.*

*As Jesus went along, he saw a man who had been blind from
birth.* His disciples asked him, 'Rabbi, who sinned, this man or
his parents, for him to have been born blind?' 'Neither he nor his
parents sinned,' Jesus answered 'he was born blind so that the
works of God might be displayed in him.

   'As long as the day lasts
   I must carry out the work of the one who sent me;
   the night will soon be here when no one can work.
   As long as I am in the world
   I am the light of the world.'

Having said this, *he spat on the ground, made a paste with
the spittle, put this over the eyes of the blind man and said to
him, 'Go and wash in the Pool of Siloam' (a name that means
'sent'). So the blind man went off and washed himself, and came
away with his sight restored.

His neighbours and people who earlier had seen him begging
said, 'Isn't this the man who used to sit and beg?' Some said,
'Yes, it is the same one.' Others said, 'No, he only looks like
him.' The man himself said, 'I am the man.'* So they said to him,
'Then how do your eyes come to be open?' 'The man called Jesus'
he answered 'made a paste, daubed my eyes with it and said to
me, "Go and wash at Siloam"; so I went, and when I washed I
could see.' They asked, 'Where is he?' 'I don't know' he
answered.

*They brought the man who had been blind to the Pharisees.

It had been a sabbath day when Jesus made the paste and opened the man's eyes, so when the Pharisees asked him how he had come to see, he said, 'He put a paste on my eyes, and I washed, and I can see.' Then some of the Pharisees said, 'This man cannot be from God: he does not keep the sabbath.' Others said, 'How could a sinner produce signs like this?' And there was disagreement among them, So they spoke to the blind man again, 'What have you to say about him yourself, now that he has opened your eyes?' 'He is a prophet' replied the man.*

However, the Jews would not believe that the man had been blind and had gained his sight, without first sending for his parents and asking them, 'Is this man really your son who you say was born blind? If so how is it that he is now able to see?' His parents answered, 'We know he is our son and we know he was born blind, but we don't know how it is that he can see now, or who opened his eyes. He is old enough: let him speak for himself.' His parents spoke like this out of fear of the Jews, who had already agreed to expel from the synagogue anyone who should acknowledge Jesus as the Christ. This was why his parents said, 'He is old enough; ask him.'

So the Jews again sent for the man and said to him, 'Give glory to God! For our part, we know that this man is a sinner.' The man answered, 'I don't know if he is a sinner; I only know that I was blind and now I can see.' They said to him, 'What did he do to you? How did he open your eyes?' He replied, 'I have told you once and you wouldn't listen. Why do you want to hear it all again? Do you want to become his disciples too?' At this they hurled abuse at him: 'You can be his disciple,' they said 'we are disciples of Moses: we know that God spoke to Moses, but as for this man, we don't know where he comes from.' The man replied, 'Now here is an astonishing thing! He has opened my eyes and you don't know where he comes from! We know that God doesn't listen to sinners, but God does listen to men who are devout and do his will. Ever since the world began it is unheard of for anyone to open the eyes of a man who was born blind; if this man were not from God, he couldn't do a thing.' *'Are you trying to teach us,' they replied 'and you a sinner through and through, since you were born!' And they drove him away.

Jesus heard they had driven him away, and when he found him he said to him, 'Do you believe in the Son of Man?' 'Sir,' the man replied 'tell me who he is so that I may believe in him.' Jesus said, 'You are looking at him; he is speaking to you.' The man

| said, 'Lord, I believe', and worshipped him.*
    Jesus said:

'It is for judgement
that I have come into this world,
so that those without sight may see
and those with sight turn blind.'

Hearing this, some Pharisees who were present said to him, 'We
are not blind, surely?' Jesus replied:

'Blind? If you were,
you would not be guilty,
but since you say, "We see",
your guilt remains.'

| *This is the Gospel of the Lord.*

*Shorter Form, verses 1. 6-9. 13-17. 34-38. Read between *

After the homily the Second Scrutiny of the candidates for
baptism may take place. The texts are given below p.192.

Prayer over the Gifts
Lord,
we offer you these gifts
which bring us peace and joy.
Increase our reverence by this eucharist,
and bring salvation to the world.

Preface of Fourth Sunday of Lent, P15

If there have been Scrutinies and Eucharistic Prayer I is used the
special forms given on Third Sunday of Lent, p.183 above, are
said.

Communion Antiphon: The Lord rubbed my eyes: I went away and
washed; then I could see, and I believed in God.

Prayer after Communion
Father,
you enlighten all who come into the world.
Fill our hearts with the light of your gospel,
that our thoughts may please you,
and our love be sincere.

An appropriate Solemn Blessing or Prayer over the People may
be used. See pp.90ff.

SECOND SCRUTINY

After the Homily the elect and their godparents come before the celebrant. He invites all to pray in silence, and the elect to show their spirit of repentance by bowing or kneeling.

A solemn intercessory *Prayer for the Elect* follows. While this prayer is being said for the elect, the godparents place their right hand on the shoulder of the one they are sponsoring.

Celebrant: Let us pray for these men and women whom God has chosen, that their lives may remain centred in him and they may offer convincing witness to the message of eternal life.

Reader: That they may find and maintain freedom of mind and heart in faithfulness to the truth of Christ, let us pray to the Lord:

℟ **Lord, hear our prayer.**

Reader: That they may prefer the foolishness of the cross to the wisdom of the world and seek happiness in God alone, let us pray to the Lord:

℟ **Lord, hear our prayer.**

Reader: That the power of the Holy Spirit may fill them with freedom and change their fear into trust, let us pray to the Lord:

℟ **Lord, hear our prayer.**

Reader: That they may become spiritual men (and women) by striving to do what is holy and just, let us pray to the Lord:

℟ **Lord, hear our prayer.**

Reader: That all who suffer for their allegiance to Christ may find their strength in him, let us pray to the Lord:

℟ **Lord, hear our prayer.**

Reader: That families and nations who are hindered from embracing the faith may be granted the freedom to believe the Gospel, let us pray to the Lord:

℟ **Lord, hear our prayer.**

Reader: That we who are immersed in the world may remain faithful to the spirit of the Gospel, let us pray to the Lord:

℟ **Lord, hear our prayer.**

Reader: That the whole world, which the Father so loves, may attain complete spiritual freedom in the Church, let us pray to the Lord:

℟ **Lord, hear our prayer.**

The celebrant may adapt the introduction and invocations according to various circumstances. The usual petition for the

needs of the Church and the entire world is added if the
catechumens are to be dismissed and the general intercessions
will be omitted in the Mass.

Exorcism

After the prayer, the celebrant turns to the elect and with hands
joined says:

Let us pray.

Father of mercy,
you helped the man born blind to believe in your Son
and through that faith to reach the light of your Kingdom.
Free your chosen ones from the falsehoods that surround and
   blind them.
Let truth be the foundation of their lives.
May they live in your light for ever.
We ask this through Christ our Lord. ℟ **Amen.**

The celebrant then lays his hand in silence on each one of the
elect, if this can be done conveniently.
Then he extends his hands over the elect and continues:

Lord Jesus,
you are the true light that enlightens all men.
By the Spirit of truth,
free all who struggle under the yoke of the father of lies.
Arouse the good will of these men (and women)
whom you have chosen for your sacraments.
Grant them to enjoy your light
like the man whose sight you once restored,
and inspire them to become fearless witnesses to the faith,
for you are Lord for ever and ever. ℟ **Amen.**

An appropriate song may be sung, for example, Psalms 6, 25, 31,
37, 38, 39, 50, 114, 129, 138, or 141.

Dismissal of the Elect

Then the celebrant dismisses the elect:

Go in peace until we meet at the next scrutiny.
May the Lord be with you always.

Elect: **Amen.**

FIFTH SUNDAY OF LENT   **A**

Christ Breathes Into Us His Living Spirit

Today we open ourselves to Christ's life-giving Spirit. We pray too for those who are to be given the new life of the Spirit in baptism this Easter.

Entrance Antiphon: Give me justice, O God, and defend my cause against the wicked; rescue me from deceitful and unjust men. You, O God, are my refuge.

The Gloria is omitted.

Opening Prayer
Let us pray
    [for the courage to follow Christ]

Father,
help us to be like Christ your Son,
who loved the world and died for our salvation.
Inspire us by his love,
guide us by his example,
who lives and reigns with you and the Holy Spirit,
one God, for ever and ever.

or

Let us pray
    [for the courage to embrace the world
    in the name of Christ]

Father in heaven,
the love of your Son led him to accept the suffering of the cross
that his brothers might glory in new life.
Change our selfishness into self-giving.
Help us to embrace the world you have given us,
that we may transform the darkness of its pain
into the life and joy of Easter.

FIRST READING

A reading from the prophet Ezekiel   37:12-14
I shall put my spirit in you, and you will live.

The Lord says this: I am now going to open your graves; I mean to raise you from your graves, my people, and lead you back to the soil of Israel. And you will know that I am the Lord, when I open your graves and raise you from your graves, my people. And I shall put my spirit in you, and you will live, and I shall resettle you on your own soil; and you will know that I, the Lord, have said and done this – it is the Lord who speaks.

This is the word of the Lord.

Responsorial Psalm Ps 129. ℟ v.7

℟ **With the Lord there is mercy
and fullness of redemption.**

1 Out of the depths I cry to you, O Lord,
Lord, hear my voice!
O let your ears be attentive
to the voice of my pleading. ℟

2 If you, O Lord, should mark our guilt,
Lord, who would survive?
But with you is found forgiveness:
for this we revere you. ℟

3 My soul is waiting for the Lord,
I count on his word.
My soul is longing for the Lord
more than watchman for daybreak.
(Let the watchman count on daybreak
and Israel on the Lord.) ℟

4 Because with the Lord there is mercy
and fullness of redemption,
Israel indeed he will redeem
from all its iniquity. ℟

SECOND READING

A reading from the letter of St Paul to the Romans 8:8-11
The Spirit of him who raised Jesus from the dead is living in you.

People who are interested only in unspiritual things can never be pleasing to God. Your interests, however, are not in the unspiritual, but in the spiritual, since the Spirit of God has made his home in you. In fact, unless you possessed the Spirit of Christ you would not belong to him. Though your body may be dead it is because of sin, but if Christ is in you then your spirit is life itself because you have been justified; and if the Spirit of him who raised Jesus from the dead is living in you, then he who raised Jesus from the dead will give life to your own mortal bodies through his Spirit living in you.

This is the word of the Lord.

Gospel Acclamation   Jn 11:25. 26
    Glory and praise to you, O Christ!
    I am the resurrection and the life, says the Lord;
    who ever believes in me will never die.
    Glory and praise to you, O Christ!

GOSPEL

A reading from the holy Gospel according to John   11:1-45
I am the resurrection and the life.

There was a man named Lazarus who lived in the village of Bethany with the two sisters, Mary and Martha, and he was ill. – It was the same Mary, the sister of the sick man Lazarus, who anointed the Lord with ointment and wiped his feet with her hair. *The sisters sent this mesage to Jesus, 'Lord, the man you love is ill.' On receiving the message, Jesus said, 'This sickness will end not in death but in God's glory, and through it the Son of God will be glorified.'

Jesus loved Martha and her sister and Lazarus, yet when he heard that Lazarus was ill he stayed where he was for two more days before saying to the disciples, 'Let us go to Judaea.'* The disciples said, 'Rabbi, it is not long since the Jews wanted to stone you; are you going back again?' Jesus replied:

    'Are there not twelve hours in the day?
    A man can walk in the daytime without stumbling
    because he has the light of this world to see by;
    but if he walks at night he stumbles,
    because there is no light to guide him'.

He said that and then added, 'Our friend Lazarus is resting, I am going to wake him.' The disciples said to him 'Lord, if he is able to rest he is sure to get better.' The phrase Jesus used referred to the death of Lazarus, but they thought that by 'rest' he meant 'sleep', so Jesus put it plainly, 'Lazarus is dead, and for your sake I am glad I was not there because now you will believe. But let us go to him.' Then Thomas – known as the Twin – said to the other disciples, 'Let us go too, and die with him.'

    *On arriving, Jesus found that Lazarus had been in the tomb

for four days already.* Bethany is only about two miles from Jerusalem, and many Jews had come to Martha and Mary to sympathise with them over their brother. *When Martha heard that Jesus had come she went to meet him. Mary remained sitting in the house. Martha said to Jesus, 'If you had been here, my brother would not have died, but I know that, even now, whatever you ask of God, he will grant you.' 'Your brother' said Jesus to her 'will rise again.' Martha said, 'I know he will rise again at the resurrection on the last day.' Jesus said:

'I am the resurrection and the life.
If anyone believes in me, even though he dies he will live,
and whoever lives and believes in me
will never die.
Do you believe this?'

'Yes Lord,' she said 'I believe that you are the Christ, the Son of God, the one who was to come into this world.'*

When she had said this, she went and called her sister Mary, saying in a low voice, 'The Master is here and wants to see you.' Hearing this, Mary got up quickly and went to him. Jesus had not yet come into the village; he was still at the place where Martha had met him. When the Jews who were in the house sympathising with Mary saw her get up so quickly and go out, they followed her, thinking that she was going to the tomb to weep there.

Mary went to Jesus, and as soon as she saw him she threw herself at his feet, saying, 'Lord if you had been here, my brother would not have died.' At the sight of her tears, and those of the Jews who followed her, *Jesus said in great distress, with a sigh that came straight from the heart, 'Where have you put him?' They said, 'Lord, come and see.' Jesus wept; and the Jews said, 'See how much he loved him!' But there were some who remarked, 'He opened the eyes of the blind man, could he not have prevented this man's death?' Still sighing, Jesus reached the tomb: it was a cave with a stone to close the opening. Jesus said, 'Take the stone away.' Martha said to him 'Lord by now he will smell; this is the fourth day.' Jesus replied 'Have I not told you that if you believe you will see the glory of God?' So they took away the stone. Then Jesus lifted up his eyes and said:

'Father, I thank you for hearing my prayer.
I knew indeed that you always hear me.
But I speak

for the sake of all these who stand round me,
so that they may believe it was you who sent me.'

When he had said this, he cried in a loud voice, 'Lazarus, here! Come out!' The dead man came out, his feet and hands bound with bands of stuff and a cloth round his face. Jesus said to them, 'Unbind him, let him go free.'

Many of the Jews who had come to visit Mary and had seen what he did believed in him.

This is the Gospel of the Lord.*

*Shorter Form, verses 3-7. 17. 20-7. 33-45. Read between *

After the homily the Third Scrutiny of candidates for baptism may take place. The texts are given below p.199.

Prayer over the Gifts
Almighty God,
may the sacrifice we offer
take away the sins of those
whom you enlighten with the Christian faith.

Preface of Fifth Sunday of Lent, P16

If there have been scrutinies and Eucharistic Prayer I is used the special forms given on Third Sunday of Lent, p.183 above, are said.

Communion Antiphon: He who lives and believes in me will not die for ever, said the Lord.

Prayer after Communion

Almighty Father,
by this sacrifice
may we always remain one with your Son, Jesus Christ,
whose body and blood we share,
for he is Lord for ever and ever.

An appropriate Solemn Blessing or Prayer over the People may be used. See pp.90ff.

THIRD SCRUTINY

After the Homily the elect and their godparents come before the celebrant. He invites all to pray in silence, and the elect to show their spirit of repentance by bowing or kneeling.

A solemn intercessory *Prayer for the Elect* follows.

While this prayer is being said for the elect, the godparents place their right hand on the shoulder of the one they are sponsoring.

Celebrant: God has chosen these men and women to serve him. Let us pray that they may be united to Christ in his death and resurrection and, by the grace of his sacraments, conquer the bitterness of death.

Reader: That their faith may strengthen them against the deceits of the world, let us pray to the Lord:

℟ **Lord, hear our prayer.**

Reader: That they may remain grateful to God who has rescued them from ignorance and opened to them the hope of salvation, let us pray to the Lord:

℟ **Lord, hear our prayer.**

Reader: That the prayers and example of catechumens who have shed their blood for Christ may arouse their hope of eternal life, let us pray to the Lord:

℟ **Lord, hear our prayer.**

Reader: That they may reject sin which destroys life, let us pray to the Lord:

℟ **Lord, hear our prayer.**

Reader: That all who are saddened by the death of their loved ones may find comfort in Christ, let us pray to the Lord:

℟ **Lord, hear our prayer.**

Reader: That we too at Easter may be strengthened by the hope of rising to life with Christ, let us pray to the Lord:

℟ **Lord, hear our prayer.**

Reader: That an increase of faith and love may give life to the whole world which God created out of love, let us pray to the Lord:

℟ **Lord, hear our prayer.**

The celebrant may adapt the introduction and invocations according to various circumstances. The usual petition for the needs of the Church and the whole world is added if the

catechumens are to be dismissed and the general intercessions
will be omitted in the Mass.

Exorcism

After the prayer, the celebrant turns to the elect and with hands
joined, says:

Let us pray.

Father of eternal life,
you are a God, not of the dead, but of the living:
you sent your Son to proclaim the good news of life,
to rescue men from the kingdom of death
and to lead them to resurrection.
Free these chosen people
from the power of the evil spirit who brings death.
May they receive new life from Christ
and bear witness to his resurrection.
We ask this through Christ our Lord.   R̸   **Amen.**

The celebrant then lays his hands in silence on each one of the
elect, if this can be done conveniently.

Then he extends his hands over the elect and continues:

Lord Jesus,
you raised Lazarus from death
as a sign that you had come to give men life in fullest measure.
Rescue from death all who seek life from your sacraments
and free them from the spirit of evil.
By your Holy Spirit fill them with life;
give them faith, hope and love
that they may live with you always
and come to share the glory of your resurrection,
for you are Lord for ever and ever.   R̸   **Amen.**

An appropriate song may be sung, for example, Psalms 6, 25, 31,
37, 38, 39, 50, 114, 129, 138, or 141.

Dismissal of the Elect

Then the celebrant dismisses the elect:

Go in peace, and may the Lord be with you always.

Elect: **Amen.**

HOLY WEEK

PASSION SUNDAY
(Palm Sunday)

A,B,C

On this day the Church celebrates Christ's entrance into Jerusalem to accomplish his paschal mystery. Accordingly, the memorial of this event is included in every Mass, with the procession or the solemn entrance before the principal Mass, with the simple entrance before the other Masses. The solemn entrance (but not the procession) may be repeated before one or other Mass that is usually well attended.

COMMEMORATION OF THE LORD'S ENTRANCE INTO JERUSALEM

First Form: The Procession

The congregation assembles in some suitable place distinct from the church to which the procession will move. The faithful carry palm branches.

The priest and ministers put on red vestments for Mass and go to the place where the people have assembled.

Meanwhile, this antiphon, or any suitable song, is sung.

Antiphon

Hosanna to the Son of David,
the King of Israel.
Blessed is he who comes
in the name of the Lord.
Hosanna in the highest.

The priest greets the people in the usual way and gives a brief introduction, inviting them to take a full part in the celebration. He may use these or similar words:

Dear friends in Christ, for five weeks of Lent we have been preparing, by works of charity and self-sacrifice, for the celebration of our Lord's paschal mystery. Today we come together to begin this solemn celebration in union with the whole Church throughout the world. Christ entered in triumph into his own city, to complete his work as our Messiah: to suffer, to die, and to rise again. Let us remember with devotion this entry which began his saving work and follow him with a lively faith. United with him in his suffering on the cross, may we share his resurrection and new life.

Afterwards the priest says one of the following prayers:

Let us pray.
Almighty God,
we pray you
bless ✠ these branches
and make them holy.
Today we joyfully acclaim Jesus our Messiah and King.
May we reach one day the happiness of the new and everlasting
    Jerusalem
by faithfully following him
who lives and reigns for ever and ever.

or

Let us pray.
Lord,
increase the faith of your people
and listen to our prayers.
Today we honour Christ our triumphant King
by carrying these branches.
May we honour you every day
by living always in him,
for he is Lord for ever and ever.

The priest sprinkles the branches with holy water in silence. The
account of the Lord's entrance into Jerusalem is proclaimed from
one of the four gospels.

Gospel A, B or C is read according to the Cycle for the Year. See
Table of Principal Celebrations.

Year A

A reading from the holy Gospel according to Matthew   21:1-11
Blessings on him who comes in the name of the Lord!

When they were near Jerusalem and had come in sight of
Bethphage on the Mount of Olives, Jesus sent two disciples,
saying to them, 'Go to the village facing you, and you will
immediately find a tethered donkey and a colt with her. Untie
them and bring them to me. If anyone says anything to you, you
are to say, "The Master needs them and will send them back
directly." ' This took place to fulfill the prophecy:

    Say to the daughter of Zion:
    Look, your king comes to you:

he is humble, he rides on a donkey
and on a colt, the foal of a beast of burden.

So the disciples went out and did as Jesus had told them. They brought the donkey and the colt, then they laid their cloaks on their backs and he sat on them. Great crowds of people spread their cloaks on the road, while others were cutting branches from the trees and spreading them in his path. The crowds who went in front of him and those who followed were all shouting:

'Hosanna to the Son of David!
Blessings on him who comes in the name of the Lord!
Hosanna in the highest heavens!'

And when he entered Jerusalem, the whole city was in turmoil. 'Who is this?' people asked, and the crowds answered, 'This is the prophet Jesus from Nazareth in Galilee.'

This is the Gospel of the Lord.

Year B

A reading from the holy Gospel according to Mark   11:1-10
Blessings on him who comes in the name of the Lord.

When they were approaching Jerusalem, in sight of Bethphage and Bethany, close by the Mount of Olives, Jesus sent two of his disciples and said to them, 'Go off to the village facing you, and as soon as you enter it you will find a tethered colt that no one has yet ridden. Untie it and bring it here. If anyone says to you, "What are you doing?" say, "The Master needs it and will send it back here directly." ' They went off and found a colt tethered near a door in the open street. As they untied it, some men standing there said, 'What are you doing, untying that colt?' They gave the answer Jesus had told them, and the men let them go. Then they took the colt to Jesus and threw their cloaks on its back, and he sat on it. Many people spread their cloaks on the road, others greenery which they had cut in the fields. And those who went in front and those who followed were all shouting, 'Hosanna! Blessings on him who comes in the name of the Lord! Blessings on the coming kingdom of our father David! Hosanna in the highest heavens!'

This is the Gospel of the Lord.

Alternative Gospel Year B

A reading from the holy Gospel according to John   12:12-16
Blessings on him who comes in the name of the Lord.

The crowds who had come up for the festival heard that Jesus was on his way to Jerusalem. They took branches of palm and went out to meet him, shouting, 'Hosanna! Blessings on the King of Israel, who comes in the name of the Lord.' Jesus found a young donkey and mounted it – as scripture says: Do not be afraid, daughter of Zion; see, your king is coming, mounted on the colt of a donkey. At the time his disciples did not understand this, but later, after Jesus had been glorified, they remembered that this had been written about him and that this was in fact how they had received him.

This is the Gospel of the Lord.

Year C

A reading from the holy Gospel according to Luke   19:28-40
Blessings on him who comes in the name of the Lord.

Jesus went on ahead, going up to Jerusalem. Now when he was near Bethphage and Bethany, close by the Mount of Olives as it is called, he sent two of the disciples, telling them, 'Go off to the village opposite, and as you enter it you will find a tethered colt that no one has yet ridden. Untie it and bring it here. If anyone asks you, "Why are you untying it?" you are to say this, "The Master needs it." ' The messengers went off and found every-thing just as he had told them. As they were untying the colt, its owner said, 'Why are you untying that colt?' and they answered, 'The Master needs it.'

So they took the colt to Jesus, and throwing their garments over its back they helped Jesus on to it. As he moved off, people spread their cloaks in the road, and now, as he was approaching the downward slope of the Mount of Olives, the whole group of disciples joyfully began to praise God at the top of their voices for all the miracles they had seen. They cried out:

'Blessings on the King who comes,
in the name of the Lord!
Peace in heaven
and glory in the highest heavens!'

Some Pharisees in the crowd said to him, 'Master, check your disciples,' but he answered, 'I tell you, if these keep silence the stones will cry out.'

This is the Gospel of the Lord.

After the gospel a brief homily may be given. Before the procession begins, the celebrant or other suitable minister may address the people in these or similar words:

Let us go forth in peace,
praising Jesus our Messiah,
as did the crowds who welcomed him to Jerusalem.

The procession to the church where Mass will be celebrated then begins. During the procession, the choir and people sing the following or other appropriate songs:

Antiphon
The children of Jerusalem
welcome Christ the King.
They carried olive branches
and loudly praised the Lord:
Hosanna in the highest.

The antiphon may be repeated between the verses of psalm 23.

Psalm 23
1   The Lord's is the earth and its fullness,
      the world and all its peoples.
      It is he who set it on the seas;
      on the waters he made it firm. (*Ant.*)

2   Who shall climb the mountain of the Lord?
      Who shall stand in his holy place?
      The man with clean hands and pure heart,
      who desires not worthless things,
      (who has not sworn so as to deceive his neighbour). (*Ant.*)

3   He shall receive blessings from the Lord
      and reward from the God who saves him.
      Such are the men who seek him,
      seek the face of the God of Jacob. (*Ant.*)

4   O gates, lift high your heads;
      grow higher, ancient doors.
      Let him enter, the king of glory. (*Ant.*)

5 Who is the king of glory?
   The Lord, the mighty, the valiant,
   the Lord, the valiant in war. (*Ant.*)

6 O gates, lift high your heads;
   grow higher, ancient doors.
   Let him enter, the king of glory! (*Ant.*)

7 Who is he, the king of glory?
   He, the Lord of armies,
   he is the king of glory. (*Ant.*)

Antiphon
The children of Jerusalem
welcomed Christ the King.
They spread their cloaks before him
and loudly praised the Lord:
Hosanna to the Son of David!
Blessed is he who comes
in the name of the Lord!

The antiphon may be repeated between the verses of Psalm 46.

Psalm 46
1 All people, clap your hands,
   cry to God with shouts of joy!
   For the Lord, the Most High, we must fear,
   great king over all the earth. (*Ant.*)

2 He subdues peoples under us
   and nations under our feet.
   Our inheritance, our glory, is from him,
   given to Jacob out of love. (*Ant.*)

3 God goes up with shouts of joy;
   the Lord goes up with trumpet blast.
   Sing praise for God, sing praise,
   sing praise to our king, sing praise. (*Ant.*)

4 God is king of all the earth.
   Sing praise with all your skill.
   God is king over the nations;
   God reigns on his holy throne. (*Ant.*)

5 The princes of the peoples are assembled
   with the people of Abraham's God.

The rulers of the earth belong to God,
to God who reigns over all. (*Ant.*)

Hymn to Christ the King

℟   All glory, praise and honour
To thee, Redeemer, King
To whom the lips of children
Made sweet hosannas ring.

Thou art the King of Israel,
Thou David's royal Son,
Who in the Lord's name comest,
The king and blessed one. ℟

The company of angels
Are praising thee on high,
And mortal men and all things
Created make reply. ℟

The people of the Hebrews
With palms before thee went;
Our praise and prayer and anthems
Before thee we present. ℟

To thee before thy Passion
They sang their hymns of praise;
To thee now high exalted
Our melody we raise. ℟

Thou didst accept their praises,
Accept the prayers we bring,
Who in all good delightest
Thou good and gracious king. ℟

Entry into the Church

As the procession enters the church, the following responsory or
another song which refers to the Lord's entrance is sung.

℟   The children of Jerusalem
welcomed Christ the King.
They proclaimed the resurrection of life,
and, waving olive branches,
they loudly praised the Lord:
Hosanna in the highest.

℣   When the people heard that Jesus
was entering Jerusalem,
they went to meet him
and, waving olive branches,
they loudly praised the Lord:
Hosanna in the highest.

When the priest comes to the altar he venerates it and may also
incense it. Then he goes to his chair and begins immediately the
opening prayer of Mass, which concludes the procession. Mass
then continues in the usual way. Turn to p.209.

Second Form: The Solemn Entrance

If the procession cannot be held outside the church, the com-
memoration of the Lord's entrance may be celebrated before the
principal Mass with the solemn entrance, which takes place
within the church.

    The faithful, holding the branches, assemble either in front of
the church door or inside the church. The priest and ministers,
with a representative group of the faithful, go to a suitable place
in the church outside the sanctuary, so that most of the people
will be able to see the rite.

    While the priest goes to the appointed place, the antiphon
Hosanna or other suitable song is sung. Then the blessing of
branches and proclamation of the gospel about the Lord's
entrance into Jerusalem take place, as above. After the gospel the
priest, with the ministers and the group of the faithful, moves
solemnly through the church to the sanctuary, while the
responsory *The Children of Jerusalem* or other appropriate song is
sung.

    When the priest comes to the altar he venerates it, goes to his
chair, and immediately begins the opening prayer of Mass,
which then continues in the usual way. See next page.

Third Form: The Simple Entrance

At all other Masses on this Sunday, if the solemn entrance is not
held, the Lord's entrance is commemorated with the following
simple entrance.

    While the priest goes to the altar, the entrance antiphon (see
below) with its psalm or another song with the same theme is
sung. After the priest venerates the altar, he goes to his chair and
greets the people. Mass continues in the usual way.

Entrance Antiphon: Six days before the solemn passover the Lord came to Jerusalem, and children waving palm branches ran out to welcome him. They loudly praised the Lord: Hosanna in the highest. Blessed are you who have come to us so rich in love and mercy.

Psalm

Psalm 23:9-10

> Open wide the doors and gates.
> Lift high the ancient portals.
> The King of glory enters.
>
> Who is this King of glory?
> He is God the mighty Lord.
>
> Hosanna in the highest.
> Blessed are you who have come to us
> so rich in love and mercy.

THE MASS

Opening Prayer

Let us pray
    [for a closer union with Christ
    during this holy season]

Almighty, ever-living God,
you have given the human race Jesus Christ our Saviour
as a model of humility.
He fulfilled your will
by becoming man and giving his life on the cross.
Help us to bear witness to you
by following his example of suffering
and make us worthy to share in his resurrection.

or

Let us pray
    [as we accompany our king to Jerusalem]

Almighty Father of our Lord Jesus Christ,
you sent your Son
to be born of woman and to die on a cross,
so that through the obedience of one man,
estrangement might be dissolved for all men.

Guide our minds by his truth
and strengthen our lives by the example of his death,
that we may live in union with you
in the kingdom of your promise.

FIRST READING

A reading from the prophet Isaiah 50:4-7
I did not cover my face against insult – I know I shall not be shamed.

The Lord has given me
a disciple's tongue.
So that I may know how to reply to the wearied
he provides me with speech.
Each morning he wakes me to hear,
to listen like a disciple.
The Lord has opened my ear.
For my part, I made no resistance,
neither did I turn away.
I offered my back to those who struck me,
my cheeks to those who tore at my beard;
I did not cover my face
against insult and spittle.
The Lord comes to my help,
so that I am untouched by the insults.
So, too, I set my face like flint;
I know I shall not be shamed.

This is the word of the Lord.

Responsorial Psalm Ps 21:8-9. 17-20. 23-24. ℟ v.2
℟ **My God, my God, why have you forsaken me?**

1 All who see me deride me.
They curl their lips, they toss their heads.
'He trusted in the Lord, let him save him;
let him release him if this is his friend.' ℟

2 Many dogs have surrounded me,
a band of the wicked beset me.
They tear holes in my hands and my feet.
I can count every one of my bones. ℟

3 They divide my clothing among them.
They cast lots for my robe.
O Lord, do not leave me alone,
my strength, make haste to help me! ℟

4 I will tell of your name to my brethren
and praise you where they are assembled.
'You who fear the Lord give him praise;
all sons of Jacob, give him glory.
Revere him, Israel's sons.' ℟

SECOND READING

A reading from the letter of St Paul to the Philippians   2:6-11
He humbled himself, but God raised him high.

His state was divine,
yet Christ Jesus did not cling
to his equality with God
but emptied himself
to assume the condition of a slave,
and became as men are,
and being as all men are,
he was humbler yet,
even to accepting death,
death on a cross.
But God raised him high
and gave him the name
which is above all other names
so that all beings
in the heavens, on earth and in the underworld,
should bend the knee at the name of Jesus
and that every tongue should acclaim
Jesus Christ as Lord,
to the glory of God the Father.

This is the word of the Lord.

Gospel Acclamation   Phil 2:8-9
Praise to you, O Christ, king of eternal glory:
Christ was humbler yet,
even to accepting death, death on a cross.
But God raised him high
and gave him the name which is above all names.
Praise to you, O Christ, king of eternal glory.

GOSPEL

Year A

The passion of our Lord Jesus Christ   26:14 – 27:66
according to Matthew

N One of the Twelve, the man called Judas Iscariot, went to the
chief priests and said:

N Narrator.   J Jesus.   O Other single speaker.
C Crowd, or more than one other speaker.

O What are you prepared to give me if I hand him over to you?
N They paid him thirty silver pieces, and from that moment he
   looked for an opportunity to betray him.
        Now on the first day of Unleavened Bread the disciples
   came to Jesus to say,
C Where do you want us to make the preparations for you to eat
   the passover?
N He replied:
J Go to so-and-so in the city and say to him, 'The Master says:
   My time is near. It is at your house that I am keeping Passover
   with my disciples'.
N The disciples did what Jesus told them and prepared the
   Passover. When the evening came he was at table with the
   twelve disciples. And while they were eating he said:
J I tell you solemnly, one of you is about to betray me.
N They were greatly distressed and started asking him in turn,
C Not I, Lord, surely?
N He answered:
J Someone who has dipped his hand into the dish with me, will
   betray me. The Son of Man is going to his fate, as the
   scriptures say he will, but alas for that man by whom the Son
   of Man is betrayed! Better for that man if he had never been
   born!
N Judas, who was to betray him, asked in his turn,
O Not I, Rabbi, surely?
N Jesus answered:
J They are your own words.
N Now as they were eating, Jesus took some bread, and when
   he had said the blessing he broke it and gave it to the disciples
   and said:
J Take it and eat; this is my body.
N Then he took a cup, and when he had returned thanks he
   gave it to them saying:
J Drink all of you from this, for this is my blood, the blood of
   the covenant, which is to be poured out for many for the
   forgiveness of sins. From now on, I tell you, I shall not drink
   wine until the day I drink the new wine with you in the
   kingdom of my Father.
N After psalms had been sung they left for the Mount of Olives.
   Then Jesus said to them,
J You will all lose faith in me this night, for the scripture says: I
   shall strike the shepherd and the sheep of the flock will be
   scattered. But after my resurrection I shall go before you to
   Galilee.

N At this, Peter said:

O Though all lose faith in you, I will never lose faith.

N Jesus answered him,

J I tell you solemnly, this very night, before the cock crows, you will have disowned me three times.

N Peter said to him,

O Even if I have to die with you, I will never disown you.

N And all the disciples said the same.

　　Then Jesus came with them to a small estate called Gethsemane; and he said to his disciples,

J Stay here while I go over there to pray.

N He took Peter and the two sons of Zebedee with him. And sadness came over him, and great distress. Then he said to them:

J My soul is sorrowful to the point of death. Wait here and keep awake with me.

N And going on a little further he fell on his face and prayed:

J My Father, if it is possible let this cup pass me by. Nevertheless, let it be as you, not I, would have it.

N He came back to the disciples and found them sleeping, and he said to Peter:

J So you had not the strength to keep awake with me one hour? You should be awake, and praying not to be put to the test. The spirit is willing, but the flesh is weak.

N Again, a second time, he went away and prayed:

J My father, if this cup cannot pass by without my drinking it, your will be done!

N And he came again back and found them sleeping, their eyes were so heavy. Leaving them there, he went away again and prayed for the third time, repeating the same words. Then he came back to the disciples and said to them,

J You can sleep on now and take your rest. Now the hour has come when the Son of Man is to be betrayed into the hands of sinners. Get up! Let us go! My betrayer is already close at hand.

N He was still speaking when Judas, one of the Twelve, appeared, and with him a large number of men armed with swords and clubs, sent by the chief priests and elders of the people. Now the traitor had arranged a sign with them. He had said:

O 'The one I kiss, he is the man. Take him in charge.'

N So he went straight up to Jesus and said:

O Greetings, Rabbi,

N and kissed him. Jesus said to him,
J My friend, do what you are here for.
N Then they came forward, seized Jesus and took him in charge. At that, one of the followers of Jesus grasped his sword and drew it; he struck out at the high priest's servant, and cut off his ear. Jesus then said:
J Put your sword back, for all who draw the sword will die by the sword. Or do you think that I cannot appeal to my Father who would promptly send more than twelve legions of angels to my defence? But then, how would the scriptures be fulfilled that say this is the way it must be?
N It was at this time that Jesus said to the crowds:
J Am I a brigand, that you had to set out to capture me with swords and clubs? I sat teaching in the Temple day after day and you never laid hands on me.
N Now all this happened to fulfil the prophecies in scripture. Then all the disciples deserted him and ran away.

The men who had arrested Jesus led him off to Caiaphas the high priest, where the scribes and the elders were assembled. Peter followed him at a distance, and when he reached the high priest's palace, he went in and sat down with the attendants to see what the end would be.

The chief priests and the whole Sanhedrin were looking for evidence against Jesus, however false, on which they might pass the death-sentence. But they could not find any, though several lying witnesses came forward. Eventually two stepped forward and made a statement,
O This man said: 'I have power to destroy the Temple of God and in three days build it up'.
N The high priest then stood up and said to him:
O Have you no answer to that? What is this evidence these men are bringing against you?
N But Jesus was silent. And the high priest said to him:
O I put you on oath by the living God to tell us if you are the Christ, the Son of God.
N Jesus answered:
J The words are your own. Moreover, I tell you that from this time onward you will see the Son of Man seated at the right hand of the Power and coming on the clouds of heaven.
N At this, the high priest tore his clothes and said:
O He has blasphemed. What need of witnesses have we now? There! You have just heard the blasphemy. What is your opinion?

N They answered:
C He deserves to die.
N Then they spat in his face and hit him with their fists; others said as they struck him:
C Play the prophet, Christ! Who hit you then?
N Meanwhile Peter was sitting outside in the courtyard, and a servant-girl came up to him and said:
O You too were with Jesus the Galilean.
N But he denied it in front of them all, saying:
O I do not know what you are talking about.
N When he went out to the gateway another servant-girl saw him and said to the people there:
O This man was with Jesus the Nazarene.
N And again, with an oath, he denied it,
O I do not know the man.
N A little later the bystanders came up and said to Peter:
C You are one of them for sure! Why, your accent gives you away.
N Then he started calling down curses on himself and swearing:
O I do not know the man.
N At that moment the cock crew, and Peter remembered what Jesus had said, 'Before the cock crows you will have disowned me three times.' And he went outside and wept bitterly.
   When morning came, all the chief priests and the elders of the people met in council to bring about the death of Jesus. They had him bound, and led him away to hand him over to Pilate, the governor. When he found that Jesus had been condemned, Judas his betrayer was filled with remorse and took the thirty pieces of silver back to the chief priests and elders, saying:
O I have sinned. I have betrayed innocent blood.
N They replied:
C What is that to us? That is your concern.
N And flinging down the silver pieces in the sanctuary he made off, and went and hanged himself. The chief priests picked up the silver pieces and said:
C It is against the Law to put this into the treasury; it is blood money.
N So they discussed the matter and bought the potter's field with it as a graveyard for foreigners, and this is why the field is called the Field of Blood today. The words of the prophet Jeremiah were then fulfilled: And they took the thirty silver pieces, the sum at which the precious One was priced

by children of Israel, and they gave them for the potter's field, just as the Lord directed me.

N Jesus, then, was brought before the governor, and the governor put to him this question:

O Are you the king of the Jews?

N Jesus replied:

J It is you who say it.

N But when he was accused by the chief priests and the elders he refused to answer at all. Pilate then said to him:

O Do you not hear how many charges they have brought against you?

N But to the governor's complete amazement, he offered no reply to any of the charges.

At festival time it was the governor's practice to release a prisoner for the people, anyone they chose. Now there was at that time a notorious prisoner whose name was Barabbas. So when the crowd gathered, Pilate said to them,

O Which do you want me to release for you: Barabbas or Jesus who is called Christ?

N For Pilate knew it was out of jealousy that they had handed him over. Now as he was seated in the chair of judgement, his wife sent him a message,

O Have nothing to do with that man; I have been upset all day by a dream I had about him.

N The chief priests and the elders, however, had persuaded the crowd to demand the release of Barabbas and the execution of Jesus. So when the governor spoke and asked them:

O Which of the two do you want me to release for you?

N They said:

C Barabbas.

N Pilate said to them:

O What am I to do with Jesus who is called Christ?

N They all said:

C Let him be crucified!

N Pilate asked:

O Why? What harm has he done?

N But they shouted all the louder,

C Let him be crucified!

N Then Pilate saw that he was making no impression, that in fact a riot was imminent. So he took some water, washed his hands in front of the crowd and said:

O I am innocent of this man's blood. It is your concern.

N And the people, to a man, shouted back:

C His blood be on us and on our children.

N Then he released Barabbas for them. He ordered Jesus to be first scourged and then handed over to be crucified.

The governor's soldiers took Jesus with them into the Praetorium and collected the whole cohort round him. Then they stripped him and made him wear a scarlet cloak, and having twisted some thorns into a crown they put this on his head and placed a reed in his right hand. To make fun of him they knelt to him saying:

C Hail, king of the Jews!

N And they spat on him and took the reed and struck him on the head with it. And when they had finished making fun of him, they took off the cloak and dressed him in his own clothes and led him away to crucify him.

On their way out, they came across a man from Cyrene, Simon by name, and enlisted him to carry his cross. When they had reached a place called Golgotha, that is, the place of the skull, they gave him wine to drink. When they had finished crucifying him they shared out his clothing by casting lots, and then sat down and stayed there keeping guard over him. Above his head was placed the charge against him; it read: 'This is Jesus, the King of the Jews'. At the same time two robbers were crucified with him, one on the right and one on the left.

The passers-by jeered at him; they shook their heads and said:

C So you would destroy the Temple and rebuild it in three days! Then save yourself! If you are God's son, come down from the cross!

N The chief priests with the scribes and elders mocked him in the same way, saying:

C He saved others; he cannot save himself. He is the King of Israel; let him come down from the cross now, and we will believe in him. He put his trust in God; now let God rescue him if he wants him. For he did say, 'I am the son of God'.

N Even the robbers who were crucified with him taunted him in the same way.

From the sixth hour there was darkness over all the land until the ninth hour. And about the ninth hour, Jesus cried out in a loud voice:

J Eli, Eli, lama sabachthani?

N That is: 'My God, my God, why have you deserted me?' When some of those who stood there heard this, they said:

C The man is calling on Elijah,

N and one of them quickly ran to get a sponge which he dipped in vinegar and, putting it on a reed, gave it him to drink. The rest of them said:

C Wait! See if Elijah will come to save him.

N But Jesus, again crying out in a loud voice, yielded up his spirit.

All kneel and pause a moment.

N At that, the veil of the Temple was torn in two from top to bottom; the earth quaked; the rocks were split; the tombs opened and the bodies of many holy men rose from the dead, and these, after his resurrection, came out of the tombs, entered the Holy City and appeared to a number of people.

Meanwhile the centurion, together with the others guarding Jesus, had seen the earthquake and all that was taking place, and they were terrified and said:

C In truth this was a son of God.

N And many women were there, watching from a distance, the same women who had followed Jesus from Galilee and looked after him. Among them were Mary of Magdala, Mary the mother of James and Joseph, and the mother of Zebedee's sons.

When it was evening, there came a rich man of Arimathaea called Joseph, who had himself become a disciple of Jesus. This man went to Pilate and asked for the body of Jesus. Pilate thereupon ordered it to be handed over. So Joseph took the body, wrapped it in a clean shroud and put it in his own new tomb which he had hewn out of the rock. He then rolled a large stone across the entrance of the tomb and went away. Now Mary of Magdala and the other Mary were there, sitting opposite the sepulchre.

Next day, that is, when Preparation Day was over, the chief priests and the Pharisees went in a body to Pilate and said to him,

C Your Excellency, we recall that this impostor said, while he was still alive, 'After three days I shall rise again'. Therefore give the order to have the sepulchre kept secure until the third day, for fear his disciples come and steal him away and tell the people, 'He has risen from the dead'. This last piece of fraud would be worse than what went before.

N Pilate said to them:

O You may have your guards. Go and make all as secure as you know how.

N So they went and made the sepulchre secure, putting seals on the stone and mounting a guard.

Year B

The passion of our Lord Jesus Christ   14:1 – 15:47
according to Mark

N It was two days before the Passover and the feast of Unleavened Bread, and the chief priests and scribes were looking for a way to arrest Jesus by some trick and have him put to death. For they said,

C It must not be during the festivities, or there will be a disturbance among the people.

N Jesus was at Bethany in the house of Simon the leper; he was at dinner when a woman came in with an alabaster jar of very costly ointment, pure nard. She broke the jar and poured the ointment on his head. Some who were there said to one another indignantly,

C Why this waste of ointment? Ointment like this could have been sold for over three hundred denarii and the money given to the poor;

N and they were angry with her. But Jesus said,

J Leave her alone. Why are you upsetting her? What she has done for me is one of the good works. You have the poor with you always and you can be kind to them whenever you wish, but you will not always have me. She has done what was in her power to do; she has anointed my body beforehand for its burial. I tell you solemnly, wherever throughout all the world the Good News is proclaimed, what she has done will be told also, in remembrance of her.

N Judas Iscariot, one of the Twelve, approached the chief priests with an offer to hand Jesus over to them. They were delighted to hear it, and promised to give him money; and he looked for a way of betraying him when the opportunity should occur.

On the first day of Unleavened Bread, when the Passover lamb was sacrificed, his disciples said to him,

C Where do you want us to go and make the preparations for you to eat the passover?

N So he sent two of his disciples, saying to them,

J Go into the city and you will meet a man carrying a pitcher of water. Follow him, and say to the owner of the house which he enters, 'The Master says: Where is my dining room in which I can eat the passover with my disciples?' He will show you a large upper room furnished with couches, all prepared. Make the preparations for us there.

N The disciples set out and went to the city and found everything as he had told them, and prepared the Passover.

When evening came he arrived with the Twelve. And while they were at table eating, Jesus said,

J I tell you solemnly, one of you is about to betray me, one of you eating with me.

N They were distressed and asked him, one after another,

O Not I, surely?

N He said to them,

J It is one of the Twelve, one who is dipping into the same dish with me. Yes, the Son of Man is going to his fate, as the scriptures say he will, but alas for that man by whom the Son of Man is betrayed! Better for that man if he had never been born!

N And as they were eating he took some bread, and when he had said the blessing he broke it and gave it to them, saying,

J Take it; this is my body.

N Then he took a cup, and when he had returned thanks he gave it to them, and all drank from it, and he said to them,

J This is my blood, the blood of the covenant, which is to be poured out for many. I tell you solemnly, I shall not drink any more wine until the day I drink the new wine in the kingdom of God.

N After psalms had been sung they left for the Mount of Olives. And Jesus said to them,

J You will all lose faith, for the scripture says, 'I shall strike the shepherd and the sheep will be scattered'. However after my resurrection I shall go before you to Galilee.

N Peter said,

O Even if all lose faith, I will not.

N And Jesus said to him,

J I tell you solemnly, this day, this very night, before the cock crows twice, you will have disowned me three times.

N But he repeated still more earnestly,

O If I have to die with you, I will never disown you.

N And they all said the same.

They came to a small estate called Gethsemane, and Jesus said to his disciples,

J Stay here while I pray.

N Then he took Peter and James and John with him. And a sudden fear came over him, and great distress. And he said to them,

J My soul is sorrowful to the point of death. Wait here, and keep awake.

N And going on a little further he threw himself on the ground and prayed that, if it were possible, this hour might pass him by. He said,

J Abba (Father)! Everything is possible for you. Take this cup away from me. But let it be as you, not I, would have it.

N He came back and found them sleeping, and he said to Peter,

J Simon, are you asleep? Had you not the strength to keep awake one hour? You should be awake, and praying not to be put to the test. The spirit is willing but the flesh is weak.

N Again he went away and prayed, saying the same words. And once more he came back and found them sleeping, their eyes were so heavy; and they could find no answer for him. He came back a third time and said to them,

J You can sleep on now and take your rest. It is all over . The hour has come. Now the Son of Man is to be betrayed into the hands of sinners. Get up! Let us go! My betrayer is close at hand already.

N Even while he was still speaking, Judas, one of the Twelve, came up with a number of men armed with swords and clubs, sent by the chief priests and the scribes and the elders. Now the traitor had arranged a signal with them. He had said,

O 'The one I kiss, he is the man. Take him in charge, and see he is well guarded when you lead him away.'

N So when the traitor came, he went straight up to Jesus and said,

O Rabbi!

N and kissed him. The others seized him and took him in charge. Then one of the bystanders drew his sword and struck out at the high priest's servant, and cut off his ear.

    Then Jesus spoke,

J Am I a brigand that you had to set out to capture me with swords and clubs? I was among you teaching in the Temple day after day and you never laid hands on me. But this is to fulfil the scriptures.

N And they all deserted him and ran away. A young man who followed him had nothing on but a linen cloth. They caught hold of him, but he left the cloth in their hands and ran away naked.

    They led Jesus off to the high priest; and all the chief priests and the elders and the scribes assembled there. Peter had followed him at a distance, right into the high priest's palace, and was sitting with the attendants warming himself at the fire.

  The chief priests and the whole Sanhedrin were looking
for evidence against Jesus on which they might pass the
death-sentence. But they could not find any. Several, indeed,
brought false evidence against him, but their evidence was
conflicting. Some stood up and submitted this false evidence
against him,

C We heard him say, 'I am going to destroy this Temple made
  by human hands, and in three days build another, not made
  by human hands'.

N But even on this point their evidence was conflicting. The
  high priest then stood up before the whole assembly and put
  this question to Jesus,

O Have you no answer to that? What is this evidence these men
  are bringing against you?

N But he was silent and made no answer at all. The high priest
  put a second question to him,

O Are you the Christ the Son of the Blessed One?

N Jesus said,

J I am, and you will see the Son of Man seated at the right hand
  of the Power and coming with the clouds of heaven.

N The high priest tore his robes, and said,

O What need of witnesses have we now? You heard the blasphemy. What is your finding?

N And they all gave their verdict: he deserved to die.
  Some of them started spitting at him and, blindfolding him,
  began hitting him with their fists and shouting,

C Play the prophet!

N And the attendants rained blows on him.
  While Peter was down below in the courtyard, one of the
  high-priest's servant-girls came up. She saw Peter warming
  himself there, stared at him and said,

O You too were with Jesus, the man from Nazareth.

N But he denied it, saying

O I do not know, I do not understand what you are talking
  about.

N And he went out into the forecourt. The servant-girl saw him
  and again started telling the bystanders,

O This fellow is one of them.

N But he again denied it. A little later the bystanders themselves
  said to Peter,

C You are one of them for sure! Why, you are a Galilean.

N But he started calling curses on himself and swearing,

O I do not know the man you speak of.

N At that moment the cock crew for the second time, and Peter recalled how Jesus had said to him, 'Before the cock crows twice, you will have disowned me three times'. And he burst into tears.

First thing in the morning, the chief priest together with the elders and scribes, in short the whole Sanhedrin, had their plan ready. They had Jesus bound and took him away and handed him over to Pilate.

Pilate questioned him,

O Are you the king of the Jews?

N He answered,

J It is you who say it.

N And the chief priests brought many accusations against him. Pilate questioned him again,

O Have you no reply at all? See how many accusations they are bringing against you!

N But to Pilate's amazement, Jesus made no further reply.

At festival time Pilate used to release a prisoner for them, anyone they asked for. Now a man called Barabbas was then in prison with the rioters who had committed murder during the uprising. When the crowd went up and began to ask Pilate the customary favour, Pilate answered them,

O Do you want me to release for you the king of the Jews?

N For he realised it was out of jealousy that the chief priests had handed Jesus over. The chief priests, however, had incited the crowd to demand that he should release Barabbas for them instead. Then Pilate spoke again.

O But in that case, what am I to do with the man you call king of the Jews?

N They shouted back.

C Crucify him!

N Pilate asked them,

O Why? What harm has he done?

N But they shouted all the louder,

C Crucify him!

N So Pilate, anxious to placate the crowd, released Barabbas for them and, having ordered Jesus to be scourged, handed him over to be crucified.

The soldiers led him away to the inner part of the palace, that is, the Praetorium, and called the whole cohort together. They dressed him up in purple, twisted some thorns into a crown and put it on him. And they began saluting him,

C Hail, king of the Jews!

N They struck his head with a reed and spat on him; and they went down on their knees to do him homage. And when they had finished making fun of him, they took off the purple and dressed him in his own clothes.

They led him out to crucify him. They enlisted a passer-by, Simon of Cyrene, father of Alexander and Rufus, who was coming in from the country, to carry his cross. They brought Jesus to the place called Golgotha, which means the place of the skull.

They offered him wine mixed with myrrh, but he refused it. Then they crucified him, and shared out his clothing, casting lots to decide what each should get. It was the third hour when they crucified him. The inscription giving the charge against him read: 'The King of the Jews.' And they crucified two robbers with him, one on his right and one on his left.

The passers-by jeered at him; they shook their heads and said,

C Aha! So you would destroy the Temple and rebuild it in three days! Then save yourself: come down from the cross!

N The chief priests and the scribes mocked him among themselves in the same way. They said,

C He saved others, he cannot save himself. Let the Christ, the king of Israel, come down from the cross now, for us to see it and believe.

N Even those who were crucified with him taunted him.

When the sixth hour came there was darkness over the whole land until the ninth hour. And at the ninth hour Jesus cried out in a loud voice,

J Eloi, Eloi, lama sabachthani?

N This means 'My God, my God, why have you deserted me?' When some of those who stood by heard this, they said,

C Listen, he is calling on Elijah.

N Someone ran and soaked a sponge in vinegar and, putting it on a reed, gave it him to drink, saying,

O Wait and see if Elijah will come to take him down.

N But Jesus gave a loud cry and breathed his last.

All kneel and pause a moment.

N And the veil of the Temple was torn in two from top to bottom. The centurion, who was standing in front of him, had seen how he had died, and he said,

O In truth this man was a son of God.
N There were some women watching from a distance. Among them were Mary of Magdala, Mary who was the mother of James the younger, and Joset, and Salome. These used to follow him and look after him when he was in Galilee. And there were many other women there who had come up to Jerusalem with him

It was now evening, and since it was Preparation Day (that is the vigil of the sabbath), there came Joseph of Arimathaea, a prominent member of the Council, who himself lived in the hope of seeing the kingdom of God, and he boldly went to Pilate and asked for the body of Jesus. Pilate, astonished that he should have died so soon, summoned the centurion and enquired if he was already dead. Having been assured of this by the centurion, he granted the corpse to Joseph who brought a shroud, took Jesus down from the cross, wrapped him in the shroud and laid him in a tomb which had been hewn out of the rock. He then rolled a stone against the entrance to the tomb. Mary of Magdala and Mary the mother of Joset were watching and took note of where he was laid.

Shorter form

The passion of our Lord Jesus Christ according to Mark   15:1-39

First thing in the morning, the chief priests together with the elders and scribes, in short the whole Sanhedrin, had their plan ready. They had Jesus bound and took him away and handed him over to Pilate.

Pilate questioned him, 'Are you the king of the Jews?' 'It is you who say it' he answered. And the chief priests brought many accusations against him. Pilate questioned him again, 'Have you no reply at all? See how many accusations they are bringing against you!' But to Pilate's amazement, Jesus made no further reply.

At festival time Pilate used to release a prisoner for them, anyone they asked for. Now a man called Barabbas was then in prison with the rioters who had committed murder during the uprising. When the crowd went up and began to ask Pilate the customary favour, Pilate answered them, 'Do you want me to release for you the king of the Jews?' For he realised it was out of jealousy that the chief priests had handed Jesus over. The chief priests, however, had incited the crowd to demand that he should release Barabbas for them instead. Then Pilate spoke again. 'But in that case,' he said to them 'what am I to do with the man you call king of the Jews?' They shouted back, 'Crucify him!' 'Why?' Pilate asked them 'What harm has he done?' But they shouted all the louder, 'Crucify him!' So Pilate, anxious to placate the crowd, released Barabbas for them and, having ordered Jesus to be scourged, handed him over to be crucified.

The soldiers led him away to the inner part of the palace, that is, the Praetorium, and called the whole cohort together. They dressed him up in purple, twisted some thorns into a crown and put it on him. And they began saluting him, 'Hail, king of the Jews!' They struck his head with a reed and spat on him; and they went down on their knees to do him homage. And when they had finished making fun of him, they took off the purple and dressed him in his own clothes.

They led him out to crucify him. They enlisted a passer-by, Simon of Cyrene, father of Alexander and Rufus, who was coming in from the country, to carry his cross. They brought Jesus to the place called Golgotha, which means the place of the skull.

They offered him wine mixed with myrrh, but he refused it. Then they crucified him, and shared out his clothing, casting lots to decide what each should get. It was the third hour when they crucified him. The inscription giving the charge against him read: 'The King of the Jews'. And they crucified two robbers with him, one on his right and one on his left.

The passers-by jeered at him; they shook their heads and said, 'Aha! So you would destroy the Temple and rebuild it in three days! Then save yourself: come down from the cross!' The chief priests and the scribes mocked him among themselves in the same way. 'He saved others,' they said 'he cannot save himself. Let the Christ, the king of Israel, come down from the cross now, for us to see it and believe.' Even those who were crucified with him taunted him.

When the sixth hour came there was darkness over the whole land until the ninth hour. And at the ninth hour Jesus cried out in a loud voice, 'Eloi, Eloi, lama sabachthani?' which means, 'My God, my God, why have you deserted me?' When some of those who stood by heard this, they said, 'Listen he is calling on Elijah'. Someone ran and soaked a sponge in vinegar and, putting it on a reed, gave it him to drink saying, 'Wait and see if Elijah will come to take him down.' But Jesus gave a loud cry and breathed his last.

All kneel and pause a moment.

And the veil of the Temple was torn in two from top to bottom. The centurion, who was standing in front of him, had seen how he had died, and he said, 'In truth this man was a son of God.'

Year C

The passion of our Lord Jesus Christ   22:14 – 23:56
according to Luke

N When the hour came Jesus took his place at table, and the apostles with him. And he said to them,

J I have longed to eat this passover with you before I suffer; because, I tell you, I shall not eat it again until it is fulfilled in the kingdom of God.

N Then, taking a cup, he gave thanks and said,

J Take this and share it among you, because from now on, I tell you, I shall not drink wine until the kingdom of God comes.

N Then he took some bread, and when he had given thanks, broke it and gave it to them, saying,

J This is my body which will be given for you; do this as a memorial of me.

N He did the same with the cup after supper, and said,

J This cup is the new covenant in my blood which will be poured out for you.

And yet, here with me on the table is the hand of the man who betrays me. The Son of Man does indeed go to his fate even as it has been decreed, but alas for that man by whom he is betrayed!

N And they began to ask one another which of them it could be who was to do this thing.

A dispute arose also between them about which should be reckoned the greatest, but he said to them,

J Among pagans it is the kings who lord it over them, and those who have authority over them are given the title Benefactor. This must not happen with you. No; the greatest among you must behave as if he were the youngest, the leader as if he were the one who serves. For who is the greater: the one at table or the one who serves? The one at table, surely? Yet here I am among you as one who serves!

You are the men who have stood by me faithfully in my trials; and now I confer a kingdom on you, just as my Father conferred one on me: you will eat and drink at my table in my kingdom, and you will sit on thrones to judge the twelve tribes of Israel.

Simon, Simon! Satan, you must know, has got his wish to sift you all like wheat; but I have prayed for you, Simon, that your faith may not fail, and once you have recovered, you in your turn must strengthen your brothers.

N He answered,

O Lord, I would be ready to go to prison with you, and to death.

N Jesus replied,

J I tell you, Peter, by the time the cock crows today you will have denied three times that you know me.

N He said to them,

J When I sent you out without purse or haversack or sandals, were you short of anything?

N They answered,

C No.

N He said to them,

J But now if you have a purse, take it: if you have a haversack, do the same; if you have no sword, sell your cloak and buy one, because I tell you these words of scripture have to be fulfilled in me: He let himself be taken for a criminal. Yes, what scripture says about me is even now reaching its fulfilment.

N They said,

C Lord, there are two swords here now.

N He said to them,

J That is enough!

N He then left the upper room to make his way as usual to the Mount of Olives, with the disciples following. When they reached the place he said to them,

J Pray not to be put to the test.

N Then he withdrew from them, about a stone's throw away, and knelt down and prayed, saying,

J Father, if you are willing, take this cup away from me. Nevertheless, let your will be done, not mine.

N Then an angel appeared to him coming from heaven to give him strength. In his anguish he prayed even more earnestly, and his sweat fell to the ground like great drops of blood.

When he rose from prayer he went to the disciples and found them sleeping for sheer grief. He said to them,

J Why are you asleep? Get up and pray not to be put to the test.
N He was still speaking when a number of men appeared, and at the head of them the man called Judas, one of the Twelve, who went up to Jesus to kiss him. Jesus said,
J Judas, are you betraying the Son of Man with a kiss?
N His followers, seeing what was happening, said,
C Lord, shall we use our swords?
N And one of them struck out at the high priest's servant, and cut off his right ear. But at this Jesus spoke,
J Leave off! That will do!
N And touching the man's ear he healed him.

Then Jesus spoke to the chief priests and captains of the Temple guard and elders who had come for him. He said.
J Am I a brigand that you had to set out with swords and clubs? When I was among you in the Temple day after day you never moved to lay hands on me. But this is your hour; this is the reign of darkness.
N They seized him then and led him away, and they took him to the high priest's house. Peter followed at a distance. They had lit a fire in the middle of the courtyard and Peter sat down among them, and as he was sitting there by the blaze a servant-girl saw him, peered at him and said,
O This person was with him too.
N But he denied it, saying,
O Woman, I do not know him.
N Shortly afterwards, someone else saw him and said,
O You are another of them.
N But Peter replied,
O I am not, my friend.
N About an hour later, another man insisted, saying,
O This fellow was certainly with him. Why, he is a Galilean.
N Peter said,
O My friend, I do not know what you are talking about.
N At that instant, while he was still speaking, the cock crew, and the Lord turned and looked straight at Peter, and Peter remembered what the Lord had said to him, 'Before the cock crows today, you will have disowned me three times'. And he went outside and wept bitterly.

Meanwhile the men who guarded Jesus were mocking and beating him. They blindfolded him and questioned him, saying,
C Play the prophet. Who hit you then?
N And they continued heaping insults on him.

When day broke there was a meeting of the elders of the
people, attended by the chief priests and scribes. He was
brought before their council, and they said to him,

C If you are the Christ, tell us.

N He replied,

J If I tell you, you will not believe me, and if I question you, you
will not answer. But from now on, the Son of Man will be
seated at the right hand of the Power of God.

N Then they all said,

C So you are the Son of God then?

N He answered,

J It is you who say I am.

N They said,

C What need of witnesses have we now? We have heard it for
ourselves from his own lips.

N The whole assembly then rose, and they brought him before
Pilate.
    They began their accusation by saying,

C We found this man inciting our people to revolt, opposing
payment of tribute to Caesar, and claiming to be Christ, a
king.

N Pilate put to him this question,

O Are you the king of the Jews?

N He replied,

J It is you who say it.

N Pilate then said to the chief priests and the crowd,

O I find no case against this man.

N But they persisted,

C He is inflaming the people with his teaching all over Judaea; it
has come all the way from Galilee, where he started, down to
here.

N When Pilate heard this, he asked if the man were a Galilean;
and finding that he came under Herod's jurisdiction he
passed him over to Herod who was also in Jerusalem at that
time.
    Herod was delighted to see Jesus; he had heard about him
and had been wanting for a long time to set eyes on him;
moreover, he was hoping to see some miracle worked by him.
So he questioned him at some length; but without getting any
reply. Meanwhile the chief priests and the scribes were there,
violently pressing their accusations. Then Herod, together
with his guards, treated him with contempt and made fun of
him; he put a rich cloak on him and sent him back to Pilate.
And though Herod and Pilate had been enemies before, they

were reconciled that same day.

Pilate then summoned the chief priests and the leading men and the people. He said,

O You brought this man before me as a political agitator. Now I have gone into the matter myself in your presence and found no case against him. Nor has Herod either, since he has sent him back to us. As you can see, the man has done nothing that deserves death, so I shall have him flogged and then let him go.

N But as one man they howled,

C Away with him! Give us Barabbas!

N This man had been thrown into prison for causing a riot in the city and for murder.

Pilate was anxious to set Jesus free and addressed them again, but they shouted back.

C Crucify him! Crucify him!

N And for the third time he spoke to them,

O Why? What harm has this man done? I have found no case against him that deserves death, so I shall have him punished and let him go.

N But they kept on shouting at the top of their voices, demanding that he should be crucified, and their shouts were growing louder.

Pilate then gave his verdict: their demand was to be granted. He released the man they asked for, who had been imprisoned for rioting and murder, and handed Jesus over to them to deal with as they pleased.

As they were leading him away they seized on a man, Simon from Cyrene, who was coming in from the country, and made him shoulder the cross and carry it behind Jesus. Large numbers of people followed him, and of women too who mourned and lamented for him. But Jesus turned to them and said,

J Daughters of Jerusalem, do not weep for me; weep rather for yourselves and for your children. For the days will surely come when people will say, 'Happy are those who are barren, the wombs that have never borne, the breasts that have never suckled!' Then they will begin to say to the mountains, 'Fall on us!'; to the hills, 'Cover us!' For if men use the green wood like this, what will happen when it is dry?

N Now with him they were also leading out two other criminals to be executed.

When they reached the place called The Skull, they cru-

cified him there and the criminals also, one on the right, the
other on the left. Jesus said,

J   Father, forgive them; they do not know what they are doing.

N   Then they cast lots to share out his clothing. The people
stayed there watching him. As for the leaders, they jeered at
him, saying,

C   He saved others; let him save himself if he is the Christ of
God, the Chosen One.

N   The soldiers mocked him too, and when they approached to
offer him vinegar they said,

C   If you are the king of the Jews, save yourself.

N   Above him there was an inscription: 'This is the King of the
Jews.'
    One of the criminals hanging there abused him, saying,

O   Are you not the Christ? Save yourself and us as well.

N   But the other spoke up and rebuked him,

O   Have you no fear of God at all? You got the same sentence as
he did, but in our case we deserved it: we are paying for what
we did. But this man has done nothing wrong. Jesus, remember me when you come into your kingdom.

N   He replied

J   Indeed, I promise you, today you will be with me in paradise.

N   It was now about the sixth hour and, with the sun eclipsed, a
darkness came over the whole land until the ninth hour. The
veil of the Temple was torn right down the middle; and when
Jesus had cried out in a loud voice, he said,

J   Father, into your hands I commit my spirit.

N   With these words he breathed his last.

All kneel and pause a moment.

    When the centurion saw what had taken place, he gave
praise to God and said,

O   This was a great and good man.

N   And when all the people who had gathered for the spectacle
saw what had happened, they went home beating their
breasts.
    All his friends stood at a distance; so also did the women
who had accompanied him from Galilee, and they saw all this
happen.
    Then a member of the council arrived, an upright and
virtuous man named Joseph. He had not consented to what
the others had planned and carried out. He came from
Arimathaea, a Jewish town, and he lived in the hope of seeing

the kingdom of God. This man went to Pilate and asked for the body of Jesus. He then took it down, wrapped it in a shroud and put him in a tomb which was hewn in stone in which no one had yet been laid. It was Preparation Day and the sabbath was imminent.

Meanwhile the women who had come from Galilee with Jesus were following behind. They took note of the tomb and of the position of the body.

Then they returned and prepared spices and ointments. And on the sabbath day they rested, as the law required.

Shorter form

The passion of our Lord Jesus Christ
according to Luke   23:1-49

The elders of the people and the chief priests and scribes rose, and they brought Jesus before Pilate.

They began their accusation by saying, 'We found this man inciting our people to revolt, opposing payment of tribute to Caesar, and claiming to be Christ, a king.' Pilate put to him this question, 'Are you the king of the Jews?' 'It is you who say it' he replied. Pilate then said to the chief priests and the crowd, 'I find no case against this man.' But they persisted, 'He is inflaming the people with his teaching all over Judaea; it has come all the way from Galilee, where he started, down to here.' When Pilate heard this, he asked if the man were a Galilean; and finding that he came under Herod's jurisdiction he passed him over to Herod who was also in Jerusalem at that time.

Herod was delighted to see Jesus; he had heard about him and had been wanting for a long time to set eyes on him; moreover, he was hoping to see some miracle worked by him. So he questioned him at some length; but without getting any reply. Meanwhile the chief priests and the scribes were there, violently pressing their accusations. Then Herod, together with his guards, treated him with contempt and made fun of him; he put a rich cloak on him and sent him back to Pilate. And though Herod and Pilate had been enemies before, they were reconciled that same day.

Pilate then summoned the chief priests and the leading men and the people. 'You brought this man before me' he said 'as a political agitator. Now I have gone into the matter myself in your presence and found no case against the man in respect of all the charges you bring against him. Nor has Herod either, since he has sent him back to us. As you can see, the man has done nothing that deserves death, so I shall have him flogged and then let him go.' But as one man they howled, 'Away with him! Give us Barabbas!' (This man had been thrown into prison for causing a riot in the city and for murder.)

Pilate was anxious to set Jesus free and addressed them again, but they shouted back, 'Crucify him! Crucify him!' And for the third time he spoke to them, 'Why? What harm has this man done? I have found no case against him that deserves death, so I shall have him punished and then let him go.' But they kept on shouting at the top of their voices, demanding that he should be crucified. And their shouts were growing louder.

Pilate then gave his verdict: their demand was to be granted. He released the man they asked for, who had been imprisoned for rioting and murder, and handed Jesus over to them to deal with as they pleased.

As they were leading him away they seized on a man, Simon from Cyrene, who was coming in from the country, and made him shoulder the cross and carry it behind Jesus. Large numbers of people followed him, and of women too, who mourned and lamented for him. But Jesus turned to them and said, 'Daughters of Jerusalem, do not weep for me; weep rather for yourselves and for your children. For the days will surely come when people will say, "Happy are those who are barren, the wombs that have never borne, the breasts that have never suckled!" Then they will begin to say to the mountains, "Fall on us!"; to the hills, "Cover us!" For if men use the green wood like this, what will happen when it is dry?' Now with him they were also leading out two other criminals to be executed.

When they reached the place called The Skull, they crucified him there and the two criminals also, one on the right, the other on the left. Jesus said, 'Father forgive them; they do not know what they are doing.' Then they cast lots to share out his clothing.

The people stayed there watching him. As for the leaders, they jeered at him. 'He saved others,' they said 'let him save himself if he is the Christ of God, the Chosen One.' The soldiers mocked him too and when they approached to offer him vinegar they said, 'If you are the king of the Jews, save yourself.' Above him there was an inscription: 'This is the King of the Jews.'

One of the criminals hanging there abused him. 'Are you not the Christ?' he said. 'Save yourself and us as well.' But the other spoke up and rebuked him. 'Have you no fear of God at all?' he said. 'You got the same sentence as he did, but in our case we deserved it; we are paying for what we did. But this man has done nothing wrong. Jesus,' he said 'remember me when you come into your kingdom.' 'Indeed, I promise you,' he replied 'today you will be with me in paradise.'

It was now about the sixth hour and, with the sun eclipsed, a darkness came over the whole land until the ninth hour. The veil of the Temple was torn right down the middle; and when Jesus had cried out in a loud voice, he said, 'Father, into your hands I commit my spirit.' With these words he breathed his last.

All kneel and pause a moment.

When the centurion saw what had taken place, he gave praise to God and said, 'This was a great and good man.' And when all the people who had gathered for the spectacle saw what had happened, they went home beating their breasts.

All his friends stood at a distance; so also did the women who had accompanied him from Galilee, and they saw all this happen.

Prayer over the Gifts

Lord,
may the suffering and death of Jesus, your only Son,
make us pleasing to you.
Alone we can do nothing,
but may this perfect sacrifice
win us your mercy and love.

Preface of Passion Sunday, P19

Communion Antiphon: Father, if this cup may not pass, but I must drink it, then your will be done.

Prayer after Communion
Lord,
you have satisfied our hunger with this eucharistic food.
The death of your Son gives us hope and strengthens our faith.
May his resurrection give us perseverance
and lead us to salvation.

Solemn Blessing
Bow your heads and pray for God's blessing.

The Father of mercies has given us an example of unselfish love

in the sufferings of his only Son.
Through your service of God and neighbour
may you receive his countless blessings.   R̷   **Amen.**
You believe that by his dying
Christ destroyed death for ever.
May he give you everlasting life.   R̷   **Amen.**

He humbled himself for our sakes.
May you follow his example
and share in his resurrection.   R̷   **Amen.**

May almighty God bless you,
the Father, and the Son, ✛ and the Holy Spirit.   R̷   **Amen.**

HOLY THURSDAY: CHRISM MASS

This Mass, which the bishop concelebrates with his presbyterium
and at which the oils are blessed, manifests the communion of
the priests with their bishop. It is thus desirable that, if possible,
all the priests take part in it and receive communion under both
kinds. To show the unity of the presbyterium, the priests who
concelebrate with the bishop should come from different parts of
the diocese.

Entrance Antiphon: Jesus Christ has made us a kingdom of priests
to serve his God and Father: glory and kingship be his for ever
and ever.

The Gloria is sung or said.

Opening Prayer
Father,
by the power of the Holy Spirit
you anointed your only Son Messiah and Lord of creation;
you have given us a share in his consecration
to priestly service in your Church.
Help us to be faithful witnesses in the world
to the salvation Christ won for all mankind.

FIRST READING

A reading from the prophet Isaiah   61:1-3. 6. 8-9
The Lord has anointed me and has sent me to bring Good News to the
poor, to give them the oil of gladness.

The spirit of the Lord has been given to me,

for the Lord has anointed me.
He has sent me to bring good news to the poor,
to bind up hearts that are broken;

to proclaim liberty to captives,
freedom to those in prison;
to proclaim a year of favour from the Lord,
a day of vengeance for our God;

to comfort all those who mourn and to give them
for ashes a garland;
for mourning robe the oil of gladness,
for despondency, praise.

But you, you will be named 'priests of the Lord',
they will call you 'ministers of our God'.
I reward them faithfully
and make an everlasting covenant with them.

Their race will be famous throughout the nations,
their descendants throughout the peoples.
All who see them will admit
that they are a race whom the Lord has blessed.

This is the word of the Lord.

Responsorial Psalm Ps 88:21-22. 25. 27. ℟ v.2
℟ **I will sing for ever of your love, O Lord.**

1 I have found David my servant
and with my holy oil anointed him.
My hand shall always be with him
and my arm shall make him strong. ℟

2 My truth and my love shall be with him;
by my name his might shall be exalted.
He will say to me: 'You are my father,
my God, the rock who saves me.' ℟

SECOND READING
A reading from the book of the Apocalypse 1:5-8
He made us a line of kings, priests to serve his God and Father.

Grace and peace to you from Jesus Christ, the faithful witness,
the First-born from the dead, the Ruler of the kings of the earth.
He loves us and has washed away our sins with his blood, and
made us a line of kings, priests to serve his God and Father; to

him, then, be glory and power for ever and ever. Amen. It is he who is coming on the clouds; everyone will see him, even those who pierced him, and all the races of the earth will mourn over him. This is the truth. Amen. 'I am the Alpha and the Omega' says the Lord God, who is, who was, and who is to come, the Almighty.

This is the word of the Lord.

Gospel Acclamation   Is 61:1 (Lk 4:18)
Praise to you, O Christ, king of eternal glory!
The spirit of the Lord has been given to me;
he has sent me to bring the good news to the poor.
Praise to you, O Christ, king of eternal glory.

GOSPEL

A reading from the holy Gospel according to Luke   4:16-21
The spirit of the Lord has been given to me, for he has anointed me.

Jesus came to Nazara, where he had been brought up, and went into the synagogue on the sabbath day as he usually did. He stood up to read, and they handed him the scroll of the prophet Isaiah. Unrolling the scroll he found the place where it is written:

The spirit of the Lord has been given to me,
for he has anointed me.
He has sent me to bring the good news to the poor,
to proclaim liberty to captives
and to the blind new sight,
to set the downtrodden free,
to proclaim the Lord's year of favour.

He then rolled up the scroll, gave it back to the assistant and sat down. And all eyes in the synagogue were fixed on him. Then he began to speak to them, 'This text is being fulfilled today even as you listen.'

This is the Gospel of the Lord.

Renewal of Commitment to Priestly Service
After the homily, the bishop speaks to the priests, inviting them to renew publicly their priestly promises. He uses these, or similar, words:

My brothers,
today we celebrate the memory of the first eucharist,

at which our Lord Jesus Christ
shared with his apostles and with us
his call to the priestly service of his Church.
Now, in the presence of your bishop and God's holy people,
are you ready to renew your own dedication to Christ
as priests of his new covenant?

Priests I am.

At your ordination
you accepted the responsibilities of the priesthood
out of love for the Lord Jesus and his Church.
Are you resolved to unite yourselves more closely to Christ
and to try to become more like him
by joyfully sacrificing your own pleasure and ambition
to bring his peace and love to your brothers and sisters?

Priests I am.

Are you resolved
to be faithful ministers of the mysteries of God,
to celebrate the eucharist and the other liturgical services
with sincere devotion?
Are you resolved to imitate Jesus Christ,
the head and shepherd of the Church,
by teaching the Christian faith
without thinking of your own profit,
solely for the well-being of the people
you were sent to serve?

Priests I am.

Then the bishop addresses the people:

My brothers and sisters,
pray for your priests.
Ask the Lord to bless them with the fullness of his love,
to help them be faithful ministers of Christ the High Priest,
so that they will be able to lead you to him,
the fountain of your salvation.

People **Lord Jesus Christ, hear us and answer our prayer.**

Pray also for me
that despite my own unworthiness
I may faithfully fulfil the office of apostle
which Jesus Christ has entrusted to me.
Pray that I may become more like
our High Priest and Good Shepherd,
the teacher and servant of all,
and so be a genuine sign

of Christ's loving presence among you.

People   **Lord Jesus Christ, hear us and answer our prayer.**

May the Lord in his love
keep you close to him always,
and may he bring all of us,
his priests and people,
to eternal life.

All   **Amen.**

The Profession of Faith and Prayer of the Faithful are omitted.

BLESSING OF OILS AND CONSECRATION OF THE CHRISM

The oils are brought in a solemn offertory procession to the
bishop who places them on a table before the altar. The entire rite
may take place immediately, or as detailed below. The Prayer
over the Gifts of the Mass is on p.246 below.

Blessing of the Oil of the Sick

Before the conclusion of the eucharistic prayer the bishop blesses
the oil held before him in a vessel:

Bishop   Lord God, loving Father,
you bring healing to the sick
through your Son Jesus Christ.
Hear us as we pray to you in faith,
and send the Holy Spirit, man's Helper and Friend,
upon this oil, which nature has provided
to serve the needs of men.
May your blessing ✢
come upon all who are anointed with this oil,
that they may be freed from pain and illness
and made well again in body, mind, and soul.
Father, may this oil be blessed for our use
in the name of our Lord Jesus Christ
(who lives and reigns with you for ever and
     ever.)   (℟   **Amen.**)

The conclusion *who lives and reigns with you* is said only when this
blessing takes place outside the eucharistic prayer.

Blessing of the Oil of Catechumens

After the prayer after communion, the bishop blesses the oils
placed on a table in the centre of the sanctuary. The conceleb-
rating priests stand on either side.

Bishop   Lord God,
protector of all who believe in you,
bless ✠ this oil
and give wisdom and strength
to all who are anointed with it
in preparation for their baptism.
Bring them to a deeper understanding of the gospel,
help them to accept the challenge of Christian living,
and lead them to the joy of new birth
in the family of your Church.
We ask this through Christ our Lord.   ℟   **Amen.**

Consecration of the Chrism

Then the bishop pours the balsam or perfume in the oil and
mixes the chrism in silence, unless this was done beforehand.

After this he sings or says the invitation:

Let us pray
that God our almighty Father
will bless this oil
so that all who are anointed with it
may be inwardly transformed
and come to share in eternal salvation.

Then the bishop may breathe over the opening of the vessel of
chrism. With his hands extended, he sings or says one of the
following consecratory prayers.

Consecratory Prayer A

God our maker,
source of all growth in holiness
accept the joyful thanks and praise
we offer in the name of your Church.

In the beginning, at your command,
the earth produced fruit-bearing trees.
From the fruit of the olive tree
you have provided us with oil for holy chrism.
The prophet David sang of the life and joy
that the oil would bring us in the sacraments of your love.

After the avenging flood,
the dove returning to Noah with an olive branch
announced your gift of peace.
This was a sign of a greater gift to come.

Now the waters of baptism wash away the sins of men,
and by the anointing with olive oil
you make us radiant with your joy.

At your command,
Aaron was washed with water,
and your servant Moses, his brother,
anointed him priest.
This too foreshadowed greater things to come.
After your Son, Jesus Christ our Lord,
asked John for baptism in the waters of Jordan,
you sent the Spirit upon him
in the form of a dove
and by the witness of your own voice
you declared him to be your only, well-beloved Son.
In this you clearly fulfilled the prophecy of David,
that Christ would be anointed with the oil of gladness
beyond his fellow men.

All the concelebrants extend their right hands towards the
chrism, without saying anything, until the end of the prayer.

And so, Father, we ask you to bless ✢ this oil you have created.
Fill it with the power of your Holy Spirit
through Christ your Son.
It is from him that chrism takes its name
and with chrism you have anointed
for yourself priests and kings,
prophets and martyrs.

Make this chrism a sign of life and salvation
for those who are to be born again in the waters of baptism.
Wash away the evil they have inherited from sinful Adam,
and when they are anointed with this holy oil
make them temples of your glory,
radiant with the goodness of life
that has its source in you.

Through this sign of chrism
grant them royal, priestly, and prophetic honour,
and clothe them with incorruption.
Let this be indeed the chrism of salvation
for those who will be born again of water and the Holy Spirit.
May they come to share eternal life
in the glory of your kingdom.

We ask this through Christ our Lord. ℟ **Amen.**

Alternative Consecratory Prayer B
Father,
we thank you for the gifts
you have given us in your love:
we thank you for life itself and for the sacraments
that strengthen it and give it fuller meaning.

In the Old Covenant you gave your people
a glimpse of the power of this holy oil
and when the fullness of time had come
you brought that mystery to perfection
in the life of our Lord Jesus Christ, your Son.

By his suffering, dying, and rising to life
he saved the human race.
He sent your Spirit to fill the Church
with every gift needed to complete your saving work.

From that time forward,
through the sign of holy chrism,
you dispense your life and love to men.
By anointing them with the Spirit,
you strengthen all who have been reborn in baptism.
Through that anointing
you transform them into the likeness of Christ your Son
and give them a share
in his royal, priestly, and prophetic work.

All the concelebrants extend their right hands towards the
chrism, without saying anything, until the end of the prayer.

And so, Father, by the power of your love,
make this mixture of oil and perfume
a sign and source ✛ of your blessing.
Pour out the gifts of your Holy Spirit
on our brothers and sisters who will be anointed with it.
Let the splendour of holiness shine on the world
from every place and thing
signed with this oil.

Above all, Father, we pray
that through this sign of your anointing
you will grant increase to your Church
until it reaches the eternal glory
where you, Father, will be the all in all,

together with Christ your Son,
in the unity of the Holy Spirit,
for ever and ever.   ℞   **Amen.**

Prayer over the Gifts
Lord God,
may the power of this sacrifice
cleanse the old weakness of our human nature.
Give us a newness of life
and bring us to salvation.

Preface of the Priesthood (Chrism Mass), P20

Communion Antiphon: For ever I will sing the goodness of the
Lord; I will proclaim your faithfulness to all generations.

Prayer after Communion
Lord God Almighty,
you have given us fresh strength
in these sacramental gifts.
Renew in us the image of Christ's goodness.

An appropriate Solemn Blessing or Prayer over the People may
be used. See pp.90ff. After the final blessing of the Mass, the
bishop puts incense in the censer, and the procession to the
sacristy is arranged.

The blessed oils are carried by the ministers immediately after
the cross, and the choir and people sing some verses of the hymn
O Redeemer or some other appropriate song.

The faithful who receive communion at this Mass may receive
communion again at the Mass of the Lord's Supper in the
evening.

UPON HIM WAS LAID THE INIQUITY OF US ALL

FAITHFUL CROSS ABOVE ALL OTHERS
ONE AND ONLY NOBLE TREE
NONE IN FOLIAGE NONE IN BLOSSOM
NONE IN FRUIT THY PEER MAY BE

The Easter Triduum, *the three days that begin on Holy Thursday with the Mass of the Lord's Supper, celebrates the paschal event, and that newness of life which flows from the crucified, buried and risen Christ.*

HOLY THURSDAY
Evening Mass of the Lord's Supper

Today we celebrate Christ's twofold giving of himself:

To his enemies, to die on the cross for the life of the world. He is the paschal victim, whose blood saves his people (see the Old Testament Reading).

To his friends and disciples, his Church – that is, to us – in the sacrament of his body and blood (see the reading from St Paul).

If we want to belong to Christ, we must follow his example of self-giving and of service – 'washing one another's feet' (see Gospel). We must be willing and ready to say with Christ, about our own selves:

'This is my body which is given up for you.'

The whole purpose of today's liturgy is to enable us to make this self-giving the real motivation for our lives.

The Mass of the Lord's Supper is celebrated in the evening, at a convenient hour, with the full participation of the whole local community and with all the priests and clergy exercising their ministry. The Order of Mass is followed.

INTRODUCTORY RITES AND
LITURGY OF THE WORD

Entrance Antiphon: We should glory in the cross of our Lord Jesus Christ, for he is our salvation, our life and our resurrection; through him we are saved and made free.

During the singing of the *Gloria*, the church bells are rung and then remain silent until the Easter Vigil, unless the conference of bishops or the Ordinary decrees otherwise.

Opening Prayer
God our Father,
we are gathered here to share in the supper
which your only Son left to his Church to reveal his love.
He gave it to us when he was about to die
and commanded us to celebrate it as the new and eternal
    sacrifice.
We pray that in this eucharist
we may find the fullness of love and life.

FIRST READING

A reading from the book of Exodus   12:1-8. 11-14
Instructions concerning the Passover meal.

The Lord said to Moses and Aaron in the land of Egypt, 'This month is to be the first of all the others for you, the first month of your year. Speak to the whole community of Israel and say, "On the tenth day of this month each man must take an animal from the flock, one for each family: one animal for each household. If the household is too small to eat the animal, a man must join with his neighbour, the nearest to his house, as the number of persons requires. You must take into account what each can eat in deciding the number for the animal. It must be an animal without blemish, a male one year old; you may take it from either sheep or goats. You must keep it till the fourteenth day of the month when the whole assembly of the community of Israel shall slaughter it between the two evenings. Some of the blood must then be taken and put on the two doorposts and the lintel of the houses where it is eaten. That night, the flesh is to be eaten, roasted over the fire; it must be eaten with unleavened bread and bitter herbs. You shall eat it like this: with a girdle round your waist, sandals on your feet, a staff in your hand. You shall eat it hastily; it is a passover in honour of the Lord. That night, I will go through the land of Egypt and strike down all the first-born in the land of Egypt, man and beast alike, and I shall deal out punishment to all the gods of Egypt, I am the Lord. The blood shall serve to mark the houses that you live in. When I see the blood I will pass over you and you shall escape the destroying plague when I strike the land of Egypt. This day is to be a day of remembrance for you, and you must celebrate it as a feast in the Lord's honour. For all generations you are to declare it a day of festival, for ever." '

This is the word of the Lord.

Responsorial Psalm   Ps 115:12-13. 15-18. ℟ cf. 1 Cor 10:16

℟ **The blessing-cup that we bless
    is a communion with the blood of Christ.**

1   How can I repay the Lord
    for his goodness to me?
    The cup of salvation I will raise;
    I will call on the Lord's name.   ℟

2 O precious in the eyes of the Lord
is the death of his faithful.
Your servant, Lord, your servant am I;
you have loosened my bonds. ℟

3 A thanksgiving sacrifice I make:
I will call on the Lord's name.
My vows to the Lord I will fulfil
before all his people. ℟

SECOND READING

A reading from the first letter of St Paul
to the Corinthians   11:23-26

Every time you eat this bread and drink this cup, you are proclaiming the death of the Lord.

This is what I received from the Lord, and in turn passed on to you: that on the same night that he was betrayed, the Lord Jesus took some bread, and thanked God for it and broke it, and he said, 'This is my body, which is for you; do this as a memorial of me.' In the same way he took the cup after supper, and said, 'This cup is the new covenant in my blood. Whenever you drink it, do this as a memorial of me.' Until the Lord comes, therefore, every time you eat this bread and drink this cup, you are proclaiming his death.

This is the word of the Lord.

Gospel Acclamation   Jn 13:34
Praise and honour to you, Lord Jesus!
I give you a new commandment:
love one another just as I have loved you, says the Lord.
Praise and honour to you, Lord Jesus!

GOSPEL

A reading from the holy Gospel according to John   13:1-15
Now he showed how perfect his love was.

It was before the festival of the Passover, and Jesus knew that the hour had come for him to pass from this world to the Father. He had always loved those who were his in the world, but now he showed how perfect his love was.

They were at supper, and the devil had already put it into the mind of Judas Iscariot son of Simon, to betray him. Jesus knew that the Father had put everything into his hands, and that he had come from God and was returning to God, and he got up from table, removed his outer garment and, taking a towel, wrapped it round his waist; he then poured water into a basin and began to wash the disciples' feet and to wipe them with the towel he was wearing.

He came to Simon Peter, who said to him, 'Lord, are you going to wash my feet?' Jesus answered, 'At the moment you do not know what I am doing, but later you will understand.' 'Never!' said Peter 'You shall never wash my feet.' Jesus replied, 'If I do not wash you, you can have nothing in common with me.' 'Then, Lord,' said Simon Peter 'not only my feet, but my hands and my head as well!' Jesus said, 'No one who has taken a bath needs washing, he is clean all over. You too are clean, though not all of you are.' He knew who was going to betray him, that was why he said, 'though not all of you are.'

When he had washed their feet and put on his clothes again he went back to the table. 'Do you understand' he said 'what I have done to you? You call me Master and Lord, and rightly; so I am. If I, then, the Lord and Master, have washed your feet, you should wash each other's feet. I have given you an example so that you may copy what I have done to you.'

This is the Gospel of the Lord.

WASHING OF FEET

The washing of feet may follow the homily.

The men who have been chosen are led by the ministers to chairs prepared in a suitable place. Then the priest goes to each man. With the help of the ministers, he pours water over each one's feet and dries them.

Meanwhile some of the following antiphons or other appropriate songs are sung.

Antiphon 1   cf. Jn 13:4.5.15
The Lord Jesus,
when he had eaten with his disciples,
poured water into a basin
and began to wash their feet, saying:
This example I leave you.

Antiphon 2   Jn 13:6.7.8
Lord, do you wash my feet?
Jesus said to him:
If I do not wash your feet,

you can have no part with me.

℣ So he came to Simon Peter,
who said to him:
Lord, do you wash my feet?

℣ Now you do not know what I am doing,
but later you will understand.
Lord, do you wash my feet?

Antiphon 3
cf. Jn 13:14

If I, your Lord and Teacher, have washed your feet,
then surely you must wash one another's feet.

Antiphon 4
Jn 13:35

If there is this love among you,
all will know that you are my disciples.

℣ Jesus said to his disciples:
If there is this love among you,
all will know that you are my disciples.

Antiphon 5
Jn 13:34

I give you a new commandment:
love one another as I have loved you, says the Lord.

Antiphon 6
1 Cor 13:13

Faith, hope, and love,
let these endure among you;
and the greatest of these is love.

The general intercessions follow the washing of feet, or, if this
does not take place, they follow the homily. The profession of
faith is not said.

THE LITURGY OF THE EUCHARIST

At the beginning of the liturgy of the eucharist, there may be a
procession of the faithful with gifts for the poor.

During the procession the following may be sung, or another
appropriate song.

Antiphon
Where charity and love are found, there is God.

℣ The love of Christ has gathered us together into one.

℣ Let us rejoice and be glad in him.
℣ Let us fear and love the living God,
℣ and love each other from the depths of our heart.

℞ Where charity and love are found, there is God.

℣ Therefore when we are together,
℣ let us take heed not to be divided in mind.
℣ Let there be an end to bitterness and quarrels, an end to strife,
℣ and in our midst be Christ our God.

℞ Where charity and love are found, there is God.

℣ And, in company with the blessed, may we see
℣ your face in glory, Christ our God,
℣ pure and unbounded joy
℣ for ever and for ever.

℞ Where charity and love are found, there is God.

Prayer over the Gifts
Lord,
make us worthy to celebrate these mysteries.
Each time we offer this memorial sacrifice
the work of our redemption is accomplished.

Preface of the Holy Eucharist I, P47

If Eucharistic Prayer I is said, the following special forms are used.

In union with the whole Church
we celebrate that day
when Jesus Christ, our Lord,
was betrayed for us.
We honour Mary,
the ever-virgin mother of Jesus Christ our Lord and God.
We honour Joseph, her husband,
the apostles and martyrs
Peter and Paul, Andrew,
(James, John, Thomas,
James, Philip,
Bartholomew, Matthew, Simon and Jude;
we honour Linus, Cletus, Clement, Sixtus,
Cornelius, Cyprian, Lawrence, Chrysogonus,
John and Paul, Cosmas and Damian)

and all the saints.
May their merits and prayers
gain us your constant help and protection.
(Through Christ our Lord.   Amen.)

Father, accept this offering
from your whole family
in memory of the day when Jesus Christ, our Lord,
gave the mysteries of his body and blood
for his disciples to celebrate.
Grant us your peace in this life,
save us from final damnation,
and count us among those you have chosen.
(Through Christ our Lord.   Amen.)

Bless and approve our offering;
make it acceptable to you,
an offering in spirit and in truth.
Let it become for us
the body and blood of Jesus Christ,
your only Son, our Lord.

The day before he suffered
to save us and all men,
that is today,
he took bread in his sacred hands
and looking up to heaven,
to you, his almighty Father,
he gave you thanks and praise.
He broke the bread,
gave it to his disciples, and said:
Take this, all of you, and eat it:
this is my body which will be given up for you.

Communion Antiphon: This body will be given for you. This is the
cup of the new covenant in my blood; whenever you receive
them, do so in remembrance of me.

After the distribution of communion, the ciborium with hosts for
Good Friday is left on the altar, and Mass concludes with the
prayer after communion.

Prayer after Communion
Almighty God,
we receive new life
from the supper your Son gave us in this world.
May we find full contentment
in the meal we hope to share
in your eternal kingdom.

TRANSFER OF THE HOLY EUCHARIST

After the prayer after communion, the priest accompanied by the ministers carries the Blessed Sacrament in procession to the place where it is to be kept until tomorrow. During the procession, the *Pange lingua* or other suitable hymn is sung.

Hymn: Pange Lingua

1   Of the glorious Body telling,
O my tongue, its mysteries sing,
And the Blood, all price excelling,
Which the world's eternal King,
In a noble womb once dwelling,
Shed for the world's ransoming.

2   Given for us, for us descending,
Of a Virgin to proceed,
Man with man in converse blending,
Scattered he the Gospel seed,
Till his sojourn drew to ending,
Which he closed in wondrous deed.

3   At the last great Supper lying
Circled by his brethren's band,
Meekly with the law complying,
First he finished its command,
Then, immortal Food supplying,
Gave himself with his own hand.

4   Word made Flesh, by word he maketh
Very bread his Flesh to be;
Man in wine Christ's Blood partaketh:
And if senses fail to see,
Faith alone the true heart waketh
To behold the mystery.

When the procession reaches the place of reposition the singing is concluded with the *Tantum ergo Sacramentum*:

5   Therefore we, before him bending,
    This great Sacrament revere;
    Types and shadows have their ending,
    For the newer rite is here;
    Faith, our outward sense befriending,
    Makes the inward vision clear.

6   Glory let us give, and blessing
    To the Father and the Son;
    Honour, might, and praise addressing,
    While eternal ages run;
    Ever too his love confessing,
    Who, from both, with both is one.
    Amen.

The tabernacle of reposition is closed.

After a period of silent adoration, the priest and ministers genuflect and return to the sacristy.

Then the altar is stripped and, if possible, the crosses are removed from the church. It is desirable to cover any crosses which remain in the church.

The faithful should be encouraged to continue adoration before the Blessed Sacrament for a suitable period of time during the night, but there should be no solemn adoration after midnight.

GOOD FRIDAY
CELEBRATION OF THE LORD'S PASSION

In this celebration of the passion and death of the Lord,
    (a) we listen to the words of scripture and strive to understand the
true meaning of his sufferings and the mind that was in him
    (b) we pray with his spirit for the needs of the whole world
    (c) we worship the cross as the symbol of his triumph
and finally
    (d) we enter into sacramental communion with him who is our
Saviour and our Life.

According to the Church's ancient tradition, the sacraments are not celebrated today or tomorrow. The altar should be completely bare, without cloths, candles, or cross. The celebration of the Lord's passion takes place in the afternoon, about three o'clock, unless pastoral reasons suggest a later hour. The celebration consists of three parts: liturgy of the word, veneration of the cross, and holy communion.

   The priest and sacred ministers, wearing red Mass vestments, go to the altar. There they make a reverence and prostrate themselves, or they may kneel.

   All pray silently for a while.

   Then the priest goes to the chair with the ministers. He faces the people and, with hands joined, says one of the following:

Prayer
Lord,
by shedding his blood for us,
your Son, Jesus Christ,
established the paschal mystery.
In your goodness, make us holy
and watch over us always.

   or

Lord,
by the suffering of Christ your Son
you have saved us all from the death
we inherited from sinful Adam.
By the law of nature
we have borne the likeness of his manhood.
May the sanctifying power of grace
help us to put on the likeness of our Lord in heaven,
who lives and reigns for ever and ever.

PART ONE: LITURGY OF THE WORD

FIRST READING

A reading from the prophet Isaiah

He was pierced through for our faults.

52:13 – 53:12

See, my servant will prosper,
he shall be lifted up, exalted, rise to great heights.

As the crowds were appalled on seeing him
– so disfigured did he look
that he seemed no longer human –
so will the crowds be astonished at him,
and kings stand speechless before him;
for they shall see something never told
and witness something never heard before:
'Who could believe what we have heard,
and to whom has the power of the Lord been revealed?'

Like a sapling he grew up in front of us,
like a root in arid ground.
Without beauty, without majesty (we saw him),
no looks to attract our eyes;
a thing despised and rejected by men,
a man of sorrows and familiar with suffering,
a man to make people screen their faces;
he was despised and we took no account of him.

And yet ours were the sufferings he bore,
ours the sorrows he carried.
But we, we thought of him as someone punished,
struck by God, and brought low.
Yet he was pierced through for our faults,
crushed for our sins.
On him lies a punishment that brings us peace,
and through his wounds we are healed.
We had all gone astray like sheep,
each taking his own way,
and the Lord burdened him
with the sins of all of us.
Harshly dealt with, he bore it humbly,
he never opened his mouth,
like a lamb that is led to the slaughter-house,
like a sheep that is dumb before its shearers
never opening its mouth

By force and by law he was taken;
would anyone plead his cause?
Yes, he was torn away from the land of the living;
for our faults struck down in death.
They gave him a grave with the wicked,
a tomb with the rich,
though he had done no wrong
and there had been no perjury in his mouth.
The Lord has been pleased to crush him with suffering.
If he offers his life in atonement,
he shall see his heirs, he shall have a long life
and through him what the Lord wishes will be done.

His soul's anguish over
he shall see the light and be content.
By his sufferings shall my servant justify many,
taking their faults on himself.

Hence I will grant whole hordes for his tribute,
he shall divide the spoil with the mighty,
for surrendering himself to death
and letting himself be taken for a sinner,
while he was bearing the faults of many
and praying all the time for sinners.

This is the word of the Lord.

Responsorial Psalm   Ps 30:2. 6. 12-13. 15-17. 25. ℟ Lk 23:46
  ℟ **Father, into your hands I commend my spirit.**

1 In you, O Lord, I take refuge.
   Let me never be put to shame.
   In your justice, set me free.
   Into your hands I commend my spirit.
   It is you who will redeem me, Lord. ℟

2 In the face of all my foes
   I am a reproach,
   an object of scorn to my neighbours
   and of fear to my friends. ℟

3 Those who see me in the street
   run far away from me.
   I am like a dead man, forgotten in men's hearts,
   like a thing thrown away. ℟

4　But as for me, I trust in you, Lord,
　　I say: 'You are my God.'
　　My life is in your hands, deliver me
　　from the hands of those who hate me. ℟

5　Let your face shine on your servant.
　　Save me in your love.
　　Be strong, let your heart take courage,
　　all who hope in the Lord. ℟

SECOND READING

A reading from the letter to the Hebrews　　4:14-16; 5:7-9

He learnt to obey through suffering and became for all who obey him the source of eternal salvation.

Since in Jesus, the Son of God, we have the supreme high priest who has gone through to the highest heaven, we must never let go of the faith that we have professed. For it is not as if we had a high priest who was incapable of feeling our weaknesses with us; but we have one who has been tempted in every way that we are, though he is without sin. Let us be confident, then, in approaching the throne of grace, that we shall have mercy from him and find grace when we are in need of help.

During his life on earth, he offered up prayer and entreaty, aloud and in silent tears, to the one who had the power to save him out of death, and he submitted so humbly that his prayer was heard. Although he was Son, he learnt to obey through suffering; but having been made perfect, he became for all who obey him the source of eternal salvation.

　　This is the word of the Lord.

Gospel Acclamation　　Phil 2:8-9
　　Glory and praise to you, O Christ!
　　Christ was humbler yet,
　　even to accepting death, death on a cross.
　　But God raised him high
　　and gave him the name which is above all names.
　　Glory and praise to you, O Christ!

GOSPEL

The passion of our Lord Jesus Christ
according to John   18:1 – 19:42

N Jesus left with his disciples and crossed the Kedron valley.
There was a garden there, and he went into it with his
disciples. Judas the traitor knew the place well, since Jesus
had often met his disciples there, and he brought the cohort to
this place together with a detachment of guards sent by the
chief priests and the Pharisees, all with lanterns and torches
and weapons. Knowing everything that was going to happen
to him, Jesus then came forward and said,

J Who are you looking for?

N They answered,

C Jesus the Nazarene.

N He said,

J I am he.

N Now Judas the traitor was standing among them. When Jesus
said, 'I am he', they moved back and fell to the ground. He
asked them a second time,

J Who are you looking for?

N They said,

C Jesus the Nazarene.

N Jesus replied,

J I have told you that I am he. If I am the one you are looking
for, let these others go.

N This was to fulfil the words he had spoken: 'Not one of those
you gave me have I lost'.

  Simon Peter, who carried a sword, drew it and wounded
the high priest's servant, cutting off his right ear. The servant's name was Malchus. Jesus said to Peter,

J Put your sword back in its scabbard; am I not to drink the cup
that the Father has given me?

N The cohort and its captain and the Jewish guards seized Jesus
and bound him. They took him first to Annas, because Annas
was the father-in-law of Caiaphas, who was high priest that
year. It was Caiaphas who had suggested to the Jews, 'It is
better for one man to die for the people'.

  Simon Peter, with another disciple, followed Jesus. This
disciple, who was known to the high priest, went with Jesus
into the high priest's palace, but Peter stayed outside the

N   Narrator.   J Jesus.   O   Other single speaker.
C   Crowd, or more than one speaker.

door. So the other disciple, the one known to the high priest, went out, spoke to the woman who was keeping the door and brought Peter in. The maid on duty at the door said to Peter,

O Aren't you another of that man's disciples?

N He answered,

O I am not.

N Now it was cold, and the servants and guards had lit a charcoal fire and were standing there warming themselves; so Peter stood there too, warming himself with the others.

The high priest questioned Jesus about his disciples and his teaching. Jesus answered,

J I have spoken openly for all the world to hear; I have always taught in the synagogue and in the Temple where all the Jews meet together: I have said nothing in secret. But why ask me? Ask my hearers what I taught: they know what I said.

N At these words, one of the guards standing by gave Jesus a slap in the face, saying,

O Is that the way to answer the high priest?

N Jesus replied,

J If there is something wrong in what I said, point it out; but if there is no offence in it, why do you strike me?

N Then Annas sent him, still bound, to Caiaphas, the high priest.

As Simon Peter stood there warming himself, someone said to him,

O Aren't you another of his disciples?

N He denied it saying,

O I am not.

N One of the high priest's servants, a relation of the man whose ear Peter had cut off, said,

O Didn't I see you in the garden with him?

N Again Peter denied it; and at once a cock crew.

They then led Jesus from the house of Caiaphas to the Praetorium. It was now morning. They did not go into the Praetorium themselves or they would be defiled and unable to eat the passover. So Pilate came outside to them and said,

O What charge do you bring against this man?

N They replied,

C If he were not a criminal, we should not be handing him over to you.

N Pilate said,

O Take him yourselves, and try him by your own Law.

N The Jews answered,

C   We are not allowed to put a man to death.

N   This was to fulfil the words Jesus had spoken indicating the way he was going to die.

     So Pilate went back into the Praetorium and called Jesus to him, and asked,

O   Are you the king of the Jews?

N   Jesus replied,

J   Do you ask this of your own accord, or have others spoken to you about me?

N   Pilate answered,

O   Am I a Jew? It is your own people and the chief priests who have handed you over to me: what have you done?

N   Jesus replied,

J   Mine is not a kingdom of this world; if my kingdom were of this world, my men would have fought to prevent me being surrendered to the Jews. But my kingdom is not of this kind.

N   Pilate said,

O   So you are a king then?

N   Jesus answered,

J   It is you who say it. Yes, I am a king. I was born for this, I came into the world for this; to bear witness to the truth, and all who are on the side of truth listen to my voice.

N   Pilate said,

O   Truth? What is that?

N   And with that he went out again to the Jews and said,

O   I find no case against him. But according to a custom of yours I should release one prisoner at the Passover; would you like me, then, to release the king of the Jews?

N   At this they shouted:

C   Not this man, but Barabbas.

N   Barabbas was a brigand.

     Pilate then had Jesus taken away and scourged; and after this, the soldiers twisted some thorns into a crown and put it on his head, and dressed him in a purple robe. They kept coming up to him and saying,

C   Hail, king of the Jews!

N   and they slapped him in the face.

     Pilate came outside again and said to them,

O   Look, I am going to bring him out to you to let you see that I find no case.

N   Jesus then came out wearing the crown of thorns and the purple robe. Pilate said,

O   Here is the man.

N When they saw him the chief priests and the guards shouted,
C Crucify him! Crucify him!
N Pilate said,
O Take him yourselves and crucify him: I can find no case against him.
N The Jews replied,
C We have a Law, and according to the Law he ought to die, because he has claimed to be the son of God.
N When Pilate heard them say this his fears increased. Re-entering the Praetorium, he said to Jesus,
O Where do you come from?
N But Jesus made no answer. Pilate then said to him,
O Are you refusing to speak to me? Surely you know I have power to release you and I have power to crucify you?
N Jesus replied
J You would have no power over me if it had not been given you from above; that is why the one who handed me over to you has the greater guilt.
N From that moment Pilate was anxious to set him free, but the Jews shouted,
C If you set him free you are no friend of Caesar's; anyone who makes himself king is defying Caesar.
N Hearing these words, Pilate had Jesus brought out, and seated himself on the chair of judgement at a place called the Pavement, in Hebrew Gabbatha. It was Passover Preparation Day, about the sixth hour. Pilate said to the Jews,
O Here is your king.
N They said,
C Take him away, take him away. Crucify him!
N Pilate said,
O Do you want me to crucify your king?
N The chief priests answered,
C We have no king except Caesar.
N So in the end Pilate handed him over to them to be crucified.

They then took charge of Jesus, and carrying his own cross he went out of the city to the place of the skull, or, as it was called in Hebrew, Golgotha, where they crucified him with two others, one on either side with Jesus in the middle. Pilate wrote out a notice and had it fixed to the cross; it ran: 'Jesus the Nazarene, King of the Jews.' This notice was read by many of the Jews, because the place where Jesus was crucified was not far from the city, and the writing was in Hebrew, Latin and Greek. So the Jewish chief priests said to Pilate,

C You should not write 'King of the Jews', but 'This man said: I am King of the Jews'.
N Pilate answered,
O What I have written, I have written.
N When the soldiers had finished crucifying Jesus they took his clothing and divided it into four shares, one for each soldier. His undergarment was seamless, woven in one piece from neck to hem; so they said to one another,
C Instead of tearing it, let's throw dice to decide who is to have it.
N In this way the words of scripture were fulfilled:

> They shared out my clothing among them.
> They cast lots for my clothes.

This is exactly what the soldiers did.

Near the cross of Jesus stood his mother and his mother's sister, Mary the wife of Clopas, and Mary of Magdala. Seeing his mother and the disciple he loved standing near her, Jesus said to his mother,
J Woman, this is your son.
N Then to the disciple he said,
J This is your mother.
N And from that moment the disciple made a place for her in his home.

After this, Jesus knew that everything had now been completed, and to fulfil the scripture perfectly he said:
J I am thirsty.
N A jar full of vinegar stood there, so putting a sponge soaked in vinegar on a hyssop stick they held it up to his mouth. After Jesus had taken the vinegar he said,
J It is accomplished;
N and bowing his head he gave up the spirit.

All kneel and pause a moment.

N It was Preparation Day, and to prevent the bodies remaining on the cross during the sabbath – since that sabbath was a day of special solemnity – the Jews asked Pilate to have the legs broken and the bodies taken away. Consequently the soldiers came and broke the legs of the first man who had been crucified with him and then of the other. When they came to Jesus, they found that he was already dead, and so instead of breaking his legs one of the soldiers pierced his side with a lance; and immediately there came out blood and water. This is the evidence of one who saw it – trustworthy evidence, and he knows he speaks the truth – and he gives it so that you may believe as well. Because all this happened to fulfil the words of scripture:

Not one bone of his will be broken,

and again, in another place scripture says:

They will look on the one whom they have pierced.

After this, Joseph of Arimathaea, who was a disciple of Jesus – though a secret one because he was afraid of the Jews – asked Pilate to let him remove the body of Jesus. Pilate gave permission, so they came and took it away. Nicodemus came as well – the same one who had first come to Jesus at night-time – and he brought a mixture of myrrh and aloes, weighing about a hundred pounds. They took the body of Jesus and wrapped it with the spices in linen cloths, following the Jewish burial custom. At the place where he had been crucified there was a garden, and in the garden a new tomb in which no one had yet been buried. Since it was the Jewish Day of Preparation and the tomb was near at hand, they laid Jesus there.

General Intercessions

The general intercessions conclude the liturgy of the word. The priest sings or says the introduction in which each intention is stated.

All kneel and pray silently for some period of time, and then the priest, with hands extended, sings or says the prayer.

The people may either kneel or stand throughout the entire period of the general intercessions.

I.   For the Church

Let us pray, dear friends,
for the holy Church of God throughout the world.
that God the almighty Father
guide it and gather it together
so that we may worship him
in peace and tranquility.

Silent prayer. Then the priest says:

Almighty and eternal God,
you have shown your glory to all nations
in Christ, your Son.
Guide the work of your Church.
Help it to persevere in faith,
proclaim your name,
and bring your salvation to people everywhere.
We ask this through Christ our Lord. ℟ **Amen.**

II.   For the pope

Let us pray
for our Holy Father, Pope N.,
that God who chose him to be bishop
may give him health and strength
to guide and govern God's holy people.

Silent prayer. Then the priest says:

Almighty and eternal God,
you guide all things by your word,
you govern all Christian people.
In your love protect the Pope you have chosen for us.
Under his leadership deepen our faith
and make us better Christians.
We ask this through Christ our Lord.   ℟ **Amen.**

III.   For the clergy and laity of the Church

Let us pray
for N., our bishop,
for all bishops, priests, and deacons;
for all who have a special ministry in the Church
and for all God's people.

Silent prayer. Then the priest says:

Almighty and eternal God,
your Spirit guides the Church
and makes it holy.
Listen to our prayers
and help each of us
in his own vocation
to do your work more faithfully.
We ask this through Christ our Lord.   ℟ **Amen.**

IV.   For those preparing for baptism

Let us pray
for those (among us) preparing for baptism,

that God in his mercy
make them responsive to his love,
forgive their sins through the waters of new birth,
and give them life in Jesus Christ our Lord.

Silent prayer. Then the priest says:
Almighty and eternal God,
you continually bless your Church with new members.
Increase the faith and understanding
of those (among us) preparing for baptism.
Give them a new birth in these living waters
and make them members of your chosen family.
We ask this through Christ our Lord.   R̸ **Amen.**

V.   For the unity of Christians
Let us pray
for all our brothers and sisters
who share our faith in Jesus Christ,
that God may gather and keep together in one Church
all those who seek the truth with sincerity.

Silent prayer. Then the priest says:
Almighty and eternal God,
you keep together all those you have united.
Look kindly on all who follow Jesus your Son.
We are all consecrated to you by our common baptism
Make us one in the fullness of faith,
and keep us one in the fellowship of love.
We ask this through Christ our Lord.   R̸ **Amen.**

VI.   For the Jewish people
Let us pray
for the Jewish people,
the first to hear the word of God,
that they may continue to grow in the love of his name
and in faithfulness to his covenant.

Silent prayer. Then the priest says:
Almighty and eternal God,
long ago you gave your promise to Abraham and his posterity.
Listen to your Church as we pray
that the people you first made your own
may arrive at the fullness of redemption.
We ask this through Christ our Lord.   R̸ **Amen.**

VII.   For those who do not believe in Christ

Let us pray
for those who do not believe in Christ,
that the light of the Holy Spirit
may show them the way to salvation.

Silent prayer. Then the priest says:

Almighty and eternal God,
enable those who do not acknowledge Christ
to find the truth
as they walk before you in sincerity of heart.
Help us to grow in love for one another,
to grasp more fully the mystery of your godhead,
and to become more perfect witnesses of your love
in the sight of men.
(We ask this) through Christ our Lord.   ℟   **Amen.**

VIII.   For those who do not believe in God

Let us pray
for those who do not believe in God,
that they may find him
by sincerely following all that is right.

Silent prayer. Then the priest says:

Almighty and eternal God,
you created mankind
so that all might long to find you
and have peace when you are found.
Grant that, in spite of the hurtful things
that stand in their way,
they may all recognise in the lives of Christians
the tokens of your love and mercy,
and gladly acknowledge you
as the one true God and Father of us all.
We ask this through Christ our Lord.   ℟   **Amen.**

IX.   For all in public office

Let us pray
for those who serve us in public office,
that God may guide their minds and hearts,
so that all men may live in true peace and freedom.

Silent prayer. Then the priest says:

Almighty and eternal God,
you know the longings of men's hearts

and you protect their rights.
In your goodness
watch over those in authority,
so that people everywhere may enjoy
religious freedom, security, and peace.
We ask this through Christ our Lord.   ℟   **Amen.**

X.   For those in special need
Let us pray, dear friends,
that God the almighty Father
may heal the sick,
comfort the dying,
give safety to travellers,
free those unjustly deprived of liberty,
and rid the world of falsehood,
hunger, and disease.

Silent prayer. Then the priest says:
Almighty, ever-living God,
you give strength to the weary
and new courage to those who have lost heart.
Hear the prayers of all who call on you in any trouble
that they may have the joy of receiving your help in their need.
We ask this through Christ our Lord.   ℟   **Amen.**

PART TWO
VENERATION OF THE CROSS

The Invitation
The cross is shown to the people three times, either from the
altar, while it is unveiled, or as it is carried in procession through
the Church to the sanctuary.

Each time, the priest, assisted by the sacred minister or by the
choir, sings, each time on a higher note:

This is the wood of the cross, on which hung the Saviour of the
world.

and the people reply:
   ℟   **Come, let us worship.**

After each response, all kneel and venerate the cross briefly in
silence. Then the cross and candles are placed at the entrance to
the sanctuary.

Veneration of the Cross

The priest, clergy, and faithful approach to venerate the cross in a kind of procession. They make a simple genuflection or perform some other appropriate sign of reverence according to local custom, for example, kissing the cross. During the veneration the antiphon *We worship you, Lord,* the Improperia (*Reproaches*) or other suitable songs are sung. All who have venerated the cross return to their places and sit. The faithful may, where necessary, venerate the cross in silence, without leaving their places. After the veneration, the cross is carried to its place at the altar, and the lighted candles are placed around the altar or near the cross.

Songs at the Veneration of the Cross

Individual parts are indicated by No. 1 (first choir) and No. 2 (second choir); parts sung by both choirs together are indicated by Nos. 1 and 2.

1.   Antiphon

1 and 2:   We worship you, Lord,
we venerate your cross,
we praise your resurrection.
Through the cross you brought joy to the world.

1:   May God be gracious and bless us;
and let his face shed its light upon us.

1 and 2:   We worship you, Lord,
we venerate your cross,
we praise your resurrection.
Through the cross you brought joy to the world.

2.   The Reproaches

I

1 and 2:   My people, what have I done to you?
How have I offended you? Answer me!

1:   I led you out of Egypt, from slavery to freedom,
but you led your Saviour to the cross.

2:   My people, what have I done to you?
How have I offended you? Answer me!

1:   Holy is God!

2:   Holy and strong!

1:   Holy immortal One,
have mercy on us!

1 and 2: For forty years I led you safely through the desert.
         I fed you with manna from heaven,
         and brought you to a land of plenty;
         but you led your Saviour to the cross.

1:       Holy is God!
2:       Holy and strong!
1:       Holy immortal One,
         have mercy on us!

1 and 2: What more could I have done for you?
         I planted you as my fairest vine,
         but you yielded only bitterness:
         when I was thirsty you gave me vinegar to drink,
         and you pierced your Saviour with a lance.

1:       Holy is God!
2:       Holy and strong!
1:       Holy immortal One,
         have mercy on us!

II

1: For your sake I scourged your captors and their firstborn sons,
   but you brought your scourges down on me.
2: My people, what have I done to you?
   How have I offended you? Answer me!

1: I led you from slavery to freedom
   and drowned your captors in the sea,
   but you handed me over to your high priests.
2: My people, what have I done to you?
   How have I offended you? Answer me!

1: I opened the sea before you,
   but you opened my side with a spear.
2: My people, what have I done to you?
   How have I offended you? Answer me!

1: I led you on your way in a pillar of cloud,
   but you led me to Pilate's court.
2: My people, what have I done to you?
   How have I offended you? Answer me!

1: I bore you up with manna in the desert,
   but you struck me down and scourged me.
2: My people, what have I done to you?
   How have I offended you? Answer me!

1: I gave you saving water from the rock,
    but you gave me gall and vinegar to drink.
2: My people, what have I done to you?
    How have I offended you? Answer me!

1: For you I struck down the kings of Canaan,
    but you struck my head with a reed.
2: My people, what have I done to you?
    How have I offended you? Answer me!

1: I gave you a royal sceptre,
    but you gave me a crown of thorns.
2: My people, what have I done to you?
    How have I offended you? Answer me!

1: I raised you to the height of majesty,
    but you have raised me high on a cross.
2: My people, what have I done to you?
    How have I offended you? Answer me!

3.   Hymn

A. Faithful Cross! above all other
    One and only noble tree!
    None in foliage, none in blossom,
    None in fruit thy peer may be;
B. Sweetest wood and sweetest nails,
    Sweetest weight is hung on thee.

1 Sing, my tongue, the glorious battle,
    Sing the ending of the fray;
    Now above the Cross, the trophy,
    Sound the loud triumphant lay:
    Tell how Christ the world's Redeemer,
    As a Victim won the day.
        A.   Faithful Cross, etc. (*first four lines only*)

2 God in pity saw man fallen,
    Shamed and sunk in misery,
    When he fell on death by tasting
    Fruit of the forbidden tree;
    Then another tree was chosen
    Which the world from death should free.
        B.   Sweetest wood, etc. (*last two lines only*)

3 Thus the scheme of our salvation
    Was of old in order laid,

That the manifold deceiver's
Art by art might be outweighed,
And the lure the foe put forward
Into means of healing made.
    A.   Faithful Cross, etc.

4 Therefore when the appointed fullness
Of the holy time was come,
He was sent who maketh all things
Forth from God's eternal home;
Thus he came to earth, incarnate,
Offspring of a maiden's womb.
    B.   Sweetest wood, etc.

5 Hear the helpless baby crying
Where the narrow manger stands;
See how she, his Virgin Mother,
Ties his limbs with slender bands,
Swaddling clothes she wraps about him,
And confines God's feet and hands!
    A.   Faithful Cross, etc.

6 Thirty years among us dwelling,
His appointed time fulfilled,
Born for this, he meets his Passion,
For that this he freely willed,
On the Cross the Lamb is lifted
Where his life-blood shall be spilled.
    B.   Sweetest wood, etc.

7 He endured the nails, the spitting,
Vinegar, and spear, and reed;
From that holy Body broken
Blood and water forth proceed:
Earth, and stars, and sky, and ocean
By that flood from stain are freed.
    A.   Faithful Cross, etc.

8 Bend thy boughs, O Tree of Glory!
Thy relaxing sinews bend;
For a while the ancient rigour
That thy birth bestowed, suspend;
And the King of heavenly beauty
On thy bosom gently tend!
    B.   Sweetest wood, etc.

9 Thou alone wast counted worthy
  This world's ransom to uphold;
  For a ship-wreck'd race preparing
  Harbour, like the Ark of old;
  With the sacred Blood anointed
  From the smitten Lamb that rolled.
  A.   Faithful Cross, etc.

10 To the Trinity be glory
   Everlasting, as is meet;
   Equal to the Father, equal
   To the Son, and Paraclete:
   Trinal Unity, whose praises
   All created things repeat. Amen.
   B.   Sweetest wood, etc.

PART THREE: HOLY COMMUNION

The altar is covered with a cloth and the corporal and book are placed on it. Then the deacon or the priest brings the ciborium with the Blessed Sacrament from the place of reposition to the altar without any procession, while all stand in silence. Two ministers with lighted candles accompany him and they place their candles near the altar or on it.

C. Let us pray with confidence to the Father
    in the words our Saviour gave us:

He extends his hands and continues, with all present:

    Our Father . . .
C. Deliver us, Lord, from every evil,
    and grant us peace in our day.
    In your mercy keep us free from sin
    and protect us from all anxiety
    as we wait in joyful hope
    for the coming of our Saviour, Jesus Christ.

All **For the kingdom, the power, and the glory are yours,
    now and for ever.**

The celebrant says quietly:

Lord Jesus Christ, with faith in your love and mercy I eat your
    body and drink your blood.
Let it not bring me condemnation, but health in mind and body.

Facing the people, he says aloud:

This is the Lamb of God
who takes away the sins of the world.
Happy are those who are called to his supper.
All   **Lord, I am not worthy to receive you,
but only say the word and I shall be healed.**

Then communion is distributed to the faithful. Any appropriate
song may be sung during communion.

A period of silence may now be observed. The celebrant then
says the following prayer:

Let us pray.
Almighty and eternal God,
you have restored us to life
by the triumphant death and resurrection of Christ.
Continue this healing work within us.
May we who participate in this mystery
never cease to serve you.

For the dismissal the celebrant faces the people, and says:

Prayer over the People
Lord,
send down your abundant blessing
upon your people who have devoutly recalled the death of your
    Son
in the sure hope of the resurrection.
Grant them pardon; bring them comfort.
May their faith grow stronger
and their eternal salvation be assured.

All depart in silence.

HOLY SATURDAY

On Holy Saturday the Church waits at the Lord's tomb, meditating on his suffering and death. The altar is left bare, and the
sacrifice of the mass is not celebrated. Only after the solemn vigil
during the night, held in anticipation of the resurrection, does
the Easter celebration begin, with a spirit of joy that overflows
into the following period of fifty days.

GOD RAISED GLORIFIED HIS SON

ALLELUIA ALLELUIA ALLELUIA ALLELUIA

EASTER SUNDAY
During the Night
THE EASTER VIGIL

*In accord with ancient tradition, this night is one of vigil for the Lord
(Exodus 12:42). The Gospel of Luke (12:35ff) is a reminder to the faithful
to have their lamps burning ready, to be like men awaiting their master's
return, so that when he arrives he will find them wide awake and seat
them at his table.*

The night vigil is arranged in four parts:

Part One: *a brief* service of light

Part Two: *the* liturgy of the word – *the Church meditates on all the
wonderful things God has done for his people from the beginning*

Part Three: *the* liturgy of baptism – *as the day of resurrection
approaches, new members of the Church are reborn in baptism; and all
renew their baptismal promises*

Part Four: *the* liturgy of the eucharist – *the whole Church is called
to the table which the Lord prepared for his people through his death and
resurrection.*

The entire celebration of the Easter Vigil takes place at night. It
should not begin before nightfall; it should end before daybreak
on Sunday.

Even if the vigil Mass takes place before midnight, the Easter
Mass of the resurrection is celebrated.

Those who participate in the Mass at night may receive
communion again at the second Mass of Easter Sunday.

PART ONE
SOLEMN BEGINNING OF THE VIGIL
THE SERVICE OF LIGHT

All the lights in the church are put out.

A large fire is prepared in a suitable place outside the church.
When the people have assembled, the priest goes there with the
ministers, one of whom carries the Easter candle.

Where it may be difficult to have a large fire, the blessing of the fire is adapted to the circumstances. When the people have assembled in the church as on other occasions, the priest goes with ministers (carrying the Easter candle) to the church door. If possible, the people turn to face the priest.

The priest greets the congregation in the usual manner and briefly instructs them about the vigil in these or similar words:

Dear friends in Christ,
on this most holy night,
when our Lord Jesus Christ passed from death to life,
the Church invites her children throughout the world
to come together in vigil and prayer.
This is the passover of the Lord:
if we honour the memory of his death and resurrection
by hearing his word and celebrating his mysteries,
then we may be confident
that we shall share his victory over death
and live with him for ever in God.

Then the fire is blessed.

Let us pray.
Father,
we share in the light of your glory
through your Son, the light of the world.
Make this new fire ✠ holy, and inflame us with new hope.
Purify our minds by this Easter celebration
and bring us one day to the feast of eternal light.
(We ask this) through Christ our Lord.   ℟ **Amen.**

The Easter candle is lighted from the new fire.
    The procession may follow immediately (see next page) or the optional blessing of the candle may follow.

Optional Blessing of the Candle

After the blessing of the new fire, an acolyte or one of the ministers brings the Easter candle to the celebrant, who cuts a cross in the wax with a stylus. Then he traces the Greek letter alpha above the cross, the letter omega below, and the numerals of the current year between the arms of the cross. Meanwhile he says:

1. Christ yesterday and today
2. the beginning and the end,
3. Alpha,
4. and Omega;
5. all time belongs to him,
6. and all the ages;
7. to him be glory and power,
8. through every age for ever. Amen.

When the cross and other marks have been made, the priest may insert five grains of incense in the candle. He does this in the form of a cross, saying:

1. By his holy
2. and glorious wounds
3. may Christ our Lord
4. guard us
5. and keep us. Amen.

The priest lights the candle from the new fire, saying

May the light of Christ, rising in glory,
dispel the darkness of our hearts and minds.

Procession

Then the deacon, or, if there is no deacon, the priest takes the Easter candle, lifts it high, and sings alone:

C.   Christ our light.
All   **Thanks be to God.**

Then all enter the church, led by the deacon with the Easter candle. If incense is used, the thurifer goes before the deacon.

At the church door the deacon lifts the candle high and sings a second time:

C.   Christ our light.
All   **Thanks be to God.**

All light their candles from the Easter candle and continue in the procession.

When the deacon arrives before the altar, he faces the people and sings a third time:

C.   Christ our light.
All   **Thanks be to God.**

Then the lights in the church are put on.

Easter Proclamation
When he comes to the altar, the priest goes to his chair. The
deacon places the Easter candle on a stand in the middle of the
sanctuary or near the lectern. If incense is used, the priest puts
some in the thurible as at the gospel during Mass.

The book and candle may be incensed. Then the deacon or, if
there is no deacon, the priest sings the Easter proclamation at the
lectern or pulpit. All stand and hold lighted candles.

If necessary, one who is not a deacon may sing the Easter
proclamation, omitting the sections in brackets.

1.   Long Form of the Easter Proclamation (Exsultet)
Rejoice, heavenly powers! Sing, choirs of angels!
      Exult, all creation around God's throne!
      Jesus Christ, our King, is risen!
      Sound the trumpet of salvation!

Rejoice, O earth, in shining splendour,
      radiant in the brightness of your King!
      Christ has conquered! Glory fills you!
      Darkness vanishes for ever!

Rejoice, O Mother Church! Exult in glory!
      The risen Saviour shines upon you!
      Let this place resound with joy,
      echoing the mighty song of all God's people!

(My dearest friends, standing with me in this holy light,
      join me in asking God for mercy,
      that he may give his unworthy minister
      grace to sing his Easter praises.)

(℣ The Lord be with you.
  ℟ **And also with you.)***
  ℣ Lift up your hearts.
  ℟ **We lift them up to the Lord.**
  ℣ Let us give thanks to the Lord our God.
  ℟ **It is right to give him thanks and praise.**

It is truly right
      that with full hearts and minds and voices
      we should praise the unseen God, the all-powerful Father,
      and his only Son, our Lord Jesus Christ.

*These words are omitted if the proclamation is sung by one who is not a
deacon.

For Christ has ransomed us with his blood,
    and paid for us the price of Adam's sin
      to our eternal Father!

This is our passover feast,
    when Christ, the true Lamb, is slain,
      whose blood consecrates the homes of all believers.

This is the night when first you saved our fathers:
    you freed the people of Israel from their slavery
    and led them dry-shod through the sea.

This is the night when the pillar of fire
    destroyed the darkness of sin!

This is the night when Christians everywhere,
    washed clean of sin
    and freed from all defilement,
    are restored to grace and grow together in holiness.

This is the night when Jesus Christ
    broke the chains of death
    and rose triumphant from the grave.

What good would life have been to us,
    had Christ not come as our Redeemer?

Father, how wonderful your care for us!
    How boundless your merciful love!
    To ransom a slave
    you gave away your Son.

O happy fault, O necessary sin of Adam,
    which gained for us so great a Redeemer!
    Most blessed of all nights, chosen by God
    to see Christ rising from the dead!

Of this night scripture says:
    'The night will be as clear as day:
    it will become my light, my joy.'

The power of this holy night
    dispels all evil, washes guilt away,
    restores lost innocence, brings mourners joy;
    it casts out hatred, brings us peace, and humbles earthly
      pride.

Night truly blessed when heaven is wedded to earth
    and man is reconciled with God!

Therefore, heavenly Father, in the joy of this night,
   receive our evening sacrifice of praise,
   your Church's solemn offering.

Accept this Easter candle,
   a flame divided but undimmed,
   a pillar of fire that glows to the honour of God.

Let it mingle with the lights of heaven
   and continue bravely burning
   to dispel the darkness of this night!

May the Morning Star which never sets find this flame still
      burning:
   Christ, that Morning Star, who came back from the dead,
   and shed his peaceful light on all mankind,
   your Son who lives and reigns for ever and ever.

℟   **Amen.**

Turn to p.286.

or

2.   **Short Form of the Easter Proclamation (Exsultet)**

Rejoice, heavenly powers! Sing, choirs of angels!
   Exult, all creation around God's throne!
   Jesus Christ, our King, is risen!
   Sound the trumpet of salvation!

Rejoice, O earth, in shining splendour,
   radiant in the brightness of your King!
   Christ has conquered! Glory fills you!
   Darkness vanishes for ever!

Rejoice, O Mother Church! Exult in glory!
   The risen Saviour shines upon you!
   Let this place resound with joy,
   echoing the mighty song of all God's people!

(℣   The Lord be with you.
   ℟   **And also with you.**)*
   ℣   Lift up your hearts.
   ℟   **We lift them up to the Lord.**
   ℣   Let us give thanks to the Lord our God.
   ℟   **It is right to give him thanks and praise.**

*These words are omitted if the proclamation is sung by one who is not a
deacon.

It is truly right
that with full hearts and minds and voices
we should praise the unseen God, the all-powerful Father,
and his only Son, our Lord Jesus Christ.

For Christ has ransomed us with his blood,
 and paid for us the price of Adam's sin
 to our eternal Father.

This is our passover feast,
 when Christ, the true Lamb, is slain,
 whose blood consecrates the homes of all believers.

This is the night when first you saved our fathers:
 you freed the people of Israel from their slavery
 and led them dry-shod through the sea.

This is the night when Christians everywhere,
 washed clean of sin
 and freed from all defilement,
 are restored to grace and grow together in holiness.

This is the night when Jesus Christ
 broke the chains of death
 and rose triumphant from the grave.

Father, how wonderful your care for us!
 How boundless your merciful love!
 To ransom a slave
 you gave away your Son.

O happy fault, O necessary sin of Adam,
 which gained for us so great a Redeemer!

The power of this holy night
 dispels all evil, washes guilt away,
 restores lost innocence, brings mourners joy.

Night truly blessed when heaven is wedded to earth
 and man is reconciled with God!

Therefore, heavenly Father, in the joy of this night,
 receive our evening sacrifice of praise,
 your Church's solemn offering.

Accept this Easter candle.
 May it always dispel the darkness of this night!

May the Morning Star which never sets find this flame still
 burning:

Christ, that Morning Star, who came back from the dead,
and shed his peaceful light on all mankind,
your Son who lives and reigns for ever and ever.
℟   **Amen.**

PART TWO: LITURGY OF THE WORD

After the Easter proclamation, the candles are put aside and all sit
down. Before the readings begin, the priest speaks to the people
in these or similar words:

Dear friends in Christ,
we have begun our solemn vigil.
Let us now listen attentively to the word of God,
recalling how he saved his people throughout history
and, in the fullness of time,
sent his own Son to be our Redeemer.

Through this Easter celebration,
may God bring to perfection
the saving work he has begun in us.

The readings follow. A reader goes to the lectern and proclaims
the first reading. Then the cantor leads the psalm and the people
respond. All rise and the priest sings or says *Let us pray*. When all
have prayed silently for a while, he sings or says the prayer.

   Instead of the responsorial psalm a period of silence may be
observed. In this case the pause after *Let us pray* is omitted.

Nine readings, seven from the Old Testament and two from the
New, are proposed for the Easter Vigil. The number of readings
may be reduced if circumstances demand it for special reasons.
But there should be at least three readings from the Old Testament (though these may be reduced to two in special cases)
before the Epistle and Gospel. The account of the Crossing of the
Red Sea (Third Reading) must always be read.

FIRST READING

A reading from the book of Genesis   1:1 – 2:2
God saw all he had made, and indeed it was very good.

| *In the beginning God created the heavens and the earth.* Now
the earth was a formless void, there was darkness over the deep,
and God's spirit hovered over the water.

God said, 'Let there be light', and there was light. God saw that light was good, and God divided light from darkness. God called light 'day', and darkness he called 'night'. Evening came and morning came: the first day.

God said, 'Let there be a vault in the waters to divide the waters in two.' And so it was. God made the vault, and it divided the waters above the vault from the waters under the vault. God called the vault 'heaven'. Evening came and morning came: the second day.

God said, 'Let the waters under heaven come together into a single mass, and let dry land appear.' And so it was. God called the dry land 'earth' and the mass of waters 'seas', and God saw that it was good.

God said, 'Let the earth produce vegetation: seed-bearing plants, and fruit trees bearing fruit with their seed inside, on the earth.' And so it was. The earth produced vegetation: plants bearing seed in their several kinds, and trees bearing fruit with their seed inside in their several kinds. God saw that it was good. Evening came and morning came: the third day.

God said, 'Let there be lights in the vault of heaven to divide day from night, and let them indicate festivals, days and years. Let them be lights in the vault of heaven to shine on the earth.' And so it was. God made the two great lights: the greater light to govern the day, the smaller light to govern the night, and the stars. God set them in the vault of heaven to shine on the earth, to govern the day and the night and to divide light from darkness. God saw that it was good. Evening came and morning came: the fourth day.

God said, 'Let the waters teem with living creatures, and let birds fly above the earth within the vault of heaven.' And so it was. God created great sea-serpents and every kind of living creature with which the waters teem, and every kind of winged creature. God saw that it was good. God blessed them, saying 'Be fruitful, multiply, and fill the waters of the seas; and let the birds multiply upon the earth.' Evening came and morning came: the fifth day.

God said, 'Let the earth produce every kind of living creature: cattle, reptiles, and every kind of wild beast.' And so it was. God made every kind of wild beast, every kind of cattle, and every kind of land reptile. God saw that it was good.

God said, 'Let us make man in our own image, in the likeness of ourselves, and let them be masters of the fish of the sea, the birds of heaven, the cattle, all the wild beasts and all the reptiles that crawl upon the earth.'

God created man in the image of himself,
in the image of God he created him,
male and female he created them.

God blessed them, saying to them, 'Be fruitful, multiply, fill
the earth and conquer it. Be masters of the fish of the sea, the
birds of heaven and all living animals on the earth.' God said,
'See, I give you all the seed-bearing plants that are upon the
whole earth, and all the trees with seed-bearing fruit; this shall be
your food. To all wild beasts, all birds of heaven and all living
reptiles on the earth I give all the foliage of plants for food.' And
so it was. God saw all he had made, and indeed it was very good.
Evening came and morning came: the sixth day.

Thus heaven and earth were completed with all their array.
On the seventh day God completed the work he had been doing.
He rested on the seventh day after all the work he had been
doing.

This is the word of the Lord.*

Shorter Form, verses 1. 26-31. Read between.

Responsorial Psalm   Ps 103:1-2. 5-6. 10. 12-14. 24. 35. ℟ cf. v.30

℟ **Send forth your spirit, O Lord,
and renew the face of the earth.**

1   Bless the Lord, my soul!
Lord God, how great you are,
clothed in majesty and glory,
wrapped in light as in a robe! ℟

2   You founded the earth on its base,
to stand firm from age to age.
You wrapped it with the ocean like a cloak:
the waters stood higher than the mountains. ℟

3   You make springs gush forth in the valleys:
they flow in between the hills.
On their banks dwell the birds of heaven;
from the branches they sing their song. ℟

4   From your dwelling you water the hills;
earth drinks its fill of your gift.
You make the grass grow for the cattle

and the plants to serve man's needs. ℟

5 How many are your works, O Lord!
In wisdom you have made them all.
The earth is full of your riches.
Bless the Lord, my soul! ℟

Alternative Psalm Ps 32:4-7. 12-13. 20. 22. ℟ v.5

℟ **The Lord fills the earth with his love.**

1 The word of the Lord is faithful
and all his works to be trusted.
The Lord loves justice and right
and fills the earth with his love. ℟

2 By his word the heavens were made,
by the breath of his mouth all the stars.
He collects the waves of the ocean;
he stores up the depths of the sea. ℟

3 They are happy, whose God is the Lord,
the people he has chosen as his own.
From the heavens the Lord looks forth,
he sees all the children of men. ℟

4 Our soul is waiting for the Lord.
The Lord is our help and our shield.
May your love be upon us, O Lord,
as we place all our hope in you. ℟

Prayer
Let us pray.
Almighty and eternal God,
you created all things in wonderful beauty and order.
Help us now to perceive
how still more wonderful is the new creation
by which in the fullness of time
you redeemed your people
through the sacrifice of our passover, Jesus Christ,
who lives and reigns for ever and ever. ℟ **Amen.**

or

Let us pray.
Lord God,

the creation of man was a wonderful work,
his redemption still more wonderful.
May we persevere in right reason
against all that entices to sin
and so attain to everlasting joy.
We ask this through Christ our Lord.   R℣ **Amen.**

SECOND READING

A reading from the book of Genesis   22:1-18
The sacrifice of Abraham, our father in faith.

*God put Abraham to the test. 'Abraham, Abraham,' he called.
'Here I am' he replied. 'Take your son,' God said 'your only child
Isaac, whom you love, and go to the land of Moriah. There you
shall offer him as a burnt offering, on a mountain I will point out
to you.'*

Rising early next morning Abraham saddled his ass and took
with him two of his servants and his son Isaac. He chopped
wood for the burnt offering and started on his journey to the
place God had pointed out to him. On the third day Abraham
looked up and saw the place in the distance. Then Abraham said
to his servants, 'Stay here with the donkey. The boy and I will go
over there; we will worship and come back to you.'

Abraham took the wood for the burnt offering, loaded it on
Isaac, and carried in his own hands the fire and the knife. Then
the two of them set out together. Isaac spoke to his father
Abraham, 'Father' he said. 'Yes, my son' he replied. 'Look,' he
said 'here are the fire and the wood, but where is the lamb for the
burnt offering?' Abraham answered, 'My son, God himself will
provide the lamb for the burnt offering.' Then the two of them
went on together.

*When they arrived at the place God had pointed out to him,
Abraham built an altar there, and arranged the wood. Then he
bound his son Isaac and put him on the altar on top of the wood.
Abraham stretched out his hand and seized the knife to kill his
son.

But the angel of the Lord called to him from heaven,
'Abraham, Abraham' he said. 'I am here' he replied. 'Do not raise
your hand against the boy' the angel said. 'Do not harm him, for
now I know you fear God. You have not refused me your son,
your only son.' Then looking up, Abraham saw a ram caught by
its horns in a bush. Abraham took the ram and offered it as a

burnt-offering in place of his son.*

Abraham called this place 'The Lord provides', and hence the saying today: On the mountain the Lord provides.

*The angel of the Lord called Abraham a second time from heaven. 'I swear by my own self – it is the Lord who speaks – because you have done this, because you have not refused me your son, your only son, I will shower blessings on you, I will make your descendants as many as the stars of heaven and the grains of sand on the seashore. Your descendants shall gain possession of the gates of their enemies. All the nations of the earth shall bless themselves by your descendants, as a reward for your obedience.'

This is the word of the Lord.*

*Shorter Form, verses 1-2. 9-13. 15-18. Read between *

Responsorial Psalm

Ps 15:5. 8-11. ℟ v.1

℟ **Preserve me, God, I take refuge in you.**

1   O Lord, it is you who are my portion and cup;
      it is you yourself who are my prize.
      I keep the Lord ever in my sight:
      since he is at my right hand, I shall stand firm.   ℟

2   And so my heart rejoices, my soul is glad;
      even my body shall rest in safety.
      For you will not leave my soul among the dead,
      nor let your beloved know decay.   ℟

3   You will show me the path of life,
      the fullness of joy in your presence,
      at your right hand happiness for ever.   ℟

Prayer

Let us pray.
God and Father of all who believe in you,
you promised Abraham that he would become the father of all
   nations,
and through the death and resurrection of Christ
you fulfil that promise:
everywhere throughout the world you increase your chosen
   people.
May we respond to your call
by joyfully accepting your invitation to the new life of grace.
We ask this through Christ our Lord.   ℟ **Amen.**

The following reading must always be read.

THIRD READING

A reading from the book of Exodus   14:15 – 15:1

The sons of Israel went on dry ground right into the sea.

The Lord said to Moses, 'Why do you cry to me so? Tell the sons of Israel to march on. For yourself, raise your staff and stretch out your hand over the sea and part it for the sons of Israel to walk through the sea on dry ground. I for my part will make the heart of the Egyptians so stubborn that they will follow them. So shall I win myself glory at the expense of Pharaoh, of all his army, his chariots, his horsemen. And when I have won glory for myself, at the expense of Pharaoh and his chariots and his army, the Egyptians will learn that I am the Lord.'

Then the angel of the Lord, who marched at the front of the army of Israel, changed station and moved to their rear. The pillar of cloud changed station from the front to the rear of them, and remained there. It came between the camp of the Egyptians and the camp of Israel. The cloud was dark, and the night passed without the armies drawing any closer the whole night long. Moses stretched out his hand over the sea. The Lord drove back the sea with a strong easterly wind all night, and he made dry land of the sea. The waters parted and the sons of Israel went on dry ground right into the sea, walls of water to right and to left of them. The Egyptians gave chase: after them they went, right into the sea, all Pharaoh's horses, his chariots, and his horsemen. In the morning watch, the Lord looked down on the army of the Egyptians from the pillar of fire and of cloud, and threw the army into confusion. He so clogged their chariot wheels that they could scarcely make headway. 'Let us flee from the Israelites,' the Egyptians cried 'the Lord is fighting for them against the Egyptians!' 'Stretch out your hand over the sea,' the Lord said to Moses 'that the waters may flow back on the Egyptians and their chariots and their horsemen.' Moses stretched out his hand over the sea and, as day broke, the sea returned to its bed. The fleeing Egyptians marched right into it, and the Lord overthrew the Egyptians in the very middle of the sea. The returning waters overwhelmed the chariots and the horsemen of Pharaoh's whole army, which had followed the Israelites into the sea; not a single one of them was left. But the sons of Israel had marched through the sea on dry ground, walls of water to right and to left of them. That day, the Lord rescued Israel from the Egyptians, and Israel saw the Egyptians lying dead on the shore. Israel witnessed the great act that the Lord had performed against the Egyptians, and the people venerated the Lord; they put their faith in the Lord and in Moses, his servant.

It was then that Moses and the sons of Israel sang this song in honour of the Lord:

The choir takes up the Responsorial Psalm immediately.

Responsorial Psalm   Ex 15:1-6. 17-18. ℟ v.1

℟   **I will sing to the Lord, glorious his triumph!**

1   I will sing to the Lord, glorious his triumph!
    Horse and rider he has thrown into the sea!
    The Lord is my strength, my song, my salvation.
    This is my God and I extol him,
    my father's God and I give him praise.   ℟

2   The Lord is a warrior! The Lord is his name.
    The chariots of Pharaoh he hurled into the sea,
    the flower of his army is drowned in the sea.
    The deeps hide them; they sank like a stone.   ℟

3   Your right hand, Lord, glorious in its power,
    your right hand, Lord, has shattered the enemy.
    In the greatness of your glory you crushed the foe.   ℟

4   You will lead your people and plant them on your mountain,
    the place, O Lord, where you have made your home,
    the sanctuary, Lord, which your hands have made.
    The Lord will reign for ever and ever.   ℟

Prayer
Let us pray.
Father,
even today we see the wonders
of the miracles you worked long ago.
You once saved a single nation from slavery,
and now you offer that salvation to all through baptism.
May the peoples of the world become true sons of Abraham
and prove worthy of the heritage of Israel.
We ask this through Christ our Lord.   ℟   **Amen.**

or

Let us pray.
Lord God,
in the new covenant
you shed light on the miracles you worked in ancient times:
the Red Sea is a symbol of our baptism,
and the nation you freed from slavery
is a sign of your Christian people.
May every nation
share the faith and privilege of Israel
and come to new birth in the Holy Spirit.
We ask this through Christ our Lord. R/ **Amen.**

FOURTH READING

A reading from the prophet Isaiah   54:5-14
With everlasting love the Lord your redeemer has taken pity on you.

Thus says the Lord:

Now your creator will be your husband,
his name, the Lord of hosts;
your redeemer will be the Holy One of Israel,
he is called the God of the whole earth.
Yes, like a forsaken wife, distressed in spirit,
the Lord calls you back.
Does a man cast off the wife of his youth?
says your God.

I did forsake you for a brief moment,
but with great love will I take you back.
In excess of anger, for a moment
I hid my face from you.
But with everlasting love I have taken pity on you,
says the Lord, your redeemer.

I am now as I was in the days of Noah
when I swore that Noah's waters
should never flood the world again.
So now I swear concerning my anger with you
and the threats I made against you;

for the mountains may depart,
the hills be shaken,
but my love for you will never leave you
and my covenant of peace with you will never be shaken,
says the Lord who takes pity on you.

Unhappy creature, storm-tossed, disconsolate,
see, I will set your stones on carbuncles
and your foundations on sapphires.
I will make rubies your battlements,
your gates crystal,
and your entire wall precious stones.
Your sons will all be taught by the Lord.
The prosperity of your sons will be great.
You will be founded on integrity;
remote from oppression, you will have nothing to fear;
remote from terror, it will not approach you.

This is the word of the Lord.

Responsorial Psalm   Ps 29:2. 4-6. 11-13. ℟ v.2

℟   **I will praise you, Lord, you have rescued me.**

1   I will praise you, Lord, you have rescued me
    and have not let my enemies rejoice over me.
    O Lord, you have raised my soul from the dead,
    restored me to life from those who sink into the grave.   ℟

2   Sing psalms to the Lord, you who love him,
    give thanks to his holy name.
    His anger lasts but a moment; his favour through life.
    At night there are tears, but joy comes with dawn.   ℟

3   The Lord listened and had pity.
    The Lord came to my help.
    For me you have changed my mourning into dancing,
    O Lord my God, I will thank you for ever.   ℟

Prayer
Let us pray.
Almighty and eternal God,
glorify your name by increasing your chosen people
as you promised long ago.
In reward for their trust,
may we see in the Church the fulfilment of your promise.
We ask this through Christ our Lord.   ℟   **Amen.**

Prayers may also be chosen from those given after the following
readings, if the readings are omitted.

FIFTH READING

A reading from the prophet Isaiah 55:1-11

Come to me and your soul will live, and I will make an everlasting covenant with you.

Thus says the Lord:

Oh, come to the water all you who are thirsty;
though you have no money, come!
Buy corn without money, and eat,
and, at no cost, wine and milk.
Why spend money on what is not bread,
your wages on what fails to satisfy?
Listen, listen to me, and you will have good things to eat
and rich food to enjoy.
Pay attention, come to me;
listen, and your soul will live.

With you I will make an everlasting covenant
out of the favours promised to David.
See, I have made of you a witness to the peoples,
a leader and a master of the nations.
See, you will summon a nation you never knew,
those unknown will come hurrying to you,
for the sake of the Lord your God,
of the Holy One of Israel who will glorify you.

Seek the Lord while he is still to be found,
call to him while he is still near.
Let the wicked man abandon his way,
the evil man his thoughts.
Let him turn back to the Lord who will take pity on him,
to our God who is rich in forgiving;
for my thoughts are not your thoughts,
my ways not your ways – it is the Lord who speaks.
Yes, the heavens are as high above earth
as my ways are above your ways,
my thoughts above your thoughts.

Yes, as the rain and the snow come down from the heavens and do not return without watering the earth, making it yield and giving growth to provide seed for the sower and bread for the eating, so the word that goes from my mouth does not return to me empty, without carrying out my will and succeeding in what it was sent to do.

This is the word of the Lord.

Responsorial Psalm   Is 12:2-6. ℟ v.3

℟ **With joy you will draw water from the wells of salvation.**

1 Truly God is my salvation,
   I trust, I shall not fear.
   For the Lord is my strength, my song,
   he became my saviour.
   With joy you will draw water
   from the wells of salvation.   ℟

2 Give thanks to the Lord, give praise to his name!
   Make his mighty deeds known to the peoples,
   declare the greatness of his name.   ℟

3 Sing a psalm to the Lord
   for he has done glorious deeds,
   make them known to all the earth!
   People of Zion, sing and shout for joy
   for great in your midst is the Holy One of Israel.   ℟

Prayer
Let us pray.
Almighty, ever-living God,
only hope of the world,
by the preaching of the prophets
you proclaimed the mysteries we are celebrating tonight.
Help us to be your faithful people,
for it is by your inspiration alone
that we can grow in goodness.
We ask this through Christ our Lord.   ℟ **Amen.**

SIXTH READING

A reading from the prophet Baruch   3:9-15. 32 – 4:4

In the radiance of the Lord make your way to light.

Listen, Israel, to commands that bring life;
hear, and learn what knowledge means.
Why, Israel, why are you in the country of your enemies,
growing older and older in an alien land,
sharing defilement with the dead,
reckoned with those who go to Sheol?
Because you have forsaken the fountain of wisdom.
Had you walked in the way of God,

you would have lived in peace for ever.
Learn where knowledge is, where strength,
where understanding, and so learn
where length of days is, where life,
where the light of the eyes and where peace.
But who has found out where she lives,
who has entered her treasure house?

But the One who knows all knows her,
he has grasped her with his own intellect,
he has set the earth firm for ever
and filled it with four-footed beasts,
he sends the light – and it goes,
he recalls it – and trembling it obeys;
the stars shine joyfully at their set times:
when he calls them, they answer, 'Here we are';
they gladly shine for their creator.
It is he who is our God,
no other can compare with him.
He has grasped the whole way of knowledge,
and confided it to his servant Jacob,
to Israel his well-beloved;
so causing her to appear on earth
and move among men.

This is the book of the commandments of God,
the Law that stands for ever;
those who keep her live,
those who desert her die.
Turn back, Jacob, seize her,
in her radiance make your way to light:
do not yield your glory to another,
your privilege to a people not your own.
Israel, blessed are we:
what pleases God has been revealed to us.

This is the word of the Lord.

Responsorial Psalm   Ps 18:8-11. R̷ Jn 6:69
    R̷ **You have the message of eternal life, O Lord.**

1   The law of the Lord is perfect,
    it revives the soul.
    The rule of the Lord is to be trusted,
    it gives wisdom to the simple. R̷

2 The precepts of the Lord are right,
  they gladden the heart.
  The command of the Lord is clear,
  it gives light to the eyes. ℟

3 The fear of the Lord is holy,
  abiding for ever.
  The decrees of the Lord are truth
  and all of them just. ℟

4 They are more to be desired than gold,
  than the purest of gold
  and sweeter are they than honey,
  than honey from the comb. ℟

Prayer

Let us pray.
Father,
you increase your Church
by continuing to call all people to salvation.
Listen to our prayers
and always watch over those you cleanse in baptism.
We ask this through Christ our Lord. ℟ **Amen.**

SEVENTH READING

A reading from the prophet Ezekiel 36:16-28
I shall pour clean water over you, and I shall give you a new heart.

The word of the Lord was addressed to me as follows: 'Son of man, the members of the House of Israel used to live in their own land, but they defiled it by their conduct and actions. I then discharged my fury at them because of the blood they shed in their land and the idols with which they defiled it. I scattered them among the nations and dispersed them in foreign countries. I sentenced them as their conduct and actions deserved. And now they have profaned my holy name among the nations where they have gone, so that people say of them, "These are the people of the Lord; they have been exiled from his land." But I have been concerned about my holy name, which the House of Israel has profaned among the nations where they have gone. And so, say to the House of Israel, "The Lord says this: I am not doing this for my sake, House of Israel, but for the sake of my holy name, which you have profaned among the nations where you have gone. I mean to display the holiness of my great name, which has been profaned among the nations, which you have profaned among them. And the nations will learn that I am the Lord – it is the Lord who speaks – when I display my holiness for your sake before their eyes. Then I am going to take you from among the nations and gather you together from all the foreign countries, and bring you home to your own land. I shall pour clean water over you and you will be cleansed; I shall cleanse you of all your defilement and all your idols. I shall give you a new heart, and put a new spirit in you; I shall remove the heart of stone from your bodies and give you a heart of flesh instead. I shall put my spirit in you, and make you keep my laws and sincerely respect my observances. You will live in the land which I gave your ancestors. You shall be my people and I will be your God." '

This is the word of the Lord.

Responsorial Psalm   Pss 41:3. 5;42:3. 4. R⁄ 41:2
   R⁄   **Like the deer that yearns for running streams,**
       so my soul is yearning for you, my God.

1   My soul is thirsting for God.
    the God of my life;
    when can I enter and see
    the face of God?   R⁄

2   These things will I remember
    as I pour out my soul:
    how I would lead the rejoicing crowd
    into the house of God,
    amid cries of gladness and thanksgiving,
    the throng wild with joy.   R⁄

3   O send forth your light and your truth;
    let these be my guide.
    Let them bring me to your holy mountain
    to the place where you dwell.   R⁄

4   And I will come to the altar of God,
    the God of my joy.
    My redeemer, I will thank you on the harp,
    O God, my God.   R⁄

If a Baptism takes place the Responsorial Psalm which follows the Fifth reading above, p.297 is used, or Ps 50 as follows:

Responsorial Psalm   Ps 50:12-15. 18. 19. ℟ v.12

   ℟   **A pure heart create for me, O God.**

1   A pure heart create for me, O God,
    put a steadfast spirit within me.
    Do not cast me away from your presence,
    nor deprive me of your holy spirit.   ℟

2   Give me again the joy of your help;
    with a spirit of fervour sustain me,
    that I may teach transgressors your ways
    and sinners may return to you.   ℟

3   For in sacrifice you take no delight,
    burnt offering from me you would refuse,
    my sacrifice, a contrite spirit.
    A humbled, contrite heart you will not spurn.   ℟

Prayer
Let us pray.
God of unchanging power and light,
look with mercy and favour on your entire Church.
Bring lasting salvation to mankind,
so that the world may see
the fallen lifted up,
the old made new,
and all things brought to perfection,
through him who is their origin,
our Lord Jesus Christ,
who lives and reigns for ever and ever.   ℟   **Amen.**

or

Let us pray.
Father,
you teach us in both the Old and the New Testament
to celebrate this passover mystery.
Help us to understand your great love for us.
May the goodness you now show us
confirm our hope in your future mercy.
We ask this through Christ our Lord.   ℟   **Amen.**

or

Let us pray.
Almighty and eternal God,

be present in this sacrament of your love.
Send your Spirit of adoption
on those to be born again in baptism.
And may the work of our humble ministry
be brought to perfection by your mighty power.
We ask this through Christ our Lord. ℟ **Amen.**

THE MASS OF EASTER NIGHT

After the last reading from the Old Testament with its responsory and prayer, the altar candles are lighted, and the priest intones the *Gloria*, which is taken up by all present. The church bells are rung, according to local custom.

At the end of the *Gloria*, the priest sings or says the opening prayer in the usual way.

Opening Prayer
Let us pray.
Lord God,
you have brightened this night
with the radiance of the risen Christ.
Quicken the spirit of sonship in your Church;
renew us in mind and body
to give you whole-hearted service.

FIRST READING

A reading from the letter of St Paul to the Romans 6:3-11
Christ, having been raised from the dead, will never die again.

When we were baptised in Christ Jesus we were baptised in his death; in other words, when we were baptised we went into the tomb with him and joined him in death, so that as Christ was raised from the dead by the Father's glory, we too might live a new life.

If in union with Christ we have imitated his death, we shall also imitate him in his resurrection. We must realise that our former selves have been crucified with him to destroy this sinful body and to free us from the slavery of sin. When a man dies, of course, he has finished with sin.

But we believe that having died with Christ we shall return to life with him: Christ, as we know, having been raised from the dead will never die again. Death has no power over him any more. When he died, he died, once for all, to sin, so his life now is life with God; and in that way, you too must consider yourselves to be dead to sin but alive for God in Christ Jesus.

This is the word of the Lord.

After the epistle all rise, and the priest solemnly intones the Alleluia which is repeated by all present.

Responsorial Psalm Ps 117:1-2. 16-17. 22-23

℞ **Alleluia, alleluia, alleluia!**

1 Give thanks to the Lord for he is good,
   for his love has no end.
   Let the sons of Israel say:
   'His love has no end.'   ℞

2 The Lord's right hand has triumphed;
   his right hand raised me up.
   I shall not die, I shall live
   and recount his deeds.   ℞

3 The stone which the builders rejected
   has become the corner stone.
   This is the work of the Lord,
   a marvel in our eyes.   ℞

GOSPEL

Year A

A reading from the holy Gospel according to Matthew 28:1-10

He has risen from the dead and now he is going before you into Galilee.

After the sabbath, and towards dawn on the first day of the week, Mary of Magdala and the other Mary went to visit the sepulchre. And all at once there was a violent earthquake, for the angel of the Lord, descending from heaven, came and rolled away the stone and sat on it. His face was like lightning, his robe white as snow. The guards were so shaken, so frightened of him, that they were like dead men. But the angel spoke; and he said to the women, 'There is no need for you to be afraid. I know you are looking for Jesus, who was crucified. He is not here, for he has risen, as he said he would. Come and see the place where he lay, then go quickly and tell his disciples, "He has risen from the dead and now he is going before you to Galilee; it is there you will see him." Now I have told you.' Filled with awe and great joy the women came quickly away from the tomb and ran to tell the disciples.

And there, coming to meet them, was Jesus. 'Greetings' he said. And the women came up to him and, falling down before him, clasped his feet. Then Jesus said to them, 'Do not be afraid; go and tell my brothers that they must leave for Galilee; they will see me there.'

This is the Gospel of the Lord.

Year B

A reading from the holy Gospel according to Mark 16:1-7

Jesus of Nazareth, who was crucified, has risen.

When the sabbath was over, Mary of Magdala, Mary the mother of James, and Salome, bought spices with which to go and anoint him. And very early in the morning on the first day of the week they went to the tomb, just as the sun was rising.

They had been saying to one another, 'Who will roll away the stone for us from the entrance to the tomb?' But when they looked they could see that the stone – which was very big – had already been rolled back. On entering the tomb they saw a young man in a white robe seated on the right-hand side, and they were struck with amazement. But he said to them, 'There is no need for alarm. You are looking for Jesus of Nazareth, who was crucified: he has risen, he is not here. See, here is the place where they laid him. But you must go and tell his disciples and Peter, "He is going before you to Galilee; it is there you will see him, just as he told you." '

This is the Gospel of the Lord.

Year C

A reading from the holy Gospel according to Luke 24:1-12

Why look among the dead for someone who is alive?

On the first day of the week, at the first sign of dawn, the women went to the tomb with the spices they had prepared. They found that the stone had been rolled away from the tomb, but on entering discovered that the body of the Lord Jesus was not there. As they stood there not knowing what to think, two men in brilliant clothes suddenly appeared at their side. Terrified, the women lowered their eyes. But the two men said to them, 'Why look among the dead for someone who is alive? He is not here; he has risen. Remember what he told you when he was still in Galilee: that the Son of Man had to be handed over into the power of sinful men and be crucified, and rise again on the third day?' And they remembered his words.

When the women returned from the tomb they told all this to the Eleven and to all the others. The women were Mary of Magdala, Joanna, and Mary the mother of James. The other women with them also told the apostles, but this story of theirs seemed pure nonsense, and they did not believe them.

Peter, however, went running to the tomb. He bent down and saw the binding cloths, but nothing else; he then went back home, amazed at what had happened.

This is the Gospel of the Lord.

Homily

A homily should follow the readings.

PART THREE: LITURGY OF BAPTISM

A. When there is a baptism

(If there is no baptism, turn to p.311.)

The priest goes with the ministers to the baptismal font, if this can be seen by all. Otherwise a vessel of water is placed in the sanctuary.

If there are candidates to be baptised, they are called forward and presented by their godparents. If they are children, the parents and godparents bring them forward in front of the congregation.

Then the priest speaks to the people in these or similar words:

Dear friends in Christ,
as our brothers and sisters approach the waters of rebirth,
let us help them by our prayers
and ask God, our almighty Father,
to support them with his mercy and love.

Litany

The litany is sung by two cantors. In the litany some saints' names may be added, especially the titular of the church, the local patrons, and the saints of those to be baptised. All present stand (as is customary during the Easter season) and answer.

If there is to be a procession of some length to the baptistery, the litany is sung during the procession. In this case those who are to be baptised are first called forward. Then the procession begins: the Easter candle is carried first, followed by the candidates with their godparents, and the priest with the ministers.

Lord, have mercy	Lord, have mercy
Christ, have mercy	Christ, have mercy
Lord, have mercy	Lord, have mercy
Holy Mary, Mother of God	pray for us
Saint Michael	pray for us
Holy angels of God	pray for us
Saint John the Baptist	pray for us
Saint Joseph	pray for us
Saint Peter and Saint Paul	pray for us
Saint Andrew	pray for us
Saint John	pray for us
Saint Mary Magdalene	pray for us
Saint Stephen	pray for us
Saint Ignatius	pray for us
Saint Lawrence	pray for us
Saint Perpetua and Saint Felicity	pray for us
Saint Agnes	pray for us
Saint Gregory	pray for us
Saint Augustine	pray for us
Saint Athanasius	pray for us
Saint Basil	pray for us
Saint Martin	pray for us
Saint Benedict	pray for us
Saint Francis and Saint Dominic	pray for us
Saint Francis Xavier	pray for us
Saint John Vianney	pray for us
Saint Catherine	pray for us
Saint Teresa	pray for us
All holy men and women	pray for us
Lord, be merciful	Lord, save your people
From all evil	Lord, save your people
From every sin	Lord, save your people
From everlasting death	Lord, save your people
By your coming as man	Lord, save your people
By your death and rising to new life	Lord, save your people
By your gift of the Holy Spirit	Lord, hear our prayer
Be merciful to us sinners	Lord, save your people
Give new life to these chosen ones by the grace of baptism	Lord, hear our prayer
	Lord, hear our prayer
Jesus Son of the living God	Lord, hear our prayer
Christ, hear us	Christ, hear us

Lord Jesus, hear our prayer

Lord Jesus, hear our prayer

Blessing of Water
The priest then blesses the baptismal water.

Father, you give us grace through sacramental signs,
  which tell us of the wonders of your unseen power.

In baptism we use your gift of water,
  which you have made a rich symbol
  of the grace you give us in this sacrament.

At the very dawn of creation
  your Spirit breathed on the waters,
  making them the wellspring of all holiness.

The waters of the great flood
  you made a sign of the waters of baptism,
  that make an end of sin and a new beginning of goodness.

Through the waters of the Red Sea
  you led Israel out of slavery,
  to be an image of God's holy people,
  set free from sin by baptism.

In the waters of the Jordan
  your Son was baptised by John
  and anointed with the Spirit.

Your Son willed that water and blood
  should flow from his side
  as he hung upon the cross.

After his resurrection he told his disciples:
  'Go out and teach all nations,
  baptising them in the name of the Father
  and of the Son and of the Holy Spirit.'

Father, look now with love upon your Church,
  and unseal for her the fountain of baptism.

By the power of the Spirit
  give to the water of this font
  the grace of your Son.

You created man in your own likeness:
  cleanse him from sin in a new birth of innocence
  by water and the Spirit.

The priest may lower the Easter candle into the water either once or three times, as he continues:

We ask you, Father, with your Son
  to send the Holy Spirit upon the waters of this font.

He holds the candle in the water:
May all who are buried with Christ
  in the death of baptism
  rise also with him to newness of life.
We ask this through Christ our Lord.
℟   **Amen.**

Then the candle is taken out of the water as the people sing the acclamation:

Springs of water, bless the Lord.
Give him glory and praise for ever.

Any other appropriate acclamation may be sung.

The rites of Baptism and Confirmation follow.

Baptism
Candidates to be baptised renounce the devil individually. Then they are questioned about their faith and are baptised.

Priest:	Do you reject Satan?
Candidates:	**I do.**
Priest:	And all his works?
Candidates:	**I do.**
Priest:	And all his empty promises?
Candidates:	**I do.**

or

Priest:	Do you reject sin, so as to live in the freedom of God's children?
Candidates:	**I do.**
Priest:	Do you reject the glamour of evil, and refuse to be mastered by sin?
Candidates:	**I do.**
Priest:	Do you reject Satan, father of sin and prince of darkness?
Candidates:	**I do.**

According to circumstances, this second form may be adapted to local needs by the conferences of bishops.

Then the priest continues:

Priest:	Do you believe in God, the Father almighty, creator of heaven and earth?
Candidates:	**I do.**
Priest:	Do you believe in Jesus Christ, his only Son, our Lord,
	who was born of the Virgin Mary,
	was crucified, died, and was buried,
	rose from the dead,
	and is now seated at the right hand of the Father?
Candidates:	**I do.**
Priest:	Do you believe in the Holy Spirit,
	the holy catholic Church, the communion of saints,
	the forgiveness of sins, the resurrection of the body,
	and life everlasting?
Candidates:	**I do.**

The candidates are then baptised by the priest who says:

Priest: N., I baptise you in the name of the Father, and of the Son, and of the Holy Spirit.

An acclamation may be sung, for example one of the following:

Rejoice, you newly baptised,
chosen members of the Kingdom.
Buried with Christ in death,
you are reborn in him by faith.

or

Blessed be God who chose you in Christ.

Confirmation

Adults are confirmed immediately after baptism if a bishop or a priest with the faculty to confirm is present.
The neophyte stands in front of the celebrant, who speaks to him in these or similar words:

N., born again in Christ by baptism, you have become a member of Christ and of his priestly people. Now you are to share in the outpouring of the Holy Spirit among us, the Spirit sent by the Lord upon his apostles at Pentecost and given by them and their successors to be baptised.

The promised strength of the Holy Spirit which you are to receive will make you more like Christ and help you to be a witness to his suffering, death, and resurrection. It will strengthen you to be an active member of the Church and to build up the Body of Christ in faith and love.

Then the celebrant stands and faces the people and says:

Let us pray, dear friends,
to God the all-powerful Father
that he will pour out the Holy Spirit
on the newly baptised,
to strengthen him (her) with his abundant gifts
and anoint him (her) to be more like Christ, his Son.

All pray in silence for a short time.
Then the celebrant lays hands upon the candidate and says:

All-powerful God, Father of our Lord Jesus Christ,
by water and the Holy Spirit
you freed your son (daughter) from sin
and gave him (her) new life.
Spend your Holy Spirit upon him (her)
to be his (her) Helper and Guide.
Give him (her) the spirit of wisdom and understanding,
the spirit of right judgment and courage,
the spirit of knowledge and reverence.
Fill him (her) with the spirit of wonder and awe in your presence.
We ask this through Christ our Lord. ℞ **Amen.**

The candidate goes to the celebrant. The godparent places his right hand on the candidate's shoulder and gives the candidate's name to the celebrant, or the candidate may give his own name. The celebrant dips his right thumb in the chrism and makes the sign of the cross on the forehead of the one to be confirmed saying:

Celebrant: N., be sealed with the gift of the Holy Spirit.
Newly confirmed: **Amen.**
Celebrant: Peace be with you.
Newly confirmed: **And also with you.**

When the rite of baptism (and confirmation) has been completed, all present stand with lighted candles and renew their baptismal profession of faith (see p.313.)

B. When there is no baptism

(If there is no baptism, and no font to be blessed, see p312.)
The priest speaks to the people in these or similar words:

Dear friends in Christ,
let us ask God, the almighty Father,
to bless this font,
that those reborn in it
may be made one with his adopted children in Christ.

Litany

The litany is sung by two cantors. In the litany some saints'
names may be added, especially the titular of the church, and the
local patrons. All stand and answer.

Lord, have mercy	Lord, have mercy
Christ, have mercy	Christ, have mercy
Lord, have mercy	Lord, have mercy
Holy Mary, Mother of God	pray for us
Saint Michael	pray for us
Holy angels of God	pray for us
Saint John the Baptist	pray for us
Saint Joseph	pray for us
Saint Peter and Saint Paul	pray for us
Saint Andrew	pray for us
Saint John	pray for us
Saint Mary Magdalene	pray for us
Saint Stephen	pray for us
Saint Ignatius	pray for us
Saint Lawrence	pray for us
Saint Perpetua and Saint Felicity	pray for us
Saint Agnes	pray for us
Saint Gregory	pray for us
Saint Augustine	pray for us
Saint Athanasius	pray for us
Saint Basil	pray for us
Saint Martin	pray for us
Saint Benedict	pray for us
Saint Francis and Saint Dominic	pray for us
Saint Francis Xavier	pray for us
Saint John Vianney	pray for us
Saint Catherine	pray for us
Saint Teresa	pray for us
All holy men and women	pray for us

Lord, be merciful	Lord, save your people
From all evil	Lord, save your people
From every sin	Lord, save your people
From everlasting death	Lord, save your people
By your coming as man	Lord, save your people
By your death and rising to new life	Lord, save your people
By your gift of the Holy Spirit	Lord, hear our prayer
Be merciful to us sinners	Lord, save your people
By your grace bless this font where your children will be reborn	Lord, hear our prayer
Jesus Son of the living God	Lord, hear our prayer
Christ, hear us	Christ, hear us
Lord Jesus, hear our prayer	Lord Jesus, hear our prayer

Blessing of water

See above, p.307.

Blessing of Water

To be used when there is to be no baptism, and no blessing of the font.

My brothers and sisters,
let us ask the Lord our God
to bless this water he has created,
which we shall use to recall our baptism.
May he renew us
and keep us faithful to the Spirit
we have all received.

All pray silently for a short while. With hands joined, the priest continues:

Lord our God,
this night your people keep prayerful vigil.
Be with us as we recall the wonder of our creation
and the greater wonder of our redemption.
Bless this water: it makes the seed to grow,
it refreshes us and makes us clean.
You have made of it a servant of your loving kindness:
through water you set your people free,
and quenched their thirst in the desert.
With water the prophets announced a new covenant
that you would make with man.

By water, made holy by Christ in the Jordan,
you made our sinful nature new
in the bath that gives rebirth.
Let this water remind us of our baptism;
let us share the joys of our brothers
who are baptised this Easter.
We ask this through Christ our Lord. ℟ **Amen.**

Renewal of Baptismal Promises

All present stand with lighted candles and renew their baptismal profession of faith.

The priest speaks to the people in these or similar words:

Dear friends,
through the paschal mystery
we have been buried with Christ in baptism,
so that we may rise with him to a new life.
Now that we have completed our lenten observance,
let us renew the promises we made in baptism
when we rejected Satan and his works,
and promised to serve God faithfully
in his holy Catholic Church.
And so:

Priest:	Do you reject Satan?
All:	**I do.**
Priest:	And all his works?
All:	**I do.**
Priest:	And all his empty promises?
All:	**I do.**

or

Priest:	Do you reject sin, so as to live in the freedom of God's children?
All:	**I do.**
Priest:	Do you reject the glamour of evil, and refuse to be mastered by sin?
All:	**I do.**
Priest:	Do you reject Satan, father of sin and prince of darkness?
All:	**I do.**

According to circumstances, this second form may be adapted to local needs by the conferences of bishops.

Then the priest continues:

Priest: Do you believe in God, the Father almighty,
           creator of heaven and earth?
All: **I do.**
Priest: Do you believe in Jesus Christ, his only Son, our Lord,
           who was born of the Virgin Mary,
           was crucified, died, and was buried,
           rose from the dead,
           and is now seated at the right hand of the Father?
All: **I do.**
Priest: Do you believe in the Holy Spirit,
           the holy catholic Church, the communion of saints,
           the forgiveness of sins, the resurrection of the body,
           and life everlasting?
All: **I do.**

The priest concludes:

God, the all-powerful Father of our Lord Jesus Christ,
has given us a new birth by water and the Holy Spirit,
and forgiven all our sins.
May he also keep us faithful to our Lord Jesus Christ for ever and
    ever.
All: **Amen.**

The priest sprinkles the people with the blessed water, while all
sing a song which is baptismal in character, such as:

I saw water flowing
from the right side of the temple, alleluia.
It brought God's life and his salvation,
and the people sang in joyful praise:
alleluia, alleluia.

Meanwhile the newly baptised are led to their place among the
faithful.

   If the blessing of the baptismal water does not take place in
the baptistery, the ministers reverently carry the vessel of water
to the font.

   If the blessing of the font does not take place, the blessed
water is put in a convenient place.

   After the people have been sprinkled, the priest returns to the
chair. The profession of faith (creed) is omitted, and the priest
directs the general intercessions, in which the newly baptised
take part for the first time.

PART FOUR: LITURGY OF THE EUCHARIST

The priest goes to the altar and begins the liturgy of the eucharist in the usual way. (See Order of Mass, pp.35ff.)

It is fitting that the bread and wine be brought forward by the newly baptised.

Prayer over the Gifts
Lord,
accept the prayers and offerings of your people.
With your help
may this Easter mystery of our redemption
bring to perfection the saving work you have begun in us.

Preface of Easter I, P21.

When Eucharistic Prayer I is used, the special forms of *In union with the whole Church*, and, *Father, accept this offering* are said.

Communion Antiphon: Christ has become our paschal sacrifice; let us feast with the unleavened bread of sincerity and truth, alleluia.

Prayer after Communion
Lord,
you have nourished us with your Easter sacraments.
Fill us with your Spirit
and make us all one in peace and love.

The deacon (or the priest) sings or says the dismissal as follows:

Go in the peace of Christ, alleluia, alleluia.

or

The Mass is ended, go in peace, alleluia, alleluia.

or

Go in peace to love and serve the Lord, alleluia, alleluia.
℟ **Thanks be to God, alleluia, alleluia.**

EASTER SUNDAY
Mass of the Day

Alleluia!

This Mass is our Alleluia; our song of praise to the risen Christ who is our life and whose triumph over death we proclaim to all the world.

Entrance Antiphon: I have risen: I am with you once more; you placed your hand on me to keep me safe. How great is the depth of your wisdom, alleluia!

or

The Lord has indeed risen, alleluia. Glory and kingship be his for ever and ever.

Opening Prayer
Let us pray
    [that the risen Christ will raise us up
    and renew our lives]

God our Father,
by raising Christ your Son
you conquered the power of death
and opened for us the way to eternal life.
Let our celebration today
raise us up and renew our lives
by the Spirit that is within us.

or

Let us pray
    [on this Easter morning for the life
    that never again shall see darkness]

God our Father, creator of all,
today is the day of Easter joy.
This is the morning on which the Lord appeared to men
who had begun to lose hope
and opened their eyes to what the scriptures foretold:
that first he must die, and then he would rise
and ascend into his Father's glorious presence.

May the risen Lord
breathe on our minds and open our eyes
that we may know him in the breaking of bread,
and follow him in his risen life.

FIRST READING

A reading from the Acts of the Apostles 10:34. 37-43
We have eaten and drunk with him after his resurrection.

Peter addressed Cornelius and his household: 'You must have heard about the recent happenings in Judaea; about Jesus of Nazareth and how he began in Galilee, after John had been preaching baptism. God had anointed him with the Holy Spirit and with power, and because God was with him, Jesus went about doing good and curing all who had fallen into the power of the devil. Now I, and those with me, can witness to everything he did throughout the countryside of Judaea and in Jerusalem itself: and also to the fact that they killed him by hanging him on a tree, yet three days afterwards God raised him to life and allowed him to be seen, not by the whole people but only by certain witnesses God had chosen beforehand. Now we are those witnesses – we have eaten and drunk with him after his resurrection from the dead – and he has ordered us to proclaim this to his people and to tell them that God has appointed him to judge everyone, alive or dead. It is to him that all the prophets bear this witness: that all who believe in Jesus will have their sins forgiven through his name.'

This is the word of the Lord.

Responsorial Psalm Ps 117:1-2. 16-17. 22-23. ℟ v.24
℟ **This day was made by the Lord;
we rejoice and are glad.**

or

℟ **Alleluia, alleluia, alleluia!**

1 Give thanks to the Lord for he is good,
for his love has no end.
Let the sons of Israel say:
'His love has no end.' ℟

2 The Lord's right hand has triumphed;
his right hand raised me up.
I shall not die, I shall live
and recount his deeds. ℟

3 The stone which the builders rejected
has become the corner stone.
This is the work of the Lord,
a marvel in our eyes. ℟

SECOND READING

A reading from the letter of St Paul to the Colossians   3:1-4

You must look for the things that are in heaven, where Christ is.

Since you have been brought back to true life with Christ, you must look for the things that are in heaven, where Christ is, sitting at God's right hand. Let your thoughts be on heavenly things, not on the things that are on the earth, because you have died, and now the life you have is hidden with Christ in God. But when Christ is revealed – and he is your life – you too will be revealed in all your glory with him.

This is the word of the Lord.

Alternative Reading

A reading from the first letter of St Paul   5:6-8
to the Corinthians

Get rid of the old yeast, make yourselves into a completely new batch of bread.

You must know how even a small amount of yeast is enough to leaven all the dough, so get rid of all the old yeast, and make yourselves into a completely new batch of bread, unleavened as you are meant to be. Christ, our passover, has been sacrificed; let us celebrate the feast, by getting rid of all the old yeast of evil and wickedness, having only the unleavened bread of sincerity and truth.

This is the word of the Lord.

The sequence is said or sung on this day. On the weekdays of the Octave of Easter, its use is optional.

SEQUENCE

Christians, to the Paschal Victim offer sacrifice and praise.
The sheep are ransomed by the Lamb;
and Christ, the undefiled,
hath sinners to his Father reconciled.
Death with life contended: combat strangely ended!
Life's own Champion, slain, yet lives to reign.
Tell us, Mary: say what thou didst see upon the way.
The tomb the Living did enclose;

I saw Christ's glory as he rose!
The angels there attesting;
shroud with grave-clothes resting.
Christ, my hope, has risen: he goes before you into Galilee.
That Christ is truly risen from the dead we know.
Victorious king, thy mercy show!
Amen.

Gospel Acclamation 1 Cor 5:7-8
Alleluia, alleluia!
Christ, our passover, has been sacrificed;
let us celebrate the feast then, in the Lord.
Alleluia!

GOSPEL

A reading from the holy Gospel according to John 20:1-9
He must rise from the dead.

It was very early on the first day of the week and still dark, when Mary of Magdala came to the tomb. She saw that the stone had been moved away from the tomb and came running to Simon Peter and the other disciple, the one Jesus loved. 'They have taken the Lord out of the tomb' she said 'and we don't know where they have put him.'

So Peter set out with the other disciple to go to the tomb. They ran together, but the other disciple, running faster than Peter, reached the tomb first; he bent down and saw the linen cloths lying on the ground, but did not go in. Simon Peter who was following now came up, went right into the tomb, saw the linen cloths on the ground, and also the cloth that had been over his head; this was not with the linen cloths but rolled up in a place by itself. Then the other disciple who had reached the tomb first also went in; he saw and he believed. Till this moment they had failed to understand the teaching of scripture, that he must rise from the dead.

This is the Gospel of the Lord.

As an alternative, the Gospel of the Mass of Easter Night, pp.303ff. above, may be read.

At an evening Mass, Luke 24:13-35, p.328 below, may be used as an alternative.

Renewal of Baptismal Promises

In Easter Sunday Masses which are celebrated with a congregation, the rite of the renewal of baptismal promises may be repeated after the homily. See above, pp.313ff.

When this is done, the Profession of Faith is omitted.

Prayer over the Gifts

Lord,
with Easter joy we offer you the sacrifice
by which your Church is reborn and nourished
through Christ our Lord.

Preface of Easter I, P21.

When Eucharistic Prayer I is used, the special Easter forms of *In union with the whole Church* and *Father, accept this offering* are said.

Communion Antiphon: Christ has become our paschal sacrifice; let us feast with the unleavened bread of sincerity and truth, alleluia.

Prayer after Communion

Father of love,
watch over your Church
and bring us to the glory of the resurrection
promised by this Easter sacrament.

Solemn Blessing

Bow your heads and pray for God's blessing.

May almighty God bless you on this solemn feast of Easter,
    and may he protect you against all sin.   ℟   **Amen.**

Through the resurrection of his Son
God has granted us healing.
May he fulfil his promises,
and bless you with eternal life.   ℟   **Amen.**

You have mourned for Christ's sufferings;
now you celebrate the joy of his resurrection.
May you come with joy to the feast which lasts for ever.
℟   **Amen.**

May almighty God bless you,
the Father, and the Son, ✛ and the Holy Spirit.   ℟   **Amen.**

The Dismissal is sung or recited as at the Easter Vigil, see p.315.

CHRIST RISEN
OF ALL THOSE FALLEN ASLEEP
THE FIRST FRUITS

THE SEASON OF EASTER

SECOND SUNDAY OF EASTER A

Our Easter Joy

Today as we hail Christ as our Lord and God we are filled with the joy of the disciples in seeing the risen Lord. In this season of renewal we are like those early Christians who were 'filled with a joy so glorious that it cannot be described.'

Entrance Antiphon: Like newborn children you should thirst for milk, on which your spirit can grow to strength, alleluia.

or

Rejoice to the full in the glory that is yours, and give thanks to God who called you to his kingdom, alleluia.

Opening Prayer
Let us pray
  [for a deeper awareness of our Christian baptism]

God of mercy,
you wash away our sins in water,
you give us new birth in the Spirit,
and redeem us in the blood of Christ.
As we celebrate Christ's resurrection
increase our awareness of these blessings,
and renew your gift of life within us.

or

Let us pray
  [as Christians thirsting for the risen life]

Heavenly Father and God of mercy,
we no longer look for Jesus among the dead,

for he is alive and has become the Lord of life.
From the waters of death you raise us with him
and renew your gift of life within us.

Increase in our minds and hearts
the risen life we share with Christ
and help us to grow as your people
toward the fullness of eternal life with you.

FIRST READING

A reading from the Acts of the Apostles   2:42-47
The faithful all lived together and owned everything in common.

The whole community remained faithful to the teaching of the
apostles, to the brotherhood, to the breaking of bread and to the
prayers.
    The many miracles and signs worked through the apostles
made a deep impression on everyone.
    The faithful all lived together and owned everything in
common; they sold their goods and possessions and shared out
the proceeds among themselves according to what each one
needed.
    They went as a body to the Temple every day but met in their
houses for the breaking of bread; they shared their food gladly
and generously; they praised God and were looked up to by
everyone. Day by day the Lord added to their community those
destined to be saved.

    This is the word of the Lord.

Responsorial Psalm   Ps 117:2-4. 13-15. 22-24. ℟ v.1
    ℟   **Give thanks to the Lord for he is good,**
        for his love has no end.

or

    ℟   **Alleluia, alleluia, alleluia!**

1   Let the sons of Israel say:
    'His love has no end.'
    Let the sons of Aaron say:
    'His love has no end,'
    Let those who fear the Lord say:
    'His love has no end.'   ℟

2   I was thrust, thrust down and falling
    but the Lord was my helper.

The Lord is my strength and my song;
he was my saviour.
There are shouts of joy and victory
in the tents of the just. ℟

3   The stone which the builders rejected
has become the corner stone.
This is the work of the Lord,
a marvel in our eyes.
This day was made by the Lord;
we rejoice and are glad. ℟

SECOND READING

A reading from the first letter of St Peter   1:3-9
In his great mercy he has given us a new birth as his sons by raising Jesus from the dead.

Blessed be God the Father of our Lord Jesus Christ, who in his great mercy has given us a new birth as his sons, by raising Jesus Christ from the dead, so that we have a sure hope and the promise of an inheritance that can never be spoilt or soiled and never fade away, because it is being kept for you in the heavens. Through your faith, God's power will guard you until the salvation which had been prepared is revealed at the end of time. This is a cause of great joy for you, even though you may for a short time have to bear being plagued by all sorts of trials; so that, when Jesus Christ is revealed, your faith will have been tested and proved like gold – only it is more precious than gold, which is corruptible even though it bears testing by fire – and then you will have praise and glory and honour. You did not see him, yet you love him; and still without seeing him, you are already filled with a joy so glorious that it cannot be described, because you believe; and you are sure of the end to which your faith looks forward, that is, the salvation of your souls.

This is the word of the Lord.

Gospel Acclamation   Jn 20:29
Alleluia, alleluia!
Jesus said: 'You believe because you can see me.
Happy are those who have not seen and yet believe.'
Alleluia!

GOSPEL

A reading from the holy Gospel according to John   20:19-31

Eight days later, Jesus came.

In the evening of that same day, the first day of the week, the doors were closed in the room where the disciples were, for fear of the Jews. Jesus came and stood among them. He said to them, 'Peace be with you,' and showed them his hands and his side. The disciples were filled with joy when they saw the Lord, and he said to them again, 'Peace be with you.

'As the Father sent me,
so am I sending you.'

After saying this he breathed on them and said:

'Receive the Holy Spirit.
For those whose sins you forgive,
they are forgiven;
for those whose sins you retain,
they are retained.'

Thomas, called the Twin, who was one of the Twelve, was not with them when Jesus came. When the disciples said, 'We have seen the Lord,' he answered, 'Unless I see the holes that the nails made in his hands and can put my finger into the holes they made, and unless I can put my hand into his side, I refuse to believe.' Eight days later the disciples were in the house again and Thomas was with them. The doors were closed, but Jesus came in and stood among them. 'Peace be with you,' he said. Then he spoke to Thomas, 'Put your finger here; look, here are my hands. Give me your hand; put it into my side. Doubt no longer but believe.' Thomas replied, 'My Lord and my God!'
Jesus said to him:

'You believe because you can see me.
Happy are those who have not seen and yet believe.'

There were many other signs that Jesus worked and the disciples saw, but they are not recorded in this book. These are recorded so that you may believe that Jesus is the Christ, the Son of God, and that believing this you may have life through his name.

This is the Gospel of the Lord.

Prayer over the Gifts
Lord,
through faith and baptism
we have become a new creation.
Accept the offerings of your people
(and of those born again in baptism)
and bring us to eternal happiness.

Preface of Easter I, P21

When Eucharistic Prayer I is used, the special Easter forms of *In union with the whole Church* and *Father, accept this offering* are said.

Communion Antiphon: Jesus spoke to Thomas: Put your hand here, and see the place of the nails. Doubt no longer, but believe, alleluia.

Prayer after Communion
Almighty God,
may the Easter sacraments we have received
live for ever in our minds and hearts.

An appropriate Solemn Blessing or Prayer over the People may be used. See pp.90ff.

THIRD SUNDAY OF EASTER   A

Christ With Us On The Way Of Life

Christ has made known to us the true way of life and ransomed us from the useless way of life handed down to us. He is with us today in the breaking of bread.

Entrance Antiphon: Let all the earth cry out to God with joy; praise the glory of his name; proclaim his glorious praise, alleluia.

Opening Prayer
Let us pray
    [that Christ will give us
    a share in the glory of his unending life]

God our Father,
may we look forward with hope to our resurrection,
for you have made us your sons and daughters,
and restored the joy of our youth.

or

Let us pray
[in confident peace and Easter hope]

Father in heaven, author of all truth,
a people once in darkness has listened to your Word
and followed your Son as he rose from the tomb.

Hear the prayer of this newborn people
and strengthen your Church to answer your call.
May we rise and come forth into the light of day
to stand in your presence until eternity dawns.

FIRST READING

A reading from the Acts of the Apostles   2:14. 22-33

It was impossible for him to be held in the power of Hades.

On the day of Pentecost Peter stood up with the Eleven and
addressed the crowd in a loud voice: 'Men of Israel, listen to what
I am going to say: Jesus the Nazarene was a man commended to
you by God by the miracles and portents and signs that God
worked
through him when he was among you, as you all know. This
man, who was put into your power by the deliberate intention
and foreknowledge of God, you took and had crucified by men
outside the Law. You killed him, but God raised him to life,
freeing him from the pangs of Hades; for it was impossible for
him to be held in its power since, as David says of him:

I saw the Lord before me always,
for with him at my right hand nothing can shake me.
So my heart was glad
and my tongue cried out with joy:
my body, too, will rest in the hope
that you will not abandon my soul to Hades
nor allow your holy one to experience corruption.
You have made known the way of life to me,
you will fill me with gladness through your presence.'

'Brothers, no one can deny that the patriarch David himself is
dead and buried: his tomb is still with us. But since he was a
prophet, and knew that God had sworn him an oath to make one
of his descendants succeed him on the throne, what he foresaw
and spoke about was the resurrection of the Christ: he is the one
who was not abandoned to Hades, and whose body did not

experience corruption. God raised this man Jesus to life, and all of us are witnesses to that. Now raised to the heights by God's right hand, he has received from the Father the Holy Spirit, who was promised, and what you see and hear is the outpouring of that Spirit.'

This is the word of the Lord.

Responsorial Psalm   Ps 15:1-2. 5. 7-11. ℟ v.11

℟ **Show us, Lord, the path of life.**

or

℟ **Alleluia!**

1   Preserve me, God, I take refuge in you.
     I say to the Lord: 'You are my God.
     O Lord, it is you who are my portion and cup;
     it is you yourself who are my prize.'   ℟

2   I will bless the Lord who gives me counsel,
     who even at night directs my heart.
     I keep the Lord ever in my sight:
     since he is at my right hand, I shall stand firm.   ℟

3   And so my heart rejoices, my soul is glad;
     even my body shall rest in safety.
     For you will not leave my soul among the dead,
     nor let your beloved know decay.   ℟

4   You will show me the path of life,
     the fullness of joy in your presence,
     at your right hand happiness for ever.   ℟

SECOND READING
A reading from the first letter of St Peter   1:17-21
Your ransom was paid in the precious blood of a lamb without spot or stain, namely, Christ.

If you are acknowledging as your Father one who has no favourites and judges everyone according to what he has done, you must be scrupulously careful as long as you are living away from your home. Remember, the ransom that was paid to free you from the useless way of life your ancestors handed down was not paid in anything corruptible, neither in silver nor gold, but in the precious blood of a lamb without spot or stain, namely Christ; who, though known since before the world was made, has been revealed only in our time, the end of the ages, for your sake. Through him you now have faith in God, who raised him from the dead and gave him glory for that very reason – so that you would have faith and hope in God.

This is the word of the Lord.

Gospel Acclamation   cf. Lk 24:32
Alleluia, alleluia!
Lord Jesus, explain the scriptures to us.
Make our hearts burn within us as you talk to us.
Alleluia!

GOSPEL

A reading from the holy Gospel according to Luke   24:13-35
They recognised him at the breaking of bread.

Two of the disciples of Jesus were on their way to a village called Emmaus, seven miles from Jerusalem, and they were talking together about all that had happened. Now as they talked this over, Jesus himself came up and walked by their side; but something prevented them from recognising him. He said to them, 'What matters are you discussing as you walk along?' They stopped short, their faces downcast.

Then one of them, called Cleopas answered him, 'You must be the only person staying in Jerusalem who does not know the things that have been happening there these last few days.' 'What things?' he asked. 'All about Jesus of Nazareth' they answered 'who proved he was a great prophet by the things he said and did in the sight of God and of the whole people; and how our chief priests and our leaders handed him over to be sentenced to death, and had him crucified. Our own hope had been that he would be the one to set Israel free. And this is not all: two whole days have gone by since it all happened; and some women from our group have astounded us: they went to the tomb in the early morning, and when they did not find the body, they came back to tell us they had seen a vision of angels who declared he was alive. Some of our friends went to the tomb and found everything exactly as the women had reported, but of him they saw nothing.'

Then he said to them, 'You foolish men! So slow to believe the full message of the prophets! Was it not ordained that the Christ should suffer and so enter into his glory?' Then, starting with Moses and going through all the prophets, he explained to them the passages throughout the scriptures that were about himself.

When they drew near to the village to which they were going, he made as if to go on; but they pressed him to stay with them. 'It is nearly evening' they said 'and the day is almost over.' So he went in to stay with them. Now while he was with them at the table, he took the bread and said the blessing; then he broke it and handed it to them. And their eyes were opened and they recognised him; but he had vanished from their sight. Then they said to each other, 'Did not our hearts burn within us as he talked to us on the road and explained the scriptures to us?'

They set out that instant and returned to Jerusalem. There they found the Eleven assembled together with their companions, who said to them, 'Yes, it is true. The Lord has risen and has appeared to Simon.' Then they told their story of what had happened on the road and how they had recognised him at the breaking of bread.

This is the Gospel of the Lord.

Prayer over the Gifts

Lord,
receive these gifts from your Church.
May the great joy you give us
come to perfection in heaven.

Preface of Easter II-V, P22-P25

Communion Antiphon: The disciples recognised the Lord Jesus in the breaking of bread, alleluia.

Prayer after Communion

Lord,
look on your people with kindness
and by these Easter mysteries
bring us to the glory of the resurrection.

An appropriate Solemn Blessing or Prayer over the People may be used. See pp.90ff.

FOURTH SUNDAY OF EASTER   A

The Shepherd And Guardian Of Our Souls

Today we rejoice in the Lord, our Shepherd, who calls us to himself.

Entrance Antiphon: The earth is full of the goodness of the Lord;
by the word of the Lord the heavens were made, alleluia.

Opening Prayer
Let us pray
    [that Christ our shepherd
    will lead us through the difficulties of this life]

Almighty and ever-living God,
give us new strength
from the courage of Christ our shepherd,
and lead us to join the saints in heaven,
where he lives and reigns with you and the Holy Spirit,
one God, for ever and ever.

or

Let us pray
    [to God our helper in time of distress]

God and Father of our Lord Jesus Christ,
though your people walk in the valley of darkness,
no evil should they fear;
for they follow in faith the call of the shepherd
whom you have sent for their hope and strength.
Attune our minds to the sound of his voice,
lead our steps in the path he has shown,
that we may know the strength of his outstretched arm
and enjoy the light of your presence for ever.

FIRST READING

A reading from the Acts of the Apostles   2:14. 36-41
God has made him both Lord and Christ.

On the day of Pentecost Peter stood up with the Eleven and
addressed the crowd with a loud voice: 'The whole House of
Israel can be certain that God has made this Jesus whom you
crucified both Lord and Christ.'

    Hearing this, they were cut to the heart and said to Peter and
the apostles, 'What must we do, brothers?' 'You must repent,'
Peter answered 'and every one of you must be baptised in the
name of Jesus Christ for the forgiveness of your sins, and you

will receive the gift of the Holy Spirit. The promise that was made is for you and your children, and for all those who are far away, for all those whom the Lord our God will call to himself.' He spoke to them for a long time using many arguments, and he urged them, 'Save yourselves from this perverse generation.' They were convinced by his arguments, and they accepted what he said and were baptised. That very day about three thousand were added to their number.

This is the word of the Lord.

Responsorial Psalm   Ps 22:1-6. ℟ v.1

> ℟ **The Lord is my shepherd;**
>   **there is nothing I shall want.**

or

> ℟ **Alleluia!**

1   The Lord is my shepherd;
    there is nothing I shall want.
    Fresh and green are the pastures
    where he gives me repose.
    Near restful waters he leads me,
    to revive my drooping spirit.   ℟

2   He guides me along the right path;
    he is true to his name.
    If I should walk in the valley of darkness
    no evil would I fear.
    You are there with your crook and your staff;
    with these you give me comfort.   ℟

3   You have prepared a banquet for me
    in the sight of my foes.
    My head you have anointed with oil;
    my cup is overflowing.   ℟

4   Surely goodness and kindness shall follow me
    all the days of my life.
    In the Lord's own house shall I dwell
    for ever and ever.   ℟

SECOND READING

A reading from the first letter of St Peter   2:20-25
You have come back to the shepherd of your souls.

The merit, in the sight of God, is in bearing punishment patiently when you are punished after doing your duty.

This, in fact, is what you were called to do, because Christ suffered for you and left an example for you to follow the way he took. He had not done anything wrong, and there had been no perjury in his mouth. He was insulted and did not retaliate with insults; when he was tortured he made no threats but he put his trust in the righteous judge. He was bearing our faults in his own body on the cross, so that we might die to our faults and live for holiness; through his wounds you have been healed. You had gone astray like sheep but now you have come back to the shepherd and guardian of your souls.

This is the word of the Lord.

Gospel Acclamation   Jn 10:14
   Alleluia, alleluia!
   I am the good shepherd, says the Lord;
   I know my own sheep and my own know me.
   Alleluia!

GOSPEL

A reading from the holy Gospel according to John   10:1-10
I am the gate of the sheepfold.

Jesus said: 'I tell you most solemnly, anyone who does not enter the sheepfold through the gate, but gets in some other way is a thief and a brigand. The one who enters through the gate is the shepherd of the flock; the gatekeeper lets him in, the sheep hear his voice, one by one he calls his own sheep and leads them out. When he has brought out his flock, he goes ahead of them, and the sheep follow because they know his voice. They never follow a stranger but run away from him: they do not recognise the voice of strangers.'

Jesus told them this parable but they failed to understand what he meant by telling it to them.

So Jesus spoke to them again:

'I tell you most solemnly,
I am the gate of the sheepfold.
All others who have come
are thieves and brigands;
but the sheep took no notice of them.
I am the gate.
Anyone who enters through me will be safe:
he will go freely in and out

or

℟ **Alleluia!**

1 Ring out your joy to the Lord, O you just;
   for praise is fitting for loyal hearts.
   Give thanks to the Lord upon the harp,
   with a ten-stringed lute sing him songs. ℟

2 For the word of the Lord is faithful
   and all his works to be trusted.
   The Lord loves justice and right
   and fills the earth with his love. ℟

3 The Lord looks on those who revere him,
   on those who hope in his love,
   to rescue their souls from death,
   to keep them alive in famine. ℟

SECOND READING

A reading from the first letter of St Peter   2:4-9
But you are a chosen race, a royal priesthood.

The Lord is the living stone, rejected by men but chosen by God
and precious to him; set yourselves close to him so that you too,
the holy priesthood that offers the spiritual sacrifices which Jesus
Christ has made acceptable to God, may be living stones making
a spiritual house. As scripture says: See how I lay in Zion a
precious cornerstone that I have chosen and the man who rests
his trust on it will not be disappointed. That means that for you
who are believers, it is precious; but for unbelievers, the stone
rejected by the builders has proved to be the keystone, a stone to
stumble over, a rock to bring men down. They stumble over it
because they do not believe in the word; it was the fate in store
for them.

But you are a chosen race, a royal priesthood, a consecrated
nation, a people set apart to sing the praises of God who called
you out of the darkness into his wonderful light.

This is the word of the Lord.

Gospel Acclamation   Jn 14:6
    Alleluia, alleluia!
    Jesus said: 'I am the Way, the Truth and the Life.
    No one can come to the Father except through me.'
    Alleluia!

GOSPEL

A reading from the holy Gospel according to John   14:1-12

I am the Way, the Truth and the Life.

Jesus said to his disciples:

'Do not let your hearts be troubled.
Trust in God still, and trust in me.
There are many rooms in my Father's house;
if there were not, I should have told you.
I am now going to prepare a place for you,
and after I have gone and prepared you a place,
I shall return to take you with me;
so that where I am
you may be too.
You know the way to the place where I am going.'

Thomas said, 'Lord, we do not know where you are going, so how can we know the way?' Jesus said:

'I am the Way, the Truth and the Life.
No one can come to the Father except through me.
If you know me, you know my Father too.
From this moment you know him and have seen him.'

Philip said, 'Lord, let us see the Father and then we shall be satisfied.' 'Have I been with you all this time, Philip,' said Jesus to him 'and you still do not know me?

'To have seen me is to have seen the Father,
so how can you say, "Let us see the Father"?
Do you not believe
that I am in the Father and the Father is in me?
The words I say to you I do not speak as from myself:
it is the Father, living in me, who is doing this work.
You must believe me when I say
that I am in the Father and the Father is in me;
believe it on the evidence of this work, if for no other reason.

'I tell you most solemnly,
whoever believes in me
will perform the same works as I do myself,
he will perform even greater works,
because I am going to the Father.'

This is the Gospel of the Lord.

Prayer over the Gifts
Lord God,
by this holy exchange of gifts
you share with us your divine life.
Grant that everything we do
may be directed by the knowledge of your truth.

Preface of Easter II-V, P22-P25

Communion Antiphon: I am the vine and you are the branches,
says the Lord; he who lives in me, and I in him, will bear much
fruit, alleluia!

Prayer after Communion
Merciful Father,
may these mysteries give us new purpose
and bring us to a new life in you.

An appropriate Solemn Blessing or Prayer over the People may
be used. See pp.90ff.

SIXTH SUNDAY OF EASTER   A

The Spirit Of Truth

*We celebrate the coming of Christ's Spirit of truth on the Church, the
source of the Churchs' proclamation of the Christian message to the
world.*

Entrance Antiphon: Speak out with a voice of joy; let it be heard to
the ends of the earth: The Lord has set his people free, alleluia.

Opening Prayer
Let us pray
    [that we may practise in our lives
    the faith we profess]

Ever-living God,
help us to celebrate our joy
in the resurrection of the Lord
and to express in our lives
the love we celebrate.

or

Let us pray
    [in silence, reflecting on the joy of Easter]

God our Father, maker of all,
the crown of your creation was the Son of Man,
born of a woman, but without beginning;
he suffered for us but lives for ever.

May our mortal lives be crowned with the ultimate joy
of rising with him,
who is Lord for ever and ever.

FIRST READING

A reading from the Acts of the Apostles　　　　8:5-8. 14-17
They laid hands on them, and they received the Holy Spirit.

Philip went to a Samaritan town and proclaimed the Christ to
them. The people united in welcoming the message Philip
preached, either because they had heard of the miracles he
worked or because they saw them for themselves. There were,
for example, unclean spirits that came shrieking out of many who
were possessed, and several paralytics and cripples were cured.
As a result there was great rejoicing in that town.

When the apostles in Jerusalem heard that Samaria had
accepted the word of God, they sent Peter and John to them, and
they went down there, and prayed for the Samaritans to receive
the Holy Spirit, for as yet he had not come down on any of them:
they had only been baptised in the name of the Lord Jesus. Then
they laid hands on them, and they received the Holy Spirit.

This is the word of the Lord.

Responsorial Psalm　　　　　　　　Ps 65:1-7. 16. 20. R̊ v.1

　　R̊　**Cry out with joy to God all the earth.**

or

　　R̊　**Alleluia!**

1　Cry out with joy to God all the earth,
　　O sing to the glory of his name.
　　O render him glorious praise.
　　Say to God: 'How tremendous your deeds!　R̊

2　'Before you all the earth shall bow;
　　shall sing to you, sing to your name!'
　　Come and see the works of God,
　　tremendous his deeds among men.　R̊

3   He turned the sea into dry land,
     they passed through the river dry-shod.
     Let our joy then be in him;
     he rules for ever by his might.   R̸

4   Come and hear, all who fear God.
     I will tell what he did for my soul:
     Blessed be God who did not reject my prayer
     nor withhold his love from me.   R̸

SECOND READING

A reading from the first letter of St Peter   3:15-18
In the body he was put to death, in the spirit he was raised to life.

Reverence the Lord Christ in your hearts, and always have your
answer ready for people who ask you the reason for the hope
that you all have. But give it with courtesy and respect and with a
clear conscience, so that those who slander you when you are
living a good life in Christ may be proved wrong in the accusations that they bring. And if it is the will of God that you should
suffer, it is better to suffer for doing right than for doing
wrong.

   Why, Christ himself, innocent though he was, had died once
for sins, died for the guilty, to lead us to God. In the body he was
put to death, in the spirit he was raised to life.

   This is the word of the Lord.

Gospel Acclamation   Jn 14:23
     Alleluia, alleluia!
     Jesus said: 'If anyone loves me he will keep my word,
     and my Father will love him, and we shall come to him.'
     Alleluia!

GOSPEL

A reading from the holy Gospel according to John   14:15-21
I shall ask the Father, and he will give you another Advocate.

Jesus said to his disciples:

   'If you love me you will keep my commandments.
   I shall ask the Father,
   and he will give you another Advocate
   to be with you for ever,
   that Spirit of truth
   whom the world can never receive

since it neither sees nor knows him;
but you know him,
because he is with you, he is in you.
I will not leave you orphans;
I will come back to you.
In a short time the world will no longer see me;
but you will see me,
because I live and you will live.
On that day
you will understand that I am in my Father
and you in me and I in you.
Anybody who receives my commandments and keeps them
will be one who loves me;
and anybody who loves me will be loved by my Father,
and I shall love him and show myself to him.'

This is the Gospel of the Lord.

When the Ascension of the Lord is celebrated on the Seventh
Sunday of Easter, the Second Reading and Gospel assigned to
the Seventh Sunday (see below, p.346ff.) may be read on the
Sixth Sunday.

Prayer over the Gifts
Lord,
accept our prayers and offerings.
Make us worthy of your sacraments of love
by granting us your forgiveness.

Preface of Easter II-V, P22-P25

Communion Antiphon: If you love me, keep my commandments,
says the Lord. The Father will send you the Holy Spirit, to be
with you for ever, alleluia.

Prayer after Communion
Almighty and ever-living Lord,
you restored us to life
by raising Christ from death.
Strengthen us by this Easter sacrament;
may we feel its saving power in our daily life.

An appropriate Solemn Blessing or Prayer over the People may
be used. See pp.90ff.

THE ASCENSION OF THE LORD   **A**

Christ's Eternal Glory

We celebrate today Christ's ascension to his eternal glory in heaven and express our Christian hope that where he, our Head, has gone before us, we, his Body, will one day follow, to live for ever in the Kingdom of our Father.

Entrance Antiphon: Men of Galilee, why do you stand looking in the sky? The Lord will return, just as you have seen him ascend, alleluia.

Opening Prayer
Let us pray
    [that the risen Christ
    will lead us to eternal life]

God our Father,
make us joyful in the ascension of your Son Jesus Christ.
May we follow him into the new creation,
for his ascension is our glory and our hope.

or

Let us pray
    [on this day of Ascension
    as we watch and wait for Jesus' return]

Father in heaven,
our minds were prepared for the coming of your kingdom
when you took Christ beyond our sight
so that we might seek him in his glory.

May we follow where he has led
and find our hope in his glory.
for he is Lord for ever.

FIRST READING
A reading from the Acts of the Apostles   1:1-11
He was lifted up while they looked on.

In my earlier work, Theophilus, I dealt with everything Jesus had done and taught from the beginning until the day he gave his instructions to the apostles he had chosen through the Holy Spirit, and was taken up to heaven. He had shown himself alive to them after his Passion by many demonstrations: for forty days he had continued to appear to them and tell them about the kingdom of God. When he had been at table with them, he had told them not to leave Jerusalem, but to wait there for what the Father had promised. 'It is' he had said 'what you have heard me speak about: John baptised with water but you, not many days from now, will be baptised with the Holy Spirit.'

Now having met together, they asked him, 'Lord, has the time come? Are you going to restore the kingdom to Israel?' He replied, 'It is not for you to know times or dates that the Father has decided by his own authority, but you will receive power when the Holy Spirit comes on you, and then you will be my witnesses not only in Jerusalem but throughout Judaea and Samaria, and indeed to the ends of the earth.'

As he said this he was lifted up while they looked on, and a cloud took him from their sight. They were still staring into the sky when suddenly two men in white were standing near them and they said, 'Why are you men from Galilee standing here looking into the sky? Jesus who has been taken up from you into heaven, this same Jesus will come back in the same way as you have seen him go there.'

This is the word of the Lord.

Responsorial Psalm   Ps 46:2-3. 6-9. R/ v.6

> R/ **God goes up with shouts of joy;**
> **the Lord goes up with trumpet blast.**

or

> R/ **Alleluia!**

1   All peoples, clap your hands,
    cry to God with shouts of joy!
    For the Lord, the Most High, we must fear,
    great king over all the earth.   R/

2   God goes up with shouts of joy;
    the Lord goes up with trumpet blast.
    Sing praise for God, sing praise,
    sing praise to our king, sing praise.   R/

3   God is king of all the earth.
    Sing praise with all your skill.
    God is king over the nations;
    God reigns on his holy throne.   R/

SECOND READING

A reading from the letter of St Paul to the Ephesians   1:17-23

He made him sit at his right hand in heaven.

May the God of our Lord Jesus Christ, the Father of glory, give you a spirit of wisdom and perception of what is revealed, to bring you to full knowledge of him. May he enlighten the eyes of your mind so that you can see what hope his call holds for you, what rich glories he has promised the saints will inherit and how infinitely great is the power that he has exercised for us believers. This you can tell from the strength of his power at work in Christ, when he used it to raise him from the dead and to make him sit at his right hand, in heaven, far above every Sovereignty, Authority, Power, or Domination, or any other name that can be named, not only in this age, but also in the age to come. He has put all things under his feet, and made him as the ruler of everything, the head of the Church; which is his body, the fullness of him who fills the whole creation.

This is the word of the Lord.

Gospel Acclamation   Mt 28:19.20
Alleluia, alleluia!
Go, make disciples of all the nations;
I am with you always; yes, to the end of time.
Alleluia!

GOSPEL

A reading from the holy Gospel according to Matthew   28:16-20

All authority in heaven and on earth has been given to me.

The eleven disciples set out for Galilee, to the mountain where Jesus had arranged to meet them. When they saw him they fell down before him, though some hesitated. Jesus came up and spoke to them. He said, 'All authority in heaven and on earth has been given to me. Go, therefore, make disciples of all the nations; baptise them in the name of the Father and of the Son and of the Holy Spirit, and teach them to observe all the commands I gave you. And know that I am with you always; yes, to the end of time.'

This is the Gospel of the Lord.

Prayer over the Gifts
Lord,
receive our offering

as we celebrate the ascension of Christ your Son.
May his gifts help us rise with him
to the joys of heaven,
where he lives and reigns for ever and ever.

Preface of Ascension I or II, P26 or P27

Communion Antiphon: I, the Lord, am with you always, until the end of the world, alleluia.

Prayer after Communion

Father,
in this eucharist
we touch the divine life you give to the world.
Help us to follow Christ with love
to eternal life where he is Lord for ever and ever.

Solemn Blessing

Bow your heads and pray for God's blessing.

May almighty God bless you on this day
when his only Son ascended into heaven
to prepare a place for you.   ℟   **Amen.**

After his resurrection, Christ was seen by his disciples.
When he appears as judge
may you be pleasing for ever in his sight.   ℟   **Amen.**

You believe that Jesus has taken his seat in majesty
at the right hand of the Father.
May you have the joy of experiencing
that he is also with you to the end of time,
according to his promise.   ℟   **Amen.**

May almighty God bless you,
the Father, and the Son, ✛ and the Holy Spirit.   ℟   **Amen.**

SEVENTH SUNDAY OF EASTER　　　A

Where the Ascension of the Lord is celebrated on this day, the readings given for Ascension, see above pp.341ff. are used.

The Spirit Of Prayer And Praise

Christ prayed in the Spirit, and the Holy Spirit is the source of the prayer and praise of the whole Church. The Spirit of God is resting on us as we offer this sacrifice of praise today.

Entrance Antiphon: Lord, hear my voice when I call to you. My heart has prompted me to seek your face; I seek it, Lord; do not hide from me, alleluia.

Opening Prayer

Let us pray
　　[that we may recognise
　　the presence of Christ in our midst]

Father,
help us keep in mind that Christ our Saviour
lives with you in glory
and promised to remain with us until the end of time.
　or

Let us pray
　　[to our Father
　　who has raised us to life in Christ]

Eternal Father,
reaching from end to end of the universe,
and ordering all things with your mighty arm:
for you, time is the unfolding of truth that already is,
the unveiling of beauty that is yet to be.

Your Son has saved us in history
by rising from the dead,
so that transcending time he might free us from death.
May his presence among us
lead to the vision of unlimited truth
and unfold the beauty of your love.

FIRST READING

A reading from the Acts of the Apostles　　　　1:12-14
All joined in continuous prayer.

After Jesus was taken up into heaven, the apostles went back from the Mount of Olives, as it is called, to Jerusalem, a short distance away, no more than a sabbath walk; and when they reached the city they went to the upper room where they were staying; there were Peter and John, James and Andrew, Philip and Thomas, Bartholomew and Matthew, James son of Alphaeus and Simon the Zealot, and Jude son of James. All these joined in continuous prayer, together with several women, including Mary the mother of Jesus, and with his brothers.

This is the word of the Lord.

Responsorial Psalm　　　　Ps 26:1. 4. 7-8. R̸ v.13

R̸　**I am sure I shall see the Lord's goodness**
　　in the land of the living.

or

R̸　**Alleluia!**

1　The Lord is my light and my help;
　　whom shall I fear?
　　The Lord is the stronghold of my life;
　　before whom shall I shrink?　R̸

2　There is one thing I ask of the Lord,
　　for this I long,
　　to live in the house of the Lord,
　　all the days of my life,
　　to savour the sweetness of the Lord,
　　to behold his temple.　R̸

3　O Lord, hear my voice when I call;
　　have mercy and answer.
　　Of you my heart has spoken;
　　'Seek his face.'　R̸

SECOND READING

A reading from the first letter of St Peter　　　　4:13-16
It is a blessing for you when they insult you for bearing the name of Christ.

If you can have some share in the sufferings of Christ, be glad, because you will enjoy a much greater gladness when his glory is revealed. It is a blessing for you when they insult you for bearing the name of Christ, because it means that you have the Spirit of glory, the Spirit of God resting on you. None of you should ever deserve to suffer for being a murderer, a thief, a criminal or an informer; but if anyone of you should suffer for being a Christian, then he is not to be ashamed of it; he should thank God that he has been called one.

This is the word of the Lord.

Gospel Acclamation cf. Jn 14:18
Alleluia, alleluia!
I will not leave you orphans, says the Lord;
I will come back to you, and your hearts will be full of joy.
Alleluia!

GOSPEL

A reading from the holy Gospel according to John 17:1-11
Father, glorify your Son.

Jesus raised his eyes to heaven and said:

'Father, the hour has come:
glorify your Son
so that your Son may glorify you;
and, through the power over all mankind that you have given him,
let him give eternal life to all those you have entrusted to him.
And eternal life is this:
to know you,
the only true God,
and Jesus Christ whom you have sent.
I have glorified you on earth
and finished the work
that you gave me to do.
Now, Father, it is time for you to glorify me
with that glory I had with you
before ever the world was.
I have made your name known
to the men you took from the world to give me.
They were yours and you gave them to me,
and they have kept your word.
Now at last they know

that all you have given me comes indeed from you;
for I have given them
the teaching you gave to me,
and they have truly accepted this, that I came from you,
and have believed that it was you who sent me.
I pray for them;
I am not praying for the world
but for those you have given me,
because they belong to you:
all I have is yours
and all you have is mine,
and in them I am glorified.
I am not in the world any longer,
but they are in the world,
and I am coming to you.'

This is the Gospel of the Lord.

Prayer over the Gifts
Lord,
accept the prayers and gifts
we offer in faith and love.
May this eucharist
bring us to your glory.
Preface of Ascension I or II, P26-P27

Communion Antiphon: This is the prayer of Jesus: that his believers
may become one as he is one with the Father, alleluia.

Prayer after Communion
God our Saviour,
hear us,
and through this holy mystery give us hope
that the glory you have given Christ
will be given to the Church, his body,
for he is Lord for ever and ever.

An appropriate Solemn Blessing or Prayer over the People may
be used. See pp.90ff.

PENTECOST SUNDAY
Vigil Mass
A,B,C

This Mass is celebrated on Saturday evening, before or after Evening Prayer I of Pentecost.

The Spirit Of Life

The Spirit gives unity to our separation, life to our dry bones, hope to our weakness. By the work of the Spirit we are renewed.

Entrance Antiphon: The love of God has been poured into our hearts by his Spirit living in us, alleluia.

Opening Prayer
Let us pray
 [that the Holy Spirit
 may bring peace and unity to all mankind]

Almighty and ever-living God,
you fulfilled the Easter promise
by sending us your Holy Spirit.
May that Spirit unite the races and nations on earth
to proclaim your glory.

or

God our Father,
you have given us new birth.
Strengthen us with your Holy Spirit
and fill us with your light.

or

Let us pray
 [that the flame of the Spirit will descend upon us]

Father in heaven,
fifty days have celebrated the fullness
of the mystery of your revealed love.
See your people gathered in prayer,
open to receive the Spirit's flame.
May it come to rest in our hearts
and disperse the divisions of word and tongue.
With one voice and one song
may we praise your name in joy and thanksgiving.

The Gloria is said.

Any of these readings from the Old Testament may be chosen.

FIRST READING

1

A reading from the book of Genesis   11:1-9

It was named Babel because there the language of the whole earth was confused.

Throughout the earth men spoke the same language, with the same vocabulary. Now as they moved eastwards they found a plain in the land of Shinar where they settled. They said to one another, 'Come, let us make bricks and bake them in the fire.' – For stone they used bricks, and for mortar they used bitumen. – 'Come,' they said 'let us build ourselves a town and a tower with its top reaching heaven. Let us make a name for ourselves, so that we may not be scattered about the whole earth.'

Now the Lord came down to see the town and the tower that the sons of man had built. 'So they are all a single people with a single language!' said the Lord. 'This is but the start of their undertakings! There will be nothing too hard for them to do. Come, let us go down and confuse their language on the spot so that they can no longer understand one another.' The Lord scattered them thence over the whole face of the earth, and they stopped building the town. It was named Babel therefore, because there the Lord confused the language of the whole earth. It was from there that the Lord scattered them over the whole face of the earth.

This is the word of the Lord.

2

A reading from the book of Exodus   19:3-8. 16-20

The Lord came down on the mountain of Sinai before all the people.

Moses went up to God, and the Lord called to him from the mountain, saying, 'Say this to the House of Jacob, declare this to the sons of Israel, ''You yourselves have seen what I did with the Egyptians, how I carried you on eagle's wings and brought you to myself. From this you know that now, if you obey my voice and hold fast to my covenant, you of all the nations shall be my very own, for all the earth is mine. I will count you a kingdom of priests, a consecrated nation.'' Those are the words you are to speak to the sons of Israel.' So Moses went and summoned the elders of the people, putting before them all that the Lord had bidden him. Then all the people answered as one, 'All that the Lord has said, we will do.'

Now at daybreak on the third day there were peals of thunder on the mountain and lightning flashes, a dense cloud, and a loud trumpet blast, and inside the camp all the people trembled. Then Moses led the people out of the camp to meet God; and they stood at the bottom of the mountain. The mountain of Sinai was entirely wrapped in smoke, because the Lord had descended on it in the form of fire. Like smoke from a furnace the smoke went up, and the whole mountain shook violently. Louder and louder grew the sound of the trumpet. Moses spoke, and God answered him with peals of thunder. The Lord came down on the mountain of Sinai, on the mountain top, and the Lord called Moses to the top of the mountain.

This is the word of the Lord.

3

A reading from the prophet Ezekiel 37:1-14

Dry bones, I am going to make the breath enter you, and you will live.

The hand of the Lord was laid on me, and he carried me away by the spirit of the Lord and set me down in the middle of a valley, a valley full of bones. He made me walk up and down among them. There were vast quantities of these bones on the ground the whole length of the valley; and they were quite dried up. He said to me, 'Son of man, can these bones live?' I said, 'You know, Lord.' He said, 'Prophesy over these bones. Say, "Dry bones, hear the word of the Lord. The Lord says this to these bones: I am now going to make the breath enter you, and you will live. I shall put sinews on you, I shall make flesh grow on you, I shall cover you with skin and give you breath, and you will live; and you will learn that I am the Lord."' I prophesied as I had been ordered. While I was prophesying, there was a noise, a sound of clattering; and the bones joined together. I looked, and saw that they were covered with sinews; flesh was growing on them and skin was covering them, but there was no breath in them. He said to me, 'Prophesy to the breath; prophesy, son of man. Say to the breath, "The Lord says this: Come from the four winds, breath; breathe on these dead; let them live!"' I prophesied as he had ordered me, and the breath entered them; they came to life again and stood up on their feet, a great, an immense army.

Then he said, 'Son of man, these bones are the whole House of Israel. They keep saying, "Our bones are dried up, our hope

has gone; we are as good as dead.'' So prophesy. Say to them,
"The Lord says this: I am now going to open your graves; I mean
to raise you from your graves, my people, and lead you back to
the soil of Israel. And you will know that I am the Lord, when I
open your graves and raise you from your graves, my people.
And I shall put my spirit in you, and you will live, and I shall
resettle you on your own soil; and you will know that I, the Lord,
have said and done this – it is the Lord who speaks."'

This is the word of the Lord.

4

A reading from the prophet Joel   3:1-5
I will pour out my spirit on all people.

Thus says the Lord:

'I will pour out my spirit on all mankind.
Your sons and daughters shall prophesy,
your old men shall dream dreams,
and your young men see visions.
Even on the slaves, men and women,
will I pour out my spirit in those days.
I will display portents in heaven and on earth.
blood and fire and columns of smoke.'

The sun will be turned into darkness,
and the moon into blood,
before the day of the Lord dawns,
that great and terrible day.
All who call on the name of the Lord will be saved,
for on Mount Zion there will be some who have escaped,
as the Lord has said,
and in Jerusalem some survivors whom the Lord will call.

This is the word of the Lord.

Responsorial Psalm   Ps 103:1-2. 24. 27-30. 35. ℟ cf. v.30

> ℟ **Send forth your Spirit, O Lord,
> and renew the face of the earth.**

or

> ℟ **Alleluia!**

1 Bless the Lord, my soul!
   Lord God, how great you are,

clothed in majesty and glory,
wrapped in light as in a robe!   ℟

2   How many are your works, O Lord!
In wisdom you have made them all.
The earth is full of your riches.
Bless the Lord, my soul.   ℟

3   All of these look to you
to give them their food in due season.
You give it, they gather it up:
you open your hand, they have their fill.   ℟

4   You take back your spirit, they die,
returning to the dust from which they came.
You send forth your spirit, they are created;
and you renew the face of the earth.   ℟

SECOND READING

A reading from the letter of St Paul to the Romans   8:22-27
The Spirit himself expresses our plea in a way that could never be put into words.

From the beginning till now the entire creation, as we know, has been groaning in one great act of giving birth; and not only creation, but all of us who possess the first-fruits of the Spirit, we too groan inwardly as we wait for our bodies to be set free. For we must be content to hope that we shall be saved – our salvation is not in sight, we should not have to be hoping for it if it were – but, as I say, we must hope to be saved since we are not saved yet – it is something we must wait for with patience.

The Spirit too comes to help us in our weakness. For when we cannot choose words in order to pray properly, the Spirit himself expresses our plea in a way that could never be put into words, and God who knows everything in our hearts knows perfectly well what he means, and that the pleas of the saints expressed by the Spirit are according to the mind of God.

This is the word of the Lord.

Gospel Acclamation
Alleluia, alleluia!
Come, Holy Spirit, fill the hearts of your faithful
and kindle in them the fire of your love.
Alleluia!

GOSPEL

A reading from the holy Gospel according to John 7:37-39
From his breast shall flow fountains of living water.

On the last day and greatest day of the festival, Jesus stood there and cried out:
'If any man is thirsty, let him come to me!
Let the man come and drink who believes in me!'

As scripture says: From his breast shall flow fountains of living water.
He was speaking of the Spirit which those who believed in him were to receive; for there was no Spirit as yet because Jesus had not yet been glorified.

This is the Gospel of the Lord.

Prayer over the Gifts
Lord,
send your Spirit on these gifts
and through them help the Church you love
to show your salvation to all the world.

Preface of Pentecost, P28

Communion Antiphon: On the last day of the festival, Jesus stood and cried aloud: If anyone is thirsty, let him come to me and drink, alleluia.

Prayer after Communion
Lord,
through this eucharist,
send the Holy Spirit of Pentecost into our hearts
to keep us always in your love.

PENTECOST SUNDAY

A

Mass during the Day

The Day Of Pentecost

Today we celebrate the great day of Pentecost when Christ filled the Church with the power of his Spirit and sent it out into the world to bring his peace, joy and forgiveness to all mankind.

Entrance Antiphon: The Spirit of the Lord fills the whole world. It holds all things together and knows every word spoken by man, alleluia.

or

The love of God has been poured into our hearts by his Spirit living in us, alleluia.

Opening Prayer
Let us pray
   [that the Spirit will work through our lives
   to bring Christ to the world]

God our Father,
let the Spirit you sent on your Church
to begin the teaching of the gospel
continue to work in the world
through the hearts of all who believe.

or

Let us pray
   [in the Spirit who dwells within us]

Father of light, from whom every good gift comes,
send your Spirit into our lives
with the power of a mighty wind,
and by the flame of your wisdom
open the horizons of our minds.

Loosen our tongues to sing your praise
in words beyond the power of speech,
for without your Spirit
man could never raise his voice in words of peace
or announce the truth that Jesus is Lord,
who lives and reigns with you and the Holy Spirit,
one God, for ever and ever.

FIRST READING

A reading from the Acts of the Apostles   2:1-11
They were all filled with the Holy Spirit and began to speak.

When Pentecost day came round, the apostles had all met in one
room, when suddenly they heard what sounded like a powerful
wind from heaven, the noise of which filled the entire house in
which they were sitting; and something appeared to them that
seemed like tongues of fire; these separated and came to rest on
the head of each of them. They were all filled with the Holy
Spirit, and began to speak foreign languages as the Spirit gave
them the gift of speech.

Now there were devout men living in Jerusalem from every
nation under heaven, and at this sound they all assembled, each
one bewildered to hear these men speaking his own language.
They were amazed and astonished. 'Surely' they said 'all these
men speaking are Galileans? How does it happen that each of us
hears them in his own native language? Parthians, Medes and
Elamites; people from Mesopotamia, Judaea and Cappadocia,
Pontus and Asia, Phrygia and Pamphylia, Egypt and the parts of
Libya round Cyrene; as well as visitors from Rome – Jews and
proselytes alike – Cretans and Arabs; we hear them preaching in
our own language about the marvels of God.'

This is the word of the Lord.

Responsorial Psalm   Ps 103:1. 24. 29-31. 34. ℟ cf v.30
  ℟   **Send forth your Spirit, O Lord,**
       and renew the face of the earth.

or

  ℟   **Alleluia.**

1   Bless the Lord, my soul!
    Lord God, how great you are,
    How many are your works, O Lord!
    The earth is full of your riches. ℟

2   You take back your spirit, they die,
    returning to the dust from which they came.
    You send forth your spirit, they are created;
    and you renew the face of the earth. ℟

3   May the glory of the Lord last for ever!
    May the Lord rejoice in his works!
    May my thoughts be pleasing to him.
    I find my joy in the Lord. ℟

SECOND READING

A reading from the first letter of St Paul
to the Corinthians   12:3-7. 12-13

In the one Spirit we were all baptised.

No one can say, 'Jesus is Lord' unless he is under the influence of
the Holy Spirit.

There is a variety of gifts but always the same Spirit; there are
all sorts of service to be done, but always to the same Lord;
working in all sorts of different ways in different people, it is the
same God who is working in all of them. The particular way in
which the Spirit is given to each person is for a good purpose.

Just as a human body, though it is made up of many parts, is a
single unit because all these parts, though many, make one body,
so it is with Christ. In the one Spirit we were all baptised, Jews as
well as Greeks, slaves as well as citizens, and one Spirit was
given to us all to drink.

This is the word of the Lord.

SEQUENCE

The sequence may be said or sung.

Holy Spirit, Lord of light,
From the clear celestial height
Thy pure beaming radiance give.

Come, thou Father of the poor,
Come with treasures which endure;
Come, thou light of all that live!

Thou, of all consolers best,
Thou, the soul's delightful guest,
Dost refreshing peace bestow;

Thou in toil art comfort sweet;
Pleasant coolness in the heat;
Solace in the midst of woe.

Light immortal, light divine,
Visit thou these hearts of thine,
And our inmost being fill:

If thou take thy grace away,
Nothing pure in man will stay;
All his good is turned to ill.

Heal our wounds, our strength renew;

On our dryness pour thy dew;
    Wash the stains of guilt away:

Bend the stubborn heart and will;
    Melt the frozen, warm the chill;
Guide the steps that go astray.

Thou, on us who evermore
    Thee confess and thee adore,
With thy sevenfold gifts descend:

Give us comfort when we die;
    Give us life with thee on high;
Give us joys that never end.

Gospel Acclamation
Alleluia, alleluia!
Come, Holy Spirit, fill the hearts of your faithful
and kindle in them the fire of your love.
Alleluia!

GOSPEL

A reading from the holy Gospel according to John   20:19-23
As the Father sent me, so am I sending you: receive the Holy Spirit.

In the evening of the first day of the week, the doors were closed in the room where the disciples were, for fear of the Jews. Jesus came and stood among them. He said to them, 'Peace be with you,' and showed them his hands and his side. The disciples were filled with joy when they saw the Lord, and he said to them again, 'Peace be with you.

'As the Father sent me,
so am I sending you.'

After saying this he breathed on them and said:

'Receive the Holy Spirit.
For those whose sins you forgive,
they are forgiven;
for those whose sins you retain,
they are retained.'

This is the Gospel of the Lord.

Prayer over the Gifts
Lord,
may the Spirit you promised
lead us into all truth
and reveal to us the full meaning of this sacrifice.

Preface of Pentecost, P28

Communion Antiphon: They were all filled with the Holy Spirit,
and they spoke of the great things God had done, alleluia.

Prayer after Communion
Father,
may the food we receive in the eucharist
help our eternal redemption.
Keep within us the vigour of your Spirit
and protect the gifts you have given to your Church.

Solemn Blessing

Bow your heads and pray for God's blessing.

This day the Father of light
has enlightened the minds of the disciples
by the outpouring of the Holy Spirit.
May he bless you
and give you the gifts of the Spirit for ever.   ℟   **Amen.**

May that fire which hovered over the disciples
as tongues of flame
burn out all evil from your hearts
and make them glow with pure light.   ℟   **Amen.**

God inspired speech in different tongues
to proclaim one faith.
May he strengthen your faith
and fulfil your hope to see him face to face.   ℟   **Amen.**

May almighty God bless you,
the Father, and the Son, ✠ and the Holy Spirit.   ℟   **Amen.**

SOLEMNITIES OF THE LORD IN ORDINARY TIME

Sunday after Pentecost
THE MOST HOLY TRINITY **A**
Solemnity

The God Of Love And Peace

Our celebration today is a song of praise to God who has taken us up to share in the very life of the Trinity. The grace of the Lord Jesus Christ, the love of God and the fellowship of the Holy Spirit is with us all.

Entrance Antiphon: Blessed be God the Father and his only-begotten Son and the Holy Spirit: for he has shown that he loves us.

Opening Prayer
Let us pray
    [to the one God, Father, Son and Spirit,
    that our lives may bear witness to our faith]

Father,
you sent your Word to bring us truth
and your Spirit to make us holy.
Through them we come to know the mystery of your life.
Help us to worship you, one God in three Persons,
by proclaiming and living our faith in you.

or
Let us pray
    [to our God who is Father, Son, and Holy Spirit]

God, we praise you:
Father all-powerful, Christ Lord and Saviour, Spirit of love.
You reveal yourself in the depths of our being,
drawing us to share in your life and your love.
One God, three Persons,
be near to the people formed in your image,
close to the world your love brings to life.

FIRST READING

A reading from the book of Exodus 34:4-6. 8-9
Lord, Lord, a God of tenderness and compassion.

With the two tablets of stone in his hands, Moses went up the mountain of Sinai in the early morning as the Lord had commanded him. And the Lord descended in the form of a cloud, and Moses stood with him there.

He called on the name of the Lord. The Lord passed before him and proclaimed, 'Lord, Lord, a God of tenderness and compassion, slow to anger, rich in kindness and faithfulness.' And Moses bowed down to the ground at once and worshipped. 'If I have indeed won your favour, Lord,' he said 'let my Lord come with us, I beg. True, they are a headstrong people, but forgive us our faults and our sins, and adopt us as your heritage.'

This is the word of the Lord.

Responsorial Psalm Dan 3:52-56. ℟ v.52

1 You are blest, Lord God of our fathers.
℟ **To you glory and praise for evermore.**
Blest your glorious holy name.
℟ **To you glory and praise for evermore.**

2 You are blest in the temple of your glory.
℟ **To you glory and praise for evermore.**
You are blest on the throne of your kingdom.
℟ **To you glory and praise for evermore.**

3 You are blest who gaze into the depths.
℟ **To you glory and praise for evermore.**
You are blest in the firmament of heaven.
℟ **To you·glory and praise for evermore.**

SECOND READING

A reading from the second letter of St Paul 13:11-13
to the Corinthians
The grace of Jesus Christ, the love of God, and the fellowship of the Holy Spirit.

Brothers, we wish you happiness; try to grow perfect; help one another. Be united; live in peace, and the God of love and peace will be with you.

Greet one another with the holy kiss. All the saints send you greetings.

The grace of the Lord Jesus Christ, the love of God and the

fellowship of the Holy Spirit be with you all.

This is the word of the Lord.

Gospel Acclamation

cf. Apoc 1:8

Alleluia, alleluia!
Glory be to the Father, and to the Son, and to the Holy Spirit,
the God who is, who was, and who is to come.
Alleluia!

GOSPEL

A reading from the holy Gospel according to John   3:16-18

God sent his Son so that through him the world might be saved.

Jesus said to Nicodemus,

'God loved the world so much
that he gave his only Son,
so that everyone who believes in him may not be lost
but may have eternal life.
For God sent his Son into the world
not to condemn the world,
but so that through him the world might be saved.
No one who believes in him will be condemned;
but whoever refuses to believe is condemned already,
because he has refused to believe
in the name of God's only Son.'

This is the Gospel of the Lord.

Prayer over the Gifts

Lord our God,
make these gifts holy,
and through them
make us a perfect offering to you.

Preface of the Holy Trinity, P43

Communion Antiphon: You are the sons of God, so God has given
you the Spirit of his Son to form your hearts and make you cry
out: Abba, Father.

Prayer after Communion

Lord God,
we worship you, a Trinity of Persons, one eternal God.
May our faith and the sacrament we receive
bring us health of mind and body.

Thursday after Trinity Sunday

THE BODY AND BLOOD OF CHRIST A
Solemnity

The Food And Drink Of Eternal Life

God kept his people alive in the desert by giving them food and drink from heaven. The food and drink he gives us in this sacrament is the body and blood of his Son, given for the life of the world.

Entrance Antiphon: The Lord fed his people with the finest wheat and honey; their hunger was satisfied.

Opening Prayer
Let us pray
    [to the Lord who gives himself in the eucharist,
    that this sacrament may bring us salvation
    and peace]

Lord Jesus Christ,
you gave us the eucharist
as the memorial of your suffering and death.
May our worship of this sacrament of your body and blood
help us to experience the salvation you won for us
and the peace of the kingdom
where you live with the Father and the Holy Spirit,
one God, for ever and ever.

    or

Let us pray
    [for the willingness to make present in our world
    the love of Christ shown to us in the eucharist]

Lord Jesus Christ,
we worship you living among us
in the sacrament of your body and blood.

May we offer to our Father in heaven
a solemn pledge of undivided love.
May we offer to our brothers and sisters
a life poured out in loving service of that kingdom
where you live with the Father and the Holy Spirit,
one God, for ever and ever.

FIRST READING

A reading from the book of Deuteronomy   8:2-3. 14-16
He fed you with manna which neither you nor your fathers had known.

Moses said to the people: 'Remember how the Lord your God led you for forty years in the wilderness, to humble you, to test you and know your inmost heart – whether you would keep his commandments or not. He humbled you, he made you feel hunger, he fed you with manna which neither you nor your fathers had known, to make you understand that man does not live on bread alone but that man lives on everything that comes from the mouth of the Lord.

'Do not then forget the Lord your God who brought you out of the land of Egypt, out of the house of slavery: who guided you through this vast and dreadful wilderness, a land of fiery serpents, scorpions, thirst; who in this waterless place brought you water from the hardest rock; who in this wilderness fed you with manna that your fathers had not known.'

This the word of the Lord.

Responsorial Psalm   Ps 147:12-15. 19-20. ℟ v.12
     ℟ **O praise the Lord, Jerusalem!**

or

     ℟ **Alleluia!**

1 O praise the Lord, Jerusalem!
    Zion, praise your God!
    He has strengthened the bars of your gates,
    he has blessed the children within you. ℟

2 He established peace on your borders,
    he feeds you with finest wheat.
    He sends out his word to the earth
    and swiftly runs his command. ℟

3 He makes his word known to Jacob,
    to Israel his laws and decrees.
    He has not dealt thus with other nations;
    he has not taught them his decrees. ℟

SECOND READING

A reading from the first letter of St Paul to the Corinthians 10:16-17

That there is only one loaf means that, though there are many of us, we form a single body.

The blessing-cup that we bless is a communion with the blood of Christ, and the bread that we break is a communion with the body of Christ. The fact that there is only one loaf means that, though there are many of us, we form a single body because we all have a share in this one loaf.

This is the word of the Lord.

SEQUENCE

The sequence may be said or sung in full, or using the shorter form indicated by the asterisked verses.

Sing forth, O Zion, sweetly sing
The praises of thy Shepherd-King,
   In hymns and canticles divine;
Dare all thou canst, thou hast no song
Worthy his praises to prolong,
   So far surpassing powers like thine.

Today no theme of common praise
Forms the sweet burden of thy lays –
   The living, life-dispensing food –
That food which at the sacred board
Unto the brethren twelve our Lord
   His parting legacy bestowed.

Then be the anthem clear and strong,
Thy fullest note, thy sweetest song,
   The very music of the breast:
For now shines forth the day sublime
That brings remembrance of the time
   When Jesus first his table blessed.

Within our new King's banquet-hall
They meet to keep the festival
   That closed the ancient paschal rite:
The old is by the new replaced;
The substance hath the shadow chased;
   And rising day dispels the night.

Christ willed what he himself had done
Should be renewed while time should run,
    In memory of his parting hour:
Thus, tutored in his school divine,
We consecrate the bread and wine;
    And lo – a Host of saving power.

This faith to Christian men is given –
Bread is made flesh by words from heaven:
    Into his blood the wine is turned:
What though it baffles nature's powers
Of sense and sight? This faith of ours
    Proves more than nature e'er discerned.

Concealed beneath the two-fold sign,
Meet symbols of the gifts divine,
    There lie the mysteries adored:
The living body is our food;
Our drink the ever-precious blood;
    In each, one undivided Lord.

Not he that eateth it divides
The sacred food, which whole abides
    Unbroken still, nor knows decay;
Be one, or be a thousand fed,
They eat alike that living bread
    Which, still received, ne'er wastes away.

The good, the guilty share therein,
With sure increase of grace or sin,
    The ghostly life, or ghostly death:
Death to the guilty; to the good
Immortal life. See how one food
    Man's joy or woe accomplisheth.

We break the Sacrament; but bold
And firm thy faith shall keep its hold;
Deem not the whole doth more enfold
    Than in the fractured part resides:
Deem not that Christ doth broken lie;
'Tis but the sign that meets the eye;
The hidden deep reality
    In all its fullness still abides.

*Behold the bread of angels, sent
For pilgrims in their banishment,

The bread for God's true children meant,
    That may not unto dogs be given:
Oft in the olden types foreshowed;
In Isaac on the altar bowed,
And in the ancient paschal food,
    And in the manna sent from heaven.

* Come then, good shepherd, bread divine,
Still show to us thy mercy sign;
Oh, feed us still, still keep us thine;
So may we see thy glories shine
    In fields of immortality;

* O thou, the wisest, mightiest, best,
Our present food, our future rest,
Come, make us each thy chosen guest,
Co-heirs of thine, and comrades blest
    With saints whose dwelling is with thee.

Gospel Acclamation   Jn 6:51-52
    Alleluia, alleluia!
    I am the living bread which has come down from heaven,
    says the Lord.
    Anyone who eats this bread will live for ever.
    Alleluia!

GOSPEL

A reading from the holy Gospel according to John   6:51-58
My flesh is real food and my blood is real drink.

Jesus said to the Jews:
    'I am the living bread which has come down from heaven.
    Anyone who eats this bread will live for ever;
    and the bread that I shall give
    is my flesh, for the life of the world.'

Then the Jews started arguing with one another: 'How can
this man give us his flesh to eat?' they said. Jesus replied:

    'I tell you most solemnly,
    if you do not eat the flesh of the Son of Man
    and drink his blood,
    you will not have life in you.
    Anyone who does eat my flesh and drink my blood
    has eternal life,

and I shall raise him up on the last day.
For my flesh is real food
and my blood is real drink.
He who eats my flesh and drinks my blood
lives in me
and I live in him.
As I, who am sent by the living Father,
myself draw life from the Father,
so whoever eats me will draw life from me.
This is the bread come down from heaven;
not like the bread our ancestors ate:
they are dead,
but anyone who eats this bread will live for ever.'

This is the Gospel of the Lord.

Prayer over the Gifts
Lord,
may the bread and cup we offer
bring your Church the unity and peace they signify.

Preface of the Holy Eucharist I-II, P47-P48

Communion Antiphon: Whoever eats my flesh and drinks my blood will live in me and I in him, says the Lord.

Prayer after Communion

Lord Jesus Christ,
you give us your body and blood in the eucharist
as a sign that even now we share your life.
May we come to possess it completely in the kingdom
where you live for ever and ever.

Friday after the Second Sunday after Pentecost

THE SACRED HEART OF JESUS   A
Solemnity

The Heart Of Christ

God who is love has set his heart on his people and given us his Son, the gentle and humble at heart.

Entrance Antiphon: The thoughts of his heart last through every generation, that he will rescue them from death and feed them in time of famine.

Opening Prayer
Let us pray
   [that we will respond to the love of Christ]

Father,
we rejoice in the gifts of love
we have received from the heart of Jesus your Son.
Open our hearts to share his life
and continue to bless us with his love.

or

Father,
we have wounded the heart of Jesus your Son,
but he brings us forgiveness and grace.
Help us to prove our grateful love
and make amends for our sins.

or

Let us pray
   [that the love of Christ's heart
   may touch the world with healing and peace]

Father,
we honour the heart of your Son
broken by man's cruelty,
yet symbol of love's triumph,
pledge of all that man is called to be.

Teach us to see Christ in the lives we touch,
to offer him living worship
by love-filled service to our brothers and sisters.

FIRST READING
A reading from the book of Deuteronomy   7:6-11
The Lord set his heart on you and chose you.

Moses said to the people: 'You are a people consecrated to the
Lord your God; it is you that the Lord our God has chosen to be
his very own people out of all the peoples on the earth.
   'If the Lord set his heart on you and chose you, it was not
because you outnumbered other peoples: you were the least of all
peoples. It was for love of you and to keep the oath he swore to
your fathers that the Lord brought you out with his mighty hand
and redeemed you from the house of slavery, from the power of
Pharaoh king of Egypt. Know then that the Lord your God is God
indeed, the faithful God who is true to his covenant and his

graciousness for a thousand generations towards those who love him and keep his commandments, but who punishes in their own persons those that hate him; he makes him work out his punishment in person. You are therefore to keep and observe the commandments and statutes and ordinances that I lay down for you today.'

This is the word of the Lord.

Responsorial Psalm   Ps 102:1-4. 6-8. 10. ℟ v.17

℟   **The love of the Lord is everlasting**
    upon those who hold him in fear.

1   My soul, give thanks to the Lord,
    all my being, bless his holy name.
    My soul, give thanks to the Lord
    and never forget all his blessings.   ℟

2   It is he who forgives all your guilt,
    who heals every one of your ills,
    who redeems your life from the grave,
    who crowns you with love and compassion.   ℟

3   The Lord does deeds of justice,
    gives judgement for all who are oppressed.
    He made known his ways to Moses
    and his deeds to Israel's sons.   ℟

4   The Lord is compassion and love,
    slow to anger and rich in mercy.
    He does not treat us according to our sins
    nor repay us according to our faults.   ℟

SECOND READING

A reading from the first letter of St John   4:7-16
Love comes from God.

My dear people,
let us love one another
since love comes from God
and everyone who loves is begotten by God and knows God.
Anyone who fails to love can never have known God,
because God is love.
God's love for us was revealed
when God sent into the world his only Son
so that we could have life through him;

this is the love I mean:
not our love for God,
but God's love for us when he sent his Son
to be the sacrifice that takes our sins away.
My dear people,
since God has loved us so much,
we too should love one another.
No one has ever seen God;
but as long as we love one another
God will live in us
and his love will be complete in us.
We can know that we are living in him
and he is living in us
because he lets us share his Spirit.
We ourselves saw and we testify
that the Father sent his Son
as saviour of the world.
If anyone acknowledges that Jesus is the Son of God,
God lives in him, and he in God.
We ourselves have known and put our faith in
God's love towards ourselves.
God is love
and anyone who lives in love lives in God,
and God lives in him.

This is the word of the Lord.

Gospel Acclamation   Mt 11:29
Alleluia, alleluia!
Shoulder my yoke and learn from me,
for I am gentle and humble in heart.
Alleluia!

GOSPEL

A reading from the holy Gospel according to Matthew   11:25-30
I am gentle and humble in heart.

Jesus exclaimed, 'I bless you, Father, Lord of heaven and of earth, for hiding these things from the learned and the clever and revealing them to mere children. Yes, Father, for that is what it pleased you to do. Everything has been entrusted to me by my Father; and no one knows the Son except the Father, just as no one knows the Father except the Son and those to whom the Son chooses to reveal him.

'Come to me, all you who labour and are overburdened, and I will give you rest. Shoulder my yoke and learn from me, for I am gentle and humble in heart, and you will find rest for your souls. Yes, my yoke is easy and my burden light.'

This is the Gospel of the Lord.

Prayer over the Gifts
Lord,
look on the heart of Christ your Son
filled with love for us.
Because of his love
accept our eucharist and forgive our sins.

Preface of the Sacred Heart, P45

Communion Antiphon: The Lord says: If anyone is thirsty, let him come to me; whoever believes in me, let him drink. Streams of living water shall flow out from within him.

or

One of the soldiers pierced Jesus' side with a lance, and at once there flowed out blood and water.

Prayer after Communion

Father,
may this sacrament fill us with love.
Draw us closer to Christ your Son
and help us to recognise him in others.

SUNDAYS IN ORDINARY TIME
Year A

The readings for the Sundays in Ordinary Time follow a three year cycle.

The Masses for Cycle A are given in the following pages. The Masses for Cycle B are on pp.584ff, and for Cycle C on pp.793ff. To know which cycle is being used in a particular calendar year, see the Table of Principal Celebrations, p.19.

The cycle of Sundays in Ordinary Time runs from the end of the Christmas Season to the beginning of Lent; it recommences after Trinity Sunday, and runs until the beginning of Advent. The number of Sundays in Ordinary Time before Lent, and between Trinity Sunday and Advent, varies: see the Table of Principal Celebrations.

The first week of Ordinary Time begins on the Monday following the Feast of the Baptism of the Lord.

In Cycle A, the Gospel Readings are taken mainly from the Gospel According to St Matthew.

First Sunday in Ordinary Time
THE BAPTISM OF THE LORD
Feast

See above, p.158.

SECOND SUNDAY IN ORDINARY TIME   **A**

The Lamb Of God

We celebrate the Servant of God who came to do the Father's will in perfect obedience. Yet he was more than a servant. John the Baptist calls him the Lamb, the chosen one of God.

Entrance Antiphon: May all the earth give you worship and praise, and break into song to your name, O God, Most High.

Opening Prayer

Let us pray
   [to our Father for the gift of peace]

Father of heaven and earth,
hear our prayers,
and show us the way to peace in the world.

or

Let us pray
   [for the gift of peace]

Almighty and ever-present Father,
your watchful care reaches from end to end
and orders all things in such power
that even the tensions and the tragedies of sin
cannot frustrate your loving plans.

Help us to embrace your will,
give us the strength to follow your call,
so that your truth may live in our hearts
and reflect peace to those who believe in your love.

FIRST READING

A reading from the prophet Isaiah   49:3. 5-6
I will make you the light of the nations so that my salvation may reach to the ends of the earth.

The Lord said to me, 'You are my servant, Israel,
in whom I shall be glorified';
I was honoured in the eyes of the Lord,
my God was my strength.
And now the Lord has spoken,
he who formed me in the womb to be his servant,
to bring Jacob back to him,

to gather Israel to him:

'It is not enough for you to be my servant,
to restore the tribes of Jacob and bring back the survivors of
   Israel;
I will make you the light of the nations
so that my salvation may reach to the ends of the earth.'

This is the word of the Lord.

Responsorial Psalm   Ps 39:2. 4. 7-10. ℟ vv.8. 9

℟   **Here I am, Lord!**
     I come to do your will.

1 I waited, I waited for the Lord
   and he stooped down to me;
   he heard my cry.
   He put a new song into my mouth,
   praise of our God.   ℟

2 You do not ask for sacrifice and offerings,
   but an open ear.
   You do not ask for holocaust and victim.
   Instead, here am I.   ℟

3 In the scroll of the book it stands written
   that I should do your will.
   My God, I delight in your law
   in the depth of my heart.   ℟

4 Your justice I have proclaimed
   in the great assembly.
   My lips I have not sealed;
   you know it, O Lord.   ℟

SECOND READING

A reading from the first letter of St Paul to the
Corinthians
                                                          1:1-3
May God our Father and the Lord Jesus Christ send you grace and peace.

I, Paul, appointed by God to be an apostle, together with brother
Sosthenes, send greetings to the church of God in Corinth, to the
holy people of Jesus Christ, who are called to take their place
among all the saints everywhere who pray to our Lord Jesus
Christ; for he is their Lord no less than ours. May God our Father
and the Lord Jesus Christ send you grace and peace.

This is the word of the Lord.

FIRST READING

A reading from the prophet Isaiah 8:23 – 9:3

In Galilee of the nations the people has seen a great light.

In days past the Lord humbled the land of Zebulun and the land
of Naphtali, but in days to come he will confer glory on the Way
of the Sea on the far side of Jordan, province of the nations.

The people that walked in darkness
has seen a great light;
on those who live in a land of deep shadow
a light has shone.
You have made their gladness greater,
you have made their joy increase;
they rejoice in your presence
as men rejoice at harvest time,
as men are happy when they are dividing the spoils.

For the yoke that was weighing on him,
the bar across his shoulders,
the rod of his oppressor,
these you break as on the day of Midian.

This is the word of the Lord.

Responsorial Psalm Ps 26:1. 4. 13-14. R℣ v.1

R℣ **The Lord is my light and my help.**

1 The Lord is my light and my help;
 whom shall I fear?
 The Lord is the stronghold of my life;
 before whom shall I shrink? R℣

2 There is one thing I ask of the Lord,
 for this I long,
 to live in the house of the Lord,
 all the days of my life,
 to savour the sweetness of the Lord,
 to behold his temple. R℣

3 I am sure I shall see the Lord's goodness
 in the land of the living.
 Hope in him, hold firm and take heart.
 Hope in the Lord! R℣

SECOND READING

A reading from the first letter of St Paul   1:10-13. 17
to the Corinthians

Make up the differences between you instead of disagreeing among yourselves.

I appeal to you, brothers, for the sake of our Lord Jesus Christ, to make up the differences between you, and instead of disagreeing among yourselves, to be united again in your belief and practice. From what Chloe's people have been telling me, my dear brothers, it is clear that there are serious differences among you. What I mean are all these slogans that you have, like: 'I am for Paul,' 'I am for Apollos,' 'I am for Cephas,' 'I am for Christ.' Has Christ been parcelled out? Was it Paul that was crucified for you? Were you baptised in the name of Paul?

For Christ did not send me to baptise, but to preach the Good News, and not to preach that in the terms of philosophy in which the crucifixion of Christ cannot be expressed.

This is the word of the Lord.

Gospel Acclamation   Mt 4:23
Alleluia, alleluia!
Jesus proclaimed the Good News of the kingdom,
and cured all kinds of sickness among the people.
Alleluia!

GOSPEL

A reading from the holy Gospel according to Matthew   4:12-23

He went and settled in Capernaum: in this way the prophecy of Isaiah was to be fulfilled.

*Hearing that John had been arrested Jesus went back to Galilee, and leaving Nazareth he went and settled in Capernaum, a lakeside town on the borders of Zebulun and Naphtali. In this way the prophecy of Isaiah was to be fulfilled:

Land of Zebulun! Land of Naphtali!
Way of the sea on the far side of Jordan,
Galilee of the nations!
The people that lived in darkness
has seen a great light;
on those who dwell in the land and shadow of death
a light has dawned.

From that moment Jesus began his preaching with the message,

'Repent, for the kingdom of heaven is close at hand.'*

As he was walking by the Sea of Galilee he saw two brothers, Simon, who was called Peter, and his brother Andrew; they were making a cast in the lake with their net, for they were fishermen. And he said to them, 'Follow me and I will make you fishers of men.' And they left their nets at once and followed him.

Going on from there he saw another pair of brothers, James son of Zebedee and his brother John; they were in their boat with their father Zebedee, mending their nets, and he called them. At once, leaving the boat and their father, they followed him.

He went round the whole of Galilee teaching in their synagogues, proclaiming the Good News of the kingdom and curing all kinds of diseases and sickness among the people.

This is the Gospel of the Lord.

*Shorter Form, verses 12-17. Read between *

Prayer over the Gifts
Lord,
receive our gifts.
Let our offerings make us holy
and bring us salvation.

Preface of Sundays in Ordinary Time I-VIII, P29-P36

Communion Antiphon: Look up at the Lord with gladness and smile; your face will never be ashamed.

or

I am the light of the world, says the Lord; the man who follows me will have the light of life.

Prayer after Communion
God, all-powerful Father,
may the new life you give us increase our love
and keep us in the joy of your kingdom.

FOURTH SUNDAY IN ORDINARY TIME   A

Our Nothingness

Yes, we can celebrate today our nothingness in the eyes of the world, because God has looked on our humility and lowliness and given us the wisdom, virtue and holiness of Christ. He alone is our boast.

Entrance Antiphon: Save us, Lord our God, and gather us together from the nations, that we may proclaim your holy name and glory in your praise.

Opening Prayer
Let us pray
   [for a greater love of God
   and of our fellow men]

Lord our God,
help us to love you with all our hearts
and to love all men as you love them.

or

Let us pray
   [joining in the praise of the living God
   for we are his people]

Father in heaven,
from the days of Abraham and Moses
until this gathering of your Church in prayer,
you have formed a people in the image of your Son.

Bless this people with the gift of your kingdom.
May we serve you with our every desire
and show love for one another
even as you have loved us.

FIRST READING

A reading from the prophet Zephaniah   2:3; 3:12-13
In your midst I will leave a humble and lowly people.

Seek the Lord
all you, the humble of the earth,
who obey his commands.
Seek integrity,
seek humility:
you may perhaps find shelter

on the day of the anger of the Lord.
In your midst I will leave
a humble and lowly people,
and those who are left in Israel will seek refuge in the name of the
    Lord.
They will do no wrong,
will tell no lies;
and the perjured tongue will no longer
be found in their mouths.
But they will be able to graze and rest
with no one to disturb them.

This is the word of the Lord.

Responsorial Psalm   Ps 145:7-10. R̷ Mt 5:3
    R̷ **How happy are the poor in spirit;**
        theirs is the kingdom of heaven.

or

    R̷ **Alleluia!**

1 It is the Lord who keeps faith for ever,
    who is just to those who are oppressed.
    It is he who gives bread to the hungry,
    the Lord, who sets prisoners free. R̷

2 It is the Lord who gives sight to the blind,
    who raises up those who are bowed down,
    the Lord, who protects the stranger
    and upholds the widow and orphan. R̷

3 It is the Lord who loves the just
    but thwarts the path of the wicked.
    The Lord will reign for ever,
    Zion's God, from age to age. R̷

SECOND READING

A reading from the first letter of St Paul   1:26-31
to the Corinthians
God chose what is foolish by human reckoning.

Take yourselves, brothers, at the time when you were called:
how many of you were wise in the ordinary sense of the word,
how many were influential people, or came from noble families?
No, it was to shame the wise that God chose what is foolish by
human reckoning, and to shame what is strong that he chose

what is weak by human reckoning; those whom the world thinks common and contemptible are the ones that God has chosen – those who are nothing at all to show up those who are everything. The human race has nothing to boast about to God, but you, God has made members of Christ Jesus and by God's doing he has become our wisdom, and our virtue, and our holiness, and our freedom. As scripture says: if anyone wants to boast, let him boast about the Lord.

This is the word of the Lord.

Gospel Acclamation   Mt 11:25
    Alleluia, alleluia!
    Blessed are you, Father,
    Lord of heaven and earth,
    for revealing the mysteries of the kingdom
    to mere children.
    Alleluia!

or   Mt 5:12

    Alleluia, alleluia!
    Rejoice and be glad:
    your reward will be great in heaven.
    Alleluia!

GOSPEL

A reading from the holy Gospel according to Matthew   5:1-12
How happy are the poor in spirit.

Seeing the crowds, Jesus went up the hill. There he sat down and was joined by his disciples. Then he began to speak. This is what he taught them:

    'How happy are the poor in spirit;
    theirs is the kingdom of heaven.
    Happy the gentle:
    they shall have the earth for their heritage.
    Happy those who mourn:
    they shall be comforted.
    Happy those who hunger and thirst for what is right:
    they shall be satisfied.
    Happy the merciful:
    they shall have mercy shown them.
    Happy the pure in heart:
    they shall see God.

Happy the peacemakers:
they shall be called sons of God.
Happy those who are persecuted in the cause of right:
theirs is the kingdom of heaven.

'Happy are you when people abuse you and persecute you and speak all kinds of calumny against you on my account. Rejoice and be glad, for your reward will be great in heaven.'

This is the Gospel of the Lord.

Prayer over the Gifts
Lord,
be pleased with the gifts we bring to your altar,
and make them the sacrament of our salvation.

Preface of Sundays in Ordinary Time I-VIII, P29-P36

Communion Antiphon: Let your face shine on your servant, and save me by your love. Lord, keep me from shame, for I have called to you.

or

Happy are the poor in spirit; the kingdom of heaven is theirs!
Happy are the lowly; they shall inherit the land.

Prayer after Communion
Lord,
you invigorate us with this help to our salvation.
By this eucharist give the true faith continued growth
throughout the world.

FIFTH SUNDAY IN ORDINARY TIME   A

Christ's Church: A Light In The Darkness

The Church is a light shining in the darkness of the world. But today's celebration is overshadowed by a great If. How much more brightly would that light shine if we who are Christians were really like Christ.

Entrance Antiphon: Come, let us worship the Lord. Let us bow down in the presence of our maker, for he is the Lord our God.

Opening Prayer
Let us pray
    [that God will watch over us and protect us]

Father,
watch over your family
and keep us safe in your care,
for all our hope is in you.

or

Let us pray
   [with reverence in the presence of the living God]

In faith and love we ask you, Father,
to watch over your family gathered here.
In your mercy and loving kindness
no thought of ours is left unguarded,
no tear unheeded, no joy unnoticed.

Through the prayer of Jesus
may the blessings promised to the poor in spirit
lead us to the treasures of your heavenly kingdom.

FIRST READING

A reading from the prophet Isaiah   58:7-10
Then will your light shine like the dawn.

Thus says the Lord:

   Share your bread with the hungry,
   and shelter the homeless poor,
   clothe the man you see to be naked
   and turn not from your own kin.
   Then will your light shine like the dawn
   and your wound be quickly healed over.

   Your integrity will go before you
   and the glory of the Lord behind you.
   Cry, and the Lord will answer;
   call, and he will say, 'I am here.'

   If you do away with the yoke,
   the clenched fist, the wicked word,
   if you give your bread to the hungry,
   and relief to the oppressed,
   your light will rise in the darkness,
   and your shadows become like noon.

   This is the word of the Lord.

Responsorial Psalm   Ps 111:4-9. ℞ v.4

   ℞ **The good man is a light in the darkness for the upright.**

or

   ℞ **Alleluia!**

1   He is a light in the darkness for the upright:
     he is generous, merciful and just.
     The good man takes pity and lends,
     he conducts his affairs with honour. ℞

2   The just man will never waver:
     he will be remembered for ever.
     He has no fear of evil news;
     with a firm heart he trusts in the Lord. ℞

3   With a steadfast heart he will not fear;
     open-handed, he gives to the poor;
     his justice stands firm for ever.
     His head will be raised in glory. ℞

SECOND READING

A reading from the first letter of St Paul to the
Corinthians   2:1-5
*During my stay with you, the only knowledge I claimed to have was
about Jesus as the crucified Christ.*

When I came to you, brothers, it was not with any show of
oratory or philosophy, but simply to tell you what God had
guaranteed. During my stay with you, the only knowledge I
claimed to have was about Jesus, and only about him as the
crucified Christ. Far from relying on any power of my own, I
came among you in great 'fear and trembling' and in my
speeches and the sermons that I gave, there were none of the
arguments that belong to philosophy; only a demonstration of
the power of the Spirit. And I did this so that your faith should
not depend on human philosophy but on the power of God.

   This is the word of the Lord.

Gospel Acclamation   Jn 8:12
   Alleluia, alleluia!
   I am the light of the world, says the Lord,
   anyone who follows me
   will have the light of life.
   Alleluia!

GOSPEL

A reading from the holy Gospel according to Matthew   5:13-16
You are the light of the world.

Jesus said to his disciples: 'You are the salt of the earth. But if salt becomes tasteless, what can make it salty again? It is good for nothing, and can only be thrown out to be trampled underfoot by men.

'You are the light of the world. A city built on a hill-top cannot be hidden. No one lights a lamp to put it under a tub; they put it on the lamp-stand where it shines for everyone in the house. In the same way your light must shine in the sight of men, so that, seeing your good works, they may give the praise to your Father in heaven.'

This is the Gospel of the Lord.

Prayer over the Gifts
Lord our God,
may the bread and wine
you give us for our nourishment on earth
become the sacrament of our eternal life.

Preface of Sundays in Ordinary Time I-VIII, P29-36

Communion Antiphon: Give praise to the Lord for his kindness, for his wonderful deeds toward men. He has filled the hungry with good things, he has satisfied the thirsty.

or

Happy are the sorrowing; they shall be consoled. Happy those who hunger and thirst for what is right; they shall be satisfied.

Prayer after Communion
God our Father,
you give us a share in the one bread and the one cup
and make us one in Christ.
Help us to bring your salvation and joy
to all the world.

# SIXTH SUNDAY IN ORDINARY TIME	A

The Law Of Christ

The law of Christ is unlike any man-made law; it contains the hidden wisdom of God. It is a law given by love, and can only be fulfilled by genuine love and true concern for others.

Entrance Antiphon: Lord, be my rock of safety, the stronghold that saves me. For the honour of your name, lead me and guide me.

Opening Prayer
Let us pray
   [that everything we do
    will be guided by God's law of love]

God our Father,
you have promised to remain for ever
with those who do what is just and right.
Help us to live in your presence.

or

Let us pray
   [for the wisdom that is greater than human words]

Father in heaven,
the loving plan of your wisdom took flesh in Jesus Christ,
and changed mankind's history
by his command of perfect love.

May our fulfilment of his command reflect your wisdom
and bring your salvation to the ends of the earth.

FIRST READING

A reading from the book of Ecclesiasticus	15:15-20
He never commanded anyone to be godless.

If you wish, you can keep the commandments,
to behave faithfully is within your power.
He has set fire and water before you;
put out your hand to whichever you prefer.
Man has life and death before him;
whichever a man likes better will be given him.
For vast is the wisdom of the Lord;
he is almighty and all-seeing.
His eyes are on those who fear him,
he notes every action of man.

He never commanded anyone to be godless,
he has given no one permission to sin.

This is the word of the Lord.

Responsorial Psalm   Ps 118:1-2. 4-5. 17-18. 33-34. ℟ v.1
℟ **They are happy who follow God's law!**

1 They are happy whose life is blameless,
   who follow God's law!
   They are happy those who do his will,
   seeking him with all their hearts. ℟

2 You have laid down your precepts
   to be obeyed with care.
   May my footsteps be firm
   to obey your statutes. ℟

3 Bless your servant and I shall live
   and obey your word.
   Open my eyes that I may consider
   the wonders of your law. ℟

4 Teach me the demands of your statutes
   and I will keep them to the end.
   Train me to observe your law,
   to keep it with my heart. ℟

SECOND READING

A reading from the first letter of St Paul   2:6-10
to the Corinthians
God predestined wisdom to be for our glory before the ages began.

We have a wisdom to offer those who have reached maturity: not
a philosophy of our age, it is true, still less of the masters of our
age, which are coming to their end. The hidden wisdom of God
which we teach in our mysteries is the wisdom that God
predestined to be for our glory before the ages began. It is a
wisdom that none of the masters of this age have ever known, or
they would not have crucified the Lord of Glory; we teach what
scripture calls: the things that no eye has seen and no ear has
heard, things beyond the mind of man, all that God has prepared
for those who love him.

These are the very things that God has revealed to us through
the Spirit, for the Spirit reaches the depths of everything, even
the depths of God.

This is the word of the Lord.

Gospel Acclamation 1 Sam 3:9; Jn 6:68
Alleluia, alleluia!
Speak, Lord, your servant is listening:
you have the message of eternal life.
Alleluia!

or cf. Mt 11:25

Alleluia, alleluia!
Blessed are you, Father,
Lord of heaven and earth,
for revealing the mysteries of the kingdom
to mere children.
Alleluia!

GOSPEL

A reading from the holy Gospel according to Matthew 5:17-37
You have learnt how it was said to our ancestors; but I say this to you.

Jesus said to his disciples: 'Do not imagine that I have come to abolish the Law or the Prophets. I have come not to abolish them but to complete them. I tell you solemnly, till heaven and earth disappear, not one dot, one little stroke, shall disappear from the Law until its purpose is achieved. Therefore, the man who infringes even one of the least of these commandments and teaches others to do the same will be considered the least in the kingdom of heaven; but the man who keeps them and teaches them will be considered great in the kingdom of heaven.

*For I tell you, if your virtue goes no deeper than that of the scribes and Pharisees, you will never get into the kingdom of heaven.

'You have learnt how it was said to our ancestors: You must not kill; and if anyone does kill he must answer for it before the court. But I say this to you: anyone who is angry with his brother will answer for it before the court;* if a man calls his brother "Fool" he will answer for it before the Sanhedrin; and if a man calls him "Renegade" he will answer for it in hell fire. So then, if you are bringing your offering to the altar and there remember that your brother has something against you, leave your offering there before the altar, go and be reconciled with your brother first, and then come back and present your offering. Come to terms with your opponent in good time while you are still on the way to the court with him, or he may hand you over to the judge and the judge to the officer, and you will be thrown into prison. I tell you solemnly, you will not get out till you have paid the last penny.

*'You have learnt how it was said: You must not commit adultery. But I say this to you: if a man looks at a woman lustfully, he has already committed adultery with her in his heart. *If your right eye should cause you to sin, tear it out and throw it away; for it will do you less harm to lose one part of you than to have your whole body thrown into hell. And if your right hand should cause you to sin, cut it off and throw it away; for it will do you less harm to lose one part of you than to have your whole body go to hell.

'It has also been said: Anyone who divorces his wife must give her a writ of dismissal. But I say this to you: everyone who divorces his wife, except for the case of fornication, makes her an adulteress; and anyone who marries a divorced woman commits adultery.

*'Again, you have learnt how it was said to our ancestors: You must not break your oath, but must fulfil your oaths to the Lord. But I say this to you: do not swear at all, *either by heaven, since that is God's throne; or by the earth, since that is his footstool; or by Jerusalem, since that is the city of the great king. Do not swear by your own head either, since you cannot turn a single hair white or black. *All you need say is "Yes" if you mean yes, "No" if you mean no; anything more than this comes from the evil one.'

This is the Gospel of the Lord.*

*Shorter Form, verses 20-22. 27-28. 33-34. 37. Read between *

Prayer over the Gifts
Lord,
we make this offering in obedience to your word.
May it cleanse and renew us,
and lead us to our eternal reward.

Preface of Sundays in Ordinary Time I-VIII, P29-P36

Communion Antiphon: They ate and were filled; the Lord gave them what they wanted: they were not deprived of their desire.
or

God loved the world so much, he gave his only Son, that all who believe in him might not perish, but might have eternal life.

Prayer after Communion
Lord,
you give us food from heaven.
May we always hunger
for the bread of life.

SEVENTH SUNDAY IN ORDINARY TIME   A

The Lord Is Compassion And Love

We cannot celebrate the Lord of love without resolving to be more like him; for we are built into him like stones into a Temple erected to give glory to God. We belong to him.

Entrance Antiphon: Lord, your mercy is my hope, my heart rejoices in your saving power. I will sing to the Lord, for his goodness to me.

Opening Prayer
Let us pray
    [that God will make us more like Christ, his Son]

Father,
keep before us the wisdom and love
you have revealed in your Son.
Help us to be like him
in word and deed,
for he lives and reigns with you and the Holy Spirit,
one God, for ever and ever.

    or

Let us pray
    [to the God of power and might,
    for his mercy is our hope]

Almighty God,
Father of our Lord Jesus Christ,
faith in your word is the way to wisdom,
and to ponder your divine plan is to grow in the truth.

Open our eyes to your deeds,
our ears to the sound of your call,
so that our every act may increase our sharing
in the life you have offered us.

FIRST READING

A reading from the book of Leviticus   19:1-2. 17-18
You must love your neighbour as yourself.

The Lord spoke to Moses; he said: 'Speak to the whole community of the sons of Israel and say to them: "Be holy, for I, the Lord your God, am holy.

   "You must not bear hatred for your brother in your heart. You must openly tell him, your neighbour, of his offence; this way you will not take a sin upon yourself. You must not exact vengeance, nor must you bear a grudge against the children of your people. You must love your neighbour as yourself. I am the Lord." '

   This is the word of the Lord.

Responsorial Psalm   Ps 102:1-4. 8. 10. 12-13. ℟ v.8
   ℟ **The Lord is compassion and love.**

1 My soul, give thanks to the Lord,
  all my being, bless his holy name.
  My soul, give thanks to the Lord
  and never forget all his blessings.   ℟

2 It is he who forgives all your guilt,
  who heals every one of your ills,
  who redeems your life from the grave,
  who crowns you with love and compassion.   ℟

3 The Lord is compassion and love,
  slow to anger and rich in mercy.
  He does not treat us according to our sins
  nor repay us according to our faults.   ℟

4 As far as the east is from the west
  so far does he remove our sins.
  As a father has compassion on his sons,
  the Lord has pity on those who fear him.   ℟

SECOND READING

A reading from the first letter of St Paul   3:16-23
to the Corinthians

All are your servants, but you belong to Christ and Christ belongs to God.

Didn't you realise that you were God's temple and that the Spirit of God was living among you? If anybody should destroy the temple of God, God will destroy him, because the temple of God is sacred; and you are that temple.

Make no mistake about it: if any one of you thinks of himself as wise, in the ordinary sense of the word, then he must learn to be a fool before he really can be wise. Why? Because the wisdom of this world is foolishness to God. As scripture says: The Lord knows wise men's thoughts: he knows how useless they are, or again: God is not convinced by the arguments of the wise. So there is nothing to boast about in anything human: Paul, Apollos, Cephas, the world, life and death, the present and the future, are all your servants; but you belong to Christ and Christ belongs to God.

This is the word of the Lord.

Gospel Acclamation   Jn 14:23
Alleluia, alleluia!
If anyone loves me he will keep my word,
and my Father will love him,
and we shall come to him.
Alleluia!

or   1 Jn 2:5

Alleluia, alleluia!
When anyone obeys what Christ has said,
God's love comes to perfection in him.
Alleluia!

GOSPEL

A reading from the holy Gospel according to Matthew   5:38-48
Love your enemies.

Jesus said to his disciples: 'You have learnt how it was said: Eye for eye and tooth for tooth. But I say this to you: offer the wicked man no resistance. On the contrary, if anyone hits you on the right cheek, offer him the other as well; if a man takes you to law and would have your tunic, let him have your cloak as well. And if anyone orders you to go one mile, go two miles with him. Give to anyone who asks, and if anyone wants to borrow, do not turn away.

'You have learnt how it was said: You must love your neighbour and hate your enemy. But I say this to you: love your enemies and pray for those who persecute you; in this way you will be sons of your Father in heaven, for he causes his sun to rise

on bad men as well as good, and his rain to fall on honest and
dishonest men alike. For if you love those who love you, what
right have you to claim any credit? Even the tax collectors do as
much, do they not? And if you save your greetings for your
brothers, are you doing anything exceptional? Even the pagans
do as much, do they not? You must therefore be perfect just as
your heavenly Father is perfect.'

This is the Gospel of the Lord.

Prayer over the Gifts
Lord,
as we make this offering,
may our worship in Spirit and truth
bring us salvation.

Preface of Sundays in Ordinary Time I-VIII, P29-P36

Communion Antiphon: I will tell all your marvellous works, I will
rejoice and be glad in you, and sing to your name, Most High.
or

Lord, I believe that you are the Christ, the Son of God, who was
to come into this world.

Prayer after Communion
Almighty God,
help us to live the example of love
we celebrate in this eucharist
that we may come to its fulfilment in your presence.

EIGHTH SUNDAY IN ORDINARY TIME   A

The Tremendous Love Of God

*We are cherished by the tremendous love of God, tender and forgiving
above every human love. We pray that we may be able to surrender to
this love in perfect trust.*

Entrance Antiphon: The Lord has been my strength; he has led me
into freedom. He saved me because he loves me.

Opening Prayer
Let us pray
   [that God will bring peace to the world
   and freedom to his Church]

Lord,
guide the course of world events
and give your Church the joy and peace
of serving you in freedom.

or

Let us pray
[that the peace of Christ
may find welcome in the world]

Father in heaven,
form in us the likeness of your Son
and deepen his life within us.
Send us as witnesses of gospel joy
into a world of fragile peace and broken promises.
Touch the hearts of all men with your love
that they in turn may love one another.

FIRST READING

A reading from the prophet Isaiah   49:14-15
I will never forget you.

Zion was saying, 'The Lord has abandoned me,
the Lord has forgotten me.'
Does a woman forget her baby at the breast,
or fail to cherish the son of her womb?
Yet even if these forget,
I will never forget you.

     This is the word of the Lord.

Responsorial Psalm   Ps 61:2-3. 6-9. ℟ v.6
   ℟ **In God alone is my soul at rest.**

1   In God alone is my soul at rest;
    my help comes from him.
    He alone is my rock, my stronghold,
    my fortress: I stand firm.   ℟

2   In God alone be at rest, my soul;
    for my hope comes from him.
    He alone is my rock, my stronghold,
    my fortress: I stand firm.   ℟

3   In God is my safety and glory,
    the rock of my strength.

Take refuge in God all you people.
Trust him at all times.
Pour out your hearts before him.   ℟

SECOND READING

A reading from the first letter of St Paul
to the Corinthians   4:1-5
The Lord will reveal the secret intentions of men's hearts.

People must think of us as Christ's servants, stewards entrusted
with the mysteries of God. What is expected of stewards is that
each one should be found worthy of his trust. Not that it makes
the slightest difference to me whether you, or indeed any human
tribunal, find me worthy or not. I will not even pass judgement
on myself. True, my conscience does not reproach me at all, but
that does not prove that I am acquitted; the Lord alone is my
judge. There must be no passing of premature judgement. Leave
that until the Lord comes: he will light up all that is hidden in the
dark and reveal the secret intentions of men's hearts. Then will
be the time for each one to have whatever praise he deserves,
from God.

This is the word of the Lord.

Gospel Acclamation   Jn 17:17
Alleluia, alleluia!
Your word is truth, O Lord,
consecrate us in the truth.
Alleluia!

or   Heb 4:12

Alleluia, alleluia!
The word of God is something alive and active;
it can judge secret emotions and thoughts.
Alleluia!

GOSPEL

A reading from the holy Gospel according to Matthew   6:24-34
Do not worry about tomorrow.

Jesus said to his disciples: 'No one can be the slave of two
masters: he will either hate the first and love the second, or treat
the first with respect and the second with scorn. You cannot be
the slave both of God and of money.

'That is why I am telling you not to worry about your life and

what you are to eat, nor about your body and how you are to
clothe it. Surely life means more than food, and the body more
than clothing! Look at the birds in the sky. They do not sow or
reap or gather into barns; yet your heavenly Father feeds them.
Are you not worth much more than they are? Can any of you, for
all his worrying, add one single cubit to his span of life? And why
worry about clothing? Think of the flowers growing in the fields;
they never have to work or spin; yet I assure you that not even
Solomon in all his regalia was robed like one of these. Now if that
is how God clothes the grass in the field which is there today and
thrown into the furnace tomorrow, will he not much more look
after you, you men of little faith? So do not worry; do not say,
"What are we to eat? What are we to drink? How are we to be
clothed?" It is the pagans who set their hearts on all these things.
Your heavenly Father knows you need them all. Set your hearts
on his kingdom first, and on his righteousness, and all these
other things will be given you as well. So do not worry about
tomorrow; tomorrow will take care of itself. Each day has enough
trouble of its own.'

    This is the Gospel of the Lord.

Prayer over the Gifts
God our Creator,
may this bread and wine we offer
as a sign of our love and worship
lead us to salvation.

Preface of Sundays in Ordinary Time I-VIII, P29-P36

Communion Antiphon: I will sing to the Lord for his goodness to
me, I will sing the name of the Lord, Most High.

or

I, the Lord, am with you always, until the end of the world.

Prayer after Communion
God of salvation,
may this sacrament which strengthens us here on earth
bring us to eternal life.

NINTH SUNDAY IN ORDINARY TIME   **A**

Christ, Our Rock Of Refuge

It is through Christ alone that we can keep our side of the covenant, which is to love God with all our heart and keep his commandments so as to gain his blessing.

Entrance Antiphon: O look at me and be merciful, for I am wretched and alone. See my hardship and my poverty, and pardon all my sins.

Opening Prayer

Let us pray

    [for God's care and protection]

Father,
your love never fails.
Hear our call.
Keep us from danger
and provide for all our needs.

or

Let us pray

    [for the confidence born of faith]

God our Father,
teach us to cherish the gifts that surround us.
Increase our faith in you
and bring our trust to its promised fulfilment
in the joy of your kingdom.

FIRST READING

A reading from the book of Deuteronomy   11:18. 26-28. 32
See, I set before you today a blessing and a curse.

Moses said to the people: 'Let these words of mine remain in your heart and in your soul; fasten them on your hand as a sign and on your forehead as a circlet.

    'See, I set before you today a blessing and a curse: a blessing, if you obey the commandments of the Lord our God that I enjoin on you today; a curse, if you disobey the commandments of the Lord your God and leave the way I have marked out for you today, by going after other gods you have not known. You must keep and observe all the laws and customs that I set before you today.'

    This is the word of the Lord.

Responsorial Psalm   Ps 30:2-4. 17. 25. ℟ v.3

℟ **Be a rock of refuge for me, O Lord.**

1 In you, O Lord, I take refuge.
   Let me never be put to shame.
   In your justice, set me free,
   hear me and speedily rescue me.   ℟

2 Be a rock of refuge to me,
   a mighty stronghold to save me,
   for you are my rock, my stronghold.
   For your name's sake, lead me and guide me.   ℟

3 Let your face shine on your servant.
   Save me in your love.
   Be strong, let your heart take courage,
   all who hope in the Lord.   ℟

SECOND READING

A reading from the letter of St Paul to the Romans   3:21-25. 28
*A man is justified by faith and not by doing something the Law tells him
to do.*

God's justice that was made known through the Law and the
Prophets has now been revealed outside the Law, since it is the
same justice of God that comes through faith to everyone, Jew
and pagan alike, who believes in Jesus Christ. Both Jew and
pagan sinned and forfeited God's glory, and both are justified
through the free gift of his grace by being redeemed in Christ
Jesus who was appointed by God to sacrifice his life so as to win
reconciliation through faith since, as we see it, a man is justified
by faith and not by doing something the Law tells him to do.

This is the word of the Lord.

Gospel Acclamation   Jn 14:23
   Alleluia, alleluia!
   If anyone loves me he will keep my word,
   and my Father will love him,
   and we shall come to him.
   Alleluia!

or   Jn 15:5

   Alleluia, alleluia!
   I am the vine, you are the branches,
   says the Lord.

Whoever remains in me, with me in him,
bears fruit in plenty.
Alleluia!

GOSPEL

A reading from the holy Gospel according to Matthew   7:21-27
The house built on rock and the house built on sand.

Jesus said to his disciples: 'It is not those who say to me, "Lord, Lord", who will enter the kingdom of heaven, but the person who does the will of my Father in heaven. When the day comes many will say to me, "Lord, Lord, did we not prophesy in your name, cast out demons in your name, work many miracles in your name?" Then I shall tell them to their faces: I have never known you; away from me, you evil men!

'Therefore, everyone who listens to these words of mine and acts on them will be like a sensible man who built his house on rock. Rain came down, floods rose, gales blew and hurled themselves against that house, and it did not fall: it was founded on rock. But everyone who listens to these words of mine and does not act on them will be like a stupid man who built his house on sand. Rain came down, floods rose, gales blew and struck that house, and it fell; and what a fall it had!'

This is the Gospel of the Lord.

Prayer over the Gifts
Lord,
as we gather to offer our gifts
confident in your love,
make us holy by sharing your life with us
and by this eucharist forgive our sins.

Preface of Sundays in Ordinary Time I-VIII, P29-P36

Communion Antiphon: I call upon you, God, for you will answer me; bend your ear and hear my prayer.

or

I tell you solemnly, whatever you ask for in prayer, believe that you have received it, and it will be yours, says the Lord.

Prayer after Communion
Lord,
as you give us the body and blood of your Son,

guide us with your Spirit
that we may honour you
not only with our lips,
but also with the lives we lead,
and so enter your kingdom.

TENTH SUNDAY IN ORDINARY TIME   A

Our Sacrifice Of Praise And Thanksgiving

*Our love of God is like the morning dew, it evaporates so quickly. We
tend to reduce religion to a mere formality. Today we renew our love
and, approaching God with the sincerity and faith of Abraham, we offer
the one sacrifice of praise and thanksgiving which gives glory to God.*

Entrance Antiphon: The Lord is my light and my salvation. Who
shall frighten me? The Lord is the defender of my life. Who shall
make me tremble?

Opening Prayer
Let us pray
   [for the guidance of the Holy Spirit]

God of wisdom and love,
source of all good,
send your Spirit to teach us your truth
and guide our actions
in your way of peace.

or

Let us pray
   [to our Father
   who calls us to freedom in Jesus his Son]

Father in heaven,
words cannot measure the boundaries of love
for those born to new life in Christ Jesus.
Raise us beyond the limits this world imposes,
so that we may be free to love as Christ teaches
and find our joy in your glory.

FIRST READING

A reading from the prophet Hosea   6:3-6
What I want is love, not sacrifice.

Let us set ourselves to know the Lord;
that he will come is as certain as the dawn
his judgement will rise like the light,
he will come to us as showers come,
like spring rains watering the earth.

What am I to do with you, Ephraim?
What am I to do with you, Judah?
This love of yours is like a morning cloud,
like the dew that quickly disappears.
This is why I have torn them to pieces by the prophets,
why I slaughtered them with the words from my mouth,
since what I want is love, not sacrifice;
knowledge of God, not holocausts.

   This is the word of the Lord.

Responsorial Psalm   Ps 49:1. 8. 12-15. Ry v.23
   Ry **I will show God's salvation to the upright.**

1   The God of gods, the Lord,
    has spoken and summoned the earth,
    from the rising of the sun to its setting.
    'I find no fault with your sacrifices,
    your offerings are always before me.   Ry

2   'Were I hungry, I would not tell you,
    for I own the world and all it holds.
    Do you think I eat the flesh of bulls,
    or drink the blood of goats?   Ry

3   'Pay your sacrifice of thanksgiving to God
    and render him your votive offerings.
    Call on me in the day of distress.
    I will free you and you shall honour me.'   Ry

SECOND READING

A reading from the letter of St Paul to the Romans   4:18-25
Abraham drew strength from faith and gave glory to God.

Though it seemed Abraham's hope could not be fulfilled, he
hoped and he believed, and through doing so he did become the

father of many nations exactly as he had been promised: Your descendants will be as many as the stars. Even the thought that his body was past fatherhood – he was about a hundred years old – and Sarah too old to become a mother, did not shake his belief. Since God had promised it, Abraham refused either to deny it or even to doubt it, but drew strength from faith and gave glory to God, convinced that God had power to do what he had promised. This is the faith that was 'considered as justifying him'. Scripture however does not refer only to him but to us as well when it says that his faith was thus 'considered'; our faith too will be 'considered' if we believe in him who raised Jesus our Lord from the dead, Jesus who was put to death for our sins and raised to life to justify us.

This is the word of the Lord.

Gospel Acclamation   cf. Acts 16:14
Alleluia, alleluia!
Open our heart, O Lord,
to accept the words of your Son.
Alleluia!

or   Lk 4:18

Alleluia, alleluia!
The Lord has sent me to bring the good news to the poor,
to proclaim liberty to captives.
Alleluia!

GOSPEL

A reading from the holy Gospel according to Matthew   9:9-13
I did not come to call the virtuous, but sinners.

As Jesus was walking on he saw a man named Matthew sitting by the customs house, and he said to him, 'Follow me.' And he got up and followed him.

While he was at dinner in the house it happened that a number of tax collectors and sinners came to sit at the table with Jesus and his disciples. When the Pharisees saw this, they said to his disciples, 'Why does your master eat with tax collectors and sinners?' When he heard this he replied, 'It is not the healthy who need the doctor, but the sick. Go and learn the meaning of the words: What I want is mercy, not sacrifice. And indeed I did not come to call the virtuous, but sinners.'

This is the Gospel of the Lord.

Prayer over the Gifts
Lord,
look with love on our service.
Accept the gifts we bring
and help us grow in Christian love.

Preface of Sundays in Ordinary Time I-VIII, P29-P36

Communion Antiphon: I can rely on the Lord; I can always turn to
him for shelter. It was he who gave me my freedom. My God,
you are always there to help me!
or

God is love, and he who lives in love, lives in God, and God in
him.

Prayer after Communion
Lord,
may your healing love
turn us from sin
and keep us on the way that leads to you.

ELEVENTH SUNDAY IN ORDINARY TIME   A

Our Calling

*God has made us his own. He reconciles us in Christ and calls each of us
by name to be a people consecrated to him. As his priestly people we offer
this sacrifice today, filled with joyful trust in him.*

Entrance Antiphon: Lord, hear my voice when I call to you. You
are my help; do not cast me off, do not desert me, my Saviour
God.

Opening Prayer
Let us pray
    [for the grace to follow Christ more closely]

Almighty God,
our hope and our strength,
without you we falter.
Help us to follow Christ
and to live according to your will.

or

Let us pray
   [to the Father
   whose love gives us strength to follow his Son]

God our Father,
we rejoice in the faith that draws us together,
aware that selfishness can drive us apart.
Let your encouragement be our constant strength.
Keep us one in the love that has sealed our lives,
help us to live as one family
the gospel we profess.

FIRST READING

A reading from the book of Exodus   19:2-6
I will count you a kingdom of priests, a consecrated nation.

From Rephidim the Israelites set out again; and when they
reached the wilderness of Sinai, there in the wilderness they
pitched their camp; there facing the mountain Israel pitched
camp.
     Moses then went up to God, and the Lord called to him from
the mountain, saying, 'Say this to the House of Jacob, declare this
to the sons of Israel, "You yourselves have seen what I did with
the Egyptians, how I carried you on eagle's wings and brought
you to myself. From this you know that now, if you obey my
voice and hold fast to my covenant, you of all the nations shall be
my very own, for all the earth is mine. I will count you a kingdom
of priests, a consecrated nation."'

     This is the word of the Lord.

Responsorial Psalm   Ps 99:2-3. 5. R℣ v.3
   R℣ **We are his people:**
        the sheep of his flock.

1   Cry out with joy to the Lord, all the earth.
    Serve the Lord with gladness.
    Come before him, singing for joy.   R℣

2   Know that he, the Lord, is God.
    He made us, we belong to him,
    we are his people, the sheep of his flock.   R℣

3   Indeed, how good is the Lord,

eternal his merciful love.
He is faithful from age to age. ℟

SECOND READING

A reading from the letter of St Paul to the Romans 5:6-11

Now that we have been reconciled by the death of his Son, surely we may count on being saved by the life of his Son.

We were still helpless when at his appointed moment Christ died for sinful men. It is not easy to die even for a good man – though of course for someone really worthy, a man might be prepared to die – but what proves that God loves us is that Christ died for us while we were still sinners. Having died to make us righteous, is it likely that he would now fail to save us from God's anger? When we were reconciled to God by the death of his Son, we were still enemies; now that we have been reconciled surely we may count on being saved by the life of his Son? Not merely because we have been reconciled but because we are filled with joyful trust in God through our Lord Jesus Christ, through whom we have already gained our reconciliation.

This is the word of the Lord.

Gospel Acclamation Jn 10:27
Alleluia, alleluia!
The sheep that belong to me listen to my voice,
says the Lord,
I know them and they follow me.
Alleluia!

or Mk 1:15

Alleluia, alleluia!
The kingdom of God is close at hand.
Repent, and believe the Good News.
Alleluia!

GOSPEL

A reading from the holy Gospel according to Matthew 9:36 – 10:8

He summoned his twelve disciples and sent them out.

When Jesus saw the crowds he felt sorry for them because they were harassed and dejected, like sheep without a shepherd. Then he said to his disciples, 'The harvest is rich but the labourers are few, so ask the Lord of the harvest to send labourers to his harvest.'

He summoned his twelve disciples, and gave them authority over unclean spirits with power to cast them out and to cure all kinds of diseases and sickness.

These are the names of the twelve apostles: first, Simon who is called Peter, and his brother Andrew; James the son of Zebedee, and his brother John; Philip and Bartholomew; Thomas, and Matthew the tax collector; James the son of Alphaeus, and Thaddaeus; Simon the Zealot and Judas Iscariot, the one who was to betray him. These twelve Jesus sent out, instructing them as follows:

'Do not turn your steps to pagan territory, and do not enter any Samaritan town; go rather to the lost sheep of the House of Israel. And as you go, proclaim that the kingdom of heaven is close at hand. Cure the sick, raise the dead, cleanse the lepers, cast out devils. You received without charge, give without charge.'

This is the Gospel of the Lord.

Prayer over the Gifts
Lord God,
in this bread and wine
you give us food for body and spirit.
May the eucharist renew our strength
and bring us health of mind and body.

Preface of Sundays in Ordinary Time I-VIII, P29-P36

Communion Antiphon: One thing I seek: to dwell in the house of the Lord all the days of my life.

or

Father, keep in your name those you have given me, that they may be one as we are one, says the Lord.

Prayer after Communion
Lord,
may this eucharist
accomplish in your Church
the unity and peace it signifies.

TWELFTH SUNDAY IN ORDINARY TIME   **A**

The Lord At Our Side

Faced with all the evil in the world and the fearful consequences of sin, we might well be afraid did we not have Christ as a mighty hero at our side, the source of divine grace.

Entrance Antiphon: God is the strength of his people. In him, we his chosen live in safety. Save us, Lord, who share in your life, and give us your blessing; be our shepherd for ever.

Opening Prayer
Let us pray
   [that we may grow in the love of God]

Father,
guide and protector of your people,
grant us an unfailing respect for your name,
and keep us always in your love.

or

Let us pray
   [to God whose fatherly love keeps us safe]

God of the universe,
we worship you as Lord.
God, ever close to us,
we rejoice to call you Father.
From this world's uncertainty we look to your covenant.
Keep us one in your peace, secure in your love.

FIRST READING

A reading from the prophet Jeremiah   20:10-13
He has delivered the soul of the needy from the hands of evil men.

Jeremiah said:

   I hear so many disparaging me,
   ' "Terror from every side!"
   Denounce him! Let us denounce him!'
   All those who used to be my friends
   watched for my downfall,
   'Perhaps he will be seduced into error.
   Then we will master him
   and take our revenge!'

But the Lord is at my side, a mighty hero;
my opponents will stumble, mastered,
confounded by their failure;
everlasting, unforgettable disgrace will be theirs.
But you, Lord of Hosts, you who probe with justice,
who scrutinise the loins and heart,
let me see the vengeance you will take on them,
for I have committed my cause to you.
Sing to the Lord,
praise the Lord,
for he has delivered the soul of the needy
from the hands of evil men.

This is the word of the Lord.

Responsorial Psalm   Ps 68:8-10. 14. 17. 33-35. R/ v.14

℟   **In your great love, answer me, O God.**

1   It is for you that I suffer taunts,
    that shame covers my face,
    that I have become a stranger to my brothers,
    an alien to my own mother's sons.
    I burn with zeal for your house
    and taunts against you fall on me.   ℟

2   This is my prayer to you,
    my prayer for your favour.
    In your great love, answer me, O God,
    with your help that never fails:
    Lord, answer, for your love is kind;
    in your compassion, turn towards me.   ℟

3   The poor when they see it will be glad
    and God-seeking hearts will revive;
    for the Lord listens to the needy
    and does not spurn his servants in their chains.
    Let the heavens and the earth give him praise,
    the sea and all its living creatures.   ℟

SECOND READING

A reading from the letter of St Paul to the Romans   5:12-15
The gift considerably outweighed the fall.

Sin entered the world through one man, and through sin death,
and thus death has spread through the whole human race

because everyone has sinned. Sin existed in the world long before the Law was given. There was no law and so no one could be accused of the sin of 'law-breaking', yet death reigned over all from Adam to Moses, even though their sin, unlike that of Adam, was not a matter of breaking a law.

Adam prefigured the One to come, but the gift itself considerably outweighed the fall. If it is certain that through one man's fall so many died, it is even more certain that divine grace, coming through the one man, Jesus Christ, came to so many as an abundant free gift.

This is the word of the Lord.

Gospel Acclamation   Jn 1:14.12
Alleluia, alleluia!
The Word was made flesh and lived among us;
to all who did accept him
he gave power to become children of God.
Alleluia!

or   Jn 15:26. 27

Alleluia, alleluia!
The Spirit of truth will be my witness;
and you too will be my witnesses.
Alleluia!

GOSPEL

A reading from the holy Gospel according to Matthew   10:26-33
Do not be afraid of those who kill the body.

Jesus instructed the Twelve as follows: 'Do not be afraid. For everything that is now covered will be uncovered, and everything now hidden will be made clear. What I say to you in the dark, tell in the daylight; what you hear in whispers, proclaim from the house-tops.

'Do not be afraid of those who kill the body but cannot kill the soul; fear him rather who can destroy both body and soul in hell. Can you not buy two sparrows for a penny? And yet not one falls to the ground without your Father knowing. Why, every hair on your head has been counted. So there is no need to be afraid; you are worth more than hundreds of sparrows.

'So if anyone declares himself for me in the presence of men, I will declare myself for him in the presence of my Father in heaven. But the one who disowns me in the presence of men, I will disown in the presence of my Father in heaven.'

This is the Gospel of the Lord.

Prayer over the Gifts

Lord,
receive our offering,
and may this sacrifice of praise
purify us in mind and heart
and make us always eager to serve you.

Preface of Sundays in Ordinary Time I-VIII, P29-P36

Communion Antiphon: The eyes of all look to you, O Lord, and you
give them food in due season.

or

I am the Good Shepherd; I give my life for my sheep, says the
Lord.

Prayer after Communion

Lord,
you give us the body and blood of your Son
to renew your life within us.
In your mercy, assure our redemption
and bring us to the eternal life
we celebrate in this eucharist.

THIRTEENTH SUNDAY IN ORDINARY TIME   A

Welcoming Christ

*We welcome Christ today as the woman of Shunem welcomed the prophet
Elisha. But the Christ we welcome is the Christ who gave his life for
others, and our celebration would be a mockery if we were not prepared to
welcome him in one another, even in the least of his brethren.*

Entrance Antiphon: All nations, clap your hands. Shout with a
voice of joy to God.

Opening Prayer

Let us pray
    [that Christ may be our light]

Father,
you call your children
to walk in the light of Christ.

Free us from darkness
and keep us in the radiance of your truth.

or

Let us pray
[for the strength to reject the darkness of sin]

Father in heaven,
the light of Jesus
has scattered the darkness of hatred and sin.
Called to that light
we ask for your guidance.
Form our lives in your truth, our hearts in your love.

FIRST READING

A reading from the second book of the Kings   4:8-11. 14-16
This is a holy man of God, let him rest there.

One day as Elisha was on his way to Shunem, a woman of rank who lived there pressed him to stay and eat there. After this he always broke his journey for a meal when he passed that way. She said to her husband, 'Look, I am sure the man who is constantly passing our way must be a holy man of God. Let us build him a small room on the roof, and put him a bed in it, and a table and chair and lamp; whenever he comes to us he can rest there.'

One day when he came, he retired to the upper room and lay down. 'What can be done for her?' he asked. Gehazi, his servant, answered, 'Well, she has no son and her husband is old.' Elisha said, 'Call her.' The servant called her and she stood at the door. 'This time next year,' Elisha said 'you will hold a son in your arms.'

This is the word of the Lord.

Responsorial Psalm   Ps 88:2-3. 16-19. ℞ v.2
   ℞   **I will sing for ever of your love, O Lord.**

1   I will sing for ever of your love, O Lord;
    through all ages my mouth will proclaim your truth.
    Of this I am sure, that your love lasts for ever,
    that your truth is firmly established as the heavens.   ℞

2   Happy the people who acclaim such a king,
    who walk, O Lord, in the light of your face,   (continued)

who find their joy every day in your name,
who make your justice the source of their bliss.

℟ **I will sing for ever of your love, O Lord.**

3 For it is you, O Lord, who are the glory of their strength;
   it is by your favour that our might is exalted:
   for our ruler is in the keeping of the Lord;
   our king in the keeping of the Holy One of Israel. ℟

SECOND READING

A reading from the letter of St Paul to the Romans   6:3-4. 8-11
When we were baptised we went into the tomb with Christ, so that we too
might live a new life.

When we were baptised in Christ Jesus we were baptised in his
death; in other words, when we were baptised we went into the
tomb with him and joined him in death, so that as Christ was
raised from the dead by the Father's glory, we too might live a
new life.

But we believe that having died with Christ we shall return to
life with him: Christ, as we know, having been raised from the
dead will never die again. Death has no power over him any
more. When he died, he died, once for all, to sin, so his life now
is life with God; and in that way, you too must consider
yourselves to be dead to sin but alive for God in Christ Jesus.

This is the word of the Lord.

Gospel Acclamation   cf. Acts 16:14
   Alleluia, alleluia!
   Open our heart, O Lord,
   to accept the words of your Son.
   Alleluia!

or   1 Peter 2:9

   Alleluia, alleluia!
   You are a chosen race, a royal priesthood, a people set apart
   to sing the praises of God
   who called you out of darkness into his wonderful light.
   Alleluia!

GOSPEL

A reading from the holy Gospel according to Matthew   10:37-42

Anyone who does not take his cross is not worthy of me. Anyone who welcomes you welcomes me.

Jesus instructed the Twelve as follows: 'Anyone who prefers father or mother to me is not worthy of me. Anyone who prefers son or daughter to me is not worthy of me. Anyone who does not take his cross and follow in my footsteps is not worthy of me. Anyone who finds his life will lose it; anyone who loses his life for my sake will find it.

'Anyone who welcomes you welcomes me; and those who welcome me welcome the one who sent me.

'Anyone who welcomes a prophet because he is a prophet will have a prophet's reward; and anyone who welcomes a holy man because he is a holy man will have a holy man's reward.

'If anyone gives so much as a cup of cold water to one of these little ones because he is a disciple, then I tell you solemnly, he will most certainly not lose his reward.'

This is the Gospel of the Lord.

Prayer over the Gifts

Lord God,
through your sacraments
you give us the power of your grace.
May this eucharist
help us to serve you faithfully.

Preface of Sundays in Ordinary Time I-VIII, P29-P36

Communion Antiphon: O, bless the Lord, my soul, and all that is within me bless his holy name.

or

Father, I pray for them: may they be one in us, so that the world may believe it was you who sent me.

Prayer after Communion

Lord,
may this sacrifice and communion
give us a share in your life
and help us bring your love to the world.

FOURTEENTH SUNDAY IN ORDINARY TIME A

The Lord Who Is Kind And Full Of Compassion

Our Lord has every claim to the title and majesty of kingship, and yet he comes to us in humility and gentleness. We pray that this spirit of Christ may also be in us.

Entrance Antiphon: Within your temple, we ponder your loving kindness, O God. As your name, so also your praise reaches to the ends of the earth; your right hand is filled with justice.

Opening Prayer

Let us pray
    [for forgiveness through the grace of Jesus Christ]

Father,
through the obedience of Jesus,
your servant and your Son,
you raised a fallen world.
Free us from sin
and bring us the joy that lasts for ever.

or

Let us pray
    [for greater willingness
    to serve God and our fellow man]

Father,
in the rising of your Son
death gives birth to new life.
The sufferings he endured restored hope to a fallen world.
Let sin never ensnare us
with empty promises of passing joy.
Make us one with you always,
so that our joy may be holy,
and our love may give life.

FIRST READING

A reading from the prophet Zechariah   9:9-10
See now, your king comes humbly to you.

The Lord says this:
    'Rejoice heart and soul, daughter of Zion!
    Shout with gladness, daughter of Jerusalem!

See now, your king comes to you;
he is victorious, he is triumphant,
humble and riding on a donkey,
on a colt, the foal of a donkey.
He will banish chariots from Ephraim
and horses from Jerusalem;
the bow of war will be banished.
He will proclaim peace for the nations.
His empire shall stretch from sea to sea,
from the River to the ends of the earth.'

This is the word of the Lord.

Responsorial Psalm   Ps 144:1-2. 8-11. 13-14. ℟ v.1
  ℟ **I will bless your name for ever,
       O God my King.**

or

  ℟ **Alleluia!**

1 I will give you glory, O God my King,
   I will bless your name for ever.
   I will bless you day after day
   and praise your name for ever. ℟

2 The Lord is kind and full of compassion,
   slow to anger, abounding in love.
   How good is the Lord to all,
   compassionate to all his creatures. ℟

3 All your creatures shall thank you, O Lord,
   and your friends shall repeat their blessing.
   They shall speak of the glory of your reign
   and declare your might, O God. ℟

4 The Lord is faithful in all his words
   and loving in all his deeds.
   The Lord supports all who fall
   and raises all who are bowed down. ℟

SECOND READING

A reading from the letter of St Paul to the Romans   8:9. 11-13
If by the Spirit you put an end to the misdeeds of the body you will live.

Your interests are not in the unspiritual, but in the spiritual, since
the Spirit of God has made his home in you. In fact, unless you

possessed the Spirit of Christ you would not belong to him, and if the Spirit of him who raised Jesus from the dead is living in you, then he who raised Jesus from the dead will give life to your own mortal bodies through his Spirit living in you.

So then, my brothers, there is no necessity for us to obey our unspiritual selves or to live unspiritual lives. If you do live in that way, you are doomed to die; but if by the Spirit you put an end to the misdeeds of the body you will live.

This is the word of the Lord.

Gospel Acclamation   cf. Mt 11:25
Alleluia, alleluia!
Blessed are you, Father, Lord of heaven and earth,
for revealing the mysteries of the kingdom to mere children.
Alleluia!

GOSPEL

A reading from the holy Gospel according to Matthew   11:25-30
I am gentle and humble in heart.

Jesus exclaimed, 'I bless you, Father, Lord of heaven and of earth, for hiding these things from the learned and the clever and revealing them to mere children. Yes, Father, for that is what it pleased you to do. Everything has been entrusted to me by my Father; and no one knows the Son except the Father, just as no one knows the Father except the Son and those to whom the Son chooses to reveal him.

'Come to me, all you who labour and are overburdened, and I will give you rest. Shoulder my yoke and learn from me, for I am gentle and humble in heart, and you will find rest for your souls. Yes, my yoke is easy and my burden light.'

This is the Gospel of the Lord.

Prayer over the Gifts
Lord,
let this offering to the glory of your name
purify us and bring us closer to eternal life.

Preface of Sundays in Ordinary Time I-VIII, P29-P36

Communion Antiphon: Taste and see the goodness of the Lord; blessed is he who hopes in God.

or

Come to me, all you that labour and are burdened, and I will give you rest, says the Lord.

Prayer after Communion
Lord,
may we never fail to praise you
for the fullness of life and salvation
you give us in this eucharist.

FIFTEENTH SUNDAY IN ORDINARY TIME   A

Christ, The Sower

We celebrate Christ who came to sow the seed of God's word in the world, and we rejoice with him as we see everywhere around us the first-fruits of the Spirit.

Entrance Antiphon: In my justice I shall see your face, O Lord; when your glory appears, my joy will be full.

Opening Prayer
Let us pray
[that the gospel may be our rule of life]

God our Father,
your light of truth
guides us to the way of Christ.
May all who follow him
reject what is contrary to the gospel.

or

Let us pray
[to be faithful to the light we have received,
to the name we bear]

Father,
let the light of your truth
guide us to your kingdom
through a world filled with lights contrary to your own.
Christian is the name and the gospel we glory in.
May your love make us what you have called us to be.

FIRST READING

A reading from the prophet Isaiah   55:10-11
The rain makes the earth give growth.

Thus says the Lord: 'As the rain and the snow come down from the heavens and do not return without watering the earth, making it yield and giving growth to provide seed for the sower and bread for the eating, so the word that goes from my mouth does not return to me empty, without carrying out my will and succeeding in what it was sent to do.'

This is the word of the Lord.

Responsorial Psalm   Ps 64:10-14. R̷ Lk 8:8

> R̷ **Some seed fell into rich soil
> and produced its crop.**

1 You care for the earth, give it water,
  you fill it with riches.
  Your river in heaven brims over
  to provide its grain.   R̷

2 And thus you provide for the earth;
  you drench its furrows,
  you level it, soften it with showers,
  you bless its growth.   R̷

3 You crown the year with your goodness.
  Abundance flows in your steps,
  in the pastures of the wilderness it flows.   R̷

4 The hills are girded with joy,
  the meadows covered with flocks;
  the valleys are decked with wheat.
  They shout for joy, yes, they sing.   R̷

SECOND READING

A reading from the letter of St Paul to the Romans   8:18-23

The whole creation is eagerly waiting for God to reveal his sons.

I think that what we suffer in this life can never be compared to the glory, as yet unrevealed, which is waiting for us. The whole creation is eagerly waiting for God to reveal his sons. It was not for any fault on the part of creation that it was made unable to attain its purpose, it was made so by God; but creation still retains the hope of being freed, like us, from its slavery to decadence, to enjoy the same freedom and glory as the children of God. From the beginning till now the entire creation, as we know, has been groaning in one great act of giving birth; and not only creation, but all of us who possess the first-fruits of the Spirit, we too groan inwardly as we wait for our bodies to be set free.

This is the word of the Lord.

Gospel Acclamation   1 Sam 3:9; Jn 6:68
Alleluia, alleluia!
Speak, Lord, your servant is listening;
you have the message of eternal life.
Alleluia!

or

Alleluia, alleluia!
The seed is the word of God, Christ the sower;
whoever finds this seed will remain for ever.
Alleluia!

GOSPEL

A reading from the holy Gospel according to Matthew   13:1-23
A sower went out to sow.

*Jesus left the house and sat by the lakeside, but such crowds gathered round him that he got into a boat and sat there. The people all stood on the beach, and he told them many things in parables.

He said, 'Imagine a sower going out to sow. As he sowed, some seeds fell on the edge of the path, and the birds came and ate them up. Others fell on patches of rock where they found little soil and sprang up straight away, because there was no depth of earth; but as soon as the sun came up they were scorched and, not having any roots, they withered away. Others fell among thorns, and the thorns grew up and choked them. Others fell on rich soil and produced their crop, some a hundredfold, some sixty, some thirty. Listen, anyone who has ears!'*

Then the disciples went up to him and asked, 'Why do you talk to them in parables?' 'Because' he replied 'the mysteries of the kingdom of heaven are revealed to you, but they are not revealed to them. For anyone who has will be given more, and he will have more than enough; but from anyone who has not, even what he has will be taken away. The reason I talk to them in parables is that they look without seeing and listen without hearing or understanding. So in their case this prophecy of Isaiah is being fulfilled:

You will listen and listen again, but not understand,
see and see again, but not perceive.

For the heart of this nation has grown coarse,
their ears are dull of hearing, and they have shut their eyes,
for fear they should see with their eyes,
hear with their ears,
understand with their heart,
and be converted
and be healed by me.

'But happy are your eyes because they see, your ears because
they hear! I tell you solemnly, many prophets and holy men
longed to see what you see, and never saw it; to hear what you
hear, and never heard it.

'You, therefore, are to hear the parable of the sower. When
anyone hears the word of the kingdom without understanding,
the evil one comes and carries off what was sown in his heart:
this is the man who received the seed on the edge of the path.
The one who received it on patches of rock is the man who hears
the word and welcomes it at once with joy. But he has no root in
him, he does not last; let some trial come, or some persecution on
account of the word, and he falls away at once. The one who
received the seed in thorns is the man who hears the word but
the worries of this world and the lure of riches choke the word
and so he produces nothing. And the one who received the seed
in rich soil is the man who hears the word and understands it; he
is the one who yields a harvest and produces now a hundredfold,
now sixty, now thirty.'

This is the Gospel of the Lord.

*Shorter Form, verses 1-9. Read between *

Prayer over the Gifts
Lord,
accept the gifts of your Church.
May this eucharist
help us grow in holiness and faith.

Preface of Sundays in Ordinary Time I-VIII, P29-P36

Communion Antiphon: The sparrow even finds a home, the
swallow finds a nest wherein to place her young, near to your
altars, Lord of hosts, my King, my God! How happy they who
dwell in your house! For ever they are praising you.

or

Whoever eats my flesh and drinks my blood will live in me and I
in him, says the Lord.

Prayer after Communion
Lord,
by our sharing in the mystery of this eucharist,
let your saving love grow within us.

SIXTEENTH SUNDAY IN ORDINARY TIME   A

The Lord, Our Merciful Judge

*We stand in continual need of the mercy and forgiveness of God; and we
are assured of his forgiveness when we repent, because he has sent us the
Spirit of his Son to help us and to plead for us in our weakness.*

Entrance Antiphon: God himself is my help. The Lord upholds my
life. I will offer you a willing sacrifice; I will praise your name, O
Lord, for its goodness.

Opening Prayer
Let us pray
    [to be kept faithful in the service of God]

Lord,
be merciful to your people.
Fill us with your gifts
and make us always eager to serve you
in faith, hope, and love.

or

Let us pray
    [that God will continue to bless us
    with his compassion and love]

Father,
let the gift of your life
continue to grow in us,
drawing us from death to faith, hope, and love.
Keep us alive in Christ Jesus.
Keep us watchful in prayer
and true to his teaching
till your glory is revealed in us.

FIRST READING

A reading from the book of Wisdom   12:13. 16-19

After sin you will grant repentance.

There is no god, other than you, who cares for everything,
to whom you might have to prove that you never judged
    unjustly.
Your justice has its source in strength,
your sovereignty over all makes you lenient to all.
You show your strength when your sovereign power is
    questioned
and you expose the insolence of those who know it;
but, disposing of such strength, you are mild in judgement,
you govern us with great lenience,
for you have only to will, and your power is there.
By acting thus you have taught a lesson to your people
how the virtuous man must be kindly to his fellow men,
and you have given your sons the good hope
that after sin you will grant repentance.

This is the word of the Lord.

Responsorial Psalm   Ps 85:5-6. 9-10. 15-16. R⟩ v.5
    R⟩ **O Lord, you are good and forgiving.**

1 O Lord, you are good and forgiving,
       full of love to all who call.
       Give heed, O Lord, to my prayer
       and attend to the sound of my voice.   R⟩

2 All the nations shall come to adore you
       and glorify your name, O Lord:
       for you are great and do marvellous deeds,
       you who alone are God.   R⟩

3 But you, God of mercy and compassion,
       slow to anger, O Lord,
       abounding in love and truth,
       turn and take pity on me.   R⟩

SECOND READING

A reading from the letter of St Paul to the Romans   8:26-27

The Spirit expresses our plea in a way that could never be put into words.
The Spirit comes to help us in our weakness. For when we cannot
choose words in order to pray properly, the Spirit himself
expresses our plea in a way that could never be put into words,

and God who knows everything in our hearts knows perfectly well what he means, and that the pleas of the saints expressed by the Spirit are according to the mind of God.

This is the word of the Lord.

Gospel Acclamation   cf. Eph 1:17. 18
> Alleluia, alleluia!
> May the Father of our Lord Jesus Christ
> enlighten the eyes of our mind,
> so that we can see what hope his call holds for us.
> Alleluia!

or   cf. Mt 11:25

> Alleluia, alleluia!
> Blessed are you, Father,
> Lord of heaven and earth,
> for revealing the mysteries of the kingdom
> to mere children.
> Alleluia!

GOSPEL

A reading from the holy Gospel according to Matthew   13:24-43
Let them both grow till the harvest.

Jesus put a parable before the crowds, 'The kingdom of heaven may be compared to a man who sowed good seed in his field. While everybody was asleep his enemy came, sowed darnel all among the wheat, and made off. When the new wheat sprouted and ripened, the darnel appeared as well. The owner's servants went to him and said, "Sir, was it not good seed that you sowed in your field? If so, where does the darnel come from?" "Some enemy has done this" he answered. And the servants said, "Do you want us to go and weed it out?" But he said, "No, because when you weed out the darnel you might pull up the wheat with it. Let them both grow till the harvest; and at harvest time I shall say to the reapers: First collect the darnel and tie it in bundles to be burnt, then gather the wheat into my barn." '

He put another parable before them, 'The kingdom of heaven is like a mustard seed which a man took and sowed in his field. It is the smallest of all the seeds, but when it has grown it is the biggest shrub of all and becomes a tree so that the birds of the air come and shelter in its branches.'

He told them another parable, 'The kingdom of heaven is like the yeast a woman took and mixed in with three measures of flour till it was leavened all through.'

In all this Jesus spoke to the crowds in parables; indeed, he would never speak to them except in parables. This was to fulfill the prophecy:

I will speak to you in parables
and expound things hidden since the foundation of the
world.

Then, leaving the crowds, he went to the house; and his disciples came to him and said, 'Explain the parable about the darnel in the field to us.' He said in reply, 'The sower of the good seed is the Son of Man. The field is the world; the good seed is the subjects of the kingdom; the darnel, the subjects of the evil one; the enemy who sowed them, the devil; the harvest is the end of the world; the reapers are the angels. Well then, just as the darnel is gathered up and burnt in the fire, so it will be at the end of time. The Son of Man will send his angels and they will gather out of his kingdom all things that provoke offences and all who do evil, and throw them into the blazing furnace, where there will be weeping and grinding of teeth. Then the virtuous will shine like the sun in the kingdom of their Father. Listen, anyone who has ears!'

This is the Gospel of the Lord.

*Shorter Form, verses 24-30. Read between *

Prayer over the Gifts
Lord,
bring us closer to salvation
through these gifts which we bring in your honour.
Accept the perfect sacrifice you have given us,
bless it as you blessed the gifts of Abel.

Preface of Sundays in Ordinary Time I-VIII, P29-P36

Communion Antiphon: The Lord keeps in our minds the wonderful things he has done. He is compassion and love; he always provides for his faithful.

or

I stand at the door and knock, says the Lord. If anyone hears my voice and opens the door, I will come in and sit down to supper with him, and he with me.

Prayer after Communion
Merciful Father,
may these mysteries
give us new purpose
and bring us to a new life in you.

SEVENTEENTH SUNDAY IN ORDINARY TIME A

The Treasure We Have Found

Solomon prayed for the wisdom to discern the true value of things. We scarcely need the wisdom of Solomon to realise that in finding the love of God and the kingdom of God we have found a treasure beyond price. It is in the joy of this realisation that we hold our celebration today.

Entrance Antiphon: God is in his holy dwelling; he will give a home to the lonely, he gives power and strength to his people.

Opening Prayer
Let us pray
   [that we will make good use of the gifts
   that God has given us]

God our Father and protector,
without you nothing is holy,
nothing has value.
Guide us to everlasting life
by helping us to use wisely
the blessings you have given to the world.

or

Let us pray
   [for the faith to recognise God's presence in our world]

God our Father,
open our eyes to see your hand at work
in the splendour of creation,
in the beauty of human life.
Touched by your hand our world is holy.
Help us to cherish the gifts that surround us,
to share your blessings with our brothers and sisters,
and to experience the joy of life in your presence.

FIRST READING

A reading from the first book of the Kings   3:5. 7-12

You have asked for a discerning judgement for yourself.

The Lord appeared to Solomon in a dream and said, 'Ask what you would like me to give you.' Solomon replied, 'Lord, my God, you have made your servant king in succession to David my father.
But I am a very young man, unskilled in leadership. Your servant finds himself in the midst of this people of yours that you have chosen, a people so many its numbers cannot be counted or reckoned. Give your servant a heart to understand how to discern between good and evil, for who could govern this people of yours that is so great?' It pleased the Lord that Solomon should have asked for this. 'Since you have asked for this' the Lord said 'and not asked for long life for yourself or riches or the lives of your enemies, but have asked for a discerning judgement for yourself, here and now I do what you ask. I give you a heart wise and shrewd as none before you has had and none will have after you.'

This is the word of the Lord.

Responsorial Psalm   Ps 118:57. 72. 76-77. 127-130. ℟ v.97

℟   **Lord how I love your law!**

1   My part, I have resolved, O Lord,
    is to obey your word.
    The law from your mouth means more to me
    than silver and gold.   ℟

2   Let your love be ready to console me
    by your promise to your servant.
    Let your love come to me and I shall live
    for your law is my delight.   ℟

3   That is why I love your commands
    more than finest gold.
    That is why I rule my life by your precepts:
    I hate false ways.   ℟

4   Your will is wonderful indeed;
    therefore I obey it.
    The unfolding of your word gives light
    and teaches the simple.   ℟

SECOND READING

A reading from the letter of St Paul to the Romans 8:28-30

God intended us to become true images of his Son.

We know that by turning everything to their good God co-operates with all those who love him, with all those that he has called according to his purpose. They are the ones he chose specially long ago and intended to become true images of his Son, so that his Son might be the eldest of many brothers. He called those he intended for this; those he called he justified, and with those he justified he shared his glory.

This is the word of the Lord

Gospel Acclamation   Jn 15:15

Alleluia, alleluia!
I call you friends, says the Lord,
because I have made known to you
everything I have learnt from my Father.
Alleluia!

or   cf. Mt 11:25

Alleluia, alleluia!
Blessed are you, Father,
Lord of heaven and earth,
for revealing the mysteries of the kingdom
to mere children.
Alleluia!

GOSPEL

A reading from the holy Gospel according to Matthew 13:44-52

He sells everything he owns and buys the field.

*Jesus said to the crowds, 'The kingdom of heaven is like treasure hidden in a field which someone has found; he hides it again, goes off happy, sells everything he owns and buys the field.

'Again, the kingdom of heaven is like a merchant looking for fine pearls; when he finds one of great value he goes and sells everything he owns and buys it. *

'Again, the kingdom of heaven is like a dragnet cast into the sea that brings in a haul of all kinds. When it is full, the fishermen haul it ashore; then, sitting down, they collect the good ones in a basket and throw away those that are no use. This is how it will be at the end of time: the angels will appear and separate the

wicked from the just to throw them into the blazing furnace
where there will be weeping and grinding of teeth.

'Have you understood all this?' They said 'Yes.' And he said
to them, 'Well then, every scribe who becomes a disciple of the
kingdom of heaven is like a householder who brings out from his
storeroom things both new and old.'

This is the Gospel of the Lord.

*Shorter Form, verses 44-46. Read between *

Prayer over the Gifts
Lord,
receive these offerings
chosen from your many gifts.
May these mysteries make us holy
and lead us to eternal joy.

Preface of Sundays in Ordinary Time I-VIII, P29-P36

Communion Antiphon: O bless the Lord, my soul, and remember
all his kindness.

or

Happy are those who show mercy; mercy shall be theirs. Happy
are the pure of heart, for they shall see God.

Prayer after Communion
Lord,
we receive the sacrament
which celebrates the memory
of the death and resurrection of Christ your Son.
May this gift bring us closer to our eternal salvation.

EIGHTEENTH SUNDAY IN ORDINARY TIME A

The Lord Who Feeds Us

*Today we celebrate the great love of God that not only gives us life, but
also sustains that life with the food of the eucharist, the love of God made
visible in Christ our Lord.*

Entrance Antiphon: God, come to my help. Lord, quickly give me
assistance. You are the one who helps me and sets me free: Lord,
do not be long in coming.

Opening Prayer

Let us pray
　　[for the gift of God's forgiveness and love]

Father of everlasting goodness,
our origin and guide,
be close to us
and hear the prayers of all who praise you.
Forgive our sins and restore us to life.
Keep us safe in your love.

or

Let us pray
　　[to the Father whose kindness never fails]

God our Father,
gifts without measure flow from your goodness
to bring us your peace.
Our life is your gift.
Guide our life's journey,
for only your love makes us whole.
Keep us strong in your love.

FIRST READING

A reading from the prophet Isaiah　　　　　　　55:1-3
Come and eat.

Thus says the Lord:

　　Oh, come to the water all you who are thirsty;
　　though you have no money, come!
　　Buy corn without money, and eat,
　　and, at no cost, wine and milk.
　　Why spend money on what is not bread,
　　your wages on what fails to satisfy?
　　Listen, listen to me and you will have good things to eat
　　and rich food to enjoy.
　　Pay attention, come to me;
　　listen, and your soul will live.
　　With you I will make an everlasting covenant
　　out of the favours promised to David.

This is the word of the Lord.

Responsorial Psalm   Ps 144:8-9. 15-18. ℟ v.16

> ℟ **You open wide your hand, O Lord,**
>   **you grant our desires.**

1 The Lord is kind and full of compassion,
    slow to anger, abounding in love.
    How good is the Lord to all,
    compassionate to all his creatures. ℟

2 The eyes of all creatures look to you
    and you give them their food in due time.
    You open wide your hand,
    grant the desires of all who live. ℟

3 The Lord is just in all his ways
    and loving in all his deeds.
    He is close to all who call him,
    call on him from their hearts. ℟

SECOND READING

A reading from the letter of St Paul to the Romans   8:35. 37-39

*No created thing can ever come between us and the love of God made
visible in Christ.*

Nothing can come between us and the love of Christ, even if we
are troubled or worried, or being persecuted, or lacking food or
clothes, or being threatened or even attacked. These are the trials
through which we triumph, by the power of him who loved us.

    For I am certain of this: neither death nor life, no angel, no
prince, nothing that exists, nothing still to come, not any power,
or height or depth, nor any created thing, can ever come between
us and the love of God made visible in Christ Jesus our Lord.

    This is the word of the Lord.

Gospel Acclamation   Lk 19:38; 2:14
    Alleluia, alleluia!
    Blessings on the King who comes,
    in the name of the Lord!
    Peace in heaven
    and glory in the highest heavens!
    Alleluia!

or   Mt 4:4

    Alleluia, alleluia!
    Man does not live on bread alone,
    but on every word that comes from the mouth of God.
    Alleluia!

GOSPEL

A reading from the holy Gospel according to Matthew   14:13-21
They all ate as much as they wanted.

When Jesus received the news of John the Baptist's death he withdrew by boat to a lonely place where they could be by themselves. But the people heard of this and, leaving the towns, went after him on foot. So as he stepped ashore he saw a large crowd; and he took pity on them and healed their sick.

When evening came, the disciples went to him and said, 'This is a lonely place, and the time has slipped by; so send the people away, and they can go to the villages to buy themselves some food.' Jesus replied, 'There is no need for them to go: give them something to eat yourselves.' 'But they answered, 'All we have with us is five loaves and two fish.' 'Bring them here to me,' he said. He gave orders that the people were to sit down on the grass; then he took the five loaves and the two fish, raised his eyes to heaven and said the blessing. And breaking the loaves he handed them to his disciples who gave them to the crowds. They all ate as much as they wanted, and they collected the scraps remaining, twelve baskets full. Those who ate numbered about five thousand men, to say nothing of women and children.

This is the Gospel of the Lord.

Prayer over the Gifts
Merciful Lord,
make holy these gifts,
and let our spiritual sacrifice
make us an everlasting gift to you.

Preface of Sundays in Ordinary Time I-VIII, P29-P36

Communion Antiphon: You gave us bread from heaven, Lord: a sweet-tasting bread that was very good to eat.
or
The Lord says: I am the bread of life. A man who comes to me will not go away hungry, and no one who believes in me will thirst.

Prayer after Communion
Lord,
you give us the strength of new life
by the gift of the eucharist.
Protect us with your love
and prepare us for eternal redemption.

NINETEENTH SUNDAY IN ORDINARY TIME A

His Voice That Speaks Of Peace

In times of great anguish, such as St Paul himself experienced, Christ is always with us, calming the storm and bringing peace.

Entrance Antiphon: Lord, be true to your covenant, forget not the life of your poor ones for ever. Rise up, O God, and defend your cause; do not ignore the shouts of your enemies.

Opening Prayer

Let us pray
    [in the Spirit
    that we may grow in the love of God]

Almighty and ever-living God,
your Spirit made us your children,
confident to call you Father.
Increase your Spirit within us
and bring us to our promised inheritance.

or

Let us pray
    [that through us
    others may find the way to life in Christ]

Father,
we come, reborn in the Spirit,
to celebrate our sonship in the Lord Jesus Christ.
Touch our hearts,
help them grow toward the life you have promised.
Touch our lives,
make them signs of your love for all men.

FIRST READING

A reading from the first book of the Kings   19:9. 11-13
Stand on the mountain before the Lord.

When Elijah reached Horeb, the mountain of God, he went into the cave and spent the night in it. Then he was told, 'Go out and stand on the mountain before the Lord.' Then the Lord himself went by. There came a mighty wind, so strong it tore the mountains and shattered the rocks before the Lord. But the Lord was not in the wind. After the wind came an earthquake. But the Lord was not in the earthquake. After the earthquake came a fire. But the Lord was not in the fire. And after the fire there came the sound of a gentle breeze. And when Elijah heard this, he covered his face with his cloak and went out and stood at the entrance of the cave.

This is the word of the Lord.

Responsorial Psalm   Ps 84:9-14. ℟ v. 8

℟ **Let us see, O Lord, your mercy
   and give us your saving help.**

1   I will hear what the Lord God has to say,
    a voice that speaks of peace.
    His help is near for those who fear him
    and his glory will dwell in our land.   ℟

2   Mercy and faithfulness have met;
    justice and peace have embraced.
    Faithfulness shall spring from the earth
    and justice look down from heaven.   ℟

3   The Lord will make us prosper
    and our earth shall yield its fruit.
    Justice shall march before him
    and peace shall follow his steps.   ℟

SECOND READING

A reading from the letter of St Paul to the Romans   9:1-5
I would willingly be condemned if it could help my brothers.

What I want to say is no pretence; I say it in union with Christ – it is the truth – my conscience in union with the Holy Spirit assures me of it too. What I want to say is this: my sorrow is so great, my mental anguish so endless, I would willingly be condemned and be cut off from Christ if it could help my brothers of Israel, my own flesh and blood. They were adopted as sons, they were given the glory and the covenants; the Law and the ritual were drawn up for them, and the promises were made to them. They are descended from the patriarchs and from their flesh and blood came Christ who is above all, God for ever blessed! Amen.

This is the word of the Lord.

Gospel Acclamation   Lk 19:38

    Alleluia, alleluia!
    Blessings on the King who comes, in the name of the Lord!
    Peace in heaven and glory in the highest heavens!
    Alleluia!

or   Ps 129:5

    Alleluia, alleluia!
    My soul is waiting for the Lord,
    I count on his word.
    Alleluia!

GOSPEL

A reading from the holy Gospel according to Matthew   14:22-33
Tell me to come to you across the water.

Jesus made the disciples get into the boat and go on ahead to the
other side while he would send the crowds away. After sending
the crowds away he went up into the hills by himself to pray.
When evening came, he was there alone, while the boat, by now
far out on the lake, was battling with a heavy sea, for there was a
headwind. In the fourth watch of the night he went towards
them, walking on the lake, and when the disciples saw him
walking on the lake they were terrified. 'It is a ghost' they said,
and cried out in fear. But at once Jesus called out to them, saying,
'Courage! It is I! Do not be afraid.' It was Peter who answered.
'Lord ', he said 'if it is you, tell me to come to you across the
water.' 'Come' said Jesus. Then Peter got out of the boat and
started walking towards Jesus across the water, but as soon as he
felt the force of the wind, he took fright and began to sink. 'Lord!
Save me!' he cried. Jesus put out his hand at once and held him.
'Man of little faith,' he said 'why did you doubt?' And as they got
into the boat the wind dropped. The men in the boat bowed
down before him and said, 'Truly, you are the Son of God.'

    This is the Gospel of the Lord.

Prayer over the Gifts
God of power,
giver of the gifts we bring,
accept the offering of your Church
and make it the sacrament of our salvation.

Preface of Sundays in Ordinary Time I-VIII, P29-P36

Communion Antiphon: Praise the Lord, Jerusalem; he feeds you with the finest wheat.

or

The bread I shall give is my flesh for the life of the world, says the Lord.

Prayer after Communion
Lord,
may the eucharist you give us
bring us to salvation
and keep us faithful to the light of your truth.

TWENTIETH SUNDAY IN ORDINARY TIME   A

Mercy To All Mankind

We tend to think of God as exclusively our own property. But he is God of all the world, of Christians and non-Christians alike; and today we celebrate his mercies to others who are not of our faith.

Entrance Antiphon: God, our protector, keep us in mind; always give strength to your people. For if we can be with you even one day, it is better than a thousand without you.

Opening Prayer
Let us pray
   [that the love of God
   may raise us beyond what we see
   to the unseen glory of his kingdom]

God our Father,
may we love you in all things and above all things
and reach the joy you have prepared for us
beyond all our imagining.

or

Let us pray
   [with humility and persistence]

Almighty God, ever-loving Father,
your care extends beyond the boundaries of race and nation
to the hearts of all who live.

May the walls, which prejudice raises between us,
crumble beneath the shadow of your outstretched arm.

FIRST READING

A reading from the prophet Isaiah   56:1. 6-7
I will bring foreigners to my holy mountain.

Thus says the Lord: Have a care for justice, act with integrity, for
soon my salvation will come and my integrity be manifest.

Foreigners who have attached themselves to the Lord to serve
him and to love his name and be his servants – all who observe
the sabbath, not profaning it, and cling to my covenant – these I
will bring to my holy mountain. I will make them joyful in my
house of prayer. Their holocausts and their sacrifices will be
accepted on my altar, for my house will be called a house of
prayer for all the peoples.

This is the word of the Lord.

Responsorial Psalm   Ps 66:2-3. 5-6. 8. Ry v.4
  Ry **Let the peoples praise you, O God;
      let all the peoples praise you.**

1   O God, be gracious and bless us
    and let your face shed its light upon us.
    So will your ways be known upon earth
    and all nations learn your saving help.   Ry

2   Let the nations be glad and exult
    for you rule the world with justice.
    With fairness you rule the peoples,
    you guide the nations on earth.   Ry

3   Let the peoples praise you, O God;
    let all the peoples praise you.
    May God still give us his blessing
    till the ends of the earth revere him.   Ry

SECOND READING

A reading from the letter of St Paul to the Romans 11:13-15. 29-32
With Israel, God never takes back his gifts or revokes his choice.

Let me tell you pagans this: I have been sent to the pagans as
their apostle, and I am proud of being sent, but the purpose of it
is to make my own people envious of you, and in this way save

some of them. Since their rejection meant the reconciliation of the world, do you know what their admission will mean? Nothing less than a resurrection from the dead! God never takes back his gifts or revokes his choice.

Just as you changed from being disobedient to God, and now enjoy mercy because of their disobedience, so those who are disobedient now – and only because of the mercy shown to you – will also enjoy mercy eventually. God has imprisoned all men in their own disobedience only to show mercy to all mankind.

This is the word of the Lord.

Gospel Acclamation   Jn 10:27
> Alleluia, alleluia!
> The sheep that belong to me listen to my voice,
> says the Lord,
> I know them and they follow me.
> Alleluia!

or   cf. Mt 4:23

> Alleluia, alleluia!
> Jesus proclaimed the Good News of the kingdom,
> and cured all kinds of sickness among the people.
> Alleluia!

GOSPEL

A reading from the holy Gospel according to Matthew   15:21-28
Woman, you have great faith.

Jesus left Gennesaret and withdrew to the region of Tyre and Sidon. Then out came a Canaanite woman from that district and started shouting, 'Sir, Son of David, take pity on me. My daughter is tormented by a devil.' But he answered her not a word. And his disciples went and pleaded with him. 'Give her what she wants,' they said 'because she is shouting after us.' He said in reply, 'I was sent only to the lost sheep of the House of Israel.' But the woman had come up and was kneeling at his feet. 'Lord,' she said 'help me.' He replied, 'It is not fair to take the children's food and throw it to the house-dogs.' She retorted, 'Ah yes, sir; but even house-dogs can eat the scraps that fall from their master's table.' Then Jesus answered her, 'Woman, you have great faith. Let your wish be granted.' And from that moment her daughter was well again.

This is the Gospel of the Lord.

Prayer over the Gifts
Lord,
accept our sacrifice
as a holy exchange of gifts.
By offering what you have given us
may we receive the gift of yourself.

Preface of Sundays in Ordinary Time I-VIII, P29-P36

Communion Antiphon: With the Lord there is mercy, and fullness
of redemption.

or

I am the living bread from heaven, says the Lord; if anyone eats
this bread he will live for ever.

Prayer after Communion
God of mercy,
by this sacrament you make us one with Christ.
By becoming more like him on earth,
may we come to share his glory in heaven,
where he lives and reigns for ever and ever.

TWENTY-FIRST SUNDAY IN ORDINARY TIME A

Peter The Rock

*We rejoice today that Christ chose Peter in spite of his human failings to
be the rock on which he built his Church. The reason for that choice lies in
the unfathomable depth of God's wisdom. 'The Lord is high, yet he looks
on the lowly.'*

Entrance Antiphon: Listen, Lord, and answer me. Save your
servant who trusts in you. I call to you all day long, have mercy
on me, O Lord.

Opening Prayer
Let us pray
[that God will make us one in mind and heart]

Father,
help us to seek the values
that will bring us lasting joy in this changing world.
In our desire for what you promise
make us one in mind and heart.

or

Let us pray
[with minds fixed on eternal truth]

Lord our God,
all truth is from you,
and you alone bring oneness of heart.

Give your people the joy
of hearing your word in every sound
and of longing for your presence more than for life itself.
May all the attractions of a changing world
serve only to bring us
the peace of your kingdom which this world does not give.

FIRST READING

A reading from the prophet Isaiah   22:19-23

I place the key of the House of David on his shoulder.

Thus says the Lord of hosts to Shebna, the master of the palace:

I dismiss you from your office,
I remove you from your post,
and the same day I call on my servant
Eliakim son of Hilkiah.
I invest him with your robe,
gird him with your sash,
entrust him with your authority;
and he shall be a father
to the inhabitants of Jerusalem
and to the House of Judah.
I place the key of the House of David
on his shoulder;
should he open, no one shall close,
should he close, no one shall open.
I drive him like a peg
into a firm place;
he will become a throne of glory
for his father's house.

This is the word of the Lord.

Responsorial Psalm   Ps 137:1-3. 6. 8. R℣ v. 8

 R℣ **Your love, O Lord, is eternal,**
    discard not the work of your hands.

1 I thank you, Lord, with all my heart,
  you have heard the words of my mouth.
  Before the angels I will bless you.
  I will adore before your holy temple. R℣

2 I thank you for your faithfulness and love
  which excel all we ever knew of you.
  On the day I called, you answered;
  you increased the strength of my soul. R℣

3 The Lord is high yet he looks on the lowly
  and the haughty he knows from afar.
  Your love, O Lord, is eternal,
  discard not the work of your hands. R℣

SECOND READING

A reading from the letter of St Paul to the Romans 11:33-36
All that exists comes from him; all is by him and from him.

How rich are the depths of God – how deep his wisdom and
knowledge – and how impossible to penetrate his motives or
understand his methods! Who could ever know the mind of the
Lord? Who could ever be his counsellor? Who could ever give
him anything or lend him anything? All that exists comes from
him; all is by him and for him. To him be glory for ever! Amen.

 This is the word of the Lord.

Gospel Acclamation   2 Cor 5:19
 Alleluia, alleluia!
 God in Christ was reconciling the world to himself,
 and he has entrusted to us the news that they are reconciled.
 Alleluia!

or   Mt 16:18

 Alleluia, alleluia!
 You are Peter
 and on this rock I will build my Church.
 And the gates of the underworld can never hold out against it.
 Alleluia!

GOSPEL

A reading from the holy Gospel according to Matthew   16:13-20
You are Peter, and I will give you the keys of the kingdom of heaven.

When Jesus came to the region of Caesarea Philippi he put this question to his disciples, 'Who do people say the Son of Man is?' And they said, 'Some say he is John the Baptist, some Elijah, and others Jeremiah or one of the prophets.' 'But you,' he said, 'who do you say I am?' Then Simon Peter spoke up, 'You are the Christ,' he said, 'the Son of the living God.' Jesus replied, 'Simon son of Jonah, you are a happy man! Because it was not flesh and blood that revealed this to you but my Father in heaven. So I now say to you: You are Peter and on this rock I will build my Church. And the gates of the underworld can never hold out against it. I will give you the keys of the kingdom of heaven; whatever you bind on earth shall be considered bound in heaven; whatever you loose on earth shall be considered loosed in heaven.' Then he gave the disciples strict orders not to tell anyone that he was the Christ.

This is the Gospel of the Lord.

Prayer over the Gifts
Merciful God,
the perfect sacrifice of Jesus Christ
made us your people.
In your love,
grant peace and unity to your Church.

Preface of Sundays in Ordinary Time I-VIII, P29-P36

Communion Antiphon: Lord, the earth is filled with your gift from heaven; man grows bread from earth, and wine to cheer his heart.

or

The Lord says: The man who eats my flesh and drinks my blood will live for ever; I shall raise him to life on the last day.

Prayer after Communion
Lord,
may this eucharist increase within us
the healing power of your love.
May it guide and direct our efforts
to please you in all things.

TWENTY-SECOND SUNDAY
IN ORDINARY TIME   A

Christ Who Overcame The Reluctance Of The Flesh

It comes to us as no surprise that the Prophet Jeremiah should have felt reluctance to offer himself as a living sacrifice to God's will, because we all experience the same reluctance to accept the cross. But what consolation it is to know that Christ experienced the same reluctance of the flesh and had to struggle to overcome it.

Entrance Antiphon: I call to you all day long, have mercy on me, O Lord. You are good and forgiving, full of love for all who call to you.

Opening Prayer
Let us pray
   [that God will increase our faith
   and bring to perfection the gifts he has given us]

Almighty God,
every good thing comes from you.
Fill our hearts with love for you,
increase our faith,
and by your constant care
protect the good you have given us.

or

Let us pray
   [to God who forgives all who call upon him]

Lord God of power and might,
nothing is good which is against your will,
and all is of value which comes from your hand.
Place in our hearts a desire to please you
and fill our minds with insight into love,
so that every thought may grow in wisdom
and all our efforts may be filled with your peace.

FIRST READING

A reading from the prophet Jeremiah   20:7-9
The word of the Lord has meant insult for me.

You have seduced me, Lord, and I have let myself be seduced;
you have overpowered me: you were the stronger.
I am a daily laughing-stock,

everybody's butt.
Each time I speak the word, I have to howl
and proclaim: 'Violence and ruin!'
The word of the Lord has meant for me
insult, derision, all day long.
I used to say, 'I will not think about him,
I will not speak in his name any more.'
Then there seemed to be a fire burning in my heart,
imprisoned in my bones.
The effort to restrain it wearied me,
I could not bear it.

This is the word of the Lord

Responsorial Psalm   Ps 62:2-6. 8-9. R̷ v.2
   R̷ **For you my soul is thirsting, O Lord my God.**

1   O God, you are my God, for you I long;
    for you my soul is thirsting.
    My body pines for you
    like a dry, weary land without water.   R̷

2   So I gaze on you in the sanctuary
    to see your strength and your glory.
    For your love is better than life,
    my lips will speak your praise.   R̷

3   So I will bless you all my life,
    in your name I will lift up my hands.
    My soul shall be filled as with a banquet,
    my mouth shall praise you with joy.   R̷

4   For you have been my help;
    in the shadow of your wings I rejoice.
    My soul clings to you;
    your right hand holds me fast.   R̷

SECOND READING
A reading from the letter of St Paul to the Romans   12:1-2
Offer your bodies as a living sacrifice.

Think of God's mercy, my brothers, and worship him, I beg you,
in a way that is worthy of thinking beings, by offering your living
bodies as a holy sacrifice, truly pleasing to God. Do not model
yourselves on the behaviour of the world around you, but let
your behaviour change, modelled by your new mind. This is the
only way to discover the will of God and know what is good,

what it is that God wants, what is the perfect thing to do.

This is the word of the Lord.

Gospel Acclamation   cf. Eph 1:17.18
Alleluia, alleluia!
May the Father of our Lord Jesus Christ
enlighten the eyes of our mind,
so that we can see
what hope his call holds for us.
Alleluia!

GOSPEL

A reading from the holy Gospel according to Matthew   16:21-27
If anyone wants to be a follower of mine, let him renounce himself.

Jesus began to make it clear to his disciples that he was destined to go to Jerusalem and suffer grievously at the hands of the elders and chief priests and scribes, to be put to death and to be raised up on the third day. Then, taking him aside, Peter started to remonstrate with him. 'Heaven preserve you, Lord,' he said. 'This must not happen to you.' But he turned and said to Peter, 'Get behind me, Satan! You are an obstacle in my path, because the way you think is not God's way but man's.'

Then Jesus said to his disciples, 'If anyone wants to be a follower of mine, let him renounce himself and take up his cross and follow me. For anyone who wants to save his life will lose it; but anyone who loses his life for my sake will find it. What, then, will a man gain if he wins the whole world and ruins his life? Or what has a man to offer in exchange for his life?

'For the Son of Man is going to come in the glory of his Father with his angels, and, when he does, he will reward each one according to his behaviour.'

This is the Gospel of the Lord.

Prayer over the Gifts
Lord,
may this holy offering
bring us your blessing
and accomplish within us
its promise of salvation.

Preface of Sundays in Ordinary Time I-VIII, P29-P36

Communion Antiphon: O Lord, how great is the depth of the

kindness which you have shown to those who love you.

or

Happy are the peacemakers; they shall be called sons of God. Happy are they who suffer persecution for justice' sake; the kingdom of heaven is theirs.

Prayer after Communion
Lord,
you renew us at your table with the bread of life.
May this food strengthen us in love
and help us to serve you in each other.

TWENTY-THIRD SUNDAY IN ORDINARY TIME A

Christ Who Paid The Debt Of Love

Christ became our brother and made himself responsible for us, his brothers and sisters. He contracted the debt of mutual love. All he asks of us is that we should do the same.

Entrance Antiphon: Lord, you are just, and the judgements you make are right. Show mercy when you judge me, your servant.

Opening Prayer
Let us pray
    [that we may realise the freedom God has given us
    in making us his sons and daughters]

God our Father,
you redeem us
and make us your children in Christ.
Look upon us,
give us true freedom
and bring us to the inheritance you promised.

or

Let us pray
    [to our just and merciful God]

Lord our God,
in you justice and mercy meet.
With unparalleled love you have saved us from death
and drawn us into the circle of your life.

Open our eyes to the wonders this life sets before us,
that we may serve you free from fear
and address you as God our Father.

FIRST READING

A reading from the prophet Ezekiel   33:7-9

If you do not speak to the wicked man, I will hold you responsible for his death.

The word of the Lord was addressed to me as follows, 'Son of man, I have appointed you as sentry to the House of Israel. When you hear a word from my mouth, warn them in my name. If I say to a wicked man: Wicked wretch, you are to die, and you do not speak to warn the wicked man to renounce his ways, then he shall die for his sin, but I will hold you responsible for his death. If, however, you do warn a wicked man to renounce his ways and repent, and he does not repent, then he shall die for his sin, but you yourself will have saved your life.'

This is the word of the Lord.

Responsorial Psalm   Ps 94:1-2. 6-9. ℟ v.8

℟   **O that today you would listen to his voice!**
    Harden not your hearts.

1   Come, ring out our joy to the Lord;
    hail the rock who saves us.
    Let us come before him, giving thanks,
    with songs let us hail the Lord.   ℟

2   Come in; let us bow and bend low;
    let us kneel before the God who made us
    for he is our God and we
    the people who belong to his pasture,
    the flock that is led by his hand.   ℟

3   O that today you would listen to his voice!
    'Harden not your hearts as at Meribah,
    as on that day at Massah in the desert
    when your fathers put me to the test;
    when they tried me, though they saw my work.   ℟

SECOND READING

A reading from the letter of St Paul to the Romans 13:8-10

Love is the answer to every one of the commandments.

Avoid getting into debt, except the debt of mutual love. If you love your fellow men you have carried out your obligations. All the commandments: You shall not commit adultery, you shall not kill, you shall not steal, you shall not covet, and so on, are summed up in this single command: You must love your neighbour as yourself. Love is the one thing that cannot hurt your neighbour; that is why it is the answer to every one of the commandments.

This is the word of the Lord.

Gospel Acclamation Jn 17:17

Alleluia, alleluia!
Your word is truth, O Lord,
consecrate us in the truth.
Alleluia!

or 2 Cor 5:19

Alleluia, alleluia!
God in Christ was reconciling the world to himself,
and he has entrusted to us the news that they are reconciled.
Alleluia!

GOSPEL

A reading from the holy Gospel according to Matthew 18:15-20

If he listens to you, you have won back your brother.

Jesus said to his disciples: If your brother does something wrong, go and have it out with him alone, between your two selves. If he listens to you, you have won back your brother. If he does not listen, take one or two others along with you: the evidence of two or three witnesses is required to sustain any charge. But if he refuses to listen to these, report it to the community; and if he refuses to listen to the community, treat him like a pagan or a tax collector.

'I tell you solemnly, whatever you bind on earth shall be considered bound in heaven; whatever you loose on earth shall be considered loosed in heaven.

'I tell you solemnly once again, if two of you on earth agree to ask anything at all, it will be granted to you by my Father in heaven. For where two or three meet in my name, I shall be there with them.'

This is the Gospel of the Lord.

Prayer over the Gifts
God of peace and love,
may our offering bring you true worship
and make us one with you.

Preface of Sundays in Ordinary Time I-VIII, P29-P36

Communion Antiphon: Like a deer that longs for running streams,
my soul longs for you, my God. My soul is thirsting for the living
God.

or

I am the light of the world, says the Lord; the man who follows
me will have the light of life.

Prayer after Communion
Lord,
your word and your sacrament
give us food and life.
May this gift of your Son
lead us to share his life for ever.

TWENTY-FOURTH SUNDAY IN ORDINARY TIME A

Our Forgiving Lord

*We cannot celebrate today the Lord of compassion and love, the Lord who
died for us and who lives to intercede for us, unless each of us has
forgiven his brother from his heart.*

Entrance Antiphon: Give peace, Lord, to those who wait for you
and your prophets will proclaim you as you deserve. Hear the
prayers of your servant and of your people Israel.

Opening Prayer
Let us pray
    [that God will keep us faithful in his service]

Almighty God,
our creator and guide,
may we serve you with all our heart
and know your forgiveness in our lives.

or

Let us pray

[for the peace which is born of faith and hope]

Father in heaven, Creator of all,
look down upon your people in their moments of need,
for you alone are the source of our peace.
Bring us to the dignity which distinguishes the poor in spirit
and show us how great is the call to serve,
that we may share in the peace of Christ
who offered his life in the service of all.

FIRST READING

A reading from the book of Ecclesiasticus   27:30 – 28:7

*Forgive your neighbour the hurt he does you, and when you pray, your
sins will be forgiven.*

Resentment and anger, these are foul things,
and both are found with the sinner.
He who exacts vengeance will experience the vengeance of the
  Lord,
who keeps strict account of sin.
Forgive your neighbour the hurt he does you,
and when you pray, your sins will be forgiven.
If a man nurses anger against another,
can he then demand compassion from the Lord?
Showing no pity for a man like himself,
can he then plead for his own sins?
Mere creature of flesh, he cherishes resentment;
who will forgive him his sins?
Remember the last things, and stop hating,
remember dissolution and death, and live by the
  commandments.
Remember the commandments, and do not bear your neighbour
  ill-will;
remember the covenant of the Most High, and overlook the
  offence.

This is the word of the Lord.

Responsorial Psalm   Ps 102:1-4. 9-12. R℣ v.8

  R℣ **The Lord is compassion and love,
      slow to anger and rich in mercy.**

1 My soul, give thanks to the Lord,
   all my being, bless his holy name.
   My soul, give thanks to the Lord
   and never forget all his blessings. R℣

(continued)

2 It is he who forgives all your guilt,
who heals every one of your ills,
who redeems your life from the grave,
who crowns you with love and compassion.

℟ **The Lord is compassion and love,
slow to anger and rich in mercy.**

3 His wrath will come to an end;
he will not be angry for ever.
He does not treat us according to our sins
nor repay us according to our faults. ℟

4 For as the heavens are high above the earth
so strong is his love for those who fear him.
As far as the east is from the west
so far does he remove our sins. ℟

SECOND READING

A reading from the letter of St Paul to the Romans 14:7-9
Alive or dead we belong to the Lord.

The life and death of each of us has its influence on others; if we
live, we live for the Lord; and if we die, we die for the Lord, so
that alive or dead we belong to the Lord. This explains why
Christ both died and came to life, it was so that he might be Lord
both of the dead and of the living.

This is the word of the Lord.

Gospel Acclamation 1 Sam 3:9; Jn 6:68
Alleluia, alleluia!
Speak, Lord, your servant is listening:
you have the message of eternal life.
Alleluia!

or Jn 13:34

Alleluia, alleluia!
I give you a new commandmant:
love one another, just as I have loved you,
says the Lord.
Alleluia!

GOSPEL

A reading from the holy Gospel according to Matthew   18:21-35
I do not tell you to forgive seven times, but seventy-seven times.

Peter went up to Jesus and said, 'Lord, how often must I forgive my brother if he wrongs me? As often as seven times?' Jesus answered, 'Not seven, I tell you, but seventy-seven times.

'And so the kingdom of heaven may be compared to a king who decided to settle his accounts with his servants. When the reckoning began, they brought him a man who owed ten thousand talents; but he had no means of paying, so his master gave orders that he should be sold, together with his wife and children and all his possessions, to meet the debt. At this, the servant threw himself down at his master's feet. "Give me time," he said, "and I will pay the whole sum." And the servant's master felt so sorry for him that he let him go and cancelled the debt. Now as this servant went out, he happened to meet a fellow servant who owed him one hundred denarii; and he seized him by the throat and began to throttle him. "Pay what you owe me," he said. His fellow servant fell at his feet and implored him, saying, "Give me time and I will pay you." But the other would not agree; on the contrary, he had him thrown into prison till he should pay the debt. His fellow servants were deeply distressed when they saw what had happened, and they went to their master and reported the whole affair to him. Then the master sent for him. "You wicked servant," he said, "I cancelled all that debt of yours when you appealed to me. Were you not bound, then, to have pity on your fellow servant just as I had pity on you?" And in his anger the master handed him over to the torturers till he should pay all his debt. And that is how my heavenly Father will deal with you unless you each forgive your brother from your heart.'

This is the Gospel of the Lord.

Prayer over the Gifts
Lord,
hear the prayers of your people
and receive our gifts.
May the worship of each one here
bring salvation to all.

Preface of Sundays in Ordinary Time I-VIII, P29-P36

Communion Antiphon: O God, how much we value your mercy!
All mankind can gather under your protection.

or

The cup that we bless is a communion with the blood of Christ; and the bread that we break is a communion with the body of the Lord.

Prayer after Communion

Lord,
may the eucharist you have given us
influence our thoughts and actions.
May your Spirit guide and direct us in your way.

TWENTY-FIFTH SUNDAY IN ORDINARY TIME A

The Generous Love Of God

The love of God cannot be measured by any human standard. It is incalculable. By human reckoning it must even appear foolish. What sensible employer would behave like the man in the Gospel parable? We see a reflection of that love in St Paul's dilemma. He loved so much that he could not decide whether it was better to live or to die.

Entrance Antiphon: I am the Saviour of all people, says the Lord. Whatever their troubles, I will answer their cry, and I will always be their Lord.

Opening Prayer

Let us pray
    [that we will grow in the love of God
    and of one another]

Father,
guide us, as you guide creation
according to your law of love.
May we love one another
and come to perfection
in the eternal life prepared for us.

or

Let us pray
    [to the Lord who is a God of love to all peoples]

Father in heaven,
the perfection of justice is found in your love
and all mankind is in need of your law.

Help us to find this love in each other
that justice may be attained
through obedience to your law.

FIRST READING

A reading from the prophet Isaiah 55:6-9
My thoughts are not your thoughts.

Seek the Lord while he is still to be found,
call to him while he is still near.
Let the wicked man abandon his way,
the evil man his thoughts.
Let him turn back to the Lord who will take pity on him,
to our God who is rich in forgiving;
for my thoughts are not your thoughts,
my ways not your ways – it is the Lord who speaks.
Yes, the heavens are as high above earth
as my ways are above your ways,
my thoughts above your thoughts.

This is the word of the Lord.

Responsorial Psalm Ps 144:2-3, 8-9, 17-18. R̷ v.18
R̷ **The Lord is close to all who call him.**

1 I will bless you day after day
   and praise your name for ever.
   The Lord is great, highly to be praised,
   his greatness cannot be measured. R̷

2 The Lord is kind and full of compassion,
   slow to anger, abounding in love.
   How good is the Lord to all,
   compassionate to all his creatures. R̷

3 The Lord is just in all his ways
   and loving in all his deeds.
   He is close to all who call him,
   who call on him from their hearts. R̷

SECOND READING

A reading from the letter of St Paul to the Philippians 1:20-24. 27
Life to me is Christ.

Christ will be glorified in my body, whether by my life or by my
death. Life to me, of course, is Christ, but then death would

bring me something more; but then again, if living in this body
means doing work which is having good results – I do not know
what I should choose. I am caught in this dilemma: I want to be
gone and be with Christ, which would be very much the better,
but for me to stay alive in this body is a more urgent need for
your sake.

Avoid anything in your everyday lives that would be
unworthy of the gospel of Christ.

This is the word of the Lord.

Gospel Acclamation   Lk 19:38
Alleluia, alleluia!
Blessings on the King who comes,
in the name of the Lord!
Peace in heaven
and glory in the highest heavens!
Alleluia!

or   cf. Acts 16:14

Alleluia, alleluia!
Open our heart, O Lord,
to accept the words of your Son.
Alleluia!

GOSPEL

A reading from the holy Gospel according to Matthew   20:1-16
Why be envious because I am generous?

Jesus said to his disciples: 'The kingdom of heaven is like a
landowner going out at daybreak to hire workers for his vineyard. He made an agreement with the workers for one denarius a
day, and sent them to his vineyard. Going out at about the third
hour he saw others standing idle in the market place and said to
them, "You go to my vineyard too and I will give you a fair
wage." So they went. At about the sixth hour and again at about
the ninth hour, he went out and did the same. Then at about the
eleventh hour he went out and found more men standing round,
and he said to them, "Why have you been standing here idle all
day?" "Because no one has hired us" they answered. He said to
them, "You go into my vineyard too". In the evening, the owner
of the vineyard said to his bailiff, "Call the workers and pay them
their wages, starting with the last arrivals and ending with the
first." So those who were hired at about the eleventh hour

came forward and received one denarius each. When the first came, they expected to get more, but they too received one denarius each. They took it, but grumbled at the landowner. "The men who came last" they said "have done only one hour, and you have treated them the same as us, though we have done a heavy day's work in all the heat." He answered one of them and said, "My friend, I am not being unjust to you; did we not agree on one denarius? Take your earnings and go. I choose to pay the last-comer as much as I pay you. Have I no right to do what I like with my own? Why be envious because I am generous?" Thus the last will be first, and the first, last.'

This is the Gospel of the Lord.

Prayer over the Gifts
Lord,
may these gifts which we now offer
to show our belief and our love
be pleasing to you.
May they become for us
the eucharist of Jesus Christ your Son,
who is Lord for ever and ever.

Preface of Sundays in Ordinary Time I-VIII, P29-P36

Communion Antiphon: You have laid down your precepts to be faithfully kept. May my footsteps be firm in keeping your commands.

or

I am the Good Shepherd, says the Lord; I know my sheep, and mine know me.

Prayer after Communion
Lord,
help us with your kindness
Make us strong through the eucharist.
May we put into action
the saving mystery we celebrate.

TWENTY-SIXTH SUNDAY IN ORDINARY TIME A

Christ Obedient Unto Death
We celebrate Christ who obeyed his Father's will not only in word but also in deed. And Christ assures us that it is not too late to turn to God and to do his will.

Entrance Antiphon: O Lord, you had just cause to judge men as you did: because we sinned against you and disobeyed your will. But now show us your greatness of heart, and treat us with your unbounded kindness.

Opening Prayer
Let us pray
    [for God's forgiveness
    and for the happiness it brings]

Father,
you show your almighty power
in your mercy and forgiveness.
Continue to fill us with your gifts of love.
Help us to hurry toward the eternal life you promise
and come to share in the joys of your kingdom.

or

Let us pray
    [for the peace of the kingdom
    which we have been promised]

Father of our Lord Jesus Christ,
in your unbounded mercy
you have revealed the beauty of your power
through your constant forgiveness of our sins.

May the power of this love be in our hearts
to bring your pardon and your kingdom to all we meet.

FIRST READING
A reading from the prophet Ezekiel   18:25-28
When the sinner renounces sin, he shall certainly live.

The word of the Lord was addressed to me as follows: 'You object, "What the Lord does is unjust." Listen, you House of Israel: is what I do unjust? Is it not what you do that is unjust? When the upright man renounces his integrity to commit sin and dies because of this, he dies because of the evil that he himself has committed. When the sinner renounces sin to become law-abiding and honest, he deserves to live. He has chosen to renounce all his previous sins; he shall certainly live; he shall not die.'

This is the word of the Lord.

Responsorial Psalm   Ps 24:4-9. ℟ v.6
 ℟ **Remember your mercy, Lord.**

1 Lord, make me know your ways.
  Lord, teach me your paths.
  Make me walk in your truth, and teach me:
  for you are God my saviour. ℟

2 Remember your mercy, Lord,
  and the love you have shown from of old.
  Do not remember the sins of my youth.
  In your love remember me,
  because of your goodness, O Lord. ℟

3 The Lord is good and upright.
  He shows the path to those who stray,
  he guides the humble in the right path;
  he teaches his way to the poor. ℟

SECOND READING

A reading from the letter of St Paul to the Philippians   2:1-11
In your minds you must be the same as Christ Jesus.

If our life in Christ means anything to you, if love can persuade at all, or the Spirit that we have in common, or any tenderness and sympathy, then be united in your convictions and united in your love, with a common purpose and a common mind. That is the one thing which would make me completely happy. There must be no competition among you, no conceit; but everybody is to be self-effacing. Always consider the other person to be better than your self, so that nobody thinks of his own interests first but everybody thinks of other people's interests instead. In your minds you must be the same as Christ Jesus:

 His state was divine,
 yet he did not cling
 to his equality with God
 but emptied himself

to assume the condition of a slave,
and became as men are;
and being as all men are,
he was humbler yet,
even to accepting death,
death on a cross.
But God raised him high
and gave him the name
which is above all other names
so that all beings
in the heavens, on earth and in the underworld,
should bend the knee at the name of Jesus
and that every tongue should acclaim
Jesus Christ as Lord,
to the glory of God the Father.

This is the word of the Lord.

*Shorter Form, verses 1-5. Read between *

Gospel Acclamation   Jn 14:23
    Alleluia, alleluia!
    If anyone loves me he will keep my word.
    and my Father will love him,
    and we shall come to him.
    Alleluia!

or   Jn 10:27

    Alleluia, alleluia!
    The sheep that belong to me listen to my voice,
    says the Lord,
    I know them and they follow me.
    Alleluia!

GOSPEL

A reading from the holy Gospel according to Matthew   21:28-32
He thought better of it and went. Tax collectors and prostitutes are
making their way into the kingdom of God before you.

Jesus said to the chief priests and the elders of the people, 'What
is your opinion? A man had two sons. He went and said to the
first, "My boy, you go and work in the vineyard today." He
answered, "I will not go", but afterwards thought better of it and
went. The man then went and said the same thing to the second
who answered, "Certainly, sir", but did not go. Which of the two

did the father's will?' 'The first' they said. Jesus said to them, 'I tell you solemnly, tax collectors and prostitutes are making their way into the kingdom of God before you. For John came to you, a pattern of true righteousness, but you did not believe him, and yet the tax collectors and prostitutes did. Even after seeing that, you refused to think better of it and believe in him.'

This is the Gospel of the Lord.

Prayer over the Gifts
God of mercy,
accept our offering
and make it a source of blessing for us.

Preface of Sundays in Ordinary Time I-VIII, P29-P36

Communion Antiphon: O Lord, remember the words you spoke to me, your servant, which made me live in hope and consoled me when I was downcast.
or

This is how we know what love is: Christ gave up his life for us; and we too must give up our lives for our brothers.

Prayer after Communion
Lord,
may this eucharist
in which we proclaim the death of Christ
bring us salvation
and make us one with him in glory,
for he is Lord for ever and ever.

TWENTY-SEVENTH SUNDAY   A
IN ORDINARY TIME

The Vineyard Of The Lord

The Church rejoices in being the vineyard of the Lord. At the same time we have cause here for much heart-searching and prayer.

Entrance Antiphon: O Lord, you have given everything its place in the world, and no one can make it otherwise. For it is your creation, the heavens and the earth and the stars: you are the Lord of all.

Opening Prayer
Let us pray
    [that God will forgive our failings
    and bring us peace]

Father,
your love for us
surpasses all our hopes and desires.
Forgive our failings,
keep us in your peace
and lead us in the way of salvation.

or

Let us pray
    [before the face of God, in trusting faith]

Almighty and eternal God,
Father of the world to come,
your goodness is beyond what our spirit can touch
and your strength is more than the mind can bear.
Lead us to seek beyond our reach
and give us the courage to stand before your truth.

FIRST READING

A reading from the prophet Isaiah   5:1-7
The vineyard of the Lord of hosts is the House of Lords.

Let me sing to my friend
the song of his love for his vineyard.
My friend had a vineyard
on a fertile hillside.
He dug the soil, cleared it of stones,
and planted choice vines in it.
In the middle he built a tower,
he dug a press there too.
He expected it to yield grapes,
but sour grapes were all that it gave.

And now, inhabitants of Jerusalem
and men of Judah,
I ask you to judge
between my vineyard and me.
What could I have done for my vineyard
that I have not done?
I expected it to yield grapes.

Why did it yield sour grapes instead?

Very well, I will tell you
what I am going to do to my vineyard:
I will take away its hedge for it to be grazed on,
and knock down its wall for it to be trampled on.
I will lay it waste, unpruned, undug;
overgrown by the briar and the thorn.
I will command the clouds
to rain no rain on it.
Yes, the vineyard of the Lord of hosts
is the House of Israel,
and the men of Judah
that chosen plant.
He expected justice, but found bloodshed,
integrity, but only a cry of distress.

   This is the word of the Lord.

Responsorial Psalm   Ps 79:9. 12-16. 19-20. ℟ Is 5:7
   ℟   **The vineyard of the Lord is the House of Israel.**

1   You brought a vine out of Egypt;
    to plant it you drove out the nations.
    It stretched out its branches to the sea,
    to the Great River it stretched out its shoots.   ℟

2   Then why have you broken down its walls?
    It is plucked by all who pass by.
    It is ravaged by the boar of the forest,
    devoured by the beasts of the field.   ℟

3   God of hosts, turn again, we implore,
    look down from heaven and see.
    Visit this vine and protect it,
    the vine your right hand has planted.   ℟

4   And we shall never forsake you again:
    give us life that we may call upon your name.
    God of hosts, bring us back;
    let your face shine on us and we shall be saved.   ℟

SECOND READING

A reading from the letter of St Paul to the Philippians   4:6-9
The God of peace will be with you.

There is no need to worry; but if there is anything you need, pray for it, asking God for it with prayer and thanksgiving, and that peace of God, which is so much greater than we can understand, will guard your hearts and your thoughts, in Christ Jesus. Finally, brothers, fill your minds with everything that is true, everything that is noble, everything that is good and pure, everything that we love and honour, and everything that can be thought virtuous or worthy of praise. Keep doing all the things that you learnt from me and have been taught by me and have heard or seen that I do. Then the God of peace will be with you.

This is the word of the Lord.

Gospel Acclamation   Jn 15:15

Alleluia, alleluia!
I call you friends, says the Lord,
because I have made known to you
everything I have learnt from my Father.
Alleluia!

or   cf. Jn 15:16

Alleluia, alleluia!
I chose you from the world
to go out and bear fruit,
fruit that will last,
says the Lord.
Alleluia!

GOSPEL

A reading from the holy Gospel according to Matthew   21:33-43
He will lease the vineyard to other tenants.

Jesus said to the chief priests and the elders of the people, 'Listen to another parable. There was a man, a landowner, who planted a vineyard; he fenced it round, dug a winepress in it and built a tower; then he leased it to tenants and went abroad. When vintage time drew near he sent his servants to the tenants to collect his produce. But the tenants seized his servants, thrashed one, killed another and stoned a third. Next he sent some more servants, this time a larger number, and they dealt with them in the same way. Finally he sent his son to them. "They will respect my son" he said. But when the tenants saw the son, they said to each other, "This is the heir. Come on, let us kill him and take over his inheritance." So they seized him and threw him out of the vineyard and killed him. Now when the owner of the vineyard comes, what will he do to those tenants?' They answered, 'He will bring those wretches to a wretched end and lease the vineyard to other tenants who will deliver the produce to him when the season arrives.' Jesus said to them, 'Have you never read in the scriptures:

> It was the stone rejected by the builders
> that became the keystone.
> This was the Lord's doing
> and it is wonderful to see?

'I tell you, then, that the kingdom of God will be taken from you and given to a people who will produce its fruit.'

This is the Gospel of the Lord.

Prayer over the Gifts
Father,
receive these gifts
which our Lord Jesus Christ
has asked us to offer in his memory.
May our obedient service
bring us to the fullness of your redemption.
Preface of Sundays in Ordinary Time I-VIII, P29-P36

Communion Antiphon: The Lord is good to those who hope in him, to those who are searching for his love.

or

Because there is one bread, we, though many, are one body, for we all share in the one loaf and in the one cup.

Prayer after Communion
Almighty God,
let the eucharist we share
fill us with your life.
May the love of Christ
which we celebrate here
touch our lives and lead us to you.

TWENTY-EIGHTH SUNDAY IN ORDINARY TIME A

The Lord's Wedding Feast

In Christ Jesus, God fulfils all our needs, as lavishly as only God can. All of us, no matter how unworthy we may be, are invited to the wedding feast of his Son. We have only to enter.

Entrance Antiphon: If you, O Lord, laid bare our guilt, who could endure it? But you are forgiving, God of Israel.

Opening Prayer

Let us pray
   [that God will help us to love one another]

Lord,
our help and guide,
make your love the foundation of our lives.
May our love for you express itself
in our eagerness to do good for others.

or

Let us pray
   [in quiet for the grace of sincerity]

Father in heaven,
the hand of your loving kindness
powerfully yet gently guides all the moments of our day.

Go before us in our pilgrimage of life,
anticipate our needs and prevent our falling.
Send your Spirit to unite us in faith,
that sharing in your service,
we may rejoice in your presence.

FIRST READING

A reading from the prophet Isaiah   25:6-10
The Lord will prepare a banquet, and will wipe away tears from every cheek.

On this mountain,
the Lord of hosts will prepare for all people
a banquet of rich food, a banquet of fine wines,
of food rich and juicy, of fine strained wines.
On this mountain he will remove
the mourning veil covering all peoples,
and the shroud enwrapping all nations,

he will destroy Death for ever.
The Lord will wipe away
the tears from every cheek;
he will take away his people's shame
everywhere on earth,
for the Lord has said so.
That day, it will be said: See, this is our God
in whom we hoped for salvation;
the Lord is the one in whom we hoped.
We exult and we rejoice
that he has saved us;
for the hand of the Lord
rests on this mountain.

This is the word of the Lord.

Responsorial Psalm   Ps 22. ℟ v. 6
  ℟   **In the Lord's own house shall I dwell**
      for ever and ever.

1   The Lord is my shepherd;
    there is nothing I shall want.
    Fresh and green are the pastures
    where he gives me repose.
    Near restful waters he leads me,
    to revive my drooping spirit.   ℟

2   He guides me along the right path;
    he is true to his name.
    If I should walk in the valley of darkness
    no evil would I fear.
    You are there with your crook and your staff;
    with these you give me comfort.   ℟

3   You have prepared a banquet for me
    in the sight of my foes.
    My head you have anointed with oil;
    my cup is overflowing.   ℟

4   Surely goodness and kindness shall follow me
    all the days of my life
    In the Lord's own house shall I dwell
    for ever and ever.   ℟

SECOND READING

A reading from the letter of St Paul
to the Philippians

4:12-14. 19-20

There is nothing I cannot master with the help of the One who gives me strength.

I know how to be poor and I know how to be rich too. I have been through my initiation and now I am ready for anything anywhere: full stomach or empty stomach, poverty or plenty. There is nothing I cannot master with the help of the One who gives me strength. All the same, it was good of you to share with me in my hardships. In return my God will fulfil all your needs, in Christ Jesus, as lavishly as only God can. Glory to God, our Father, for ever and ever. Amen.

This is the word of the Lord.

Gospel Acclamation   Jn 1:12. 14
     Alleluia, alleluia!
     The Word was made flesh and lived among us;
     to all who did accept him
     he gave power to become children of God.
     Alleluia!

or   cf. Eph 1:17.18

     Alleluia, alleluia!
     May the Father of our Lord Jesus Christ
     enlighten the eyes of our mind,
     so that we can see what hope his call holds for us.
     Alleluia!

GOSPEL

A reading from the holy Gospel according to Matthew   22:1-14
Invite everyone you can find to the wedding.

Jesus said to the chief priests and elders of the people: 'The kingdom of heaven may be compared to a king who gave a feast for his son's wedding. He sent his servants to call those who had been invited, but they would not come. Next he sent some more servants. "Tell those who have been invited" he said "that I have my banquet all prepared, my oxen and fattened cattle have been slaughtered, everything is ready. Come to the wedding." But they were not interested: one went off to his farm, another to his business, and the rest seized his servants, maltreated them and killed them. The king was furious. He despatched his troops, destroyed those murderers and burnt their town. Then he said to his servants, ''The wedding is ready; but as those who were invited proved to be unworthy, go to the crossroads in the town and invite everyone you can find to the wedding.'' So these servants went out on to the roads and collected together every-one they could find, bad and good alike; and the wedding hall was filled with guests. When the king came in to look at the guests he noticed one man who was not wearing a wedding garment, and said to him, ''How did you get in here, my friend, without a wedding garment?'' And the man was silent. Then the king said to the attendants, ''Bind him hand and foot and throw him out into the dark, where there will be weeping and grinding of teeth.'' For many are called, but few are chosen.'

This is the Gospel of the Lord.

*Shorter Form, verses 1-10. Read between *

Prayer over the Gifts
Lord,
accept the prayers and gifts
we offer in faith and love.
May this eucharist bring us to your glory.

Preface of Sundays in Ordinary Time I-VIII, P29-P36

Communion Antiphon: The rich suffer want and go hungry, but nothing shall be lacking to those who fear the Lord.
or

When the Lord is revealed we shall be like him, for we shall see him as he is.

Prayer after Communion
Almighty Father,
may the body and blood of your Son
give us a share in his life,
for he is Lord for ever and ever.

TWENTY-NINTH SUNDAY IN ORDINARY TIME A

The Lord Of History

God is king. Earthly rulers, political regimes, Cyrus or Caesar, are called by God to reveal something of his power and majesty and his plan for the human race. But they only hold their power for a day. Our concern is not with them, but with God whom we worship in this celebration.

Entrance Antiphon: I call upon you, God, for you will answer me; bend your ear and hear my prayer. Guard me as the pupil of your eye; hide me in the shade of your wings.

Opening Prayer
Let us pray
   [for the gift of simplicity and joy
   in our service of God and man]

Almighty and ever-living God,
our source of power and inspiration,
give us strength and joy
in serving you as followers of Christ,
who lives and reigns with you and the Holy Spirit,
one God, for ever and ever.

or

Let us pray
   [to the Lord who bends close to hear our prayer]

Lord our God, Father of all,
you guard us under the shadow of your wings
and search into the depths of our hearts.

Remove the blindness that cannot know you
and relieve the fear that would hide us from your sight.

FIRST READING

A reading from the prophet Isaiah   45:1. 4-6
I have taken Cyrus by his right hand to subdue nations before him.

Thus says the Lord to his anointed, to Cyrus,
whom he has taken by his right hand
to subdue nations before him
and strip the loins of kings,
to force gateways before him
that their gates be closed no more:

   It is for the sake of my servant Jacob,
   of Israel my chosen one,
   that I have called you by your name,
   conferring a title though you do not know me.
   I am the Lord, unrivalled;
   there is no other God besides me.
   Though you do not know me, I arm you

that men may know from the rising to the setting of the sun that, apart from me, all is nothing.

This is the word of the Lord.

Responsorial Psalm   Ps 95:1. 3-5. 7-10. ℟ v.7

℟   **Give the Lord glory and power.**

1   O sing a new song to the Lord,
    sing to the Lord all the earth.
    Tell among the nations his glory
    and his wonders among all the peoples.   ℟

2   The Lord is great and worthy of praise,
    to be feared above all gods;
    the gods of the heathens are naught.
    It was the Lord who made the heavens.   ℟

3   Give the Lord, you families of peoples,
    give the Lord glory and power,
    give the Lord the glory of his name.
    Bring an offering and enter his courts.   ℟

4   Worship the Lord in his temple.
    O earth, tremble before him.
    Proclaim to the nations: 'God is king.'
    He will judge the peoples in fairness.   ℟

SECOND READING

A reading from the first letter of St Paul   1:1-5
to the Thessalonians
We constantly remember your faith, your love and your hope.

From Paul, Silvanus and Timothy, to the Church in Thessalonika which is in God the Father and the Lord Jesus Christ; wishing you grace and peace from God the Father and the Lord Jesus Christ.

We always mention you in our prayers and thank God for you all, and constantly remember before God our Father how you have shown your faith in action, worked for love and persevered through hope, in our Lord Jesus Christ.

We know, brothers, that God loves you and that you have been chosen, because when we brought the Good News to you, it came to you not only as words, but as power and as the Holy Spirit and as utter conviction.

This is the word of the Lord.

Gospel Acclamation   Jn 17:17
  Alleluia, alleluia!
  Your word is truth, O Lord,
  consecrate us in the truth.
  Alleluia!

or   Phil 2:15-16

  Alleluia, alleluia!
  You will shine in the world like bright stars
  because you are offering it the word of life.
  Alleluia!

                        GOSPEL
A reading from the holy Gospel according to Matthew   22:15-21
*Give back to Caesar what belongs to Caesar – and to God what belongs to
God.*

The Pharisees went away to work out between them how to trap
Jesus in what he said. And they sent their disciples to him,
together with the Herodians, to say, 'Master, we know that you
are an honest man and teach the way of God in an honest way,
and that you are not afraid of anyone, because a man's rank
means nothing to you. Tell us your opinion, then. Is it permiss-
ible to pay taxes to Caesar or not?' But Jesus was aware of their
malice and replied, 'You hypocrites! Why do you set this trap for
me? Let me see the money you pay the tax with.' They handed
him a denarius and he said, 'Whose head is this? Whose name?'
'Caesar's' they replied. He then said to them, 'Very well, give
back to Caesar what belongs to Caesar – and to God what belongs
to God.'

    This is the Gospel of the Lord.

Prayer over the Gifts
Lord God,
may the gifts we offer
bring us your love and forgiveness
and give us freedom to serve you with our lives.

Preface of Sundays in Ordinary Time I-VIII, P29-P36

Communion Antiphon: See how the eyes of the Lord are on those
who fear him, on those who hope in his love; that he may rescue
them from death and feed them in time of famine.

or

The Son of Man came to give his life as a ransom for many.

Prayer after Communion
Lord,
may this eucharist help us to remain faithful.
May it teach us the way to eternal life.

THIRTIETH SUNDAY IN ORDINARY TIME   A

The Commandment Of Love

Today, through the strength that Christ gives us, we can celebrate with the joy of the Holy Spirit that great commandment of love which once had to be imposed on men under threat of God's avenging anger.

Entrance Antiphon: Let hearts rejoice who search for the Lord. Seek the Lord and his strength, seek always the face of the Lord.

Opening Prayer
Let us pray
   [for the strength to do God's will]

Almighty and ever-living God,
strengthen our faith, hope, and love.
May we do with loving hearts
what you ask of us
and come to share the life you promise.

or

Let us pray
   [in humble hope for salvation]

Praised be you, God and Father of our Lord Jesus Christ.
There is no power for good
which does not come from your covenant,
and no promise to hope in
that your love has not offered.
Strengthen our faith to accept your covenant
and give us the love to carry out your command.

FIRST READING

A reading from the book of Exodus   22:20-26
If you are harsh with the widow, or with the orphan, my anger will flare against you.

The Lord said to Moses, 'Tell the sons of Israel this, "You must not molest the stranger or oppress him, for you lived as strangers in the land of Egypt. You must not be harsh with the widow, or with the orphan; if you are harsh with them, they will surely cry out to me, and be sure I shall hear their cry; my anger will flare and I shall kill you with the sword, your own wives will be widows, your own children orphans.

"If you lend money to any of my people, to any poor man among you, you must not play the usurer with him: you must not demand interest from him.

"If you take another's cloak as a pledge, you must give it back to him before sunset. It is all the covering he has; it is the cloak he wraps his body in; what else would he sleep in? If he cries to me, I will listen, for I am full of pity."'

This is the word of the Lord.

Responsorial Psalm   Ps 17:2-4. 47. 51. R̲ v.2
     R̲ **I love you, Lord, my strength.**

1 I love you, Lord, my strength,
    my rock, my fortress, my saviour.
    My God is the rock where I take refuge;
    my shield, my mighty help, my stronghold.
    The Lord is worthy of all praise:
    when I call I am saved from my foes. R̲

2 Long life to the Lord, my rock!
    Praised be the God who saves me.
    He has given great victories to his king
    and shown his love for his anointed. R̲

SECOND READING

A reading from the first letter of St Paul   1:5-10
to the Thessalonians

You broke with idolatry and became servants of God; you are now
waiting for his Son.

You observed the sort of life we lived when we were with you, which was for your instruction, and you were led to become imitators of us, and of the Lord; and it was with the joy of the Holy Spirit that you took to the gospel, in spite of the great opposition all round you. This has made you the great example to all believers in Macedonia and Achaia since it was from you that the word of the Lord started to spread – and not only throughout Macedonia and Achaia, for the news of your faith in God has spread everywhere. We do not need to tell other people about it: other people tell us how we started the work among you, how you broke with idolatry when you were converted to God and became servants of the real, living God; and how you are now waiting for Jesus, his Son, whom he raised from the dead, to come from heaven to save us from the retribution which is coming.

This is the word of the Lord.

Gospel Acclamation   cf. Acts 16:14
Alleluia, alleluia!
Open our heart, O Lord,
to accept the words of your Son.
Alleluia!

or   Jn 14:23
Alleluia, alleluia!
If anyone loves me he will keep my word,
and my Father will love him,
and we shall come to him.
Alleluia!

GOSPEL
A reading from the holy Gospel according to Matthew   22:34-40
You must love the Lord your God and your neighbour as yourself.

When the Pharisees heard that Jesus had silenced the Sadducees they got together and, to disconcert him, one of them put a question, 'Master, which is the greatest commandment of the Law?' Jesus said, 'You must love the Lord your God with all your heart, with all your soul, and with all your mind. This is the greatest and the first commandment. The second resembles it: you must love your neighbour as yourself. On these two commandments hang the whole Law, and the Prophets also.'

This is the Gospel of the Lord.

Prayer over the Gifts
Lord God of power and might,
receive the gifts we offer
and let our service give you glory.

Preface of Sundays in Ordinary Time I-VIII, P29-P36

Communion Antiphon: We will rejoice at the victory of God and make our boast in his great name.

or

Christ loved us and gave himself up for us a fragrant offering to
God.

Prayer after Communion
Lord,
bring to perfection within us
the communion we share in this sacrament.
May our celebration have an effect in our lives.

THIRTY-FIRST SUNDAY IN ORDINARY TIME A

God's Message Of Eternal Life

*How easy it is for human pride to falsify God's message, to make capital
out of it. Today let us honour God in humility, sincerity and truth.*

Entrance Antiphon: Do not abandon me, Lord. My God, do not go
away from me! Hurry to help me, Lord, my Saviour.

Opening Prayer
Let us pray
    [that our lives will reflect our faith]

God of power and mercy,
only with your help
can we offer you fitting service and praise.
May we live the faith we profess
and trust your promise of eternal life.

or

Let us pray
    [in the presence of God, the source of every good]

Father in heaven, God of power and Lord of mercy,
from whose fullness we have received,
direct our steps in our everyday efforts.
May the changing moods of the human heart
and the limits which our failings impose on hope
never blind us to you, source of every good.

Faith gives us the promise of peace
and makes known the demands of love.
Remove the selfishness that blurs the vision of faith.

FIRST READING

A reading from the prophet Malachi   1:14–2:2. 8-10

You have strayed from the way; you have caused many to stumble by your teaching.

I am a great king, says the Lord of hosts, and my name is feared throughout the nations. And now, priests, this warning is for you. If you do not listen, if you do not find it in your heart to glorify my name, says the Lord of hosts, I will send the curse on you and curse your very blessing. You have strayed from the way; you have caused many to stumble by your teaching. You have destroyed the covenant of Levi, says the Lord of hosts. And so I in my turn have made you contemptible and vile in the eyes of the whole people in repayment for the way you have not kept to my paths but have shown partiality in your administration.

Have we not all one Father? Did not one God create us? Why, then, do we break faith with one another, profaning the covenant of our ancestors?

This is the word of the Lord.

Responsorial Psalm   Ps 130

℟ **Keep my soul in peace before you, O Lord.**

1   O Lord, my heart is not proud
    nor haughty my eyes.
    I have not gone after things too great
    nor marvels beyond me. ℟

2   Truly I have set my soul
    in silence and peace.
    A weaned child on its mother's breast,
    even so is my soul. ℟

3   O Israel, hope in the Lord
    both now and for ever. ℟

SECOND READING

A reading from the first letter of St Paul
to the Thessalonians   2:7-9. 13

We were eager to hand over to you not only the Good News but our whole lives as well.

Like a mother feeding and looking after her own children, we felt so devoted and protective towards you, and had come to love you so much, that we were eager to hand over to you not only the Good News but our whole lives as well. Let me remind you, brothers, how hard we used to work, slaving night and day so as not to be a burden on any one of you while we were proclaiming God's Good News to you.

Another reason why we constantly thank God for you is that as soon as you heard the message that we brought you as God's message, you accepted it for what it really is, God's message and not some human thinking; and it is still a living power among you who believe it.

This is the word of the Lord.

Gospel Acclamation   1 Sam 3:9; Jn 6:68

Alleluia, alleluia!
Speak, Lord, your servant is listening:
you have the message of eternal life.
Alleluia!

or   Mt 23:9. 10

Alleluia, alleluia!
You have only one Father, and he is in heaven;
you have only one Teacher, the Christ!
Alleluia!

GOSPEL

A reading from the holy Gospel according to Matthew   23:1-12
They do not practise what they preach.

Addressing the people and his disciples Jesus said, 'The scribes and the Pharisees occupy the chair of Moses. You must therefore do what they tell you and listen to what they say; but do not be guided by what they do: since they do not practise what they preach. They tie up heavy burdens and lay them on men's shoulders, but will they lift a finger to move them? Not they! Everything they do is done to attract attention, like wearing broader phylacteries and longer tassels, like wanting to take the place of honour at banquets and the front seats in the syna-gogues, being greeted obsequiously in the market squares and having people call them Rabbi.

'You, however, must not allow yourselves to be called Rabbi, since you have only one Master, and you are all brothers. You must call no one on earth your father, since you have only one Father, and he is in heaven. Nor must you allow yourselves to be called teachers, for you have only one Teacher, the Christ. The greatest among you must be your servant. Anyone who exalts himself will be humbled, and anyone who humbles himself will be exalted.'

This is the Gospel of the Lord.

Prayer over the Gifts
God of mercy,
may we offer a pure sacrifice
for the forgiveness of our sins.

Preface of Sundays in Ordinary Time I-VIII, P29-P36

Communion Antiphon: Lord, you will show me the path of life and fill me with joy in your presence.

or

As the living Father sent me, and I live because of the Father, so he who eats my flesh and drinks my blood will live because of me.

Prayer after Communion
Lord,
you give us new hope in this eucharist.
May the power of your love
continue its saving work among us
and bring us to the joy you promise.

THIRTY-SECOND SUNDAY IN ORDINARY TIME A

The Bridegroom Is Here!

The whole of the Christian life, our response to the love of Christ, our waiting with joyful hope for his coming, is summed up in today's celebration in a single word: Wisdom.

Entrance Antiphon: Let my prayer come before you, Lord; listen, and answer me.

Opening Prayer
Let us pray
[for health of mind and body]

God of power and mercy,
protect us from all harm.
Give us freedom of spirit
and health in mind and body
to do your work on earth.

or

Let us pray
[that our prayer rise like incense
in the presence of the Lord]

Almighty Father,
strong is your justice and great is your mercy.
Protect us in the burdens and challenges of life.
Shield our minds from the distortion of pride
and enfold our desire with the beauty of truth.

Help us to become more aware of your loving design
so that we may more willingly give our lives in service to all.

FIRST READING

A reading from the book of Wisdom   6:12-16
Wisdom is found by those who look for her.

Wisdom is bright, and does not grow dim.
By those who love her she is readily seen,
and found by those who look for her.
Quick to anticipate those who desire her, she makes herself
     known to them.
Watch for her early and you will have no trouble;
you will find her sitting at your gates.
Even to think about her is understanding fully grown;
be on the alert for her and anxiety will quickly leave you.
She herself walks about looking for those who are worthy of her
and graciously shows herself to them as they go,
in every thought of theirs coming to meet them.

     This is the word of the Lord.

Responsorial Psalm   Ps 62:2–8. ℟ v.2
     ℟ **For you my soul is thirsting, O God, my God.**

1   O God, you are my God, for you I long;
       for you my soul is thirsting.
       My body pines for you
       like a dry, weary land without water.   ℟

2 So I gaze on you in the sanctuary
   to see your strength and your glory.
   For your love is better than life,
   my lips will speak your praise.   ℟

3 So I will bless you all my life,
   in your name I will lift up my hands.
   My soul shall be filled as with a banquet,
   my mouth shall praise you with joy.   ℟

4 On my bed I remember you.
   On you I muse through the night
   for you have been my help;
   in the shadow of your wings I rejoice.   ℟

SECOND READING

A reading from the first letter of St Paul   4:13-18
to the Thessalonians
God will bring with him those who have died in Jesus.

*We want you to be quite certain, brothers, about those who have
died, to make sure that you do not grieve about them, like the
other people who have no hope. We believe that Jesus died and
rose again, and that it will be the same for those who have died in
Jesus: God will bring them with him.* We can tell you this from
the Lord's own teaching, that any of us who are left alive until
the Lord's coming will not have any advantage over those who
have died. At the trumpet of God, the voice of the archangel will
call out the command and the Lord himself will come down from
heaven; those who have died in Christ will be the first to rise, and
then those of us who are still alive will be taken up in the clouds,
together with them, to meet the Lord in the air. So we shall stay
with the Lord for ever. With such thoughts as these you should
comfort one another.

   This is the word of the Lord.

*Shorter Form, verses 13-14. Read between *

Gospel Acclamation   Mt 24:42. 44
   Alleluia, alleluia!
   Stay awake and stand ready,
   because you do not know the hour
   when the Son of Man is coming.
   Alleluia!

GOSPEL

A reading from the holy Gospel according to Matthew   25:1-13
The bridegroom is here! Go out and meet him.

Jesus told this parable to his disciples: 'The kingdom of heaven will be like this: Ten bridesmaids took their lamps and went to meet the bridegroom. Five of them were foolish and five were sensible: the foolish ones did take their lamps, but they brought no oil, whereas the sensible ones took flasks of oil as well as their lamps. The bridegroom was late, and they all grew drowsy and fell asleep. But at midnight there was a cry, "The bridegroom is here! Go out and meet him." At this, all those bridesmaids woke up and trimmed their lamps, and the foolish ones said to the sensible ones, "Give us some of your oil: our lamps are going out." But they replied, "There may not be enough for us and for you; you had better go to those who sell it and buy some for yourselves." They had gone off to buy it when the bridegroom arrived. Those who were ready went in with him to the wedding hall and the door was closed. The other bridesmaids arrived later. "Lord, Lord," they said "open the door for us." But he replied, "I tell you solemnly, I do not know you." So stay awake, because you do not know either the day or the hour.'

This is the Gospel of the Lord.

Prayer over the Gifts
God of mercy,
in this eucharist we proclaim the death of the Lord.
Accept the gifts we present
and help us follow him with love,
for he is Lord for ever and ever.

Preface of Sundays in Ordinary Time I-VIII, P29-P36

Communion Antiphon: The Lord is my shepherd; there is nothing I shall want. In green pastures he gives me rest, he leads me beside the waters of peace.
or
The disciples recognised the Lord Jesus in the breaking of bread.

Prayer after Communion
Lord,
we thank you for the nourishment you give us
through your holy gift.
Pour out your Spirit upon us

and in the strength of this food from heaven
keep us single-minded in your service.

THIRTY-THIRD SUNDAY IN ORDINARY TIME A

Christ, The Head Of His Household

*Christ's family, the Church, today holds festival in honour of its Head,
and brings to him the talents of a good wife, devoted sons, and faithful
servants.*

Entrance Antiphon: The Lord says: my plans for you are peace and
not disaster; when you call to me, I will listen to you, and I will
bring you back to the place from which I exiled you.

Opening Prayer
Let us pray
   [that God will help us to be faithful]

Father of all that is good,
keep us faithful in serving you,
for to serve you is our lasting joy.
or
Let us pray
   [with hearts that long for peace]

Father in heaven,
ever-living source of all that is good,
from the beginning of time you promised man salvation
through the future coming of your Son, our Lord Jesus Christ.

Help us to drink of his truth
and expand our hearts with the joy of his promises,
so that we may serve you in faith and in love
and know for ever the joy of your presence.

FIRST READING

A reading from the book of Proverbs   31:10-13. 19-20. 30-31
A perfect wife – who can find her?

A perfect wife – who can find her?
She is far beyond the price of pearls.
Her husband's heart has confidence in her,
from her he will derive no little profit.
Advantage and not hurt she brings him

all the days of her life.
She is always busy with wool and with flax,
she does her work with eager hands.
She sets her hands to the distaff,
her fingers grasp the spindle.
She holds out her hand to the poor,
she opens her arms to the needy.
Charm is deceitful, and beauty empty;
the woman who is wise is the one to praise.
Give her a share in what her hands have worked for,
and let her works tell her praises at the city gates.

This is the word of the Lord.

Responsorial Psalm   Ps 127:1-5. R̥ v.1
R̥   **O blessed are those who fear the Lord.**

1   O blessed are those who fear the Lord
and walk in his ways!
By the labour of your hands you shall eat.
You will be happy and prosper.   R̥

2   Your wife like a fruitful vine
in the heart of your house;
your children like shoots of the olive,
around your table.   R̥

3   Indeed thus shall be blessed
the man who fears the Lord.
May the Lord bless you from Zion
in a happy Jerusalem
all the days of your life.   R̥

SECOND READING

A reading from the first letter of St Paul   5:1-6
to the Thessalonians
Let not the Day of the Lord overtake you like a thief.

You will not be expecting us to write anything to you, brothers,
about 'times and seasons', since you know very well that the Day
of the Lord is going to come like a thief in the night. It is when
people are saying, 'How quiet and peaceful it is' that the worst
suddenly happens, as suddenly as labour pains come on a
pregnant woman; and there will be no way for anybody to evade
it.

But it is not as if you live in the dark, my brothers, for that

Day to overtake you like a thief. No, you are all sons of light and sons of the day: we do not belong to the night or to darkness, so we should not go on sleeping, as everyone else does, but stay wide awake and sober.

This the word of the Lord.

Gospel Acclamation   Apoc 2:10
    Alleluia, alleluia!
    Even if you have to die, says the Lord,
    keep faithful, and I will give you
    the crown of life.
    Alleluia!

or   Jn 15:4.5

    Alleluia, alleluia!
    Make your home in me, as I make mine in you,
    says the Lord.
    Whoever remains in me bears fruit in plenty.
    Alleluia!

GOSPEL

A reading from the holy Gospel according to Matthew   25:14-30
You have been faithful in small things; come and join in your master's happiness.

Jesus spoke this parable to his disciples: 'The kingdom of heaven is like a man on his way abroad who summoned his servants and entrusted his property to them. To one he gave five talents, to another two, to a third one; each in proportion to his ability. Then he set out.

The man who had received the five talents promptly went and traded with them and made five more. The man who had received two made two more in the same way. But the man who had received one went off and dug a hole in the ground and hid his master's money.

Now a long time after, the master of those servants came back and went through his accounts with them. The man who had received the five talents came forward bringing five more. "Sir," he said " you entrusted me with five talents; here are five more than I have made."

His master said to him, "Well done, good and faithful servant; you have shown you can be faithful in small things, I will trust you with greater; come and join in your master's happiness." Next the man with the two talents came forward. "Sir," he said "you entrusted me with two talents; here are two more that I have made." His master said to him, "Well done, good and faithful servant; you have shown you can be faithful in small things, I will trust you with greater; come and join in your master's happiness." Last came forward the man who had the one talent. "Sir," said he "I had heard you were a hard man, reaping where you have not sown and gathering where you have not scattered; so I was afraid, and I went off and hid your talent in the ground. Here it is; it was yours, you have it back. " But his master answered him, "You wicked and lazy servant! So you knew that I reap where I have not sown and gather where I have not scattered? Well then, you should have deposited my money with the bankers, and on my return I would have recovered my capital with interest. So now, take the talent from him and give it to the man who has the five talents. For to everyone who has will be given more, and he will have more than enough; but from the man who has not, even what he has will be taken away. As for this good-for-nothing servant, throw him out into the dark, where there will be weeping and grinding of teeth." '

　　This is the Gospel of the Lord.

*Shorter Form, verses 14-15, 19-20. Read between *

Prayer over the Gifts
Lord God,
may the gifts we offer
increase our love for you
and bring us to eternal life.

Preface of Sundays in Ordinary Time I-VIII, P29-P36

Communion Antiphon: It is good for me to be with the Lord and to put my hope in him.

or

I tell you solemnly, whatever you ask for in prayer, believe that you have received it, and it will be yours, says the Lord.

Prayer after Communion
Father,
may we grow in love
by the eucharist we have celebrated
in memory of the Lord Jesus,
who is Lord for ever and ever.

Thirty-fourth or Last Sunday in Ordinary Time
OUR LORD JESUS CHRIST, UNIVERSAL KING A
Solemnity

Christ, The King

*Christ is a King on the model of the homeric kings who called themselves
'shepherds of the people'. As a royal shepherd he is leading us to the
Kingdom of his Father.*

Entrance Antiphon: The Lamb who was slain is worthy to receive
strength and divinity, wisdom and power and honour: to him be
glory and power for ever.

Opening Prayer
Let us pray
    [that all men will acclaim Jesus as Lord]

Almighty and merciful God,
you break the power of evil
and make all things new
in your Son Jesus Christ, the King of the universe.
May all in heaven and earth acclaim your glory
and never cease to praise you.

or

Let us pray
    [that the kingdom of Christ
    may live in our hearts and come to our world]

Father all-powerful, God of love,
you have raised our Lord Jesus Christ from death to life,
resplendent in glory as King of creation.

Open our hearts,
free all the world to rejoice in his peace,
to glory in his justice, to live in his love.
Bring all mankind together in Jesus Christ your Son,
whose kingdom is with you and the Holy Spirit,
one God, for ever and ever.

FIRST READING
A reading from the prophet Ezekiel   34:11-12. 15-17
As for you, my sheep, I will judge between sheep and sheep.

The Lord says this: I am going to look after my flock myself and keep all of it in view. As a shepherd keeps all his flock in view when he stands up in the middle of his scattered sheep, so shall I keep my sheep in view. I shall rescue them from wherever they have been scattered during the mist and darkness. I myself will pasture my sheep, I myself will show them where to rest – it is the Lord who speaks. I shall look for the lost one, bring back the stray, bandage the wounded and make the weak strong. I shall watch over the fat and healthy. I shall be a true shepherd to them.

As for you, my sheep, the Lord says this: I will judge between sheep and sheep, between rams and he-goats.

This is the word of the Lord.

Responsorial Psalm   Ps 22:1-3. 5-6. ℟ v.1

℟   **The Lord is my shepherd;**
there is nothing I shall want.

1   The Lord is my shepherd;
there is nothing I shall want.
Fresh and green are the pastures
where he gives me repose.   ℟

2   Near restful waters he leads me,
to revive my drooping spirit.
He guides me along the right path;
he is true to his name.   ℟

3   You have prepared a banquet for me
in the sight of my foes.
My head you have anointed with oil;
my cup is overflowing.   ℟

4   Surely goodness and kindness shall follow me
all the days of my life.
In the Lord's own house shall I dwell
for ever and ever.   ℟

SECOND READING

A reading from the first letter of St Paul   15:20-26. 28
to the Corinthians

He will hand over the kingdom to God the Father; so that God may be all in all.

Christ has been raised from the dead, the first-fruits of all who have fallen asleep. Death came through one man and in the same way the resurrection of the dead has come through one man. Just as all men die in Adam, so all men will be brought to life in Christ; but all of them in their proper order: Christ as the first-fruits and then, after the coming of Christ, those who belong to him. After that will come the end, when he hands over the kingdom to God the Father, having done away with every sovereignty, authority and power. For he must be king until he has put all his enemies under his feet and the last of the enemies to be destroyed is death. And when everything is subjected to him, then the Son himself will be subject in his turn to the One who subjected all things to him, so that God may be all in all.

This is the word of the Lord.

Gospel Acclamation   Mk 11:10
    Alleluia, alleluia!
    Blessings on him who comes in the name of the Lord!
    Blessings on the coming kingdom of our father David!
    Alleluia!

GOSPEL

A reading from the holy Gospel according to Matthew   25:31-46
He will take his seat on his throne of glory, and he will separate men one from another.

Jesus said to his disciples: 'When the Son of Man comes in his glory, escorted by all the angels, then he will take his seat on his throne of glory. All the nations will be assembled before him and he will separate men one from another as the shepherd separates sheep from goats. He will place the sheep on his right hand and the goats on his left. Then the King will say to those on his right hand, "Come, you whom my Father has blessed, take for your heritage the kingdom prepared for you since the foundation of the world. For I was hungry and you gave me food; I was thirsty and you gave me drink; I was a stranger and you made me welcome; naked and you clothed me, sick and you visited me, in prison and you came to see me." Then the virtuous will say to him in reply, "Lord, when did we see you hungry and feed you; or thirsty and give you drink? When did we see you a stranger and make you welcome; naked and clothe you; sick or in prison and go to see you?" And the King will answer, "I tell you solemnly, in so far as you did this to one of the least of these brothers of mine, you did it to me." Next he will say to those on his left hand, "Go away from me, with your curse upon you, to the eternal fire prepared for the devil and his angels. For I was hungry and you never gave me food; I was thirsty and you never gave me anything to drink; I was a stranger and you never made me welcome, naked and you never clothed me, sick and in prison and you never visited me." Then it will be their turn to ask, "Lord, when did we see you hungry or thirsty, a stranger or naked, sick or in prison, and did not come to your help?" Then he will answer, "I tell you solemnly, in so far as you neglected to do this to one of the least of these, you neglected to do it to me." And they will go away to eternal punishment, and the virtuous to eternal life.'

This is the Gospel of the Lord.

Prayer over the Gifts
Lord,
we offer you the sacrifice
by which your Son reconciles mankind.
May it bring unity and peace to the world.
Preface of Christ the King, P51

Communion Antiphon: The Lord will reign for ever and will give his people the gift of peace.

Prayer after Communion
Lord,
you give us Christ, the King of all creation,
as food for everlasting life.
Help us to live by his gospel
and bring us to the joy of his kingdom,
where he lives and reigns for ever and ever.

THIS IS THE GOOD NEWS ABOUT JESUS CHRIST THE SON OF GOD:

THE SEASON OF ADVENT

FIRST SUNDAY OF ADVENT   B

Waiting For The Lord

*Our life is a long vigil, waiting for the Lord to be revealed in all his gory.
We wait with longing and with 'joyful hope', for his Spirit is with us,
and we know that God is faithful to his promises.*

Entrance Antiphon: To you, my God, I lift my soul, I trust in you;
let me never come to shame. Do not let my enemies laugh at me.
No one who waits for you is ever put to shame.

The Gloria is omitted.

Opening Prayer
Let us pray
    [that we may take Christ's coming seriously]

All-powerful God,
increase our strength of will for doing good
that Christ may find an eager welcome at his coming
and call us to his side in the kingdom of heaven
where he lives and reigns with you and the Holy Spirit,
one God, for ever and ever.

or

Let us pray
    [in Advent time
    with longing and waiting
    for the coming of the Lord]

Father in heaven,
our hearts desire the warmth of your love
and our minds are searching for the light of your Word.

Increase our longing for Christ our Saviour
and give us the strength to grow in love,
that the dawn of his coming
may find us rejoicing in his presence
and welcoming the light of his truth.

FIRST READING

A reading from the prophet Isaiah   63:16-17; 64:1. 3-8
Oh, that you would tear the heavens open and come down.

You, Lord, yourself are our Father,
Our Redeemer is your ancient name.
Why, Lord, leave us to stray from your ways
and harden our hearts against fearing you?
Return, for the sake of your servants,
the tribes of your inheritance.
Oh, that you would tear the heavens open and come down
– at your Presence the mountains would melt.
No ear has heard,
no eye has seen
any god but you act like this
for those who trust him.
You guide those who act with integrity
and keep your ways in mind.
You were angry when we were sinners;
we had long been rebels against you.
We were all like men unclean,
all that integrity of ours like filthy clothing.
We have all withered like leaves
and our sins blew us away like the wind.
No one invoked your name
or roused himself to catch hold of you.
For you hid your face from us
and gave us up to the power of our sins.
And yet, Lord, you are our Father;
we the clay, you the potter,
we are all the work of your hand.

    This is the word of the Lord.

Responsorial Psalm   Ps 79:2-3. 15-16. 18-19. ℟. v. 4

℟ **God of hosts, bring us back;**
let your face shine on us and we shall be saved.

1 O shepherd of Israel, hear us,
shine forth from your cherubim throne.
O Lord, rouse up your might,
O Lord, come to our help. ℟

2 God of hosts, turn again, we implore,
look down from heaven and see.
Visit this vine and protect it,
the vine your right hand has planted. ℟

3 May your hand be on the man you have chosen,
the man you have given your strength.
And we shall never forsake you again:
give us life that we may call upon your name. ℟

SECOND READING

A reading from the first letter of St Paul
to the Corinthians   1:3-9
We are waiting for our Lord Jesus Christ to be revealed.

May God our Father and the Lord Jesus Christ send you grace
and peace.

I never stop thanking God for all the graces you have received
through Jesus Christ. I thank him that you have been enriched in
so many ways, especially in your teachers and preachers; the
witness to Christ has indeed been strong among you so that you
will not be without any of the gifts of the Spirit while you are
waiting for our Lord Jesus Christ to be revealed; and he will keep
you steady and without blame until the last day, the day of our
Lord Jesus Christ, because God by calling you has joined you to
his Son, Jesus Christ; and God is faithful.

This is the word of the Lord.

Gospel Acclamation   Ps 84:8
Alleluia, alleluia!
Let us see, O Lord, your mercy
and give us your saving help.
Alleluia!

GOSPEL

A reading from the holy Gospel according to Mark 13:33-37
Stay awake, because you do not know when the master of the house is coming.

Jesus said to his disciples: 'Be on your guard, stay awake, because you never know when the time will come. It is like a man travelling abroad: he has gone from home, and left his servants in charge, each with his own task; and he has told the doorkeeper to stay awake. So stay awake, because you do not know when the master of the house is coming, evening, midnight, cockcrow, dawn; if he comes unexpectedly, he must not find you asleep. And what I say to you I say to all: Stay awake!'

This is the Gospel of the Lord.

Prayer over the Gifts
Father,
from all you give us
we present this bread and wine.
As we serve you now,
accept our offering
and sustain us with your promise of eternal life.

Preface of Advent I, P1

Communion Antiphon: The Lord will shower his gifts, and our land will yield its fruit.

Prayer after Communion
Father,
may our communion
teach us to love heaven.
May its promise and hope
guide our way on earth.

An appropriate Solemn Blessing or Prayer over the People may be used. See pp.90ff.

SECOND SUNDAY OF ADVENT   B

The Good News

Today we celebrate the Good News of God's incredible love for all his people. Every messenger of this Good News says the same thing: he is coming to save you; he will make all things new; prepare a way for him; take him to your heart.

Entrance Antiphon: People of Zion, the Lord will come to save all nations, and your hearts will exult to hear his majestic voice.

The Gloria is omitted.

Opening Prayer
Let us pray
    [that nothing may hinder us
    from receiving Christ with joy]

God of power and mercy,
open our hearts in welcome.
Remove the things that hinder us from receiving Christ with joy,
so that we may share his wisdom
and become one with him
when he comes in glory,
for he lives and reigns with you and the Holy Spirit,
one God, for ever and ever.
or
Let us pray
    [in Advent time
    for the coming Saviour to teach us wisdom]

Father in heaven,
the day draws near when the glory of your Son
will make radiant the night of the waiting world.

May the lure of greed not impede us from the joy
which moves the hearts of those who seek him.
May the darkness not blind us
to the vision of wisdom
which fills the minds of those who find him.

FIRST READING

A reading from the prophet Isaiah   40:1-5. 9-11
Prepare a way for the Lord

'Console my people, console them'

says your God.
'Speak to the heart of Jerusalem
and call to her
that her time of service is ended,
that her sin is atoned for,
that she has received from the hand of the Lord
double punishment for all her crimes.'

A voice cries, 'Prepare in the wilderness
a way for the Lord.
Make a straight highway for our God
across the desert.
Let every valley be filled in,
every mountain and hill be laid low,
let every cliff become a plain,
and the ridges a valley;
then the glory of the Lord shall be revealed
and all mankind shall see it;
for the mouth of the Lord has spoken.'

Go up on a high mountain,
joyful messenger to Zion.
Shout with a loud voice,
joyful messenger to Jerusalem.
Shout without fear,
say to the towns of Judah,
'Here is your God.'

Here is the Lord coming with power,
his arm subduing all things to him.
The prize of his victory is with him,
his trophies all go before him.
He is like a shepherd feeding his flock,
gathering lambs in his arms,
holding them against his breast
and leading to their rest the mother ewes.

This is the word of the Lord.

Responsorial Psalm   Ps 84:9-14. ℟ v.8

   ℟ **Let us see, O Lord, your mercy
      and give us your saving help.**

1   I will hear what the Lord God has to say,
      a voice that speaks of peace,
      peace for his people.

His help is near for those who fear him
and his glory will dwell in our land.   ℟

2   Mercy and faithfulness have met;
    justice and peace have embraced.
    Faithfulness shall spring from the earth
    and justice look down from heaven.   ℟

3   The Lord will make us prosper
    and our earth shall yield its fruit.
    Justice shall march before him
    and peace shall follow his steps.   ℟

SECOND READING

A reading from the second letter of St Peter   3:8-14
We are waiting for the new heavens and new earth.

There is one thing, my friends, that you must never forget: that
with the Lord, 'a day' can mean a thousand years, and a
thousand years is like a day. The Lord is not being slow to carry
out his promises, as anybody else might be called slow; but he is
being patient with you all, wanting nobody to be lost and
everybody to be brought to change his ways. The Day of the Lord
will come like a thief, and then with a roar the sky will vanish,
the elements will catch fire and fall apart, the earth and all that it
contains will be burnt up.

Since everything is coming to an end like this, you should be
living holy and saintly lives while you wait and long for the Day
of God to come, when the sky will dissolve in flames and the
elements melt in the heat. What we are waiting for is what he
promised; the new heavens and new earth, the place where
righteousness will be at home. So then, my friends, while you are
waiting, do your best to live lives without spot or stain so that he
will find you at peace.

This is the word of the Lord.

Gospel Acclamation   Lk 3:4.6
    Alleluia, alleluia!
    Prepare a way for the Lord.
    make his paths straight,
    and all mankind shall see the salvation of God.
    Alleluia!

GOSPEL

A reading from the holy Gospel according to Mark   1:1-8
Make his paths straight.

The beginning of the Good News about Jesus Christ, the Son of God. It is written in the book of the prophet Isaiah:

Look, I am going to send my messenger before you;
he will prepare your way.
A voice cries in the wilderness:
Prepare a way for the Lord,
make his paths straight,

and so it was that John the Baptist appeared in the wilderness, proclaiming a baptism of repentance for the forgiveness of sins. All Judaea and all the people of Jerusalem made their way to him, and as they were baptised by him in the river Jordan they confessed their sins. John wore a garment of camel-skin, and he lived on locusts and wild honey. In the course of his preaching he said, 'Someone is following me, someone who is more powerful than I am, and I am not fit to kneel down and undo the strap of his sandals. I have baptised you with water, but he will baptise you with the Holy Spirit.'

This is the Gospel of the Lord.

Prayer over the Gifts
Lord,
we are nothing without you.
As you sustain us with your mercy,
receive our prayers and offerings.

Preface of Advent I, P1

Communion Antiphon: Rise up, Jerusalem, stand on the heights, and see the joy that is coming to you from God.

Prayer after Communion
Father,
you give us food from heaven.
By our sharing in this mystery,
teach us to judge wisely the things of earth
and to love the things of heaven.

An appropriate Solemn Blessing or Prayer over the People may be used. See pp.90ff.

THIRD SUNDAY OF ADVENT   **B**

Our Joy In Christ

We celebrate our joy in Christ's redeeming work among us, realising that he who is to come is indeed already with us, 'unknown to us.'

Entrance Antiphon: Rejoice in the Lord always; again I say, rejoice! The Lord is near.

The Gloria is omitted.

Opening Prayer
Let us pray
    [that God will fill us with joy
    at the coming of Christ]

Lord God,
may we, your people,
who look forward to the birthday of Christ
experience the joy of salvation
and celebrate that feast with love and thanksgiving.

or

Let us pray
    [this Advent
    for joy and hope in the coming Lord]

Father of our Lord Jesus Christ,
ever faithful to your promises
and ever close to your Church:
the earth rejoices in hope of the Saviour's coming
and looks forward with longing
to his return at the end of time.

Prepare our hearts and remove the sadness
that hinders us from feeling the joy and hope
which his presence will bestow,
for he is Lord for ever and ever.

FIRST READING
A reading from the prophet Isaiah   61:1-2. 10-11
I exult for joy in the Lord.

The spirit of the Lord has been given to me,
for the Lord has anointed me.

He has sent me to bring good news to the poor,
to bind up hearts that are broken;

to proclaim liberty to captives,
freedom to those in prison;
to proclaim a year of favour from the Lord.

'I exult for joy in the Lord,
my soul rejoices in my God,
for he has clothed me in the garments of salvation,
he has wrapped me in the cloak of integrity,
like a bridegroom wearing his wreath,
like a bride adorned in her jewels.

'For as the earth makes fresh things grow,
as a garden makes seeds spring up,
so will the Lord make both integrity and praise
spring up in the sight of the nations.'

This is the word of the Lord.

Responsorial Psalm   Lk 1:46-50. 53-54. R̸ Is 61:10
    R̸ **My soul rejoices in my God.**

1   My soul glorifies the Lord,
    my spirit rejoices in God, my Saviour.
    He looks on his servant in her nothingness;
    henceforth all ages will call me blessed. R̸

2   The Almighty works marvels for me.
    Holy his name!
    His mercy is from age to age,
    on those who fear him. R̸

3   He fills the starving with good things,
    sends the rich away empty.
    He protects Israel, his servant,
    remembering his mercy. R̸

SECOND READING

A reading from the first letter of St Paul   5:16-24
to the Thessalonians
*May you all be kept safe, spirit, soul and body, for the coming of the
Lord.*

Be happy at all times; pray constantly; and for all things give
thanks to God, because this is what God expects you to do in

Christ Jesus.

Never try to suppress the Spirit or treat the gift of prophecy with contempt; think before you do anything – hold on to what is good and avoid every form of evil.

May the God of peace make you perfect and holy; and may you all be kept safe and blameless, spirit, soul and body, for the coming of our Lord Jesus Christ. God has called you and he will not fail you.

This is the word of the Lord.

Gospel Acclamation   Is 61:1 (Lk 4:18)
Alleluia, alleluia!
The spirit of the Lord has been given to me.
He has sent me to bring good news to the poor.
Alleluia!

GOSPEL

A reading from the holy Gospel according to John   1:6-8. 19-28
There stands among you – unknown to you – the one who is coming after me.

A man came, sent by God.
His name was John.
He came as a witness,
as a witness to speak for the light,
so that everyone might believe through him.
He was not the light,
only a witness to speak for the light.
This is how John appeared as a witness. When the Jews sent priests and Levites from Jerusalem to ask him, 'Who are you?' he not only declared, but he declared quite openly, 'I am not the Christ.' 'Well then,' they asked 'are you Elijah?' 'I am not' he said. 'Are you the Prophet?' He answered, 'No.' So they said to him, 'Who are you? We must take back an answer to those who sent us. What have you to say about yourself ?' So John said, 'I am, as Isaiah prophesied:

a voice that cries in the wilderness:
Make a straight way for the Lord.'

Now these men had been sent by the Pharisees, and they put this further question to him, 'Why are you baptising if you are not the Christ, and not Elijah, and not the prophet?' John replied, 'I baptise with water; but there stands among you – unknown to you – the one who is coming after me; and I am not fit to undo his sandal-strap.' This happened at Bethany, on the far side of the Jordan, where John was baptising.

This is the Gospel of the Lord.

Prayer over the Gifts
Lord,
may the gift we offer in faith and love
be a continual sacrifice in your honour
and truly become our eucharist and our salvation.
Preface of Advent I or II, P1 or P2

Communion Antiphon: Say to the anxious: be strong and fear not, our God will come to save us.

Prayer after Communion
God of mercy,
may this eucharist bring us your divine help,
free us from our sins,
and prepare us for the birthday of our Saviour,
who is Lord for ever and ever.

An appropriate Solemn Blessing or Prayer over the People may be used. See pp. 90ff.

FOURTH SUNDAY OF ADVENT B

Mary, The Ark Of God's Covenant

Today's Mass is a great song to the everlasting love of God revealed in his covenant (love-pact) with his people. We praise the mystery of his love kept secret for endless ages, but now revealed through a new ark of the covenant, Mary of Nazareth.

Entrance Antiphon: Let the clouds rain down the Just One, and the earth bring forth a Saviour.

The Gloria is omitted.

Opening Prayer
Let us pray
    [as Advent draws to a close,
    that Christ will truly come into our hearts]

Lord,
fill our hearts with your love,
and as you revealed to us by an angel
the coming of your Son as man,
so lead us through his suffering and death
to the glory of his resurrection,
for he lives and reigns with you and the Holy Spirit,
one God, for ever and ever.

or

Let us pray
[as Advent draws to a close
for the faith that opens our lives
to the Spirit of God]

Father, all-powerful God,
your eternal Word took flesh on our earth
when the Virgin Mary placed her life
at the service of your plan.

Lift our minds in watchful hope
to hear the voice which announces his glory
and open our minds to receive the Spirit
who prepares us for his coming.

FIRST READING

A reading from the second book of Samuel   7:1-5. 8-12. 14. 16
The kingdom of David will always stand secure before the Lord.

Once David had settled into his house and the Lord had given
him rest from all the enemies surrounding him, the king said to
the prophet Nathan, 'Look, I am living in a house of cedar while
the ark of God dwells in a tent.' Nathan said to the king, 'Go and
do all that is in your mind, for the Lord is with you.'

But that very night the word of the Lord came to Nathan:

'Go and tell my servant David, "Thus the Lord speaks: Are
you the man to build me a house to dwell in? I took you from the
pasture, from following the sheep, to be leader of my people
Israel; I have been with you on all your expeditions; I have cut off
all your enemies before you. I will give you fame as great as the
fame of the greatest on earth. I will provide a place for my people
Israel; I will plant them there and they shall dwell in that place
and never be disturbed again; nor shall the wicked continue to
oppress them as they did, in the days when I appointed judges

over my people Israel; I will give them rest from all their enemies.
The Lord will make you great; the Lord will make you a House.
And when your days are ended and you are laid to rest with your
ancestors, I will preserve the offspring of your body after you and
make his sovereignty secure. I will be a father to him and he a son
to me. Your House and your sovereignty will always stand
secure before me and your throne be established for ever." '

This is the word of the Lord.

Responsorial Psalm   Ps 88:2-5. 27. 29. ℟ cf. v.2
   ℟ **I will sing for ever of your love, O Lord.**

1   I will sing for ever of your love, O Lord;
     through all ages my mouth will proclaim your truth.
     Of this I am sure, that your love lasts for ever,
     that your truth is firmly established as the heavens.   ℟

2   'I have made a covenant with my chosen one;
     I have sworn to David my servant:
     I will establish your dynasty for ever
     and set up your throne through all ages.'   ℟

3   He will say to me: 'You are my father,
     my God, the rock who saves me.'
     I will keep my love for him always;
     for him my covenant shall endure.   ℟

SECOND READING

A reading from the letter of St Paul to the Romans   16:25-27
The mystery, which was kept secret for endless ages, is now made clear.

Glory to him who is able to give you the strength to live
according to the Good News I preach, and in which I proclaim
Jesus Christ, the revelation of a mystery kept secret for endless
ages, but now so clear that it must be broadcast to pagans
everywhere to bring them to the obedience of faith. This is only
what scripture has predicted, and it is all part of the way the
eternal God wants things to be. He alone is wisdom; give glory
therefore to him through Jesus Christ for ever and ever. Amen.

This is the word of the Lord.

Gospel Acclamation   Lk 1:38
   Alleluia, alleluia!
   I am the handmaid of the Lord:

let what you have said be done to me.
Alleluia!

GOSPEL

A reading from the holy Gospel according to Luke   1:26-38

Listen! You are to conceive and bear a son.

The angel Gabriel was sent by God to a town in Galilee called
Nazareth, to a virgin betrothed to a man named Joseph, of the
House of David; and the virgin's name was Mary. He went in
and said to her, 'Rejoice, so highly favoured! The Lord is with
you.' She was deeply disturbed by these words and asked herself
what this greeting could mean, but the angel said to her, 'Mary,
do not be afraid; you have won God's favour. Listen! You are to
conceive and bear a son, and you must name him Jesus. He will
be great and will be called Son of the Most High. The Lord God
will give him the throne of his ancestor David; he will rule over
the House of Jacob for ever and his reign will have no end.' Mary
said to the angel, 'But how can this come about, since I am a
virgin?' 'The Holy Spirit will come upon you' the angel answered
'and the power of the Most High will cover you with its shadow.
And so the child will be holy and will be called Son of God. Know
this too: your kinswoman Elizabeth has, in her old age, herself
conceived a son, and she whom people called barren is now in
her sixth month, for nothing is impossible to God.' 'I am the
handmaid of the Lord,' said Mary 'let what you have said be
done to me.' And the angel left her.

This is the Gospel of the Lord.

Prayer over the Gifts
Lord,
may the power of the Spirit,
which sanctified Mary the mother of your Son,
make holy the gifts we place upon this altar.

Preface of Advent II, P2

Communion Antiphon: The Virgin is with child, and shall bear a
son, and she will call him Emmanuel.

Prayer after Communion
Lord,
in this sacrament

we receive the promise of salvation;
as Christmas draws near
make us grow in faith and love
to celebrate the coming of Christ our Saviour,
who is Lord for ever and ever.

An appropriate Solemn Blessing or Prayer over the People may be used. See pp.90ff.

THE SEASON OF CHRISTMAS

CHRISTMAS DAY: VIGIL MASS

See above, pp.126ff.

CHRISTMAS DAY

See above, pp.138ff.

Sunday in the Octave of Christmas

THE HOLY FAMILY OF JESUS, MARY AND JOSEPH   B

Where there is no Sunday occurring between 25 December and 1 January, this feast is celebrated on 30 December, with one reading only before the Gospel.

Holy Family

We celebrate the Holy Family of Nazareth which is the model for all who fear the Lord and walk in his ways.

Entrance Antiphon: The shepherds hastened to Bethlehem, where they found Mary and Joseph, and the baby lying in a manger.

Opening Prayer
Let us pray
   [for peace in our families]

Father,
help us to live as the holy family,

united in respect and love.
Bring us to the joy and peace of your eternal home.

or

Let us pray
[as the family of God,
who share in his life]

Father in heaven, creator of all,
you ordered the earth to bring forth life
and crowned its goodness by creating the family of man.
In history's moment when all was ready,
you sent your Son to dwell in time,
obedient to the laws of life in our world.

Teach us the sanctity of human love,
show us the value of family life,
and help us to live in peace with all men
that we may share in your life for ever.

The First Reading, Psalm, Second Reading and Gospel Acclamation given for Year A, pp.144ff., may be used, with the Gospel below. Or the alternative readings given below may be used.

FIRST READING

A reading from the book of Genesis   15:1-6. 21:1-3
Your heir shall be your own flesh and blood.

The word of the Lord was spoken to Abram in a vision, 'Have no fear, Abram, I am your shield; your reward will be very great'.

'My Lord,' Abram replied 'what do you intend to give me? I go childless...' Then Abram said, 'See, you have given me no descendants; some man of my household will be my heir'. And then this word of the Lord was spoken to him, 'He shall not be your heir; your heir shall be of your own flesh and blood'. Then taking him outside he said, 'Look up to heaven and count the stars if you can. Such will be your descendants' he told him. Abram put his faith in the Lord, who counted this as making him justified.

The Lord dealt kindly with Sarah as he had said, and did what he had promised her. So Sarah conceived and bore a son to Abraham in his old age, at the time God had promised. Abraham named the son born to him Isaac, the son to whom Sarah had given birth.

This is the word of the Lord.

Responsorial Psalm   Ps 104:1-6. 8-9. ℟ vv.7.8

℟   **He, the Lord, is our God.**
      He remembers his covenant for ever.

1   Give thanks to the Lord, tell his name,
      make known his deeds among the peoples.
      O sing to him, sing his praise;
      tell all his wonderful works!   ℟

2   Be proud of his holy name,
      let the hearts that seek the Lord rejoice.
      Consider the Lord and his strength;
      constantly seek his face.   ℟

3   Remember the wonders he has done,
      his miracles, the judgements he spoke.
      O children of Abraham, his servant,
      O sons of the Jacob he chose.   ℟

4   He remembers his covenant for ever,
      his promise for a thousand generations,
      the covenant he made with Abraham,
      the oath he swore to Isaac.   ℟

SECOND READING

A reading from the letter to the Hebrews   11:8. 11-12. 17-19
The faith of Abraham, Sarah, and Isaac.

It was by faith that Abraham obeyed the call to set out for a
country that was the inheritance given to him and his descendants, and that he set out without knowing where he was going.

It was equally by faith that Sarah, in spite of being past the
age, was made able to conceive, because she believed that he
who had made the promise would be faithful to it. Because of
this, there came from one man, and one who was already as good
as dead himself, more descendants than could be counted, as
many as the stars of heaven or the grains of sand on the seashore.

It was by faith that Abraham, when put to the test, offered up
Isaac. He offered to sacrifice his only son even though the
promises had been made to him and he had been told: It is
through Isaac that your name will be carried on. He was
confident that God had the power even to raise the dead; and so,
figuratively speaking, he was given back Isaac from the dead.

This is the word of the Lord.

Gospel Acclamation   Heb 1:1-2
> Alleluia, alleluia!
> At various times in the past
> and in various different ways,
> God spoke to our ancestors through the prophets;
> but in our own time, the last days,
> he has spoken to us through his Son.
> Alleluia!

GOSPEL

A reading from the holy Gospel according to Luke   2:22-40
The child grew, filled with wisdom.

When the day came for them to be purified as laid down by the Law of Moses, the parents of Jesus took him up to Jerusalem to present him to the Lord – observing what stands written in the law of the Lord: Every first-born male must be consecrated to the Lord – and also to offer in sacrifice, in accordance with what is said in the Law of the Lord, a pair of turtledoves or two young pigeons. Now in Jerusalem there was a man named Simeon. He was an upright and devout man; he looked forward to Israel's comforting and the Holy Spirit rested on him. It had been revealed to him by the Holy Spirit that he would not see death until he had set eyes on the Christ of the Lord. Prompted by the Spirit he came to the Temple; and when the parents brought in the child Jesus to do for him what the Law required, he took him into his arms and blessed God; and he said:

> 'Now, Master, you can let your servant go in peace,
> just as you promised;
> because my eyes have seen the salvation
> which you have prepared for all the nations to see,
> a light to enlighten the pagans
> and the glory of your people Israel.'

As the child's father and mother stood there wondering at the things that were being said about him, Simeon blessed them and said to Mary his mother, 'You see this child: he is destined for the fall and for the rising of many in Israel, destined to be a sign that is rejected – and a sword will pierce your own soul too – so that the secret thoughts of many may be laid bare.'

There was a prophetess also, Anna, the daughter of Phanuel, of the tribe of Asher. She was well on in years. Her days of girlhood over, she had been married for seven years before becoming a widow. She was now eighty-four years old and never left the Temple, serving God night and day with fasting and prayer. She came by just at that moment and began to praise God; and she spoke of the child to all who looked forward to the deliverance of Jerusalem.

*When they had done everything the Law of the Lord required, they went back to Galilee, to their own town of Nazareth. Meanwhile the child grew to maturity, and he was filled with wisdom; and God's favour was with him

This is the Gospel of the Lord.*

*Shorter Form, verses 22. 39-40. Read between *

Prayer over the Gifts
Lord,
accept this sacrifice
and through the prayers of Mary, the virgin Mother of God,
and of her husband, Joseph,
unite our families in peace and love.

Preface of Christmas I-III, P3-P5

Communion Antiphon: Our God has appeared on earth, and lived among men.

Prayer after Communion
Eternal Father,
we want to live as Jesus, Mary, and Joseph,
in peace with you and one another.
May this communion strengthen us
to face the troubles of life.

1 January: Octave of Christmas
SOLEMNITY OF MARY, MOTHER OF GOD

See above, pp.146ff.

SECOND SUNDAY AFTER CHRISTMAS

See above, pp.149ff.

6 January (or Sunday between 2 January and 8 January)

THE EPIPHANY OF THE LORD

See above, pp.154ff.

Sunday after 6 January

THE BAPTISM OF THE LORD **B**
First Sunday in Ordinary Time
Feast

This feast is omitted when the Epiphany is celebrated on this Sunday.

The Baptism Of The Lord

The Father anointed his beloved son, Jesus, with the Holy Spirit and with power, to bring healing and peace to all the nations.

Entrance Antiphon: When the Lord had been baptised, the heavens opened, and the Spirit came down like a dove to rest on him. Then the voice of the Father thundered: This is my beloved Son, with him I am well pleased.

Opening Prayer
Let us pray
    [that we will be faithful to our baptism]

Almighty, eternal God,
when the Spirit descended upon Jesus
at his baptism in the Jordan,
you revealed him as your own beloved Son.
Keep us, your children born of water and the Spirit,
faithful to our calling.

or

Father,
your only Son revealed himself to us by becoming man.
May we who share his humanity
come to share his divinity,
for he lives and reigns with you and the Holy Spirit,
one God, for ever and ever.

or

Let us pray
[as we listen to the voice of God's Spirit]

Father in heaven,
you revealed Christ as your Son
by the voice that spoke over the waters of the Jordan.

May all who share in the sonship of Christ
follow in his path of service to man,
and reflect the glory of his kingdom
even to the ends of the earth,
for he is Lord for ever and ever.

The First Reading, Psalm, Second Reading and Gospel Acclamation given for Year A, pp.159ff., may be used, with the Gospel given below. Or the alternative readings given below may be used.

FIRST READING

A reading from the prophet Isaiah   55:1-11

Come to the water. Listen and your soul will live.

Oh, come to the water all you who are thirsty;
though you have no money, come!
Buy corn without money, and eat,
and, at no cost, wine and milk.
Why spend money on what is not bread,
your wages on what fails to satisfy?
Listen, listen to me, and you will have good things to eat
and rich food to enjoy.
Pay attention, come to me;
listen, and your soul will live.

With you I will make an everlasting covenant
out of the favours promised to David.
See, I have made of you a witness to the peoples,
a leader and a master of the nations.
See, you will summon a nation you never knew,
those unknown will come hurrying to you,
for the sake of the Lord your God,
of the Holy One of Israel who will glorify you.

Seek the Lord while he is still to be found,
call to him while he is still near.

Let the wicked man abandon his way,
the evil man his thoughts.
Let him turn back to the Lord who will take pity on him,
to our God who is rich in forgiving;
for my thoughts are not your thoughts,
my ways not your ways – it is the Lord who speaks.
Yes, the heavens are as high above earth
as my ways are above your ways,
my thoughts above your thoughts.

Yes, as the rain and the snow come down from the heavens and
do not return without watering the earth, making it yield and
giving growth to provide seed for the sower and bread for the
eating, so the word that goes from my mouth does not return to
me empty, without carrying out my will and succeeding in what
it was sent to do.

This is the word of the Lord.

Responsorial Psalm   Is 12:2-6. ℟ v.3
   ℟ **With joy you will draw water
      from the wells of salvation.**

1   Truly, God is my salvation,
    I trust, I shall not fear.
    For the Lord is my strength, my song,
    he became my saviour.
    With joy you will draw water
    from the wells of salvation.   ℟

2   Give thanks to the Lord, give praise to his name!
    Make his mighty deeds known to the peoples!
    Declare the greatness of his name.   ℟

3   Sing a psalm to the Lord
    for he has done glorious deeds,
    make them known to all the earth!
    People of Zion, sing and shout for joy
    for great in your midst is the Holy One of Israel.   ℟

SECOND READING

A reading from the first letter of St John   5:1-9
The Spirit and water and blood.

Whoever believes that Jesus is the Christ
has been begotten by God;

and whoever loves the Father that begot him
loves the child whom he begets.
We can be sure that we love God's children
if we love God himself and do what he has commanded us;
this is what loving God is –
keeping his commandments;
and his commandments are not difficult,
because anyone who has been begotten by God
has already overcome the world;
this is the victory over the world –
our faith.
Who can overcome the world?
Only the man who believes that Jesus is the Son of God:
Jesus Christ who came by water and blood,
not with water only,
but with water and blood;
with the Spirit as another witness –
since the Spirit is the truth –
so that there are three witnesses,
the Spirit, the water and the blood,
and all three of them agree.
We accept the testimony of human witnesses,
but God's testimony is much greater,
and this is God's testimony,
given as evidence for his Son.

This is the word of the Lord.

Gospel Acclamation   cf. Jn 1:29
Alleluia, alleluia!
John saw Jesus coming towards him, and said:
This is the Lamb of God who takes away the sin of the world.
Alleluia!

GOSPEL

A reading from the holy Gospel according to Mark   1:7-11

You are my Son, the Beloved; my favour rests on you.

In the course of his preaching John the Baptist said, 'Someone is following me, someone who is more powerful than I am, and I am not fit to kneel down and undo the strap of his sandals. I have baptised you with water, but he will baptise you with the Holy Spirit.'

It was at this time that Jesus came from Nazareth in Galilee and was baptised in the Jordan by John. No sooner had he come up out of the water than he saw the heavens torn apart and the Spirit, like a dove, descending on him. And a voice came from heaven, 'You are my Son, the Beloved; my favour rests on you.'

This is the Gospel of the Lord.

Prayer over the Gifts

Lord,
we celebrate the revelation of Christ your Son
who takes away the sins of the world.
Accept our gifts
and let them become one with his sacrifice,
for he is Lord for ever and ever.

Preface of the Baptism of the Lord, P7

Communion Antiphon: This is he of whom John said: I have seen and have given witness that this is the Son of God.

Prayer after Communion

Lord,
you feed us with bread from heaven.
May we hear your Son with faith
and become your children in name and in fact.

An appropriate Solemn Blessing or Prayer over the People may be used. See pp.90ff.

After the Baptism of the Lord, until Lent, the cycle of Sundays in Ordinary Time begins. The number of Sundays between the Baptism of the Lord and the First Sunday of Lent varies: see the Table of Principal Celebrations.

For the Sundays in Ordinary Time, Year B, see below, pp.584ff.

THE SEASON OF LENT

For a Note on Preparation for Baptism, see above, p.162.

ASH WEDNESDAY

See above, pp.163ff.

FIRST SUNDAY OF LENT   **B**

The Good News Of The Covenant

At the beginning of Lent we renew our response to the Covenant, the pact of love that God made with each of us at our baptism. Imagine what good news it must have been to Noah, alone in a drowned world, when he learned that God's love had not abandoned, nor ever would abandon, the earth and its creatures.

Entrance Antiphon: When he calls to me, I will answer; I will rescue him and give him honour. Long life and contentment will be his.

The Gloria is omitted.

Opening Prayer

Let us pray
    [that this Lent will help us reproduce in our lives
    the self-sacrificing love of Christ]

Father,
through our observance of Lent,
help us to understand the meaning
of your Son's death and resurrection,
and teach us to reflect it in our lives.

or

Let us pray
　　[at the beginning of Lent
　　for the spirit of repentance]

Lord our God,
you formed man from the clay of the earth
and breathed into him the spirit of life,
but he turned from your face and sinned.

In this time of repentance
we call out for your mercy.
Bring us back to you
and to the life your Son won for us
by his death on the cross
for he lives and reigns for ever and ever.

FIRST READING

A reading from the book of Genesis　　　　　9:8-15

God's covenant with Noah after he had saved him from the waters of the flood.

God spoke to Noah and his sons, 'See, I establish my Covenant with you, and with your descendants after you; also with every living creature to be found with you, birds, cattle and every wild beast with you: everything that came out of the ark, everything that lives on the earth. I establish my Covenant with you: no thing of flesh shall be swept away again by the waters of the flood. There shall be no flood to destroy the earth again.'

　　God said, 'Here is the sign of the Covenant I make between myself and you and every living creature with you for all generations: I set my bow in the clouds and it shall be a sign of the Covenant between me and the earth. When I gather the clouds over the earth and the bow appears in the clouds, I will recall the Covenant between myself and you and every living creature of every kind. And so the waters shall never again become a flood to destroy all things of flesh.'

　　This is the word of the Lord.

Responsorial Psalm　　　　　Ps 24:4-9. ℟ cf. v.10
　　℟　**Your ways, Lord, are faithfulness and love**
　　　　for those who keep your covenant.

1　Lord, make me know your ways.
　　Lord, teach me your paths.

Make me walk in your truth, and teach me:
for you are God my saviour.   ℟

2 Remember your mercy, Lord,
and the love you have shown from of old.
In your love remember me,
because of your goodness, O Lord.   ℟

3 The Lord is good and upright.
He shows the path to those who stray,
he guides the humble in the right path;
he teaches his way to the poor.   ℟

SECOND READING

A reading from the first letter of St Peter   3:18-22
That water is a type of the baptism which saves you now.

Christ himself, innocent though he was, died once for sins, died
for the guilty, to lead us to God. In the body he was put to death,
in the spirit he was raised to life, and, in the spirit, he went to
preach to the spirits in prison. Now it was long ago, when Noah
was still building that ark which saved only a small group of eight
people 'by water', and when God was still waiting patiently, that
these spirits refused to believe. That water is a type of the
baptism which saves you now, and which is not the washing off
of physical dirt but a pledge made to God from a good conscience, through the resurrection of Jesus Christ, who has
entered heaven and is at God's right hand, now that he has made
the angels of the Dominations and Powers his subjects.

This is the word of the Lord.

Gospel Acclamation   Mt 4:4
Praise to you, O Christ, king of eternal glory!
Man does not live on bread alone,
but on every word that comes from the mouth of God.
Praise to you, O Christ, king of eternal glory!

GOSPEL

A reading from the holy Gospel according to Mark   1:12-15
Jesus was tempted by Satan, and the angels looked after him.

The Spirit drove Jesus out into the wilderness and he remained
there for forty days, and was tempted by Satan. He was with the
wild beasts, and the angels looked after him.

After John had been arrested, Jesus went into Galilee. There he proclaimed the Good News from God. 'The time has come' he said 'and the kingdom of God is close at hand. Repent, and believe the Good News.'

This is the Gospel of the Lord.

After the Homily, the Election or Enrolment of Candidates for Baptism may take place. See above, pp.173ff.

Prayer over the Gifts

Lord,
make us worthy to bring you these gifts.
May this sacrifice
help to change our lives.

Preface the First Sunday of Lent, P12 or Lent I or II, P8 or P9

Communion Antiphon: Man does not live on bread alone, but on every word that comes from the mouth of God.

or

The Lord will overshadow you, and you will find refuge under his wings.

Prayer after Communion

Father,
you increase our faith and hope,
you deepen our love in this communion.
Help us to live by your words
and to seek Christ, our bread of life,
who is Lord for ever and ever.

An appropriate Solemn Blessing or Prayer over the People may be used. See pp.90ff.

SECOND SUNDAY OF LENT   B

God's Gift To Us: His Son

Abraham was prepared to give God his only son, Isaac, in sacrifice. God would do no less. 'This is my Son, the Beloved,' he says to us. 'Listen to him.'

Entrance Antiphon: Remember your mercies, Lord, your tenderness from ages past. Do not let our enemies triumph over us; O

God, deliver Israel from all her distress.

or

My heart has prompted me to seek your face; I seek it, Lord; do not hide from me.

The Gloria is omitted.

Opening Prayer
Let us pray
     [for the grace to respond
     to the Word of God]

God our Father,
help us to hear your Son.
Enlighten us with your word,
that we may find the way to your glory.

or

Let us pray
     [in this season of Lent
     for the gift of integrity]

Father of light,
in you is found no shadow of change
but only the fullness of life and limitless truth.

Open our hearts to the voice of your Word
and free us from the original darkness that shadows our vision.
Restore our sight that we may look upon your Son
who calls us to repentance and a change of heart,
for he lives and reigns with you for ever and ever.

FIRST READING

A reading from the book of Genesis   22:1-2. 9-13. 15-18
The sacrifice of Abraham, our father in faith.

God put Abraham to the test. 'Abraham, Abraham' he called. 'Here I am' he replied. 'Take your son,' God said 'your only child Isaac, whom you love, and go to the land of Moriah. There you shall offer him as a burnt offering, on a mountain I will point out to you.'

   When they arrived at the place God had pointed out to him, Abraham built an altar there and arranged the wood. Then he stretched out his hand and seized the knife to kill his son.

   But the angel of the Lord called to him from heaven. 'Abraham, Abraham' he said. 'I am here' he replied. 'Do not raise your hand against the boy' the angel said. 'Do not harm him, for now I know you fear God. You have not refused me your son, your only son.' Then looking up, Abraham saw a ram caught by its horns in a bush. Abraham took the ram and offered it as a burnt-offering in place of his son.

The angel of the Lord called Abraham a second time from heaven. 'I swear by my own self – it is the Lord who speaks – because you have done this, because you have not refused me your son, your only son, I will shower blessings on you, I will make your descendants as many as the stars of heaven and the grains of sand on the seashore. Your descendants shall gain possession of the gates of their enemies. All the nations of the earth shall bless themselves by your descendants, as a reward for your obedience.'

This is the word of the Lord.

Responsorial Psalm   Ps 115:10. 15-19. ℟ Ps 114:9

   ℟   **I will walk in the presence of the Lord**
        in the land of the living.

1   I trusted, even when I said:
    'I am sorely afflicted.'
    O precious in the eyes of the Lord
    is the death of his faithful.   ℟

2   Your servant, Lord, your servant am I;
    you have loosened my bonds.
    A thanksgiving sacrifice I make:
    I will call on the Lord's name.   ℟

3   My vows to the Lord I will fulfil
    before all his people,
    in the courts of the house of the Lord,
    in your midst, O Jerusalem.   ℟

SECOND READING

A reading from the letter of St Paul to the Romans   8:31-34
God did not spare his own Son.

With God on our side who can be against us? Since God did not spare his own Son, but gave him up to benefit us all, we may be certain, after such a gift, that he will not refuse anything he can give. Could anyone accuse those that God has chosen? When God acquits, could anyone condemn? Could Christ Jesus? No! He not only died for us – he rose from the dead, and there at

God's right hand he stands and pleads for us.

This is the word of the Lord.

Gospel Acclamation   Mt 17:5
Glory and praise to you, O Christ!
From the bright cloud the Father's voice was heard:
'This is my Son, the Beloved. Listen to him!'
Glory and praise to you, O Christ!

GOSPEL
A reading from the holy Gospel according to Mark   9:2-10
This is my Son, the Beloved.

Jesus took with him Peter and James and John and led them up a
high mountain where they could be alone by themselves. There
in their presence he was transfigured: his clothes became dazzlingly white, whiter than any earthly bleacher could make them.
Elijah appeared to them with Moses; and they were talking with
Jesus. Then Peter spoke to Jesus. 'Rabbi', he said 'it is wonderful
for us to be here; so let us make three tents, one for you, one for
Moses and one for Elijah.' He did not know what to say; they
were so frightened. And a cloud came, covering them in shadow;
and there came a voice from the cloud, 'This is my Son, the
Beloved. Listen to him.' Then suddenly, when they looked
round, they saw no one with them any more but only Jesus.

As they came down the mountain he warned them to tell no
one what they had seen, until after the Son of Man had risen
from the dead. They observed the warning faithfully, though
among themselves they discussed what 'rising from the dead'
could mean.

This is the Gospel of the Lord.

Prayer over the Gifts
Lord,
make us holy.
May this eucharist take away our sins
that we may be prepared
to celebrate the resurrection.

Preface of Second Sunday of Lent, P13, or Preface of Lent I or II,
P8 or P9

Communion Antiphon: This is my Son, my beloved, in whom is all my delight: listen to him.

Prayer after Communion
Lord,
we give thanks for these holy mysteries
which bring to us here on earth
a share in the life to come,
through Christ our Lord.

An appropriate Solemn Blessing or Prayer over the People may
be used. See pp.90ff.

THIRD SUNDAY OF LENT   **B**

Christ, The Wisdom Of God
Today, we celebrate the foolishness of God that is wiser than any human
wisdom: the utter folly of his love that allowed the destruction of the
temple of the body of his Son. And we dedicate ourselves anew to the Law
of the Lord which gives wisdom to the simple.

Entrance Antiphon: My eyes are ever fixed on the Lord, for he
releases my feet from the snare. O look at me and be merciful, for
I am wretched and alone.
or
I will prove my holiness through you. I will gather you from the
ends of the earth; I will pour clean water on you and wash away
all your sins. I will give you a new spirit within you, says the
Lord.

The Gloria is omitted.

Opening Prayer
Let us pray
[for confidence in the love of God
and the strength to overcome all our weakness]

Father,
you have taught us to overcome our sins
by prayer, fasting and works of mercy.
When we are discouraged by our weakness,
give us confidence in your love.
or
Let us pray
[to the Father and ask him
to form a new heart within us]

God of all compassion, Father of all goodness,
to heal the wounds our sins and selfishness bring upon us
you bid us turn to fasting, prayer, and sharing with our brothers.
We acknowledge our sinfulness, our guilt is ever before us:
when our weakness causes discouragement,
let your compassion fill us with hope
and lead us through a Lent of repentance to the beauty of Easter
    joy.

The readings for Year A may be used as alternative readings, see above, pp.179ff. If this is done, the Preface and Communion Antiphon as at Year A are also used. If a pre-baptismal scrutiny is held today, the readings for Year A are mandatory.

FIRST READING

A reading from the book of Exodus   20:1-17
The Law was given through Moses.

*God spoke all these words. He said, 'I am the Lord your God who brought you out of the land of Egypt, out of the house of slavery.

'You shall have no gods except me.*

'You shall not make yourself a carved image or any likeness of anything in heaven or on earth beneath or in the waters under the earth; you shall not bow down to them or serve them. For I, the Lord your God, am a jealous God and I punish the father's fault in the sons, the grandsons, and the great-grandsons of those who hate me; but I show kindness to thousands of those who love me and keep my commandments.

* 'You shall not utter the name of the Lord your God to misuse it, for the Lord will not leave unpunished the man who utters his name to misuse it.*

'Remember the sabbath day and keep it holy. For six days you shall labour and do all your work, but the seventh day is a sabbath for the Lord your God. You shall do no work that day, neither you nor your son nor your daughter nor your servants, men or women, nor your animals nor the stranger who lives with you. For in six days the Lord made the heavens and the earth and the sea and all that these hold, but on the seventh day he rested; that is why the Lord has blessed the sabbath day and made it sacred.

* 'Honour your father and your mother so that you may have a long life in the land that the Lord your God has given to you.

'You shall not kill.

'You shall not commit adultery.

'You shall not steal.

'You shall not bear false witness against your neighbour.

'You shall not covet your neighbour's house. You shall not covet your neighbour's wife, or his servant, man or woman, or his ox, or his donkey, or anything that is his.'

This is the word of the Lord.*

*Shorter Form, verses 1-3. 7-8. 12-17. Read between *

Responsorial Psalm   Ps 18:8-11. ℟ Jn 6:68

℟   **You, Lord, have the message of eternal life.**

1   The law of the Lord is perfect,
    it revives the soul.
    The rule of the Lord is to be trusted,
    it gives wisdom to the simple.   ℟

2   The precepts of the Lord are right,
    they gladden the heart.
    The command of the Lord is clear,
    it gives light to the eyes.   ℟

3   The fear of the Lord is holy,
    abiding for ever.
    The decrees of the Lord are truth
    and all of them just.   ℟

4   They are more to be desired than gold,
    than the purest of gold
    and sweeter are they than honey,
    than honey from the comb.   ℟

SECOND READING

A reading from the first letter of St Paul   1:22-25
to the Corinthians

Here we are preaching a crucified Christ, an obstacle to men, but to those who are called, the wisdom of God.

While the Jews demand miracles and the Greeks look for wisdom, here are we preaching a crucified Christ; to the Jews an obstacle that they cannot get over, to the pagans madness, but to those who have been called, whether they are Jews or Greeks, a Christ who is the power and the wisdom of God. For God's foolishness is wiser than human wisdom, and God's weakness is stronger than human strength.

This is the word of the Lord.

Gospel Acclamation Jn 11:25. 26
> Praise to you, O Christ, king of eternal glory!
> I am the resurrection and the life, says the Lord,
> whoever believes in me will never die.
> Praise to you, O Christ, king of eternal glory!

or Jn 3:16
> Praise to you, O Christ, king of eternal glory!
> God loved the world so much that he gave his only Son;
> everyone who believes in him has eternal life.
> Praise to you, O Christ, king of eternal glory!

GOSPEL

A reading from the holy Gospel according to John 2:13-25

Destroy this sanctuary, and in three days I will raise it up.

Just before the Jewish Passover Jesus went up to Jerusalem, and in the Temple he found people selling cattle and sheep and pigeons, and the money changers sitting at their counters there. Making a whip out of some cord, he drove them all out of the Temple, cattle and sheep as well, scattered the money changers' coins, knocked their tables over and said to the pigeon-sellers, 'Take all this out of here and stop turning my Father's house into a market.' Then his disciples remembered the words of scripture: Zeal for your house will devour me. The Jews intervened and said, 'What sign can you show us to justify what you have done?' Jesus answered, 'Destroy this sanctuary, and in three days I will raise it up.' The Jews replied, 'It has taken forty-six years to build this sanctuary: are you going to raise it up in three days?' But he was speaking of the sanctuary that was his body, and when Jesus rose from the dead, his disciples remembered that he had said this, and they believed the scripture and the words he had said.

During his stay in Jerusalem for the Passover many believed in his name when they saw the signs that he gave, but Jesus knew them all and did not trust himself to them; he never needed evidence about any man; he could tell what a man had in him.

This is the Gospel of the Lord.

After the Homily, the First Scrutiny of Candidates for Baptism may take place. See above, pp.184ff.

Prayer over the Gifts
Lord,
by the grace of this sacrifice
may we who ask forgiveness
be ready to forgive one another.

Preface of Lent I or II, P8 or P9

Communion Antiphon: The sparrow even finds a home, the
swallow finds a nest wherein to place her young, near to your
altars, Lord of hosts, my King, my God! How happy they who
dwell in your house! For ever they are praising you.

Prayer after Communion
Lord,
in sharing this sacrament
may we receive your forgiveness
and be brought together in unity and peace.

An appropriate Solemn Blessing or Prayer over the People may
be used. See pp.90ff.

FOURTH SUNDAY OF LENT   **B**

Christ the Redeemer

*Our sins had made us exiles from God's kingdom. But just as God sent
Cyrus, the King of Persia, to bring his people back from Babylon, so in
his great love he sent his Son, Jesus Christ, to bring us back to the new
Jerusalem 'to live the good life as from the beginning he had meant us to
live it'.*

Entrance Antiphon: Rejoice, Jerusalem! Be glad for her, you who
love her; rejoice with her, you who mourned for her, and you
will find contentment at her consoling breasts.

The Gloria is omitted.

Opening Prayer
Let us pray
        [for a greater faith and love]

Father of peace,
we are joyful in your Word,
your Son Jesus Christ,
who reconciles us to you.

Let us hasten toward Easter
with the eagerness of faith and love.

or

Let us pray
   [that by growing in love this lenten season
   we may bring the peace of Christ to our world]

God our Father,
your Word, Jesus Christ, spoke peace to a sinful world
and brought mankind the gift of reconciliation
by the suffering and death he endured.

Teach us, the people who bear his name,
to follow the example he gave us:
may our faith, hope, and charity
turn hatred to love, conflict to peace, death to eternal life.

The readings for Year A may be used as alternative readings, see
above, pp.187ff. If this is done, the Preface and Communion
Antiphon as at Year A are also used. If a pre-baptismal scrutiny is
held today, the readings for Year A are mandatory.

FIRST READING

A reading from the second book of Chronicles   36:14-16. 19-23

*The wrath and mercy of God are revealed in the exile and in the release of
his people.*

All the heads of the priesthood, and the people too, added
infidelity to infidelity, copying all the shameful practices of the
nations and defiling the Temple that the Lord had consecrated
for himself in Jerusalem. The Lord, the God of their ancestors,
tirelessly sent them messenger after messenger, since he wished
to spare his people and his house. But they ridiculed the
messengers of God, they despised his words, they laughed at his
prophets, until at last the wrath of the Lord rose so high against
his people that there was no further remedy.

   Their enemies burned down the Temple of God, demolished
the walls of Jerusalem, set fire to all its palaces, and destroyed
everything of value in it. The survivors were deported by
Nebuchadnezzar to Babylon; they were to serve him and his sons
until the kingdom of Persia came to power. This is how the word
of the Lord was fulfilled that he spoke through Jeremiah, 'Until
this land has enjoyed its sabbath rest, until seventy years have
gone by, it will keep sabbath throughout the days of its

desolation.'

And in the first year of Cyrus king of Persia, to fulfil the word of the Lord that was spoken through Jeremiah, the Lord roused the spirit of Cyrus king of Persia to issue a proclamation and to have it publicly displayed throughout his kingdom: 'Thus speaks Cyrus king of Persia, "The Lord, the God of heaven, has given me all the kingdoms of the earth; he has ordered me to build him a Temple in Jerusalem, in Judah. Whoever there is among you of all his people, may his God be with him! Let him go up."'

This is the word of the Lord.

Responsorial Psalm   Ps 136:1-6. ℟ v.6

   ℟   **O let my tongue**
       cleave to my mouth
       if I remember you not!

1   By the rivers of Babylon
    there we sat and wept,
    remembering Zion;
    on the poplars that grew there
    we hung up our harps. ℟

2   For it was there that they asked us,
    our captors, for songs,
    our oppressors, for joy.
    'Sing to us,' they said,
    'one of Zion's songs.' ℟

3   O how could we sing
    the song of the Lord
    on alien soil?
    If I forget you, Jerusalem,
    let my right hand wither! ℟

4   O let my tongue
    cleave to my mouth
    if I remember you not,
    if I prize not Jerusalem
    above all my joys! ℟

SECOND READING

A reading from the letter of St Paul to the Ephesians   2:4-10
You who were dead through your sins have been saved through grace.

God loved us with so much love that he was generous with his mercy: when we were dead through our sins, he brought us to life with Christ – it is through grace that you have been saved – and raised us up with him and gave us a place with him in heaven, in Christ Jesus.

This was to show for all ages to come, through his goodness towards us in Christ Jesus, how infinitely rich he is in grace. Because it is by grace that you have been saved, through faith; not by anything of your own, but by a gift from God; not by anything that you have done, so that nobody can claim the credit. We are God's work of art, created in Christ Jesus to live the good life as from the beginning he had meant us to live it.

This is the word of the Lord.

Gospel Acclamation   Jn 3:16
> Glory and praise to you, O Christ!
> God loved the world so much that he gave his only Son;
> everyone who believes in him has eternal life.
> Glory and praise to you, O Christ!

GOSPEL

A reading from the holy Gospel according to John   3:14-21
God send his Son so that through him the world might be saved.

Jesus said to Nicodemus:

> 'The Son of Man must be lifted up
> as Moses lifted up the serpent in the desert,
> so that everyone who believes may have eternal life in him.
> Yes, God loved the world so much
> that he gave his only Son,
> so that everyone who believes in him may not be lost
> but may have eternal life.
> For God sent his Son into the world
> not to condemn the world,
> but so that through him the world might be saved.
> No one who believes in him will be condemned;
> but whoever refuses to believe is condemned already,
> because he has refused to believe
> in the name of God's only Son.
> On these grounds is sentence pronounced:
> that though the light has come into the world
> men have shown they prefer
> darkness to the light

because their deeds were evil.
And indeed, everybody who does wrong
hates the light and avoids it,
for fear his actions should be exposed;
but the man who lives by the truth
comes out into the light,
so that it may be plainly seen that what he does is done in
  God.'

This is the Gospel of the Lord.

After the Homily, the Second Scrutiny of Candidates for Baptism
may take place. See above, pp.192ff.

Prayer over the Gifts
Lord,
we offer you these gifts
which bring us peace and joy.
Increase our reverence by this eucharist,
and bring salvation to the world.

Preface of Lent I or II, P8 or P9

Communion Antiphon: To Jerusalem, that binds them together in
unity, the tribes of the Lord go up to give him praise.

Prayer after Communion
Father,
you enlighten all whom come into the world.
Fill our hearts with the light of your gospel,
that our thoughts may please you,
and our love be sincere.

An appropriate Solemn Blessing or Prayer over the People may
be used. See pp.90ff.

FIFTH SUNDAY OF LENT   B

Entrance Antiphon: Give me justice, O God, and defend my cause
against the wicked; rescue me from deceitful and unjust men.
You, O God, are my refuge.

The Gloria is omitted.

Opening Prayer

Let us pray
   [for the courage to follow Christ]

Father,
help us to be like Christ your Son,
who loved the world and died for our salvation.
Inspire us by his love,
guide us by his example,
who lives and reigns with you and the Holy Spirit,
one God, for ever and ever.

or

Let us pray
   [for the courage to embrace the world
   in the name of Christ]

Father in heaven,
the love of your Son led him to accept the suffering of the cross
that his brothers might glory in new life.
Change our selfishness into self-giving.
Help us to embrace the world you have given us,
that we may transform the darkness of its pain
into the life and joy of Easter.

The readings for Year A may be used as alternative readings, see
above, pp.194ff. If this is done, the Preface and Communion
Antiphon as at Year A are used. If a pre-baptismal scrutiny is
held today, the readings for Year A are mandatory.

FIRST READING

A reading from the prophet Jeremiah   31:31-34
I will make a new covenant and never call their sin to mind.

See, the days are coming – it is the Lord who speaks – when I will
make a new covenant with the House of Israel and the House of
Judah, but not a covenant like the one I made with their ancestors
on the day I took them by the hand to bring them out of the land
of Egypt. They broke that covenant of mine, so I had to show
them who was master. It is the Lord who speaks. No, this is the
covenant I will make with the House of Israel when those days
arrive – it is the Lord who speaks. Deep within them I will

plant my Law, writing it on their hearts. Then I will be their God and they shall be my people. There will be no further need for neighbour to try to teach neighbour, or brother to say to brother, 'Learn to know the Lord!' No, they will all know me, the least no less than the greatest – it is the Lord who speaks – since I will forgive their iniquity and never call their sin to mind.

This is the word of the Lord.

Responsorial Psalm Ps 50:3-4. 12-15. ℟ v.12

℟ **A pure heart create for me, O God.**

1 Have mercy on me, God, in your kindness.
   In your compassion blot out my offence.
   O wash me more and more from my guilt
   and cleanse me from my sin. ℟

2 A pure heart create for me, O God,
   put a steadfast spirit within me.
   Do not cast me away from your presence,
   nor deprive me of your holy spirit. ℟

3 Give me again the joy of your help;
   with a spirit of fervour sustain me,
   that I may teach transgressors your ways
   and sinners may return to you. ℟

SECOND READING

A reading from the letter to the Hebrews 5:7-9
He learnt to obey and became the source of eternal salvation.

During his life on earth, Christ offered up prayer and entreaty, aloud and in silent tears, to the one who had the power to save him out of death, and he submitted so humbly that his prayer was heard. Although he was Son, he learnt to obey through suffering; but having been made perfect, he became for all who obey him the source of eternal salvation.

This is the word of the Lord.

Gospel Acclamation Jn 12:26

Glory to you, O Christ, you are the Word of God!
If a man serves me, says the Lord, he must follow me;
wherever I am, my servant will be there too.
Glory to you, O Christ, you are the Word of God!

GOSPEL

A reading from the holy Gospel according to John   12:20-30

If a grain of wheat falls on the ground and dies, it yields a rich harvest.

Among those who went up to worship at the festival were some Greeks. These approached Philip, who came from Bethsaida in Galilee, and put this request to him, 'Sir, we should like to see Jesus.' Philip went to tell Andrew, and Andrew and Philip together went to tell Jesus. Jesus replied to them:

'Now the hour has come
for the Son of Man to be glorified.
I tell you, most solemnly,
unless a wheat grain falls on the ground and dies,
it remains only a single grain;
but if it dies,
it yields a rich harvest.
Anyone who loves his life loses it;
anyone who hates his life in this world
will keep it for the eternal life.
If a man serves me, he must follow me,
wherever I am, my servant will be there too.
If anyone serves me, my Father will honour him.
Now my soul is troubled.
What shall I say:
Father, save me from this hour?
But it was for this very reason that I have come to this hour.
Father, glorify your name!'

A voice came from heaven, 'I have glorified it, and I will glorify it again.'

People standing by, who heard this, said it was a clap of thunder; others said, 'It was an angel speaking to him.' Jesus answered, 'It was not for my sake that this voice came, but for yours.

'Now sentence is being passed on this world;
now the prince of this world is to be overthrown.
And when I am lifted up from the earth,
I shall draw all men to myself.'

By these words he indicated the kind of death he would die.

This is the Gospel of the Lord.

After the Homily, the Third Scrutiny of Candidates for Baptism may take place. See above, pp.199ff.

Prayer over the Gifts

Almighty God,
may the sacrifice we offer
take away the sins of those
whom you enlighten with the Christian faith.

Preface of Lent I or II, P8 or P9

Communion Antiphon: I tell you solemnly: Unless a grain of wheat falls on the ground and dies, it remains a single grain; but if it dies, it yields a rich harvest.

Prayer after Communion

Almighty Father,
by this sacrifice
may we always remain one with your Son, Jesus Christ,
whose body and blood we share,
for he is Lord for ever and ever.

An appropriate Solemn Blessing or Prayer over the People may be used. See pp.90ff.

HOLY WEEK

PASSION SUNDAY (PALM SUNDAY)

See above, pp.201ff.

HOLY THURSDAY: CHRISM MASS

See above, pp.238ff.

THE EASTER TRIDUUM

HOLY THURSDAY
(Mass of the Lord's Supper)

See above, pp.249ff.

GOOD FRIDAY
(Celebration of the Lord's Passion)

See above, pp.258ff.

THE EASTER VIGIL

See above, pp.279ff.

EASTER DAY

See above, pp.316ff.

CHRIST RISEN THE FIRST FRUITS OF ALL THOSE FALLEN ASLEEP

THE SEASON OF EASTER

SECOND SUNDAY OF EASTER　　　　B

Faith: Our Victory Over The World

We come together today like that first group of believers, united heart and soul, and celebrating our victory over the world through our faith in Christ, the Son of God.

Entrance Antiphon: Like newborn children you should thirst for milk, on which your spirit can grow to strength, alleluia.

or

Rejoice to the full in the glory that is yours, and give thanks to God who called you to his kingdom, alleluia.

Opening Prayer
Let us pray
　　[for a deeper awareness of our Christian baptism]

God of mercy,
you wash away our sins in water,
you give us new birth in the Spirit
and redeem us in the blood of Christ.
As we celebrate Christ's resurrection
increase our awareness of these blessings,
and renew your gift of life within us.

or

Let us pray
　　[as Christians thirsting for the risen life]

Heavenly Father and God of mercy,
we no longer look for Jesus among the dead,
for he is alive and has become the Lord of life.

From the waters of death you raise us with him
and renew your gift of life within us.

Increase in our minds and hearts
the risen life we share with Christ
and help us to grow as your people
toward the fullness of eternal life with you.

FIRST READING

A reading from the Acts of the Apostles   4:32-35
United, heart and soul.

The whole group of believers was united, heart and soul; no one
claimed for his own use anything that he had, as everything they
owned was held in common.

The apostles continued to testify to the resurrection of the
Lord Jesus with great power, and they were all given great
respect.

None of their members was ever in want, as all those who
owned land or houses would sell them, and bring the money
from them, to present it to the apostles; it was then distributed to
any members who might be in need.

This is the word of the Lord.

Responsorial Psalm   Ps 117:2-4. 15-18. 22-24. ℟ v.1
   ℟ **Give thanks to the Lord for he is good,**
      for his love has no end.

or

   ℟ **Alleluia, alleluia, alleluia!**

1 Let the sons of Israel say:
   'His love has no end.'
   Let the sons of Aaron say:
   'His love has no end.'
   Let those who fear the Lord say:
   'His love has no end.' ℟

2 The Lord's right hand has triumphed;
   his right hand raised me up.
   I shall not die, I shall live
   and recount his deeds.
   I was punished, I was punished by the Lord,
   but not doomed to die. ℟

(continued)

3   The stone which the builders rejected
has become the corner stone.
This is the work of the Lord,
a marvel in our eyes.
This day was made by the Lord;
we rejoice and are glad.

℟   **Give thanks to the Lord for he is good,
for his love has no end.**

or

℟   **Alleluia, alleluia, alleluia!**

SECOND READING

A reading from the first letter of St John   5:1-6
Anyone who has been begotten by God has already overcome the world.

Whoever believes that Jesus is the Christ
has been begotten by God;
and whoever loves the Father that begot him
loves the child whom he begets.
We can be sure that we love God's children
if we love God himself and do what he has commanded us;
this is what loving God is –
keeping his commandments;
and his commandments are not difficult,
because anyone who has been begotten by God
has already overcome the world;
this is the victory over the world –
our faith.
Who can overcome the world?
only the man who believes that Jesus is the Son of God;
Jesus Christ who came by water and blood,
not with water only,
but with water and blood;
with the Spirit as another witness –
since the Spirit is the truth.

    This is the word of the Lord.

Gospel Acclamation   Jn 20:29
    Alleluia, alleluia!
    Jesus said: 'You believe because you can see me.
    Happy are those who have not seen and yet believe.'
    Alleluia!

GOSPEL

A reading from the holy Gospel according to John   20:19-31

Eight days later, Jesus came.

In the evening of that same day, the first day of the week, the doors were closed in the room where the disciples were, for fear of the Jews. Jesus came and stood among them. He said to them, 'Peace be with you,' and showed them his hands and his side. The disciples were filled with joy when they saw the Lord, and he said to them again, 'Peace be with you.

'As the Father sent me,
  so am I sending you,'

After saying this he breathed on them and said:

'Receive the Holy Spirit.
For those whose sins you forgive,
they are forgiven;
for those whose sins you retain,
they are retained.'

Thomas, called the Twin, who was one of the Twelve, was not with them when Jesus came. When the disciples said, 'We have seen the Lord,' he answered, 'Unless I see the holes that the nails made in his hands and can put my finger into the holes they made, and unless I can put my hand into his side, I refuse to believe.' Eight days later the disciples were in the house again and Thomas was with them. The doors were closed, but Jesus came in and stood among them. 'Peace be with you,' he said. Then he spoke to Thomas, 'Put your finger here; look, here are my hands. Give me your hand; put it into my side. Doubt no longer but believe.' Thomas replied, 'My Lord and my God!' Jesus said to him:

'You believe because you can see me.
Happy are those who have not seen and yet believe.'

There were many other signs that Jesus worked and the disciples saw, but they are not recorded in this book. These are recorded so that you may believe that Jesus is the Christ, the Son of God, and that believing this you may have life through his name.

This is the Gospel of the Lord.

Prayer over Gifts

Lord,
through faith and baptism
we have become a new creation.
Accept the offerings of your people
(and of those born again in baptism)
and bring us to eternal happiness.

Preface of Easter I, P21

Communion Antiphon: Jesus spoke to Thomas: Put your hand here, and see the place of the nails. Doubt no longer, but believe, alleluia.

Prayer after Communion

Almighty God,
may the Easter sacraments we have received
live for ever in our minds and hearts.

An appropriate Solemn Blessing or Prayer over the People may be used. See pp.90ff.

THIRD SUNDAY OF EASTER   **B**

Our Advocate With The Father

We celebrate with the living Christ, our advocate with the Father, in whose name repentance for the forgiveness of sins is preached to all the world.

Entrance Antiphon: Let all the earth cry out to God with joy; praise the glory of his name; proclaim his glorious praise, alleluia.

Opening Prayer
Let us pray
    [that Christ will give us
    a share in the glory of his unending life]

God our Father,
may we look forward with hope to our resurrection,
for you have made us your sons and daughters,
and restored the joy of our youth.

or

Let us pray
    [in confident peace and Easter hope]

Father in heaven, author of all truth,
a people once in darkness has listened to your Word
and followed your Son as he rose from the tomb.

Hear the prayer of this newborn people
and strengthen your Church to answer your call.
May we rise and come forth into the light of day
to stand in your presence until eternity dawns.

FIRST READING

A reading from the Acts of the Apostles   3:13-15. 17-19
You killed the prince of life. God, however, raised him from the dead.

Peter said to the people: 'You are Israelites, and it is the God of Abraham, Isaac and Jacob, the God of our ancestors, who has glorified his servant Jesus, the same Jesus you handed over and then disowned in the presence of Pilate, after Pilate had decided to release him. It was you who accused the Holy One, the Just One, you who demanded the reprieve of a murderer while you killed the prince of life. God, however, raised him from the dead, and to that fact we are the witnesses.

'Now I know, brothers, that neither you nor your leaders had any idea what you were really doing; this was the way God carried out what he had foretold, when he said through all his prophets that his Christ would suffer. Now you must repent and turn to God, so that your sins may be wiped out.'

This is the word of the Lord.

Responsorial Psalm   Ps 4:2. 4. 7. 9. ℟ v.7

℟   **Lift up the light of your face on us, O Lord.**

or

℟   **Alleluia!**

1   When I call, answer me, O God of justice;
    from anguish you released me, have mercy and hear me!   ℟

2   It is the Lord who grants favours to those whom he loves;
    the Lord hears me whenever I call him.   ℟

3   'What can bring us happiness?' many say.
    Lift up the light of your face on us, O Lord.   ℟

4   I will lie down in peace and sleep comes at once,
    for you alone, Lord, make me dwell in safety.   ℟

SECOND READING

A reading from the first letter of St John   2:1-5

He is the sacrifice that takes our sins away, and not only ours, but the whole world's.

I am writing this, my children,
to stop you sinning;
but if anyone should sin,
we have our advocate with the Father,
Jesus Christ, who is just;
he is the sacrifice that takes our sins away,
and not only ours,
but the whole world's.
We can be sure that we know God
only by keeping his commandments.
Anyone who says, 'I know him',
and does not keep his commandments,
is a liar,
refusing to admit the truth.
But when anyone does obey what he has said,

God's love comes to perfection in him.

This is the word of the Lord.

Gospel Acclamation   cf. Lk 24:32
Alleluia, alleluia!
Lord Jesus, explain the scriptures to us.
Make our hearts burn within us as you talk to us.
Alleluia!

GOSPEL

A reading from the holy Gospel according to Luke   24:35-48
So you see how it is written that the Christ would suffer and on the third day rise from the dead.

The disciples told their story of what had happened on the road and how they had recognised Jesus at the breaking of bread.

They were still talking about this when Jesus himself stood among them and said to them, 'Peace be with you!' In a state of alarm and fright, they thought they were seeing a ghost. But he said, 'Why are you so agitated, and why are these doubts rising in your hearts? Look at my hands and feet; yes, it is I indeed. Touch me and see for yourselves; a ghost has no flesh and bones as you can see I have.' And as he said this he showed them his hands and feet. Their joy was so great that they could not believe it, and they stood dumbfounded; so he said to them, 'Have you anything here to eat?' And they offered him a piece of grilled fish, which he took and ate before their eyes.

Then he told them, 'This is what I meant when I said, while I was still with you, that everything written about me in the Law of Moses, in the Prophets and in the Psalms, has to be fulfilled.' He then opened their minds to understand the scriptures, and he said to them, 'So you see how it is written that the Christ would suffer and on the third day rise from the dead, and that, in his name, repentance for the forgiveness of sins would be preached to all the nations, beginning from Jerusalem. You are witnesses to this.'

This is the Gospel of the Lord.

Prayer over the Gifts
Lord,
receive these gifts from your Church.
May the great joy you give us
come to perfection in heaven.

Preface of Easter II-V, P22-P25

Communion Antiphon: Christ had to suffer and to rise from the dead on the third day. In his name penance for the remission of sins is to be preached to all nations, alleluia.

Prayer after Communion

Lord,
look on your people with kindness
and by these Easter mysteries
bring us to the glory of the resurrection.

An appropriate Solemn Blessing or Prayer over the People may be used. See pp. 90ff.

FOURTH SUNDAY OF EASTER   B

The Good Shepherd

Christ, the Good Shepherd, went before us through suffering and death, so that we could follow in safety and be with him in his heavenly kingdom.

Entrance Antiphon: The earth is full of the goodness of the Lord; by the word of the Lord the heavens were made, alleluia.

Opening Prayer

Let us pray
    [that Christ our shepherd
    will lead us through the difficulties of this life]

Almighty and ever-living God,
give us new strength
from the courage of Christ our shepherd,
and lead us to join the saints in heaven,
where he lives and reigns with you and the Holy Spirit,
one God, for ever and ever.

or

Let us pray
    [to God our helper in time of distress]

God and Father of our Lord Jesus Christ,
though your people walk in the valley of darkness,
no evil should they fear;
for they follow in faith the call of the shepherd

whom you have sent for their hope and strength.

Attune our minds to the sound of his voice,
lead our steps in the path he has shown,
that we may know the strength of his outstretched arm
and enjoy the light of your presence for ever.

FIRST READING
A reading from the Acts of the Apostles   4:8-12
This is the only name by which we can be saved.

Filled with the Holy Spirit, Peter said: 'Rulers of the people, and
elders! If you are questioning us today about an act of kindness to
a cripple, and asking us how he was healed, then I am glad to tell
you all, and would indeed be glad to tell the whole people of
Israel, that it was by the name of Jesus Christ the Nazarene, the
one you crucified, whom God raised from the dead, by this name
and by no other that this man is able to stand up perfectly
healthy, here in your presence today. This is the stone rejected
by you the builders, but which has proved to be the keystone.
For of all the names in the world given to men, this is the only
one by which we can be saved.'

This is the word of the Lord.

Responsorial Psalm   Ps 117:1. 8-9. 21-23. 26. 28-29. ℟ v.22

℟ **The stone which the builders rejected
has become the corner stone.**

or

℟ **Alleluia!**

1   Give thanks to the Lord for he is good,
for his love has no end.
It is better to take refuge in the Lord
than to trust in men:
it is better to take refuge in the Lord
than to trust in princes. ℟

2   I will thank you for you have given answer
and you are my saviour.
The stone which the builders rejected
has become the corner stone.
This is the work of the Lord,
a marvel in our eyes. ℟

(continued)

3   Blessed in the name of the Lord
    is he who comes.
    We bless you from the house of the Lord;
    I will thank you for you have given answer
    and you are my saviour.
    Give thanks to the Lord for he is good;
    for his love has no end.

  ℟   **The stone which the builders rejected
        has become the corner stone.**

or
  ℟   **Alleluia!**

SECOND READING

A reading from the first letter of St John   3:1-2
We shall see God as he really is.

Think of the love that the Father has lavished on us,
by letting us be called God's children;
and that is what we are.
Because the world refused to acknowledge him,
therefore it does not acknowledge us.
My dear people, we are already the children of God
but what we are to be in the future has not yet been revealed;
all we know is, that when it is revealed
we shall be like him
because we shall see him as he really is.

    This is the word of the Lord.

Gospel Acclamation   Jn 10:14
    Alleluia, alleluia!
    I am the good shepherd, says the Lord;
    I know my own sheep and my own know me.
    Alleluia!

GOSPEL

A reading from the holy Gospel according to John   10:11-18
The good shepherd is one who lays down his life for his sheep.

Jesus said:

    'I am the good shepherd:
    the good shepherd is one who lays down his life for his sheep.
    The hired man, since he is not the shepherd
    and the sheep do not belong to him,

abandons the sheep and runs away
as soon as he sees a wolf coming,
and then the wolf attacks and scatters the sheep;
this is because he is only a hired man
and has no concern for the sheep.
I am the good shepherd;
I know my own
and my own know me,
just as the Father knows me
and I know the Father;
and I lay down my life for my sheep.
And there are other sheep I have
that are not of this fold,
and these I have to lead as well.
They too will listen to my voice,
and there will be only one flock
and one shepherd.
The Father loves me,
because I lay down my life
in order to take it up again.
No one takes it from me;
I lay it down of my own free will,
and as it is in my power to lay it down,
so it is in my power to take it up again;
and this is the command I have been given by my Father.'

This is the Gospel of the Lord.

Prayer over the Gifts
Lord,
restore us by these Easter mysteries.
May the continuing work of our redeemer
bring us eternal joy.

Preface of Easter II-V, P22-P25

Communion Antiphon: The Good Shepherd is risen! He who laid
down his life for his sheep, who died for his flock, he is risen,
alleluia.

Prayer after Communion
Father, eternal shepherd,
watch over the flock redeemed by the blood of Christ
and lead us to the promised land.

An appropriate Solemn Blessing or Prayer over the People may be used. See pp.90ff.

FIFTH SUNDAY OF EASTER   **B**

Christ The True Vine

When, like St Paul, we 'believe in the name of Jesus Christ', God lives in us and we in him. We become branches of the true vine, Jesus Christ.

Entrance Antiphon: Sing to the Lord a new song, for he has done marvellous deeds; he has revealed to the nations his saving power, alleluia.

Opening Prayer
Let us pray
    [that we may enjoy true freedom]

God our Father,
look upon us with love.
You redeem us and make us your children in Christ.
Give us true freedom
and bring us to the inheritance you promised.

or

Let us pray
    [in the freedom of the sons of God]

Father of our Lord Jesus Christ,
you have revealed to the nations your saving power
and filled all ages with the words of a new song.
Hear the echo of this hymn.
Give us voice to sing your praise
throughout this season of joy.

FIRST READING

A reading from the Acts of the Apostles   9:26-31
Barnabas explained how the Lord had appeared to Saul on his journey.

When Saul got to Jerusalem he tried to join the disciples, but they were all afraid of him: they could not believe he was really a disciple. Barnabas, however, took charge of him, introduced him to the apostles, and explained how the Lord had appeared to Saul and spoken to him on his journey, and how he had preached boldly at Damascus in the name of Jesus. Saul now started to go round with them in Jerusalem, preaching fearlessly in the name of the Lord. But after he had spoken to the Hellenists, and argued with them, they became determined to kill him. When the brothers knew, they took him to Caesarea, and sent him off from there to Tarsus.

The churches throughout Judaea, Galilee and Samaria were now left in peace, building themselves up, living in the fear of the Lord, and filled with the consolation of the Holy Spirit.

This is the word of the Lord.

Responsorial Psalm   Ps 21:26-28. 30-32. ℟ v.26

    ℟ **You, Lord, are my praise in the great assembly.**

or

    ℟ **Alleluia!**

1   My vows I will pay before those who fear him.
    The poor shall eat and shall have their fill.
    They shall praise the Lord, those who seek him.
    May their hearts live for ever and ever! ℟

2   All the earth shall remember and return to the Lord,
    all families of the nations worship before him.
    They shall worship him, all the mighty of the earth;
    before him shall bow all who go down to the dust. ℟

3   And my soul shall live for him, my children serve him.
    They shall tell of the Lord to generations yet to come,
    declare his faithfulness to peoples yet unborn:
    'These things the Lord has done.' ℟

SECOND READING

A reading from the first letter of St John   3:18-24

His commandments are these: that we believe in his Son and that we love one another.

My children,
our love is not to be just words or mere talk,
but something real and active;
only by this can we be certain
that we are the children of the truth
and be able to quieten our conscience in his presence,
whatever accusations it may raise against us,
because God is greater than our conscience and he knows
    everything.
My dear people,

if we cannot be condemned by our own conscience,
we need not be afraid in God's presence,
and whatever we ask him,
we shall receive,
because we keep his commandments
and live the kind of life that he wants.
His commandments are these:
that we believe in the name of his Son Jesus Christ
and that we love one another
as he told us to.
Whoever keeps his commandments
lives in God and God lives in him.
We know that he lives in us
by the Spirit that he has given us.

This is the word of the Lord.

Gospel Acclamation   Jn 15:4.5
    Alleluia, alleluia!
    Make your home in me, as I make mine in you.
    Whoever remains in me bears fruit in plenty.
    Alleluia!

GOSPEL

A reading from the holy Gospel according to John   15:1-8
Whoever remains in me, with me in him, bears fruit in plenty.

Jesus said to his disciples:

    'I am the true vine,
    and my Father is the vinedresser.
    Every branch in me that bears no fruit
    he cuts away,
    and every branch that does bear fruit he prunes
    to make it bear even more.
    You are pruned already,
    by means of the word that I have spoken to you.
    Make your home in me, as I make mine in you.
    As a branch cannot bear fruit all by itself,
    but must remain part of the vine,
    neither can you unless you remain in me.
    I am the vine,
    you are the branches.
    Whoever remains in me, with me in him,
    bears fruit in plenty;

for cut off from me you can do nothing.
Anyone who does not remain in me
is like a branch that has been thrown away
– he withers;
these branches are collected and thrown on the fire,
and they are burnt.
If you remain in me
and my words remain in you,
you may ask what you will
and you shall get it.
It is to the glory of my Father that you should bear much fruit,
and then you will be my disciples.'

This is the Gospel of the Lord.

Prayer over the Gifts
Lord God,
by this holy exchange of gifts
you share with us your divine life.
Grant that everything we do
may be directed by the knowledge of your truth.

Preface of Easter II-V, P22-P25

Communion Antiphon: I am the vine and you are the branches, says the Lord; he who lives in me, and I in him, will bear much fruit, alleluia!

Prayer after Communion
Merciful Father,
may these mysteries give us new purpose
and bring us to a new life in you.

An appropriate Solemn Blessing or Prayer over the People may be used. See pp.90ff.

SIXTH SUNDAY OF EASTER B

The Spirit of God's Love

We celebrate the coming of the Spirit of God's love on the Church. And because God does not have favourites, the Spirit is communicated through the Church to the whole world.

Entrance Antiphon: Speak out with a voice of joy; let it be heard to the ends of the earth: The Lord has set his people free, alleluia.

Opening Prayer
Let us pray
   [that we may practise in our lives
   the faith we profess]

Ever-living God,
help us to celebrate our joy
in the resurrection of the Lord
and to express in our lives
the love we celebrate.

or

Let us pray
   [in silence, reflecting on the joy of Easter]

God our Father, maker of all,
the crown of your creation was the Son of Man,
born of a woman, but without beginning;
he suffered for us but lives for ever.

May our mortal lives be crowned with the ultimate joy
of rising with him,
who is Lord for ever and ever.

FIRST READING

A reading from the Acts of the Apostles   10:25-26. 34-35. 44-48
The Holy Spirit has been poured out on the pagans too.

As Peter reached the house Cornelius went out to meet him,
knelt at his feet and prostrated himself. But Peter helped him up.
'Stand up,' he said 'I am only a man after all!'
   Then Peter addressed them: 'The truth I have now come to
realise' he said 'is that God does not have favourites, but that
anybody of any nationality who fears God and does what is right
is acceptable to him.'
   While Peter was still speaking the Holy Spirit came down on all
the listeners. Jewish believers who had accompanied Peter were
all astonished that the gift of the Holy Spirit should be poured
out on the pagans too, since they could hear them speaking
strange languages and proclaiming the greatness of God. Peter
himself then said, 'Could anyone refuse the water of baptism to
these people, now they have received the Holy Spirit just as
much as we have?' He then gave orders for them to be baptised
in the name of Jesus Christ. Afterwards they begged him to stay
on for some days.

   This is the word of the Lord.

Responsorial Psalm   Ps 97:1-4. ℟ cf. v.2
    ℟ **The Lord has shown his salvation to the nations.**

or

    ℟ **Alleluia!**

1   Sing a new song to the Lord
      for he has worked wonders.
    His right hand and his holy arm
      have brought salvation. ℟

2   The Lord has made known his salvation;
      has shown his justice to the nations.
    He has remembered his truth and love
      for the house of Israel. ℟

3   All the ends of the earth have seen
      the salvation of our God.
    Shout to the Lord all the earth,
      ring out your joy. ℟

When the Ascension of the Lord is celebrated on the Seventh
Sunday of Easter, the Second Reading and Gospel assigned to
the Seventh Sunday (see below, pp.565ff.) may be read on the
Sixth Sunday.

SECOND READING

A reading from the first letter of St John   4:7-10
God is love.

My dear people,
let us love one another
since love comes from God
and everyone who loves is begotten by God and knows God.
Anyone who fails to love can never have known God,
because God is love.
God's love for us was revealed
when God sent into the world his only Son
so that we could have life through him;
this is the love I mean:
not our love for God,
but God's love for us when he sent his Son
to be the sacrifice that takes our sins away.

    This is the word of the Lord.

Gospel Acclamation   Jn 14:23
    Alleluia, alleluia!
    Jesus said: 'If anyone loves me he will keep my word,
    and my Father will love him, and we shall come to him.
    Alleluia!

GOSPEL

A reading from the holy Gospel according to John   15:9-17
A man can have no greater love than to lay down his life for his friends.

Jesus said to his disciples:

    'As the Father has loved me,
    so I have loved you.
    Remain in my love.
    If you keep my commandments
    you will remain in my love,
    just as I have kept my Father's commandments
    and remain in his love.
    I have told you this
    so that my own joy may be in you
    and your joy be complete.
    This is my commandment:
    love one another,
    as I have loved you.
    A man can have no greater love
    than to lay down his life for his friends.
    You are my friends,
    if you do what I command you.
    I shall not call you servants any more,
    because a servant does not know
    his master's business;
    I call you friends,
    because I have made known to you
    everything I have learnt from my Father.
    You did not choose me,
    no, I chose you;
    and I commissioned you
    to go out and to bear fruit,
    fruit that will last;
    and then the Father will give you
    anything you ask him in my name.
    What I command you
    is to love one another.'

This is the Gospel of the Lord.

Prayer over the Gifts

Lord,
accept our prayers and offerings.
Make us worthy of your sacraments of love
by granting us your forgiveness.

Preface of Easter I-V, P22-P25

Communion Antiphon: If you love me, keep my commandments,
says the Lord. The Father will send you the Holy Spirit, to be
with you for ever, alleluia.

Prayer after Communion

Almighty and ever-living Lord,
you restored us to life
by raising Christ from the death.
Strengthen us by this Easter sacrament;
may we feel its saving power in our daily life.

An appropriate Solemn Blessing or Prayer over the People may
be used. See pp.90ff.

THE ASCENSION OF THE LORD   B

Christ's Eternal Glory

*We celebrate today Christ's ascension to his eternal glory in heaven and
express our Christian hope that where he, our Head, has gone before us,
his Body, we will one day follow, to live for ever in the Kingdom of our
Father.*

Entrance Antiphon: Men of Galilee, why do you stand looking in
the sky? The Lord will return, just as you have seen him ascend,
alleluia.

Opening Prayer

Let us pray
   [that the risen Christ
   will lead us to eternal life]

God our Father,
make us joyful in the ascension of your Son Jesus Christ.
May we follow him into the new creation,
for his ascension is our glory and our hope.

or

Let us pray
  [on this day of Ascension
  as we watch and wait for Jesus' return]

Father in heaven,
our minds were prepared for the coming of your kingdom
when you took Christ beyond our sight
so that we might seek him in his glory.

May we follow where he has led
and find our hope in his glory,
for he is Lord for ever.

FIRST READING

A reading from the Acts of the Apostles 1:1-11
He was lifted up while they looked on.

In my earlier work, Theophilus, I dealt with everything Jesus had
done and taught from the beginning until the day he gave his
instructions to the apostles he had chosen through the Holy
Spirit, and was taken up to heaven. He had shown himself alive
to them after his Passion by many demonstrations: for forty days
he had continued to appear to them and tell them about the
kingdom of God. When he had been at table with them, he had
told them not to leave Jerusalem, but to wait there for what the
Father had promised. 'It is,' he had said, 'what you have heard
me speak about: John baptised with water but you, not many
days from now, will be baptised with the Holy Spirit.'

Now having met together, they asked him, 'Lord, has the
time come? Are you going to restore the kingdom to Israel?' He
replied, 'It is not for you to know times or dates that the Father
has decided by his own authority, but you will receive power
when the Holy Spirit comes on you, and then you will be my
witnesses not only in Jerusalem but throughout Judaea and
Samaria, and indeed to the ends of the earth.'

As he said this he was lifted up while they looked on, and a
cloud took him from their sight. They were still staring into the
sky when suddenly two men in white were standing near them
and they said, 'Why are you men from Galilee standing here
looking into the sky? Jesus who has been taken up from you into
heaven, this same Jesus will come back in the same way as you
have seen him go there.'

This is the word of the Lord.

Responsorial Psalm   Ps 46:2-3. 6-9. ℟v. 6

℟   **God goes up with shouts of joy;**
     the Lord goes up with trumpet blast.

or

℟   **Alleluia!**

1   All peoples, clap your hands,
     cry to God with shouts of joy!
     For the Lord, the Most High, we must fear,
     great king over all the earth. ℟

2   God goes up with shouts of joy;
     the Lord goes up with trumpet blast.
     Sing praise for God, sing praise,
     sing praise to our king, sing praise. ℟

3   God is king of all the earth.
     Sing praise with all your skill.
     God is king over the nations;
     God reigns on his holy throne. ℟

SECOND READING

The reading of Year A, Eph 1:17-23, p.343 (above), may be used
in place of the following.

A reading from the letter of St Paul to the Ephesians   4:1-13
Fully mature with the fullness of Christ.

*I, the prisoner in the Lord, implore you to lead a life worthy of
your vocation. Bear with one another charitably, in complete
selflessness, gentleness and patience. Do all you can to preserve
the unity of the Spirit by the peace that binds you together. There
is one Body, one Spirit, just as you were all called into one and
the same hope when you were called. There is one Lord, one
faith, one baptism, and one God who is Father of all, over all,
through all and within all.

Each one of us, however, has been given his own share of
grace, given as Christ allotted it.* It was said that he would:

When he ascended to the height, he captured prisoners,
he gave gifts to men.

When it says, 'he ascended', what can it mean if not that he
descended right down to the lower regions of the earth? The one
who rose higher than all the heavens to fill all things is none
other than the one who descended. And * to some, his gift was

that they should be apostles; to some, prophets; to some, evangelists; to some, pastors and teachers; so that the saints together make a unity in the work of service, building up the body of Christ. In this way we are all to come to unity in our faith and in our knowledge of the Son of God, until we become the perfect Man, fully mature with the fullness of Christ himself.

This is the word of the Lord.*

*Shorter Form, verses 1-7. 11-13. Read between *

Gospel Acclamation Mt 28:19. 20
Alleluia, alleluia!
Go, make disciples of all the nations;
I am with you always; yes, to the end of time.
Alleluia!

GOSPEL

A reading from the holy Gospel according to Mark 16:15-20
He was taken up into heaven: there at the right hand of God he took his place.

Jesus showed himself to the Eleven, and said to them, 'Go out to the whole world; proclaim the Good News to all creation. He who believes and is baptised will be saved; he who does not believe will be condemned. These are the signs that will be associated with believers: in my name they will cast out devils; they will have the gift of tongues; they will pick up snakes in their hands, and be unharmed should they drink deadly poison; they will lay their hands on the sick, who will recover.'

And so the Lord Jesus, after he had spoken to them, was taken up into heaven: there at the right hand of God he took his place, while they, going out, preached everywhere, the Lord working with them and confirming the word by the signs that accompanied it.

This is the Gospel of the Lord.

Prayer over the Gifts
Lord,
receive our offering
as we celebrate the ascension of Christ your Son.
May his gifts help us rise with him
to the joys of heaven,
where he lives and reigns for ever and ever.

Preface of Ascension I or II, P26 or P27

Communion Antiphon: I, the Lord, am with you always, until the end of the world, alleluia.

Prayer after Communion
Father,
in this eucharist
we touch the divine life you give to the world.
Help us to follow Christ with love
to eternal life where he is Lord for ever and ever.

Solemn Blessing
Bow your heads and pray for God's blessing.

May almighty God bless you on this day
when his only Son ascended into heaven
to prepare a place for you.   ℟   **Amen.**

After his resurrection, Christ was seen by his disciples.
When he appears as judge
may you be pleasing for ever in his sight.   ℟   **Amen.**

You believe that Jesus has taken his seat in majesty
at the right hand of the Father.
May you have the joy of experiencing
that he is also with you to the end of time,
according to his promise.   ℟   **Amen.**

May almighty God bless you,
the Father, and the Son, ✠ and the Holy Spirit.   ℟   **Amen.**

SEVENTH SUNDAY OF EASTER   B

Where the Ascension is not a holiday of obligation, it is celebrated on this Sunday.

The Spirit of God's Life

The Holy Spirit is the soul of the Church, the principle of its life and unity. God is living in us because he lets us share his Spirit.

Entrance Antiphon: Lord, hear my voice when I call to you. My heart has prompted me to seek your face; I seek it, Lord; do not hide from me, alleluia.

Opening Prayer
Let us pray
    [that we may recognise
    the presence of Christ in our midst]

Father,
help us keep in mind that Christ our Saviour
lives with you in glory
and promised to remain with us until the end of time.

or

Let us pray
    [to our Father
    who has raised us to life in Christ]

Eternal Father,
reaching from end to end of the universe,
and ordering all things with your mighty arm:
for you, time is the unfolding of truth that already is,
the unveiling of beauty that is yet to be.

Your Son has saved us in history
by rising from the dead,
so that transcending time he might free us from death.
May his presence among us
lead to the vision of unlimited truth
and unfold the beauty of your love.

FIRST READING

A reading from the Acts of the Apostles   1:15-17.20-26
We must choose one of these to be a witness to his resurrection with us.

One day Peter stood up to speak to the brothers – there were
about a hundred and twenty persons in the congregation:
'Brothers, the passage of scripture had to be fulfilled in which the
Holy Spirit, speaking through David, foretells the fate of Judas,
who offered himself as a guide to the men who arrested Jesus –
after having been one of our number and actually sharing this
ministry of ours.

    'In the Book of Psalms it says:

    Let someone else take his office.

    'We must therefore choose someone who has been with us
the whole time that the Lord Jesus was travelling around with us,
someone who was with us right from the time when John was
baptising until the day when he was taken up from us – and he
can act with us as a witness to his resurrection.'

Having nominated two candidates, Joseph known as Barsabbas, whose surname was Justus, and Matthias, they prayed, 'Lord, you can read everyone's heart; show us therefore which of these two you have chosen to take over this ministry and apostolate, which Judas abandoned to go to his proper place.' They then drew lots for them, and as the lot fell to Matthias, he was listed as one of the twelve apostles.

This is the word of the Lord.

Responsorial Psalm   Ps 102:1-2. 11-12. 19-20. R℣ v.19
   R℣ **The Lord has set his sway in heaven.**

or

   R℣ **Alleluia!**

1   My soul, give thanks to the Lord;
     all my being, bless his holy name.
     My soul, give thanks to the Lord
     and never forget all his blessings.   R℣

2   For as the heavens are high above the earth
     so strong is his love for those who fear him.
     As far as the east is from the west
     so far does he remove our sins.   R℣

3   The Lord has set his sway in heaven
     and his kingdom is ruling over all.
     Give thanks to the Lord, all his angels,
     mighty in power, fulfilling his word.   R℣

SECOND READING

A reading from the first letter of St John   4:11-16
Anyone who lives in love lives in God, and God lives in him.

My dear people,
since God has loved us so much,
we too should love one another.
No one has ever seen God;
but as long as we love one another
God will live in us
and his love will be complete in us.
We can know that we are living in him
and he is living in us
because he lets us share his Spirit.
We ourselves saw and we testify

that the Father sent his Son
as saviour of the world.
If anyone acknowledges that Jesus is the Son of God,
God lives in him, and he in God.
We ourselves have known and put our faith in
God's love towards ourselves.
God is love
and anyone who lives in love lives in God,
and God lives in him.

This is the word of the Lord.

Gospel Acclamation   cf. Jn 14:18
Alleluia, alleluia!
I will not leave your orphans, says the Lord;
I will come back to you, and your hearts will be full of joy.
Alleluia!

GOSPEL

A reading from the holy Gospel according to John   17:11-19
That they may be one like us!

Jesus raised his eyes to heaven and said:

'Holy Father,
keep those you have given me true to your name,
so that they may be one like us.
While I was with them,
I kept those you had given me true to your name.
I have watched over them and not one is lost
except the one who chose to be lost,
and this was to fulfil the scriptures.
But now I am coming to you
and while still in the world I say these things
to share my joy with them to the full.
I passed your word on to them,
and the world hated them,
because they belong to the world
no more than I belong to the world.
I am not asking you to remove them from the world,
but to protect them from the evil one.
They do not belong to the world
any more than I belong to the world.
Consecrate them in the truth;
your word is truth.

As you sent me into the world,
I have sent them into the world,
and for their sake I consecrate myself
so that they too may be consecrated in truth.'

This is the Gospel of the Lord.

Prayer over the Gifts
Lord,
accept the prayers and gifts
we offer in faith and love.
May this eucharist
bring us to your glory.

Preface of Ascension I or II, P26-P27

Communion Antiphon: This is the prayer of Jesus: that his believers may become one as he is one with the Father, alleluia.

Prayer after Communion
God our Saviour,
hear us,
and through this holy mystery give us hope
that the glory you have given Christ
will be given to the Church, his body,
for he is Lord for ever and ever.

An appropriate Solemn Blessing or Prayer over the People may be used. See pp.90ff.

PENTECOST SUNDAY

The Vigil Mass, which is celebrated on Saturday evening, will be found under Year A, pp.349ff.

Mass During the Day

The Day of Pentecost

Today we celebrate the great day of Pentecost when Christ filled the Church with the power of his spirit and sent it out into the world to bring his peace, joy and forgiveness to all mankind.

Entrance Antiphon: The Spirit of the Lord fills the whole world. It holds all things together and knows every word spoken by man, alleluia.

or

The love of God has been poured into our hearts by his Spirit
living in us, alleluia.

Opening Prayer
Let us pray
    [that the Spirit will work through our lives
    to bring Christ to the world]
God our Father,
let the Spirit you sent on your Church
to begin the teaching of the gospel
continue to work in the world
through the hearts of all who believe.

or

Let us pray
    [in the Spirit who dwells within us]

Father of light, from whom every good gift comes,
send your Spirit into our lives
with the power of a mighty wind,
and by the flame of your wisdom
open the horizons of our minds.

Loosen our tongues to sing your praise
in words beyond the power of speech,
for without your Spirit
man could never raise his voice in words of peace
or announce the truth that Jesus is Lord,
who lives and reigns with you and the Holy Spirit,
one God, for ever and ever.

FIRST READING

A reading from the Acts of the Apostles   2:1-11
They were all filled with the Holy Spirit and began to speak.

When Pentecost day came round, the apostles had all met in one
room, when suddenly they heard what sounded like a powerful
wind from heaven, the noise of which filled the entire house in
which they were sitting; and something appeared to them that
seemed like tongues of fire; these separated and came to rest on
the head of each of them. They were all filled with the Holy
Spirit, and began to speak foreign languages as the Spirit gave
them the gift of speech.
    Now there were devout men living in Jerusalem from every

nation under heaven, and at this sound they all assembled, each one bewildered to hear these men speaking his own language. They were amazed and astonished. 'Surely' they said 'all these men speaking are Galileans? How does it happen that each of us hears them in his own native language? Parthians, Medes and Elamites; people from Mesopotamia, Judaea and Cappadocia, Pontus and Asia, Phrygia and Pamphylia, Egypt and the parts of Libya round Cyrene; as well as visitors from Rome – Jews and proselytes alike – Cretans and Arabs; we hear them preaching in our own language about the marvels of God.'

This is the word of the Lord.

Responsorial Psalm   Ps 103:1. 24. 29-31. 34. R̸ cf v.30

R̸ **Send forth your Spirit, O Lord,
and renew the face of the earth.**

or

R̸ **Alleluia.**

1 Bless the Lord, my soul!
   Lord God, how great you are,
   How many are your works, O Lord!
   The earth is full of your riches.   R̸

2 You take back your spirit, they die,
   returning to the dust from which they came.
   You send forth your spirit, they are created;
   and you renew the face of the earth.   R̸

3 May the glory of the Lord last for ever!
   May the Lord rejoice in his works!
   May my thoughts be pleasing to him.
   I find my joy in the Lord.   R̸

The Second Reading and the Gospel may be taken from Year A, see above, pp.357ff. Alternatively, the Second Reading and the Gospel given below may be used.

SECOND READING

A reading from the letter of St Paul to the Galatians   5:16-25
The fruit of the Spirit.

If you are guided by the Spirit you will be in no danger of yielding to self-indulgence, since self-indulgence is the opposite of the Spirit, the Spirit is totally against such a thing, and it is precisely because the two are so opposed that you do not always carry out your good intentions. If you are led by the Spirit, no law can touch you. When self-indulgence is at work the results are obvious: fornication, gross indecency and sexual irresponsibility; idolatry and sorcery; feuds and wrangling, jealousy, bad temper and quarrels; disagreements, factions, envy; drunkenness, orgies and similar things. I warn you now, as I warned you before: those who behave like this will not inherit the kingdom of God. What the Spirit brings is very different: love, joy, peace, patience, kindness, goodness, trustfulness, gentleness and self-control. There can be no law against things like that, of course. You cannot belong to Christ Jesus unless you crucify all self-indulgent passions and desire.

Since the Spirit is our life, let us be directed by the Spirit.

This is the word of the Lord.

SEQUENCE

The sequence may be said or sung.

Holy Spirit, Lord of light,
  From the clear celestial height
Thy pure beaming radiance give.

Come, thou Father of the poor,
  Come with treasures which endure;
Come, thou light of all that live!

Thou, of all consolers best,
  Thou, the soul's delightful guest,
Dost refreshing peace bestow;

Thou in toil art comfort sweet;
  Pleasant coolness in the heat;
Solace in the midst of woe.

Light immortal, light divine,
  Visit thou these hearts of thine,
And our inmost being fill:

If thou take thy grace away,
  Nothing pure in man will stay;
All his good is turned to ill.

Heal our wounds, our strength renew;
  On our dryness pour thy dew;
Wash the stains of guilt away:

Bend the stubborn heart and will;

Melt the frozen, warm the chill;
Guide the steps that go astray.

Thou, on us who evermore
    Thee confess and thee adore,
With thy sevenfold gifts descend:

Give us comfort when we die;
    Give us life with thee on high;
Give us joys that never end.

Gospel Acclamation

Alleluia, alleluia!
Come, Holy Spirit, fill the hearts of your faithful
and kindle in them the fire of your love.
Alleluia!

GOSPEL

A reading from the holy Gospel according to John

15:26-27; 16:12-15

The Spirit of truth will lead you to the complete truth.

Jesus said to his disciples:

'When the Advocate comes,
whom I shall send to you from the Father,
the Spirit of truth who issues from the Father,
he will be my witness.
And you too will be witnesses,
because you have been with me from the outset.

I still have many things to say to you
but they would be too much for you now.
But when the Spirit of truth comes
he will lead you to the complete truth,
since he will not be speaking as from himself
but will say only what he has learnt;
and he will tell you of the things to come
He will glorify me,
since all he tells you
will be taken from what is mine.
Everything the Father has is mine;
that is why I said:
All he tells you
will be taken from what is mine.'

This is the Gospel of the Lord.

Prayer over the Gifts
Lord,
may the Spirit you promised
lead us into all truth
and reveal to us the full meaning of this sacrifice.

Preface of Pentecost, P28
Communion Antiphon: They were all filled with the Holy Spirit,
and they spoke of the great things God had done, alleluia.

Prayer after Communion
Father,
may the food we receive in the eucharist
help our eternal redemption.
Keep within us the vigour of your Spirit
and protect the gifts you have given to your Church.

Solemn Blessing
Bow your heads and pray for God's blessing.

This day the Father of light
has enlightened the minds of the disciples
by the outpouring of the Holy Spirit.
May he bless you
and give you the gifts of the Spirit for ever.   ℞   **Amen.**

May that fire which hovered over the disciples
as tongues of flame
burn out all evil from your hearts
and make them glow with pure light.   ℞   **Amen.**

God inspired speech in different tongues
to proclaim one faith.
May he strengthen your faith
and fulfil your hope to see him face to face.   ℞
May almighty God bless you,
the Father, and the Son, ✠ and the Holy Spirit.   ℞

SOLEMNITIES OF THE LORD IN ORDINARY TIME

Sunday after Pentecost

THE MOST HOLY TRINITY   B
Solemnity

Abba, Father!

We celebrate our baptism in the name of the Trinity as a result of which we have received the spirit of sons and are privileged to call the great God of glory and majesty our Father.

Entrance Antiphon: Blessed be God the Father and his only-begotten Son and the Holy Spirit: for he has shown that he loves us.

Opening Prayer
Let us pray
    [to the one God, Father, Son and Spirit,
      that our lives may bear witness to our faith]

Father,
you sent your Word to bring us truth
and your Spirit to make us holy.
Through them we come to know the mystery of your life.
Help us to worship you, one God in three Persons,
by proclaiming and living our faith in you.

or

Let us pray
    [to our God who is Father, Son, and Holy Spirit]

God, we praise you:
Father all-powerful, Christ Lord and Saviour, Spirit of love.
You reveal yourself in the depths of our being,
drawing us to share in your life and your love.
One God, three Persons,
be near to the people formed in your image,
close to the world your love brings to life.

FIRST READING
A reading from the book of Deuteronomy   4:32-34. 39-40
The Lord is God indeed, in heaven above as on earth beneath, he and no other.

Moses said to the people: 'Put this question to the ages that are past, that went before you, from the time God created man on earth: Was there ever a word so majestic, from one end of heaven to the other? Was anything ever heard? Did ever a people hear the voice of the living God speaking from the heart of the fire, as you heard it, and remain alive? Has any god ventured to take to himself one nation from the midst of another by ordeals, signs, wonders, war with mighty hand and outstretched arm, by fearsome terrors – all this that the Lord your God did for you before your eyes in Egypt?

'Understand this today, therefore, and take it to heart: The Lord is God indeed, in heaven above as on earth beneath, he and no other. Keep his laws and commandments as I give them to you today so that you and your children may prosper and live long in the land that the Lord your God gives you for ever.'

This is the word of the Lord.

Responsorial Psalm   Ps 32:4-6. 9. 18-20. 22. ℟ v.12

℟   **Happy the people the Lord has chosen as his own.**

1   The word of the Lord is faithful
    and all his works to be trusted.
    The Lord loves justice and right
    and fills the earth with his love.   ℟

2   By his word the heavens were made,
    by the breath of his mouth all the stars.
    He spoke; and they came to be.
    He commanded; they sprang into being.   ℟

3   The Lord looks on those who revere him,
    on those who hope in his love,
    to rescue their souls from death,
    to keep them alive in famine.   ℟

4   Our soul is waiting for the Lord.
    The Lord is our help and our shield.
    May your love be upon us, O Lord,
    as we place all our hope in you.   ℟

SECOND READING

A reading from the letter of St Paul to the Romans   8:14-17
You received the spirit of sons, and it makes us cry out, 'Abba, Father!'

Everyone moved by the Spirit is a son of God. The spirit you received is not the spirit of slaves bringing fear into your lives again; it is the spirit of sons, and it makes us cry out, 'Abba, Father!' The Spirit himself and our spirit bear united witness that we are children of God. And if we are children we are heirs as well: heirs of God and coheirs with Christ, sharing his sufferings so as to share his glory.

This is the word of the Lord.

Gospel Acclamation   cf Apoc 1:8
Alleluia, alleluia!
Glory be to the Father, and to the Son, and to the Holy Spirit, the God who is, who was, and who is to come.
Alleluia!

GOSPEL
A reading from the holy Gospel according to Matthew   28:16-20
Baptise them in the name of the Father and of the Son and of the Holy Spirit.

The eleven disciples set out for Galilee, to the mountain where Jesus had arranged to meet them. When they saw him they fell down before him, though some hesitated. Jesus came up and spoke to them. He said, 'All authority in heaven and on earth has been given to me. Go, therefore, make disciples of all the nations; baptise them in the name of the Father and of the Son and of the Holy Spirit, and teach them to observe all the commands I gave you. And know that I am with you always; yes, to the end of time.'

This is the Gospel of the Lord.

Prayer over the Gifts
Lord our God,
make these gifts holy,
and through them
make us a perfect offering to you.

Preface of the Holy Trinity, P43

Communion Antiphon: You are the sons of God, so God has given you the Spirit of his Son to form your hearts and make you cry out: Abba, Father.

Prayer after Communion
Lord God,

we worship you, a Trinity of Persons, one eternal God.
May our faith and the sacrament we receive
bring us health of mind and body.

Thursday after Trinity Sunday
THE BODY AND BLOOD OF CHRIST
Solemnity

The Blood Of The Covenant

The old covenant was sealed with the blood of the sacrifice which Moses sprinkled on the people. The new covenant was sealed with the blood of Christ who offered himself as a perfect sacrifice to God.

Entrance Antiphon: The Lord fed his people with the finest wheat and honey; their hunger was satisfied.

Opening Prayer
Let us pray
    [to the Lord who gives himself in the eucharist,
    that this sacrament may bring us salvation
    and peace]

Lord Jesus Christ,
you gave us the eucharist
as the memorial of your suffering and death.
May our worship of this sacrament of your body and blood
help us to experience the salvation you won for us
and the peace of the kingdom
where you live with the Father and the Holy Spirit,
one God, for ever and ever.
    or
Let us pray
    [for the willingness to make present in our world
    the love of Christ shown to us in the eucharist]

Lord Jesus Christ,
we worship you living among us
in the sacrament of your body and blood.

May we offer to our Father in heaven
a solemn pledge of undivided love.
May we offer to our brothers and sisters
a life poured out in loving service of that kingdom

where you live with the Father and the Holy Spirit,
one God, for ever and ever.

FIRST READING

A reading from the book of Exodus 24:3-8

This is the blood of the Covenant that the Lord has made with you.

Moses went and told the people all the commands of the Lord
and all the ordinances. In answer, all the people said with one
voice, 'We will observe all the commands that the Lord has
decreed.' Moses put all the commands of the Lord into writing,
and early next morning he built an altar at the foot of the
mountain, with twelve standing-stones for the twelve tribes of
Israel. Then he directed certain young Israelites to offer holocausts and to immolate bullocks to the Lord as communion
sacrifices. Half of the blood Moses took up and put into basins,
the other half he cast on the altar. And taking the Book of the
Covenant he read it to the listening people, and they said, 'We
will observe all that the Lord has decreed; we will obey.' Then
Moses took the blood and cast it towards the people. 'This' he
said 'is the blood of the Covenant that the Lord has made with
you, containing all these rules.'

This is the word of the Lord.

Responsorial Psalm Ps 115:12-13. 15-18 ℟ v.13

℟ **The cup of salvation I will raise;**
I will call on the Lord's name.

or

℟ **Alleluia!**

1 How can I repay the Lord
for his goodness to me?
The cup of salvation I will raise;
I will call on the Lord's name. ℟

2 O precious in the eyes of the Lord
is the death of his faithful.
Your servant, Lord, your servant am I;
you have loosened my bonds. ℟

3 A thanksgiving sacrifice I make:
I will call on the Lord's name.
My vows to the Lord I will fulfil
before all his people. ℟

SECOND READING

A reading from the letter to the Hebrews 9:11-15

The blood of Christ can purify our inner self from dead actions.

Now Christ has come, as the high priest of all the blessings which were to come. He has passed through the greater, the more perfect tent, which is better than one made by men's hands because it is not of this created order; and he has entered the sanctuary once and for all, taking with him not the blood of goats and bull calves, but his own blood, having won an eternal redemption for us. The blood of goats and bulls and the ashes of a heifer are sprinkled on those who have incurred defilement and they restore the holiness of their outward lives; how much more effectively the blood of Christ, who offered himself as the perfect sacrifice to God through the eternal Spirit, can purify our inner self from dead actions so that we do our service to the living God.

He brings a new covenant, as the mediator, only so that the people who were called to an eternal inheritance may actually receive what was promised: his death took place to cancel the sins that infringed the earlier covenant.

This is the word of the Lord.

The Sequence, *Sing forth, O Zion*, may be said or sung in its longer or shorter form. See above, pp.365ff.

Gospel Acclamation Jn 6:51-52
Alleluia, alleluia!
I am the living bread which has come down from heaven, says the Lord.
Anyone who eats this bread will live for ever.
Alleluia!

GOSPEL

A reading from the holy Gospel according to Mark 14:12-16. 22-26
This is my body. This is my blood.

On the first day of Unleavened Bread, when the Passover lamb was sacrificed, his disciples said to Jesus, 'Where do you want us to go and make the preparations for you to eat the passover?' So he sent two of his disciples, saying to them, 'Go into the city and you will meet a man carrying a pitcher of water. Follow him, and say to the owner of the house which he enters, "The Master says: Where is my dining room in which I can eat the passover with my disciples?" He will show you a large upper room furnished with couches, all prepared. Make the preparations for us there.' The disciples set out and went to the city and found everything as he had told them, and prepared the Passover.

And as they were eating he took some bread, and when he had said the blessing he broke it and gave it to them, 'Take it,' he said 'this is my body.' Then he took a cup, and when he had returned thanks he gave it to them, and all drank from it, and he said to them, 'This is my blood, the blood of the covenant, which is to be poured out for many. I tell you solemnly, I shall not drink any more wine until the day I drink the new wine in the kingdom of God.'

After psalms had been sung they left for the Mount of Olives.

This is the Gospel of the Lord.

Prayer over the Gifts
Lord,
may the bread and cup we offer
bring your Church the unity and peace they signify.

Preface of the Holy Eucharist I or II, P47 or P48

Communion Antiphon: Whoever eats my flesh and drinks my blood will live in me and I in him, says the Lord.

Prayer after Communion
Lord Jesus Christ,
you give us your body and blood in the eucharist
as a sign that even now we share your life.
May we come to possess it completely in the kingdom
where you live for ever and ever.

Friday after the Second Sunday after Pentecost
THE SACRED HEART OF JESUS   B

The Heart That Was Pierced

Man's rejection of God's love is tragically symbolised by the piercing of the heart of Christ on the cross.

Entrance Antiphon: The thoughts of his heart last through every generation, that he will rescue them from death and feed them in time of famine.

Opening Prayer
Let us pray
[that we will respond to the love of Christ]

Father,
we rejoice in the gifts of love
we have received from the heart of Jesus your Son.
Open our hearts to share his life
and continue to bless us with his love.

or

Father,
we have wounded the heart of Jesus your Son,
but he brings us forgiveness and grace.
Help us to prove our grateful love
and make amends for our sins.

or

Let us pray
[that the love of Christ's heart
may touch the world with healing and peace]

Father,
we honour the heart of your Son
broken by man's cruelty,
yet symbol of love's triumph,
pledge of all that man is called to be.

Teach us to see Christ in the lives we touch,
to offer him living worship
by love-filled service to our brothers and sisters.

FIRST READING

A reading from the prophet Hosea   11:1.3-4. 8-9
My heart recoils from it.

Listen to the word of the Lord:

When Israel was a child I loved him,
and I called my son out of Egypt.
I myself taught Ephraim to walk,
I took them in my arms;
yet they have not understood that I was the one looking after
    them.
I led them with reins of kindness,
with leading-strings of love.
I was like someone who lifts an infant close against his cheek;

stooping down to him I gave him his food.
How could I treat you like Admah,
or deal with you like Zeboiim?
My heart recoils from it,
my whole being trembles at the thought.
I will not give rein to my fierce anger,
I will not destroy Ephraim again,
for I am God, not man:
I am the Holy One in your midst
and have no wish to destroy.

This is the word of the Lord.

Responsorial Psalm   Is 12:2-6. R⩗ v.3
  R⩗ **With joy you will draw water**
      from the wells of the Saviour.

1   Truly God is my salvation,
    I trust, I shall not fear.
    For the Lord is my strength, my song,
    he became my saviour.
    With joy you will draw water
    from the wells of salvation.   R⩗

2   Give thanks to the Lord, give praise to his name!
    Make his mighty deeds known to the peoples!
    Declare the greatness of his name.   R⩗

3   Sing a psalm to the Lord
    for he has done glorious deeds;
    make them known to all the earth!
    People of Zion, sing and shout for joy
    for great in your midst is the Holy One of Israel.   R⩗

SECOND READING
A reading from the letter of St Paul to the Ephesians 3:8-12. 14-19
The love of Christ is beyond all knowledge.

I, Paul, who am less than the least of all the saints, have been
entrusted with this special grace, not only of proclaiming to the
pagans the infinite treasure of Christ but also of explaining how
the mystery is to be dispensed. Through all the ages, this has
been kept hidden in God, the creator of everything. Why? So that
the Sovereignties and Powers should learn only now, through
the Church, how comprehensive God's wisdom really is, exactly
according to the plan which he had had from all eternity in Christ

Jesus our Lord. This is why we are bold enough to approach God in complete confidence, through our faith in him.

This, then, is what I pray, kneeling before the Father, from whom every family, whether spiritual or natural, takes its name:

Out of his infinite glory, may he give you the power through his Spirit for your hidden self to grow strong, so that Christ may live in your hearts through faith, and then, planted in love and built on love, you will with all the saints have strength to grasp the breadth and the length, the height and the depth; until, knowing the love of Christ, which is beyond all knowledge, you are filled with the utter fullness of God.

This is the word of the Lord.

Gospel Acclamation   Mt 11:29
    Alleluia, alleluia!
    Shoulder my yoke and learn from me,
    for I am gentle and humble in heart.
    Alleluia!

Alternative Gospel Acclamation   1 Jn 4:10
    Alleluia, alleluia!
    This is the love I mean:
    God's love for us when he sent his Son
    to be the sacrifice that takes our sins away.
    Alleluia!

GOSPEL

A reading from the holy Gospel according to John   19:31-37
One of the soldiers pierced his side and there came out blood and water.

It was Preparation Day, and to prevent the bodies remaining on the cross during the sabbath since that sabbath was a day of special solemnity – the Jews asked Pilate to have the legs broken and the bodies taken away. Consequently the soldiers came and broke the legs of the first man who had been crucified with him and then of the other. When they came to Jesus, they found he was already dead, and so instead of breaking his legs one of the soldiers pierced his side with a lance; and immediately there came out blood and water. This is the evidence of one who saw it – trustworthy evidence, and he knows he speaks the truth – and he gives it so that you may believe as well. Because all this happened to fulfil the words of scripture:

Not one bone of his will be broken;

and again, in another place scripture says:

> They will look on the one whom they have pierced.

This is the Gospel of the Lord.

Prayer over the Gifts
Lord,
look on the heart of Christ your Son
filled with love for us.
Because of his love
accept our eucharist and forgive our sins.
Preface of the Sacred Heart, P45

Communion Antiphon: The Lord says: If anyone is thirsty, let him come to me; whoever believes in me, let him drink. Streams of living water shall flow out from within him.

or

One of the soldiers pierced Jesus' side with a lance, and at once there flowed out blood and water.

Prayer after Communion
Father,
may this sacrament fill us with love.
Draw us closer to Christ your Son
and help us to recognise him in others.

THE BREAD WE BREAK

BECAUSE THERE IS ONE BREAD WE WHO ARE MANY ARE ONE BODY

SUNDAYS IN ORDINARY TIME

Year B

The cycle of Sundays in Ordinary Time runs from the end of the Christmas season to the beginning of Lent; it recommences after Trinity Sunday, and runs until the beginning of Advent. The number of Sundays in Ordinary Time before Lent, and between Trinity Sunday and Advent, varies: see the Table of Principal Celebrations.

The first week of Ordinary Time begins on the Monday following the Feast of the Baptism of the Lord.

In Cycle B, the Gospel Readings are taken mainly from the Gospel according to St Mark.

First Sunday in Ordinary Time

THE BAPTISM OF THE LORD

See above, p.158.

SECOND SUNDAY IN ORDINARY TIME   B

Answering God's Call

Christ calls each of us by name. In this celebration we listen to what he has to say to us, prepared to use in his service the body that he has given us for the glory of God. We say with him, 'This is my body which is given up for you.'

Entrance Antiphon: May all the earth give you worship and praise, and break into song to your name, O God, Most High.

Opening Prayer
Let us pray
   [to our Father for the gift of peace]

Father of heaven and earth,
hear our prayers,
and show us the way to peace in the world.

or

Let us pray
   [for the gift of peace]

Almighty and ever-present Father,
your watchful care reaches from end to end
and orders all things in such power
that even the tensions and the tragedies of sin
cannot frustrate your loving plans.

Help us to embrace your will,
give us the strength to follow your call,
so that your truth may live in our hearts
and reflect peace to those who believe in your love.

FIRST READING
A reading from the first book of Samuel   3:3-10. 19
Speak, Lord, your servant is listening.

Samuel was lying in the sanctuary of the Lord where the ark of
God was, when the Lord called, 'Samuel! Samuel!' He answered,
'Here I am.' Then he ran to Eli and said, 'Here I am, since you
called me.' Eli said, 'I did not call. Go back and lie down.' So he
went and lay down. Once again the Lord called, 'Samuel!
Samuel!' Samuel got up and went to Eli and said, 'Here I am,
since you called me.' He replied, 'I did not call you, my son; go
back and lie down.' Samuel had as yet no knowledge of the Lord
and the word of the Lord had not yet been revealed to him. Once
again the Lord called, the third time. He got up and went to Eli
and said, 'Here I am, since you called me.' Eli then understood
that it was the Lord who was calling the boy, and he said to
Samuel, 'Go and lie down, and if someone calls say, "Speak,
Lord, your servant is listening." ' So Samuel went and lay down
in his place.

   The Lord then came and stood by, calling as he had done
before, 'Samuel! Samuel!' Samuel answered, 'Speak, Lord, your
servant is listening.'

   Samuel grew up and the Lord was with him and let no word

of his fall to the ground.

This is the word of the Lord.

Responsorial Psalm   Ps 39:2. 4. 7-10. ℟ vv. 8. 9
> ℟ **Here I am, Lord!**
> **I come to do your will.**

1   I waited, I waited for the Lord
      and he stooped down to me;
      he heard my cry.
      He put a new song into my mouth,
      praise of our God.   ℟

2   You do not ask for sacrifice and offerings,
      but an open ear.
      You do not ask for holocaust and victim.
      Instead, here am I.   ℟

3   In the scroll of the book it stands written
      that I should do your will.
      My God, I delight in your law
      in the depth of my heart.   ℟

4   Your justice I have proclaimed
      in the great assembly.
      My lips I have not sealed;
      you know it, O Lord.   ℟

SECOND READING

A reading from the first letter of St Paul   6:13-15. 17-20
to the Corinthians
Your bodies are members making up the body of Christ.

The body is not meant for fornication; it is for the Lord, and the Lord for the body. God who raised the Lord from the dead, will by his power raise us up too.

You know, surely, that your bodies are members making up the body of Christ; anyone who is joined to the Lord is one spirit with him.

Keep away from fornication. All the other sins are committed outside the body; but to fornicate is to sin against your own body. Your body, you know, is the temple of the Holy Spirit, who is in you since you received him from God. You are not your own property; you have been bought and paid for. That is why you should use your body for the glory of God.

This is the word of the Lord.

Gospel Acclamation   1 Sam 3:9; Jn 6:68
    Alleluia, alleluia!
    Speak, Lord, your servant is listening:
    you have the message of eternal life.
    Alleluia!

or   Jn 1:41.17

    Alleluia, alleluia!
    We have found the Messiah – which means the Christ –
    grace and truth have come through him.
    Alleluia!

GOSPEL

A reading from the holy Gospel according to John   1:35-42
They saw where he lived, and stayed with him.

As John stood with two of his disciples, Jesus passed, and John
stared hard at him and said, 'Look, there is the lamb of God.'
Hearing this, the two disciples followed Jesus. Jesus turned
round, saw them following and said, 'What do you want?' They
answered, 'Rabbi,' – which means Teacher – 'where do you live?'
'Come and see' he replied; so they went and saw where he lived,
and stayed with him the rest of that day. It was about the tenth
hour.

    One of these two who became followers of Jesus after hearing
what John had said was Andrew, the brother of Simon Peter.
Early next morning, Andrew met his brother and said to him,
'We have found the Messiah' – which means the Christ – and he
took Simon to Jesus. Jesus looked hard at him and said, 'You are
Simon son of John; you are to be called Cephas' – meaning Rock.

    This is the Gospel of the Lord.

Prayer over the Gifts
Father,
may we celebrate the eucharist
with reverence and love,
for when we proclaim the death of the Lord
you continue the work of his redemption,
who is Lord for ever and ever.

Preface of Sundays in Ordinary Time I-VIII, P29-P36

Communion Antiphon: The Lord has prepared a feast for me: given
wine in plenty for me to drink.

or

We know and believe in God's love for us.

Prayer after Communion
Lord,
you have nourished us with bread from heaven.
Fill us with your Spirit,
and make us one in peace and love.

THIRD SUNDAY IN ORDINARY TIME   B

The Lord Who Teaches Us His Ways

Like Jonah, Christ was sent to preach repentance. He calls us to change our ways. We are not to become engrossed in the world, but to believe the good news and live for the kingdom of God.

Entrance Antiphon: Sing a new song to the Lord! Sing to the Lord, all the earth. Truth and beauty surround him, he lives in holiness and glory.

Opening Prayer
Let us pray
    [for unity and peace]

All-powerful and ever-living God,
direct your love that is within us,
that our efforts in the name of your Son
may bring mankind to unity and peace.

    or

Let us pray
    [pleading that our vision
    may overcome our weakness]

Almighty Father,
the love you offer
always exceeds the furthest expression of our human longing,
for you are greater than the human heart.

Direct each thought, each effort of our life,
so that the limits of our faults and weaknesses
may not obscure the vision of your glory
or keep us from the peace you have promised.

FIRST READING

A reading from the prophet Jonah   3:1-5. 10

The people of Nineveh renounce their evil behaviour.

The word of the Lord was addressed to Jonah: 'Up!' he said 'Go to Nineveh, the great city, and preach to them as I told you to.' Jonah set out and went to Nineveh in obedience to the word of the Lord. Now Nineveh was a city great beyond compare: it took three days to cross it. Jonah went on into the city, making a day's journey. He preached in these words, 'Only forty days more and Nineveh is going to be destroyed.' And the people of Nineveh believed in God; they proclaimed a fast and put on sackcloth, from the greatest to the least.

God saw their efforts to renounce their evil behaviour. And God relented: he did not inflict on them the disaster which he had threatened.

This is the word of the Lord.

Responsorial Psalm   Ps 24:4-9. R℣ v.4

℟ **Lord, make me know your ways.**

1 Lord, make me know your ways.
   Lord, teach me your paths.
   Make me walk in your truth, and teach me:
   for you are God my saviour.   ℟

2 Remember your mercy, Lord,
   and the love you have shown from of old.
   In your love remember me,
   because of your goodness, O Lord.   ℟

3 The Lord is good and upright.
   He shows the path to those who stray,
   he guides the humble in the right path;
   he teaches his way to the poor.   ℟

SECOND READING

A reading from the first letter of St Paul   7:29-31
to the Corinthians

The world as we know it is passing away.

Brothers: our time is growing short. Those who have wives should live as though they had none, and those who mourn should live as though they had nothing to mourn for; those who are enjoying life should live as though there were nothing to laugh about; those whose life is buying things should live as though they had nothing of their own; and those who have to deal with the world should not become engrossed in it. I say this because the world as we know it is passing away.

This is the word of the Lord.

Gospel Acclamation   Mk 1:15
Alleluia, alleluia!
The kingdom of God is close at hand;
believe the Good News.
Alleluia!

GOSPEL

A reading from the holy Gospel according to Mark   1:14-20
Repent, and believe the Good News.

After John had been arrested, Jesus went into Galilee. There he proclaimed the Good News from God. 'The time has come' he said 'and the kingdom of God is close at hand. Repent, and believe the Good News.'

As he was walking along by the Sea of Galilee he saw Simon and his brother Andrew casting a net in the lake – for they were fishermen. And Jesus said to them, 'Follow me and I will make you into fishers of men.' And at once they left their nets and followed him.

Going on a little further, he saw James son of Zebedee and his brother John; they too were in their boat, mending their nets. He called them at once and, leaving their father Zebedee in the boat with the men he employed, they went after him.

This is the Gospel of the Lord.

Prayer over the Gifts
Lord,
receive our gifts.
Let our offerings make us holy
and bring us salvation.

Preface of Sundays in Ordinary Time I-VIII, P29-P36

Communion Antiphon: Look up at the Lord with gladness and smile; your face will never be ashamed.

or

I am the light of the world, says the Lord; the man who follows me will have the light of life.

Prayer after Communion
God, all-powerful Father,
may the new life you give us increase our love
and keep us in the joy of your kingdom.

FOURTH SUNDAY IN ORDINARY TIME B

The Lord, Our Teacher
Today we celebrate him who speaks with authority and to whom we must
give our undivided attention.

Entrance Antiphon: Save us, Lord our God, and gather us together
from the nations, that we may proclaim your holy name and
glory in your praise.

Opening Prayer
Let us pray
    [for a greater love of God
    and of our fellow men]

Lord our God,
help us to love you with all our hearts
and to love all men as you love them.

or

Let us pray
    [joining in the praise of the living God
    for we are his people]

Father in heaven,
from the days of Abraham and Moses
until this gathering of your Church in prayer,
you have formed a people in the image of your Son.

Bless this people with the gift of your kingdom.
May we serve you with our every desire
and show love for one another
even as you have loved us.

FIRST READING
A reading from the book of Deuteronomy   18:15-20
I will raise up a prophet and I will put my words into his mouth.

Moses said to the people: 'Your God will raise up for you a

prophet like myself, from among yourselves, from your own brothers; to him you must listen. This is what you yourselves asked of the Lord your God at Horeb on the day of the Assembly. "Do not let me hear again" you said "the voice of the Lord my God, nor look any longer on this great fire, or I shall die"; and the Lord said to me, "All they have spoken is well said. I will raise up a prophet like yourself for them from their own brothers; I will put my words into his mouth and he shall tell them all I command him. The man who does not listen to my words that he speaks in my name, shall be held answerable to me for it. But the prophet who presumes to say in my name a thing I have not commanded him to say, or who speaks in the name of other gods, that prophet shall die." '

This is the word of the Lord.

Responsorial Psalm   Ps 94:1-2. 6-9. R℣ v.9

℟   **O that today you would listen to his voice!**
    Harden not your hearts.

1   Come, ring out our joy to the Lord;
    hail the rock who saves us.
    Let us come before him, giving thanks,
    with songs let us hail the Lord.   ℟

2   Come in; let us kneel and bend low;
    let us kneel before the God who made us
    for he is our God and we
    the people who belong to his pasture,
    the flock that is led by his hand.   ℟

3   O that today you would listen to his voice!
    'Harden not your hearts as at Meribah,
    as on that day at Massah in the desert
    when your fathers put me to the test;
    when they tried me, though they saw my work.'   ℟

SECOND READING

A reading from the first letter of St Paul   7:32-35
to the Corinthians

An unmarried woman can devote herself to the Lord's affairs; all she need worry about is being holy.

I would like to see you free from all worry. An unmarried man can devote himself to the Lord's affairs, all he need worry about is pleasing the Lord; but a married man has to bother about the world's affairs and devote himself to pleasing his wife: he is torn two ways. In the same way an unmarried woman, like a young girl, can devote herself to the Lord's affairs; all she need worry about is being holy in body and spirit. The married woman, on the other hand, has to worry about the world's affairs and devote herself to pleasing her husband. I say this only to help you, not to put a halter round your necks, but simply to make sure that everything is as it should be, and that you give your undivided attention to the Lord.

This is the word of the Lord.

Gospel Acclamation   cf. Mt 11:25
Alleluia, alleluia!
Blessed are you, Father,
Lord of heaven and earth,
for revealing the mysteries of the kingdom
to mere children.
Alleluia!

or   Mt 4:16

Alleluia, alleluia!
The people that lived in darkness
has seen a great light;
on those who dwell in the land and shadow of death
a light has dawned.
Alleluia!

GOSPEL

A reading from the holy Gospel according to Mark   1:21-28
He taught them with authority.

Jesus and his followers went as far as Capernaum, and as soon as the sabbath came Jesus went to the synagogue and began to teach. And his teaching made a deep impression on them because, unlike the scribes, he taught them with authority.

In their synagogue just then there was a man possessed by an unclean spirit, and it shouted, 'What do you want with us, Jesus of Nazareth? Have you come to destroy us? I know who you are: the Holy One of God.' But Jesus said sharply, 'Be quiet! Come out of him!' And the unclean spirit threw the man into convulsions and with a loud cry went out of him. The people were so astonished that they started asking each other what it all meant. 'Here is a teaching that is new' they said 'and with authority behind it: he gives orders even to unclean spirits and they obey him.' And his reputation rapidly spread everywhere, through all the surrounding Galilean countryside.

This is the Gospel of the Lord.

Prayer over the Gifts
Lord,
be pleased with the gifts we bring to your altar,
and make them the sacrament of our salvation.

Preface of Sundays in Ordinary Time I-VIII, P29-P36

Communion Antiphon: Let your face shine on your servant, and save me by your love. Lord, keep me from shame, for I have called to you.

or

Happy are the poor in spirit; the kingdom of heaven is theirs! Happy are the lowly; they shall inherit the land.

Prayer after Communion
Lord,
you invigorate us with this help to our salvation.
By this eucharist give the true faith continued growth
throughout the world.

FIFTH SUNDAY IN ORDINARY TIME   B

Christ Who Makes Us Free To Serve

Without Christ our lives would be pure drudgery. We would be like slaves, or like workmen with nothing to look forward to but our wages. But the healing power of Christ has transformed our lives: now we are free to make ourselves like him, the slaves of everyone, offering men the good news without asking for anything in return.

Entrance Antiphon: Come, let us worship the Lord. Let us bow down in the presence of our maker, for he is the Lord our God.

Opening Prayer
Let us pray
    [that God will watch over us and protect us]

Father,
watch over your family
and keep us safe in your care,
for all our hope is in you.

or

Let us pray
    [with reverence in the presence of the living God]

In faith and love we ask you, Father,
to watch over your family gathered here.
In your mercy and loving kindness
no thought of ours is left unguarded,
no tear unheeded, no joy unnoticed.

Through the prayer of Jesus
may the blessings promised to the poor in spirit
lead us to the treasures of your heavenly kingdom.

FIRST READING

A reading from the book of Job   7:1-4. 6-7
Restlessly I fret till twilight falls.

Job began to speak:

Is not man's life on earth nothing more than pressed service,
his time no better than hired drudgery?
Like the slave, sighing for the shade,
or the workman with no thought but his wages,
months of delusion I have assigned to me,
nothing for my own but nights of grief.
Lying in bed I wonder, 'When will it be day?'
Risen I think, 'How slowly evening comes!'
Restlessly I fret till twilight falls.
Swifter than a weaver's shuttle my days have passed,
and vanished, leaving no hope behind.
Remember that my life is but a breath,
and that my eyes will never again see joy.

This is the word of the Lord.

Responsorial Psalm   Ps 146:1-6. ℟ v.3

  ℟ **Praise the Lord who heals the broken-hearted.**

or

  ℟ **Alleluia!**

1 Praise the Lord for he is good;
   sing to our God for he is loving:
   to him our praise is due.   ℟

2 The Lord builds up Jerusalem
   and brings back Israel's exiles,
   he heals the broken-hearted,
   he binds up all their wounds.
   He fixes the number of the stars;
   he calls each one by its name.   ℟

3 Our Lord is great and almighty;
   his wisdom can never be measured.
   The Lord raises the lowly;
   he humbles the wicked to the dust.   ℟

SECOND READING

A reading from the first letter of St Paul   9:16-19. 22-23
to the Corinthians
I should be punished if I did not preach the Gospel.

I do not boast of preaching the gospel, since it is a duty which has
been laid on me; I should be punished if I did not preach it! If I
had chosen this work myself, I might have been paid for it, but as
I have not, it is a responsibility which has been put into my
hands. Do you know what my reward is? It is this: in my
preaching, to be able to offer the Good News free, and not insist
on the rights which the gospel gives me.

So though I am not a slave of any man I have made myself the
slave of everyone so as to win as many as I could. For the weak I
made myself weak. I made myself all things to all men in order to
save some at any cost; and I still do this, for the sake of the
gospel, to have a share in its blessing.

This is the word of the Lord.

Gospel Acclamation   Jn 8:12
    Alleluia, alleluia!
    I am the light of the world, says the Lord,
    anyone who follows me

will have the light of life.
Alleluia!

or

Mt 8:17

Alleluia, alleluia!
He took our sicknesses away,
and carried our diseases for us.
Alleluia!

GOSPEL

A reading from the holy Gospel according to Mark 1:29-39
He cured many who were suffering from diseases of one kind or another.

On leaving the synagogue, Jesus went with James and John straight to the house of Simon and Andrew. Now Simon's mother-in-law had gone to bed with fever, and they told him about her straightaway. He went to her, took her by the hand and helped her up. And the fever left her and she began to wait on them.

That evening, after sunset, they brought to him all who were sick and those who were possessed by devils. The whole town came crowding round the door, and he cured many who were suffering from diseases of one kind or another; he also cast out many devils, but he would not allow them to speak, because they knew who he was.

In the morning, long before dawn, he got up and left the house, and went off to a lonely place and prayed there. Simon and his companions set out in search of him, and when they found him they said, 'Everybody is looking for you.' He answered, 'Let us go elsewhere, to the neighbouring country towns, so that I can preach there too, because that is why I came.' And he went all through Galilee, preaching in their synagogues and casting out devils.

This is the Gospel of the Lord.

Prayer over the Gifts
Lord our God,
may the bread and wine
you give us for our nourishment on earth
become the sacrament of our eternal life.

Preface of Sundays in Ordinary Time I-VIII, P29-36

Communion Antiphon: Give praise to the Lord for his kindness, for his wonderful deeds towards men. He has filled the hungry with good things, he has satisfied the thirsty.

or

Happy are the sorrowing; they shall be consoled. Happy those who hunger and thirst for what is right; they shall be satisfied.

Prayer after Communion
God our Father,
you give us a share in the one bread and the one cup
and make us one in Christ.
Help us to bring your salvation and joy
to all the world.

SIXTH SUNDAY IN ORDINARY TIME   B

Jesus, Friend Of Outcasts

To bring help to outcasts, Jesus himself had to become an outcast and 'stay outside in places where nobody lived'.

Entrance Antiphon: Lord, be my rock of safety, the stronghold that saves me. For the honour of your name, lead me and guide me.

Opening Prayer
Let us pray
   [that everything we do
   will be guided by God's law of love]

God our Father,
you have promised to remain for ever
with those who do what is just and right.
Help us to live in your presence.
or
Let us pray
   [for the wisdom that is greater than human words]

Father in heaven,
the loving plan of your wisdom took flesh in Jesus Christ,
and changed mankind's history
by his command of perfect love.

May our fulfilment of his command reflect your wisdom
and bring your salvation to the ends of the earth.

FIRST READING

A reading from the book of Leviticus   13:1-2. 44-46
The leper must live apart: he must live outside the camp.

The Lord said to Moses and Aaron, 'If a swelling or scab or shiny spot appears on a man's skin, a case of leprosy of the skin is to be suspected. The man must be taken to Aaron, the priest, or to one of the priests who are his sons.

'The man is leprous: he is unclean. The priest must declare him unclean; he is suffering from leprosy of the head. A man infected with leprosy must wear his clothing torn and his hair disordered; he must shield his upper lip and cry, "Unclean, unclean." As long as the disease lasts he must be unclean; and therefore he must live apart; he must live outside the camp.'

This is the word of the Lord.

Responsorial Psalm   Ps 31:1-2. 5. 11. ℟ v.7

℟ **You are my refuge, O Lord;**
    you fill me with the joy of salvation.

1   Happy the man whose offence is forgiven,
    whose sin is remitted.
    O happy the man to whom the Lord
    imputes no guilt,
    in whose spirit is no guile. ℟

2   But now I have acknowledged my sins;
    my guilt I did not hide.
    I said: 'I will confess
    my offence to the Lord.'
    And you, Lord, have forgiven
    the guilt of my sin. ℟

3   Rejoice, rejoice in the Lord,
    exult, you just!
    O come, ring out your joy,
    all you upright of heart. ℟

SECOND READING

A reading from the first letter of St Paul   10:31 – 11:1
to the Corinthians

Take me for your model, as I take Christ.

Whatever you eat, whatever you drink, whatever you do at all, do it for the glory of God. Never do anything offensive to anyone – to Jews or Greeks or to the Church of God; just as I try to be helpful to everyone at all times, not anxious for my own advantage but for the advantage of everybody else, so that they may be saved.

Take me for your model, as I take Christ.

This is the word of the Lord.

Gospel Acclamation   cf. Eph 1:17. 18
    Alleluia, alleluia!
    May the Father of our Lord Jesus Christ
    enlighten the eyes of our mind,
    so that we can see what hope his call holds for us.
    Alleluia!

or   Lk 7:16

    Alleluia, alleluia!
    A great prophet has appeared among us;
    God has visited his people.
    Alleluia!

GOSPEL

A reading from the holy Gospel according to Mark   1:40-45
The leprosy left him at once and he was cured.

A leper came to Jesus and pleaded on his knees: 'If you want to'
he said 'you can cure me.' Feeling sorry for him, Jesus stretched
out his hand and touched him. 'Of course I want to!' he said. 'Be
cured!' And the leprosy left him at once and he was cured. Jesus
immediately sent him away and sternly ordered him, 'Mind you
say nothing to anyone, but go and show yourself to the priest,
and make the offering for your healing prescribed by Moses as
evidence of your recovery.' The man went away, but then started
talking about it freely and telling the story everywhere, so that
Jesus could no longer go openly into any town, but had to stay
outside in places where nobody lived. Even so, people from all
around would come to him.

    This is the Gospel of the Lord.

Prayer over the Gifts
Lord,
we make this offering in obedience to your word.
May it cleanse and renew us,
and lead us to our eternal reward.

Preface of Sundays in Ordinary Time I-VIII, P29-P36

Communion Antiphon: They ate and were filled; the Lord gave
them what they wanted: they were not deprived of their desire.

or

God loved the world so much, he gave his only Son, that all who
believe in him might not perish, but might have eternal life.

Prayer after Communion
Lord,
you give us food from heaven.
May we always hunger
for the bread of life.

SEVENTH SUNDAY IN ORDINARY TIME   B

Christ Forgives Our Sins

*Today we say Yes to the Lord who comes to forgive us our sins, and we
praise him who shows such mercy to the poor and the weak.*

Entrance Antiphon: Lord, your mercy is my hope, my heart
rejoices in your saving power. I will sing to the Lord for his
goodness to me.

Opening Prayer
Let us pray
   [that God will make us more like Christ, his Son]

Father,
keep before us the wisdom and love
you have revealed in your Son.
Help us to be like him
in word and deed,
for he lives and reigns with you and the Holy Spirit,
one God, for ever and ever.
  or

Let us pray
   [to the God of power and might,
   for his mercy is our hope]

Almighty God,
Father of our Lord Jesus Christ,
faith in your word is the way to wisdom,
and to ponder your divine plan is to grow in the truth.

Open our eyes to your deeds,

our ears to the sound of your call,
so that our every act may increase our sharing
in the life you have offered us.

FIRST READING

A reading from the prophet Isaiah   43:18-19. 21-22. 24-25

I it is who must blot out everything.

Thus says the Lord:
   No need to recall the past,
   no need to think about what was done before.
   See, I am doing a new deed,
   even now it comes to light; can you not see it?
   Yes, I am making a road in the wilderness,
   paths in the wilds.
   The people I have formed for myself
   will sing my praises.
   Jacob, you have not invoked me,
   you have not troubled yourself, Israel, on my behalf.
   Instead you have burdened me with your sins,
   troubled me with your iniquities.
   I it is, I it is, who must blot out everything
   and not remember your sins.

   This is the word of the Lord.

Responsorial Psalm   Ps 40:2-5. 13-14. R̸ v.5
   R̸ **Heal my soul for I have sinned against you.**

1   Happy the man who considers the poor and the weak.
   The Lord will save him in the day of evil,
   will guard him, give him life, make him happy in the land
   and will not give him up to the will of his foes.   R̸

2   The Lord will help him on his bed of pain,
   he will bring him back from sickness to health.
   As for me, I said: 'Lord, have mercy on me,
   heal my soul for I have sinned against you.'   R̸

3   If you uphold me I shall be unharmed
   and set in your presence for evermore.
   Blessed be the Lord, the God of Israel
   from age to age. Amen. Amen.   R̸

SECOND READING

A reading from the second letter of St Paul   1:18-22
to the Corinthians

Jesus was never Yes and No: with him it was always Yes.

I swear by God's truth, there is no Yes and No about what we say
to you. The Son of God, the Christ Jesus that we proclaimed
among you – I mean Silvanus and Timothy and I – was never Yes
and No: with him it was always Yes, and however many the
promises God made, the Yes to them all is in him. That is why it
is 'through him' that we answer Amen to the praise of God.
Remember it is God himself who assures us all, and you, of our
standing in Christ, and has anointed us, marking us with his seal
and giving us the pledge, the Spirit, that we carry in our hearts.

This is the word of the Lord.

Gospel Acclamation   Jn 1:14. 12
Alleluia, alleluia!
The Word was made flesh and lived among us;
to all who did accept him
he gave power to become children of God.
Alleluia!

or   cf Lk 4:18

Alleluia, alleluia!
The Lord has sent me to bring the good news to the poor,
to proclaim liberty to captives.
Alleluia!

GOSPEL

A reading from the holy Gospel according to Mark   2:1-12
The Son of Man has authority on earth to forgive sins.

When Jesus returned to Capernaum, word went round that he
was back; and so many people collected that there was no room
left, even in front of the door. He was preaching the word to
them when some people came bringing him a paralytic carried by
four men, but as the crowds made it impossible to get the man to
him, they stripped the roof over the place where Jesus was; and
when they had made an opening, they lowered the stretcher on
which the paralytic lay. Seeing their faith, Jesus said to the
paralytic, 'My child, your sins are forgiven.' Now some scribes
were sitting there, and they thought to themselves, 'How can
this man talk like that? He is blaspheming. Who can forgive sins

but God?' Jesus, inwardly aware that this was what they were thinking, said to them, 'Why do you have these thoughts in your hearts? Which of these is easier: to say to the paralytic, "Your sins are forgiven" or to say, "Get up, pick up your stretcher and walk?" But to prove to you that the Son of Man has authority on earth to forgive sins,' – he said to the paralytic – 'I order you: get up, pick up your stretcher, and go off home.' And the man got up, picked up his stretcher at once and walked out in front of everyone, so that they were all astounded and praised God saying, 'We have never seen anything like this.'

This is the Gospel of the Lord.

Prayer over the Gifts
Lord,
as we make this offering,
may our worship in Spirit and truth
bring us salvation.
Preface of Sundays in Ordinary Time I-VIII, P29-P36

Communion Antiphon: I will tell all your marvellous works. I will rejoice and be glad in you, and sing to your name, Most High.
or

Lord, I believe that you are the Christ, the Son of God, who was to come into this world.

Prayer after Communion
Almighty God,
help us to live the example of love
we celebrate in this eucharist,
that we may come to its fulfilment in your presence.

EIGHTH SUNDAY IN ORDINARY TIME   B

Christ The Bridegroom
Today the love of Christ for his Church is shown to be no less than the love of a bridegroom for his bride. His love-letter is written on every Christian heart.

Entrance Antiphon: The Lord has been my strength; he has led me into freedom. He saved me because he loves me.

Opening Prayer

Let us pray
> [that God will bring peace to the world
> and freedom to his Church]

Lord,
guide the course of world events
and give your Church the joy and peace
of serving you in freedom.

or

Let us pray
> [that the peace of Christ
> may find welcome in the world]

Father in heaven,
form in us the likeness of your Son
and deepen his life within us.
Send us as witnesses of gospel joy
into a world of fragile peace and broken promises.
Touch the hearts of all men with your love
that they in turn may love one another.

FIRST READING

A reading from the prophet Hosea   2:16-17. 21-22
I will betroth you to myself for ever.

Thus says the Lord:
> I am going to lure her
> and lead her out into the wilderness
> and speak to her heart.
> There she will respond to me as she did when she was young,
> as she did when she came out of the land of Egypt.
> I will betroth you to myself for ever,
> betroth you with integrity and justice,
> with tenderness and love;
> I will betroth you to myself with faithfulness,
> and you will come to know the Lord.

This is the word of the Lord.

Responsorial Psalm   Ps 102:1-4. 8. 10. 12-13. R℣ v.8
   R℣ **The Lord is compassion and love.**

1   My soul, give thanks to the Lord,
     all my being, bless his holy name.
     My soul, give thanks to the Lord
     and never forget all his blessings. R℣

2   It is he who forgives all your guilt,
     who heals every one of your ills,
     who redeems your life from the grave,
     who crowns you with love and compassion. R℣

3   The Lord is compassion and love,
     slow to anger and rich in mercy.
     He does not treat us according to our sins
     nor repay us according to our faults. R℣

4   So far as the east is from the west
     so far does he remove our sins.
     As a father has compassion on his sons,
     the Lord has pity on those who fear him. R℣

SECOND READING

A reading from the second letter of St Paul   3:1-6
to the Corinthians
You are a letter from Christ drawn up by us.

Unlike other people, we need no letters of recommendation
either to you or from you, because you are yourselves our letter,
written in our hearts, that anybody can see and read, and it is
plain that you are a letter from Christ, drawn up by us, and
written not with ink but with the Spirit of the living God, not on
stone tablets but on the tablets of your living hearts.

   Before God, we are confident of this through Christ: not that
we are qualified in ourselves to claim anything as our own work:
all our qualifications come from God. He is the one who has
given us the qualifications to be the administrators of this new
covenant, which is not a covenant of written letters but of the
Spirit: the written letters bring death, but the Spirit gives life.

   This is the word of the Lord.

Gospel Acclamation   Jn 10:27
   Alleluia, alleluia!
   The sheep that belong to me listen to my voice,

says the Lord,
I know them and they follow me.
Alleluia!

or

James 1:18

Alleluia, alleluia!
By his own choice the Father made us his children
by the message of the truth,
so that we should be a sort of first-fruits
of all that he created.
Alleluia!

GOSPEL

A reading from the holy Gospel according to Mark 2:18-22
The bridegroom is with them.

One day when John's disciples and the Pharisees were fasting, some people came and said to Jesus, 'Why is it that John's disciples and the disciples of the Pharisees fast, but your disciples do not?' Jesus replied, 'Surely the bridegroom's attendants would never think of fasting while the bridegroom is still with them? As long as they have the bridegroom with them, they could not think of fasting. But the time will come for the bridegroom to be taken away from them, and then, on that day, they will fast. No one sews a piece of unshrunken cloth on an old cloak; if he does, the patch pulls away from it, the new from the old, and the tear gets worse. And nobody puts new wine into old wineskins; if he does, the wine will burst the skins, and the wine is lost and the skins too. No! New wine, fresh skins!'

This is the Gospel of the Lord.

Prayer over the Gifts
God our Creator,
may this bread and wine we offer
as a sign of our love and worship
lead us to salvation.

Preface of Sundays in Ordinary Time I-VIII, P29-P36

Communion Antiphon: I will sing to the Lord for his goodness to me, I will sing the name of the Lord, Most High.

or

I, the Lord, am with you always, until the end of the world.

Prayer after Communion
God of salvation,
may this sacrament which strengthens us here on earth
bring us to eternal life.

NINTH SUNDAY IN ORDINARY TIME   B

The Lord Of The Sabbath

*The Christian Sabbath is the Lord's day: the day of his triumph over sin
and death. It is our day of respite from the drabness of the daily routine,
the day on which in our mortal flesh the life of Jesus is openly shown.*

Entrance Antiphon: O look at me and be merciful, for I am
wretched and alone. See my hardship and my poverty, and
pardon all my sins.

Opening Prayer
Let us pray
[for God's care and protection]

Father,
your love never fails.
Hear our call.
Keep us from danger
and provide for all our needs.

or

Let us pray
[for the confidence born of faith]

God our Father,
teach us to cherish the gifts that surround us.
Increase our faith in you
and bring our trust to its promised fulfilment
in the joy of your kingdom.

FIRST READING

A reading from the book of Deuteronomy   5:12-15
Remember that you were a servant in the land of Egypt.

The Lord says this: 'Observe the sabbath day and keep it holy, as
the Lord your God has commanded you. For six days you shall
labour and do all your work, but the seventh day is a sabbath for

the Lord your God. You shall do no work that day, neither you nor your son nor your daughter nor your servants, men or women, nor your ox nor your donkey nor any of your animals, nor the stranger who lives with you. Thus your servant, man or woman, shall rest as you do. Remember that you were a servant in the land of Egypt, and that the Lord your God brought you out from there with mighty hand and outstretched arm; because of this, the Lord your God has commanded you to keep the sabbath day.'

This is the word of the Lord.

Responsorial Psalm   Ps 80:3-8. 10-11. ℟ v.2

℟ **Ring out your joy to God our strength.**

1   Raise a song and sound the timbrel,
    the sweet-sounding harp and the lute,
    blow the trumpet at the new moon,
    when the moon is full, on our feast.   ℟

2   For this is Israel's law,
    a command of the God of Jacob.
    He imposed it as a rule on Joseph,
    when he went out against the land of Egypt.   ℟

3   A voice I did not know said to me:
    'I freed your shoulder from the burden;
    your hands were freed from the load.
    You called in distress and I saved you.   ℟

4   'Let there be no foreign god among you,
    no worship of an alien god.
    I am the Lord your God,
    who brought you from the land of Egypt.'   ℟

SECOND READING

A reading from the second letter of St Paul   4:6-11
to the Corinthians
In our mortal flesh the life of Jesus is openly shown.

It is the same God that said, 'Let there be light shining out of darkness,' who has shone in our minds to radiate the light of the knowledge of God's glory, the glory on the face of Christ.

We are only the earthenware jars that hold this treasure, to make it clear that such an overwhelming power comes from God and not from us. We are in difficulties on all sides, but never cornered; we see no answer to our problems, but never despair; we have been persecuted, but never deserted; knocked down, but never killed; always, wherever we may be, we carry with us in our body the death of Jesus, so that the life of Jesus, too, may always be seen in our body. Indeed, while we are still alive, we are consigned to our death every day, for the sake of Jesus, so that in our mortal flesh the life of Jesus, too, may be openly shown.

This is the word of the Lord.

Gospel Acclamation   cf. Jn 6:63. 68

Alleluia, alleluia!
Your words are spirit, Lord,
and they are life:
you have the message of eternal life.
Alleluia!

or   cf. Jn 17:17

Alleluia, alleluia!
Your word is truth, O Lord,
consecrate us in the truth.
Alleluia!

GOSPEL

A reading from the holy Gospel according to Mark   2:23 – 3:6

The Son of Man is master even of the Sabbath.

*One sabbath day Jesus happened to be taking a walk through the cornfields, and his disciples began to pick ears of corn as they went along. And the Pharisees said to him, 'Look, why are they doing something on the sabbath day that is forbidden?' And he replied, 'Did you ever read what David did in his time of need when he and his followers were hungry – how he went into the house of God when Abiathar was high priest, and ate the loaves of offering which only the priests are allowed to eat, and how he also gave some to the men with him?'

And he said to them, 'The sabbath was made for man, not man for the sabbath; so the Son of Man is master even of the sabbath.'*

He went again into a synagogue, and there was a man there who had a withered hand. And they were watching him to see if he would cure him on the sabbath day, hoping for something to use against him. He said to the man with the withered hand, 'Stand up out in the middle!' Then he said to them, 'Is it against the law on the sabbath day to do good, or to do evil; to save life, or to kill?' But they said nothing. Then, grieved to find them so obstinate, he looked angrily round at them, and said to the man, 'Stretch out your hand.' He stretched it out and his hand was better. The Pharisees went out and at once began to plot with the Herodians against him, discussing how to destroy him.

This is the Gospel of the Lord.

*Shorter Form, verses 23-28, read between *

Prayer over the Gifts
Lord,
as we gather to offer our gifts
confident in your love,
make us holy by sharing your life with us
and by this eucharist forgive our sins.

Preface of Sundays in Ordinary Time I-VIII, P29-P36

Communion Antiphon: I call upon you, God, for you will answer me; bend your ear and hear my prayer.

or

I tell you solemnly, whatever you ask for in prayer, believe that you have received it, and it will be yours, says the Lord.

Prayer after Communion
Lord,
as you give us the body and blood of your Son,
guide us with your Spirit
that we may honour you
not only with our lips,
but also with the lives we lead,
and so enter your kingdom.

TENTH SUNDAY IN ORDINARY TIME   **B**

Mary, The Type Of The Church

In Mary, we see the fullness of redemption. Today we celebrate with her, who did the will of God throughout her life and who was the first whom God raised with Jesus and put by his side.

Entrance Antiphon: The Lord is my light and my salvation. Who shall frighten me? The Lord is the defender of my life. Who shall make me tremble?

Opening Prayer
Let us pray
    [for the guidance of the Holy Spirit]

God of wisdom and love,
source of all good,
send your Spirit to teach us your truth
and guide our actions
in your way of peace.

or

Let us pray
    [to our Father
      who calls us to freedom in Jesus his Son]

Father in heaven,
words cannot measure the boundaries of love
for those born to new life in Christ Jesus.
Raise us beyond the limits this world imposes,
so that we may be free to love as Christ teaches
and find our joy in your glory.

FIRST READING

A reading from the book of Genesis   3:9-15

I will make you enemies of each other: you and the woman, your offspring and her offspring.

The Lord God called to the man after he had eaten of the tree. 'Where are you?' he asked. 'I heard the sound of you in the garden;' he replied 'I was afraid because I was naked, so I hid.' 'Who told you that you were naked?' he asked. 'Have you been eating of the tree I forbade you to eat?' The man replied, 'It was the woman you put with me; she gave me the fruit, and

I ate it.' Then the Lord God asked the woman, 'What is this you have done?' The woman replied, 'The serpent tempted me and I ate.'

Then the Lord God said to the serpent, 'Because you have done this,

'Be accursed beyond all cattle,
all wild beasts.
You shall crawl on your belly and eat dust
every day of your life.
I will make you enemies of each other:
you and the woman,
your offspring and her offspring.
It will crush your head
and you will strike its heel.'

This is the word of the Lord.

Responsorial Psalm   Ps 129. ℟ v.7

   ℟ **With the Lord there is mercy
       and fullness of redemption.**

1 Out of the depths I cry to you, O Lord,
   Lord, hear my voice!
   O let your ears be attentive
   to the voice of my pleading.   ℟

2 If you, O Lord, should mark our guilt,
   Lord, who would survive?
   But with you is found forgiveness:
   for this we revere you.   ℟

3 My soul is waiting for the Lord,
   I count on his word.
   My soul is longing for the Lord
   more than watchman for daybreak.   ℟

4 Because with the Lord there is mercy
   and fullness of redemption,
   Israel indeed he will redeem
   from all its iniquity.   ℟

SECOND READING

A reading from the second letter of St Paul   4:13 – 5:1
to the Corinthians
We believe and therefore we also speak.

As we have the same spirit of faith that is mentioned in scripture

– I believed, and therefore I spoke – we too believe and therefore we too speak, knowing that he who raised the Lord Jesus to life will raise us with Jesus in our turn, and put us by his side and you with us. You see, all this is for your benefit, so that the more grace is multiplied among people, the more thanksgiving there will be, to the glory of God.

That is why there is no weakening on our part, and instead, though this outer man of ours may be falling into decay, the inner man is renewed day by day. Yes, the troubles which are soon over, though they weigh little, train us for the carrying of a weight of eternal glory which is out of all proportion to them. And so we have no eyes for things that are visible, but only for things that are invisible; for visible things last only for a time, and the invisible things are eternal.

For we know that when the tent that we live in on earth is folded up, there is a house built by God for us, an everlasting home not made by human hands, in the heavens.

This is the word of the Lord.

Gospel Acclamation　　　　　　　　　　　　　　Jn 14:23
Alleluia, alleluia!
If anyone loves me he will keep my word,
and my Father will love him,
and we shall come to him.
Alleluia!

or　　　　　　　　　　　　　　　　　　　　　　Jn 12:31.32

Alleluia, alleluia!
Now the prince of this world is to be overthrown,
says the Lord.
And when I am lifted up from the earth,
I shall draw all men to myself.
Alleluia!

GOSPEL

A reading from the holy Gospel according to Mark　　3:20-35
It is the end of Satan.

Jesus went home with his disciples, and such a crowd collected that they could not even have a meal. When his relatives heard of this, they set out to take charge of him, convinced he was out of his mind.

The scribes who had come down from Jerusalem were saying,

'Beelzebul is in him,' and, 'It is through the prince of devils that he casts devils out.' So he called them to him and spoke to them in parables, 'How can Satan cast out Satan? If a kingdom is divided against itself, that kingdom cannot last. And if a house-hold is divided against itself, that household can never stand. Now if Satan has rebelled against himself and is divided, he cannot stand either – it is the end of him. But no one can make his way into a strong man's house and burgle his property unless he has tied up the strong man first. Only then can he burgle his house.

'I tell you solemnly, all men's sins will be forgiven, and all their blasphemies; but let anyone blaspheme against the Holy Spirit and he will never have forgiveness: he is guilty of an eternal sin.' This was because they were saying, 'An unclean spirit is in him.'

His mother and brothers now arrived and, standing outside, sent in a message asking for him. A crowd was sitting round him at the time the message was passed to him, 'Your mother and brothers and sisters are outside asking for you.' He replied, 'Who are my mother and my brothers?' And looking round at those sitting in a circle about him, he said, 'Here are my mother and my brothers. Anyone who does the will of God, that person is my brother and sister and mother.'

This is the Gospel of the Lord.

Prayer over the Gifts
Lord,
look with love on our service.
Accept the gifts we bring
and help us grow in Christian love.

Preface of Sundays in Ordinary Time I-VIII, P29-P36

Communion Antiphon: I can rely on the Lord; I can always turn to him for shelter. It was he who gave me my freedom. My God, you are always there to help me!

or

God is love, and he who lives in love, lives in God, and God in him.

Prayer after Communion
Lord,
may your healing love
turn us from sin
and keep us on the way that leads to you.

ELEVENTH SUNDAY IN ORDINARY TIME **B**

The Cedar Of Lebanon

The Church of Christ is like a tree that God planted in the world. From the smallest of seeds it became the noblest of trees and filled the earth. We are like the birds of the air who make their home in him.

Entrance Antiphon: Lord, hear my voice when I call to you. You are my help; do not cast me off, do not desert me, my Saviour God.

Opening Prayer

Let us pray
    [for the grace to follow Christ more closely]

Almighty God,
our hope and our strength,
without you we falter.
Help us to follow Christ
and to live according to your will.
    or

Let us pray
    [to the Father
    whose love gives us strength to follow his Son]

God our Father,
we rejoice in the faith that draws us together,
aware that selfishness can drive us apart.
Let your encouragement be our constant strength.
Keep us one in the love that has sealed our lives,
help us to live as one family
the gospel we profess.

FIRST READING

A reading from the prophet Ezekiel   17:22-24
I make low trees grow.

The Lord says this:

'From the top of the cedar,
from the highest branch I will take a shoot
and plant it myself on a very high mountain.
I will plant it on the high mountain of Israel.
It will sprout branches and bear fruit,

and become a noble cedar.
Every kind of bird will live beneath it,
every winged creature rest in the shade of its branches.
And every tree of the field will learn that I, the Lord, am the
    one
who stunts tall trees and makes the low ones grow,
who withers green trees and makes the withered green.
I, the Lord, have spoken, and I will do it.'

 This is the word of the Lord.

Responsorial Psalm   Ps 91:2-3. 13-16. R℣ cf. v.2
    R℣ **It is good to give you thanks, O Lord.**

1 It is good to give thanks to the Lord
   to make music to your name, O Most High,
   to proclaim your love in the morning
   and your truth in the watches of the night.   R℣

2 The just will flourish like the palm-tree
   and grow like a Lebanon cedar.   R℣

3 Planted in the house of the Lord
   they will flourish in the courts of our God,
   still bearing fruit when they are old,
   still full of sap, still green,
   to proclaim that the Lord is just.
   In him, my rock, there is no wrong.   R℣

SECOND READING

A reading from the second letter of St Paul   5:6-10
to the Corinthians

Whether we are living in the body or exiled from it, we are intent on
pleasing the Lord.

We are always full of confidence when we remember that to live
in the body means to be exiled from the Lord, going as we do by
faith and not by sight – we are full of confidence, I say, and
actually want to be exiled from the body and make our home
with the Lord. Whether we are living in the body or exiled from
it, we are intent on pleasing him. For all the truth about us will be
brought out in the law court of Christ, and each of us will get
what he deserves for the things he did in the body, good or bad.

 This is the word of the Lord.

Gospel Acclamation   Jn 15:15
>   Alleluia, alleluia!
>   I call you friends, says the Lord,
>   because I have made known to you
>   everything I have learnt from my Father.
>   Alleluia!

or

>   Alleluia, alleluia!
>   The seed is the word of God, Christ the sower;
>   whoever finds the seed will remain for ever.
>   Alleluia!

GOSPEL

A reading from the holy Gospel according to Mark   4:26-34

It is the smallest of all the seeds; yet it grows into the biggest shrub of them all.

Jesus said to the crowds: 'This is what the kingdom of God is like. A man throws seed on the land. Night and day, while he sleeps, when he is awake, the seed is sprouting and growing; how, he does not know. Of its own accord the land produces first the shoot, then the ear, then the full grain in the ear. And when the crop is ready, he loses no time: he starts to reap because the harvest has come.'

He also said, 'What can we say the kingdom of God is like? What parable can we find for it? It is like a mustard seed which at the time of its sowing in the soil is the smallest of all the seeds on earth; yet once it is sown it grows into the biggest shrub of them all and puts out big branches so that the birds of the air can shelter in its shade.'

Using many parables like these, he spoke the word to them, so far as they were capable of understanding it. He would not speak to them except in parables, but he explained everything to his disciples when they were alone.

> This is the Gospel of the Lord.

Prayer over the Gifts
Lord God,
in this bread and wine
you give us food for body and spirit.
May the eucharist renew our strength
and bring us health of mind and body.

Preface of Sundays in Ordinary Time I-VIII, P29-P36

Communion Antiphon: **One thing I seek: to dwell in the house of the Lord all the days of my life.**

or

Father, keep in your name those you have given me, that they may be one as we are one, says the Lord.

Prayer after Communion
Lord,
may this eucharist
accomplish in your Church
the unity and peace it signifies.

TWELFTH SUNDAY IN ORDINARY TIME   B

The Lord Of The Storm

Just to know that Christ is with us amid all the turbulence of life is a great cause for celebration and thanksgiving. With Christ the turbulence can become the birth pangs of a new creation.

Entrance Antiphon: **God is the strength of his people. In him, we his chosen live in safety. Save us, Lord, who share in your life, and give us your blessing; be our shepherd for ever.**

Opening Prayer
Let us pray
   [that we may grow in the love of God]

Father,
guide and protector of your people,
grant us an unfailing respect for your name,
and keep us always in your love.

or

Let us pray
   [to God whose fatherly love keeps us safe]

God of the universe,
we worship you as Lord.
God, ever close to us,
we rejoice to call you Father.
From this world's uncertainty we look to your covenant.
Keep us one in your peace, secure in your love.

FIRST READING

A reading from the book of Job   3:1.8-11
Here your proud waves shall break.

From the heart of tempest the Lord gave Job his answer. He said:

> Who pent up the sea behind closed doors
> when it leapt tumultuous out of the womb,
> when I wrapped it in a robe of mist
> and made black clouds its swaddling bands;
> when I marked the bounds it was not to cross
> and made it fast with a bolted gate?
> Come thus far, I said, and no farther:
> here your proud waves shall break.

This is the word of the Lord.

Responsorial Psalm   Ps 106:23-26. 28-31. ℟ v.1
　℟　**O give thanks to the Lord,**
　　for his love endures for ever.

or

　℟　**Alleluia!**

1　Some sailed to the sea in ships
　　to trade on the mighty waters.
　　These men have seen the Lord's deeds,
　　the wonders he does in the deep.　℟

2　For he spoke; he summoned the gale.
　　tossing the waves of the sea
　　up to heaven and back into the deep;
　　their soul melted away in their distress.　℟

3　Then they cried to the Lord in their need
　　and he rescued them from their distress
　　He stilled the storm to a whisper:
　　all the waves of the sea were hushed.　℟

4　They rejoiced because of the calm
　　and he led them to the haven they desired.
　　Let them thank the Lord for his love,
　　the wonders he does for men.　℟

SECOND READING

A reading from the second letter of St Paul 5:14-17
to the Corinthians
Now the new creation is here.

The love of Christ overwhelms us when we reflect that if one
man has died for all, then all men should be dead; and the reason
he died for all was so that living men should live no longer for
themselves, but for him who died and was raised to life for them.

From now onwards, therefore, we do not judge anyone by
the standards of the flesh. Even if we did once know Christ in the
flesh, that is not how we know him now. And for anyone who is
in Christ, there is a new creation; the old creation has gone, and
now the new one is here.

This is the word of the Lord.

Gospel Acclamation cf. Eph 1:17. 18
Alleluia, alleluia!
May the Father of our Lord Jesus Christ
enlighten the eyes of our mind,
so that we can see what hope his call holds for us.
Alleluia!

or Lk 7:16

Alleluia, alleluia!
A great prophet has appeared among us;
God has visited his people.
Alleluia!

GOSPEL

A reading from the holy Gospel according to Mark 4:35-41
Who can this be? Even the wind and the sea obey him.

With the coming of evening, Jesus said to his disciples, 'Let us
cross over to the other side.' And leaving the crowd behind they
took him, just as he was, in the boat; and there were other boats
with him. Then it began to blow a gale and the waves were
breaking into the boat so that it was almost swamped. But he was
in the stern, his head on the cushion, asleep. They woke him and
said to him, 'Master, do you not care? We are going down!' And
he woke up and rebuked the wind and said to the sea, 'Quiet
now! Be calm!' And the wind dropped, and all was calm again.
Then he said to them, 'Why are you so frightened? How is it that
you have no faith?' They were filled with awe and said to one

another, 'Who can this be? Even the wind and the sea obey him.'

This is the Gospel of the Lord.

Prayer over the Gifts
Lord,
receive our offering,
and may this sacrifice of praise
purify us in mind and heart
and make us always eager to serve you.

Preface of Sundays in Ordinary Time I-VIII, P29-P36

Communion Antiphon: The eyes of all look to you, O Lord, and you give them food in due season.

or

I am the Good Shepherd; I give my life for my sheep, says the Lord.

Prayer after Communion
Lord,
you give us the body and blood of your Son
to renew your life within us.
In your mercy, assure our redemption
and bring us to the eternal life
we celebrate in this eucharist.

THIRTEENTH SUNDAY IN ORDINARY TIME   B
The Lord Who Gives Life

The Lord made us to live. Death is totally opposed to God, who is life itself. And yet Christ accepted death in order that we might live. He took our poverty to make us rich.

Entrance Antiphon: All nations, clap your hands. Shout with a voice of joy to God.

Opening Prayer
Let us pray
[that Christ may be our light]

Father,
you call your children
to walk in the light of Christ.
Free us from darkness
and keep us in the radiance of your truth.

or

Let us pray
　　[for the strength to reject the darkness of sin]

Father in heaven,
the light of Jesus
has scattered the darkness of hatred and sin.
Called to that light
we ask for your guidance.
Form our lives in your truth, our hearts in your love.

FIRST READING

A reading from the book of Wisdom　　　1:13-15; 2:23-24
It was the devil's envy that brought death into the world.

Death was not God's doing,
he takes no pleasure in the extinction of the living.
To be – for this he created all;
the world's created things have health in them,
in them no fatal poison can be found,
and Hades holds no power on earth;
for virtue is undying.
Yet God did make man imperishable,
he made him in the image of his own nature;
it was the devil's envy that brought death into the world,
as those who are his partners will discover.

　　This is the word of the Lord.

Responsorial Psalm　　　　　Ps 29:2. 4-6. 11-13. ℟ v.2
　　℟　**I will praise you, Lord, you have rescued me.**

1　I will praise you, Lord, you have rescued me
　　and have not let my enemies rejoice over me.
　　O Lord, you have raised my soul from the dead,
　　restored me to life from those who sink into the grave.　℟

2　Sing psalms to the Lord, you who love him,
　　give thanks to his holy name.

(continued)

His anger lasts but a moment; his favour through life.
At night there are tears, but joy comes with dawn.

℟ **I will praise you, Lord, you have rescued me.**

3   The Lord listened and had pity.
The Lord came to my help.
For me you have changed my mourning into dancing,
O Lord my God, I will thank you for ever.   ℟

SECOND READING

A reading from the second letter of St Paul   8:7. 9. 13-15
to the Corinthians

In giving relief to others, balance what happens to be your surplus now
against their present need.

You always have the most of everything – of faith, of eloquence,
of understanding, of keenness for any cause, and the biggest
share of our affection – so we expect you to put the most into this
work of mercy too. Remember how generous the Lord Jesus was:
he was rich, but he became poor for your sake, to make you rich
out of his poverty. This does not mean that to give relief to others
you ought to make things difficult for yourselves: it is a question
of balancing what happens to be your surplus now against their
present need, and one day they may have something to spare
that will supply your own need. That is how we strike a balance:
as scripture says: The man who gathered much had none too
much, the man who gathered little did not go short.

This is the word of the Lord.

Gospel Acclamation   cf. Jn 6:63. 68
Alleluia, alleluia!
Your words are spirit, Lord,
and they are life:
you have message of eternal life.
Alleluia!

or   cf. 2 Tim 1:10

Alleluia, alleluia!
Our Saviour Christ Jesus abolished death,
and he has proclaimed life through the Good News.
Alleluia!

GOSPEL

A reading from the holy Gospel according to Mark   5:21-43

Little girl, I tell you to get up.

When Jesus had crossed in the boat to the other side, a large crowd gathered round him and he stayed by the lakeside. Then one of the synagogue officials came up, Jairus by name, and seeing him, fell at his feet and pleaded with him earnestly, saying, 'My little daughter is desperately sick. Do come and lay your hands on her to make her better and save her life.' Jesus went with him and a large crowd followed him; they were pressing all round him.

Now there was a woman who had suffered from a haemorrhage for twelve years; after long and painful treatment under various doctors, she had spent all she had without being any the better for it, in fact, she was getting worse. She had heard about Jesus, and she came up behind him through the crowd and touched his cloak. 'If I can touch even his clothes,' she had told herself 'I shall be well again.' And the source of the bleeding dried up instantly, and she felt in herself that she was cured of her complaint. Immediately aware that power had gone out from him Jesus turned round in the crowd and said, 'Who touched my clothes?' His disciples said to him, 'You see how the crowd is pressing round you and yet you say, "Who touched me?" ' But he continued to look all round to see who had done it. Then the woman came forward, frightened and trembling because she knew what had happened to her, and she fell at his feet and told him the whole truth. 'My daughter,' he said 'your faith has restored you to health; go in peace and be free from your complaint.'

While he was still speaking some people arrived from the house of the synagogue offical to say, 'Your daughter is dead: why put the Master to any further trouble?' But Jesus had overheard this remark of theirs and he said to the official, 'Do not be afraid; only have faith.' And he allowed no one to go with him except Peter and James and John the brother of James. So they came to the official's house and Jesus noticed all the commotion, with people weeping and wailing unrestrainedly. He went in and said to them, 'Why all this commotion and crying? The child is not dead, but asleep.' But they laughed at him. So he turned them all out and, taking with him the child's father and mother and his own companions, he went into the place where the child lay. And taking the child by the hand he said to her, 'Talitha, kum!' which means, 'Little girl, I tell you to get up.' The little girl got up at once and began to walk about, for she was twelve years old. At this they were overcome with astonishment, and he ordered them strictly not to let anyone know about it, and told them to give her something to eat.

This is the Gospel of the Lord.*

*Shorter Form, verses 21-24. 35-43. Read between *

Prayer over the Gifts
Lord God,
through your sacraments
you give us the power of your grace.
May this eucharist
help us to serve you faithfully.

Preface of Sundays in Ordinary Time I-VIII, P29-P36

Communion Antiphon: O, bless the Lord, my soul, and all that is within me bless his holy name.

or

Father, I pray for them: may they be one in us, so that the world may believe it was you who sent me.

Prayer after Communion
Lord,
may this sacrifice and communion
give us a share in your life
and help us bring your love to the world.

FOURTEENTH SUNDAY IN ORDINARY TIME B

The Church As Prophet of God

The Church rejoices in the spirit of prophecy, even though the exercise of that charism does not bring her any honour from the world. It is exercised in weakness.

Entrance Antiphon: Within your temple, we ponder your loving kindness, O God. As your name, so also your praise reaches to the ends of the earth; your right hand is filled with justice.

Opening Prayer
Let us pray
[for forgiveness through the grace of Jesus Christ]

Father,
through the obedience of Jesus,
your servant and your Son,
you raised a fallen world.
Free us from sin
and bring us the joy that lasts for ever.

or

Let us pray
    [for greater willingness
    to serve God and our fellow man]

Father,
in the rising of your Son
death gives birth to new life.
The sufferings he endured restored hope to a fallen world.

Let sin never ensnare us
with empty promises of passing joy.
Make us one with you always,
so that our joy may be holy,
and our love may give life.

FIRST READING

A reading from the prophet Ezekiel   2:2-5
*The sons are defiant and obstinate and they shall know that there is a
prophet among them.*

The spirit came into me and made me stand up, and I heard the
Lord speaking to me. He said, 'Son of man, I am sending you to
the Israelites, to the rebels who have turned against me. Till now
they and their ancestors have been in revolt against me. The sons
are defiant and obstinate; I am sending you to them, to say, "The
Lord says this." Whether they listen or not, this set of rebels shall
know there is a prophet among them.'

This is the word of the Lord.

Responsorial Psalm   Ps 122. R̥ v.2
    R̥ **Our eyes are on the Lord**
        till he show us his mercy.

1   To you have I lifted up my eyes,
    you who dwell in the heavens:
    my eyes, like the eyes of slaves
    on the hand of their lords. R̥

2   Like the eyes of a servant
    on the hand of her mistress,
    so our eyes are on the Lord our God
    till he show us his mercy.

    ℟   **Our eyes are on the Lord
    till he shows us his mercy.**

3   Have mercy on us, Lord, have mercy.
    We are filled with contempt.
    Indeed all too full is our soul
    with the scorn of the rich,
    with the proud man's disdain.   ℟

SECOND READING

A reading from the second letter of St Paul   12:7-10
to the Corinthians
I shall be very happy to make my weaknesses my special boast so that the
power of Christ may stay over me.

In view of the extraordinary nature of these revelations, to stop
me from getting too proud I was given a thorn in the flesh, an
angel of Satan to beat me and stop me from getting too proud!
About this thing, I have pleaded with the Lord three times for it
to leave me, but he has said, 'My grace is enough for you: my
power is at its best in weakness.' So I shall be very happy to make
my weaknesses my special boast so that the power of Christ may
stay over me, and that is why I am quite content with my
weaknesses, and with insults, hardships, persecutions, and the
agonies I go through for Christ's sake. For it is when I am weak
that I am strong.

    This is the word of the Lord.

Gospel Acclamation   Jn 1:14. 12
    Alleluia, alleluia!
    The Word was made flesh and lived among us;
    to all who did accept him
    he gave power to become children of God.
    Alleluia!

or   cf. Lk 4:18

    Alleluia, alleluia!
    The Lord has sent me to bring the good news to the poor,
    to proclaim liberty to captives.
    Alleluia!

GOSPEL

A reading from the holy Gospel according to Mark 6:1-6
A prophet is only despised in his own country.

Jesus went to his home town and his disciples accompanied him. With the coming of the sabbath he began teaching in the synagogue and most of them were astonished when they heard him. They said, 'Where did the man get all this? What is this wisdom that has been granted him, and these miracles that are worked through him? This is the carpenter, surely, the son of Mary, the brother of James and Joset and Jude and Simon? His sisters, too, are they not here with us?' And they would not accept him. And Jesus said to them, 'A prophet is only despised in his own country among his own relations and in his own house'; and he could work no miracle there, though he cured a few sick people by laying his hands on them. He was amazed at their lack of faith.

This is the Gospel of the Lord.

Prayer over the Gifts
Lord,
let this offering to the glory of your name
purify us and bring us closer to eternal life.

Preface of Sundays in Ordinary Time I-VIII, P29-P36

Communion Antiphon: Taste and see the goodness of the Lord; blessed is he who hopes in God.

or

Come to me, all you that labour and are burdened, and I will give you rest, says the Lord.

Prayer after Communion
Lord,
may we never fail to praise you
for the fullness of life and salvation
you give us in this eucharist.

FIFTEENTH SUNDAY IN ORDINARY TIME **B**

The Missionary Church

'Go, tell my people,' is the command we have been given by God. And the message is the most stupendous one imaginable: that God has blessed us with all the spiritual blessings from heaven in Christ.

Entrance Antiphon: In my justice I shall see your face, O Lord; when your glory appears, my joy will be full.

Opening Prayer
Let us pray
    [that the gospel may be our rule of life]

God our Father,
your light of truth
guides us to the way of Christ.
May all who follow him
reject what is contrary to the gospel.

or

Let us pray
    [to be faithful to the light we have received,
    to the name we bear]

Father,
let the light of your truth
guide us to your kingdom
through a world filled with lights contrary to your own.
Christian is the name and the gospel we glory in.
May your love make us what you have called us to be.

FIRST READING

A reading from the prophet Amos   7:12-15
Go, prophesy to my people.

Amaziah, the priest of Bethel, said to Amos, 'Go away, seer; get back to the land of Judah; earn your bread there, do your prophesying there. We want no more prophesying in Bethel; this is the royal sanctuary, the national temple.' 'I was no prophet, neither did I belong to any of the brotherhoods of prophets,' Amos replied to Amaziah. 'I was a shepherd, and looked after sycamores: but it was the Lord who took me from herding the flock, and the Lord who said, "Go, prophesy to my people

Israel." '

This is the word of the Lord.

Responsorial Psalm   Ps 84:9-14. R℣ v.8
R℣ **Let us see, O Lord, your mercy
    and give us your saving help.**

1 I will hear what the Lord God has to say,
   a voice that speaks of peace,
   peace for his people.
   His help is near for those who fear him
   and his glory will dwell in our land.   R℣

2 Mercy and faithfulness have met;
   justice and peace have embraced.
   Faithfulness shall spring from the earth
   and justice look down from heaven.   R℣

3 The Lord will make us prosper
   and our earth shall yield its fruit.
   Justice shall march before him
   and peace shall follow his steps.   R℣

SECOND READING
A reading from the letter of St Paul to the Ephesians   1:3-14
Before the world was made, God chose us.

*Blessed be God the Father of our Lord Jesus Christ,
who has blessed us with all the spiritual blessings of heaven in
    Christ.
Before the world was made, he chose us, chose us in Christ,
to be holy and spotless, and to live through love in his presence,
determining that we should become his adopted sons, through
    Jesus Christ
for his own kind purposes,
to make us praise the glory of his grace,
his free gift to us in the Beloved
in whom, through his blood, we gain our freedom, the
    forgiveness of our sins.
Such is the richness of the grace
which he has showered on us
in all wisdom and insight.
He has let us know the mystery of his purpose,
the hidden plan he so kindly made in Christ from the beginning

to act upon when the times had run their course to the end:
that he would bring everything together under Christ, as head,
everything in the heavens and everything on earth.*

And it is in him that we were claimed as God's own,
chosen from the beginning,
under the predetermined plan of the one who guides all things
as he decides by his own will;
chosen to be,
for his greater glory,
the people who would put their hopes in Christ before he came.
Now you too, in him,
have heard the message of the truth and the good news of your
    salvation,
and have believed it:
and you too have been stamped with the seal of the Holy Spirit of
    the Promise,
the pledge of our inheritance
which brings freedom for those whom God has taken for his
    own,
to make his glory praised.

   This is the word of the Lord.

*Shorter Form, verses 3-10. Read between *

Gospel Acclamation   cf. Jn 6:63. 68
    Alleluia, alleluia!
    Your words are spirit, Lord,
    and they are life:
    you have the message of eternal life.
    Alleluia!

or   cf. Eph 1:17.18

    Alleluia, alleluia!
    May the Father of our Lord Jesus Christ
    enlighten the eyes of our mind,
    so that we can see what hope his call holds for us.
    Alleluia!

GOSPEL
A reading from the holy Gospel according to Mark   6:7-13
He began to send them out.

Jesus summoned the Twelve and began to send them out in pairs giving them authority over the unclean spirits. And he instructed them to take nothing for the journey except a staff – no bread, no haversack, no coppers for their purses. They were to wear sandals but, he added, 'Do not take a spare tunic.' And he said to them, 'If you enter a house anywhere, stay there until you leave the district. And if any place does not welcome you and people refuse to listen to you, as you walk away shake off the dust from under your feet as a sign to them.' So they set off to preach repentance; and they cast out many devils, and anointed many sick people with oil and cured them.

This is the Gospel of the Lord.

Prayer over the Gifts
Lord,
accept the gifts of your Church.
May this eucharist
help us grow in holiness and faith.

Preface of Sundays in Ordinary Time I-VIII, P29-P36

Communion Antiphon: The sparrow even finds a home, the swallow finds a nest wherein to place her young, near to your altars, Lord of hosts, my King, my God! How happy they who dwell in your house! For ever they are praising you.

or

Whoever eats my flesh and drinks my blood will live in me and I in him, says the Lord.

Prayer after Communion
Lord,
by our sharing in the mystery of this eucharist,
let your saving love grow within us.

SIXTEENTH SUNDAY IN ORDINARY TIME   B

Christ The Good Shepherd

Today we celebrate the Shepherd who leads all men to the Father, however far apart they may be in race or culture.

Entrance Antiphon: God himself is my help. The Lord upholds my life. I will offer you a willing sacrifice; I will praise your name, O Lord, for its goodness.

Opening Prayer

Let us pray
    [to be kept faithful in the service of God]

Lord,
be merciful to your people.
Fill us with your gifts
and make us always eager to serve you
in faith, hope, and love.

or

Let us pray
    [that God will continue to bless us
    with his compassion and love]

Father,
let the gift of your life
continue to grow in us,
drawing us from death to faith, hope, and love.
Keep us alive in Christ Jesus.
Keep us watchful in prayer
and true to his teaching
till your glory is revealed in us.

FIRST READING

A reading from the prophet Jeremiah   23:1-6
*The remnant of my flock I will gather and I will raise up shepherds to look
after them.*

'Doom for the shepherds who allow the flock of my pasture to be
destroyed and scattered – it is the Lord who speaks! This,
therefore, is what the Lord, the God of Israel, says about the
shepherds in charge of my people: You have let my flock be
scattered and go wandering and have not taken care of them.
Right, I will take care of you for your misdeeds – it is the Lord
who speaks! But the remnant of my flock I myself will gather
from all the countries where I have dispersed them, and will
bring them back to their pastures: they shall be fruitful and
increase in numbers. I will raise up shepherds to look after them
and pasture them; no fear, no terror for them any more; not one
shall be lost – it is the Lord who speaks!

'See, the days are coming – it is the Lord who speaks –
when I will raise a virtuous Branch for David,
who will reign as true king and be wise,

practising honesty and integrity in the land.
In his days Judah will be saved
and Israel dwell in confidence.
And this is the name he will be called:
The Lord-our-integrity.'

This is the word of the Lord.

Responsial Psalm   Ps 22. ℟ v.1

℟ **The Lord is my shepherd;
    there is nothing I shall want.**

1 The Lord is my shepherd;
   there is nothing I shall want.
   Fresh and green are the pastures
   where he gives me repose.
   Near restful waters he leads me,
   to revive my drooping spirit.   ℟

2 He guides me along the right path;
   he is true to his name.
   If I should walk in the valley of darkness
   no evil would I fear.
   You are there with your crook and your staff;
   with these you give me comfort.   ℟

3 You have prepared a banquet for me
   in the sight of my foes.
   My head you have anointed with oil;
   my cup is overflowing.   ℟

4 Surely goodness and kindness shall follow me
   all the days of my life.
   In the Lord's own house shall I dwell
   for ever and ever.   ℟

SECOND READING
A reading from the letter of St Paul to the Ephesians   2:13-18
Christ Jesus is the peace between us, and has made the two into one.

In Christ Jesus, you that used to be so far apart from us have been
brought very close, by the blood of Christ. For he is the peace
between us, and has made the two into one and broken down the
barrier which used to keep them apart, actually destroying in his
own person the hostility caused by the rules and decrees of the
Law. This was to create one single New Man in himself out of the

two of them and by restoring peace through the cross, to unite them both in a single Body and reconcile them with God. In his own person he killed the hostility. Later he came to bring the good news of peace, peace to you who were far away and peace to those who were near at hand. Through him, both of us have in the one Spirit our way to come to the Father.

This is the word of the Lord.

Gospel Acclamation   Jn 10:27
Alleluia, alleluia!
The sheep that belong to me listen to my voice,
says the Lord,
I know them and they follow me.
Alleluia!

GOSPEL

A reading from the holy Gospel according to Mark   6:30-34
They were like sheep without a shepherd.

The apostles rejoined Jesus and told him all they had done and taught. Then he said to them, 'You must come away to some lonely place all by yourselves and rest for a while'; for there were so many coming and going that the apostles had no time even to eat. So they went off in a boat to a lonely place where they could be by themselves. But people saw them going, and many could guess where; and from every town they all hurried to the place on foot and reached it before them. So as he stepped ashore he saw a large crowd; and he took pity on them because they were like sheep without a shepherd, and he set himself to teach them at some length.

This is the Gospel of the Lord.

Prayer over the Gifts
Lord,
bring us closer to salvation
through these gifts which we bring in your honour.
Accept the perfect sacrifice you have given us,
bless it as you blessed the gifts of Abel.

Preface of Sundays in Ordinary Time I-VIII, P29-P36

Communion Antiphon: The Lord keeps in our minds the wonderful things he has done. He is compassion and love; he always provides for his faithful.

or

I stand at the door and knock, says the Lord. If anyone hears my voice and opens the door, I will come in and sit down to supper with him, and he with me.

Prayer after Communion
Merciful Father,
may these mysteries
give us new purpose
and bring us to a new life in you.

SEVENTEENTH SUNDAY IN ORDINARY TIME B

Christ Who Feeds Us

We celebrate today the new Elisha who feeds his people and makes us one body, one spirit, in himself.

Entrance Antiphon: God is in his holy dwelling; he will give a home to the lonely, he gives power and strength to his people.

Opening Prayer
Let us pray
　[that we will make good use of the gifts
　that God has given us]

God our Father and protector,
without you nothing is holy,
nothing has value.
Guide us to everlasting life
by helping us to use wisely
the blessings you have given to the world.
or

Let us pray
　[for the faith to recognise God's presence in our world]

God our Father,
open our eyes to see your hand at work
in the splendour of creation,
in the beauty of human life.
Touched by your hand our world is holy.
Help us to cherish the gifts that surround us,
to share your blessings with our brothers and sisters,
and to experience the joy of life in your presence.

FIRST READING

A reading from the second book of the Kings   4:42-44

They will eat and have some left over.

A man came from Baal-shalishah, bringing Elisha, the man of God, bread from the first-fruits, twenty barley loaves and fresh grain in the ear. 'Give it to the people to eat,' Elisha said. But his servant replied, 'How can I serve this to a hundred men?' 'Give it to the people to eat' he insisted 'for the Lord says this, "They will eat and have some left over." ' He served them; they ate and had some over, as the Lord had said.

This is the word of the Lord.

Responsorial Psalm   Ps 144:10-11. 15-18. ℟ v. 16

℟ **You open wide your hand, O Lord,
    and grant our desires.**

1 All your creatures shall thank you, O Lord,
   and your friends shall repeat their blessing.
   They shall speak of the glory of your reign
   and declare your might, O God. ℟

2 The eyes of all creatures look to you
   and you give them their food in due time.
   You open wide your hand,
   grant the desires of all who live. ℟

3 The Lord is just in all his ways
   and loving in all his deeds.
   He is close to all who call him,
   who call on him from their hearts. ℟

SECOND READING

A reading from the letter of St Paul to the Ephesians   4:1-6

One Body, one Lord, one faith, one baptism.

I, the prisoner in the Lord, implore you to lead a life worthy of your vocation. Bear with one another charitably, in complete selflessness, gentleness and patience. Do all you can to preserve the unity of the Spirit by the peace that binds you together. There is one Body, one Spirit, just as you were all called into one and the same hope when you were called. There is one Lord, one faith, one baptism, and one God who is Father of all, through all and within all.

This is the word of the Lord.

Gospel Acclamation cf. Jn 6:63. 68

Alleluia, alleluia!
Your words are spirit, Lord,
and they are life:
you have the message of eternal life.
Alleluia!

or Lk 7:16

Alleluia, alleluia!
A great prophet has appeared among us;
God has visited his people.
Alleluia!

GOSPEL

A reading from the holy Gospel according to John 6:1-15
Jesus gave out as much as was wanted to all who were sitting ready.

Jesus went off to the other side of the Sea of Galilee – or of Tiberias – and a large crowd followed him, impressed by the signs he gave by curing the sick. Jesus climbed the hillside, and sat down there with his disciples. It was shortly before the Jewish feast of Passover.

Looking up, Jesus saw the crowds approaching and said to Philip, 'Where can we buy some bread for these people to eat?' He only said this to test Philip; he himself knew exactly what he was going to do. Philip answered, 'Two hundred denarii would only buy enough to give them a small piece each.' One of his disciples, Andrew, Simon Peter's brother, said, 'There is a small boy here with five barley loaves and two fish; but what is that between so many?' Jesus said to them, 'Make the people sit down.' There was plenty of grass there, and as many as five thousand men sat down. Then Jesus took the loaves, gave thanks, and gave them out to all who were sitting ready; he then did the same with the fish, giving out as much as was wanted. When they had eaten enough he said to the disciples, 'Pick up the pieces left over, so that nothing gets wasted.' So they picked them up, and filled twelve hampers with scraps left over from the meal of five barley loaves. The people, seeing this sign that he had given, said, 'This really is the prophet who is to come into the world.' Jesus, who could see they were about to come and take him by force and make him king, escaped back to the hills by himself.

This is the Gospel of the Lord.

Prayer over the Gifts

Lord,
receive these offerings
chosen from your many gifts.
May these mysteries make us holy
and lead us to eternal joy.

Preface of Sundays in Ordinary Time I-VIII, P29-P36

Communion Antiphon: O, bless the Lord, my soul, and remember
all his kindness.

or

Happy are those who show mercy; mercy shall be theirs. Happy
are the pure of heart, for they shall see God.

Prayer after Communion

Lord,
we receive the sacrament
which celebrates the memory
of the death and resurrection of Christ your Son.
May this gift bring us closer to our eternal salvation.

EIGHTEENTH SUNDAY IN ORDINARY TIME   B

Bread From Heaven

*Through Christ we have undergone what St Paul calls a spiritual
revolution and we can no longer be satisfied with material things. We
need the food that comes from heaven, the bread of life which we receive at
this Mass.*

Entrance Antiphon: God, come to my help. Lord, quickly give me
assistance. You are the one who helps me and sets me free: Lord,
do not be long in coming.

Opening Prayer

Let us pray
    [for the gift of God's forgiveness and love]

Father of everlasting goodness,
our origin and guide,
be close to us
and hear the prayers of all who praise you.

Forgive our sins and restore us to life.
Keep us safe in your love.

or

Let us pray

[to the Father whose kindness never fails]

God our Father,
gifts without measure flow from your goodness
to bring us your peace.
Our life is your gift.
Guide our life's journey,
for only your love makes us whole.
Keep us strong in your love.

FIRST READING

A reading from the first book of Exodus   16:2-4
I will rain down bread for you from the heavens.

The whole community of the sons of Israel began to complain
against Moses and Aaron in the wilderness and said to them,
'Why did we not die at the Lord's hand in the land of Egypt,
when we were able to sit down to pans of meat and could eat
bread to our heart's content! As it is, you have brought us to this
wilderness to starve this whole company to death!'

Then the Lord said to Moses, 'Now I will rain down bread for
you from the heavens. Each day the people are to go out and
gather the day's portion; I propose to test them in this way to see
whether they will follow my law or not.'

'I have heard the complaints of the sons of Israel. Say this to
them, "Between the two evenings you shall eat meat, and in the
morning you shall have bread to your heart's content. Then you
will learn that I, the Lord, am your God." ' And so it came about:
quails flew up in the evening, and they covered the camp; in the
morning there was a coating of dew all round the camp. When
the coating of dew lifted, there on the surface of the desert was a
thing delicate, powdery, as fine as hoarfrost on the ground.
When they saw this, the sons of Israel said to one another, 'What
is that?' not knowing what it was. 'That' said Moses to them 'is
the bread the Lord gives you to eat.'

This is the word of the Lord.

Responsorial Psalm   Ps 77:3-4. 23-25. 54. ℟ v.24

   ℟ **The Lord gave them bread from heaven.**

1 The things we have heard and understood,
   the things our fathers have told us,
   we will tell to the next generation:
   the glories of the Lord and his might. ℟

2 He commanded the clouds above
   and opened the gates of heaven.
   He rained down manna for their food,
   and gave them bread from heaven. ℟

3 Mere men ate the bread of angels.
   He sent them abundance of food.
   He brought them to his holy land,
   to the mountain which his right hand had won. ℟

SECOND READING

A reading from the letter of St Paul to the Ephesians 4:17. 20-24
Put on the new self that has been created in God's way.

I want to urge you in the name of the Lord, not to go on living the
aimless kind of life that pagans live. Now that is hardly the way
you have learnt from Christ, unless you failed to hear him
properly when you were taught what the truth is in Jesus. You
must give up your old way of life; you must put aside your old
self, which gets corrupted by following illusory desires. Your
mind must be renewed by a spiritual revolution so that you can
put on the new self that has been created in God's way, in the
goodness and holiness of the truth.

   This is the word of the Lord.

Gospel Acclamation   Jn 14:5

   Alleluia, alleluia!
   I am the Way, the Truth and the Life, says the Lord;
   no one can come to the Father except through me.
   Alleluia!

or   Mt 4:4

   Alleluia, alleluia!
   Man does not live on bread alone,
   but on every word that comes from the mouth of God.
   Alleluia!

GOSPEL

A reading from the holy Gospel according to John   6:24-35

He who comes to me will never be hungry; he who believes in me will never thirst.

When the people saw that neither Jesus nor his disciples were there, they got into boats and crossed to Capernaum to look for Jesus. When they found him on the other side, they said to him, 'Rabbi, when did you come here?' Jesus answered:

'I tell you most solemnly,
you are not looking for me
because you have seen the signs
but because you had all the bread you wanted to eat.
Do not work for food that cannot last,
but work for food that endures to eternal life,
the kind of food the Son of Man is offering you,
for on him the Father, God himself, has set his seal.'

Then they said to him, 'What must we do if we are to do the works that God wants?' Jesus gave them this answer, 'This is working for God: you must believe in the one he has sent.' So they said, 'What sign will you give to show us that we should believe in you? What work will you do? Our fathers had manna to eat in the desert; as scripture says: He gave them bread from heaven to eat.'

Jesus answered:

'I tell you most solemnly,
it was not Moses who gave you bread from heaven,
it is my Father who gives you the bread from heaven,
the true bread;
for the bread of God
is that which comes down from heaven
and gives life to the world.'

'Sir,' they said 'give us that bread always.' Jesus answered:

'I am the bread of life.
He who comes to me will never be hungry;
he who believes in me will never thirst.'

This is the Gospel of the Lord.

Prayer over the Gifts
Merciful Lord,

make holy these gifts,
and let our spiritual sacrifice
make us an everlasting gift to you.

Preface of Sundays in Ordinary Time I-VIII, P29-P36

Communion Antiphon: You gave us bread from heaven, Lord: a
sweet-tasting bread that was very good to eat.

or

The Lord says: I am the bread of life. A man who comes to me
will not go away hungry, and no one who believes in me will
thirst.

Prayer after Communion
Lord,
you give us the strength of new life
by the gift of the eucharist.
Protect us with your love
and prepare us for eternal redemption.

NINETEENTH SUNDAY IN ORDINARY TIME   B

The Father Who Draws Us To Himself

*Elijah was drawn to the mountain of God by the Lord who gave him food
and drink. The Father is drawing us to himself by offering us the bread of
life at this Mass.*

Entrance Antiphon: Lord, be true to your covenant, forget not the
life of your poor ones for ever. Rise up, O God, and defend your
cause; do not ignore the shouts of your enemies.

Opening Prayer
Let us pray
    [in the Spirit
    that we may grow in the love of God]

Almighty and ever-living God,
your Spirit made us your children,
confident to call you Father.
Increase your Spirit within us
and bring us to our promised inheritance.

or

Let us pray

[that through us
others may find the way to life in Christ]

Father,
we come, reborn in the Spirit,
to celebrate our sonship in the Lord Jesus Christ.
Touch our hearts,
help them grow towards the life you have promised.
Touch our lives,
make them signs of your love for all men.

FIRST READING

A reading from the first book of Kings   19:4-8

Strengthened by the food he walked until he reached the mountain of God.

Elijah went into the wilderness, a day's journey, and sitting under a furze bush wished he were dead. 'Lord,' he said 'I have had enough. Take my life; I am no better than my ancestors.' Then he lay down and went to sleep. But an angel touched him and said, 'Get up and eat.' He looked round, and there at his head was a scone baked on hot stones, and a jar of water. He ate and drank and then lay down again. But the angel of the Lord came back a second time and touched him and said, 'Get up and eat, or the journey will be too long for you.' So he got up and ate and drank, and strengthened by that food he walked for forty days and forty nights until he reached Horeb, the mountain of God.

This is the word of the Lord.

Responsorial Psalm   Ps 33:2-9. ℟ v.9

℟   **Taste and see that the Lord is good.**

1   I will bless the Lord at all times,
his praise always on my lips;
in the Lord my soul shall make its boast.
The humble shall hear and be glad.   ℟

2   Glorify the Lord with me.
Together let us praise his name.
I sought the Lord and he answered me;
from all my terrors he set me free.   ℟

3   Look towards him and be radiant;
let your faces not be abashed.
This poor man called; the Lord heard him
and rescued him from all his distress.   ℟ (continued)

4   The angel of the Lord is encamped
    around those who revere him, to rescue them.
    Taste and see that the Lord is good.
    He is happy who seeks refuge in him.

    ℟   **Taste and see that the Lord is good.**

SECOND READING

A reading from the letter of St Paul to the Ephesians   4:30 – 5:2
Follow Christ by loving as he loved you.

Do not grieve the Holy Spirit of God who has marked you with
his seal for you to be set free when the day comes. Never have
grudges against others, or lose your temper, or raise your voice
to anybody, or call each other names, or allow any sort of
spitefulness. Be friends with one another, and kind, forgiving
each other as readily as God forgave you in Christ.

Try, then, to imitate God, as children of his that he loves, and
follow Christ by loving as he loved you, giving himself up in our
place as a fragrant offering and a sacrifice to God.

This is the word of the Lord.

Gospel Acclamation   Jn 14:23
    Alleluia, alleluia!
    If anyone loves me he will keep my word,
    and my Father will love him,
    and we shall come to him.
    Alleluia!

or   Jn 6:51

    Alleluia, alleluia!
    I am the living bread which has come down from heaven,
    says the Lord.
    Anyone who eats this bread will live for ever.
    Alleluia!

GOSPEL

A reading from the holy Gospel according to John   6:41-51
I am the living bread which has come down from heaven.

The Jews were complaining to each other about Jesus, because he
had said, 'I am the bread that came down from heaven.' 'Surely
this is Jesus son of Joseph' they said. 'We know his father and
mother. How can he now say, "I have come down from
heaven"?' Jesus said in reply, 'Stop complaining to each other.

'No one can come to me
unless he is drawn by the Father who sent me,
and I will raise him up at the last day.
It is written in the prophets:
They will all be taught by God,
and to hear the teaching of the Father,
and learn from it,
is to come to me.
Not that anybody has seen the Father,
except the one who comes from God:
he has seen the Father.
I tell you most solemnly,
everybody who believes has eternal life.
I am the bread of life.
Your fathers ate the manna in the desert
and they are dead;
but this is the bread that comes down from heaven,
so that a man may eat it and not die.
I am the living bread which has come down from heaven.
Anyone who eats this bread will live for ever;
and the bread that I shall give
is my flesh, for the life of the world.'

This is the Gospel of the Lord.

Prayer over the Gifts
God of power,
giver of the gifts we bring,
accept the offering of your Church
and make it the sacrament of our salvation.

Preface of Sundays in Ordinary Time I-VIII, P29-P36

Communion Antiphon: Praise the Lord, Jerusalem; he feeds you
with the finest wheat.
or
The bread I shall give is my flesh for the life of the world, says the
Lord.

Prayer after Communion
Lord,
may the eucharist you give us
bring us to salvation
and keep us faithful to the light of your truth.

TWENTIETH SUNDAY IN ORDINARY TIME   B

Our Eucharist: Thanksgiving

*Eucharist means thanksgiving. Today, filled with the Spirit, we make
thanksgiving to God for the bread of life.*

Entrance Antiphon: God, our protector, keep us in mind; always
give strength to your people. For if we can be with you even one
day, it is better than a thousand without you.

Opening Prayer

Let us pray
    [that the love of God
    may raise us beyond what we see
    to the unseen glory of his kingdom]

God our Father,
may we love you in all things and above all things
and reach the joy you have prepared for us
beyond all our imagining.

or

Let us pray
    [with humility and persistence]

Almighty God, ever-loving Father,
your care extends beyond the boundaries of race and nation
to the hearts of all who live.

May the walls, which prejudice raises between us,
crumble beneath the shadow of your outstretched arm.

FIRST READING

A reading from the book of Proverbs   9:1-6
Eat my bread, drink the wine I have prepared for you.

Wisdom has built herself a house,
she has erected her seven pillars,
she has slaughtered her beasts, prepared her wine,
she has laid her table.
She has despatched her maidservants
and proclaimed from the city's heights:
'Who is ignorant? Let him step this way.'
To the fool she says,

'Come and eat my bread,
drink the wine I have prepared!
Leave your folly and you will live,
walk in the ways of perception.'

This is the word of the Lord.

Responsorial Psalm   Ps 33:2-3. 10-15. ℞ v.9

℞ **Taste and see that the Lord is good.**

1 I will bless the Lord at all times,
   his praise always on my lips;
   in the Lord my soul shall make its boast.
   The humble shall hear and be glad.   ℞

2 Revere the Lord, you his saints.
   They lack nothing, those who revere him.
   Strong lions suffer want and go hungry
   but those who seek the Lord lack no blessing.   ℞

3 Come, children, and hear me
   that I may teach you the fear of the Lord.
   Who is he who longs for life
   and many days, to enjoy his prosperity?   ℞

4 Then keep your tongue from evil
   and your lips from speaking deceit.
   Turn aside from evil and do good;
   seek and strive after peace.   ℞

SECOND READING

A reading from the letter of St Paul to the Ephesians   5:15-20
Recognise what is the will of God.

Be very careful about the sort of lives you lead, like intelligent
and not like senseless people. This may be a wicked age, but your
lives should redeem it. And do not be thoughtless but recognise
what is the will of the Lord. Do not drug yourselves with wine,
this is simply dissipation; be filled with the Spirit. Sing the words
and tunes of the psalms and hymns when you are together, and
go on singing and chanting to the Lord in your hearts, so that
always and everywhere you are giving thanks to God who is our
Father in the name of our Lord Jesus Christ.

This is the word of the Lord.

Gospel Acclamation   Jn 1:14. 12

    Alleluia, alleluia!
    The Word was made flesh and lived among us;
    to all who did accept him
    he gave power to become children of God.
    Alleluia!

or   Jn 6:56

    Alleluia, alleluia!
    He who eats my flesh and drinks my blood
    lives in me, and I live in him,
    says the Lord.
    Alleluia!

GOSPEL

A reading from the holy Gospel according to John   6:51-58
My flesh is real food and my blood is real drink.

Jesus said to the crowd:

    'I am the living bread which has come down from heaven.
    Anyone who eats this bread will live for ever;
    and the bread that I shall give
    is my flesh, for the life of the world.'

Then the Jews started arguing with one another: 'How can this
man give us his flesh to eat?' they said. Jesus replied:

    'I tell you most solemnly,
    if you do not eat the flesh of the Son of Man
    and drink his blood,
    you will not have life in you.
    Anyone who does eat my flesh and drink my blood
    has eternal life,
    and I shall raise him up on the last day.
    For my flesh is real food
    and my blood is real drink.
    He who eats my flesh and drinks my blood
    lives in me
    and I live in him.
    As I, who am sent by the living Father,
    myself draw life from the Father,
    so whoever eats me will draw life from me.
    This is the bread come down from heaven;
    not like the bread our ancestors ate:

they are dead,
but anyone who eats this bread will live for ever.'

This is the Gospel of the Lord.

Prayer over the Gifts
Lord,
accept our sacrifice
as a holy exchange of gifts.
By offering what you have given us
may we receive the gift of yourself.

Preface of Sundays in Ordinary Time I-VIII, P29-P36

Communion Antiphon: With the Lord there is mercy, and fullness
of redemption.

or

I am the living bread from heaven, says the Lord; if anyone eats
this bread he will live for ever.

Prayer after Communion

God of mercy,
by this sacrament you make us one with Christ.
By becoming more like him on earth,
may we come to share his glory in heaven,
where he lives and reigns for ever and ever.

TWENTY-FIRST SUNDAY IN ORDINARY TIME   B

The Holy One of God

*Today, as we celebrate the marriage feast of Christ with his Church, we
consciously choose him who is the Holy One of God.*

Entrance Antiphon: Listen Lord, and answer me. Save your
servant who trusts in you. I call to you all day long, have mercy
on me, O Lord.

Opening Prayer
Let us pray
    [that God will make us one in mind and heart]

Father,
help us to see the values

that will bring us lasting joy in this changing world.
In our desire for what you promise
make us one in mind and heart.

or

Let us pray
[with minds fixed on eternal truth]

Lord our God,
all truth is from you,
and you alone bring oneness of heart.

Give your people the joy
of hearing your word in every sound
and of longing for your presence more than for life itself.
May all the attractions of a changing world
serve only to bring us
the peace of your kingdom which this world does not give.

FIRST READING

A reading from the book of Joshua   24:1-2. 15-18
We will serve the Lord, for he is our God.

Joshua gathered all the tribes of Israel together at Shechem; then
he called the elders, leaders, judges and scribes of Israel, and
they presented themselves before God. Then Joshua said to all
the people: 'If you will not serve the Lord, choose today whom
you wish to serve, whether the gods that your ancestors served
beyond the River, or the gods of the Amorites in whose land you
are now living. As for me and my House, we will serve the Lord.'

The people answered, 'We have no intention of deserting the
Lord our God and serving other gods. Was it not the Lord our
God who brought us and our ancestors out of the land of Egypt,
the house of slavery, who worked those great wonders before our
eyes and preserved us all along the way we travelled and among
all the peoples through whom we journeyed. We too will serve
the Lord, for he is our God.'

This is the word of the Lord.

Responsorial Psalm   Ps 33:2-3. 16-23. ℟ v.9
   ℟ **Taste and see that the Lord is good.**

1   I will bless the Lord at all times,
      his praise always on my lips;
      in the Lord my soul shall make its boast.
      The humble shall hear and be glad.   ℟

2 The Lord turns his face against the wicked
   to destroy their remembrance from the earth.
   The Lord turns his eyes to the just
   and his ears to their appeal. ℟

3 They call and the Lord hears
   and rescues them in all their distress.
   The Lord is close to the broken-hearted;
   those whose spirit is crushed he will save. ℟

4 Many are the trials of the just man
   but from them all the Lord will rescue him.
   He will keep guard over all his bones,
   not one of his bones shall be broken. ℟

5 Evil brings death to the wicked;
   those who hate the good are doomed.
   The Lord ransoms the souls of his servants.
   Those who hide in him shall not be condemned. ℟

SECOND READING

A reading from the letter of St Paul to the Ephesians   5:21-32
This mystery has many implications for Christ and his Church.

Give way to one another in obedience to Christ. Wives should
regard their husbands as they regard the Lord, since as Christ is
head of the Church and saves the whole body, so is a husband
the head of his wife; and as the Church submits to Christ, so
should wives to their husbands, in everything. Husbands should
love their wives just as Christ loved the Church and sacrificed
himself for her to make her holy. He made her clean by washing
her in water with a form of words, so that when he took her to
himself she would be glorious, with no speck or wrinkle or
anything like that, but holy and faultless. In the same way,
husbands must love their wives as they love their own bodies; for
a man to love his wife is for him to love himself. A man never
hates his own body, but he feeds it and looks after it; and that is
the way Christ treats the Church, because it is his body – and we
are its living parts. For this reason, a man must leave his father
and mother and be joined to his wife, and the two will become
one body. This mystery has many implications; but I am saying it
applies to Christ and the Church.

   This is the word of the Lord.

Gospel Acclamation　　　　　　　　　　　　　cf. Jn 6:63. 68
　　Alleluia, alleluia!
　　Your words are spirit, Lord,
　　and they are life:
　　you have the message of eternal life.
　　Alleluia!

GOSPEL

A reading from the holy Gospel according to John　　6:60-69
Who shall we go to? You have the message of eternal life.

After hearing his doctrine many of the followers of Jesus said,
'This is intolerable language. How could anyone accept it?' Jesus
was aware that his followers were complaining about it and said,
'Does this upset you? What if you should see the Son of Man
ascend to where he was before?

　　'It is the spirit that gives life,
　　the flesh has nothing to offer.
　　The words I have spoken to you are spirit
　　and they are life.

　　'But there are some of you who do not believe.' For Jesus
knew from the outset those who did not believe, and who it was
that would betray him. He went on, 'This is why I told you that
no one could come to me unless the Father allows him.' After
this, many of his disciples left him and stopped going with him.

　　Then Jesus said to the Twelve, 'What about you, do you want
to go away too?' Simon Peter answered, 'Lord, who shall we go
to? You have the message of eternal life, and we believe; we
know that you are the Holy One of God.'

　　This is the Gospel of the Lord.

Prayer over the Gifts
Merciful God,
the perfect sacrifice of Jesus Christ
made us your people.
In your love,
grant peace and unity to your Church.

Preface of Sundays in Ordinary Time I-VIII, P29-P36

Communion Antiphon: Lord, the earth is filled with your gift from
heaven; man grows bread from earth, and wine to cheer his
heart.

or

The Lord says: The man who eats my flesh and drinks my blood
will live for ever; I shall raise him to life on the last day.

Prayer after Communion

Lord,
may this eucharist increase within us
the healing power of your love.
May it guide and direct our efforts
to please you in all things.

TWENTY-SECOND SUNDAY   B
IN ORDINARY TIME

The Commandments Of Life

*We rejoice in the Law of God which is pure religion, totally different from
any man-made law or human tradition. It is fulfilled in this sacrament of
love.*

Entrance Antiphon: I call to you all day long, have mercy on me, O
Lord. You are good and forgiving, full of love for all who call to
you.

Opening Prayer
Let us pray
    [that God will increase our faith
    and bring to perfection the gifts he has given us]

Almighty God,
every good thing comes from you.
Fill our hearts with love for you,
increase our faith,
and by your constant care
protect the good you have given us.

or

Let us pray
    [to God who forgives all who call upon him]

Lord God of power and might,
nothing is good which is against your will,
and all is of value which comes from your hand.
Place in our hearts a desire to please you
and fill our minds with insight into love,

so that every thought may grow in wisdom
and all our efforts may be filled with your peace.

FIRST READING

A reading from the book of Deuteronomy   4:1-2. 6-8

Add nothing to what I command you, keep the commandments of the Lord.

Moses said to the people: 'Now, Israel, take notice of the laws and customs that I teach you today, and observe them, that you may have life and may enter and take possession of the land that the Lord the God of your fathers is giving you. You must add nothing to what I command you, and take nothing from it, but keep the commandments of the Lord your God just as I lay them down for you. Keep them, observe them, and they will demonstrate to the peoples your wisdom and understanding. When they come to know of all these laws they will exclaim, "No other people is as wise and prudent as this great nation." And indeed, what great nation is there that has its gods so near as the Lord our God is to us whenever we call to him? And what great nation is there that has laws and customs to match this whole Law that I put before you today?'

This is the word of the Lord.

Responsorial Psalm   Ps 14:2-5. ℟ v.1

℟   **The just will live in the presence of the Lord.**

1   Lord, who shall dwell on your holy mountain?
    He who walks without fault;
    he who acts with justice
    and speaks the truth from his heart.   ℟

2   He who does no wrong to his brother,
    who casts no slur on his neighbour,
    who holds the godless in disdain,
    but honours those who fear the Lord.   ℟

3   He who keeps his pledge, come what may;
    who takes no interest on a loan
    and accepts no bribes against the innocent.
    Such a man will stand firm for ever.   ℟

SECOND READING

A reading from the letter of St James   1:17-18. 21-22. 27

You must do what the word tells you.

It is all that is good, everything that is perfect, which is given us from above; it comes down from the Father of all light; with him there is no such thing as alteration, no shadow of a change. By his own choice he made us his children by the message of the truth so that we should be a sort of first-fruits of all that he had created.

Accept and submit to the word which has been planted in you and can save your souls. But you must do what the word tells you, and not just listen to it and deceive yourselves.

Pure unspoilt religion, in the eyes of God our Father is this: coming to the help of orphans and widows when they need it, and keeping oneself uncontaminated by the world.

This is the word of the Lord.

Gospel Acclamation   cf. Jn 6:63. 68
Alleluia, alleluia!
Your words are spirit, Lord,
and they are life:
you have the message of eternal life.
Alleluia!

or

James 1:18

Alleluia, alleluia!
By his own choice the Father made us his children
by the message of the truth,
so that we should be a sort of first-fruits
of all that he created.
Alleluia!

GOSPEL

A reading from the holy Gospel according to Mark
7:1-8. 14-15. 21-23

You put aside the commandment of God to cling to human traditions.

The Pharisees and some of the scribes who had come from Jerusalem gathered round Jesus, and they noticed that some of his disciples were eating with unclean hands, that is, without washing them. For the Pharisees, and the Jews in general, follow the tradition of the elders and never eat without washing their arms as far as the elbow; and on returning from the market place they never eat without first sprinkling themselves.

There are also many other observances which have been handed down to them concerning the washing of cups and pots and bronze dishes. So these Pharisees and scribes asked him, 'Why do your disciples not respect the tradition of the elders but eat their food with unclean hands?' He answered, 'It was of you hypocrites that Isaiah so rightly prophesied in this passage of scripture:

This people honours me only with lip-service,
while their hearts are far from me.
The worship they offer me is worthless,
the doctrines they teach are only human regulations.

You put aside the commandment of God to cling to human traditions.'
He called the people to him again and said, 'Listen to me, all of you, and understand. Nothing that goes into a man from outside can make him unclean; it is the things that come out of a man that make him unclean. For it is from within, from men's hearts, that evil intentions emerge: fornication, theft, murder, adultery, avarice, malice, deceit, indecency, envy, slander, pride, folly. All these evil things come from within and make a man unclean.'

This is the Gospel of the Lord.

Prayer over the Gifts
Lord,
may this holy offering
bring us your blessing
and accomplish within us
its promise of salvation.

Preface of Sundays in Ordinary Time I-VIII, P29-P36

Communion Antiphon: O Lord, how great is the depth of the kindness which you have shown to those who love you.
or
Happy are the peacemakers; they shall be called sons of God. Happy are they who suffer persecution for justice' sake; the kingdom of heaven is theirs.

Prayer after Communion
Lord,
you renew us at your table with the bread of life.
May this food strengthen us in love
and help us to serve you in each other.

TWENTY-THIRD SUNDAY IN ORDINARY TIME   **B**

The Lord Who Does All Things Well

Today we celebrate our 'unbounded admiration' for the Lord who makes no distinctions between classes of people, but makes the poor rich in faith, the deaf hear and the dumb speak.

Entrance Antiphon: Lord, you are just, and the judgements you make are right. Show mercy when you judge me, your servant.

Opening Prayer
Let us pray
   [that we may realise the freedom God has given us
   in making us his sons and daughters]

God our Father,
you redeem us
and make us your children in Christ.
Look upon us,
give us true freedom
and bring us to the inheritance you promised.

or

Let us pray
   [to our just and merciful God]

Lord our God,
in you justice and mercy meet.
With unparalleled love you have saved us from death
and drawn us into the circle of your life.

Open our eyes to the wonders this life sets before us,
that we may serve you free from fear
and address you as God our Father.

FIRST READING
A reading from the prophet Isaiah   35:4-7
The ears of the deaf shall be unsealed and the tongues of the dumb shall be loosed.

Say to all faint hearts,
'Courage! Do not be afraid.

'Look, your God is coming,
vengeance is coming,

the retribution of God;
he is coming to save you.'

Then the eyes of the blind shall be opened,
the ears of the deaf unsealed,
then the lame shall leap like a deer
and the tongues of the dumb sing for joy;

for water gushes in the desert,
streams in the wasteland,
the scorched earth becomes a lake,
the parched land springs of water.

This is the word of the Lord.

Responsorial Psalm   Ps 145:7-10. ℟ v.1
 ℟ **My soul, give praise to the Lord.**

or

 ℟ **Alleluia!**

1   It is the Lord who keeps faith for ever,
     who is just to those who are oppressed.
     It is he who gives bread to the hungry,
     the Lord, who sets prisoners free.   ℟

2   It is the Lord who gives sight to the blind,
     who raises up those who are bowed down,
     the Lord who loves the just,
     the Lord, who protects the stranger.   ℟

3   The Lord upholds the widow and orphan,
     but thwarts the path of the wicked.
     The Lord will reign for ever,
     Zion's God, from age to age.   ℟

SECOND READING

A reading from the letter of St James   2:1-5
God chose the poor to be the heirs to the kingdom.

My brothers, do not try to combine faith in Jesus Christ, our
glorified Lord, with the making of distinctions between classes of
people. Now suppose a man comes into your synagogue, beauti-
fully dressed and with a gold ring on, and at the same time a poor
man comes in, in shabby clothes, and you take notice of the
well-dressed man, and say, 'Come this way to the best seats;'
then you tell the poor man, 'Stand over there' or 'You can sit on

the floor by my foot-rest.' Can't you see that you have used two different standards in your mind, and turned yourselves into judges, and corrupt judges at that?

Listen, my dear brothers: it was those who are poor according to the world that God chose, to be rich in faith and to be the heirs to the kingdom which he promised to those who love him.

This is the word of the Lord.

Gospel Acclamation   1 Sam 3:9; Jn 6:68
Alleluia, alleluia!
Speak, Lord, your servant is listening:
you have the message of eternal life.
Alleluia!

or   cf. Mt 4:23

Alleluia, alleluia!
Jesus proclaimed the Good News of the kingdom,
and cured all kinds of sickness among the people.
Alleluia!

GOSPEL

A reading from the holy Gospel according to Mark   7:31-37
He makes the deaf hear and the dumb speak.

Returning from the district of Tyre, Jesus went by way of Sidon towards the Sea of Galilee, right through the Decapolis region. And they brought him a deaf man who had an impediment in his speech; and they asked him to lay his hand on him. He took him aside in private, away from the crowd, put his fingers into the man's ears and touched his tongue with spittle. Then looking up to heaven he sighed; and he said to him, 'Ephphatha,' that is, 'Be opened.' And his ears were opened, and the ligament of his tongue was loosened and he spoke clearly. And Jesus ordered them to tell no one about it, but the more he insisted, the more widely they published it. Their admiration was unbounded. 'He has done all things well,' they said 'he makes the deaf hear and the dumb speak.'

This is the Gospel of the Lord.

Prayer over the Gifts
God of peace and love,
may our offering bring you true worship
and make us one with you.

Preface of Sundays in Ordinary Time I-VIII, P29-P36

Communion Antiphon: Like a deer that longs for running streams, my soul longs for you, my God. My soul is thirsting for the living God.

or

I am the light of the world, says the Lord; the man who follows me will have the light of life.

Prayer after Communion

Lord,
your word and your sacrament
give us food and life.
May this gift of your Son
lead us to share his life for ever.

TWENTY-FOURTH SUNDAY IN ORDINARY TIMEB

Christ, The Son Of Man

We worship the man Christ, who accepted every weakness of our human condition, renouncing himself and taking up the cross.

Entrance Antiphon: Give peace, Lord, to those who wait for you, and your prophets will proclaim you as you deserve. Hear the prayers of your servant and of your people Israel.

Opening Prayer

Let us pray
[that God will keep us faithful in his service]

Almighty God,
our creator and guide,
may we serve you with all our heart
and know your forgiveness in our lives.

or

Let us pray
[for the peace which is born of faith and hope]

Father in heaven, Creator of all,
look down upon your people in their moments of need,
for you alone are the source of our peace.
Bring us to the dignity which distinguishes the poor in spirit

and show us how great is the call to serve,
that we may share in the peace of Christ
who offered his life in the service of all.

FIRST READING

A reading from the prophet Isaiah   50:5-9

I offered my back to those who struck me.

The Lord has opened my ear.

For my part, I made no resistance,
neither did I turn away.
I offered my back to those who struck me,
my cheeks to those who tore at my beard;
I did not cover my face
against insult and spittle.

The Lord comes to my help,
so that I am untouched by the insults.
So, too, I set my face like flint;
I know I shall not be shamed.

My vindicator is here at hand. Does anyone start proceedings
    against me?
Then let us go to court together.
Who thinks he has a case against me?
Let him approach me.
The Lord is coming to my help,
who dare condemn me?

This is the word of the Lord.

Responsorial Psalm   Ps 114:1-6. 8-9. ℟ v.9

℟ **I will walk in the presence of the Lord,
    in the land of the living.**

or

℟ **Alleluia!**

1 I love the Lord for he has heard
   the cry of my appeal;
   for he turned his ear to me
   in the day when I called him. ℟

2 They surrounded me, the snares of death,
   with the anguish of the tomb;
   they caught me, sorrow and distress. (continued)

I called on the Lord's name.
O Lord my God, deliver me!

℟ **I will walk in the presence of the Lord,
in the land of the living.**

or

℟ **Alleluia!**

3 How gracious is the Lord, and just;
our God has compassion.
The Lord protects the simple hearts;
I was helpless so he saved me.   ℟

4 He has kept my soul from death,
my eyes from tears
and my feet from stumbling.
I will walk in the presence of the Lord
in the land of the living.   ℟

SECOND READING

A reading from the letter of St James   2:14-18

If good works do not go with faith, it is quite dead.

Take the case, my brothers, of someone who has never done a
single good act but claims that he has faith. Will that faith save
him? If one of the brothers or one of the sisters is in need of
clothes and has not enough food to live on, and one of you says
to them, 'I wish you well; keep yourself warm and eat plenty,'
without giving them these bare necessities of life, then what
good is that? Faith is like that: if good works do not go with it, it is
quite dead.

This is the way to talk to people of that kind: 'You say you
have faith and I have good deeds; I will prove to you that I have
faith by showing you my good deeds – now you prove to me that
you have faith without any good deeds to show.'

This is the word of the Lord.

Gospel Acclamation   Jn 14:5
Alleluia, alleluia!
I am the Way, the Truth and the Life, says the Lord;
no one can come to the Father except through me.
Alleluia!

or   Gal 6:14

Alleluia, alleluia!
The only thing I can boast about is the cross of our Lord,

through whom the world is crucified to me, and I to the
world.
Alleluia!

GOSPEL

A reading from the holy Gospel according to Mark   8:27-35
You are the Christ. The Son of Man is destined to suffer grievously.

Jesus and his disciples left for the villages round Caesarea
Philippi. On the way he put this question to his disciples, 'Who
do people say I am?' And they told him. 'John the Baptist,' they
said 'others Elijah; others again, one of the prophets.' 'But you,'
he asked 'who do you say I am?' Peter spoke up and said to him,
'You are the Christ.' And he gave them strict orders not to tell
anyone about him.

And he began to teach them that the Son of Man was destined
to suffer grievously, to be rejected by the elders and the chief
priests and the scribes, and to be put to death, and after three
days to rise again; and he said all this quite openly. Then, taking
him aside, Peter started to remonstrate with him. But, turning
and seeing his disciples, he rebuked Peter and said to him, 'Get
behind me, Satan! Because the way you think is not God's way
but man's.'

He called the people and his disciples to him and said, 'If
anyone wants to be a follower of mine, let him renounce himself
and take up his cross and follow me. For anyone who wants to
save his life will lose it; but anyone who loses his life for my sake,
and for the sake of the gospel, will save it.'

This is the Gospel of the Lord.

Prayer over the Gifts
Lord,
hear the prayers of your people
and receive our gifts.
May the worship of each one here
bring salvation to all.

Preface of Sundays in Ordinary Time I-VIII, P29-P36

Communion Antiphon: O God, how much we value your mercy!
All mankind can gather under your protection.

or

The cup that we bless is a communion with the blood of Christ;
and the bread that we break is a communion with the body of the
Lord.

Prayer after Communion
Lord,
may the eucharist you have give us
influence our thoughts and actions.
May your Spirit guide and direct us in your way.

TWENTY-FIFTH SUNDAY IN ORDINARY TIME   B

Christ, The Son Of God

We worship the Son of God, the wisdom that came down from above and became the servant of men.

Entrance Antiphon: I am the Saviour of all people, says the Lord. Whatever their troubles, I will answer their cry, and I will always be their Lord.

Opening Prayer
Let us pray
    [that we will grow in the love of God
    and of one another]

Father,
guide us, as you guide creation
according to your law of love.
May we love one another
and come to perfection
in the eternal life prepared for us.

or

Let us pray
    [to the Lord who is a God of love to all peoples]

Father in heaven,
the perfection of justice is found in your love
and all mankind is in need of your law.

Help us to find this love in each other
that justice may be attained
through obedience to your law.

FIRST READING

A reading from the book of Wisdom   2:12. 17-20
Let us condemn him to a shameful death.

The godless say to themselves,

'Let us lie in wait for the virtuous man, since he annoys us
and opposes our way of life,
reproaches us for our breaches of the law
and accuses us of playing false to our upbringing.
Let us see if what he says is true,
let us observe what kind of end he himself will have.
If the virtuous man is God's son, God will take his part
and rescue him from the clutches of his enemies.
Let us test him with cruelty and with torture,
and thus explore this gentleness of his
and put his endurance to the proof.
Let us condemn him to a shameful death
since he will be looked after – we have his word for it.'

This is the word of the Lord.

Responsorial Psalm   Ps 53:3-6. 8. R℣ v.6
  R℣ **The Lord upholds my life.**

1   O God, save me by your name;
    by your power, uphold my cause.
    O God, hear my prayer;
    listen to the words of my mouth.   R℣

2   For proud men have risen against me,
    ruthless men seek my life.
    They have no regard for God.   R℣

3   But I have God for my help.
    The Lord upholds my life.
    I will sacrifice to you with willing heart
    and praise your name for it is good.   R℣

SECOND READING
A reading from the letter of St James   3:16 – 4:3
*Peacemakers, when they work for peace, sow the seeds which will bear
fruit in holiness.*

Wherever you find jealousy and ambition, you find disharmony,
and wicked things of every kind being done; whereas the
wisdom that comes down from above is essentially something
pure; it also makes for peace, and is kindly and considerate; it is
full of compassion and shows itself by doing good; nor is there
any trace of partiality or hypocrisy in it. Peacemakers, when they
work for peace, sow the seeds which will bear fruit in holiness.

Where do these wars and battles between yourselves first start? Isn't it precisely in the desires fighting inside your own selves? You want something and you haven't got it; so you are prepared to kill. You have an ambition that you cannot satisfy; so you fight to get your way by force. Why you don't have what you want is because you don't pray for it; when you do pray and don't get it, it is because you have not prayed properly, you have prayed for something to indulge your own desires.

This is the word of the Lord.

Gospel Acclamation   Jn 8:12
Alleluia, alleluia!
I am the light of the world, says the Lord,
anyone who follows me
will have the light of life.
Alleluia!

or   cf. 2 Thess 2:14

Alleluia, alleluia!
Through the Good News God called us
to share the glory of our Lord Jesus Christ.
Alleluia!

GOSPEL
A reading from the holy Gospel according to Mark   9:30-37
The Son of Man will be delivered. If anyone wants to be first, he must make himself servant of all.

After leaving the mountain Jesus and his disciples made their way through Galilee; and he did not want anyone to know, because he was instructing his disciples; he was telling them, 'The Son of Man will be delivered into the hands of men; they will put him to death; and three days after he has been put to death he will rise again.' But they did not understand what he said and were afraid to ask him.

They came to Capernaum, and when he was in the house he asked them, 'What were you arguing about on the road?' They said nothing because they had been arguing which of them was the greatest. So he sat down, called the Twelve to him and said, 'If anyone wants to be first, he must make himself last of all and servant of all.' He then took a little child, set him in front of them, put his arms round him, and said to them, 'Anyone who welcomes one of these little children in my name, welcomes me; and anyone who welcomes me welcomes not me but the one who sent me.'

This is the Gospel of the Lord.

Prayer over the Gifts
Lord,
may these gifts which we now offer
to show our belief and our love
be pleasing to you.
May they become for us
the eucharist of Jesus Christ your Son,
who is Lord for ever and ever.

Preface of Sundays in Ordinary Time I-VIII, P29-P36

Communion Antiphon: You have laid down your precepts to be faithfully kept. May my footsteps be firm in keeping your commands.

or

I am the Good Shepherd, says the Lord; I know my sheep, and mine know me.

Prayer after Communion
Lord,
help us with your kindness
Make us strong through the eucharist.
May we put into action
the saving mystery we celebrate.

TWENTY-SIXTH SUNDAY IN ORDINARY TIME   B

God's Spirit In The World

We praise God for all his prophets: men and women of every nation and creed who have resisted evil and manifested the Spirit in their lives.

Entrance Antiphon: O Lord, you had just cause to judge men as you did: because we sinned against you and disobeyed your will. But now show us your greatness of heart, and treat us with your unbounded kindness.

Opening Prayer
Let us pray
  [for God's forgiveness
  and for the happiness it brings]

Father,
you show your almighty power
in your mercy and forgiveness.
Continue to fill us with your gifts of love.
Help us to hurry toward the eternal life you promise
and come to share in the joys of your kingdom.

  or

Let us pray
  [for the peace of the kingdom
  which we have been promised]

Father of our Lord Jesus Christ,
in your unbounded mercy
you have revealed the beauty of your power
through your constant forgiveness of our sins.
May the power of this love be in our hearts
to bring your pardon and your kingdom to all we meet.

FIRST READING

A reading from the book of Numbers   11:25-29
Are you jealous on my account? If only the whole people of the Lord were prophets!

The Lord came down in the Cloud. He spoke with Moses, but took some of the spirit that was on him and put it on the seventy elders. When the spirit came on them they prophesied, but not again.

Two men had stayed back in the camp; one was called Eldad and the other Medad. The spirit came down on them; though they had not gone to the Tent, their names were enrolled among the rest. These began to prophesy in the camp. The young man ran to tell this to Moses, 'Look,' he said 'Eldad and Medad are prophesying in the camp.' Then said Joshua the son of Nun, who had served Moses from his youth, 'My Lord Moses, stop them!' Moses answered him, 'Are you jealous on my account? If only the whole people of the Lord were prophets, and the Lord gave his Spirit to them all!'

This is the word of the Lord.

Responsorial Psalm   Ps 18:8. 10. 12-14. ℟ v.9

  ℟   **The precepts of the Lord gladden the heart.**

1   The law of the Lord is perfect,
    it revives the soul.
    The rule of the Lord is to be trusted,
    it gives wisdom to the simple.   ℟

2   The fear of the Lord is holy,
    abiding for ever.
    The decrees of the Lord are truth
    and all of them just.   ℟

3   So in them your servant finds instruction;
    great reward is in their keeping.
    But who can detect all his errors?
    From hidden faults acquit me.   ℟

4   From presumption restrain your servant
    and let it not rule me.
    Then shall I be blameless,
    clean from grave sin.   ℟

SECOND READING

A reading from the letter of St James   5:1-6
Your wealth is all rotting.

An answer for the rich. Start crying, weep for the miseries that
are coming to you. Your wealth is all rotting, your clothes are all
eaten up by moths. All your gold and your silver are corroding
away, and the same corrosion will be your own sentence, and eat
into your body. It was a burning fire that you stored up as your
treasure for the last days. Labourers mowed your fields, and you
cheated them – listen to the wages that you kept back, calling out;
realise that the cries of the reapers have reached the ears of the
Lord of hosts. On earth you have had a life of comfort and
luxury; in the time of slaughter you went on eating to your
heart's content. It was you who condemned the innocent and
killed them; they offered you no resistance.

  This is the word of the Lord.

Gospel Acclamation   cf. Jn 17:17
    Alleluia, alleluia!
    Your word is truth, O Lord,
    consecrate us in the truth.
    Alleluia!

GOSPEL

A reading from the holy Gospel 9:38-43. 45. 47-48
according to Mark

Anyone who is not against us is for us. If your hand should cause you to sin, cut it off.

John said to Jesus, 'Master, we saw a man who is not one of us casting out devils in your name; and because he was not one of us we tried to stop him.' But Jesus said, 'You must not stop him: no one who works a miracle in my name is likely to speak evil of me. Anyone who is not against us is for us.

'If anyone gives you a cup of water to drink just because you belong to Christ, then I tell you solemnly, he will most certainly not lose his reward.

'But anyone who is an obstacle to bring down one of these little

ones who have faith, would be better thrown into the sea with a great millstone round his neck. And if your hand should cause you to sin, cut it off; it is better for you to enter into life crippled, than to have two hands and go to hell, into the fire that cannot be put out. And if your foot should cause you to sin, cut it off; it is better for you to enter into life lame, than to have two feet and be thrown into hell. And if your eye should cause you to sin, tear it out; it is better for you to enter into the kingdom of God with one eye, than to have two eyes and be thrown into hell where their worm does not die nor their fire go out.'

This is the Gospel of the Lord.

Prayer over the Gifts
God of mercy,
accept our offering
and make it a source of blessing for us.

Preface of Sundays in Ordinary Time I-VIII, P29-P36

Communion Antiphon: O Lord, remember the words you spoke to me, your servant, which made me live in hope and consoled me when I was downcast.

or

This is how we know what love is: Christ gave up his life for us; and we too must give up our lives for our brothers.

Prayer after Communion
Lord,

may this eucharist
in which we proclaim the death of Christ
bring us salvation
and make us one with him in glory,
for he is Lord for ever and ever.

TWENTY-SEVENTH SUNDAY
IN ORDINARY TIME   **B**

The Family Of God

*We celebrate today our belonging together as the family of God. Christ
has made us his brothers and sisters, and children of our heavenly
Father. The love and respect we show for each other in this celebration
will be largely dependent on the love and respect that exists in our own
human families.*

Entrance Antiphon: O Lord, you have given everything its place in
the world, and no one can make it otherwise. For it is your
creation, the heavens and the earth and the stars: you are the
Lord of all.

Opening Prayer

Let us pray
   [that God will forgive our failings
   and bring us peace]

Father,
your love for us
surpasses all our hopes and desires.
Forgive our failings,
keep us in your peace
and lead us in the way of salvation.
or

Let us pray
   [before the face of God, in trusting faith]

Almighty and eternal God,
Father of the world to come,
your goodness is beyond what our spirit can touch
and your strength is more than the mind can bear.
Lead us to seek beyond our reach
and give us the courage to stand before your truth.

FIRST READING

A reading from the book of Genesis   2:18-24

They become one body.

The Lord God said, 'It is not good that the man should be alone. I will make him a helpmate.' So from the soil the Lord God fashioned all the wild beasts and all the birds of heaven. These he brought to the man to see what he would call them; each one was to bear the name the man would give it. The man gave names to all the cattle, all the birds of heaven and all the wild beasts. But no helpmate suitable for man was found for him. So the Lord God made the man fall into a deep sleep. And while he slept, he took one of his ribs and enclosed it in flesh. The Lord God built the rib he had taken from the man into a woman, and brought her to the man. The man exclaimed:

'This at last is bone from my bones
and flesh from my flesh!
This is to be called woman,
for this was taken from man.'

This is why a man leaves his father and mother and joins himself to his wife, and they become one body.

This is the word of the Lord.

Responsorial Psalm   Ps 127.℟ v.5

℟   **May the Lord bless us
all the days of our life.**

1   O blessed are those who fear the Lord
and walk in his ways!
by the labour of your hands you shall eat.
You will be happy and prosper.   ℟

2   Your wife will be like a fruitful vine
in the heart of your house;
your children like shoots of the olive,
around your table.   ℟

3   Indeed thus shall be blessed
the man who fears the Lord.
May the Lord bless you from Zion
in a happy Jerusalem
all the days of your life!
May you see your children's children.
On Israel, peace!   ℟

SECOND READING

A reading from the letter to the Hebrews   2:9-11
The one who sanctifies, and the ones who are sanctified, are of the same stock.

We see in Jesus one who was for a short while made lower than the angels and is now crowned with glory and splendour because he submitted to death; by God's grace he had to experience death for all mankind.

    As it was his purpose to bring a great many of his sons into glory, it was appropriate that God, for whom everything exists and through whom everything exists, should make perfect, through suffering, the leader who would take them to their salvation. For the one who sanctifies, and the ones who are sanctified, are of the same stock; that is why he openly calls them brothers.

    This is the word of the Lord.

Gospel Acclamation   cf. Jn 17:17
    Alleluia, alleluia!
    Your word is truth, O Lord,
    consecrate us in the truth.
    Alleluia!

or   1 Jn 4:12

    Alleluia, alleluia!
    As long as we love one another
    God will live in us
    and his love will be complete in us.
    Alleluia!

GOSPEL

A reading from the holy Gospel according to Mark   10:2-16
What God has united, man must not divide.

Some Pharisees approached Jesus and asked, 'Is it against the law for a man to divorce his wife?' They were testing him. He answered them, 'What did Moses command you?' 'Moses allowed us' they said 'to draw up a writ of dismissal and so to divorce.' Then Jesus said to them, 'It was because you were so unteachable that he wrote this commandment for you. But from the beginning of creation God made them male and female. This is why a man must leave father and mother, and the two become one body. They are no longer two, therefore, but one body. So then, what God has united, man must not divide.' Back in the house the disciples questioned him again about this, and he said to them, 'The man who divorces his wife and marries another is guilty of adultery against her. And if a woman divorces her husband and marries another she is guilty of adultery too.'

People were bringing little children to him, for him to touch them. The disciples turned them away, but when Jesus saw this he was indignant and said to them, 'Let the little children come to me; do not stop them; for it is to such as these that the kingdom of God belongs. I tell you solemnly, anyone who does not welcome the kingdom of God like a little child will never enter it.' Then he put his arms round them, laid his hands on them and gave them his blessing.

This is the Gospel of the Lord.

*Shorter Form, verses 2-12. Read between *

Prayer over the Gifts
Father,
receive these gifts
which our Lord Jesus Christ
has asked us to offer in his memory.
May our obedient service
bring us to the fullness of your redemption.

Preface of Sundays in Ordinary Time I-VIII, P29-P36
Communion Antiphon: The Lord is good to those who hope in him, to those who are searching for his love.

or

Because there is one bread, we, though many, are one body, for we all share in the one loaf and in the one cup.

Prayer after Communion

Almighty God,
let the eucharist we share
fill us with your life.
May the love of Christ
which we celebrate here
touch our lives and lead us to you.

TWENTY-EIGHTH SUNDAY
IN ORDINARY TIME

B

Christ, Our Wealth

Even though we had nothing in this world that we could call our own, in having Christ, the wisdom of God, we possess all things; we are rich in him. He is the word of God that is alive and active in our hearts.

Entrance Antiphon: If you, O Lord, laid bare our guilt, who could endure it? But you are forgiving, God of Israel.

Opening Prayer

Let us pray

[that God will help us to love one another]

Lord,
our help and guide,
make your love the foundation of our lives.
May our love for you express itself
in our eagerness to do good for others.

or

Let us pray

[in quiet for the grace of sincerity]

Father in heaven,
the hand of your loving kindness
powerfully yet gently guides all the moments of our day.

Go before us in our pilgrimage of life,
anticipate our needs and prevent our falling.
Send your Spirit to unite us in faith,
that sharing in your service,
we may rejoice in your presence.

FIRST READING

A reading from the book of Wisdom   7:7-11
Compared with wisdom, I held riches as nothing.

I prayed, and understanding was given me;
I entreated, and the spirit of Wisdom came to me.
I esteemed her more than sceptres and thrones;
compared with her, I held riches as nothing.
I reckoned no priceless stone to be her peer,
for compared with her, all gold is a pinch of sand,
and beside her silver ranks as mud.

I loved her more than health or beauty,
preferred her to the light,
since her radiance never sleeps.
In her company all good things came to me,
at her hands riches not to be numbered.

This is the word of the Lord.

Responsorial Psalm Ps 89:12-17. ℟ v.14

℟ **Fill us with your love that we may rejoice.**

1 Make us know the shortness of our life
   that we may gain wisdom of heart.
   Lord, relent! Is your anger for ever?
   Show pity to your servants. ℟

2 In the morning, fill us with your love;
   we shall exult and rejoice all our days.
   Give us joy to balance our affliction
   for the years when we knew misfortune. ℟

3 Show forth your work to your servants;
   let your glory shine on their children.
   Let the favour of the Lord be upon us:
   give success to the work of our hands. ℟

SECOND READING

A reading from the letter to the Hebrews 4:12-13
The word of God can judge secret emotions and thoughts.

The word of God is something alive and active: it cuts like any
double-edged sword but more finely: it can slip through the place
where the soul is divided from the spirit, or joints from the
marrow; it can judge the secret emotions and thoughts. No
created thing can hide from him; everything is uncovered and
open to the eyes of the one to whom we must give account of
ourselves.

This is the word of the Lord.

Gospel Acclamation cf. Mt 11:25
Alleluia, alleluia!
Blessed are you, Father,
Lord of heaven and earth,
for revealing the mysteries of the kingdom
to mere children.
Alleluia!

or

Alleluia, alleluia!
How happy are the poor in spirit;
theirs is the kingdom of heaven.
Alleluia!

GOSPEL

A reading from the holy Gospel according to Mark   10:17-30
Go and sell everything you own and follow me.

*Jesus was setting out on a journey when a man ran up, knelt before him and put this question to him, 'Good master, what must I do to inherit eternal life?' Jesus said to him, 'Why do you call me good? No one is good but God alone. You know the commandments: You must not kill; You must not commit adultery; You must not steal; You must not bring false witness; You must not defraud; Honour your father and mother.' And he said to him, 'Master, I have kept all these from my earliest days.' Jesus looked steadily at him and loved him, and he said, 'There is one thing you lack. Go and sell everything you own and give the money to the poor, and you will have treasure in heaven; then come, follow me.' But his face fell at these words and he went away sad, for he was a man of great wealth.

Jesus looked round and said to his disciples, 'How hard it is for those who have riches to enter the kingdom of God!' The disciples were astounded by these words, but Jesus insisted, 'My children,' he said to them, 'how hard it is to enter the kingdom of God! It is easier for a camel to pass through the eye of a needle than for a rich man to enter the kingdom of God.' They were more astonished than ever. 'In that case' they said to one another 'who can be saved?' Jesus gazed at them. 'For men' he said 'it is impossible, but not for God: because everything is possible for God.'*

Peter took this up. 'What about us?' he asked him. 'We have left everything and followed you.' Jesus said, 'I tell you solemnly, there is no one who has left house, brothers, sisters, father, children or land for my sake and for the sake of the gospel who will not be repaid a hundred times over, houses, brothers, sisters, mothers, children and land – not without persecutions – now in this present time and, in the world to come, eternal life.'

This is the Gospel of the Lord.

*Shorter Form, verses 17-27. Read between *

Prayer over the Gifts
Lord,
accept the prayers and gifts
we offer in faith and love.
May this eucharist bring us to your glory.

Preface of Sundays in Ordinary Time I-VIII, P29-P36

Communion Antiphon: The rich suffer want and go hungry, but nothing shall be lacking to those who fear the Lord.

or

When the Lord is revealed we shall be like him, for we shall see him as he is.

Prayer after Communion
Almighty Father,
may the body and blood of your Son
give us a share in his life,
for he is Lord for ever and ever.

TWENTY-NINTH SUNDAY IN ORDINARY TIME B

Christ The Suffering Servant Of God

Today we celebrate the Christ who gives meaning to all human suffering. By taking on himself the role of a servant and redeeming us by his sufferings, he has turned all our human values upside down. It is the weak who have become strong.

Entrance Antiphon: I call upon you, God, for you will answer me; bend your ear and hear my prayer. Guard me as the pupil of your eye; hide me in the shade of your wings.

Opening Prayer
Let us pray
    [for the gift of simplicity and joy
    in our service of God and man]

Almighty and ever-living God,
our source of power and inspiration,
give us strength and joy
in serving you as followers of Christ,
who lives and reigns with you and the Holy Spirit,
one God, for ever and ever.

or

Let us pray
    [to the Lord who bends close to hear our prayer]

Lord our God, Father of all,
you guard us under the shadow of your wings
and search into the depths of our hearts.

Remove the blindness that cannot know you
and relieve the fear that would hide us from your sight.

FIRST READING

A reading from the prophet Isaiah   53:10-11

*If he offers his life in atonement, he shall see his heirs, he shall have a long
life.*

The Lord has been pleased to crush his servant with suffering.
If he offers his life in atonement,
he shall see his heirs, he shall have a long life
and through him what the Lord wishes will be done.
His soul's anguish over
he shall see the light and be content.
By his sufferings shall my servant justify many,
taking their faults on himself.

    This is the word of the Lord.

Responsorial Psalm   Ps 32:4-5. 18-20. 22. ℟ v.22
    ℟ **May your love be upon us, O Lord,**
        as we place all our hope in you.

1   The word of the Lord is faithful
    and all his works to be trusted.
    The Lord loves justice and right
    and fills the earth with his love.   ℟

2   The Lord looks on those who revere him,
    on those who hope in his love,
    to rescue their souls from death,
    to keep them alive in famine.   ℟

3   Our soul is waiting for the Lord.
    The Lord is our help and our shield.
    May your love be upon us, O Lord,
    as we place all our hope in you.   ℟

SECOND READING

A reading from the letter to the Hebrews   4:14-16
Let us be confident in approaching the throne of grace.

Since in Jesus, the Son of God, we have the supreme high priest
who has gone through to the highest heaven, we must never let
go of the faith that we have professed. For it is not as if we had a
high priest who was incapable of feeling our weaknesses with us;
but we have one who has been tempted in every way that we are,
though he is without sin. Let us be confident, then, in approaching the throne of grace, that we shall have mercy from him and
find grace when we are in need of help.

This is the word of the Lord.

Gospel Acclamation   Jn 14:6
    Alleluia, alleluia!
    I am the Way, the Truth and the Life, says the Lord;
    no one can come to the Father except through me.
    Alleluia!

or   Mk 10:45

    Alleluia, alleluia!
    The Son of Man came to serve,
    and to give his life as a ransom for many.
    Alleluia!

GOSPEL

A reading from the holy Gospel according to Mark   10:35-45
The Son of Man came to give his life as a ransom for many.

James and John, the sons of Zebedee, approached Jesus.
'Master,' they said to him 'we want you to do us a favour.' He
said to them, 'What is it you want me to do for you?' They said to
him, 'Allow us to sit one at your right hand and the other at your
left in your glory.' 'You do not know what you are asking' Jesus
said to them. 'Can you drink the cup that I must drink, or be
baptised with the baptism with which I must be baptised?' They
replied, 'We can.' Jesus said to them, 'The cup that I must drink
you shall drink, and with the baptism with which I must be
baptised you shall be baptised, but as for seats at my right hand
or my left, these are not mine to grant; they belong to those to
whom they have been allotted.'

   When the other ten heard this they began to feel indignant
with James and John, so *Jesus called them to him and said to
them, 'You know that among the pagans their so-called rulers

lord it over them, and their great men make their authority felt. This is not to happen among you. No; anyone who wants to become great among you must be your servant, and anyone who wants to be first among you must be slave to all. For the Son of Man himself did not come to be served but to serve, and to give his life as a ransom for many.'*

This is the Gospel of the Lord.*

*Shorter Form, verses 42-45. Read between *

Prayer over the Gifts
Lord God,
may the gifts we offer
bring us your love and forgiveness
and give us freedom to serve you with our lives.

Preface of Sundays in Ordinary Time I-VIII, P29-P36

Communion Antiphon: See how the eyes of the Lord are on those who fear him, on those who hope in his love, that he may rescue them from death and feed them in time of famine.

or

The Son of Man came to give his life as a ransom for many.

Prayer after Communion
Lord,
may this eucharist help us to remain faithful.
May it teach us the way to eternal life.

THIRTIETH SUNDAY IN ORDINARY TIME   B

The Lord Who Works Marvels

We worship Christ who opens our eyes to see the marvels that he has done for us as our high priest and mediator with the Father.

Entrance Antiphon: Let hearts rejoice who search for the Lord. Seek the Lord and his strength, seek always the face of the Lord.

Opening Prayer
Let us pray
    [for the strength to do God's will]

Almighty and ever-living God,
strengthen our faith, hope, and love.
May we do with loving hearts
what you ask of us
and come to share the life you promise.

or

Let us pray
[in humble hope for salvation]

Praised be you, God and Father of our Lord Jesus Christ.
There is no power for good
which does not come from your covenant,
and no promise to hope in
that your love has not offered.
Strengthen our faith to accept your covenant
and give us the love to carry out your command.

FIRST READING

A reading from the prophet Jeremiah   31:7-9
I will comfort the blind and the lame as I lead them back.

The Lord says this:

Shout with joy for Jacob!
Hail the chief of nations!
Proclaim! Praise! Shout!
'The Lord has saved his people,
the remnant of Israel!'
See, I will bring them back
from the land of the North
and gather them from the far ends of earth;
all of them: the blind and the lame,
women with child, women in labour:
a great company returning here.
They had left in tears,
I will comfort them as I lead them back;
I will guide them to streams of water,
by a smooth path where they will not stumble.
For I am a father to Israel,
and Ephraim is my first-born son.

This is the word of the Lord.

Responsorial Psalm   Ps 125. R℣ v. 3

R℣ **What marvels the Lord worked for us!**
     Indeed we were glad.

1 When the Lord delivered Zion from bondage,
   it seemed like a dream.
   Then was our mouth filled with laughter,
   on our lips there were songs.   R℣

2 The heathens themselves said: 'What marvels
   the Lord worked for them!'
   What marvels the Lord worked for us!
   Indeed we were glad.   R℣

3 Deliver us, O Lord, from our bondage
   as streams in dry land.
   Those who are sowing in tears
   will sing when they reap.   R℣

4 They go out, they go out, full of tears,
   carrying seed for the sowing:
   they come back, they come back, full of song,
   carrying their sheaves.   R℣

SECOND READING

A reading from the letter to the Hebrews   5:1-6
You are a priest of the order of Melchizedek, and for ever.

Every high priest has been taken out of mankind and is
appointed to act for men in their relations with God, to offer gifts
and sacrifices for sins; and so he can sympathise with those who
are ignorant or uncertain because he too lives in the limitations of
weakness. That is why he has to make sin offerings for himself as
well as for the people. No one takes this honour on himself, but
each one is called by God, as Aaron was. Nor did Christ give
himself the glory of becoming high priest, but he had it from the
one who said to him: You are my son, today I have become your
father, and in another text: You are a priest of the order of
Melchizedek, and for ever.

  This is the word of the Lord.

Gospel Acclamation   Jn 8:12
   Alleluia, alleluia!
   I am the light of the world, says the Lord,
   anyone who follows me
   will have the light of life.
   Alleluia!

or   cf. 2 Tim 1:10

Alleluia, alleluia!
Our Saviour Christ Jesus abolished death,
and he has proclaimed life through the Good News.
Alleluia!

GOSPEL

A reading from the holy Gospel according to Mark   10:46-52
Master, let me see again.

As Jesus left Jericho with his disciples and a large crowd,
Bartimaeus (that is, the son of Timaeus), a blind beggar, was
sitting at the side of the road. When he heard that it was Jesus of
Nazareth, he began to shout and to say, 'Son of David, Jesus,
have pity on me.' And many of them scolded him and told him to
keep quiet, but he only shouted all the louder, 'Son of David,
have pity on me.' Jesus stopped and said, 'Call him here.' So they
called the blind man. 'Courage,' they said 'get up; he is calling
you.' So throwing off his cloak, he jumped up and went to Jesus.
Then Jesus spoke, 'What do you want me to do for you?'
'Rabbuni,' the blind man said to him 'Master, let me see again.'
Jesus said to him, 'Go; your faith has saved you.' And immediately his sight returned and he followed him along the road.

This is the Gospel of the Lord.

Prayer over the Gifts
Lord God of power and might,
receive the gifts we offer
and let our service give you glory.

Preface of Sundays in Ordinary Time I-VIII, P29-P36

Communion Antiphon: We will rejoice at the victory of God and
make our boast in his great name.

or

Christ loved us and gave himself up for us as a fragrant offering
to God.

Prayer after Communion
Lord,
bring to perfection within us
the communion we share in this sacrament.
May our celebration have an effect in our lives.

THIRTY-FIRST SUNDAY IN ORDINARY TIME B

Christ The Priest Of The New Covenant

Through, with, and in Christ we offer the sacrifice of the new covenant which gives perfect glory to the Father and enables us to give him a fitting return of love.

Entrance Antiphon: Do not abandon me, Lord. My God, do not go away from me! Hurry to help me, Lord, my Saviour.

Opening Prayer
Let us pray
    [that our lives will reflect our faith]

God of power and mercy,
only with your help
can we offer you fitting service and praise.
May we live the faith we profess
and trust your promise of eternal life.

or

Let us pray
    [in the presence of God, the source of every good]

Father in heaven, God of power and Lord of mercy,
from whose fullness we have received,
direct our steps in our everyday efforts.
May the changing moods of the human heart
and the limits which our failings impose on hope
never blind us to you, source of every good.

Faith gives us the promise of peace
and makes known the demands of love.
Remove the selfishness that blurs the vision of faith.

FIRST READING

A reading from the book of Deuteronomy   6:2-6
Listen, Israel: You shall love the Lord Your God with all your heart.
Moses said to the people: 'If you fear the Lord your God all the days of your life and if you keep all his laws and commandments which I lay on you, you will have a long life, you and your son and your grandson. Listen then, Israel, keep and observe what will make you prosper and give you great increase, as the Lord

God of your fathers has promised you, giving you a land where milk and honey flow.

'Listen, Israel: The Lord our God is the one Lord. You shall love the Lord your God with all your heart, with all your soul, with all your strength. Let these words I urge on you today be written on your heart.'

This is the word of the Lord.

Responsorial Psalm   Ps 17:2-4. 47. 51. R̷ v.2
   R̷ **I love you, Lord, my strength.**

1   I love you, Lord, my strength,
    my rock, my fortress, my saviour.
    My God is the rock where I take refuge;
    my shield, my mighty help, my stronghold.
    The Lord is worthy of all praise:
    when I call I am saved from my foes.   R̷

2   Long life to the Lord, my rock!
    Praised be the God who saves me.
    He has given great victories to his king
    and shown his love for his anointed.   R̷

SECOND READING

A reading from the letter to the Hebrews   7:23-28

Because he remains for ever, Christ can never lose his priesthood.

There used to be a great number of priests under the former covenant, because death put an end to each one of them; but this one, Christ, because he remains for ever, can never lose his priesthood. It follows then, that his power to save is utterly certain, since he is living for ever to intercede for all who come to God through him.

To suit us, the ideal high priest would have to be holy, innocent and uncontaminated, beyond the influence of sinners, and raised up above the heavens; one who would not need to offer sacrifices every day, as the other high priests do for their own sins and then for those of the people, because he has done this once and for all by offering himself. The Law appoints high priests who are men subject to weakness; but the promise on oath, which came after the Law, appointed the Son who is made perfect for ever.

This is the word of the Lord.

Gospel Acclamation   cf. Jn 6:63.68
> Alleluia, alleluia!
> Your words are spirit, Lord,
> and they are life:
> you have the message of eternal life.
> Alleluia!

or   Jn 14:23

> Alleluia, alleluia!
> If anyone loves me he will keep my word,
> and my Father will love him,
> and we shall come to him.
> Alleluia!

GOSPEL

A reading from the holy Gospel according to Mark   12:28-34
This is the first commandment. The second is like it.

One of the scribes came up to Jesus and put a question to him, 'Which is the first of all the commandments?' Jesus replied, 'This is the first: Listen, Israel, the Lord our God is the one Lord, and you must love the Lord your God with all your heart, with all your soul, with all your mind and with all your strength. The second is this: You must love your neighbour as yourself. There is no commandment greater than these.' The scribe said to him, 'Well spoken, Master; what you have said is true: that he is one and there is no other. To love with all your heart, with all your understanding and strength and to love your neighbour as yourself, this is far more important than any holocaust or sacrifice.' Jesus, seeing how wisely he had spoken said, 'You are not far from the kingdom of God.' And after that no one dared to question him any more.

This is the Gospel of the Lord.

Prayer over the Gifts
God of mercy,
may we offer a pure sacrifice
for the forgiveness of our sins.

Preface of Sundays in Ordinary Time I-VIII, P29-P36

Communion Antiphon: Lord, you will show me the path of life and fill me with joy in your presence.

or

As the living Father sent me, and I live because of the Father, so
he who eats my flesh and drinks my blood will live because of
me.

Prayer after Communion
Lord,
you give us new hope in this eucharist.
May the power of your love
continue its saving work among us
and bring us to the joy you promise.

THIRTY-SECOND SUNDAY IN ORDINARY TIME B

God In Whom We Trust

*We must not be afraid to give, for Christ gave himself completely and
will reward with salvation all those who are waiting for him.*

Entrance Antiphon: Let my prayer come before you, Lord; listen,
and answer me.

Opening Prayer
Let us pray
    [for health of mind and body]

God of power and mercy,
protect us from all harm.
Give us freedom of spirit
and health in mind and body
to do your work on earth.

or

Let us pray
    [that our prayer rise like incense
    in the presence of the Lord]

Almighty Father,
strong is your justice and great is your mercy.
Protect us in the burdens and challenges of life.
Shield our minds from the distortion of pride
and enfold our desire with the beauty of truth.

Help us to become more aware of your loving design
so that we may more willingly give our lives in service to all.

FIRST READING

A reading from the first book of the Kings   17:10-16

The widow made a little scone from her meal and brought it to Elijah.

Elijah the Prophet went off to Sidon. And when he reached the city gate, there was a widow gathering sticks; addressing her he said, 'Please bring a little water in a vessel for me to drink.' She was setting off to bring it when he called after her. 'Please' he said 'bring me a scrap of bread in your hand.' 'As the Lord your God lives,' she replied 'I have no baked bread, but only a handful of meal in a jar and a little oil in a jug; I am just gathering a stick or two to go and prepare this for myself and my son to eat, and then we shall die.' But Elijah said to her, 'Do not be afraid, go and do as you have said; but first make a little scone of it for me and bring it to me, and then make some for yourself and for your son. For thus the Lord speaks, the God of Israel:

"Jar of meal shall not be spent,
jug of oil shall not be emptied,
before the day when the Lord sends
rain on the face of the earth." '

The woman went and did as Elijah told her and they ate the food, she, himself and her son. The jar of meal was not spent nor the jug of oil emptied, just as the Lord had foretold through Elijah.

This is the word of the Lord.

Responsorial Psalm   Ps 145:7-10. R℣ v.2
    R℣ **My soul, give praise to the Lord.**
or
    R℣ **Alleluia!**

1 It is the Lord who keeps faith for ever,
    who is just to those who are oppressed.
    It is he who gives bread to the hungry,
    the Lord, who sets prisoners free.   R℣

2 It is the Lord who gives sight to the blind,
    who raises up those who are bowed down.
    It is the Lord who loves the just,
    the Lord, who protects the stranger.   R℣

3 The Lord upholds the widow and orphan
    but thwarts the path of the wicked.
    The Lord will reign for ever,
    Zion's God, from age to age.   R℣

SECOND READING

A reading from the letter to the Hebrews   9:24-28
Christ offers himself only once to take the faults of many on himself.

It is not as though Christ had entered a man-made sanctuary which was only modelled on the real one; but it was heaven itself, so that he could appear in the actual presence of God on our behalf. And he does not have to offer himself again and again, like the high priest going into the sanctuary year after year with the blood that is not his own, or else he would have had to suffer over and over again since the world began. Instead of that, he has made his appearance once and for all, now at the end of the last age, to do away with sin by sacrificing himself. Since men only die once, and after that comes judgement, so Christ, too, offers himself only once to take the faults of many on himself, and when he appears a second time, it will not be to deal with sin but to reward with salvation those who are waiting for him.

This is the word of the Lord.

Gospel Acclamation   Apoc 2:10
Alleluia, alleluia!
Even if you have to die, says the Lord,
keep faithful, and I will give you
the crown of life.
Alleluia!

or   Mt 5:3

Alleluia, alleluia!
How happy are the poor in spirit;
theirs is the kingdom of heaven.
Alleluia!

GOSPEL

A reading from the holy Gospel according to Mark   12:38-44
This poor widow has put in more than all.

In his teaching Jesus said, 'Beware of the scribes who like to walk about in long robes, to be greeted obsequiously in the market squares, to take the front seats in the synagogues and the places of honour at banquets; these are the men who swallow the property of widows, while making a show of lengthy prayers. The more severe will be the sentence they receive.'

*He sat down opposite the treasury and watched the people putting money into the treasury, and many of the rich put in a great deal. A poor widow came and put in two small coins, the equivalent of a penny. Then he called his disciples and said to them, 'I tell you solemnly, this poor widow has put more in than all who have contributed to the treasury; for they have all put in money they had over, but she from the little she had has put in everything she possessed, all she had to live on.'

This is the Gospel of the Lord.*

*Shorter Form, verses 41-44. Read between *

Prayer over the Gifts
God of mercy,
in this eucharist we proclaim the death of the Lord.
Accept the gifts we present
and help us follow him with love,
for he is Lord for ever and ever.

Preface of Sundays in Ordinary Time I-VIII, P29-P36

Communion Antiphon: The Lord is my shepherd; there is nothing I shall want. In green pastures he gives me rest, he leads me beside the waters of peace.

or

The disciples recognized the Lord Jesus in the breaking of bread.

Prayer after Communion
Lord,
we thank you for the nourishment you give us
through your holy gift.
Pour out your Spirit upon us
and in the strength of this food from heaven
keep us single-minded in your service.

THIRTY-THIRD SUNDAY IN ORDINARY TIME B

The Eternal Perfection Of All Whom Christ Is Sanctifying

We celebrate today the final consummation at the end of time. Each Mass continues Christ's redemptive work in the world and brings us nearer to the final Mass when that work of sanctification will be complete.

Entrance Antiphon: The Lord says: my plans for you are peace and not disaster; when you call to me, I will listen to you, and I will bring you back to the place from which I exiled you.

Opening Prayer
Let us pray
　　[that God will help us to be faithful]

Father of all that is good,
keep us faithful in serving you,
for to serve you is our lasting joy.

or

Let us pray
　　[with hearts that long for peace]

Father in heaven,
ever-living source of all that is good,
from the beginning of time you promised man salvation
through the future coming of your Son, our Lord Jesus Christ.

Help us to drink of his truth
and expand our hearts with the joy of his promises,
so that we may serve you in faith and in love
and know for ever the joy of your presence.

FIRST READING

A reading from the prophet Daniel   12:1-13
When that time comes, your own people will be spared.

'At that time Michael will stand up, the great prince who mounts
guard over your people. There is going to be a time of great
distress, unparalleled since nations first came into existence.
When that time comes, your own people will be spared, all those
whose names are found written in the Book. Of those who lie
sleeping in the dust of the earth many will awake, some to
everlasting life, some to shame and everlasting disgrace. The
learned will shine as brightly as the vault of heaven, and those
who have instructed many in virtue, as bright as stars for all
eternity.'

　　This is the word of the Lord.

Responsorial Psalm   Ps 15:5. 8-11. ℟ v.1
　　℟   **Preserve me, God, I take refuge in you.**

1   O Lord, it is you who are my portion and cup;
　　it is you yourself who are my prize.
　　I keep the Lord ever in my sight:
　　since he is at my right hand, I shall stand firm.   ℟

2 And so my heart rejoices, my soul is glad;
 even my body shall rest in safety.
 For you will not leave my soul among the dead,
 nor let your beloved know decay. ℟

3 You will show me the path of life,
 the fullness of joy in your presence,,
 at your right hand happiness for ever. ℟

SECOND READING

A reading from the letter to the Hebrews   10:11-14. 18

By virtue of one single offering, he has achieved the eternal perfection of all whom he is sanctifying.

All the priests stand at their duties every day, offering over and over again the same sacrifices which are quite incapable of taking sins away. Christ, on the other hand, has offered one single sacrifice for sins, and then taken his place for ever, at the right hand of God, where he is now waiting until his enemies are made into a footstool for him. By virtue of that one single offering, he has achieved the eternal perfection of all whom he is sanctifying. When all sins have been forgiven, there can be no more sin offerings.

This is the word of the Lord.

Gospel Acclamation   Mt 24:42. 44

Alleluia, alleluia!
Stay awake and stand ready,
because you do not know the hour
when the Son of Man is coming.
Alleluia!

or   Lk 21:36

Alleluia, alleluia!
Stay awake, praying at all times
for the strength to stand with confidence
before the Son of Man.
Alleluia!

GOSPEL

A reading from the holy Gospel according to Mark   13:24-32

He will gather his chosen from the four winds.

Jesus said to his disciples: 'In those days, after the time of distress, the sun will be darkened, the moon will lose its brightness, the stars will come falling from heaven and the powers in the heavens will be shaken. And then they will see the Son of Man coming in the clouds with great power and glory; then too he will send the angels to gather his chosen from the four winds, from the ends of the world to the ends of heaven.

'Take the fig tree as a parable: as soon as its twigs grow supple and its leaves come out, you know that summer is near. So with you, when you see these things happening: know that he is near, at the very gates. I tell you solemnly, before this generation has passed away all these things will have taken place. Heaven and earth will pass away, but my words will not pass away.

'But as for that day or hour, nobody knows it, neither the angels of heaven, nor the Son; no one but the Father.'

This is the Gospel of the Lord.

Prayer over the Gifts
Lord God,
may the gifts we offer
increase our love for you
and bring us to eternal life.

Preface of Sundays in Ordinary Time I-VIII, P29-P36

Communion Antiphon: It is good for me to be with the Lord and to put my hope in him.

or

I tell you solemnly, whatever you ask for in prayer, believe that you have received it, and it will be yours, says the Lord.

Prayer after Communion
Father,
may we grow in love
by the eucharist we have celebrated
in memory of the Lord Jesus,
who is Lord for ever and ever.

Last Sunday in Ordinary Time
OUR LORD JESUS CHRIST, UNIVERSAL KING B
Solemnity

Christ The King

Today we celebrate Christ the universal King. He did not claim to be only the king of the Jews. His kingdom was not to be an exclusive one. He is king of all who are on the side of truth and listen to his voice.

Entrance Antiphon: **The Lamb who was slain is worthy to receive strength and divinity, wisdom and power and honour: to him be glory and power for ever.**

Opening Prayer
Let us pray
[that all men will acclaim Jesus as Lord]

Almighty and merciful God,
you break the power of evil
and make all things new
in your Son Jesus Christ, the King of the universe.
May all in heaven and earth acclaim your glory
and never cease to praise you.

or

Let us pray
[that the kingdom of Christ
may live in our hearts and come to our world]

Father all-powerful, God of love,
you have raised our Lord Jesus Christ from death to life,
resplendent in glory as King of creation.

Open our hearts,
free all the world to rejoice in his peace,
to glory in his justice, to live in his love.
Bring all mankind together in Jesus Christ your Son,
whose kingdom is with you and the Holy Spirit,
one God, for ever and ever.

FIRST READING

A reading from the prophet Daniel   7:13-14
His sovereignty is an eternal sovereignty.

I gazed into the visions of the night.

And I saw, coming on the clouds of heaven,
one like a son of man.
He came to the one of great age
and was led into his presence.
On him was conferred sovereignty,
glory and kingship,
and men of all peoples, nations and languages became his
    servants.
His sovereignty is an eternal sovereignty
which shall never pass away,
nor will his empire be destroyed.

This is the word of the the Lord.

Responsorial Psalm   Ps 92:1-2. 5. ℟ v.1
    ℟ **The Lord is king, with majesty enrobed.**

1   The Lord is king, with majesty enrobed;
    the Lord has robed himself with might,
    he has girded himself with power.   ℟

2   The world you made firm, not to be moved;
    your throne has stood firm from of old.
    From all eternity, O Lord, you are.   ℟

3   Truly your decrees are to be trusted.
    Holiness is fitting to your house,
    O Lord, until the end of time.   ℟

SECOND READING

A reading from the book of the Apocalypse   1:5-8
Ruler of the kings of the earth . . . he made us a line of kings, priests to serve his God.

Jesus Christ is the faithful witness, the First-born from the dead, the Ruler of the kings of the earth. He loves us and has washed away our sins with his blood, and made us a line of kings, priests to serve his God and Father; to him, then, be glory and power for ever and ever. Amen. It is he who is coming on the clouds; everyone will see him, even those who pierced him, and all the races of the earth will mourn over him. This is the truth. Amen. 'I am the Alpha and the Omega' says the Lord God, who is, who was, and who is to come, the Almighty.

This is the word of the Lord.

Gospel Acclamation Mk 11:9. 10
Alleluia, alleluia!
Blessings on him who comes in the name of the Lord!
Blessings on the coming kingdom of our father David!
Alleluia!

GOSPEL

A reading from the holy Gospel according to John 18:33-37
It is you who say that I am a king.

'Are you the king of the Jews?' Pilate asked. Jesus replied, 'Do you ask this of your own accord, or have others spoken to you about me?' Pilate answered, 'Am I a Jew? It is your own people and the chief priests who have handed you over to me: what have you done?' Jesus replied, 'Mine is not a kingdom of this world; if my kingdom were of this world, my men would have fought to prevent my being surrendered to the Jews. But my kingdom is not of this kind.' 'So you are a king then?' said Pilate. 'It is you who say it' answered Jesus. 'Yes, I am a king. I was born for this, I came into the world for this: to bear witness to the truth; and all who are on the side of truth listen to my voice.'

This is the Gospel of the Lord.

Prayer over the Gifts
Lord,
we offer you the sacrifice
by which your Son reconciles mankind.
May it bring unity and peace to the world.

Preface of Christ the King, P51

Communion Antiphon: The Lord will reign for ever and will give his people the gift of peace.

Prayer after Communion
Lord,
you give us Christ, the King of all creation,
as food for everlasting life.
Help us to live by his gospel
and bring us to the joy of his kingdom,
where he lives and reigns for ever and ever.

Chapter Acclamation
Alleluia, alleluia!
Blessings on him who comes in the name of the Lord!
Blessings on the coming kingdom of our father David!
Alleluia!

GOSPEL

A reading from the holy Gospel according to John

'Are you the king of the Jews?' Pilate asked. Jesus replied, 'Do you ask this of your own accord, or have others spoken to you about me?' Pilate answered, 'Am I a Jew? It is your own people and the chief priests who have handed you over to me: what have you done?' Jesus replied, 'Mine is not a kingdom of this world; if my kingdom were of this world, my men would have fought to prevent my being surrendered to the Jews. But my kingdom is not of this kind.' 'So you are a king then?' said Pilate. 'It is you who say it,' answered Jesus. 'Yes, I am a king. I was born for this, I came into the world for this: to bear witness to the truth; and all who are on the side of truth listen to my voice.'

This is the Gospel of the Lord.

Prayer over the Gifts
Lord,
we offer you the sacrifice
by which your Son reconciles mankind.
May it bring unity and peace to the world.

Preface of Christ the King (52)

Communion Antiphon. The Lord will reign for ever and will give his people the gift of peace.

Prayer after Communion
Lord,
you give us Christ, the King of all creation,
as food for everlasting life.
Help us to live by his gospel
and bring us to the joy of his kingdom,
where he lives and reigns for ever and ever.

BEHOLD I AM SENDING UPON YOU THE GIFT PROMISED BY MY FATHER

LUKE

O KEY OF DAVID OPEN GATES OF LIFE

THE SEASON OF ADVENT

FIRST SUNDAY OF ADVENT   C

Our Liberation From Fear

Fear is the most crippling of all the emotions and there are many things in life and in the world to make us afraid. We lack integrity because we are afraid to be ourselves. But today we lift up our souls to Christ who comes to deliver us from fear. We can stand erect, hold our heads high, and dwell in confidence.

Entrance Antiphon: To you, my God, I lift my soul, I trust in you; let me never come to shame. Do not let my enemies laugh at me. No one who waits for you is ever put to shame.

The Gloria is omitted.

Opening Prayer
Let us pray
    [that we may take Christ's coming seriously]

All-powerful God,
increase our strength of will for doing good
that Christ may find an eager welcome at his coming
and call us to his side in the kingdom of heaven
where he lives and reigns with you and the Holy Spirit,
one God for ever and ever.

    or

Let us pray
    [in Advent time
    with longing and waiting
    for the coming of the Lord]

Father in heaven,
our hearts desire the warmth of your love
and our minds are searching for the light of your Word.

Increase our longing for Christ our Saviour
and give us the strength to grow in love,
that the dawn of his coming
may find us rejoicing in his presence
and welcoming the light of his truth.

FIRST READING

A reading from the prophet Jeremiah   33:14-16
I will make a virtuous Branch grow for David.

See, the days are coming – it is the Lord who speaks – when I am
going to fulfil the promise I made to the House of Israel and the
House of Judah:

'In those days and at that time,
I will make a virtuous Branch grow for David,
who shall practise honesty and integrity in the land.
In those days Judah shall be saved
and Israel shall dwell in confidence.
And this is the name the city will be called:
The-Lord-our-integrity.'

This is the word of the Lord.

Responsorial Psalm   Ps 24:4-5. 8-9. 10. 14. ℟ v.1
    ℟ **To you, O Lord, I lift up my soul.**

1 Lord, make me know your ways.
   Lord, teach me your paths.
   Make me walk in your truth, and teach me:
   for you are God my saviour.   ℟

2 The Lord is good and upright.
   He shows the path to those who stray,
   he guides the humble in the right path;
   he teaches his way to the poor.   ℟

3 His ways are faithfulness and love
   for those who keep his covenant and will.
   The Lord's friendship is for those who revere him;
   to them he reveals his covenant.   ℟

SECOND READING

A reading from the first letter of St Paul 3:12 – 4:2
to the Thessalonians

May the Lord confirm your hearts in holiness when Christ comes.

May the Lord be generous in increasing your love and make you love one another and the whole human race as much as we love you. And may he so confirm your hearts in holiness that you may be blameless in the sight of our God and Father when our Lord Jesus Christ comes with all his saints.

Finally, brothers, we urge you and appeal to you in the Lord Jesus to make more and more progress in the kind of life that you are meant to live: the life that God wants, as you learnt from us, and as you are already living it. You have not forgotten the instructions we gave you on the authority of the Lord Jesus.

This is the word of the Lord.

Gospel Acclamation Ps 84:8
Alleluia, alleluia!
Let us see, O Lord, your mercy
and give us your saving help.
Alleluia!

GOSPEL

A reading from the holy Gospel according 21:25-28. 34-36
to Luke

Your liberation is near at hand.

Jesus said to his disciples: 'There will be signs in the sun and moon and stars; on earth nations in agony, bewildered by the clamour of the ocean and its waves; men dying of fear as they await what menaces the world, for the powers of heaven will be shaken. And then they will see the Son of Man coming in a cloud with power and great glory. When these things begin to take place, stand erect, hold your heads high, because your liberation is near at hand.'

'Watch yourselves, or your hearts will be coarsened with debauchery and drunkenness and the cares of life, and that day will be sprung on you suddenly, like a trap. For it will come down on every living man on the face of the earth. Stay awake, praying at all times for the strength to survive all that is going to happen, and to stand with confidence before the Son of Man.'

This is the Gospel of the Lord.

Prayer over the Gifts
Father,
from all you give us
we present this bread and wine.
As we serve you now,
accept our offering
and sustain us with your promise of eternal life.

Preface of Advent I, P1

Communion Antiphon: The Lord will shower his gifts, and our land
will yield its fruit.

Prayer after Communion
Father,
may our communion
teach us to love heaven.
May its promise and hope
guide our way on earth.

An appropriate Solemn Blessing or Prayer over the People may
be used. See pp.90ff.

SECOND SUNDAY OF ADVENT   C

The Joy Of Salvation

*We celebrate the marvels God has worked for us in sending us his mercy
and forgiveness, and calling us to share his glory. We await with joyful
hope that 'Day of the Lord' when his work in us will be complete.*

Entrance Antiphon: People of Zion, the Lord will come to save all
nations, and your hearts will exult to hear his majestic voice.

The Gloria is omitted.

Opening Prayer
Let us pray
  [that nothing may hinder us
  from receiving Christ with joy]

God of power and mercy,
open our hearts in welcome.
Remove the things that hinder us from receiving Christ with joy,
so that we may share his wisdom

and become one with him
when he comes in glory,
for he lives and reigns with you and the Holy Spirit,
one God, for ever and ever.

or

Let us pray
    [in Advent time
    for the coming Saviour to teach us wisdom]

Father in heaven,
the day draws near when the glory of your Son
will make radiant the night of the waiting world.

May the lure of greed not impede us from the joy
which moves the hearts of those who seek him.
May the darkness not blind us
to the vision of wisdom
which fills the minds of those who find him.

FIRST READING

A reading from the prophet Baruch   5:1-9
God means to show your splendour to every nation.

Jerusalem, take off your dress of sorrow and distress,
put on the beauty of the glory of God for ever,
wrap the cloak of the integrity of God around you,
put the diadem of the glory of the Eternal on your head:
since God means to show your splendour to every nation under
    heaven,
since the name God gives you for ever will be,
'Peace through integrity, and honour through devotedness'.
Arise, Jerusalem, stand on the heights
and turn your eyes to the east:
see your sons reassembled from west and east
at the command of the Holy One, jubilant that God has
    remembered them.
Though they left you on foot,
with enemies for an escort,
now God brings them back to you
like royal princes carried back in glory.
For God has decreed the flattening
of each high mountain, of the everlasting hills,
the filling of the valleys to make the ground level

so that Israel can walk in safety under the glory of God.
And the forests and every fragrant tree will provide shade
for Israel at the command of God;
for God will guide Israel in joy by the light of his glory
with his mercy and integrity for escort.

This is the word of the Lord.

Responsorial Psalm Ps 125. R/ v.3
R/ **What marvels the Lord worked for us!**
Indeed we were glad.

1 When the Lord delivered Zion from bondage,
it seemed like a dream.
Then was our mouth filled with laughter,
on our lips there were songs. R/

2 The heathens themselves said: 'What marvels
the Lord worked for them!'
What marvels the Lord worked for us!
Indeed we were glad. R/

3 Deliver us, O Lord, from our bondage
as streams in dry land.
Those who are sowing in tears
will sing when they reap. R/

4 They go out, they go out, full of tears
carrying seed for the sowing:
they come back, they come back, full of song,
carrying their sheaves. R/

SECOND READING

A reading from the letter of St Paul to 1:3-6. 8-11
the Philippians
Be pure and blameless for the day of Christ.

Every time I pray for all of you, I pray with joy, remembering
how you have helped to spread the Good News from the day you
first heard it right up to the present. I am quite certain that the
One who began this good work in you will see that it is finished
when the Day of Christ Jesus comes. God knows how much I
miss you all, loving you as Christ Jesus loves you. My prayer is
that your love for each other may increase more and more and
never stop improving your knowledge and deepening your
perception so that you can always recognise what is best. This

will help you to become pure and blameless, and prepare you for the Day of Christ, when you will reach the perfect goodness which Jesus Christ produces in us for the glory and praise of God.

This is the word of the Lord.

Gospel Acclamation   Lk 3:4. 6
Alleluia, alleluia!
Prepare a way for the Lord,
make his paths straight,
and all mankind shall see the salvation of God.
Alleluia!

GOSPEL
A reading from the holy Gospel according to Luke   3:1-6
All mankind shall see the salvation of God.

In the fifteenth year of Tiberius Caesar's reign, when Pontius Pilate was governor of Judaea, Herod tetrarch of Galilee, his brother Philip tetrarch of the lands of Ituraea and Trachonitis, Lysanias tetrarch of Abilene, during the pontificate of Annas and Caiaphas, the word of God came to John son of Zechariah, in the wilderness. He went through the whole Jordan district proclaiming a baptism of repentance for the forgiveness of sins, as it is written in the book of the sayings of the prophet Isaiah:

A voice cries in the wilderness;
Prepare a way for the Lord,
make his paths straight.
Every valley will be filled in,
every mountain and hill be laid low,
winding ways will be straightened
and rough roads made smooth.
And all mankind shall see the salvation of God.

This is the Gospel of the Lord.

Prayer over the Gifts
Lord,
we are nothing without you.
As you sustain us with your mercy,
receive our prayers and offerings.

Preface of Advent I, P1

Communion Antiphon: Rise up, Jerusalem, stand on the heights, and see the joy that is coming to you from God.

Prayer after Communion

Father,
you give us food from heaven.
By our sharing in this mystery,
teach us to judge wisely the things of earth
and to love the things of heaven

An appropriate Solemn Blessing or Prayer over the People may be used. See pp.90ff.

THIRD SUNDAY OF ADVENT   C

A Day Of Festival

Today we sing and shout for joy with Christ, the Lord of the Dance, who brings us the Good News of our redemption, and renews us by his love.

Entrance Antiphon: Rejoice in the Lord always; again I say, rejoice! The Lord is near.

The Gloria is omitted.

Opening Prayer

Let us pray
   [that God will fill us with joy
   at the coming of Christ]

Lord God,
may we, your people,
who look forward to the birthday of Christ
experience the joy of salvation
and celebrate that feast with love and thanksgiving.
   or

Let us pray
   [this Advent
   for joy and hope in the coming Lord]

Father of our Lord Jesus Christ,
ever faithful to your promises
and ever close to your Church:
the earth rejoices in hope of the Saviour's coming

and looks forward with longing
to his return at the end of time.

Prepare our hearts and remove the sadness
that hinders us from feeling the joy and hope
which his presence will bestow,
for he is Lord for ever and ever.

FIRST READING

A reading from the prophet Zephaniah 3:14-18

The Lord will dance with shouts of joy for you as on a day of festival.

Shout for joy, daughter of Zion,
Israel, shout aloud!
Rejoice, exult with all your heart,
daughter of Jerusalem!
The Lord has repealed your sentence;
he has driven your enemies away.
The Lord, the king of Israel, is in your midst;
you have no more evil to fear.
When that day comes, word will come to Jerusalem:
Zion, have no fear,
do not let your hands fall limp.
The Lord your God is in your midst,
a victorious warrior.
He will exult with joy over you,
he will renew you by his love;
he will dance with shouts of joy for you
as on a day of festival.

This is the word of the Lord.

Responsorial Psalm Is 12:2-6. R̝ v.6

R̝ **Sing and shout for joy**
for great in your midst is the Holy One of Israel.

1 Truly, God is my salvation,
 I trust, I shall not fear.
 For the Lord is my strength, my song,
 he became my saviour.
 With joy you will draw water
 from the wells of salvation. R̝

2 Give thanks to the Lord, give praise to his name!
 Make his mighty deeds known to the peoples!
 Declare the greatness of his name. R̝

(continued)

3   Sing a psalm to the Lord
    for he has done glorious deeds,
    make them known to all the earth!
    People of Zion, sing and shout for joy
    for great in your midst is the Holy One of Israel.

℟   **Sing and shout for joy**
    for great in your midst is the Holy One of Israel.

SECOND READING

A reading from the letter of St Paul to the Philippians   4:4-7
The Lord is very near.

I want you to be happy, always happy in the Lord; I repeat, what I want is your happiness. Let your tolerance be evident to everyone: the Lord is very near. There is no need to worry; but if there is anything you need, pray for it, asking God for it with prayer and thanksgiving, and that peace of God, which is so much greater than we can understand, will guard your hearts and your thoughts, in Christ Jesus.

    This is the word of the Lord.

Gospel Acclamation   Is 61:1 (Lk 4:18)
    Alleluia, alleluia!
    The spirit of the Lord has been given to me.
    He has sent me to bring good news to the poor.
    Alleluia!

GOSPEL

A reading from the holy Gospel according to Luke   3:10-18
What must we do?

When all the people asked John, 'What must we do?' he answered, 'If anyone has two tunics he must share with the man who has none, and the one with something to eat must do the same.' There were tax collectors too who came for baptism, and these said to him, 'Master what must we do?' He said to them, 'Exact no more than your rate.' Some soldiers asked him in their turn, 'What about us? What must we do?' He said to them, 'No intimidation! No extortion! Be content with your pay!'

    A feeling of expectancy had grown among the people, who were beginning to think that John might be the Christ, so John declared before them all, 'I baptise you with water, but someone is coming, someone who is more powerful than I am, and I am not fit to undo the strap of his sandals; he will baptise you with the Holy Spirit and fire. His winnowing-fan is in his hand to clear his threshing-floor and to gather the wheat into his barn; but the chaff he will burn in a fire that will never go out.' As well as this, there were many other things he said to exhort the people and to announce the Good News to them.

This is the Gospel of the Lord.

Prayer over the Gifts
Lord,
may the gift we offer in faith and love
be a continual sacrifice in your honour
and truly become our eucharist and our salvation.

Preface of Advent I or II, P1 or P2

Communion Antiphon: Say to the anxious: be strong and fear not, our God will come to save us.

Prayer after Communion
God of mercy,
may this eucharist bring us your divine help,
free us from our sins,
and prepare us for the birthday of our Saviour,
who is Lord for ever and ever.

An appropriate Solemn Blessing or Prayer over the People may be used. See pp.90ff.

FOURTH SUNDAY OF ADVENT   C

Mary's Child: The Prince Of Peace

From the least of the clans of Judah, from Mary his lowly handmaid, God prepared a body for his Christ, who comes to fill the world with his spirit of peace.

Entrance Antiphon: Let the clouds rain down the Just One, and the earth bring forth a Saviour.

The Gloria is omitted.

Opening Prayer
Let us pray
   [as Advent draws to a close,
   that Christ will truly come into our hearts]

Lord,
fill our hearts with your love,
and as you revealed to us by an angel
the coming of your Son as man,
so lead us through his suffering and death
to the glory of his resurrection,
for he lives and reigns with you and the Holy Spirit,
one God, for ever and ever.

or

Let us pray
[as Advent draws to a close
for the faith that opens our lives
to the Spirit of God]

Father, all-powerful God,
your eternal Word took flesh on our earth
when the Virgin Mary placed her life
at the service of your plan.

Lift our minds in watchful hope
to hear the voice which announces his glory
and open our minds to receive the Spirit
who prepares us for his coming.

FIRST READING

A reading from the prophet Micah   5:1-4
Out of you will be born the one who is to rule over Israel.

The Lord says this:

You, Bethlehem Ephrathah,
the least of the clans of Judah,
out of you will be born for me
the one who is to rule over Israel;
his origin goes back to the distant past,
to the days of old.
The Lord is therefore going to abandon them
till the time when she who is to give birth gives birth.
Then the remnant of his brothers will come back
to the sons of Israel.
He will stand and feed his flock
with the power of the Lord,
with the majesty of the name of his God.
They will live secure, for from then on he will extend his
    power

to the ends of the land.
He himself will be peace.

This is the word of the Lord.

Responsorial Psalm   Ps 79:2-3. 15-16. 18-19. ℟ v.4
  ℟ **God of hosts, bring us back;**
     let your face shine on us and we shall be saved.

1 O shepherd of Israel, hear us,
   shine forth from your cherubim throne.
   O Lord, rouse up your might,
   O Lord, come to our help. ℟

2 God of hosts, turn again, we implore,
   look down from heaven and see.
   Visit this vine and protect it,
   the vine your right hand has planted.℟

3 May your hand be on the man you have chosen,
   the man you have given your strength.
   And we shall never forsake you again:
   give us life that we may call upon your name. ℟

SECOND READING
A reading from the letter to the Hebrews   10:5-10
Here I am! I am coming to obey your will.

This is what Christ said, on coming into the world:

You who wanted no sacrifice or oblation,
prepared a body for me.
You took no pleasure in holocausts or sacrifices for sin;
then I said,
just as I was commanded in the scroll of the book,
'God, here I am! I am coming to obey your will.'

Notice that he says first: You did not want what the Law lays down as the things to be offered, that is: the sacrifices, the oblations, the holocausts and the sacrifices for sin, and you took no pleasure in them; and then he says: Here I am! I am coming to obey your will. He is abolishing the first sort to replace it with the second. And this will was for us to be made holy by the offering of his body made once and for all by Jesus Christ.

This is the word of the Lord.

Gospel Acclamation   Lk 1:38
Alleluia, alleluia!
I am the handmaid of the Lord:
let what you have said be done to me.
Alleluia!

GOSPEL

A reading from the holy Gospel according to Luke   1:39-44
Why should I be honoured with a visit from the mother of my Lord?

Mary set out and went as quickly as she could to a town in the hill
country of Judah. She went into Zechariah's house and greeted
Elizabeth. Now as soon as Elizabeth heard Mary's greeting, the
child leapt in her womb and Elizabeth was filled with the Holy
Spirit. She gave a loud cry and said, 'Of all women you are the
most blessed, and blessed is the fruit of your womb. Why should
I be honoured with a visit from the mother of my Lord? For the
moment your greeting reached my ears, the child in my womb
leapt for joy. Yes, blessed is she who believed that the promise
made her by the Lord would be fulfilled.'

This is the Gospel of the Lord.

Prayer over the Gifts
Lord,
may the power of the Spirit,
which sanctified Mary the mother of your Son,
make holy the gifts we place upon this altar.

Preface of Advent II, P2

Communion Antiphon: **The Virgin is with child, and shall bear a
son, and she will call him Emmanuel.**

Prayer after Communion
Lord,
in this sacrament
we receive the promise of salvation;
as Christmas draws near
make us grow in faith and love
to celebrate the coming of Christ our Saviour,
who is Lord for ever and ever.

An appropriate Solemn Blessing or Prayer over the People may
be used. See pp.90ff.

THE SEASON OF CHRISTMAS

CHRISTMAS DAY: VIGIL MASS

See above, pp.126ff.

CHRISTMAS DAY

See above, pp.131ff.

Sunday in the Octave of Christmas

THE HOLY FAMILY OF JESUS, MARY AND JOSEPH
C
Feast

Where there is no Sunday occurring between 25 December and 1 January, this feast is celebrated on 30 December, with one reading only before the Gospel.

The Holy Family

We celebrate that Holy Family of Nazareth which is the model for all who fear the Lord and walk in his ways.

Entrance Antiphon: The shepherds hastened to Bethlehem, where they found Mary and Joseph, and the baby lying in a manger.

Opening Prayer
Let us pray
[for peace in our families]

Father,
help us to live as the holy family,
united in respect and love.
Bring us to the joy and peace of your eternal home.

or

Let us pray
   [as the family of God,
   who share in his life]

Father in heaven, creator of all,
you ordered the earth to bring forth life
and crowned its goodness by creating the family of man.
In history's moment when all was ready,
you sent your Son to dwell in time,
obedient to the laws of life in our world.

Teach us the sanctity of human love,
show us the value of family life,
and help us to live in peace with all men
that we may share in your life for ever.

The First Reading, Psalm, Second Reading and Gospel Acclamation given for Year A, pp.144ff., may be used, with the Gospel below. Or the alternative readings given below may be used.

FIRST READING

A reading from the first book of Samuel   1:20-22. 24-28
Samuel is made over to the Lord for the whole of his life.

Hannah conceived and gave birth to a son, and called him Samuel 'since' she said 'I asked the Lord for him.'
    When a year had gone by, the husband Elkanah went up again with all his family to offer the annual sacrifice to the Lord and to fulfil his vow. Hannah, however, did not go up, having said to her husband, 'Not before the child is weaned. Then I will bring him and present him before the Lord and he shall stay there for ever.'
    When she had weaned him, she took him up with her together with a three-year old bull, an ephah of flour and a skin of wine, and she brought him to the temple of the Lord at Shiloh; and the child was with them. They slaughtered the bull and the child's mother came to Eli. She said, 'If you please, my lord. As you live, my lord, I am the woman who stood here beside you, praying to the Lord. This is the child I prayed for, and the Lord

granted me what I asked him. Now I make him over to the Lord
for the whole of his life. He is made over to the Lord.'
There she left him, for the Lord.

This is the word of the Lord.

Responsorial Psalm   Ps 83:2-3. 5-6. 9-10. ℟ v.5
  ℟   **They are happy who dwell in your house, O Lord.**

1   How lovely is your dwelling place,
     Lord, God of hosts.
     My soul is longing and yearning,
     is yearning for the courts of the Lord.
     My heart and my soul ring out their joy
     to God, the living God.   ℟

2   They are happy, who dwell in your house,
     for ever singing your praise.
     They are happy, whose strength is in you;
     they walk with ever growing strength.   ℟

3   O Lord, God of hosts, hear my prayer,
     give ear, O God of Jacob.
     Turn your eyes, O God, our shield,
     look on the face of your anointed.   ℟

SECOND READING

A reading from the first letter of St John   3:1-2. 21-24
We are called God's children, and that is what we are.

Think of the love that the Father has lavished on us,
by letting us be called God's children;
and that is what we are.
Because the world refused to acknowledge him,
therefore it does not acknowledge us.
My dear people, we are already the children of God
but what we are to be in the future has not yet been revealed,
 all we know is, that when it is revealed
we shall be like him
because we shall see him as he really is.

My dear people,
if we cannot be condemned by our own conscience,
we need not be afraid in God's presence,
and whatever we ask him,

we shall receive,
because we keep his commandments
and live the kind of life that he wants.
His commandments are these:
that we believe in the name of his Son Jesus Christ
and that we love one another
as he told us to.
Whoever keeps his commandments
lives in God and God lives in him.
We know that he lives in us
by the Spirit that he has given us.

This is the word of the Lord.

Gospel Acclamation   cf. Acts 16:14
Alleluia, alleluia!
Open our heart, O Lord,
to accept the words of your Son.
Alleluia!

GOSPEL

A reading from the holy Gospel according to Luke   2:41-52

Jesus is found by his parents sitting among the doctors.

Every year the parents of Jesus used to go to Jerusalem for the
feast of the Passover. When he was twelve years old, they went
up for the feast as usual. When they were on their way home
after the feast, the boy Jesus stayed behind in Jerusalem without
his parents knowing it. They assumed he was with the caravan,
and it was only after a day's journey that they went to look for
him among their relations and acquaintances. When they failed
to find him they went back to Jerusalem looking for him
everywhere.

Three days later, they found him in the Temple, sitting
among the doctors, listening to them, and asking them questions; and all those who heard him were astounded at his
intelligence and his replies. They were overcome when they saw
him, and his mother said to him, 'My child, why have you done
this to us? See how worried your father and I have been, looking
for you.' 'Why were you looking for me?' he replied. 'Did you not
know that I must be busy with my Father's affairs?' But they did
not understand what he meant.

He then went down with them and came to Nazareth and

lived under their authority. His mother stored up all these things in her heart. And Jesus increased in wisdom, in stature, and in favour with God and men.

This is the Gospel of the Lord.

Prayer over the Gifts
Lord,
accept this sacrifice
and through the prayers of Mary, the virgin Mother of God,
and of her husband, Joseph,
unite our families in peace and love.

Preface of Christmas I-III, P3-P5

Communion Antiphon: Our God has appeared on earth, and lived among men.

Prayer after Communion
Eternal Father,
we want to live as Jesus, Mary, and Joseph,
in peace with you and one another.
May this communion strengthen us
to face the troubles of life.

An appropriate Solemn Blessing or Prayer over the People may be used. See pp.90ff.

1 January: Octave of Christmas

SOLEMNITY OF MARY, MOTHER OF GOD

See above, pp.146ff.

SECOND SUNDAY AFTER CHRISTMAS

See above, pp.149ff.

6 January (or the Sunday between 2 January and 8 January)

THE EPIPHANY OF THE LORD

See above, pp.154ff.

Sunday after 6 January

THE BAPTISM OF THE LORD   C

First Sunday in Ordinary Time

Feast

This feast is omitted when the Epiphany is celebrated on this Sunday.

The Baptism of the Lord

The Father anointed his beloved son, Jesus, with the Holy Spirit and with power, to bring healing and peace to all the nations.

Entrance Antiphon: When the Lord had been baptised, the heavens opened, and the Spirit came down like a dove to rest on him. Then the voice of the Father thundered: This is my beloved Son, with him I am well pleased.

Opening Prayer

Let us pray

   [that we will be faithful to our baptism]

Almighty, eternal God,
when the Spirit descended upon Jesus
at his baptism in the Jordan,
you revealed him as your own beloved Son.
Keep us, your children born of water and the Spirit,
faithful to our calling.

or

Father,
your only Son revealed himself to us by becoming man.
May we who share his humanity
come to share his divinity,
for he lives and reigns with you and the Holy Spirit,
one God, for ever and ever.

or

Let us pray

   [as we listen to the voice of God's Spirit]

Father in heaven,
you revealed Christ as your Son
by the voice that spoke over the waters of the Jordan.

May all who share in the sonship of Christ
follow in his path of service to man,
and reflect the glory of his kingdom
even to the ends of the earth,
for he is Lord for ever and ever.

The First Reading, Psalm, Second Reading and Gospel Acclamation given for Year A, pp.159ff., may be used, with the Gospel below. Or the alternative readings given below may be used.

FIRST READING

A reading from the prophet Isaiah   40:1-5. 9-11
The glory of the Lord shall be revealed and all mankind shall see it.

'Console my people, console them'
says your God.
'Speak to the heart of Jerusalem
and call to her
that her time of service is ended,
that her sin is atoned for,
that she has received from the hand of the Lord
double punishment for all her crimes.'

A voice cries, 'Prepare in the wilderness
a way for the Lord.
Make a straight highway for our God
across the desert.
Let every valley be filled in,
every mountain and hill be laid low,
let every cliff become a plain,
and the ridges a valley;
then the glory of the Lord shall be revealed
and all mankind shall see it;
for the mouth of the Lord has spoken.'

Go up on a high mountain,
joyful messenger to Zion.
Shout with a loud voice,
joyful messenger to Jerusalem.
Shout without fear,
say to the towns of Judah,
'Here is your God.'
Here is the Lord coming with power,
his arm subduing all things to him.
The prize of his victory is with him,

his trophies all go before him.
He is like a shepherd feeding his flock,
gathering lambs in his arms,
holding them against his breast
and leading to their rest the mother ewes.

This is the word of the Lord.

Responsorial Psalm   Ps 103:1-2. 3-4. 24-25. 27-30. ℟ v.1

℟   **Bless the Lord, my soul!**
    Lord God, how great you are.

1   Lord God, how great you are,
    clothed in majesty and glory,
    wrapped in light as in a robe!
    You stretch out the heavens like a tent.   ℟

2   Above the rains you build your dwelling.
    You make the clouds your chariot,
    you walk on the wings of the wind,
    you make the winds your messengers
    and flashing fire your servants.   ℟

3   How many are your works, O Lord!
    In wisdom you have made them all.
    The earth is full of your riches.
    There is the sea, vast and wide,
    with its moving swarms past counting,
    living things great and small.   ℟

4   All of these look to you
    to give them their food in due season.
    You give it, they gather it up:
    you open your hand, they have their fill.   ℟

5   You take back your spirit, they die,
    returning to the dust from which they came.
    You send forth your spirit, they are created;
    and you renew the face of the earth.   ℟

SECOND READING

A reading from the letter of St Paul to Titus 2:11-14. 3:4-7

He saved us by the cleansing water of re-birth and by renewing us with the Holy Spirit.

God's grace has been revealed, and it has made salvation possible for the whole human race and taught us that what we have to do is to give up everything that does not lead to God, and all our worldly ambitions; we must be self-restrained and live good and religious lives here in this present world, while we are waiting in hope for the blessing which will come with the Appearing of the glory of our great God and saviour Christ Jesus. He sacrificed himself for us in order to set us free from all wickedness and to purify a people so that it could be his very own and would have no ambition except to do good.

When the kindness and love of God our saviour for mankind were revealed, it was not because he was concerned with any righteous actions we might have done ourselves; it was for no reason except his own compassion that he saved us, by means of the cleansing water of rebirth and by renewing us with the Holy Spirit which he has so generously poured over us through Jesus Christ our saviour. He did this so that we should be justified by his grace, to become heirs looking forward to inheriting eternal life.

This is the word of the Lord.

Gospel Acclamation cf. Lk 3:16
Alleluia, alleluia!
Someone is coming, said John, someone greater than I.
He will baptize you with the Holy Spirit and with fire.
Alleluia!

GOSPEL

A reading from the holy Gospel according to Luke 3:15-16. 21-22

While Jesus after his own baptism was at prayer, heaven opened.

A feeling of expectancy had grown among the people, who were beginning to think that John might be the Christ, so John declared before them all, 'I baptise you with water, but someone is coming, someone who is more powerful than I am and I am not fit to undo the strap of his sandals; he will baptise you with the Holy Spirit and fire.'

Now when all the people had been baptised and while Jesus after his own baptism was at prayer, heaven opened and the

Holy Spirit descended on him in bodily shape, like a dove. And a voice came from heaven, 'You are my Son, the Beloved; my favour rests on you'.

This is the Gospel of the Lord.

Prayer over the Gifts
Lord,
we celebrate the revelation of Christ your Son
who takes away the sins of the world.
Accept our gifts
and let them become one with his sacrifice,
for he is Lord for ever and ever.

Preface of the Baptism of the Lord, P7

Communion Antiphon: This is he of whom John said: I have seen and have given witness that this is the Son of God.

Prayer after Communion
Lord,
you feed us with bread from heaven.
May we hear your Son with faith
and become your children in name and in fact.

An appropriate Solemn Blessing or Prayer over the People may be used. See pp.90ff.

THE SEASON OF LENT

For a Note on Preparation for Baptism, see above, p.162.

ASH WEDNESDAY

See above, pp.163ff.

FIRST SUNDAY OF LENT   C

Jesus Is Lord

Today we praise God for the marvellous things he did for our fathers, for his mighty hand and outstretched arm. What he did for them he still does for us, in Jesus the Lord who conquered sin and death.

Entrance Antiphon: When he calls to me, I will answer; I will rescue him and give him honour. Long life and contentment will be his.

The Gloria is omitted.

Opening Prayer
Let us pray
  [that this Lent will help us reproduce in our lives
  the self-sacrificing love of Christ]

Father,
through our observance of Lent,
help us to understand the meaning
of your Son's death and resurrection,
and teach us to reflect it in our lives.

or

Let us pray
   [at the beginning of Lent
   for the spirit of repentance]

Lord our God,
you formed man from the clay of the earth
and breathed into him the spirit of life,
but he turned from your face and sinned.

In this time of repentance
we call out for your mercy.
Bring us back to you
and to the life your Son won for us
by his death on the cross
for he lives and reigns for ever and ever.

FIRST READING

A reading from the book of Deuteronomy   26:4-10

The creed of the chosen people.

Moses said to the people: 'The priest shall take the pannier from your hand and lay it before the altar of the Lord your God. Then, in the sight of the Lord your God, you must make this pronouncement:

"My father was a wandering Aramaean. He went down into Egypt to find refuge there, few in numbers; but there he became a nation, great, mighty, and strong. The Egyptians ill-treated us, they gave us no peace and inflicted harsh slavery on us. But we called on the Lord, the God of our fathers. The Lord heard our voice and saw our misery, our toil and our oppression; and the Lord brought us out of Egypt with mighty hand and outstretched arm, with great terror, and with signs and wonders. He brought us here and gave us this land, a land where milk and honey flow. Here then I bring the first-fruits of the produce of the soil that you, Lord, have given me." You must then lay them before the Lord your God, and bow down in the sight of the Lord your God.'

This is the word of the Lord.

Responsorial Psalm Ps 90:1-2. 10-15. ℟ v.15

℟ **Be with me, O Lord, in my distress.**

1 He who dwells in the shelter of the Most High
   and abides in the shade of the Almighty
   says to the Lord: 'My refuge,
   my stronghold, my God in whom I trust!' ℟

2 Upon you no evil shall fall,
   no plague approach where you dwell.
   For you has he commanded his angels,
   to keep you in all your ways. ℟

3 They shall bear you upon their hands
   lest you strike your foot against a stone.
   On the lion and the viper you will tread
   and trample the young lion and the dragon. ℟

4 His love he set on me, so I will rescue him;
   protect him for he knows my name.
   When he calls I shall answer: 'I am with you.'
   I will save him in distress and give him glory. ℟

SECOND READING

A reading from the letter of St Paul to the Romans 10:8-13
The creed of the Christian.

Scripture says: The word, that is the faith we proclaim, is very
near to you, it is on your lips and in your heart. If your lips
confess that Jesus is Lord and if you believe in your heart that
God raised him from the dead, then you will be saved. By
believing from the heart you are made righteous; by confessing
with your lips you are saved. When scripture says: those who
believe in him will have no cause for shame, it makes no
distinction between Jew and Greek: all belong to the same Lord
who is rich enough, however many ask for his help, for everyone
who calls on the name of the Lord will be saved.

This is the word of the Lord.

Gospel Acclamation Mt 4:4
   Praise to you, O Christ, king of eternal glory!
   Man does not live on bread alone
   but on every word that comes from the mouth of God.
   Praise to you, O Christ, king of eternal glory!

GOSPEL

A reading from the holy Gospel according to Luke   4:1-13

Jesus was led by the Spirit through the wilderness and was tempted there.

Filled with the Holy Spirit, Jesus left the Jordan and was led by the Spirit through the wilderness, being tempted there by the devil for forty days. During that time he ate nothing and at the end he was hungry. Then the devil said to him, 'If you are the Son of God, tell this stone to turn into a loaf.' But Jesus replied, 'Scripture says: Man does not live on bread alone.'

Then leading him to a height, the devil showed him in a moment of time all the kingdoms of the world and said to him, 'I will give you all this power and the glory of these kingdoms, for it has been committed to me and I give it to anyone I choose. Worship me, then, and it shall all be yours.' But Jesus answered him. 'Scripture says:

You must worship the Lord your God,
and serve him alone.'

Then he led him to Jerusalem and made him stand on the parapet of the Temple. 'If you are the Son of God', he said to him 'throw yourself down from here, for scripture says:

He will put his angels in charge of you
to guard you,

and again:

They will hold you up on their hands
in case you hurt your foot against a stone.'

But Jesus answered him, 'It has been said:

You must not put the Lord your God to the test.'

Having exhausted all these ways of tempting him, the devil left him, to return at the appointed time.

This is the Gospel of the Lord.

After the Homily, the Election or Enrolment of Candidates for Baptism may follow. See above, pp.173ff.

Prayer over the Gifts
Lord,
make us worthy to bring you these gifts.
May this sacrifice
help to change our lives.

Preface of First Sunday of Lent, P12 or Lent I or II, P8 or P9

Communion Antiphon: Man does not live on bread alone, but on every word that comes from the mouth of God.

or

The Lord will overshadow you, and you will find refuge under his wings.

Prayer after Communion
Father,
you increase our faith and hope,
you deepen our love in this communion.
Help us to live by your words
and to seek Christ, our bread of life,
who is Lord for ever and ever.

An appropriate Solemn Blessing or Prayer over the People may be used. See pp. 90ff.

SECOND SUNDAY OF LENT   C

The Lord In Whom We Put Our Faith

Like Abraham, our father in faith, we are called by God to a new homeland. We are not to rest in the material comforts of this world, but to move onwards towards the land of promise, where the Lord in whom we put our faith will transfigure our mortal bodies into the likeness of his glorified body.

Entrance Antiphon: Remember your mercies, Lord, your tenderness from ages past. Do not let our enemies triumph over us; O God, deliver Israel from all her distress.

or

My heart has prompted me to seek your face; I seek it, Lord; do not hide from me.

The Gloria is omitted.

Opening Prayer
Let us pray
  [for the grace to respond
  to the Word of God]

God our Father,
help us to hear your Son.
Enlighten us with your word,
that we may find the way to your glory.

or

Let us pray
  [in this season of Lent
  for the gift of integrity]

Father of light,
in you is found no shadow of change
but only the fullness of life and limitless truth.

Open our hearts to the voice of your Word
and free us from the original darkness that shadows our vision.
Restore our sight that we may look upon your Son
who calls us to repentance and a change of heart,
for he lives and reigns with you for ever and ever.

FIRST READING

A reading from the book of Genesis   15:5-12. 17-18
God enters into a Covenant with Abraham, the man of faith.

Taking Abram outside the Lord said, 'Look up to heaven and
count the stars if you can. Such will be your descendants' he told
him. Abram put his faith in the Lord, who counted this as
making him justified.
    'I am the Lord' he said to him 'who brought you out of Ur of
the Chaldaeans to make you heir to this land.' 'My Lord, the
Lord' Abram replied 'how am I to know that I shall inherit it?' He
said to him, 'Get me a three-year-old heifer, a three-year-old
goat, a three-year-old ram, a turtledove and a young pigeon.' He
brought him all these, cut them in half and put half on one side
and half facing it on the other; but the birds he did not cut in half.
Birds of prey came down on the carcasses but Abram drove them
off.
    Now as the sun was setting Abram fell into a deep sleep, and
terror seized him. When the sun had set and darkness had fallen,
there appeared a smoking furnace and a firebrand that went
between the halves. That day the Lord made a Covenant with

Abram in these terms:
> 'To your descendants I give this land,
> from the wadi of Egypt to the Great River.'

This is the word of the Lord.

Responsorial Psalm   Ps 26:1. 7-9. 13-14. R℣ v.1
> R℣ **The Lord is my light and my help.**

1 The Lord is my light and my help;
  whom shall I fear?
  The Lord is the stronghold of my life;
  before whom shall I shrink? R℣

2 O Lord, hear my voice when I call;
  have mercy and answer.
  Of you my heart has spoken:
  'Seek his face.' R℣

3 It is your face, O Lord, that I seek;
  hide not your face.
  Dismiss not your servant in anger;
  you have been my help. R℣

4 I am sure I shall see the Lord's goodness
  in the land of the living.
  Hope in him, hold firm and take heart.
  Hope in the Lord! R℣

SECOND READING

A reading from the letter of St Paul to the Philippians   3:17 – 4:1
Christ will transfigure our bodies into copies of his glorious body.

My brothers, be united in following my rule of life. Take as your models everybody who is already doing this and study them as you used to study us. I have told you often, and I repeat it today with tears, there are many who are behaving as the enemies of the cross of Christ. They are destined to be lost. They make foods into their god and they are proudest of something they ought to think shameful; the things they think important are earthly things. *For us, our homeland is in heaven, and from heaven comes the saviour we are waiting for, the Lord Jesus Christ, and he will transfigure these wretched bodies of ours into copies of his glorious body. He will do that by the same power with which he can subdue the whole universe.

So then, my brothers and dear friends, do not give way

but remain faithful in the Lord. I miss you very much, dear friends; you are my joy and my crown.

This is the word of the Lord.*

*Shorter Form, 3:20–4:1. Read between *

Gospel Acclamation   Mt 17:5
Glory and praise to you, O Christ!
From the bright cloud, the Father's voice was heard:
'This is my Son, the Beloved. Listen to him!'
Glory and praise to you, O Christ!

GOSPEL

A reading from the holy Gospel according to Luke   9:28-36
As Jesus prayed, the aspect of his face was changed.

Jesus took with him Peter and John and James and went up the mountain to pray. As he prayed, the aspect of his face was changed and his clothing became brilliant as lightning. Suddenly there were two men there talking to him; they were Moses and Elijah appearing in glory, and they were speaking of his passing which he was to accomplish in Jerusalem. Peter and his companions were heavy with sleep, but they kept awake and saw his glory and the two men standing with him. As these were leaving him, Peter said to Jesus, 'Master, it is wonderful for us to be here; so let us make three tents, one for you, one for Moses and one for Elijah.' – He did not know what he was saying. As he spoke, a cloud came and covered them with shadow; and when they went into the cloud the disciples were afraid. And a voice came from the cloud saying, 'This is my Son, the Chosen One. Listen to him'. And after the voice had spoken, Jesus was found alone. The disciples kept silence and, at that time, told no one what they had seen.

This is the Gospel of the Lord.

Prayer over the Gifts
Lord,
make us holy.
May this eucharist take away our sins
that we may be prepared
to celebrate the resurrection.

Preface of Second Sunday of Lent, P13, or of Lent I or II, P8 or P9

Communion Antiphon: This is my Son, my beloved, in whom is all my delight: listen to him.

Prayer after Communion
Lord,
we give thanks for these holy mysteries
which bring to us here on earth
a share in the life to come,
through Christ our Lord.

An appropriate Solemn Blessing or Prayer over the People may be used. See pp. 90ff.

THIRD SUNDAY OF LENT   C

The Lord Of Compassion And Love

We celebrate today the Lord who resolves to free us from our slavery to sin, if only we will listen to his serious warnings to us to repent.

Entrance Antiphon: My eyes are ever fixed on the Lord, for he releases my feet from the snare. O look at me and be merciful, for I am wretched and alone.

or

I will prove my holiness through you. I will gather you from the ends of the earth; I will pour clean water on you and wash away all your sins. I will give you a new spirit within you, says the Lord.

The Gloria is omitted.

Opening Prayer
Let us pray
[for confidence in the love of God
and the strength to overcome all our weakness]

Father, you have taught us to overcome our sins
by prayer, fasting and works of mercy.
When we are discouraged by our weakness,
give us confidence in your love.

or

Let us pray
[to the Father and ask him

to form a new heart within us]

God of all compassion, Father of all goodness,
to heal the wounds our sins and selfishness bring upon us
you bid us turn to fasting, prayer, and sharing with our brothers.

We acknowledge our sinfulness, our guilt is ever before us:
when our weakness causes discouragement,
let your compassion fill us with hope
and lead us through a Lent of repentance to the beauty of Easter
joy.

The readings for Cycle A may be used as alternative readings, see
above, pp.179ff. If this is done, the Preface and Communion
Antiphon as at Cycle A are also used. If a pre-baptismal scrutiny
is held today, the readings for Year A are mandatory.

FIRST READING

A reading from the book of Exodus   3:1-8. 13-15
I Am has sent me to you.

Moses was looking after the flock of Jethro, his father-in-law,
priest of Midian. He led his flock to the far side of the wilderness
and came to Horeb, the mountain of God. There the angel of the
Lord appeared to him in the shape of a flame of fire, coming from
the middle of a bush. Moses looked; there was the bush blazing
but it was not being burnt up. 'I must go and look at this strange
sight,' Moses said 'and see why the bush is not burnt.' Now the
Lord saw him go forward to look, and God called to him from the
middle of the bush. 'Moses, Moses!' he said. 'Here I am' he
answered. 'Come no nearer' he said. 'Take off your shoes, for the
place on which you stand is holy ground. I am the God of your
father,' he said 'the God of Abraham, the God of Isaac and the
God of Jacob.' At this Moses covered his face, afraid to look at
God.

And the Lord said, 'I have seen the miserable state of my
people in Egypt. I have heard their appeal to be free of their
slave-drivers. Yes, I am well aware of their sufferings. I mean to
deliver them out of the hands of the Egyptians and bring them up
out of that land to a land rich and broad, a land where milk and
honey flow.'

Then Moses said to God, 'I am to go, then, to the sons of
Israel and say to them, "The God of your fathers has sent me to
you." But if they ask me what his name is, what am I to tell
them?' And God said to Moses, 'I Am who I Am. This' he added

'is what you must say to the sons of Israel: "The Lord, the God of your fathers, the God of Abraham, the God of Isaac, and the God of Jacob, has sent me to you." This is my name for all time; by this name I shall be invoked for all generations to come.'

This is the word of the Lord.

Responsorial Psalm   Ps 102:1-4. 6-8. 11. ℟ v.8

   ℟ **The Lord is compassion and love.**

1   My soul, give thanks to the Lord,
    all my being, bless his holy name.
    My soul give thanks to the Lord
    and never forget all his blessings.   ℟

2   It is he who forgives all your guilt,
    who heals every one of your ills,
    who redeems your life from the grave,
    who crowns you with love and compassion.   ℟

3   The Lord does deeds of justice,
    gives judgement for all who are oppressed.
    He made known his ways to Moses
    and his deeds to Israel's sons.   ℟

4   The Lord is compassion and love,
    slow to anger and rich in mercy.
    For as the heavens are high above the earth
    so strong is his love for those who fear him.   ℟

SECOND READING

A reading from the first letter of St Paul   10:1-6. 10-12
to the Corinthians

The life of the people under Moses in the desert was written down to be a lesson for us.

I want to remind you, brothers, how our fathers were all guided by a cloud above them and how they all passed through the sea. They were all baptised into Moses in this cloud and in this sea; all ate the same spiritual food and all drank the same spiritual drink, since they all drank from the spiritual rock that followed them as they went, and that rock was Christ. In spite of this, most of them failed to please God and their corpses littered the desert.

These things all happened as warnings for us, not to have the wicked lusts for forbidden things that they had. You must never complain: some of them did, and they were killed by the Destroyer.

All this happened to them as a warning and it was written down to be a lesson for us who are living at the end of the age. The man who thinks he is safe must be careful that he does not fall.

This is the word of the Lord.

Gospel Acclamation   Mt 4:17
Glory to you, O Christ, you are the Word of God!
Repent, says the Lord,
for the kingdom of heaven is close at hand.
Glory to you, O Christ, you are the Word of God!

GOSPEL

A reading from the holy Gospel according to Luke   13:1-9
Unless you repent you will all perish as they did.

Some people arrived and told Jesus about the Galileans whose blood Pilate had mingled with that of their sacrifices. At this he said to them, 'Do you suppose these Galileans who suffered like that were greater sinners than any other Galileans? They were not, I tell you. No; but unless you repent you will all perish as they did. Or those eighteen on whom the tower at Siloam fell and killed them? Do you suppose that they were more guilty than all the other people living in Jerusalem? They were not, I tell you. No; but unless you repent you will all perish as they did.'

He told this parable: 'A man had a fig tree planted in his vineyard and he came looking for fruit on it but found none. He said to the man who looked after the vineyard, "Look here, for three years now I have been coming to look for fruit on this fig tree and finding none. Cut it down: why should it be taking up the ground?" "Sir," the man replied "leave it one more year and give me time to dig round it and manure it: it may bear fruit next year; if not, then you can cut it down." '

This is the Gospel of the Lord.

After the Homily, the First Scrutiny of Candidates for Baptism may follow. See above, pp.184ff.

Prayer over the Gifts
Lord,
by the grace of this sacrifice
may we who ask forgiveness
be ready to forgive one another.

Preface of Lent I or II, P8 or P9

Communion Antiphon: The sparrow even finds a home, the swallow finds a nest wherein to place her young, near to your altars, Lord of hosts, my King, my God! How happy they who dwell in your house! For ever they are praising you.

Prayer after Communion
Lord,
in sharing this sacrament
may we receive your forgiveness
and be brought together in unity and peace.

An appropriate Solemn Blessing or Prayer over the People may be used. See pp.90ff.

FOURTH SUNDAY OF LENT   C

The Lord Who Welcomes Sinners

We celebrate this Mass in the joy of forgiveness, and gratefully eat the manna, the food that our Father gives us for our journey to the kingdom where his banquet is prepared for us.

Entrance Antiphon: Rejoice, Jerusalem! Be glad for her, you who love her; rejoice with her, you who mourned for her, and you will find contentment at her consoling breasts.

The Gloria is omitted.

Opening Prayer
Let us pray
   [for a greater faith and love]

Father of peace,
we are joyful in your Word,
your Son Jesus Christ,
who reconciles us to you.
Let us hasten toward Easter
with the eagerness of faith and love.

or

Let us pray
   [that by growing in love this lenten season

we may bring the peace of Christ to our world]

God our Father,
your Word, Jesus Christ, spoke peace to a sinful world
and brought mankind the gift of reconciliation
by the suffering and death he endured.

Teach us, the people who bear his name,
to follow the example he gave us:
may our faith, hope, and charity
turn hatred to love, conflict to peace, death to eternal life.

The readings for Cycle A may be used as alternative readings, see
above, pp.187ff. If this is done, the Preface and Communion
Antiphon as at Cycle A are used. If a pre-baptismal scrutiny is
held today, the readings for Year A are mandatory.

FIRST READING

A reading from the book of Joshua   5:9-12
*The People of God keep the Passover on their entry into the promised
land.*

The Lord said to Joshua, 'Today I have taken the shame of Egypt
away from you.'
    The Israelites pitched their camp at Gilgal and kept the
Passover there on the fourteenth day of the month, at evening in
the plain of Jericho. On the morrow of the Passover they tasted
the produce of that country, unleavened bread and roasted ears
of corn, that same day. From that time, from their first eating of
the produce of that country, the manna stopped falling. And
having manna no longer, the Israelites fed from that year
onwards on what the land of Canaan yielded.

    This is the word of the Lord.

Responsorial Psalm   Ps 33:2-7. R℣ v.9
    R℣ **Taste and see that the Lord is good.**

1   I will bless the Lord at all times,
      his praise always on my lips;
      in the Lord my soul shall make its boast.
      The humble shall hear and be glad. R℣

2   Glorify the Lord with me.
      Together let us praise his name.
      I sought the Lord and he answered me;
      from all my terrors he set me free. R℣

3 Look towards him and be radiant;
   let your faces not be abashed.
   This poor man called; the Lord heard him
   and rescued him from all his distress. ℟

SECOND READING

A reading from the second letter of St Paul
to the Corinthians   5:17-21

God reconciled us to himself through Christ.

For anyone who is in Christ, there is a new creation; the old
creation has gone, and now the new one is here. It is all God's
work. It was God who reconciled us to himself through Christ
and gave us the work of handing on his reconciliation. In other
words, God in Christ was reconciling the world to himself, not
holding men's faults against them, and he has entrusted to us the
news that they are reconciled. So we are ambassadors for Christ;
it is as though God were appearing through us, and the appeal
that we make in Christ's name is: be reconciled to God. For our
sake God made the sinless one into sin, so that in him we might
become the goodness of God.

This is the word of the Lord.

Gospel Acclamation   Lk 15:18

Praise and honour to you, Lord Jesus!
I will leave this place and go to my father and say:
'Father, I have sinned against heaven and against you.'
Praise and honour to you, Lord Jesus!

GOSPEL

A reading from the holy Gospel according to Luke   15:1-3. 11- 32

Your brother here was dead and has come to life.

The tax collectors and the sinners were all seeking the company
of Jesus to hear what he had to say, and the Pharisees and the
scribes complained. 'This man' they said 'welcomes sinners and
eats with them.' So he spoke this parable to them:

'A man had two sons. The younger said to his father, "Father,
let me have the share of the estate that would come to me." So
the father divided the property between them. A few days later,
the younger son got together everything he had and left for a
distant country where he squandered his money on a life of
debauchery.

'When he had spent it all, that country experienced a severe famine, and now he began to feel the pinch, so he hired himself out to one of the local inhabitants who put him on his farm to feed the pigs. And he would willingly have filled his belly with the husks the pigs were eating but no one offered him anything. Then he came to his senses and said, "How many of my father's paid servants have more food than they want, and here am I dying of hunger! I will leave this place and go to my father and say: Father, I have sinned against heaven and against you; I no longer deserve to be called your son; treat me as one of your paid servants." So he left the place and went back to his father.

'While he was still a long way off, his father saw him and was moved with pity. He ran to the boy, clasped him in his arms and kissed him tenderly. Then his son said, "Father, I have sinned against heaven and against you. I no longer deserve to be called your son." But the father said to his servants, "Quick! Bring out the best robe and put it on him; put a ring on his finger and sandals on his feet. Bring the calf we have been fattening, and kill it; we are going to have a feast, a celebration, because this son of mine was dead and has come back to life; he was lost and is found." And they began to celebrate.

'Now the elder son was out in the fields, and on his way back, as he drew near the house, he could hear music and dancing. Calling one of the servants he asked what it was all about. "Your brother has come" replied the servant "and your father has killed the calf we had fattened because he has got him back safe and sound." He was angry then and refused to go in, and his father came out to plead with him; but he answered his father, "Look, all these years I have slaved for you and never once disobeyed your orders, yet you never offered me so much as a kid for me to celebrate with my friends. But for this son of yours, when he comes back after swallowing up your property – he and his women – you kill the calf we had been fattening."

'The father said, "My son, you are with me always and all I have is yours. But it is only right we should celebrate and rejoice, because your brother here was dead and has come to life; he was lost and is found." '

This is the Gospel of the Lord.

After the Homily, the Second Scrutiny of Candidates for Baptism may follow. See above, pp.192ff.

Prayer over the Gifts

Lord,

we offer you these gifts
which bring us peace and joy.
Increase our reverence by this eucharist,
and bring salvation to the world.

Preface of Lent I or II, P8 or P9

Communion Antiphon: My son, you should rejoice, because your
brother was dead and has come back to life; he was lost and is
found.

Prayer after Communion
Father,
you enlighten all who come into the world.
Fill our hearts with the light of your gospel,
that our thoughts may please you,
and our love be sincere.

An appropriate Solemn Blessing or Prayer over the People may
be used. See pp.90ff.

FIFTH SUNDAY OF LENT   C

The Lord Who Has Wiped Out Our Past Sinfulness

*The utter completeness of Christ's forgiveness is almost incredible. When
he says to us 'Neither do I condemn you', the past is dead, snuffed out
like a wick, forgotten. Laughter and song fill our hearts. It seems like a
dream.*

Entrance Antiphon: Give me justice, O God, and defend my cause
against the wicked; rescue me from deceitful and unjust men.
You, O God, are my refuge.

The Gloria is omitted.

Opening Prayer
Let us pray
  [for the courage to follow Christ]

Father,
help us to be like Christ your Son,
who loved the world and died for our salvation.
Inspire us by his love,
guide us by his example,
who lives and reigns with you and the Holy Spirit,

one God, for ever and ever.

or

Let us pray
  [for the courage to embrace the world
  in the name of Christ]

Father in heaven,
the love of your Son led him to accept the suffering of the cross
that his brothers might glory in new life.
Change our selfishness into self-giving.
Help us to embrace the world you have given us,
that we may transform the darkness of its pain
into the life and joy of Easter.

The readings for Cycle A may be used as alternative readings, see
above, pp.194ff. If this is done, the Preface and Communion
Antiphon as at Year A are used. If a pre-baptismal scrutiny is
held today, the readings for Year A are mandatory.

FIRST READING

A reading from the prophet Isaiah   43:16-21
See, I am doing a new deed, and I will give my chosen people drink.

Thus says the Lord,
who made a way through the sea,
a path in the great waters;
who put chariots and horse in the field
and a powerful army,
which lay there never to rise again,
snuffed out, put out like a wick:

  No need to recall the past,
  no need to think about what was done before.
  See, I am doing a new deed,
  even now it comes to light; can you not see it?
  Yes, I am making a road in the wilderness,
  paths in the wilds.

  The wild beasts will honour me,
  jackals and ostriches,
  because I am putting water in the wilderness
  (rivers in the wild)
  to give my chosen people drink.
  The people I have formed for myself

will sing my praises.

This is the word of the Lord.

Responsorial Psalm

Ps 125. ℟ v.3

℟ **What marvels the Lord worked for us!**
Indeed we were glad.

1 When the Lord delivered Zion from bondage,
   it seemed like a dream.
   Then was our mouth filled with laughter,
   on our lips there were songs. ℟

2 The heathens themselves said: 'What marvels
   the Lord worked for them!'
   What marvels the Lord worked for us!
   Indeed we were glad. ℟

3 Deliver us, O Lord, from our bondage
   as streams in dry land.
   Those who are sowing in tears
   will sing when they reap. ℟

4 They go out, they go out, full of tears,
   carrying seed for the sowing:
   they come back, they come back, full of song,
   carrying their sheaves. ℟

SECOND READING

A reading from the letter of St Paul to the Philippians 3:8-14

Reproducing the pattern of his death, I have accepted the loss of everything for Christ.

I believe nothing can happen that will outweigh the supreme advantage of knowing Christ Jesus my Lord. For him I have accepted the loss of everything, and I look on everything as so much rubbish if only I can have Christ and be given a place in him. I am no longer trying for perfection by my own efforts, the perfection that comes from the Law, but I want only the perfection that comes through faith in Christ, and is from God and based on faith. All I want is to know Christ and the power of his resurrection and to share his sufferings by reproducing the pattern of his death. That is the way I can hope to take my place in the resurrection of the dead. Not that I have become perfect yet: I have not yet won, but I am still running, trying to capture the prize for which Christ Jesus captured me. I can assure you my brothers, I am far from thinking that I have already won. All I can say is that I forget the past and I strain ahead for what is still to come; I am racing for the finish, for the prize to which God calls us upwards to receive in Christ Jesus.

This is the word of the Lord.

Gospel Acclamation   cf. Amos 5:14
Praise to you, O Christ, king of eternal glory!
Seek good and not evil so that you may live,
and that the Lord God of hosts may really be with you.
Praise to you, O Christ, king of eternal glory!

or   Joel 2:12-13

Praise to you, O Christ, king of eternal glory!
Now, now – it is the Lord who speaks –
come back to me with all your heart,
for I am all tenderness and compassion.
Praise to you, O Christ, king of eternal glory!

GOSPEL

A reading from the holy Gospel according to John   8:1-11

If there is one of you who has not sinned, let him be the first to throw a stone at her.

Jesus went to the Mount of Olives. At daybreak he appeared in the Temple again; and as all the people came to him, he sat down and began to teach them.

The scribes and Pharisees brought a woman along who had been caught committing adultery; and making her stand there in full view of everybody, they said to Jesus, 'Master, this woman was caught in the very act of committing adultery, and Moses has ordered us in the Law to condemn women like this to death by stoning. What have you to say?' They asked him this as a test, looking for something to use against him. But Jesus bent down and started writing on the ground with his finger. As they persisted with their question, he looked up and said, 'If there is one of you who has not sinned, let him be the first to throw a stone at her.' Then he bent down and wrote on the ground again. When they heard this they went away one by one, beginning with the eldest, until Jesus was left alone with the woman, who remained standing there. He looked up and said, 'Woman, where are they? Has no one condemned you?' 'No one, sir,' she replied. 'Neither do I condemn you,' said Jesus 'go away, and don't sin any more.'

This is the Gospel of the Lord.

After the Homily, the Third Scrutiny of Candidates for Baptism may follow. See above, pp.199ff.

Prayer over the Gifts

Almighty God,
may the sacrifice we offer
take away the sins of those
whom you enlighten with the Christian faith.

Preface of Lent I or II, P8 or P9

Communion Antiphon: Has no one condemned you? The woman answered: No one, Lord. Neither do I condemn you: go and do not sin again.

Prayer after Communion

Almighty Father,
by this sacrifice
may we always remain one with your Son, Jesus Christ,
whose body and blood we share,
for he is Lord for ever and ever.

An appropriate Solemn Blessing or Prayer over the People may be used. See pp.90ff.

HOLY WEEK
PASSION SUNDAY (PALM SUNDAY)

See above, pp.201ff.

HOLY THURSDAY: CHRISM MASS

See above, pp.238ff.

THE EASTER TRIDUUM
HOLY THURSDAY
(Mass of the Lord's Supper)

See above, pp.249ff.

GOOD FRIDAY
(Celebration of the Lord's Passion)

See above, pp.258ff.

EASTER VIGIL

See above, pp.279ff.

EASTER SUNDAY

See above, pp.316ff.

CHRIST RISEN THE FIRST FRUITS OF ALL THOSE FALLEN ASLEEP

THE SEASON OF EASTER

SECOND SUNDAY OF EASTER   C

The Living One

We worship Christ who was dead and is now alive for ever and ever. He is present in our midst, bringing healing and peace.

Entrance Antiphon: Like newborn children you should thirst for milk, on which your spirit can grow to strength, alleluia.

or

Rejoice to the full in the glory that is yours, and give thanks to God who called you to his kingdom, alleluia.

Opening Prayer
Let us pray
   [for a deeper awareness of our Christian baptism]

God of mercy,
you wash away our sins in water,
you give us new birth in the Spirit,
and redeem us in the blood of Christ.
As we celebrate Christ's resurrection
increase our awareness of these blessings,
and renew your gift of life within us.

or

Let us pray
   [as Christians thirsting for the risen life]

Heavenly Father and God of mercy,
we no longer look for Jesus among the dead,
for he is alive and has become the Lord of life.

From the waters of death you raise us with him
and renew your gift of life within us.

Increase in our minds and hearts
the risen life we share with Christ
and help us to grow as your people
toward the fullness of eternal life with you.

FIRST READING

A reading from the Acts of the Apostles   5:12-16

The numbers of men and women who came to believe in the Lord
increased steadily.

The faithful all used to meet by common consent in the Portico of
Solomon. No one else ever dared to join them, but the people
were loud in their praise and the numbers of men and women
who came to believe in the Lord increased steadily. So many
signs and wonders were worked among the people at the hands
of the apostles that the sick were even taken out into the streets
and laid on beds and sleeping-mats in the hope that at least the
shadow of Peter might fall across some of them as he went past.
People even came crowding in from the towns round about
Jerusalem, bringing with them their sick and those tormented by
unclean spirits, and all of them were cured.

This is the word of the Lord.

Responsorial Psalm   Ps 117:2-4. 22-27. ℟ v.1

℟ **Give thanks to the Lord for he is good,**
for his love has no end.

or

℟ **Alleluia, alleluia, alleluia!**

1 Let the sons of Israel say:
'His love has no end.'
Let the sons of Aaron say:
'His love has no end.'
Let those who fear the Lord say:
'His love has no end.'   ℟

2 The stone which the builders rejected
has become the corner stone.
This is the work of the Lord,
a marvel in our eyes.

This day was made by the Lord;
we rejoice and are glad.   ℟

3   O Lord, grant us salvation;
O Lord grant success.
Blessed in the name of the Lord
is he who comes.
We bless you from the house of the Lord;
the Lord God is our light.   ℟

SECOND READING

A reading from the book of the Apocalypse   1:9-13. 17-19
I was dead and now I am to live for ever and ever.

My name is John, and through our union in Jesus I am your
brother and share your sufferings, your kingdom, and all you
endure. I was on the island of Patmos for having preached God's
word and witnessed for Jesus; it was the Lord's day and the Spirit
possessed me, and I heard a voice behind me, shouting like a
trumpet, 'Write down all that you see in a book.' I turned round
to see who had spoken to me, and when I turned I saw seven
golden lamp-stands and, surrounded by them, a figure like a Son
of man, dressed in a long robe tied at the waist with a golden
girdle.
     When I saw him, I fell in a dead faint at his feet, but he
touched me with his right hand and said, 'Do not be afraid; it is I,
the First and the Last; I am the Living One. I was dead and now I
am to live for ever and ever, and I hold the keys of death and of
the underworld. Now write down all that you see of present
happenings and things that are still to come.'

     This is the word of the Lord.

Gospel Acclamation   Jn 20:29
     Alleluia, alleluia!
     Jesus said: 'You believe because you can see me.
     Happy are those who have not seen and yet believe.'
     Alleluia!

GOSPEL

A reading from the holy Gospel according to John   20:19-31
Eight days later, Jesus came.

In the evening of that same day, the first day of the week, the
doors were closed in the room where the disciples were, for fear

of the Jews. Jesus came and stood among them. He said to them, 'Peace be with you,' and showed them his hands and his side. The disciples were filled with joy when they saw the Lord, and he said to them again, 'Peace be with you.

'As the Father sent me,
so am I sending you.'

After saying this he breathed on them and said:

'Receive the Holy Spirit.
For those whose sins you forgive,
they are forgiven;
for those whose sins you retain,
they are retained.'

Thomas, called the Twin, who was one of the Twelve, was not with them when Jesus came. When the disciples said, 'We have seen the Lord', he answered, 'Unless I see the holes that the nails made in his hands and can put my finger into the holes they made, and unless I can put my hand into his side, I refuse to believe.' Eight days later the disciples were in the house again and Thomas was with them. The doors were closed, but Jesus came in and stood among them. 'Peace be with you' he said. Then he spoke to Thomas, 'Put your finger here; look, here are my hands. Give me your hand; put it into my side. Doubt no longer but believe.' Thomas replied, 'My Lord and my God!' Jesus said to him:

'You believe because you can see me.
Happy are those who have not seen and yet believe.'

There were many other signs that Jesus worked and the disciples saw, but they are not recorded in this book. These are recorded so that you may believe that Jesus is the Christ, the Son of God, and that believing this you may have life through his name.

This is the Gospel of the Lord.

Prayer over Gifts
Lord,
through faith and baptism
we have become a new creation.
Accept the offerings of your people
(and of those born again in baptism)
and bring us to eternal happiness.

Preface of Easter I, P21

When Eucharistic Prayer I is used, the special Easter forms of *In union with the whole Church* and *Father, accept this offering* are said.

Communion Antiphon: Jesus spoke to Thomas: Put your hand here, and see the place of the nails. Doubt no longer, but believe, alleluia.

Prayer after Communion
Almighty God,
may the Easter sacraments we have received
live for ever in our minds and hearts.

An appropriate Solemn Blessing or Prayer over the People may be used. See pp.90ff.

THIRD SUNDAY OF EASTER   C

'It Is The Lord'

In this eucharist we proclaim that Christ is the Lord, the Lamb that was sacrificed and who is worthy to be given power, riches, wisdom, strength, honour, glory and blessing. The apostles accepted every kind of humiliation rather than give up proclaiming his name.

Entrance Antiphon: Let all the earth cry out to God with joy; praise the glory of his name; proclaim his glorious praise, alleluia.

Opening Prayer
Let us pray
[that Christ will give us
a share in the glory of his unending life]

God our Father,
may we look forward with hope to our resurrection,
for you have made us your sons and daughters,
and restored the joy of our youth.

or

Let us pray
[in confident peace and Easter hope]

Father in heaven, author of all truth,
a people once in darkness has listened to your Word

and followed your Son as he rose from the tomb.

Hear the prayer of this newborn people
and strengthen your Church to answer your call.
May we rise and come forth into the light of day
to stand in your presence until eternity dawns.

FIRST READING

A reading from the Acts of the Apostles 5:27-32. 40-41
We are witnesses of all this, we and the Holy Spirit.

The high priest demanded an explanation of the apostles. 'We
gave you a formal warning,' he said 'not to preach in this name,
and what have you done? You have filled Jerusalem with your
teaching, and seem determined to fix the guilt of this man's death
on us.' In reply Peter and the apostles said, 'Obedience to God
comes before obedience to men; it was the God of our ancestors
who raised up Jesus, but it was you who had him executed by
hanging on a tree. By his own right hand God has now raised
him up to be leader and saviour, to give repentance and
forgiveness of sins through him to Israel. We are witnesses to all
this, we and the Holy Spirit whom God has given to those who
obey him.' They warned the apostles not to speak in the name of
Jesus and released them. And so they left the presence of the
Sanhedrin glad to have had the honour of suffering humiliation
for the sake of the name.

This is the word of the Lord.

Responsorial Psalm Ps 29:2. 4-6. 11-13. ℟ v.2

℟ **I will praise you, Lord,
you have rescued me.**

or

℟ **Alleluia!**

1 I will praise you, Lord, you have rescued me
and have not let my enemies rejoice over me.
O Lord, you have raised my soul from the dead,
restored me to life from those who sink into the grave. ℟

2 Sing psalms to the Lord, you who love him,
give thanks to his holy name.
His anger lasts but a moment; his favour through life.
At night there are tears, but joy comes with dawn. ℟

3 The Lord listened and had pity.
   The Lord came to my help.
   For me you have changed my mourning into dancing;
   O Lord my God, I will thank you for ever. ℟

SECOND READING

A reading from the book of the Apocalypse   5:11-14

The Lamb that was sacrificed is worthy to be given riches and power.

In my vision, I, John, heard the sound of an immense number of
angels gathered round the throne and the animals and the elders;
there were ten thousand times ten thousand of them and
thousands upon thousands, shouting, 'The Lamb that was
sacrificed is worthy to be given power, riches, wisdom, strength,
honour, glory and blessing.' Then I heard all the living things in
creation – everything that lives in the air, and on the ground, and
under the ground, and in the sea, crying, 'To the One who is
sitting on the throne and to the Lamb, be all praise, honour, glory
and power, for ever and ever.' And the four animals said,
'Amen'; and the elders prostrated themselves to worship.

This is the word of the Lord.

Gospel Acclamation   cf. Lk 24:32
    Alleluia, alleluia!
    Lord Jesus, explain the scriptures to us.
    Make our hearts burn within us as you talk to us.
    Alleluia!

or

    Alleluia, alleluia!
    Christ has risen: he who created all things,
    and has granted his mercy to men.
    Alleluia!

GOSPEL

A reading from the holy Gospel according to John   21:1-19

*Jesus stepped forward, took the bread and gave it to them, and the same
with the fish.*

*Jesus showed himself again to the disciples. It was by the Sea of
Tiberias, and it happened like this: Simon Peter, Thomas called
the Twin, Nathanael from Cana in Galilee, the sons of Zebedee
and two more of his disciples were together. Simon Peter said,
'I'm going fishing.' They replied, 'We'll come with you.' They

went out and got into the boat but caught nothing that night.

It was light by now and there stood Jesus on the shore, though the disciples did not realise that it was Jesus. Jesus called out, 'Have you caught anything, friends?' And when they answered, 'No', he said, 'Throw the net out to starboard and you'll find something.' So they dropped the net, and there were so many fish that they could not haul it in. The disciple Jesus loved said to Peter, 'It is the Lord.' At these words 'It is the Lord', Simon Peter, who had practically nothing on, wrapped his cloak round him and jumped into the water. The other disciples came on in the boat, towing the net and the fish; they were only about a hundred yards from land.

As soon as they came ashore they saw that there was some bread there, and a charcoal fire with fish cooking on it. Jesus said, 'Bring some of the fish you have just caught.' Simon Peter went aboard and dragged the net to the shore, full of big fish, one hundred and fifty-three of them; and in spite of there being so many the net was not broken. Jesus said to them, 'Come and have breakfast.' None of the disciples was bold enough to ask, 'Who are you?'; they knew quite well it was the Lord. Jesus then stepped forward, took the bread and gave it to them, and the same with the fish. This was the third time that Jesus showed himself to the disciples after rising from the dead.

After the meal Jesus said to Simon Peter, 'Simon son of John, do you love me more than these others do?' He answered, 'Yes Lord, you know I love you.' Jesus said to him, 'Feed my lambs.' A second time he said to him, 'Simon son of John, do you love me?' He replied 'Yes, Lord, you know I love you.' Jesus said to him, 'Look after my sheep.' Then he said to him a third time, 'Simon son of John, do you love me?' Peter was upset that he asked him the third time, 'Do you love me?' and said, 'Lord, you know everything; you know I love you.' Jesus said to him, 'Feed my sheep.

'I tell you most solemnly,
when you were young
you put on your own belt
and walked where you liked;
but when you grow old
you will stretch out your hands,
and somebody else will put a belt round you
and take you where you would rather not go.'

In these words he indicated the kind of death by which Peter would give glory to God. After this he said, 'Follow me.'

| *This is the Gospel of the Lord.*

*Shorter Form, verses 1-14. Read between *

Prayer over the Gifts
Lord,
receive these gifts from your Church.
May the great joy you give us
come to perfection in heaven.

Preface of Easter II-V, P22-P25

Communion Antiphon: Jesus said to his disciples: Come and eat.
And he took the bread, and gave it to them, alleluia.

Prayer after Communion
Lord,
look on your people with kindness
and by these Easter mysteries
bring us to the glory of the resurrection.

An appropriate Solemn Blessing or Prayer over the People may
be used. See pp.90ff.

FOURTH SUNDAY OF EASTER   C

The Lamb Will Be Our Shepherd

*We offer in sacrifice the Lamb that takes away the sins of the world. He
who was slain is now our Shepherd. He will lead to springs of living
water all who do not reject him.*

Entrance Antiphon: The earth is full of the goodness of the Lord;
by the word of the Lord the heavens were made, alleluia.

Opening Prayer
Let us pray
  [that Christ our shepherd
  will lead us through the difficulties of this life]

Almighty and ever-living God,
give us new strength
from the courage of Christ our shepherd,
and lead us to join the saints in heaven,

where he lives and reigns with you and the Holy Spirit,
one God, for ever and ever.

or

Let us pray
   [to God our helper in time of distress]

God and Father of our Lord Jesus Christ,
though your people walk in the valley of darkness,
no evil should they fear;
for they follow in faith the call of the shepherd
whom you have sent for their hope and strength.

Attune our minds to the sound of his voice,
lead our steps in the path he has shown,
that we may know the strength of his outstretched arm
and enjoy the light of your presence for ever.

FIRST READING

A reading from the Acts of the Apostles   13:14. 43-52

We must turn to the pagans.

Paul and Barnabas carried on from Perga till they reached
Antioch in Pisidia. Here they went to synagogue on the sabbath
and took their seats.

   When the meeting broke up, many Jews and devout converts
joined Paul and Barnabas, and in their talks with them Paul and
Barnabas urged them to remain faithful to the grace God had
given them.

   The next sabbath almost the whole town assembled to hear
the word of God. When they saw the crowds, the Jews,
prompted by jealousy, used blasphemies and contradicted everything Paul said. Then Paul and Barnabas spoke out boldly, 'We
had to proclaim the word of God to you first, but since you have
rejected it, since you do not think yourselves worthy of eternal
life, we must turn to the pagans. For this is what the Lord
commanded us to do when he said:

   I have made you a light for the nations,
   so that my salvation may reach the ends of the earth.'

   It made the pagans very happy to hear this and they thanked
the Lord for his message; all who were destined for eternal life
became believers. Thus the word of the Lord spread through the
whole countryside.

   But the Jews worked upon some of the devout women of

the upper classes and the leading men of the city and persuaded them to turn against Paul and Barnabas and expel them from their territory. So they shook the dust from their feet in defiance and went off to Iconium; but the disciples were filled with joy and the Holy Spirit.

This is the word of the Lord.

Responsorial Psalm   Ps 99:1-3. 5. ℟ v.3
   ℟ **We are his people, the sheep of his flock.**

or

   ℟ **Alleluia!**

1   Cry out with joy to the Lord, all the earth.
    Serve the Lord with gladness.
    Come before him, singing for joy.   ℟

2   Know that he, the Lord, is God.
    He made us, we belong to him,
    we are his people, the sheep of his flock.   ℟

3   Indeed, how good is the Lord,
    eternal his merciful love.
    He is faithful from age to age.   ℟

SECOND READING
A reading from the book of the Apocalypse   7:9. 14-17
The Lamb will be their shepherd and will lead them to springs of living water.

I, John, saw a huge number, impossible to count, of people from every nation, race, tribe and language; they were standing in front of the throne and in front of the Lamb, dressed in white robes and holding palms in their hands. One of the elders said to me, 'These are the people who have been through the great persecution, and because they have washed their robes white again in the blood of the Lamb, they now stand in front of God's throne and serve him day and night in his sanctuary; and the One who sits on the throne will spread his tent over them. They will never hunger or thirst again; neither the sun nor scorching wind will ever plague them, because the Lamb who is at the throne will be their shepherd and will lead them to springs of living water; and God will wipe away all tears from their eyes.'

This is the word of the Lord.

Gospel Acclamation   Jn 10:14
   Alleluia, alleluia!
   I am the good shepherd, says the Lord;
   I know my own sheep and my own know me.
   Alleluia!

GOSPEL

A reading from the holy Gospel according to John   10:27-30
I give eternal life to the sheep that belong to me.

Jesus said:

   'The sheep that belong to me listen to my voice;
   I know them and they follow me.
   I give them eternal life;
   they will never be lost
   and no one will ever steal them from me.
   The Father who gave them to me is greater than anyone,
   and no one can steal them from the Father.
   The Father and I are one.'

   This is the Gospel of the Lord.

Prayer over the Gifts
Lord,
restore us by these Easter mysteries.
May the continuing work of our Redeemer
bring us eternal joy.

Preface of Easter II-V, P22-P25

Communion Antiphon: The Good Shepherd is risen! He who laid
down his life for his sheep, who died for his flock, he is risen,
alleluia.

Prayer after Communion
Father, eternal shepherd,
watch over the flock redeemed by the blood of Christ
and lead us to the promised land.

An appropriate Solemn Blessing or Prayer over the People may
be used. See pp.90ff.

FIFTH SUNDAY OF EASTER C

The New Creation

Christ at this season puts fresh heart in us to spread his kingdom. He gives us his new commandment of love and encourages us with the promise of the new Jerusalem.

Entrance Antiphon: Sing to the Lord a new song, for he has done marvellous deeds; he has revealed to the nations his saving power, alleluia.

Opening Prayer
Let us pray
    [that we may enjoy true freedom]

God our Father,
look upon us with love.
You redeem us and make us your children in Christ.
Give us true freedom
and bring us to the inheritance you promised.
or
Let us pray
    [in the freedom of the sons of God]

Father of our Lord Jesus Christ,
you have revealed to the nations your saving power
and filled all ages with the words of a new song.
Hear the echo of this hymn.
Give us voice to sing your praise
throughout this season of joy.

FIRST READING

A reading from the Acts of the Apostles 14:21-27
They gave an account to the church of all that God had done with them.

Paul and Barnabas went back through Lystra and Iconium to Antioch. They put fresh heart into the disciples, encouraging them to persevere in the faith. 'We all have to experience many hardships' they said 'before we enter the kingdom of God.' In each of these churches they appointed elders, and with prayer and fasting they commended them to the Lord in whom they had come to believe.

They passed through Pisidia and reached Pamphylia. Then after proclaiming the word at Perga they went down to Attalia and from there sailed for Antioch, where they had originally been commended to the grace of God for the work they had now completed.

On their arrival they assembled the church and gave an account of all that God had done with them, and how he had opened the door of faith to the pagans.

This is the word of the Lord.

Responsorial Psalm   Ps 144:8-13. ℟ cf. v.1
℟ **I will bless your name for ever, O God my King.**

or

℟ **Alleluia!**

1 The Lord is kind and full of compassion,
   slow to anger, abounding in love.
   How good is the Lord to all,
   compassionate to all his creatures.   ℟

2 All your creatures shall thank you, O Lord,
   and your friends shall repeat their blessing.
   They shall speak of the glory of your reign
   and declare your might, O God,
   to make known to men your mighty deeds
   and the glorious splendour of your reign.   ℟

3 Yours is an everlasting kingdom;
   your rule lasts from age to age.   ℟

SECOND READING

A reading from the book of the Apocalypse   21:1-5
God will wipe away all tears from their eyes.

I, John, saw a new heaven and a new earth; the first heaven and the first earth had disappeared now, and there was no longer any sea. I saw the holy city, and the new Jerusalem, coming down from God out of heaven, as beautiful as a bride all dressed for her husband. Then I heard a loud voice call from the throne, 'You see this city? Here God lives among men. He will make his home among them; they shall be his people, and he will be their God; his name is God-with-them. He will wipe away all tears from their eyes; there will be no more death, and no more mourning or sadness. The world of the past has gone.'

Then the One sitting on the throne spoke: 'Now I am making the whole of creation new'.

This is the word of the Lord.

Gospel Acclamation Jn 13:34
Alleluia, alleluia!
Jesus said: 'I give you a new commandment:
love one another, just as I have loved you.'
Alleluia!

GOSPEL

A reading from the holy Gospel according to John 13:31-35
I give you a new commandment: love one another.

When Judas had gone Jesus said:

'Now has the Son of Man been glorified,
and in him God has been glorified.
If God has been glorified in him,
God will in turn glorify him in himself,
and will glorify him very soon.
My little children,
I shall not be with you much longer.
I give you a new commandment:
love one another;
just as I have loved you,
you also must love one another.
By this love you have for one another,
everyone will know that you are my disciples.'

This is the Gospel of the Lord.

Prayer over the Gifts
Lord God,
by this holy exchange of gifts
you share with us your divine life.
Grant that everything we do
may be directed by the knowledge of your truth.

Preface of Easter II-V, P22-P25

Communion Antiphon: I am the vine and you are the branches,
says the Lord; he who lives in me, and I in him, will bear much
fruit, alleluia!

Prayer after Communion
Merciful Father,
may these mysteries give us new purpose
and bring us to a new life in you.

An appropriate Solemn Blessing or Prayer over the People may
be used. See pp.90ff.

SIXTH SUNDAY OF EASTER   C

The Radiant Glory Of God

*The Holy Spirit is the radiant glory of God that enlightens the Church
and guides it on its way through the world in all its decision.*

Entrance Antiphon: Speak out with a voice of joy; let it be heard to
the ends of the earth: The Lord has set his people free, alleluia.

Opening Prayer
Let us pray
   [that we may practise in our lives
   the faith we profess]

Ever-living God,
help us to celebrate our joy
in the resurrection of the Lord
and to express in our lives
the love we celebrate.

or

Let us pray
   [in silence, reflecting on the joy of Easter]

God our Father, maker of all,
the crown of your creation was the Son of Man,
born of a woman, but without beginning;
he suffered for us but lives for ever.

May our mortal lives be crowned with the ultimate joy
of rising with him,
who is Lord for ever and ever.

FIRST READING

A reading from the Acts of the Apostles   15:1-2. 22-29
*It has been decided by the Holy Spirit and by ourselves not to saddle you
with any burden beyond these essentials.*

Some men came down from Judaea and taught the brothers,
'Unless you have yourselves circumcised in the tradition of
Moses you cannot be saved.' This led to disagreement, and after
Paul and Barnabas had had a long argument with these men it
was arranged that Paul and Barnabas and others of the church
should go up to Jerusalem and discuss the problem with the
apostles and elders.

Then the apostles and elders decided to choose delegates to send to Antioch with Paul and Barnabas; the whole church concurred with this. They chose Judas known as Barsabbas and Silas, both leading men in the brotherhood, and gave them this letter to take with them:

'The apostles and elders, your brothers, send greetings to the brothers of pagan birth in Antioch, Syria and Cilicia. We hear that some of our members have disturbed you with their demands and have unsettled your minds. They acted without any authority from us, and so we have decided unanimously to elect delegates and to send them to you with Barnabas and Paul, men we highly respect who have dedicated their lives to the name of our Lord Jesus Christ. Accordingly we are sending you Judas and Silas, who will confirm by word of mouth what we have written in this letter. It has been decided by the Holy Spirit and by ourselves not to saddle you with any burden beyond these essentials: you are to abstain from food sacrificed to idols, from blood, from the meat of strangled animals and from fornication. Avoid these, and you will do what is right. Farewell.'

This is the word of the Lord.

Responsorial Psalm   Ps 66:2-3. 5-6. 8. ℟ v.4

   ℟ **Let the peoples praise you, O God;**
       let all the peoples praise you.

or

   ℟ **Alleluia!**

1   O God, be gracious and bless us
    and let your face shed its light upon us.
    So will your ways be known upon earth.
    and all nations learn your saving help. ℟

2   Let the nations be glad and exult
    for you rule the world with justice.
    With fairness you rule the peoples,
    you guide the nations on earth. ℟

3   Let the peoples praise you, O God;
    let all the peoples praise you.
    May God still give us his blessing
    till the ends of the earth revere him. ℟

When the Ascension of the Lord is celebrated on the Seventh Sunday of Easter, the Second Reading and Gospel assigned to the Seventh Sunday (see below pp.774ff.) may be read on the Sixth Sunday.

SECOND READING

A reading from the book of the Apocalypse   21:10-14. 22-23

He showed me the holy city coming down out of heaven.

In the spirit, the angel took me to the top of an enormous high mountain and showed me Jerusalem, the holy city, coming down from God out of heaven. It had all the radiant glory of God and glittered like some precious jewel of crystal-clear diamond. The walls of it were of a great height, and had twelve gates; at each of the twelve gates there was an angel, and over the gates were written the names of the twelve tribes of Israel; on the east there were three gates, on the north three gates, on the south three gates, and on the west three gates. The city walls stood on twelve foundation stones, each one of which bore the name of one of the twelve apostles of the Lamb.

I saw that there was no temple in the city since the Lord God Almighty and the Lamb were themselves the temple, and the city did not need the sun or the moon for light, since it was lit by the radiant glory of God and the Lamb was a lighted torch for it.

This is the word of the Lord.

Gospel Acclamation   Jn 14:23
    Alleluia, alleluia!
    Jesus said: 'If anyone loves me he will keep my word,
    and my Father will love him, and we shall come to him.
    Alleluia!

GOSPEL

A reading from the holy Gospel according to John   14:23-29

The Holy Spirit will remind you of all I have said to you.

Jesus said to his disciples:

    'If anyone loves me he will keep my word,
    and my Father will love him,
    and we shall come to him
    and make our home with him.
    Those who do not love me do not keep my words.
    And my word is not my own:
    it is the word of the one who sent me.

I have said these things to you
while still with you;
but the Advocate, the Holy Spirit,
whom the Father will send in my name,
will teach you everything
and remind you of all I have said to you.
Peace I bequeath to you,
my own peace I give you,
a peace the world cannot give, this is my gift to you.
Do not let your hearts be troubled or afraid.
You heard me say:
I am going away, and shall return.
If you loved me you would have been glad to know that I am
    going to the Father,
for the Father is greater than I.
I have told you this now before it happens,
so that when it does happen you may believe.'

This is the Gospel of the Lord.

Prayer over the Gifts
Lord,
accept our prayers and offerings.
Make us worthy of your sacraments of love
by granting us your forgiveness.

Preface of Easter II-V, P22-P25

Communion Antiphon: If you love me, keep my commandments,
says the Lord. The Father will send you the Holy Spirit, to be
with you for ever, alleluia.

Prayer after Communion
Almighty and ever-living Lord,
you restored us to life
by raising Christ from death.
Strengthen us by this Easter sacrament.

An appropriate Solemn Blessing or Prayer over the People may
be used. See pp.90ff.

THE ASCENSION OF THE LORD   C

Christ's Eternal Glory

We celebrate today Christ's ascension to his eternal glory in heaven and express our Christian hope that where he, our Head, has gone before us, we, his Body, will one day follow, to live for ever in the Kingdom of our Father.

Entrance Antiphon: Men of Galilee, why do you stand looking in the sky? The Lord will return, just as you have seen him ascend, alleluia.

Opening Prayer

Let us pray
    [that the risen Christ
    will lead us to eternal life]

God our Father,
make us joyful in the ascension of your Son Jesus Christ.
May we follow him into the new creation,
for his ascension is our glory and our hope.

or

Let us pray
    [on this day of Ascension
    as we watch and wait for Jesus' return]

Father in heaven,
our minds were prepared for the coming of your kingdom
when you took Christ beyond our sight
so that we might seek him in his glory.

May we follow where he has led
and find our hope in his glory,
for he is Lord for ever.

FIRST READING

A reading from the Acts of the Apostles   1:1-11
He was lifted up while they looked on.

In my earlier work, Theophilus, I dealt with everything Jesus had done and taught from the beginning until the day he gave his instructions to the apostles he had chosen through the Holy Spirit, and was taken up to heaven. He had shown himself alive to them after his Passion by many demonstrations: for forty days he had continued to appear to them and tell them about the kingdom of God. When he had been at table with them, he had told them not to leave Jerusalem, but to wait there for what the Father had promised. 'It is,' he had said, 'what you have heard me speak about: John baptised with water but you, not many days from now, will be baptised with the Holy Spirit.'

Now having met together, they asked him, 'Lord, has the time come? Are you going to restore the kingdom to Israel?' He replied, 'It is not for you to know times or dates that the Father has decided by his own authority, but you will receive power when the Holy Spirit comes on you, and then you will be my witnesses not only in Jerusalem but throughout Judaea and Samaria, and indeed to the ends of the earth.'

As he said this he was lifted up while they looked on, and a cloud took him from their sight. They were still staring into the sky when suddenly two men in white were standing near them and they said, 'Why are you men from Galilee standing here looking into the sky? Jesus who has been taken up from you into heaven, this same Jesus will come back in the same way as you have seen him go there.'

This is the word of the Lord.

Responsorial Psalm　　　　　　　　　　Ps 46:2-3. 6-7. 8-9. ℟ v.6

℟ **God goes up with shouts of joy;**
the Lord goes up with trumpet blast.

or

℟ **Alleluia!**

1 All peoples, clap your hands,
cry to God with shouts of joy!
For the Lord, the Most High, we must fear,
great king over all the earth. ℟

2 God goes up with shouts of joy;
the Lord goes up with trumpet blast.
Sing praise for God, sing praise,
sing praise to our king, sing praise. ℟

3 God is king of all the earth.
Sing praise with all your skill.
God is king over the nations;
God reigns on his holy throne. ℟

SECOND READING

A reading from the letter of St Paul to the Ephesians 1:17-23

He made him sit at his right hand in heaven.

May the God of our Lord Jesus Christ, the Father of glory, give you a spirit of wisdom and perception of what is revealed, to bring you to full knowledge of him. May he enlighten the eyes of your mind so that you can see what hope his call holds for you, what rich glories he has promised the saints will inherit and how infinitely great is the power that he has exercised for us believers. This you can tell from the strength of his power at work in Christ, when he used it to raise him from the dead and to make him sit at his right hand, in heaven, far above every Sovereignty, Authority, Power, or Domination, or any other name that can be named, not only in this age, but also in the age to come. He has put all things under his feet, and made him, as the ruler of everything, the head of the Church; which is his body, the fullness of him who fills the whole creation.

This is the word of the Lord.

Optional Second Reading for Year C

A reading from the letter to the Hebrews 9:24-28. 10:19-23

Christ entered into heaven itself.

It is not as though Christ had entered a man-made sanctuary which was only modelled on the real one; but it was heaven itself, so that he could appear in the actual presence of God on our behalf. And he does not have to offer himself again and again, like the high priest going into the sanctuary year after year with the blood that is not his own, or else he would have had to suffer over and over again since the world began. Instead of that, he has made his appearance once and for all, now at the end of the last age, to do away with sin by sacrificing himself. Since men only die once, and after that comes judgement, so Christ, too, offers himself only once to take the faults of many on himself, and when he appears a second time, it will not be to deal with sin but to reward with salvation those who are waiting for him.

In other words, brothers, through the blood of Jesus we have the right to enter the sanctuary, by a new way which he had opened for us, a living opening through the curtain, that is to say, his body. And we have the supreme high priest over all the house of God. So as we go in, let us be sincere in heart and filled with faith, our minds sprinkled and free from any trace of bad conscience and our bodies washed with pure water. Let us keep firm in the hope we profess, because the one who made the promise is faithful.

This is the word of the Lord.

Gospel Acclamation Mt 28:19. 20
Alleluia, alleluia!
Go, make disciples of all the nations;
I am with you always; yes, to the end of time.
Alleluia!

GOSPEL

A reading from the holy Gospel according to Luke 24:46-53
As he blessed them he was carried up to heaven.

Jesus said to his disciples: 'You see how it is written that the Christ would suffer and on the third day rise from the dead, and that, in his name, repentance for the forgiveness of sins would be preached to all the nations, beginning from Jerusalem. You are witnesses to this.

'And now I am sending down to you what the Father has promised. Stay in the city then, until you are clothed with the power from on high.' Then he took them out as far as the outskirts of Bethany, and lifting up his hands he blessed them. Now as he blessed them, he withdrew from them and was carried up to heaven. They worshipped him and then went back to Jerusalem full of joy; and they were continually in the Temple praising God.

This is the Gospel of the Lord.

Prayer over the Gifts
Lord,
receive our offering
as we celebrate the ascension of Christ your Son.
May his gifts help us rise with him
to the joys of heaven,
where he lives and reigns for ever and ever.

Preface of Ascension I or II, P26 or P27

When Eucharistic Prayer I is used, the special Ascension form of
In union with the whole Church is said.

Communion Antiphon: I, the Lord, am with you always, until the
end of the world, alleluia.

Prayer after Communion
Father,
in this eucharist
we touch the divine life you give to the world.
Help us to follow Christ with love
to eternal life where he is Lord for ever and ever.

Solemn Blessing
Bow your heads and pray for God's blessing.

May almighty God bless you on this day
when his only Son ascended into heaven
to prepare a place for you.   ℟   **Amen.**

After his resurrection, Christ was seen by his disciples.
When he appears as judge
may you be pleasing for ever in his sight.   ℟   **Amen.**

You believe that Jesus has taken his seat in majesty
at the right hand of the Father.
May you have the joy of experiencing
that he is also with you to the end of time,
according to his promise.   ℟   **Amen.**

May almighty God bless you,
the Father, and the Son, ✠ and the Holy Spirit.   ℟   **Amen.**

SEVENTH SUNDAY OF EASTER   C

Where the Ascension of the Lord is celebrated on this day, the
readings given for Ascension, see above pp.768ff, are used.

The Spirit And The Bride

*The Church is wedded to Christ in the love of the Spirit and looks forward
to the final fulfilment of that love in the glory of heaven.*

Entrance Antiphon: Lord, hear my voice when I call to you. My
heart has prompted me to seek your face; I seek it, Lord; do not
hide from me, alleluia.

Opening Prayer
Let us pray
    [that we may recognise
    the presence of Christ in our midst]

Father,
help us keep in mind that Christ our Saviour
lives with you in glory
and promised to remain with us until the end of time.

or

Let us pray
    [to our Father
    who has raised us to life in Christ]

Eternal Father,
reaching from end to end of the universe,
and ordering all things with your mighty arm:
for you, time is the unfolding of truth that already is,
the unveiling of beauty that is yet to be.

Your Son has saved us in history
by rising from the dead,
so that transcending time he might free us from death.
May his presence among us
lead to the vision of unlimited truth
and unfold the beauty of your love.

FIRST READING

A reading from the Acts of the Apostles   7:55-60
I can see the Son of Man standing at the right hand of God.

Stephen, filled with the Holy Spirit, gazed into heaven and saw
the glory of God, and Jesus standing at God's right hand. 'I can
see heaven thrown open' he said 'and the Son of Man standing at
the right hand of God.' At this all the members of the council
shouted out and stopped their ears with their hands; then they
all rushed at him, sent him out of the city and stoned him. The
witnesses put down their clothes at the feet of a young man
called Saul. As they were stoning him, Stephen said in invocation, 'Lord Jesus, receive my spirit.' Then he knelt down and
said aloud, 'Lord, do not hold this sin against them'; and with
these words he fell asleep.

This is the word of the Lord.

Responsorial Psalm   Ps 96:1-2. 6-7. 9. ℟ vv.1. 9

  ℟   **The Lord is king, most high above all the earth.**

or

  ℟   **Alleluia!**

1   The Lord is king, let earth rejoice,
     the many coastlands be glad.
     His throne is justice and right.   ℟

2   The skies proclaim his justice;
     all peoples see his glory.
     All you spirits, worship him.   ℟

3   For you indeed are the Lord
     most high above all the earth
     exalted far above all spirits.   ℟

SECOND READING

A reading from the book of the Apocalypse   22:12-14. 16-17. 20
Come, Lord Jesus.

I, John, heard a voice speaking to me: 'Very soon now, I shall be with you again, bringing the reward to be given to every man according to what he deserves. I am the Alpha and the Omega, the First and the Last, the Beginning and the End. Happy are those who will have washed their robes clean, so that they will have the right to feed on the tree of life and can come through the gates into the city.'

I, Jesus, have sent my angel to make these revelations to you for the sake of the churches. I am of David's line, the root of David and the bright star of the morning.

The Spirit and the Bride say, 'Come.' Let everyone who listens answer, 'Come.' Then let all who are thirsty come; all who want it may have the water of life, and have it free.

The one who guarantees these revelations repeats his promise: I shall indeed be with you soon. Amen; come, Lord Jesus.

This is the word of the Lord.

Gospel Acclamation   cf. Jn 14:18
   Alleluia, alleluia!
   I will not leave you orphans, says the Lord;
   I will come back to you, and your hearts will be full of joy.
   Alleluia!

GOSPEL

A reading from the holy Gospel according to John   17:20-26
May they be completely one.

Jesus raised his eyes to heaven and said:

'Holy Father,
I pray not only for these,
but for those also
who through their words will believe in me.
May they all be one.
Father, may they be one in us,
as you are in me and I am in you,
so that the world may believe it was you who sent me.
I have given them the glory you gave to me,
that they may be one as we are one.
With me in them and you in me,
may they be so completely one
that the world will realise that it was you who sent me
and that I have loved them as much as you love me.
Father,
I want those you have given me
to be with me where I am,
so that they may always see the glory
you have given me
because you loved me
before the foundation of the world.
Father, Righteous One,
the world has not known you,
but I have known you,
and these have known
that you have sent me.
I have made your name known to them
and will continue to make it known,
so that the love with which you loved me may be in them,
and so that I may be in them.'

This is the Gospel of the Lord.

Prayer over the Gifts
Lord,
accept the prayers and gifts
we offer in faith and love.
May this eucharist
bring us to your glory.

Preface of Ascension I or II, P26-P27

Communion Antiphon: **This is the prayer of Jesus: that his believers may become one as he is one with the Father, alleluia.**

Prayer after Communion

God our Saviour,
hear us,
and through this holy mystery give us hope
that the glory you have given Christ
will be given to the Church, his body,
for he is Lord for ever and ever.

An appropriate Solemn Blessing or Prayer over the People may be used. See pp.90ff.

PENTECOST SUNDAY C

Vigil Mass

See above, pp.349ff.

Mass during the Day

The Day of Pentecost

Today we celebrate the great day of Pentecost when Christ filled the Church with the power of his Spirit and sent it out into the world to bring his peace, joy and forgiveness to all mankind.

Entrance Antiphon: **The Spirit of the Lord fills the whole world. It holds all things together and knows every word spoken by man, alleluia.**
or

The love of God has been poured into our hearts by his Spirit living in us, alleluia.

Opening Prayer

Let us pray
[that the Spirit will work through our lives
to bring Christ to the world]

God our Father,
let the Spirit you sent on your Church
to begin the teaching of the gospel
continue to work in the world
through the hearts of all who believe.

or

Let us pray
   [in the Spirit who dwells within us]

Father of light, from whom every good gift comes,
send your Spirit into our lives
with the power of a mighty wind,
and by the flame of your wisdom
open the horizons of our minds.

Loosen our tongues to sing your praise
in words beyond the power of speech,
for without your Spirit
man could never raise his voice in words of peace
or announce the truth that Jesus is Lord,
who lives and reigns with you and the Holy Spirit,
one God, for ever and ever.

FIRST READING

A reading from the Acts of the Apostles   2:1-11
They were all filled with the Holy Spirit and began to speak.

When Pentecost day came round, the apostles had all met in one
room, when suddenly they heard what sounded like a powerful
wind from heaven, the noise of which filled the entire house in
which they were sitting; and something appeared to them that
seemed like tongues of fire; these separated and came to rest on
the head of each of them. They were all filled with the Holy
Spirit, and began to speak foreign languages as the Spirit gave
them the gift of speech.

   Now there were devout men living in Jerusalem from every
nation under heaven, and at this sound they all assembled, each
one bewildered to hear these men speaking his own language.
They were amazed and astonished. 'Surely' they said 'all these
men speaking are Galileans? How does it happen that each of us
hears them in his own native language? Parthians, Medes and
Elamites; people from Mesopotamia, Judaea and Cappadocia,
Pontus and Asia, Phrygia and Pamphylia, Egypt and the parts of

Libya round Cyrene; as well as visitors from Rome – Jews and proselytes alike – Cretans and Arabs; we hear them preaching in our own language about the marvels of God.'

This is the word of the Lord.

Responsorial Psalm   Ps 103:1. 24. 29-31. 34. R℟ cf v.30

℟ **Send forth your Spirit, O Lord,**
and renew the face of the earth.

or

℟ **Alleluia.**

1 Bless the Lord, my soul!
Lord God, how great you are,
How many are your works, O Lord!
The earth is full of your riches. ℟

2 You take back your spirit, they die,
returning to the dust from which they came.
You send forth your spirit, they are created;
and you renew the face of the earth. ℟

3 May the glory of the Lord last for ever!
May the Lord rejoice in his works!
May my thoughts be pleasing to him.
I find my joy in the Lord. ℟

The Second Reading and Gospel may be taken from Year A, see above pp.357ff. Alternatively, the Second Reading and Gospel given below may be used.

SECOND READING

A reading from the letter of St Paul to the Romans   8:8-17

Everyone moved by the Spirit is a son of God.

People who are interested only in unspiritual things can never be pleasing to God. Your interests, however, are not in the unspiritual, but in the spiritual, since the Spirit of God has made his home in you. In fact, unless you possessed the Spirit of Christ you would not belong to him. Though your body may be dead it is because of sin, but if Christ is in you then your spirit is life itself because you have been justified; and if the Spirit of him who raised Jesus from the dead is living in you, then he who raised Jesus from the dead will give life to your own mortal bodies through his Spirit living in you.

So then, my brothers, there is no necessity for us to obey our unspiritual selves or to live unspiritual lives. If you do live in that way, you are doomed to die; but if by the Spirit you put an end to the misdeeds of the body you will live.

Everyone moved by the Spirit is a son of God. The spirit you received is not the spirit of slaves bringing fear into your lives again; it is the spirit of sons, and it makes us cry out, 'Abba, Father!' The Spirit himself and our spirit bear united witness that we are children of God. And if we are children we are heirs as well: heirs of God and coheirs with Christ, sharing his sufferings so as to share his glory.

This is the word of the Lord.

SEQUENCE

The sequence may be said or sung.

Holy Spirit, Lord of light,
From the clear celestial height
Thy pure beaming radiance give.

Come, thou Father of the poor,
Come with treasures which endure;
Come, thou light of all that live!

Thou, of all consolers best,
Thou, the soul's delightful guest,
Dost refreshing peace bestow;

Thou in toil art comfort sweet;
Pleasant coolness in the heat;
Solace in the midst of woe.

Light immortal, light divine,
Visit thou these hearts of thine,
And our inmost being fill:

If thou take thy grace away,
Nothing pure in man will stay;
All his good is turned to ill.

Heal our wounds, our strength renew;
On our dryness pour thy dew;
Wash the stains of guilt away:

Bend the stubborn heart and will;
Melt the frozen, warm the chill;
Guide the steps that go astray.

Thou, on us who evermore
  Thee confess and thee adore,
With thy sevenfold gifts descend:

Give us comfort when we die;
  Give us life with thee on high;
Give us joys that never end.

Gospel Acclamation
  Alleluia, alleluia!
  Come, Holy Spirit, fill the hearts of your faithful
  and kindle in them the fire of your love.
  Alleluia!

GOSPEL

A reading from the holy Gospel according to John 14:15-16. 23-26
The Holy Spirit will teach you everything.

Jesus said to his disciples

'If you love me you will keep my commandments.
I shall ask the Father
and he will give you another Advocate
to be with you for ever.

'If anyone loves me he will keep my word,
and my Father will love him,
and we shall come to him
and make our home with him.
Those who do not love me do not keep my words.
And my word is not my own;
it is the word of the one who sent me.
I have said these things to you
while still with you;
but the Advocate, the Holy Spirit,
whom the Father will send in my name,
will teach you everything
and remind you of all I have said to you.'

  This is the Gospel of the Lord.

Prayer over the Gifts
Lord,
may the Spirit you promised
lead us into all truth
and reveal to us the full meaning of this sacrifice.

Preface of Pentecost, P28.

When Eucharistic Prayer I is used, the special Pentecost form of *In union with the whole Church* is said.

Communion Antiphon: They were all filled with the Holy Spirit, and they spoke of the great things God had done, alleluia.

Prayer after Communion
Father,
may the food we receive in the eucharist
help our eternal redemption.
Keep within us the vigour of your Spirit
and protect the gifts you have given to your Church.

Solemn Blessing
Bow your heads and pray for God's blessing.

This day the Father of light
has enlightened the minds of the disciples
by the outpouring of the Holy Spirit.
May he bless you
and give you the gifts of the Spirit for ever.   R̸   **Amen.**

May that fire which hovered over the disciples
as tongues of flame
burn out all evil from your hearts
and make them glow with pure light.   R̸   **Amen.**

God inspired speech in different tongues
to proclaim one faith.
May he strengthen your faith
and fulfil your hope to see him face to face.   R̸   **Amen.**

May almighty God bless you,
the Father, and the Son, ✠ and the Holy Spirit.   R̸   **Amen.**

SOLEMNITIES OF THE LORD
IN ORDINARY TIME

Sunday after Pentecost

THE MOST HOLY TRINITY   C
Solemnity

Glory To The Father, The Son, And The Holy Spirit

The Spirit glorifies the Son of the eternal Father, and today we in the Spirit give glory to God, for the love of God has been poured into our hearts by the Holy Spirit who has been given to us.

Entrance Antiphon: Blessed be God the Father and his only-begotten Son and the Holy Spirit: for he has shown that he loves us.

Opening Prayer
Let us pray
   [to the one God, Father, Son and Spirit,
   that our lives may bear witness to our faith]

Father,
you sent your Word to bring us truth
and your Spirit to make us holy.
Through them we come to know the mystery of your life.
Help us to worship you, one God in three Persons,
by proclaiming and living our faith in you.

or

Let us pray
   [to our God who is Father, Son, and Holy Spirit]

God, we praise you:
Father all-powerful, Christ Lord and Saviour, Spirit of love.
You reveal yourself in the depths of our being,
drawing us to share in your life and your love.
One God, three Persons,
be near to the people formed in your image,
close to the world your love brings to life.

FIRST READING

A reading from the book of Proverbs 8:22-31

Before the earth came into being, Wisdom was born.

The Wisdom of God cries aloud:
The Lord created me when his purpose first unfolded,
before the oldest of his works.
From everlasting I was firmly set,
from the beginning, before earth came into being.
The deep was not, when I was born,
there were no springs to gush with water.
Before the mountains were settled,
before the hills, I came to birth;
before he made the earth, the countryside,
or the first grains of the world's dust.
When he fixed the heavens firm, I was there,
when he drew a ring on the surface of the deep,
when he thickened the clouds above,
when he fixed fast the springs of the deep,
when he assigned the sea its boundaries
– and the waters will not invade the shore –
when he laid down the foundations of the earth,
I was by his side, a master craftsman,
delighting him day after day,
ever at play in his presence,
at play everywhere in his world,
delighting to be with the sons of men.

This is the word of the Lord.

Responsorial Psalm Ps 8:4-9. ℟ v.2

℟ **How great is your name, O Lord our God,
through all the earth!**

1 When I see the heavens, the work of your hands,
the moon and the stars which you arranged,
what is man that you should keep him in mind,
mortal man that you care for him? ℟

2 Yet you have made him little less than a god;
with glory and honour you crowned him,
gave him power over the works of your hand,
put all things under his feet. ℟ (continued)

3   All of them, sheep and cattle,
        yes, even the savage beasts,
        birds of the air, and fish
        that make their way through the waters.

℟   **How great is your name, O Lord our God,
    through all the earth!**

SECOND READING

A reading from the letter of St Paul to the Romans   5:1-5
To God, through Christ, in the love poured out by the Spirit.

Through our Lord Jesus Christ, by faith we are judged righteous
and at peace with God, since it is by faith and through Jesus that
we have entered this state of grace in which we can boast about
looking forward to God's glory. But that is not all we can boast
about; we can boast about our sufferings. These sufferings bring
patience, as we know, and patience brings perseverance, and
perseverance brings hope, and this hope is not deceptive,
because the love of God has been poured into our hearts by the
Holy Spirit which has been given us.

        This is the word of the Lord.

Gospel Acclamation   cf. Apoc 1:8
    Alleluia, alleluia!
    Glory be to the Father, and to the Son, and to the Holy Spirit,
    the God who is, who was, and who is to come.
    Alleluia!

GOSPEL

A reading from the holy Gospel according to John   16:12-15
*Everything the Father has is mine; all the Spirit tells you will be taken
from what is mine.*

Jesus said to his disciples:

    'I still have many things to say to you
    but they would be too much for you now.
    But when the Spirit of truth comes
    he will lead you to the complete truth,
    since he will not be speaking as from himself
    but will say only what he has learnt;
    and he will tell you of the things to come.
    He will glorify me

since all he tells you
will be taken from what is mine.
Everything the Father has is mine;
that is why I said:
All he tells you
will be taken from what is mine.'

This the Gospel of the Lord.

Prayer over the Gifts
Lord our God,
make these gifts holy,
and through them
make us a perfect offering to you.

Preface of the Holy Trinity, P43

Communion Antiphon: You are the sons of God, so God has given
you the Spirit of his Son to form your hearts and make you cry
out: Abba, Father.

Prayer after Communion
Lord God,
we worship you, a Trinity of Persons, one eternal God.
May our faith and the sacrament we receive
bring us health of mind and body.

Thursday after Trinity Sunday
THE BODY AND BLOOD OF CHRIST   C
Solemnity

The Priesthood Of Melchizedek

*Like Melchizedek of old we bring bread and wine to the altar and Christ
transforms it into his own body and blood for the life of the multitude of
the redeemed.*

Entrance Antiphon: The Lord fed his people with the finest wheat
and honey; their hunger was satisfied.

Opening Prayer
Let us pray
   [to the Lord who gives himself in the eucharist,
    that this sacrament may bring us salvation
    and peace]

Lord Jesus Christ,
you gave us the eucharist
as the memorial of your suffering and death.
May our worship of this sacrament of your body and blood
help us to experience the salvation you won for us
and the peace of the kingdom
where you live with the Father and the Holy Spirit,
one God, for ever and ever.

or

Let us pray
  [for the willingness to make present in our world
  the love of Christ shown to us in the eucharist]

Lord Jesus Christ,
we worship you living among us
in the sacrament of your body and blood.

May we offer to our Father in heaven
a solemn pledge of undivided love.
May we offer to our brothers and sisters
a life poured out in loving service of that kingdom
where you live with the Father and the Holy Spirit,
one God, for ever and ever.

FIRST READING

A reading from the book of Genesis   14:18-20
He brought bread and wine.

Melchizedek king of Salem brought bread and wine; he was a
priest of God Most High. He pronounced this blessing:

  'Blessed be Abraham by God Most High, creator of heaven
    and earth,
  and blessed be God Most High for handing over your enemies
    to you.'

And Abraham gave him a tithe of everything.

  This is the word of the Lord.

Responsorial Psalm   Ps 109:1-4. ℟ v.4
  ℟ **You are a priest for ever,
      a priest like Melchizedek of old.**

1   The Lord's revelation to my Master:

'Sit on my right:
I will put your foes beneath your feet.' ℟

2 The Lord will send from Zion
your sceptre of power:
rule in the midst of all your foes. ℟

3 A prince from the day of your birth
on the holy mountains;
from the womb before the daybreak I begot you. ℟

4 The Lord has sworn an oath he will not change.
'You are a priest for ever,
a priest like Melchizedek of old.' ℟

SECOND READING

A reading from the first letter of St Paul   11:23-26
to the Corinthians

Every time you eat this bread and drink this cup, you are proclaiming the Lord's death.

This is what I received from the Lord, and in turn passed on to you: that on the same night that he was betrayed, the Lord Jesus took some bread, and thanked God for it and broke it, and he said, 'This is my body, which is for you; do this as a memorial of me.' In the same way he took the cup after supper, and said, 'This cup is the new covenant in my blood. Whenever you drink it, do this as a memorial of me.' Until the Lord comes, therefore, every time you eat this bread and drink this cup, you are proclaiming his death.

This is the word of the Lord.

The sequence, *Sing forth, O Zion,* may be said or sung in its longer or shorter form. See above, p.365ff.

Gospel Acclamation   Jn 6:51-52
Alleluia, alleluia!
I am the living bread which has come down from heaven,
says the Lord.
Anyone who eats this bread will live for ever.
Alleluia!

GOSPEL

A reading from the holy Gospel according to Luke   9:11-17
They all ate as much as they wanted.

Jesus made the crowds welcome and talked to them about the
kingdom of God; and he cured those who were in need of
healing.

It was late afternoon when the Twelve came to him and said,
'Send the people away, and they can go to the villages and farms
round about to find lodging and food; for we are in a lonely place
here.' He replied, 'Give them something to eat yourselves.' But
they said, 'We have no more than five loaves and two fish, unless
we are to go ourselves and buy food for all these people.' For
there were about five thousand men. But he said to his disciples,
'Get them to sit down in parties of about fifty.' They did so and
made them all sit down. Then he took the five loaves and the two
fish, raised his eyes to heaven, and said the blessing over them;
then he broke them and handed them to his disciples to distri-
bute among the crowd. They all ate as much as they wanted, and
when the scraps remaining were collected they filled twelve
baskets.

This is the Gospel of the Lord.

Prayer over the Gifts
Lord,
may the bread and cup we offer
bring your Church the unity and peace they signify.

Preface of the Holy Eucharist I or II, P47 or P48

Communion Antiphon: Whoever eats my flesh and drinks my
blood will live in me and I in him, says the Lord.

Prayer after Communion
Lord Jesus Christ,
you give us your body and blood in the eucharist
as a sign that even now we share your life.
May we come to possess it completely in the kingdom
where you live for ever and ever.

Friday after the Second Sunday after Pentecost

THE SACRED HEART OF JESUS C
Solemnity

The Heart Of The Shepherd

We celebrate the love of Christ the Good Shepherd who gave his life for his sheep.

Entrance Antiphon: The thoughts of his heart last through every generation, that he will rescue them from death and feed them in time of famine.

Opening Prayer

Let us pray
    [that we will respond to the love of Christ]

Father,
we rejoice in the gifts of love
we have received from the heart of Jesus your Son.
Open our hearts to share his life
and continue to bless us with his love.

or

Father,
we have wounded the heart of Jesus your Son,
but he brings us forgiveness and grace.
Help us to prove our grateful love
and make amends for our sins.

or

Let us pray
    [that the love of Christ's heart
      may touch the world with healing and peace]

Father,
we honour the heart of your Son
broken by man's cruelty,
yet symbol of love's triumph,
pledge of all that man is called to be.

Teach us to see Christ in the lives we touch,
to offer him living worship
by love-filled service to our brothers and sisters.

FIRST READING

A reading from the prophet Ezekiel   34:11-16

I myself will pasture my sheep, I myself will show them where to rest.

The Lord God says this: I am going to look after my flock myself and keep all of it in view. As a shepherd keeps all his flock in view when he stands up in the middle of his scattered sheep, so shall I keep my sheep in view. I shall rescue them from wherever they have been scattered during the mist and darkness. I shall bring them out of the countries where they are; I shall gather them together from foreign countries and bring them back to their own land. I shall pasture them on the mountains of Israel, in the ravines and in every inhabited place in the land. I shall feed them in good pasturage; the high mountains of Israel will be their grazing ground. There they will rest in good grazing ground; they will browse in rich pastures on the mountains of Israel. I myself will pasture my sheep, I myself will show them where to rest – it is the Lord who speaks. I shall look for the lost one, bring back the stray, bandage the wounded and make the weak strong. I shall watch over the fat and healthy. I shall be a true shepherd to them.

This is the word of the Lord.

Responsorial Psalm   Ps 22. ℟ v.1

   ℟   **The Lord is my shepherd;
        there is nothing I shall want.**

1   The Lord is my shepherd;
    there is nothing I shall want.
    Fresh and green are the pastures
    where he gives me repose.
    Near restful waters he leads me,
    to revive my drooping spirit.   ℟

2   He guides me along the right path;
    he is true to his name.
    If I should walk in the valley of darkness
    no evil would I fear.
    You are there with your crook and your staff;
    with these you give me comfort.   ℟

3   You have prepared a banquet for me
    in the sight of my foes.
    My head you have anointed with oil;

my cup is overflowing.   ℟

4   Surely goodness and kindness shall follow me
all the days of my life.
In the Lord's own house shall I dwell
for ever and ever.   ℟

SECOND READING

A reading from the letter of St Paul to the Romans   5:5-11

What proves that God loves us is that Christ died for us.

The love of God has been poured into our hearts by the Holy
Spirit which has been given us. We were still helpless when at his
appointed moment Christ died for sinful men. It is not easy to die
even for a good man – though of course for someone really
worthy, a man might be prepared to die – but what proves that
God loves us is that Christ died for us while we were still sinners.
Having died to make us righteous, is it likely that he would now
fail to save us from God's anger? When we were reconciled to
God by the death of his Son, we were still enemies; now that we
have been reconciled, surely we may count on being saved by the
life of his Son? Not merely because we have been reconciled but
because we are filled with joyful trust in God, through our Lord
Jesus Christ, through whom we have already gained our reconciliation.

This is the word of the Lord.

Gospel Acclamation   Mt 11:29
Alleluia, alleluia!
Shoulder my yoke and learn from me,
for I am gentle and humble in heart.
Alleluia!

Alternative Gospel Acclamation   Jn 10:14
Alleluia, alleluia!
I am the good shepherd, says the Lord;
I know my own sheep and my own know me.
Alleluia!

GOSPEL

A reading from the holy Gospel according to Luke   15:3-7
Rejoice with me, I have found my sheep that was lost.

Jesus spoke this parable to the scribes and Pharisees:

'What man among you with a hundred sheep, losing one, would not leave the ninety-nine in the wilderness and go after the missing one till he found it? And when he found it, would he not joyfully take it on his shoulders and then, when he got home, call together his friends and neighbours? "Rejoice with me," he would say "I have found my sheep that was lost." In the same way, I tell you, there will be more rejoicing in heaven over one repentant sinner than over ninety-nine virtuous men who have no need of repentance.'

This is the Gospel of the Lord.

Prayer over the Gifts
Lord,
look on the heart of Christ your Son
filled with love for us.
Because of his love
accept our eucharist and forgive our sins.
Preface of the Sacred Heart, P45

Communion Antiphon: The Lord says: If anyone is thirsty, let him come to me; whoever believes in me, let him drink. Streams of living water shall flow out from within him.

or

One of the soldiers pierced Jesus' side with a lance, and at once there flowed out blood and water.

Prayer after Communion
Father,
may this sacrament fill us with love.
Draw us closer to Christ your Son
and help us to recognise him in others.

THE BREAD WE BREAK

BECAUSE THERE IS ONE BREAD · WE WHO ARE MANY ARE ONE BODY

SUNDAYS IN ORDINARY TIME
Year C

The cycle of Sundays in Ordinary Time runs from the end of Christmastide to the beginning of Lent; it recommences after Trinity Sunday, and runs until the beginning of Advent. The number of Sundays in Ordinary Time before Lent, and between Trinity Sunday and Advent varies: see the Table of Principal Celebrations.

The first week of Ordinary Time begins on the Monday following the Feast of the Baptism of the Lord.

In Cycle C, the Gospel Readings are taken mainly from the Gospel according to St Luke.

First Sunday in Ordinary Time

THE BAPTISM OF THE LORD
Feast

See above, pp.158ff.

SECOND SUNDAY IN ORDINARY TIME   C

The Church's Bridegroom

The Church rejoices in her Bridegroom who will cherish her, lavish upon her the many gifts of his Spirit, and transform her into a new creation as he transformed water into wine.

Entrance Antiphon: May all the earth give you worship and praise, and break into song to your name, O God, Most High.

Opening Prayer
Let us pray
    [to our Father for the gift of peace]

Father of heaven and earth,
hear our prayers,
and show us the way to peace in the world.

or

Let us pray
    [for the gift of peace]

Almighty and ever-present Father,
your watchful care reaches from end to end
and orders all things in such power
that even the tensions and the tragedies of sin
cannot frustrate your loving plans.

Help us to embrace your will,
give us the strength to follow your call,
so that your truth may live in our hearts
and reflect peace to those who believe in your love.

FIRST READING

62:1-5

A reading from the prophet Isaiah
The bridegroom rejoices in his bride.

About Zion I will not be silent.
about Jerusalem I will not grow weary,
until her integrity shines out like the dawn
and her salvation flames like a torch.
The nations then will see your integrity,
all the kings your glory,
and you will be called by a new name,

one which the mouth of the Lord will confer.
You are to be a crown of splendour in the hand of the Lord,
a princely diadem in the hand of your God;
no longer are you to be named 'Forsaken',
nor your land 'Abandoned',
but you shall be called 'My Delight'
and your land 'The Wedded';
for the Lord takes delight in you
and your land will have its wedding.
Like a young man marrying a virgin,
so will the one who built you wed you,
and as the bridegroom rejoices in his bride,
so will your God rejoice in you.

This is the word of the Lord.

Responsorial Psalm   Ps 95:1-3. 7-10. ℟ v.3
   ℟ **Proclaim the wonders of the Lord**
       among all the peoples.

1   O sing a new song to the Lord,
     sing to the Lord all the earth.
     O sing to the Lord, bless his name.   ℟

2   Proclaim his help day by day,
     tell among the nations his glory
     and his wonders among all the peoples.   ℟

3   Give the Lord, you families of peoples,
     give the Lord glory and power,
     give the Lord the glory of his name.   ℟

4   Worship the Lord in his temple.
     O earth, tremble before him.
     Proclaim to the nations: 'God is king.'
     He will judge the peoples in fairness.   ℟

SECOND READING

A reading from the first letter of St Paul
to the Corinthians   12:4-11
One and the same Spirit, who distributes gifts to different people just as
he chooses.

There is a variety of gifts but always the same Spirit; there are all
sorts of service to be done, but always to the same Lord; working
in all sorts of different ways in different people, it is the same

God who is working in all of them. The particular way in which the Spirit is given to each person is for a good purpose. One may have the gift of preaching with wisdom given him by the Spirit; another may have the gift of preaching instruction given him by the same Spirit; and another the gift of faith given by the same Spirit; another again the gift of healing, through this one Spirit; one, the power of miracles; another, prophecy; another the gift of recognising spirits; another the gift of tongues and another the ability to interpret them. All these are the work of one and the same Spirit, who distributes different gifts to different people just as he chooses.

This is the word of the Lord.

Gospel Acclamation　　　　　　　　　　　　　cf. Jn 6:63. 68
　　Alleluia, alleluia!
　　Your words are spirit, Lord,
　　and they are life:
　　you have the message of eternal life.
　　Alleluia!

or　　　　　　　　　　　　　　　　　　　　　　cf. 2 Thess 2:14

　　Alleluia, alleluia!
　　Through the Good News God called us
　　to share the glory of our Lord Jesus Christ.
　　Alleluia!

GOSPEL

A reading from the holy Gospel according to John　　　2:1-11
This was the first of the signs given by Jesus: it was given at Cana in Galilee.

There was a wedding at Cana in Galilee. The mother of Jesus was there, and Jesus and his disciples had also been invited. When they ran out of wine, since the wine provided for the wedding was all finished, the mother of Jesus said to him, 'They have no wine.' Jesus said, 'Woman why turn to me? My hour has not come yet.' His mother said to the servants, 'Do whatever he tells you.' There were six stone water jars standing there, meant for the ablutions that are customary among the Jews; each could hold twenty or thirty gallons. Jesus said to the servants, 'Fill the jars with water,' and they filled them to the brim. 'Draw some out now' he told them 'and take it to the steward.' They did this; the steward tasted the water, and it had turned into wine.

Having no idea where it came from – only the servants who had drawn the water knew – the steward called the bridegroom and said, 'People generally serve the best wine first, and keep the cheaper sort till the guests have had plenty to drink; but you have kept the best wine till now.'

This was the first of the signs given by Jesus: it was given at Cana in Galilee. He let his glory be seen, and his disciples believed in him.

This is the Gospel of the Lord.

Prayer over the Gifts
Father,
may we celebrate the eucharist
with reverence and love,
for when we proclaim the death of the Lord
you continue the work of his redemption,
who is Lord for ever and ever.

Preface of Sundays in Ordinary Time I-VIII, P29-P36

Communion Antiphon: The Lord has prepared a feast for me: given wine in plenty for me to drink.

or

We know and believe in God's love for us.

Prayer after Communion
Lord,
you have nourished us with bread from heaven.
Fill us with your Spirit,
and make us one in peace and love.

THIRD SUNDAY IN ORDINARY TIME   C

The Law Of The Lord

Today is a day of rejoicing in the New Law which Christ has given us and which unites us with him, binds us together as his people, and enables us to work together for his Kingdom. We listen to the words of the Law and ponder them in our hearts.

Entrance Antiphon: Sing a new song to the Lord! Sing to the Lord, all the earth. Truth and beauty surround him, he lives in holiness and glory.

Opening Prayer
Let us pray
    [for unity and peace]

All-powerful and ever-living God,
direct your love that is within us,
that our efforts in the name of your Son
may bring mankind to unity and peace.

or

Let us pray
    [pleading that our vision
    may overcome our weakness]

Almighty Father,
the love you offer
always exceeds the furthest expression of our human longing,
for you are greater than the human heart.

Direct each thought, each effort of our life,
so that the limits of our faults and weaknesses
may not obscure the vision of your glory
or keep us from the peace you have promised.

FIRST READING

A reading from the book of Nehemiah   8:2-6. 8-10
Ezra read from the law of God and the people understood what was read.

Ezra the priest brought the Law before the assembly, consisting
of men, women, and children old enough to understand. This
was the first day of the seventh month. On the square before the
Water Gate, in the presence of the men and women, and children
old enough to understand, he read from the book from early
morning till noon; all the people listened attentively to the Book
of the Law.

    Ezra the scribe stood on a wooden dais erected for the
purpose. In full view of all the people – since he stood higher
than all the people – Ezra opened the book; and when he opened
it all the people stood up. Then Ezra blessed the Lord, the great
God, and all the people raised their hands and answered, 'Amen!
Amen!'; then they bowed down and, face to the ground, prostrated themselves before the Lord. And Ezra read from the Law
of God, translating and giving the sense, so that the people
understood what was read.

    Then Nehemiah – His Excellency – and Ezra, priest and

scribe (and the Levites who were instructing the people) said to all the people, 'This day is sacred to the Lord your God. Do not be mournful, do not weep.' For the people were all in tears as they listened to the words of the Law.

He then said, 'Go, eat the fat, drink the sweet wine, and send a portion to the man who has nothing prepared ready. For this day is sacred to our Lord. Do not be sad: the joy of the Lord is your stronghold.'

This is the word of the Lord.

Responsorial Psalm   Ps 18:8-10. 15. ℞ Jn 6:63

  ℞   **Your words are spirit, Lord,**
      and they are life.

1   The law of the Lord is perfect,
    it revives the soul.
    The rule of the Lord is to be trusted,
    it gives wisdom to the simple.   ℞

2   The precepts of the Lord are right,
    they gladden the heart.
    The command of the Lord is clear,
    it gives light to the eyes.   ℞

3   The fear of the Lord is holy,
    abiding for ever.
    The decrees of the Lord are truth
    and all of them just.   ℞

4   May the spoken words of my mouth,
    the thoughts of my heart,
    win favour in your sight, O Lord,
    my rescuer, my rock!   ℞

SECOND READING

A reading from the first letter of St Paul   12:12-30
to the Corinthians
You together are Christ's body; but each of you is a different part of it.

*Just as a human body, though it is made up of many parts is a single unit because all these parts, though many, make one body, so it is with Christ. In the one Spirit we were all baptised, Jews as well as Greeks, slaves as well as citizens, and one Spirit was given to us all to drink.

Nor is the body to be identified with any one of its many

parts.* If the foot were to say, 'I am not a hand and so I do not belong to the body', would that mean that it stopped being part of the body? If the ear were to say, 'I am not an eye, and so I do not belong to the body,' would that mean that it is not a part of the body? If your whole body was just one eye, how would you hear anything? If it was just one ear, how would you smell anything?

Instead of that, God put all the separate parts into the body on purpose. If all the parts were the same, how could it be a body? As it is, the parts are many but the body is one. The eye cannot say to the hand, 'I do not need you,' nor can the head say to the feet, 'I do not need you.'

What is more, it is precisely the parts of the body that seem to be the weakest which are the indispensable ones; and it is the least honourable parts of the body that we clothe with the greatest care. So our more improper parts get decorated in a way that our more proper parts do not need. God has arranged the body so that more dignity is given to the parts which are without it, and so that there may not be disagreements inside the body, but that each part may be equally concerned for all the others. If one part is hurt, all parts are hurt with it. If one part is given special honour, all parts enjoy it.

Now you together are Christ's body; but each of you is a different part of it. In the Church, God has given the first place to apostles, the second to prophets, the third to teachers; after them, miracles, and after them the gift of healing; helpers, good leaders, those with many languages. Are all of them apostles, or all of them prophets, or all of them teachers? Do they all have the gift of miracles, or all have the gift of healing? Do all speak strange languages, and all interpret them?

This is the word of the Lord.

*Shorter Form, verses 12-14. 17. Read between *

Gospel Acclamation   Lk 4:18
    Alleluia, alleluia!
    The Lord has sent me to bring the good news to the poor,
    to proclaim liberty to captives.
    Alleluia!

GOSPEL

A reading from the holy Gospel according to Luke   1:1-4; 4:14-21
The text is being fulfilled today.

Seeing that many others have undertaken to draw up accounts of
the events that have taken place among us, exactly as these were
handed down to us by those who from the outset were eyewit-
nesses and ministers of the word, I in my turn, after carefully
going over the whole story from the beginning, have decided to
write an ordered account for you, Theophilus, so that your
Excellency may learn how well founded the teaching is that you
have received.

Jesus, with the power of the Spirit in him, returned to Galilee;
and his reputation spread throughout the countryside. He taught
in their synagogues and everyone praised him.

He came to Nazara, where he had been brought up, and went
into the synagogue on the sabbath day as he usually did. He
stood up to read, and they handed him the scroll of the prophet
Isaiah. Unrolling the scroll he found the place where it is written:

The spirit of the Lord has been given to me, for he has
    anointed me.
He has sent me to bring the good news to the poor,
to proclaim liberty to captives
and to the blind new sight,
to set the downtrodden free,
to proclaim the Lord's year of favour.

He then rolled up the scroll, gave it back to the assistant and sat
down. And all eyes in the synagogue were fixed on him. Then he
began to speak to them, 'This text is being fulfilled today even as
you listen.'

This is the Gospel of the Lord.

Prayer over the Gifts
Lord,
receive our gifts.
Let our offerings make us holy
and bring us salvation.

Preface of Sundays in Ordinary Time I-VIII, P29-P36

Communion Antiphon: Look up at the Lord with gladness and
smile; your face will never be ashamed.

or

I am the light of the world, says the Lord; the man who follows
me will have the light of life.

Prayer after Communion
God, all-powerful Father,
may the new life you give us increase our love
and keep us in the joy of your kingdom.

FOURTH SUNDAY IN ORDINARY TIME   C

The Church As The Prophet Of God

*We are privileged to be called by God to be his prophets: to take his words
on our lips and proclaim them to the world. But the gift of prophecy is of
no avail without the gift of love: a Christ-like love of the world which is
proof even against the world's rejection of us.*

Entrance Antiphon: Save us, Lord our God, and gather us together
from the nations, that we may proclaim your holy name and
glory in your praise.

Opening Prayer
Let us pray
    [for a greater love of God
    and of our fellow men]

Lord our God,
help us to love you with all our hearts
and to love all men as you love them.
    or

Let us pray
    [joining in the praise of the living God
    for we are his people]

Father in heaven,
from the days of Abraham and Moses
until this gathering of your Church in prayer,
you have formed a people in the image of your Son.

Bless this people with the gift of your kingdom.
May we serve you with our every desire
and show love for one another
even as you have loved us.

FIRST READING

A reading from the prophet Jeremiah   1:4-5. 17-19
I have appointed you as prophet to the nations.

In the days of Josiah, the word of the Lord was addressed to me,
saying,

'Before I formed you in the womb I knew you;
before you came to birth I consecrated you;
I have appointed you as prophet to the nations.
So now brace yourself for action.
Stand up and tell them
all I command you.
Do not be dismayed at their presence,
or in their presence I will make you dismayed.
I, for my part, today will make you
into a fortified city,
a pillar of iron,
and a wall of bronze
to confront all this land:
the kings of Judah, its princes,
its priests and the country people.
They will fight against you
but shall not overcome you,
for I am with you to deliver you –
it is the Lord who speaks.'

This is the word of the Lord.

Responsorial Psalm   Ps 70:1-6. 15. 17. ℟ v.15
  ℟ **My lips will tell of your help.**

1 In you, O Lord, I take refuge;
   let me never be put to shame.
   In your justice rescue me, free me:
   pay heed to me and save me.   ℟

2 Be a rock where I can take refuge,
   a mighty stronghold to save me;
   for you are my rock, my stronghold.
   Free me from the hand of the wicked.   ℟

3 It is you, O Lord, who are my hope,
   my trust, O Lord, since my youth.
   On you I have leaned from my birth,
   from my mother's womb you have been my help.   ℟(continued)

4   My lips will tell of your justice
       and day by day of your help.
       O God, you have taught me from my youth
       and I proclaim your wonders still.

℟   **My lips will tell of your help.**

SECOND READING

A reading from the first letter of St Paul   12:31 – 13:13
to the Corinthians

There are three things that last: faith, hope and love; and the greatest of
these is love.

Be ambitious for the higher gifts. And I am going to show you a
way that is better than any of them.

   If I have all the eloquence of men or of angels, but speak
without love, I am simply a gong booming or a cymbal clashing.
If I have the gift of prophecy, understanding all the mysteries
there are, and knowing everything, and if I have faith in all its
fulness, to move mountains, but without love, then I am nothing
at all. If I give away all that I possess, piece by piece, and if I even
let them take my body to burn it, but am without love, it will do
me no good whatever.

   *Love is always patient and kind: it is never jealous; love is
never boastful or conceited; it is never rude or selfish; it does not
take offence, and is not resentful. Love takes no pleasure in other
people's sins but delights in the truth; it is always ready to
excuse, to trust, to hope, and to endure whatever comes.

   Love does not come to an end. But if there are gifts of
prophecy, the time will come when they must fail; or the gift of
languages, it will not continue for ever; and knowledge – for this,
too, the time will come when it must fail. For our knowledge is
imperfect and our prophesying is imperfect; but once perfection
comes, all imperfect things will disappear. When I was a child, I
used to talk like a child, and think like a child, and argue like a
child, but now I am a man, all childish ways are put behind me.
Now we are seeing a dim reflection in a mirror; but then we shall
be seeing face to face. The knowledge that I have now is
imperfect; but then I shall know as fully as I am known.

   In short, there are three things that last: faith, hope and love;
and the greatest of these is love.

   This is the word of the Lord.*

Shorter Form, verses 4-13, read between.

Gospel Acclamation   Jn 14:5
Alleluia, alleluia!
I am the Way, the Truth and the Life, says the Lord;
no one can come to the Father except through me.
Alleluia!

or   Lk 4:18

Alleluia, alleluia!
The Lord has sent me to bring the good news to the poor,
to proclaim liberty to captives.
Alleluia!

GOSPEL

A reading from the holy Gospel according to Luke   4:21-30
Like Elijah and Elisha, Jesus is not sent to the Jews only.

Jesus began to speak in the synagogue, 'This text is being fulfilled
today even as you listen.' And he won the approval of all, and
they were astonished by the gracious words that came from his
lips.

They said, 'This is Joseph's son, surely?' But he replied, 'No
doubt you will quote me the saying, "Physician, heal yourself"
and tell me, "We have heard all that happened in Capernaum, do
the same here in your own countryside." ' And he went on, 'I tell
you solemnly, no prophet is ever accepted in his own country.

'There were many widows in Israel, I can assure you, in
Elijah's day, when heaven remained shut for three years and six
months and a great famine raged throughout the land, but Elijah
was not sent to any one of these: he was sent to a widow at
Zarephath, a Sidonian town. And in the prophet Elisha's time
there were many lepers in Israel, but none of these was cured,
except the Syrian, Naaman.'

When they heard this everyone in the synagogue was
enraged. They sprang to their feet and hustled him out of the
town; and they took him up to the brow of the hill their town was
built on, intending to throw him down the cliff, but he slipped
through the crowd and walked away.

This is the Gospel of the Lord.

Prayer over the Gifts
Lord,
be pleased with the gifts we bring to your altar,
and make them the sacrament of our salvation.

Preface of Sundays in Ordinary Time I-VIII, P29-P36

Communion Antiphon: Let your face shine on your servant, and save me by your love. Lord, keep me from shame, for I have called to you.

or

Happy are the poor in spirit; the kingdom of heaven is theirs! Happy are the lowly; they shall inherit the land.

Prayer after Communion

Lord,
you invigorate us with this help to our salvation.
By this eucharist give the true faith continued growth
throughout the world.

FIFTH SUNDAY IN ORDINARY TIME　　C

Christ Makes Us His Apostles

We are utterly unworthy to be the apostles of Christ and yet he sends us out to be fishers of men. He cleanses us from our sins and gives us the strength to say: 'Here I am, Lord, send me.'

Entrance Antiphon: Come, let us worship the Lord. Let us bow down in the presence of our maker, for he is the Lord our God.

Opening Prayer
Let us pray
　　[that God will watch over us and protect us]

Father,
watch over your family
and keep us safe in your care,
for all our hope is in you.

or

Let us pray
　　[with reverence in the presence of the living God]

In faith and love we ask you, Father,
to watch over your family gathered here.
In your mercy and loving kindness
no thought of ours is left unguarded,
no tear unheeded, no joy unnoticed.

Through the prayer of Jesus
may the blessings promised to the poor in spirit
lead us to the treasures of your heavenly kingdom.

FIRST READING

A reading from the prophet Isaiah   6:1-8
Here I am, send me.

In the year of King Uzziah's death I saw the Lord seated on a high throne; his train filled the sanctuary; above him stood seraphs, each one with six wings.

And they cried out one to another in this way,

'Holy, holy, holy is the Lord of hosts.
His glory fills the whole earth.'

The foundations of the threshold shook with the voice of the one who cried out, and the Temple was filled with smoke. I said:

'What a wretched state I am in! I am lost,
for I am a man of unclean lips
and I live among a people of unclean lips,
and my eyes have looked at the King, the Lord of hosts.'

Then one of the seraphs flew to me, holding in his hand a live coal which he had taken from the altar with a pair of tongs. With this he touched my mouth and said:

'See now, this has touched your lips,
your sin is taken away,
your iniquity is purged.'

Then I heard the voice of the Lord saying:

'Whom shall I send? Who will be our messenger?'

I answered, 'Here I am, send me.'

This is the word of the Lord.

Responsorial Psalm   Ps 137:1-5. 7-8. ℟ v.1
  ℟ **Before the angels I will bless you, O Lord.**

1 I thank you, Lord, with all my heart,
   you have heard the words of my mouth.
   Before the angels I will bless you.
   I will adore before your holy temple.   ℟

(continued)

2   I thank you for your faithfulness and love
    which excel all we ever knew of you.
    On the day I called, you answered;
    you increased the strength of my soul.

℟   **Before the angels I will bless you, O Lord.**

3   All earth's kings shall thank you
    when they hear the words of your mouth.
    They shall sing of the Lord's ways:
    'How great is the glory of the Lord!' ℟

4   You stretch out your hand and save me,
    your hand will do all things for me.
    Your love, O Lord, is eternal,
    discard not the work of your hand. ℟

SECOND READING

A reading from the first letter of St Paul   15:1-11
to the Corinthians

I preach what they preach, and this is what you all believed.

Brothers, I want to remind you of the gospel I preached to you,
the gospel that you received and in which you are firmly
established; because the gospel will save you only if you keep
believing exactly what I preached to you – believing anything else
will not lead to anything.

    Well then, * in the first place, I taught you what I had been
taught myself, namely that Christ died for our sins, in accordance
with the scriptures; that he was buried; and that he was raised to
life on the third day, in accordance with the scriptures; that he
appeared first to Cephas and secondly to the Twelve. Next he
appeared to more than five hundred of the brothers at the same
time, most of whom are still alive, though some have died; then
he appeared to James, and then to all the apostles; and last of all
he appeared to me too; it was as though I was born when no one
expected it.*

    I am the least of the apostles; in fact, since I persecuted the
Church of God, I hardly deserve the name apostle; but by God's
grace that is what I am, and the grace that he gave me has not
been fruitless. On the contrary, I, or rather the grace of God that
is with me, have worked harder than any of the others;
* but what matters is that I preach what they preach, and this is
what you all believed.

    This is the word of the Lord.*

*Shorter Form, verses 3-8. 11, read between *

Gospel Acclamation

Jn 15:15

Alleluia, alleluia!
I call you friends, says the Lord,
because I have made known to you
everything I have learnt from my Father.
Alleluia!

or

Mt 4:19

Alleluia, alleluia!
Follow me, says the Lord,
and I will make you fishers of men.
Alleluia!

GOSPEL

A reading from the holy Gospel according to Luke   5:1-11

They left everything and followed him.

Jesus was standing one day by the lake of Gennesaret, with the crowd pressing round him listening to the word of God, when he caught sight of two boats close to the bank. The fishermen had gone out of them and were washing their nets. He got into one of the boats – it was Simon's – and asked him to put out a little from the shore. Then he sat down and taught the crowds from the boat.

When he had finished speaking he said to Simon, 'Put out into deep water and pay out your nets for a catch.' 'Master,' Simon replied 'we worked hard all night long and caught nothing, but if you say so, I will pay out the nets.' And when they had done this they netted such a huge number of fish that their nets began to tear, so they signalled to their companions in the other boats to come and help them; when these came, they filled the two boats to sinking point.

When Simon Peter saw this he fell at the knees of Jesus saying, 'Leave me, Lord; I am a sinful man.' For he and all his companions were completely overcome by the catch they had made; so also were James and John, sons of Zebedee, who were Simon's partners. But Jesus said to Simon, 'Do not be afraid; from now on it is men you will catch.' Then, bringing their boats back to land, they left everything and followed him.

This is the Gospel of the Lord.

Prayer over the Gifts

Lord our God,
may the bread and wine
you give us for our nourishment on earth
become the sacrament of our eternal life.

Preface of Sundays in Ordinary Time I-VIII, P29-36

Communion Antiphon: Give praise to the Lord for his kindness, for his wonderful deeds towards men. He has filled the hungry with good things, he has satisfied the thirsty.

or

Happy are the sorrowing; they shall be consoled. Happy those who hunger and thirst for what is right; they shall be satisfied.

Prayer after Communion

God our Father,
you give us a share in the one bread and the one cup
and make us one in Christ.
Help us to bring your salvation and joy
to all the world.

SIXTH SUNDAY IN ORDINARY TIME   C

Our Trust In The Lord

Nothing in this world can rob us of our peace of mind and interior joy, because our trust is not in man, but in the crucified and risen Christ.

Entrance Antiphon: Lord, be my rock of safety, the stronghold that saves me. For the honour of your name, lead me and guide me.

Opening Prayer

Let us pray
    [that everything we do
    will be guided by God's law of love]

God our Father,
you have promised to remain for ever
with those who do what is just and right.
Help us to live in your presence.

or

Let us pray
  [for the wisdom that is greater than human words]

Father in heaven,
the loving plan of your wisdom took flesh in Jesus Christ,
and changed mankind's history
by his command of perfect love.

May our fulfilment of his command reflect your wisdom
and bring your salvation to the ends of the earth.

FIRST READING

A reading from the prophet Jeremiah   17:5-8

*A curse on the man who puts his trust in man, a blessing on the man
who puts his trust in the Lord.*

The Lord says this:

  'A curse on the man who puts his trust in man,
  who relies on things of flesh,
  whose heart turns from the Lord.
  He is like dry scrub in the wastelands:
  if good comes, he has no eyes for it,
  he settles in the parched places of the wilderness,
  a salt land, uninhabited.

  'A blessing on the man who puts his trust in the Lord,
  with the Lord for his hope.
  He is like a tree by the waterside
  that thrusts its roots to the stream:
  when the heat comes it feels no alarm,
  its foliage stays green;
  it has no worries in a year of drought,
  and never ceases to bear fruit.'

  This is the word of the Lord.

Responsorial Psalm   Ps 1:1-4. 6. ℟ Ps 39:5
  ℟ **Happy the man who has placed
     his trust in the Lord.**

1 Happy indeed is the man
   who follows not the counsel of the wicked;
   nor lingers in the way of sinners
   nor sits in the company of scorners,

but whose delight is the law of the Lord
and who ponders his law day and night.

℟   **Happy the man who has placed
his trust in the Lord.**

2   He is like a tree that is planted
beside the flowing waters,
that yields its fruit in due season
and whose leaves shall never fade;
and all that he does shall prosper.   ℟

3   Not so are the wicked, not so!
For they like winnowed chaff
shall be driven away by the wind.
For the Lord guards the way of the just
but the way of the wicked leads to doom.   ℟

SECOND READING

A reading from the first letter of St Paul   15:12. 16-20
to the Corinthians
If Christ has not been raised, your believing is useless.

If Christ raised from the dead is what has been preached, how
can some of you be saying that there is no resurrection of the
dead? For if the dead are not raised, Christ has not been raised,
and if Christ has not been raised, you are still in your sins. And
what is more serious, all who have died in Christ have perished.
If our hope in Christ has been for this life only, we are the most
unfortunate of all people.

But Christ has in fact been raised from the dead, the first-fruits
of all who have fallen asleep.

This is the word of the Lord.

Gospel Acclamation   cf. Mt 11:25
Alleluia, alleluia!
Blessed are you, Father,
Lord of heaven and earth,
for revealing the mysteries of the kingdom
to mere children.
Alleluia!

or   Lk 6:23

Alleluia, alleluia!
Rejoice and be glad:

your reward will be great in heaven.
Alleluia!

GOSPEL

A reading from the holy Gospel according to Luke   6:17. 20-26

How happy are you who are poor. Alas for you who are rich.

Jesus came down with the Twelve and stopped at a piece of level ground where there was a large gathering of his disciples with a great crowd of people from all parts of Judaea and from Jerusalem and from the coastal region of Tyre and Sidon who had come to hear him and to be cured of their diseases.

Then fixing his eyes on his disciples he said:

'How happy are you who are poor; yours is the kingdom of God.

Happy you who are hungry now: you shall be satisfied.

Happy you who weep now: you shall laugh.

'Happy are you when people hate you, drive you out, abuse you, denounce your name as criminal, on account of the Son of Man. Rejoice when that day comes and dance for joy, for then your reward will be great in heaven. This was the way their ancestors treated the prophets.

'But alas for you who are rich: you are having your consolation now.

Alas for you who have your fill now: you shall go hungry.

Alas for you who laugh now: you shall mourn and weep.

'Alas for you when the world speaks well of you! This was the way their ancestors treated the false prophets.'

This is the Gospel of the Lord.

Prayer over the Gifts

Lord,
we make this offering in obedience to your word.
May it cleanse and renew us,
and lead us to our eternal reward.

Preface of Sundays in Ordinary Time I-VIII, P29-P36

Communion Antiphon: They ate and were filled; the Lord gave them what they wanted: they were not deprived of their desire.

or

God loved the world so much, he gave his only Son, that all who
believe in him might not perish, but might have eternal life.

Prayer after Communion
Lord,
you give us food from heaven.
May we always hunger
for the bread of life.

SEVENTH SUNDAY IN ORDINARY TIME   C

The Love Of Our Father

*God's love is so overwhelming, he loves us totally, however hateful,
sinful and unworthy we are. There is no way to express this love in our
own lives except by modelling ourselves on Christ, the heavenly man,
and loving our enemies as he loves them. It is then that we are most like
our Father in heaven.*

Entrance Antiphon: Lord, your mercy is my hope, my heart
rejoices in your saving power. I will sing to the Lord, for his
goodness to me.

Opening Prayer
Let us pray
    [that God will make us more like Christ, his Son]

Father,
keep before us the wisdom and love
you have revealed in your Son.
Help us to be like him
in word and deed,
for he lives and reigns with you and the Holy Spirit,
one God, for ever and ever.

or

Let us pray
    [to the God of power and might,
    for his mercy is our hope]

Almighty God,
Father of our Lord Jesus Christ,
faith in your word is the way to wisdom,

and to ponder your divine plan is to grow in the truth.

Open our eyes to your deeds,
our ears to the sound of your call,
so that our every act may increase our sharing
in the life you have offered us.

FIRST READING

A reading from the first book of Samuel 26:2. 7-9. 12-13. 22-23
The Lord put you in my power, but I would not raise my hand.

Saul set off and went down to the wilderness of Ziph, accompanied by three thousand men chosen from Israel to search for David in the wilderness of Ziph.

So in the dark David and Abishai made their way towards the force, where they found Saul asleep inside the camp, his spear stuck in the ground beside his head, with Abner and the troops lying round him.

Then Abishai said to David, 'Today God has put your enemy in your power; so now let me pin him to the ground with his own spear. Just one stroke! I will not need to strike him twice.' David answered Abishai, 'Do not kill him, for who can lift his hand against the Lord's anointed and be without guilt?' David took the spear and the pitcher of water from beside Saul's head, and they made off. No one saw, no one knew, no one woke up; they were all asleep, for a deep sleep from the Lord had fallen on them.

David crossed to the other side and halted on the top of the mountain a long way off; there was a wide space between them. David then called out, 'Here is the king's spear. Let one of the soldiers come across and take it. The Lord repays everyone for his uprightness and loyalty. Today the Lord put you in my power, but I would not raise my hand against the Lord's anointed.'

This is the word of the Lord.

Responsorial Psalm Ps 102:1-4. 8. 10. 12-13. ℟ v.8
℟ **The Lord is compassion and love.**

1 My soul, give thanks to the Lord,
   all my being, bless his holy name.
   My soul, give thanks to the Lord
   and never forget all his blessings. ℟

2   It is he who forgives all your guilt,
     who heals every one of your ills,
     who redeems your life from the grave,
     who crowns you with love and compassion.

     ℟   **The Lord is compassion and love.**

3   The Lord is compassion and love,
     slow to anger and rich in mercy.
     He does not treat us according to our sins
     nor repay us according to our faults.   ℟

4   As far as the east is from the west
     so far does he remove our sins.
     As a father has compassion on his sons,
     the Lord has pity on those who fear him.   ℟

SECOND READING

A reading from the first letter of St Paul   15:45-49
to the Corinthians
We who have been modelled on the earthly man will be modelled on the heavenly man.

The first man, Adam, as scripture says, became a living soul; but
the last Adam has become a life-giving spirit. That is, first the one
with the soul, not the spirit, and after that, the one with the
spirit. The first man, being from the earth, is earthly by nature;
the second man is from heaven. As this earthly man was, so are
we on earth; and as the heavenly man is, so are we in heaven.
And we, who have been modelled on the earthly man, will be
modelled on the heavenly man.

This is the word of the Lord.

Gospel Acclamation   cf. Acts 16:14
     Alleluia, alleluia!
     Open our heart, O Lord,
     to accept the words of your Son.
     Alleluia!

or   Jn 13:34

     Alleluia, alleluia!
     I give you a new commandment:
     love one another,
     just as I have loved you,
     says the Lord.
     Alleluia!

GOSPEL

A reading from the holy Gospel according to Luke   6:27-38

Be compassionate as your Father is compassionate.

Jesus said to his disciples: 'I say this to you who are listening: Love your enemies, do good to those who hate you, bless those who curse you, pray for those who treat you badly. To the man who slaps you on one cheek, present the other cheek too; to the man who takes your cloak from you, do not refuse your tunic. Give to everyone who asks you, and do not ask for your property back from the man who robs you. Treat others as you would like them to treat you. If you love those who love you, what thanks can you expect? Even sinners love those who love them. And if you do good to those who do good to you, what thanks can you expect? For even sinners do that much. And if you lend to those from whom you hope to receive, what thanks can you expect? Even sinners lend to sinners to get back the same amount. Instead, love your enemies and do good, and lend without any hope of return. You will have a great reward, and you will be sons of the Most High, for he himself is kind to the ungrateful and the wicked.

'Be compassionate as your Father is compassionate. Do not judge, and you will not be judged yourselves; do not condemn, and you will not be condemned yourselves; grant pardon, and you will be pardoned. Give, and there will be gifts for you: a full measure, pressed down, shaken together, and running over, will be poured into your lap; because the amount you measure out is the amount you will be given back.'

This is the Gospel of the Lord.

Prayer over the Gifts
Lord,
we make this offering,
may our worship in Spirit and truth
bring us salvation.

Preface of Sundays in Ordinary Time I-VIII, P29-P36

Communion Antiphon: I will tell all your marvellous works. I will rejoice and be glad in you, and sing to your name, Most High.

or

Lord, I believe that you are the Christ, the Son of God, who was to come into this world.

Prayer after Communion
Almighty God,
help us to live the example of love
we celebrate in this eucharist,
that we may come to its fulfilment in your presence.

EIGHTH SUNDAY IN ORDINARY TIME   C

Praise And Thanksgiving

*Today let our hearts be so filled with the joy of the risen Christ that we
can praise and thank him with sincerity and truth.*

Entrance Antiphon: The Lord has been my strength; he has led me
into freedom. He saved me because he loves me.

Opening Prayer
Let us pray
   [that God will bring peace to the world
   and freedom to his Church]

Lord,
guide the course of world events
and give your Church the joy and peace
of serving you in freedom.

or

Let us pray
   [that the peace of Christ
   may find welcome in the world]

Father in heaven,
form in us the likeness of your Son
and deepen his life within us.
Send us as witnesses of gospel joy
into a world of fragile peace and broken promises.
Touch the hearts of all men with your love
that they in turn may love one another.

FIRST READING

A reading from the book of Ecclesiasticus   27:4-7
Do not praise a man before he has spoken.

In a shaken sieve the rubbish is left behind,

so too the defects of a man appear in his talk.
The kiln tests the work of the potter,
the test of a man is in his conversation.
The orchard where the tree grows is judged on the quality of its
    fruit,
similarly a man's words betray what he feels.
Do not praise a man before he has spoken,
since this is the test of men.

This is the word of the Lord.

Responsorial Psalm Ps 91:2-3. 13-16. ℟ cf. v.2
  ℟ **It is good to give you thanks, O Lord.**

1   It is good to give thanks to the Lord
    to make music to your name, O Most High,
    to proclaim your love in the morning
    and your truth in the watches of the night.   ℟

2   The just will flourish like the palm-tree
    and grow like a Lebanon cedar.   ℟

3   Planted in the house of the Lord
    they will flourish in the courts of our God,
    still bearing fruit when they are old,
    still full of sap, still green,
    to proclaim that the Lord is just.
    In him, my rock, there is no wrong.   ℟

SECOND READING

A reading from the first letter of St Paul   15:54-58
to the Corinthians
He has given us the victory through our Lord Jesus Christ.

When this perishable nature has put on imperishability, and
when this mortal nature has put on immortality, then the words
of scripture will come true: Death is swallowed up in victory.
Death, where is your victory? Death, where is your sting? Now
the sting of death is sin, and sin gets its power from the Law. So
let us thank God for giving us the victory through our Lord Jesus
Christ.

Never give in then, my dear brothers, never admit defeat;
keep on working at the Lord's work always, knowing that, in the
Lord, you cannot be labouring in vain.

This is the word of the Lord.

Gospel Acclamation   cf. Acts 16:14
>Alleluia, alleluia!
>Open our hearts, O Lord,
>to accept the words of your Son.
>Alleluia!

or   Phil 2:15-16

>Alleluia, alleluia!
>You will shine in the world like bright stars
>because you are offering it the word of life.
>Alleluia!

GOSPEL

A reading from the holy Gospel according to Luke   6:39-45
A man's words flow out of what fills his heart.

Jesus told a parable to his disciples. 'Can one blind man guide another? Surely both will fall into a pit? The disciple is not superior to his teacher; the fully trained disciple will always be like his teacher. Why do you observe the splinter in your brother's eye and never notice the plank in your own? How can you say to your brother, "Brother, let me take out the splinter that is in your eye," when you cannot see the plank in your own? Hypocrite! Take the plank out of your own eye first, and then you will see clearly enough to take out the splinter that is in your brother's eye.

'There is no sound tree that produces rotten fruit, nor again a rotten tree that produces sound fruit. For every tree can be told by its own fruit; people do not pick figs from thorns, nor gather grapes from brambles. A good man draws what is good from the store of goodness in his heart; a bad man draws what is bad from the store of badness. For a man's words flow out of what fills his heart.'

This is the Gospel of the Lord.

Prayer over the Gifts
God our Creator,
may this bread and wine we offer
as a sign of our love and worship
lead us to salvation.

Preface of Sundays in Ordinary Time I-VIII, P29-P36

Communion Antiphon: I will sing to the Lord for his goodness to me, I will sing the name of the Lord, Most High.

or

I, the Lord, am with you always, until the end of the world.

Prayer after Communion
God of salvation,
may this sacrament which strengthens us here on earth
bring us to eternal life.

NINTH SUNDAY IN ORDINARY TIME   C

The Church For All Men

The Good News is that God loves all men. Any version of it which makes God's love the private possession of a coterie is all wrong. We rejoice today in the healing work of Christ everywhere throughout the world.

Opening Prayer
Let us pray
    [for God's care and protection]

Father,
your love never fails.
Hear our call.
Keep us from danger
and provide for all our needs.
    or

Let us pray
    [for the confidence born of faith]

God our Father,
teach us to cherish the gifts that surround us.
Increase our faith in you
and bring our trust to its promised fulfilment
in the joy of your kingdom.

FIRST READING
A reading from the first book of the Kings   8:41-43
If a foreigner comes, grant all he asks.

Solomon stood before the altar of the Lord and, stretching out his hands towards heaven, said:
    'If a foreigner, not belonging to your people Israel, comes from a distant country for the sake of your name – for men will

hear of your name, of your mighty hand and outstretched arm –
if he comes and prays in this Temple, hear from heaven where
your home is, and grant all the foreigner asks, so that all the
peoples of the earth may come to know your name and, like your
people Israel, revere you, and know that your name is given to
the Temple I have built.'

This is the word of the Lord.

Responsorial Psalm   Ps 116:1-2. ℟ Mk. 16:15

> ℟ **Go out to the whole world
>   and proclaim the Good News.**

or

> ℟ **Alleluia!**

1   O praise the Lord, all you nations,
    acclaim him all you peoples!   ℟

2   Strong is his love for us;
    he is faithful for ever.   ℟

SECOND READING

A reading from the letter of St Paul to the Galatians   1:1-2. 6-10

If I still wanted men's approval, I should not be a servant of Christ.

From Paul to the churches of Galatia, and from all the brothers
who are here with me, an apostle who does not owe his authority
to men or his appointment to any human being but who has been
appointed by Jesus Christ and by God the Father who raised
Jesus from the dead.

I am astonished at the promptness with which you have
turned away from the one who called you and have decided to
follow a different version of the Good News. Not that there can
be more than one Good News; it is merely that some
troublemakers among you want to change the Good News of
Christ; and let me warn you that if anyone preaches a version of
the Good News different from the one we have already preached
to you, whether it be ourselves or an angel from heaven, he is to
be condemned. I am only repeating what we told you before: if
anyone preaches a version of the Good News different from the
one you have already heard, he is to be condemned. So now
whom am I trying to please – man, or God? Would

you say it is men's approval I am looking for? If I still wanted that, I should not be what I am – a servant of Christ.

This is the word of the Lord.

Gospel Acclamation Jn 1:14. 12
Alleluia, alleluia!
The Word was made flesh and lived among us;
to all who did accept him
he gave power to become children of God.
Alleluia!

or Jn 3:16

Alleluia, alleluia!
God loved the world so much
that he gave his only Son
so that everyone who believes in him
may have eternal life.
Alleluia!

GOSPEL

A reading from the holy Gospel according to Luke 7:1-10
Not even in Israel have I found faith like this.

When Jesus had come to the end of all he wanted the people to hear, he went into Capernaum. A centurion there had a servant, a favourite of his, who was sick and near death. Having heard about Jesus he sent some Jewish elders to him to ask him to come and heal his servant. When they came to Jesus they pleaded earnestly with him. 'He deserves this of you,' they said 'because he is friendly towards our people; in fact, he is the one who built the synagogue.' So Jesus went with them, and was not very far from the house when the centurion sent word to him by some friends: 'Sir,' he said 'do not put yourself to trouble; because I am not worthy to have you under my roof; and for this same reason I did not presume to come to you myself; but give the word and let my servant be cured. For I am under authority myself, and have soldiers under me; and I say to one man: Go, and he goes; to another: Come here, and he comes; to my servant: Do this, and he does it.' When Jesus heard these words he was astonished at him and, turning round, said to the crowd following him, 'I tell you, not even in Israel have I found faith like this.' And when the messengers got back to the house they found the servant in perfect health.

This is the Gospel of the Lord.

Prayer over the Gifts

Lord,
as we gather to offer our gifts
confident in your love,
make us holy by sharing your life with us
and by this eucharist forgive our sins.
Preface of Sundays in Ordinary Time I-VIII, P29-P36

Communion Antiphon: I call upon you, God, for you will answer
me; bend your ear and hear my prayer.
or

I tell you solemnly, whatever you ask for in prayer, believe that
you have received it, and it will be yours, says the Lord.

Prayer after Communion

Lord,
as you give us the body and blood of your Son,
guide us with your Spirit
that we may honour you
not only with our lips,
but also with the lives we lead,
and so enter your kingdom.

TENTH SUNDAY IN ORDINARY TIME   C

Christ Who Restores Us To Life

*Every conversion, like St Paul's for example, is a raising to new life. It is
like Christ saying to our mother, the Church, 'Look, your son is alive
again,' and 'her mourning is changed into dancing'.*

Entrance Antiphon: The Lord is my light and my salvation. Who
shall frighten me? The Lord is the defender of my life. Who shall
make me tremble?

Opening Prayer

Let us pray
    [for the guidance of the Holy Spirit]

God of wisdom and love,
source of all good,
send your Spirit to teach us your truth
and guide our actions

in your way of peace.

or

Let us pray
    [to our Father
    who calls us to freedom in Jesus his Son]

Father in heaven,
words cannot measure the boundaries of love
for those born to new life in Christ Jesus.
Raise us beyond the limits this world imposes,
so that we may be free to love as Christ teaches
and find our joy in your glory.

FIRST READING

A reading from the first book of the Kings   17:17-24
Look, your son is alive.

The son of the mistress of the house fell sick; his illness was so severe that in the end he had no breath left in him. And the woman said to Elijah, 'What quarrel have you with me, man of God? Have you come here to bring my sins home to me and to kill my son?' 'Give me your son,' he said, and taking him from her lap, carried him to the upper room where he was staying and laid him on his own bed. He cried out to the Lord, 'Lord my God, do you mean to bring grief to the widow who is looking after me by killing her son?' He stretched himself on the child three times and cried out to the Lord, 'Lord my God, may the soul of this child, I beg you, come into him again!' The Lord heard the prayer of Elijah and the soul of the child returned to him again and he revived. Elijah took the child, brought him down from the upper room into the house, and gave him to his mother. 'Look,' Elijah said 'your son is alive.' And the woman replied, 'Now I know you are a man of God and the word of the Lord in your mouth is truth itself.'

This is the word of the Lord.

Responsorial Psalm   Ps 29:2. 4-6. 11-13. ℟ v.2
    ℟ **I will praise you, Lord,
        you have rescued me.**

1   I will praise you, Lord, you have rescued me
     and have not let my enemies rejoice over me.
     O Lord, you have raised my soul from the dead,
     restored me to life from those who sink into the grave.   ℟

2 Sing psalms to the Lord, you who love him,
   give thanks to his holy name.
   His anger lasts a moment; his favour through life.
   At night there are tears, but joy comes with dawn.

   ℟ **I will praise you, Lord,
      you have rescued me.**

3 The Lord listened and had pity.
   The Lord came to my help.
   For me you have changed my mourning into dancing;
   O Lord my God, I will thank you for ever. ℟

SECOND READING

A reading from the letter of St Paul to the Galatians 1:11-19

God revealed his Son to me, so that I might preach the Good News about him to the pagans.

The Good News I preached is not a human message that I was given by men, it is something I learnt only through a revelation of Jesus Christ. You must have heard of my career as a practising Jew, how merciless I was in persecuting the Church of God, how much damage I did to it, how I stood out among other Jews of my generation, and how enthusiastic I was for the traditions of my ancestors.

Then God, who had specially chosen me while I was still in my mother's womb, called me through his grace and chose to reveal his Son in me, so that I might preach the Good News about him to the pagans. I did not stop to discuss this with any human being, nor did I go up to Jerusalem to see those who were already apostles before me, but I went off to Arabia at once and later went straight back from there to Damascus. Even when after three years I went up to Jerusalem to visit Cephas and stayed with him for fifteen days, I did not see any of the other apostles; I only saw James, the brother of the Lord.

This is the word of the Lord.

Gospel Acclamation   cf. Eph 1:17. 18
   Alleluia, alleluia!
   May the Father of our Lord Jesus Christ
   enlighten the eyes of our mind,
   so that we can see what hope his call holds for us.
   Alleluia!

or   Lk 7:16

Alleluia, alleluia!
A great prophet has appeared among us;
God has visited his people.
Alleluia!

GOSPEL

A reading from the holy Gospel according to Luke   7:11-17
Young man, I tell you to get up.

Jesus went to a town called Nain, accompanied by his disciples
and a great number of people. When he was near the gate of the
town it happened that a dead man was being carried out for
burial, the only son of his mother, and she was a widow. And a
considerable number of the townspeople were with her. When
the Lord saw her he felt sorry for her. 'Do not cry' he said. Then
he went up and put his hand on the bier and the bearers stood
still, and he said, 'Young man, I tell you to get up.' And the dead
man sat up and began to walk, and Jesus gave him to his mother.
Everyone was filled with awe and praised God saying, 'A great
prophet has appeared among us; God has visited his people.'
And this opinion of him spread throughout Judaea and all over
the countryside.

This is the Gospel of the Lord.

Prayer over the Gifts
Lord,
look with love on our service.
Accept the gifts we bring
and help us grow in Christian love.

Preface of Sundays in Ordinary Time I-VIII, P29-P36

Communion Antiphon I can rely on the Lord; I can always turn to
him for shelter. It was he who gave me my freedom. My God,
you are always there to help me!

or

God is love, and he who lives in love, lives in God, and God in
him.

Prayer after Communion
Lord,
may your healing love

turn us from sin
and keep us on the way that leads to you.

ELEVENTH SUNDAY IN ORDINARY TIME   C

The Forgiving Christ

*With David and with Mary of Magdala we celebrate today the for-
giveness of Christ and our faith in the Son of God who loved us and who
sacrificed himself for our sake.*

Entrance Antiphon: Lord, hear my voice when I call to you. You
are my help; do not cast me off, do not desert me, my Saviour
God.

Opening Prayer
Let us pray
    [for the grace to follow Christ more closely]

Almighty God,
our hope and our strength,
without you we falter.
Help us to follow Christ
and to live according to your will.

or

Let us pray
    [to the Father
    whose love gives us strength to follow his Son]

God our Father,
we rejoice in the faith that draws us together,
aware that selfishness can drive us apart.
Let your encouragement be our constant strength.
Keep us one in the love that has sealed our lives,
help us to live as one family
the gospel we profess.

FIRST READING
A reading from the second book of Samuel   12:7-10. 13
The Lord forgives your sin; you are not to die.

Nathan said to David, 'The Lord the God of Israel says this, "I
anointed you king over Israel; I delivered you from the hands of
Saul; I gave your master's house to you, his wives into your arms;

I gave you the House of Israel and of Judah; and if this were not enough, I would add as much again for you. Why have you shown contempt for the Lord, doing what displeases him? You have struck down Uriah the Hittite with the sword, taken his wife for your own, and killed him with the sword of the Ammonites. So now the sword will never be far from your House, since you have shown contempt for me and taken the wife of Uriah the Hittite to be your wife.''′

David said to Nathan, 'I have sinned against the Lord.' Then Nathan said to David, 'The Lord, for his part, forgives your sin; you are not to die.'

This is the word of the Lord.

Responsorial Psalm   Ps 31:1-2. 5. 7. 11. ℟ cf. v.5
   ℟   **Forgive, Lord, the guilt of my sin.**

1   Happy the man whose offence is forgiven
    whose sin is remitted.
    O happy the man to whom the Lord
    imputes no guilt,
    in whose spirit is no guile.   ℟

2   But now I have acknowledged my sins:
    my guilt I did not hide.
    I said: 'I will confess
    my offence to the Lord.'
    And you, Lord, have forgiven
    the guilt of my sin.   ℟

3   You are my hiding place, O Lord;
    you save me from distress.
    You surround me with cries of deliverance.   ℟

4   Rejoice, rejoice in the Lord,
    exult, you just!
    O come, ring out your joy,
    all you upright of heart.   ℟

SECOND READING

A reading from the letter of St Paul to the Galatians   2:16. 19-21
I live now not with my own life but with the life of Christ who lives in me.

We acknowledge that what makes a man righteous is not

obedience to the Law, but faith in Jesus Christ. We had to become believers in Christ Jesus no less than you had, and now we hold that faith in Christ rather than fidelity to the Law is what justifies us, and that no one can be justified by keeping the Law. In other words, through the Law I am dead to the Law, so that now I can live for God. I have been crucified with Christ, and I live now not with my own life but with the life of Christ who lives in me. The life I now live in this body I live in faith: faith in the Son of God who loved me and who sacrificed himself for my sake. I cannot bring myself to give up God's gift: if the Law can justify us, there is no point in the death of Christ.

This is the word of the Lord.

Gospel Acclamation   Jn 14:6
Alleluia, alleluia!
I am the Way, the Truth and the Life, says the Lord;
no one can come to the Father except through me.
Alleluia!

or   1 Jn 4:10

Alleluia, alleluia!
God so loved us when he sent his Son
to be the sacrifice that takes our sins away.
Alleluia!

GOSPEL

A reading from the holy Gospel according to Luke   7:36 – 8:3
Her many sins have been forgiven, or she would not have shown such great love.

*One of the Pharisees invited Jesus to a meal. When he arrived at the Pharisee's house and took his place at table, a woman came in, who had a bad name in the town. She had heard he was dining with the Pharisee and had brought with her an alabaster jar of ointment. She waited behind him at his feet, weeping, and her tears fell on his feet, and she wiped them away with her hair; then she covered his feet with kisses and anointed them with the ointment.

When the Pharisee who had invited him saw this, he said to himself, 'If this man were a prophet, he would know who this woman is that is touching him and what a bad name she has.' Then Jesus took him up and said, 'Simon, I have something to say to you.' 'Speak Master' was the reply. 'There was once a creditor who had two men in his debt; one owed him five hundred denarii, the other fifty. They were unable to pay, so he pardoned them both. Which of them will love him more?' 'The one who was pardoned more, I suppose' answered Simon. Jesus said, 'You are right.'

Then he turned to the woman. 'Simon', he said 'you see this woman? I came into your house, and you poured no water over my feet, but she has poured out her tears over my feet and wiped them away with her hair. You gave me no kiss, but she has been covering my feet with kisses ever since I came in. You did not anoint my head with oil, but she has anointed my feet with ointment. For this reason I tell you that her sins, her many sins, must have been forgiven her, or she would not have shown such great love. It is the man who is forgiven little who shows little love.' Then he said to her, 'Your sins are forgiven.' Those who were with him at table began to say to themselves, 'Who is this man, that he even forgives sins?' But he said to the woman 'Your faith has saved you; go in peace.'*

Now after this he made his way through towns and villages, preaching, and proclaiming the Good News of the kingdom of God. With him went the Twelve, as well as certain women who had been cured of evil spirits and ailments: Mary surnamed the Magdalene, from whom seven demons had gone out, Joanna the wife of Herod's steward Chuza, Susanna, and several others who provided for them out of their own resources.

This is the Gospel of the Lord.

*Shorter Form, verses 36-50, read between *

Prayer over the Gifts
Lord God,
in this bread and wine
you give us food for body and spirit.
May the eucharist renew our strength
and bring us health of mind and body.

Preface of Sundays in Ordinary Time I-VIII, P29-P36

Communion Antiphon: One thing I seek: to dwell in the house of the Lord all the days of my life.

or

Father, keep in your name those you have given me, that they may be one as we are one, says the Lord.

Prayer after Communion
Lord,
may this eucharist
accomplish in your Church
the unity and peace it signifies.

TWELFTH SUNDAY IN ORDINARY TIME　C

The One Whom We Have Pierced

*In today's celebration, with all our differences, we become one as we gaze
in prayer on the Christ we have pierced and who gave his life for our sake.*

Entrance Antiphon: God is the strength of his people. In him, we
his chosen live in safety. Save us, Lord, who share in your life,
and give us your blessing; be our shepherd for ever.

Opening Prayer
Let us pray
　[that we may grow in the love of God]

Father,
guide and protector of your people,
grant us an unfailing respect for your name,
and keep us always in your love.

or

Let us pray
　[to God whose fatherly love keeps us safe]

God of the universe,
we worship you as Lord.
God, ever close to us,
we rejoice to call you Father.
From this world's uncertainty we look to your covenant.
Keep us one in your peace, secure in your love.

FIRST READING

A reading from the prophet Zechariah　　　　12:10-11; 13:1
They will look on the one whom they have pierced.

It is the Lord who speaks: 'Over the House of David and the
citizens of Jerusalem I will pour out a spirit of kindness and
prayer. They will look on the one whom they have pierced; they

will mourn for him as for an only son, and weep for him as people weep for a first-born child. When that day comes, there will be great mourning in Judah, like the mourning of Hadad-rimmon in the plain of Megiddo. When that day comes, a fountain will be opened for the House of David and the citizens of Jerusalem, for sin and impurity.'

This is the word of the Lord.

Responsorial Psalm   Ps 62:2-6. 8-9. ℟ v.2

> ℟ **For you my soul is thirsting,
>   O God, my God.**

1 O God, you are my God, for you I long;
   for you my soul is thirsting.
   My body pines for you
   like a dry, weary land without water.   ℟

2 So I gaze on you in the sanctuary
   to see your strength and your glory.
   For your love is better than life,
   my lips will speak your praise.   ℟

3 So I will bless you all my life,
   in your name I will lift up my hands.
   My soul shall be filled as with a banquet,
   my mouth shall praise you with joy.   ℟

4 For you have been my help;
   in the shadow of your wings I rejoice.
   My soul clings to you;
   your right hand holds me fast.   ℟

SECOND READING

A reading from the letter of St Paul to the Galatians   3:26-29
All baptised in Christ, you have all clothed yourselves in Christ.

You are, all of you, sons of God through faith in Christ Jesus. All baptised in Christ, you have all clothed yourselves in Christ, and there are no more distinctions between Jew and Greek, slave and free, male and female, but all of you are one in Christ Jesus. Merely by belonging to Christ you are the posterity of Abraham, the heirs he was promised.

This is the word of the Lord.

Gospel Acclamation   Jn 8:12
Alleluia, alleluia!
I am the light of the world, says the Lord,
anyone who follows me
will have the light of life.
Alleluia!

or   Jn 10:27

Alleluia, alleluia!
The sheep that belong to me listen to my voice,
says the Lord,
I know them and they follow me.
Alleluia!

GOSPEL

A reading from the holy Gospel according to Luke   9:18-24
*You are the Christ of God. The Son of Man is destined to suffer
grievously.*

One day when Jesus was praying alone in the presence of his
disciples he put this question to them, 'Who do the crowds say I
am?' And they answered, 'John the Baptist; others Elijah; and
others say one of the ancient prophets come back to life.' 'But
you,' he said 'who do you say I am?' It was Peter who spoke up.
'The Christ of God' he said. But he gave them strict orders not to
tell anyone anything about this.

'The Son of Man' he said 'is destined to suffer grievously, to
be rejected by the elders and chief priests and scribes and to be
put to death, and to be raised up on the third day.'

Then to all he said, 'If anyone wants to be a follower of mine,
let him renounce himself and take up his cross every day and
follow me. For anyone who wants to save his life will lose it; but
anyone who loses his life for my sake, that man will save it.'

This is the Gospel of the Lord.

Prayer over the Gifts
Lord,
receive our offering,
and may this sacrifice of praise
purify us in mind and heart
and make us always eager to serve you.

Preface of Sundays in Ordinary Time I-VIII, P29-P36

Communion Antiphon: The eyes of all look to you, O Lord, and you give them food in due season.

or

I am the Good Shepherd; I give my life for my sheep, says the Lord.

Prayer after Communion
Lord,
you give us the body and blood of your Son
to renew your life within us.
In your mercy, assure our redemption
and bring us to the eternal life
we celebrate in this eucharist.

THIRTEENTH SUNDAY IN ORDINARY TIME   C

The Lord We Serve

We acclaim Christ who is more to us than all the world and whose Spirit has made us resolve to follow him wherever he leads us.

Entrance Antiphon: All nations, clap your hands. Shout with a voice of joy to God.

Opening Prayer
Let us pray
    [that Christ may be our light]

Father,
you call your children
to walk in the light of Christ.
Free us from darkness
and keep us in the radiance of your truth.

or

Let us pray
    [for the strength to reject the darkness of sin]

Father in heaven,
the light of Jesus
has scattered the darkness of hatred and sin.
Called to that light
we ask for your guidance.
Form our lives in your truth, our hearts in your love.

FIRST READING

A reading from the first book of the Kings   19:16. 19-21
Elisha rose and followed Elijah.

The Lord said the Elijah: 'Go, you are to anoint Elisha son of
Shaphat, of Abel Meholah, as prophet to succeed you.'

Leaving there, Elijah came on Elisha son of Shaphat as he was
ploughing behind twelve yoke of oxen, he himself being with the
twelfth. Elijah passed near to him and threw his cloak over him.
Elisha left his oxen and ran after Elijah. 'Let me kiss my father
and mother, then I will follow you' he said. Elijah answered, 'Go,
go back; for have I done anything to you?' Elisha turned away,
took the pair of oxen and slaughtered them. He used the plough
for cooking the oxen, then gave to his men, who ate. He then
rose, and followed Elijah and became his servant.

This is the word of the Lord.

Responsorial Psalm   Ps 15:1-2. 5. 7-11. ℟ cf. v.5

℟   **O Lord, it is you who are my portion.**

1   Preserve me, God, I take refuge in you.
I say to the Lord: 'You are my God.'
O Lord, it is you who are my portion and cup;
it is you yourself who are my prize.   ℟

2   I will bless the Lord who gives me counsel,
who even at night directs my heart.
I keep the Lord ever in my sight:
since he is at my right hand, I shall stand firm.   ℟

3   And so my heart rejoices, my soul is glad;
even my body shall rest in safety.
For you will not leave my soul among the dead,
nor let your beloved know decay.   ℟

4   You will show me the path of life,
the fullness of joy in your presence,
at your right hand happiness for ever.   ℟

SECOND READING

A reading from the letter of St Paul to the Galatians   5:1. 13-18
You were called to liberty.

When Christ freed us, he meant us to remain free. Stand firm,
therefore, and do not submit again to the yoke of slavery.

My brothers, you were called, as you know, to liberty; but

be careful, or this liberty will provide an opening for self-indulgence. Serve one another, rather, in works of love, since the whole of the Law is summarised in a single command: Love your neighbour as yourself. If you go snapping at each other and tearing each other to pieces, you had better watch or you will destroy the whole community.

Let me put it like this: if you are guided by the Spirit you will be in no danger of yielding to self-indulgence, since self-indulgence is the opposite of the Spirit, the Spirit is totally against such a thing, and it is precisely because the two are so opposed that you do not always carry out your good intentions. If you are led by the Spirit, no law can touch you.

This is the word of the Lord.

Gospel Acclamation   1 Sam 3:9; Jn 6:68
Alleluia, alleluia!
Speak, Lord, your servant is listening:
you have the message of eternal life.
Alleluia!

GOSPEL

A reading from the holy Gospel according to Luke   9:51-62
Jesus resolutely took the road for Jerusalem. I will follow you wherever you go.

As the time drew near for him to be taken up to heaven, Jesus resolutely took the road for Jerusalem and sent messengers ahead of him. These set out, and they went into a Samaritan village to make preparations for him, but the people would not receive him because he was making for Jerusalem. Seeing this, the disciples James and John said, 'Lord, do you want us to call down fire from heaven to burn them up?' But he turned and rebuked them, and they went off to another village.

As they travelled along they met a man on the road who said to him, 'I will follow you wherever you go.' Jesus answered, 'Foxes have holes and the birds of the air have nests, but the Son of Man has nowhere to lay his head.'

Another to whom he said, 'Follow me,' replied, 'Let me go and bury my father first.' But he answered, 'Leave the dead to bury their dead; your duty is to go and spread the news of the kingdom of God.'

Another said, 'I will follow you, sir, but first let me go and say good-bye to my people at home.' Jesus said to him, 'Once the hand is laid on the plough, no one who looks back is fit for the kingdom of God.'

This is the Gospel of the Lord.

Prayer over the Gifts
Lord God,
through your sacraments
you give us the power of your grace.
May this eucharist
help us to serve you faithfully.

Preface of Sundays in Ordinary Time I-VIII, P29-P36

Communion Antiphon: O, bless the Lord, my soul, and all that is within me bless his holy name.

or

Father, I pray for them: may they be one in us, so that the world may believe it was you who sent me.

Prayer after Communion
Lord,
may this sacrifice and communion
give us a share in your life
and help us bring your love to the world.

FOURTEENTH SUNDAY IN ORDINARY TIME C

Christ Our Peace

The peace of Christ which we celebrate today should leave its mark on us so that we become messengers of peace of all around us.

Entrance Antiphon: Within your temple, we ponder your loving kindness, O God. As your name, so also your praise reaches to the ends of the earth; your right hand is filled with justice.

Opening Prayer
Let us pray
[for forgiveness through the grace of Jesus Christ]

Father,
through the obedience of Jesus,
your servant and your Son,

you raised a fallen world.
Free us from sin
and bring us the joy that lasts for ever.

or

Let us pray
  [for greater willingness
  to serve God and our fellow man]

Father,
in the rising of your Son
death gives birth to new life.
The sufferings he endured restored hope to a fallen world.
Let sin never ensnare us
with empty promises of passing joy.
Make us one with you always,
so that our joy may be holy,
and our love may give life.

FIRST READING

A reading from the prophet Isaiah   66:10-14

Towards her I send flowing peace, like a river.

Rejoice, Jerusalem,
be glad for her, all you who love her!
Rejoice, rejoice for her,
all you who mourned her!

That you may be suckled, filled,
from her consoling breast,
that you may savour with delight
her glorious breasts.

For thus says the Lord:
Now towards her I send flowing
peace, like a river,
and like a stream in spate
the glory of the nations.

At her breast will her nurslings be carried
and fondled in her lap.
Like a son comforted by his mother
will I comfort you.
And by Jerusalem you will be comforted.

At the sight your heart will rejoice,
and your bones flourish like the grass.

To his servants the Lord will reveal his hand.

   This is the word of the Lord.

Responsorial Psalm   Ps 65:1-7. 16. 20. ℟ v.1
   ℟   **Cry out with joy to God all the earth.**

1   Cry out with joy to God all the earth,
     O sing to the glory of his name.
     O render him glorious praise.
     Say to God: 'How tremendous your deeds!   ℟

2   'Before you all the earth shall bow;
     shall sing to you, sing to your name!'
     Come and see the works of God,
     tremendous his deeds among men.   ℟

3   He turned the sea into dry land,
     they passed through the river dry-shod.
     Let our joy then be in him;
     he rules for ever by his might.   ℟

4   Come and hear, all who fear God.
     I will tell what he did for my soul.
     Blessed be God who did not reject my prayer
     nor withhold his love from me.   ℟

SECOND READING

A reading from the letter of St Paul to the Galatians   6:14-18
The marks on my body are those of the Lord Jesus.

The only thing I can boast about is the cross of our Lord Jesus
Christ, through whom the world is crucified to me, and I to the
world. It does not matter if a person is circumcised or not; what
matters is for him to become an altogether new creature. Peace
and mercy to all who follow this rule, who form the Israel of God.

   I want no more trouble from anybody after this; the marks on
my body are those of Jesus. The grace of our Lord Jesus Christ be
with your spirit, my brothers. Amen.

   This is the word of the Lord.

Gospel Acclamation   Jn 15:15
     Alleluia, alleluia!
     I call you friends, says the Lord,
     because I have made known to you

everything I have learnt from my Father.
Alleluia!

or   Col 3:15. 16

Alleluia, alleluia!
May the peace of Christ
reign in your hearts,
because it is for this that you were called together
as parts of one body.
Alleluia!

GOSPEL

A reading from the holy Gospel according to Luke 10:1-12. 17-20
Your peace will rest on that man.

The Lord appointed seventy-two others and sent them out ahead of him, in pairs, to all the towns and places he himself was to visit. He said to them, 'The harvest is rich but the labourers are few, so ask the Lord of the harvest to send labourers to his harvest. Start off now, but remember, I am sending you out like lambs among wolves. Carry no purse, no haversack, no sandals. Salute no one on the road. Whatever house you go into, let your first words be, "Peace to this house!" And if a man of peace lives there, your peace will go and rest on him; if not, it will come back to you. Stay in the same house, taking what food and drink they have to offer, for the labourer deserves his wages; do not move from house to house. Whenever you go into a town where they make you welcome, eat what is set before you. Cure those in it who are sick, and say, "The kingdom of God is very near to you." But whenever you enter a town and they do not make you welcome, go out into its streets and say, "We wipe off the very dust of your town that clings to our feet, and leave it with you. Yet be sure of this: the kingdom of God is very near." I tell you, that on that day it will not go as hard with Sodom as with that town.'

The seventy-two came back rejoicing. 'Lord,' they said 'even the devils submit to us when we use your name.' He said to them, 'I watched Satan fall like lightning from heaven. Yes, I have given you power to tread underfoot serpents and scorpions and the whole strength of the enemy; nothing shall ever hurt you. Yet do not rejoice that the spirits submit to you; rejoice rather that your names are written in heaven.'

This is the Gospel of the Lord.

*Shorter Form, verses 1-9, read between *

Prayer over the Gifts

Lord,
let this offering to the glory of your name
purify us and bring us closer to eternal life.

Preface of Sundays in Ordinary Time I-VIII, P29-P36

Communion Antiphon: Taste and see the goodness of the Lord;
blessed is he who hopes in God.

or

Come to me, all you that labour and are burdened, and I will give
you rest, says the Lord.

Prayer after Communion

Lord,
may we never fail to praise you
for the fullness of life and salvation
you give us in this eucharist.

FIFTEENTH SUNDAY IN ORDINARY TIME   C

His Word Is Near

*We celebrate the nearness of the Lord to us his people. He is the Good
Samaritan who comes close to us and heals us, raising us to life as his
own body.*

Entrance Antiphon: In my justice I shall see your face, O Lord;
when your glory appears, my joy will be full.

Opening Prayer

Let us pray
      [that the gospel may be our rule of life]

God our Father,
your light of truth
guides us to the way of Christ.
May all who follow him
reject what is contrary to the gospel.

or

Let us pray
      [to be faithful to the light we have received,
      to the name we bear]

Father,
let the light of your truth

guide us to your kingdom
through a world filled with lights contrary to your own.
Christian is the name and the gospel we glory in.
May your love make us what you have called us to be.

FIRST READING

A reading from the book of Deuteronomy   30:10-14
The Word is very near to you for your observance.

Moses said to the people: 'Obey the voice of the Lord your God,
keeping those commandments and laws of his that are written in
the Book of this Law, and you shall return to the Lord your God
with all your heart and soul.

'For this Law that I enjoin on you today is not beyond your
strength or beyond your reach. It is not in heaven, so that you
need to wonder, "Who will go up to heaven for us and bring it
down to us, so that we may hear it and keep it?" Nor is it beyond
the seas, so that you need to wonder, "Who will cross the seas
for us and bring it back to us, so that we may hear it and keep it?"
No, the Word is very near to you, it is in your mouth and in your
heart for your observance.'

This is the word of the Lord.

Responsorial Psalm   Ps 68:14. 17. 30-31. 33-34. 36-37. ℟ cf. v.33

℟ **Seek the Lord, you who are poor,**
   and your hearts will revive.

1 This is my prayer to you,
   my prayer for your favour.
   In your great love, answer me, O God,
   with your help that never fails:
   Lord, answer, for your love is kind;
   in your compassion, turn towards me.   ℟

2 As for me in my poverty and pain
   let your help, O God, lift me up.
   I will praise God's name with a song;
   I will glorify him with thanksgiving.   ℟

3 The poor when they see it will be glad
   and God-seeking hearts will revive;
   for the Lord listens to the needy
   and does not spurn his servants in their chains.   ℟

4 For God will bring help to Zion
   and rebuild the cities of Judah.

(continued)

The sons of his servants shall inherit it;
those who love his name shall dwell there.

℟ **Seek the Lord, you who are poor,
and your hearts will revive.**

Alternative Responsorial Psalm   Ps 18:8-11. ℟ v.9

℟ **The precepts of the Lord
gladden the heart.**

1 The law of the Lord is perfect,
    it revives the soul.
    The rule of the Lord is to be trusted,
    it gives wisdom to the simple. ℟

2 The precepts of the Lord are right,
    they gladden the heart.
    The command of the Lord is clear,
    it gives light to the eyes. ℟

3 The fear of the Lord is holy,
    abiding for ever.
    The decrees of the Lord are truth
    and all of them just. ℟

4 They are more to be desired than gold,
    than the purest of gold
    and sweeter are they than honey,
    than honey from the comb. ℟

SECOND READING

A reading from the letter of St Paul to the Colossians   1:15-20

All things were created through Christ and for him.

Christ Jesus is the image of the unseen God
and the first-born of all creation,
for in him were created
all things in heaven and on earth:
everything visible and everything invisible,
Thrones, Dominations, Sovereignties, Powers –
all things were created through him and for him.
Before anything was created, he existed,
and he holds all things in unity.
Now the Church is his body,

he is its head.
As he is the Beginning,
he was first to be born from the dead,
so that he should be first in every way;
because God wanted all perfection
to be found in him
and all things to be reconciled through him and for him,
everything in heaven and everything on earth,
when he made peace
by his death on the cross.

This is the word of the Lord.

Gospel Acclamation   Jn 10:27
Alleluia, alleluia!
The sheep that belong to me listen to my voice,
says the Lord,
I know them and they follow me.
Alleluia!

or   cf. Jn 6:63. 68

Alleluia, alleluia!
Your words are spirit, Lord,
and they are life:
you have the message of eternal life.
Alleluia!

GOSPEL
A reading from the holy Gospel according to Luke   10:25-37
Who is my neighbour?

There was a lawyer who, to disconcert Jesus, stood up and said
to him, 'Master, what must I do to inherit eternal life?' He said to
him, 'What is written in the law? What do you read there?' He
replied, 'You must love the Lord your God with all your heart,
with all your soul, with all your strength, and with all your mind,
and your neighbour as yourself.' 'You have answered right,' said
Jesus, 'do this and life is yours.'

But the man was anxious to justify himself and said to Jesus,
'And who is my neighbour?' Jesus replied, 'A man was once on
his way down from Jerusalem to Jericho and fell into the hands of
brigands; they took all he had, beat him and then made off,
leaving him half dead. Now a priest happened to be travelling
down the same road, but when he saw the man, he passed by on
the other side. In the same way a Levite who came to the place

saw him, and passed by on the other side. But a Samaritan traveller who came upon him was moved with compassion when he saw him. He went up and bandaged his wounds, pouring oil and wine on them. He then lifted him on to his own mount, carried him to the inn and looked after him. Next day, he took out two denarii and handed them to the innkeeper. "Look after him," he said "and on my way back I will make good any extra expense you have." Which of these three, do you think, proved himself a neighbour to the man who fell into the brigands' hands?' 'The one, who took pity on him' he replied. Jesus said to him, 'Go, and do the same yourself.'

This is the Gospel of the Lord.

Prayer over the Gifts
Lord,
accept the gifts of your Church.
May this eucharist
help us grow in holiness and faith.

Preface of Sundays in Ordinary Time I-VIII, P29-P36

Communion Antiphon: The sparrow even finds a home, the swallow finds a nest wherein to place her young, near to your altars, Lord of hosts, my King, my God! How happy they who dwell in your house! For ever they are praising you.

or

Whoever eats my flesh and drinks my blood will live in me and I in him, says the Lord.

Prayer after Communion
Lord,
by our sharing in the mystery of this eucharist,
let your saving love grow within us.

SIXTEENTH SUNDAY IN ORDINARY TIME   C

Jesus Our Friend

The mystery of today's celebration is Christ among us as our friend. We welcome him as Abraham welcomed the Lord at Mamre, and Martha and Mary welcomed Christ at Bethany.

Entrance Antiphon: God himself is my help. The Lord upholds my life. I will offer you a willing sacrifice; I will praise your name, O Lord, for its goodness.

Opening Prayer
Let us pray
[to be kept faithful in the service of God]

Lord,
be merciful to your people.
Fill us with your gifts
and make us always eager to serve you
in faith, hope, and love.

or

Let us pray
[that God will continue to bless us
with his compassion and love]

Father,
let the gift of your life
continue to grow in us,
drawing us from death to faith, hope, and love.
Keep us alive in Christ Jesus.
Keep us watchful in prayer
and true to his teaching
till your glory is revealed in us.

FIRST READING

A reading from the book of Genesis   18:1-10
Lord, do not pass your servant by.

The Lord appeared to Abraham at the Oak of Mamre while he was sitting by the entrance of the tent during the hottest part of the day. He looked up, and there he saw three men standing near him. As soon as he saw them he ran from the entrance of the tent to meet them, and bowed to the ground. 'My Lord,' he said 'I beg you, if I find favour with you, kindly do not pass your servant by. A little water shall be brought; you shall wash your feet and lie down under the tree. Let me fetch a little bread and you shall refresh yourselves before going further. That is why you have come in your servant's direction.' They replied, 'Do as you say.'

Abraham hastened to the tent to find Sarah. 'Hurry,' he said 'knead three bushels of flour and make loaves.' Then running to the cattle Abraham took a fine and tender calf and gave it to the servant, who hurried to prepare it. Then taking cream, milk and the calf he had prepared, he laid all before them, and they ate while he remained standing near them under the tree.

'Where is your wife Sarah?' they asked him. 'She is in the tent' he replied. Then his guest said, 'I shall visit you again next year without fail and your wife will then have a son.'

This is the word of the Lord.

Responsorial Psalm   Ps 14:2-5. ℟ v.1
   ℟   **The just will live in the presence of the Lord.**

1   Lord, who shall dwell on your holy mountain?
      He who walks without fault;
      he who acts with justice
      and speaks the truth from his heart;
      he who does not slander with his tongue.   ℟

2   He who does no wrong to his brother,
      who casts no slur on his neighbour,
      who holds the godless in disdain,
      but honours those who fear the Lord.   ℟

3   He who keeps his pledge, come what may;
      who takes no interest on a loan
      and accepts no bribes against the innocent.
      Such a man will stand firm for ever.   ℟

SECOND READING

A reading from the letter of St Paul to the Colossians   1:24-28
A mystery hidden for centuries has now been revealed to God's saints.

It makes me happy to suffer for you, as I am suffering now, and in my body to do what I can to make up all that has still to be undergone by Christ for the sake of his body, the Church. I became the servant of the Church when God made me responsible for delivering God's message to you, the message which was a mystery hidden for generations and centuries and has now been revealed to his saints. It was God's purpose to reveal it to them and to show all the rich glory of this mystery to pagans. The mystery is Christ among you, your hope of glory: this is the Christ we proclaim, this is the wisdom in which we thoroughly train everyone and instruct everyone, to make them all perfect in Christ.

This is the word of the Lord.

Gospel Acclamation cf. Acts 16:14

Alleluia, alleluia!
Open our heart, O Lord,
to accept the words of your Son.
Alleluia!

or cf. Lk 8:15

Alleluia, alleluia!
Blessed are those who,
with a noble and generous heart,
take the word of God to themselves
and yield a harvest through their perseverance.
Alleluia!

GOSPEL

A reading from the holy Gospel according to Luke 10:38-42
Martha welcomed Jesus into her house. Mary has chosen the better part.

Jesus came to a village, and a woman named Martha welcomed him into her house. She had a sister called Mary, who sat down at the Lord's feet and listened to him speaking. Now Martha who was distracted with all the serving said, 'Lord, do you not care that my sister is leaving me to do the serving all by myself? Please tell her to help me.' But the Lord answered: 'Martha, Martha,' he said 'you worry and fret about so many things, and yet few are needed, indeed only one. It is Mary who has chosen the better part; it is not to be taken from her.'

This is the Gospel of the Lord.

Prayer over the Gifts
Lord,
bring us closer to salvation
through these gifts which we bring in your honour.
Accept the perfect sacrifice you have given us,
bless it as you blessed the gifts of Abel.

Preface of Sundays in Ordinary Time I-VIII, P29-P36

Communion Antiphon: The Lord keeps in our minds the wonderful things he has done. He is compassion and love; he always provides for his faithful.

or

I stand at the door and knock, says the Lord. If anyone hears my voice and opens the door, I will come in and sit down to supper with him, and he with me.

Prayer after Communion
Merciful Father,
may these mysteries
give us new purpose
and bring us to a new life in you.

SEVENTEENTH SUNDAY IN ORDINARY TIME C

Our Father In Heaven

Christ has given us in very truth the power to become the children of God. Compare the timidity and self-abnegation of Abraham's prayer with the confidence with which Christ teaches us to pray to our Father in heaven.

Entrance Antiphon: God is in his holy dwelling; he will give a home to the lonely, he gives power and strength to his people.

Opening Prayer
Let us pray
   [that we will make good use of the gifts
   that God has given us]

God our Father and protector,
without you nothing is holy,
nothing has value.
Guide us to everlasting life
by helping us to use wisely
the blessings you have given to the world.

or

Let us pray
   [for the faith to recognise God's presence in our world]

God our Father,
open our eyes to see your hand at work
in the splendour of creation,
in the beauty of human life.
Touched by your hand our world is holy.
Help us to cherish the gifts that surround us,
to share your blessings with our brothers and sisters,
and to experience the joy of life in your presence.

FIRST READING

A reading from the book of Genesis   18:20-32

I trust my Lord will not be angry, but give me leave to speak.

The Lord said, 'How great an outcry there is against Sodom and Gomorrah! How grievous is their sin! I propose to go down and see whether or not they have done all that is alleged in the outcry against them that has come up to me. I am determined to know.'

The men left there and went to Sodom while Abraham remained standing before the Lord. Approaching him he said, 'Are you really going to destroy the just man with the sinner? Perhaps there are fifty just men in the town. Will you really overwhelm them, will you not spare the place for the fifty just men in it? Do not think of doing such a thing: to kill the just man with the sinner, treating just and sinner alike! Do not think of it! Will the judge of the whole earth not administer justice?' The Lord replied, 'If at Sodom I find fifty just men in the town, I will spare the whole place because of them.'

Abraham replied, 'I am bold indeed to speak like this to my Lord, I who am dust and ashes. But perhaps the fifty just men lack five: will you destroy the whole city for five?' 'No,' he replied, 'I will not destroy it if I find forty-five just men there.' Again Abraham said to him, 'Perhaps there will only be forty there.' 'I will not do it' he replied 'for the sake of the forty.'

Abraham said, 'I trust my Lord will not be angry, but give me leave to speak: perhaps there will only be thirty there.' 'I will not do it' he replied 'if I find thirty there.' He said, 'I am bold indeed to speak like this, but perhaps there will only be twenty there.' 'I will not destroy it' he replied 'for the sake of the twenty.' He said, 'I trust my Lord will not be angry if I speak once more: perhaps there will only be ten.' 'I will not destroy it' he replied 'for the sake of the ten.'

This is the word of the Lord.

Responsorial Psalm   Ps 137:1-3. 6-8. R℣ v.3

R℣ **On the day I called,
you answered me, O Lord.**

1   I thank you, Lord, with all my heart,
    you have heard the words of my mouth.
    Before the angels I will bless you.
    I will adore before your holy temple.   R℣

2   I thank you for your faithfulness and love
    which excel all we ever knew of you.
    On the day I called, you answered;
    you increased the strength of my soul.

℟   **On the day I called,**
    you answered me, O Lord.

3   The Lord is high yet he looks on the lowly
    and the haughty he knows from afar.
    Though I walk in the midst of affliction
    you give me life and frustrate my foes.   ℟

4   You stretch out your hand and save me,
    your hand will do all things for me.
    Your love, O Lord, is eternal,
    discard not the work of your hands.   ℟

SECOND READING

A reading from the letter of St Paul to the Colossians   2:12-14
He has brought you to life with him, he has forgiven us all our sins.

You have been buried with Christ, when you were baptised; and
by baptism, too, you have been raised up with him through your
belief in the power of God who raised him from the dead. You
were dead, because you were sinners and had not been circumcised: he has brought you to life with him, he has forgiven us all
our sins.

He has overridden the Law, and cancelled every record of the
debt that we had to pay; he has done away with it by nailing it to
the cross.

This is the word of the Lord.

Gospel Acclamation   Jn 1:14, 12
    Alleluia, alleluia!
    The Word was made flesh and lived among us;
    to all who did accept him
    he gave power to become children of God.
    Alleluia!

or   Rom 8:15

    Alleluia, alleluia!
    The spirit you received is the spirit of sons,
    and it makes us cry out, 'Abba, Father!'
    Alleluia!

GOSPEL

A reading from the holy Gospel according to Luke   11:1-13

Ask, and it will be given to you.

Once Jesus was in a certain place praying, and when he had finished, one of his disciples said, 'Lord, teach us to pray, just as John taught his disciples.' He said to them, 'Say this when you pray:

"Father, may your name be held holy,
your kingdom come;
give us each day our daily bread,
and forgive us our sins,
for we ourselves forgive each one who is in debt to us.
And do not put us to the test." '

He also said to them, 'Suppose one of you has a friend and goes to him in the middle of the night to say, "My friend, lend me three loaves because a friend of mine on his travels has just arrived at my house and I have nothing to offer him"; and the man answers from inside the house, "Do not bother me. The door is bolted now, and my children and I are in bed; I cannot get up to give it to you," I tell you, if the man does not get up and give it him for friendship's sake, persistence will be enough to make him get up and give his friend all he wants.

'So I say to you: Ask, and it will be given to you; search, and you will find; knock, and the door will be opened to you. For the one who asks always receives; the one who searches always finds; the one who knocks will always have the door opened to him. What father among you would hand his son a stone when he asked for bread? Or hand him a snake instead of a fish? Or hand him a scorpion if he asked for an egg? If you then, who are evil, know how to give your children what is good, how much more will the heavenly Father give the Holy Spirit to those who ask him!'

This is the Gospel of the Lord.

Prayer over the Gifts
Lord,
receive these offerings
chosen from your many gifts.
May these mysteries make us holy
and lead us to eternal joy.

Preface of Sundays in Ordinary Time I-VIII, P29-P36

Communion Antiphon: O, bless the Lord, my soul, and remember all his kindness.

or

Happy are those who show mercy; mercy shall be theirs. Happy are the pure of heart, for they shall see God.

Prayer after Communion
Lord,
we receive the sacrament
which celebrates the memory
of the death and resurrection of Christ your Son.
May this gift bring us closer to our eternal salvation.

EIGHTEENTH SUNDAY IN ORDINARY TIME   C

Christ Who Is Everything And In Everything

Today our thoughts are on heavenly things, not on the things of earth where without Christ all is vanity and great injustice.

Entrance Antiphon: God, come to my help. Lord, quickly give me assistance. You are the one who helps me and sets me free: Lord, do not be long in coming.

Opening Prayer
Let us pray
  [for the gift of God's forgiveness and love]

Father of everlasting goodness,
our origin and guide,
be close to us
and hear the prayers of all who praise you.
Forgive our sins and restore us to life.
Keep us safe in your love.

or

Let us pray
  [to the Father whose kindness never fails]

God our Father,
gifts without measure flow from your goodness
to bring us your peace.
Our life is your gift.
Guide our life's journey,

for only your love makes us whole.
Keep us strong in your love.

FIRST READING

A reading from the book of Ecclesiastes 1:2; 2:21-23
What does a man gain for all his toil?

Vanity of vanities, the Preacher says. Vanity of vanities. All is vanity!

For so it is that a man who has laboured wisely, skilfully and successfully must leave what is his own to someone who has not toiled for it at all. This, too, is vanity and great injustice; for what does he gain for all the toil and strain that he has undergone under the sun? What of all his laborious days, his cares of office, his restless nights? This, too, is vanity.

This is the word of the Lord.

Responsorial Psalm Ps 89:3-6. 12-14. 17. ℟ v. 1

℟ **O Lord, you have been our refuge**
from one generation to the next.

1 You turn men back into dust
and say: 'Go back, sons of men.'
To your eyes a thousand years
are like yesterday, come and gone,
no more than a watch in the night. ℟

2 You sweep men away like a dream,
like grass which springs up in the morning.
In the morning it springs up and flowers:
by evening it withers and fades. ℟

3 Make us know the shortness of our life
that we may gain wisdom of heart.
Lord, relent! Is your anger for ever?
Show pity to your servants. ℟

4 In the morning, fill us with your love;
we shall exult and rejoice all our days.
Let the favour of the Lord be upon us:
give success to the work of our hands. ℟

Alternative Responsorial Psalm　　　Ps 94:1-2. 6-9. ℟ vv. 7-8

> ℟　**O that today you would listen to his voice!**
> **Harden not your hearts.**

1　Come, ring out our joy to the Lord;
　hail the rock who saves us.
　Let us come before him, giving thanks,
　with songs let us hail the Lord.　℟

2　Come in; let us bow and bend low;
　let us kneel before the God who made us
　for he is our God and we
　the people who belong to his pasture,
　the flock that is led by his hand.　℟

3　O that today you would listen to his voice!
　'Harden not your hearts at Meribah,
　as on that day at Massah in the desert
　when your fathers put me to the test;
　when they tried me, though they saw my work.'　℟

SECOND READING

A reading from the letter of St Paul to the Colossians　3:1-5. 9-11
You must look for the things that are in heaven, where Christ is.

Since you have been brought back to true life with Christ, you must look for the things that are in heaven, where Christ is, sitting at God's right hand. Let your thoughts be on heavenly things, not on the things that are on the earth, because you have died, and now the life you have is hidden with Christ in God. But when Christ is revealed – and he is your life – you too will be revealed in all your glory with him.

That is why you must kill everything in you that belongs only to earthly life: fornication, impurity, guilty passion, evil desires and especially greed, which is the same thing as worshipping a false god; and never tell each other lies. You have stripped off your old behaviour with your old self, and you have put on a new self which will progress towards true knowledge the more it is renewed in the image of its creator; and in that image there is no room for distinction between Greek and Jew, between the circumcised or the uncircum cised, or between barbarian and Scythian, slave and free man. There is only Christ: he is every-thing and he is in everything.

This is the word of the Lord.

Gospel Acclamation   cf. Jn 17:17
    Alleluia, alleluia!
    Your word is truth, O Lord,
    consecrate us in the truth.
    Alleluia!

or   Mt 5:3

    Alleluia, alleluia!
    How happy are the poor in spirit;
    theirs is the kingdom of heaven.
    Alleluia!

GOSPEL

A reading from the holy Gospel according to Luke   12:13-21
This hoard of yours, whose will it be?

A man in the crowd said to Jesus, 'Master, tell my brother to give
me a share of our inheritance.' 'My friend,' he replied 'who
appointed me your judge, or the arbitrator of your claims?' Then
he said to them, 'Watch, and be on your guard against avarice of
any kind, for a man's life is not made secure by what he owns,
even when he has more than he needs.'

    Then he told them a parable: 'There was once a rich man who,
having had a good harvest from his land, thought to himself,
"What am I to do? I have not enough room to store my crops."
Then he said, "This is what I will do: I will pull down my barns
and build bigger ones, and store all my grain and my goods in
them, and I will say to my soul: My soul, you have plenty of good
things laid by for many years to come; take things easy, eat,
drink, have a good time." But God said to him, "Fool! This very
night the demand will be made for your soul; and this hoard of
yours, whose will it be then?" So it is when a man stores up
treasure for himself in place of making himself rich in the sight of
God.'

    This is the Gospel of the Lord.

Prayer over the Gifts
Merciful Lord,
make holy these gifts,
and let our spiritual sacrifice
make us an everlasting gift to you.

Preface of Sundays in Ordinary Time I-VIII, P29-P36

Communion Antiphon: You gave us bread from heaven, Lord: a sweet-tasting bread that was very good to eat.

or

The Lord says: I am the bread of life. A man who comes to me will not go away hungry, and no one who believes in me will thirst.

Prayer after Communion
Lord,
you give us the strength of new life
by the gift of the eucharist.
Protect us with your love
and prepare us for eternal redemption.

NINETEENTH SUNDAY IN ORDINARY TIME   C

The Lord Our God

The Lord has chosen us to be his people. Though a little flock, our history goes back into the dim and distant past. The God we worship is the God of Abraham, Isaac and Jacob. We also look forward in hope to a glorious future in the Kingdom of our Father.

Entrance Antiphon: Lord, be true to your covenant, forget not the life of your poor ones for ever. Rise up, O God, and defend your cause; do not ignore the shouts of your enemies.

Opening Prayer
Let us pray
    [in the Spirit
    that we may grow in the love of God]

Almighty and ever-living God,
your Spirit made us your children,
confident to call you Father.
Increase your Spirit within us
and bring us to our promised inheritance.

    or

Let us pray
    [that through us
    others may find the way to life in Christ]

Father,
we come, reborn in the Spirit,
to celebrate our sonship in the Lord Jesus Christ.
Touch our hearts,
help them grow toward the life you have promised.
Touch our lives,
make them signs of your love for all men.

FIRST READING

A reading from the book of Wisdom   18:6-9

By the same act with which you took vengeance on our foes you made us glorious by calling us to you.

That night had been foretold to our ancestors, so that,
once they saw what kind of oaths they had put their trust in
they would joyfully take courage.
This was the expectation of your people,
the saving of the virtuous and the ruin of their enemies;
for by the same act with which you took vengeance on our foes
you made us glorious by calling us to you.
The devout children of worthy men offered sacrifice in secret
and this divine pact they struck with one accord:
that the saints would share the same blessings and dangers alike;
and forthwith they had begun to chant the hymns of the fathers.

This is the word of the Lord.

Responsorial Psalm   Ps 32:1. 12. 18-20. 22. ℟ v.12

℟ **Happy are the people the Lord has chosen as his own.**

1 Ring out your joy to the Lord, O you just;
   for praise is fitting for loyal hearts.
   They are happy, whose God is the Lord,
   the people he has chosen as his own. ℟

2 The Lord looks on those who revere him,
   on those who hope in his love,
   to rescue their souls from death,
   to keep them alive in famine. ℟

3 Our soul is waiting for the Lord.
   The Lord is our help and our shield.
   May your love be upon us, O Lord,
   as we place all our hope in you. ℟

SECOND READING

A reading from the letter to the Hebrews   11:1-2. 8-19

Abraham looked forward to a city founded, designed and built by God.

*Only faith can guarantee the blessings that we hope for, or prove the existence of the realities that at present remain unseen. It was for faith that our ancestors were commended.

It was by faith that Abraham obeyed the call to set out for a country that was the inheritance given to him and his descendants, and that he set out without knowing where he was going. By faith he arrived, as a foreigner, in the Promised Land, and lived there as if in a strange country, with Isaac and Jacob, who were heirs with him of the same promise. They lived there in tents while he looked forward to a city founded, designed and built by God.

It was equally by faith that Sarah, in spite of being past the age, was made able to conceive, because she believed that he who had made the promise would be faithful to it. Because of this, there came from one man, and one who was already as good as dead himself, more descendants than could be counted, as many as the stars of heaven or the grains of sand on the seashore.*

All these died in faith, before receiving any of the things that had been promised, but they saw them in the far distance and welcomed them, recognising that they were only strangers and nomads on earth. People who use such terms about themselves make it quite plain that they are in search of their real homeland. They can hardly have meant the country they came from, since they had the opportunity to go back to it; but in fact they were longing for a better homeland, their heavenly homeland. That is why God is not ashamed to be called their God, since he has founded the city for them.

It was by faith that Abraham, when put to the test, offered up Isaac. He offered to sacrifice his only son even though the promises had been made to him and he had been told: It is through Isaac that your name will be carried on. He was confident that God had the power even to raise the dead; and so, figuratively speaking, he was given back Isaac from the dead.

This is the word of the Lord.

*Shorter Form, verses 1-2, 8-12. Read between *

Gospel Acclamation   cf. Mt 11:25
    Alleluia, alleluia!
    Blessed are you, Father,
    Lord of heaven and earth,
    for revealing the mysteries of the kingdom
    to mere children.
    Alleluia!

or   Mt 24:42. 44

    Alleluia, alleluia!
    Stay awake and stand ready,
    because you do not know the hour
    when the Son of Man is coming.
    Alleluia!

GOSPEL

A reading from the holy Gospel according to Luke   12:32-48
You too must stand ready.

Jesus said to his disciples: 'There is no need to be afraid, little
flock, for it has pleased your Father to give you the kingdom.

'Sell your possessions and give alms. Get yourselves purses
that do not wear out, treasure that will not fail you, in heaven
where no thief can reach it and no moth destroy it. For where
your treasure is, there will your heart be also.

*'See that you are dressed for action and have your lamps lit.
Be like men waiting for their master to return from the wedding
feast, ready to open the door as soon as he comes and knocks.
Happy those servants whom the master finds awake when he
comes. I tell you solemnly, he will put on an apron, sit them
down at table and wait on them. It may be in the second watch he
comes, or in the third, but happy those servants if he finds them
ready. You may be quite sure of this, that if the householder had
known at what hour the burglar would come, he would not have
let anyone break through the wall of his house. You too must
stand ready, because the Son of Man is coming at an hour you do
not expect.*

Peter said, 'Lord, do you mean this parable for us, or for
everyone?' The Lord replied, 'What sort of steward, then, is
faithful and wise enough for the master to place him over his
household to give them their allowance of food at the proper
time? Happy that servant if his master's arrival finds him at this
employment. I tell you truly, he will place him over everything

he owns. But as for the servant who says to himself, "My master is taking his time coming", and sets about beating the menservants and the maids, and eating and drinking and getting drunk, his master will come on a day he does not expect and at an hour he does not know. The master will cut him off and send him to the same fate as the unfaithful.

'The servant who knows what his master wants, but has not even started to carry out those wishes, will receive very many strokes of the lash. The one who did not know, but deserves to be beaten for what he has done, will receive fewer strokes. When a man has had a great deal given him, a great deal will be demanded of him; when a man has had a great deal given him on trust, even more will be expected of him.'

This is the Gospel of the Lord.

*Shorter Form, verses 35-40. Read between *

Prayer over the Gifts
God of power,
giver of the gifts we bring,
accept the offering of your Church
and make it the sacrament of our salvation.

Preface of Sundays in Ordinary Time I-VIII, P29-P36

Communion Antiphon: Praise the Lord, Jerusalem; he feeds you with the finest wheat.

or

The bread I shall give is my flesh for the life of the world, says the Lord.

Prayer after Communion
Lord,
may the eucharist you give us
bring us to salvation
and keep us faithful to the light of your truth.

TWENTIETH SUNDAY IN ORDINARY TIME   C

Victory With Christ

Today's celebration should raise our morale in the fight against evil. Christ our Leader, who came to bring fire on the earth, communicates to us something of his tremendous zeal.

Entrance Antiphon: God, our protector, keep us in mind; always give strength to your people. For if we can be with you even one day, it is better than a thousand without you.

Opening Prayer
Let us pray
    [that the love of God
    may raise us beyond what we see
    to the unseen glory of his kingdom]

God our Father,
may we love you in all things and above all things
and reach the joy you have prepared for us
beyond all our imagining.

or

Let us pray
    [with humility and persistence]

Almighty God, ever-loving Father,
your care extends beyond the boundaries of race and nation
to the hearts of all who live.

May the walls, which prejudice raises between us,
crumble beneath the shadow of your outstretched arm.

FIRST READING

A reading from the prophet Jeremiah   38:4-6. 8-10
You have borne me to be a man of dissension for all the land.

The king's leading men spoke to the king. 'Let Jeremiah be put to death: he is unquestionably disheartening the remaining soldiers in the city, and all the people too, by talking like this. The fellow does not have the welfare of this people at heart so much as its ruin.' 'He is in your hands as you know,' King Zedekiah answered 'for the king is powerless against you.' So they took Jeremiah and threw him into the well of Prince Malchiah in the

Court of the Guard, letting him down with ropes. There was no water in the well, only mud, and into the mud Jeremiah sank.

Ebed-melech came out from the palace and spoke to the king. 'My lord king,' he said 'these men have done a wicked thing by treating the prophet Jeremiah like this: they have thrown him into the well where he will die.' At this the king gave Ebed-melech the Cushite the following order: 'Take three men with you from here and pull the prophet Jeremiah out of the well before he dies.'

This is the word of the Lord.

Responsorial Psalm   Ps 39:2-4. 18. ℟ v.14

℟ **Lord, come to my aid!**

1   I waited, I waited for the Lord
    and he stooped down to me;
    he heard my cry.   ℟

2   He drew me from the deadly pit,
    from the miry clay.
    He set my feet upon a rock
    and made my footsteps firm.   ℟

3   He put a new song into my mouth,
    praise of our God.
    Many shall see and fear
    and shall trust in the Lord.   ℟

4   As for me, wretched and poor,
    the Lord thinks of me.
    You are my rescuer, my help,
    O God, do not delay.   ℟

SECOND READING

A reading from the letter to the Hebrews   12:1-4
We shall keep running steadily in the race we have started.

With so many witnesses in a great cloud on every side of us, we too, then, should throw off everything that hinders us, especially the sin that clings so easily, and keep running steadily in the race we have started. Let us not lose sight of Jesus, who leads us in our faith and brings it to perfection: for the sake of the joy which was still in the future, he endured the cross, disregarding the shamefulness of it, and from now on has taken his place at the right of God's throne. Think of the way he stood such opposition from sinners and then you will not give up for want of courage. In the fight against sin, you have not yet had to keep fighting to the point of death.

This is the word of the Lord.

Gospel Acclamation   cf. Acts 16:14
     Alleluia, alleluia!
     Open our heart, O Lord,
     to accept the words of your Son.
     Alleluia!

or   Jn 10:27

     Alleluia, alleluia!
     The sheep that belong to me listen to my voice,
     says the Lord,
     I know them and they follow me.
     Alleluia!

GOSPEL

A reading from the holy Gospel according to Luke   12:49-53
I am not here to bring peace, but rather division.

Jesus said to his disciples: 'I have come to bring fire to the earth, and how I wish it were blazing already! There is a baptism I must still receive, and how great is my distress till it is over!

     'Do you suppose that I am here to bring peace on earth? No, I tell you, but rather division. For from now on a household of five will be divided: three against two and two against three; the father divided against the son, son against father, mother against daughter, daughter against mother, mother-in-law against daughter-in-law, daughter-in-law against mother-in-law.'

This is the Gospel of the Lord.

Prayer over the Gifts
Lord,
accept our sacrifice
as a holy exchange of gifts.
By offering what you have given us
may we receive the gift of yourself.

Preface of Sundays in Ordinary Time I-VIII, P29-P36

Communion Antiphon: With the Lord there is mercy, and fullness of redemption.

or

I am the living bread from heaven, says the Lord; if anyone eats
this bread he will live for ever.

Prayer after Communion
God of mercy,
by this sacrament you make us one with Christ.
By becoming more like him on earth,
may we come to share his glory in heaven,
where he lives and reigns for ever and ever.

TWENTY-FIRST SUNDAY IN ORDINARY TIME C

The Lord Gathers A People To Himself

*Today, as sons and daughters of God, we submit ourselves to his loving
discipline, remembering that it was not just the Jews, nor will it be just
Christians whom the Lord will gather to himself. Many more worthy
than us will come from East and West to share the banquet of his
kingdom.*

Entrance Antiphon: Listen, Lord, and answer me. Save your
servant who trusts in you. I call to you all day long, have mercy
on me, O Lord.

Opening Prayer
Let us pray
    [that God will make us one in mind and heart]

Father,
help us to seek the values
that will bring us lasting joy in this changing world.
In our desire for what you promise
make us one in mind and heart.

or

Let us pray
    [with minds fixed on eternal truth]

Lord our God,
all truth is from you,
and you alone bring oneness of heart.

Give your people the joy

of hearing your word in every sound
and of longing for your presence more than for life itself.
May all the attractions of a changing world
serve only to bring us
the peace of your kingdom which this world does not give.

FIRST READING

A reading from the prophet Isaiah   66:18-21

They will bring all your brothers from all the nations.

The Lord says this: I am coming to gather the nations of every
language. They shall come to witness my glory. I will give them a
sign and send some of their survivors to the nations: to Tarshish,
Put, Lud, Moshech, Rosh, Tubal, and Javan, to the distant
islands that have never heard of me or seen my glory. They will
proclaim my glory to the nations. As an offering to the Lord they
will bring all your brothers, in horses, in chariots, in litters, on
mules, on dromedaries, from all the nations to my holy mountain
in Jerusalem, says the Lord, like Israelites bringing oblations in
clean vessels to the Temple of the Lord. And of some of them I
will make priests and Levites, says the Lord.

This is the word of the Lord.

Responsorial Psalm   Ps 116. R℣ Mk 16:15

R℣ **Go out to the whole world;
proclaim the Good News.**

or

R℣ **Alleluia!**

1 O praise the Lord, all you nations,
acclaim him all you peoples! R℣

2 Strong is his love for us;
he is faithful for ever. R℣

SECOND READING

A reading from the letter to the Hebrews   12:5-7. 11-13

The Lord trains the one that he loves.

Have you forgotten that encouraging text in which you are
addressed as sons? My son, when the Lord corrects you, do not
treat it lightly; but do not get discouraged when he reprimands
you. For the Lord trains the ones that he loves and he punishes

all those that he acknowledges as his sons. Suffering is part of your training; God is treating you as his sons. Has there ever been any son whose father did not train him? Of course, any punishment is most painful at the time, and far from pleasant; but later, in those on whom it has been used, it bears fruit in peace and goodness. So hold up your limp arms and steady your trembling knees and smooth out the path you tread; then the injured limb will not be wrenched, it will grow strong again.

This is the word of the Lord.

Gospel Acclamation   Jn 14:23
Alleluia, alleluia!
If anyone loves me he will keep my word,
and my Father will love him,
and we shall come to him.
Alleluia!

or   Jn 14:6

Alleluia, alleluia!
I am the Way, the Truth and the Life, says the Lord;
no one can come to the Father except through me.
Alleluia!

GOSPEL

A reading from the holy Gospel according to Luke   13:22-30
Men from east and west will come to take their places at the feast in the kingdom of God.

Through towns and villages Jesus went teaching, making his way to Jerusalem. Someone said to him, 'Sir, will there be only a few saved?' He said to them, 'Try your best to enter by the narrow door, because I tell you, many will try to enter and will not succeed.

'Once the master of the house has got up and locked the door, you may find yourself knocking on the door, saying, "Lord, open to us" but he will answer, "I do not know where you come from." Then you will find yourself saying, "We once ate and drank in your company; you taught in our streets" but he will reply, "I do not know where you come from. Away from me, all you wicked men!"

'Then there will be weeping and grinding of teeth, when you see Abraham and Isaac and Jacob and all the prophets in the kingdom of God, and yourselves turned outside. And men from east and west, from north and south, will come to take their

places at the feast in the kingdom of God.
   'Yes, there are those now last who will be first, and those now first who will be last.'

   This is the Gospel of the Lord.

Prayer over the Gifts
Merciful God,
the perfect sacrifice of Jesus Christ
made us your people.
In your love,
grant peace and unity to your Church.
Preface of Sundays in Ordinary Time I-VIII, P29-P36

Communion Antiphon: Lord, the earth is filled with your gift from heaven; man grows bread from earth, and wine to cheer his heart.
   or

The Lord says: The man who eats my flesh and drinks my blood will live for ever; I shall raise him to life on the last day.

Prayer after Communion
Lord,
may this eucharist increase within us
the healing power of your love.
May it guide and direct our efforts
to please you in all things.

TWENTY-SECOND SUNDAY   C
IN ORDINARY TIME

Jesus, The Mediator Of A New Covenant

God made the new covenant of his love with the poor, the lowly, the down-trodden and the oppressed. It is therefore in a spirit of humility, the spirit of Jesus, that we make our celebration today, asking him to accept the homage of the humble.

Entrance Antiphon: I call to you all day long, have mercy on me, O Lord. You are good and forgiving, full of love for all who call to you.

Opening Prayer

Let us pray
  [that God will increase our faith
  and bring to perfection the gifts he has given us]

Almighty God,
every good thing comes from you.
Fill our hearts with love for you,
increase our faith,
and by your constant care
protect the good you have given us.

or

Let us pray
  [to God who forgives all who call upon him]

Lord God of power and might,
nothing is good which is against your will,
and all is of value which comes from your hand.
Place in our hearts a desire to please you
and fill our minds with insight into love,
so that every thought may grow in wisdom
and all our efforts may be filled with your peace.

FIRST READING

A reading from the book of Ecclesiasticus   3:17-20. 28-29
Behave humbly, and then you will find favour with the Lord.

My son, be gentle in carrying out your business,
and you will be better loved than a lavish giver.
The greater you are, the more you should behave humbly,
and then you will find favour with the Lord;
for great though the power of the Lord is,
he accepts the homage of the humble.
There is no cure for the proud man's malady,
since an evil growth has taken root in him.
The heart of a sensible man will reflect on parables,
an attentive ear is the sage's dream.

  This is the word of the Lord.

Responsorial Psalm   Ps 67:4-7. 10-11. ℟ cf. v.11
  ℟ **In your goodness, O God, you prepared a home for the poor.**

1 The just shall rejoice at the presence of God,

they shall exult and dance for joy.
O sing to the Lord, make music to his name;
rejoice in the Lord, exult at his presence.   ℟

2   Father of the orphan, defender of the widow,
such is God in his holy place.
God gives the lonely a home to live in;
he leads the prisoners forth into freedom.   ℟

3   You poured down, O God, a generous rain:
when your people were starved you gave them new life.
It was there that your people found a home,
prepared in your goodness, O God, for the poor.   ℟

SECOND READING

A reading from the letter to the Hebrews   12:18-19. 22-24
You have to come to Mount Zion and to the city of the living God.

What you have come to is nothing known to the senses: not a
blazing fire, or a gloom turning to total darkness, or a storm; or
trumpeting thunder or the great voice speaking which made
everyone that heard it beg that no more should be said to them.
But what you have come to is Mount Zion and the city of the
living God, the heavenly Jerusalem where the millions of angels
have gathered for the festival, with the whole Church in which
everyone is a 'first-born son' and a citizen of heaven. You have
come to God himself, the supreme Judge, and been placed with
spirits of the saints who have been made perfect; and to Jesus,
the mediator who brings a new covenant.

This is the word of the Lord.

Gospel Acclamation   Jn 14:23
Alleluia, alleluia!
If anyone loves me he will keep my word,
and my Father will love him,
and we shall come to him.
Alleluia!

or   Mt 11:29

Alleluia, alleluia!
Shoulder my yoke and learn from me,
for I am gentle and humble in heart.
Alleluia!

GOSPEL

A reading from the holy Gospel according to Luke   14:1. 7-14

Everyone who exalts himself will be humbled, and the man who humbles himself will be exalted.

On a sabbath day Jesus had gone for a meal to the house of one of the leading Pharisees; and they watched him closely. He then told the guests a parable, because he had noticed how they picked the places of honour. He said this, 'When someone invites you to a wedding feast, do not take your seat in the place of honour. A more distinguished person than you may have been invited, and the person who invited you both may come and say, "Give up your place to this man." And then, to your embarrassment, you would have to go and take the lowest place. No; when you are a guest, make your way to the lowest place and sit there, so that, when your host comes, he may say, "My friend, move up higher." In that way, everyone with you at the table will see you honoured. For everyone who exalts himself will be humbled, and the man who humbles himself will be exalted.'

Then he said to his host, 'When you give a lunch or a dinner, do not ask your friends, brothers, relations or rich neighbours, for fear they repay your courtesy by inviting you in return. No; when you have a party, invite the poor, the crippled, the lame, the blind; that they cannot pay you back means that you are fortunate, because repayment will be made to you when the virtuous rise again.'

This is the Gospel of the Lord.

Prayer over the Gifts
Lord,
may this holy offering
bring us your blessing
and accomplish within us
its promise of salvation.

Preface of Sundays in Ordinary Time I-VIII, P29-P36

Communion Antiphon: O Lord, how great is the depth of the kindness which you have shown to those who love you.

or

Happy are the peacemakers; they shall be called sons of God. Happy are they who suffer persecution for justice's sake; the kingdom of heaven is theirs.

Prayer after Communion

Lord,
you renew us at your table with the bread of life.
May this food strengthen us in love
and help us to serve you in each other.

TWENTY-THIRD SUNDAY IN ORDINARY TIME C

Christ Who Gave Up Everything For Our Sake

We celebrate the self-sacrificing love of Christ, the unfathomable wisdom of God, who was prepared to give up everything out of love for man. In the same spirit St Paul was prepared to send back to Philemon the dear friend of his captivity, Onesimus, a part of his own self.

Entrance Antiphon: Lord, you are just, and the judgements you make are right. Show mercy when you judge me, your servant.

Opening Prayer

Let us pray
[that we may realise the freedom God has given us
in making us his sons and daughters]

God our Father,
you redeem us
and make us your children in Christ.
Look upon us,
give us true freedom
and bring us to the inheritance you promised.
or

Let us pray
[to our just and merciful God]

Lord our God,
in you justice and mercy meet.
With unparalleled love you have saved us from death
and drawn us into the circle of your life.

Open our eyes to the wonders this life sets before us,
that we may serve you free from fear
and address you as God our Father.

FIRST READING

A reading from the book of Wisdom

9:13-18

Who can divine the will of the Lord?

What man can know the intentions of God?
Who can divine the will of the Lord?
The reasonings of mortals are unsure
and our intentions unstable;
for a perishable body presses down the soul,
and this tent of clay weighs down the teeming mind.
It is hard enough for us to work out what is on earth,
laborious to know what lies within our reach;
who, then, can discover what is in the heavens?
As for your intention, who could have learnt it, had you not
    granted Wisdom
and sent your holy spirit from above?
Thus have the paths of those on earth been straightened
and men been taught what pleases you,
and saved, by Wisdom.

This is the word of the Lord.

Responsorial Psalm   Ps 89:3-6. 12-14. 17. ℟ v.1

℟ **O Lord, you have been our refuge
    from one generation to the next.**

1 You turn men back into dust
   and say: 'Go back, sons of men.'
   To your eyes a thousand years
   are like yesterday, come and gone,
   no more than a watch in the night.   ℟

2 You sweep men away like a dream,
   like grass which springs up in the morning.
   In the morning it springs up and flowers:
   by evening it withers and fades.   ℟

3 Make us know the shortness of our life
   that we may gain wisdom of heart.
   Lord, relent! Is your anger for ever?
   Show pity to your servants.   ℟

4 In the morning, fill us with your love;
   we shall exult and rejoice all our days.
   Let the favour of the Lord be upon us:
   give success to the work of our hands.   ℟

SECOND READING

A reading from the letter of St Paul to Philemon   9-10. 12-17

Have him back, not as a slave any more, but as a dear brother.

This is Paul writing, an old man now and, what is more, still a prisoner of Christ Jesus. I am appealing to you for a child of mine, whose father I became while wearing these chains: I mean Onesimus. I am sending him back to you, and with him – I could say – a part of my own self. I should have liked to keep him with me; he could have been a substitute for you, to help me while I am in the chains that the Good News has brought me. However, I did not want to do anything without your consent; it would have been forcing your act of kindness, which should be spontaneous. I know you have been deprived of Onesimus for a time, but it was only so that you could have him back for ever, not as a slave any more, but something much better than a slave, a dear brother; especially dear to me, but how much more to you, as a blood-brother as well as a brother in the Lord. So if all that we have in common means anything to you, welcome him as you would me.

This is the word of the Lord.

Gospel Acclamation   Jn 15:15
Alleluia, alleluia!
I call you friends, says the Lord,
because I have made known to you
everything I have learnt from my Father.
Alleluia!

or   Ps 118:135

Alleluia, alleluia!
Let your face shine on your servant,
and teach me your decrees.
Alleluia!

GOSPEL

A reading from the holy Gospel according to Luke   14:25-33

None of you can be my disciple unless he gives up all his possessions.

Great crowds accompanied Jesus on his way and he turned and spoke to them. 'If any man comes to me without hating his father, mother, wife, children, brothers, sisters, yes and his own life too, he cannot be my disciple. Anyone who does not carry his cross and come after me cannot be my disciple.

'And indeed, which of you here, intending to build a tower, would not first sit down and work out the cost to see if he had enough to complete it? Otherwise, if he laid the foundation and then found himself unable to finish the work, the onlookers would all start making fun of him and saying, "Here is a man who started to build and was unable to finish." Or again, what king marching to war against another king would not first sit down and consider whether with ten thousand men he could stand up to the other who advanced against him with twenty thousand? If not, then while the other king was still a long way off, he would send envoys to sue for peace. So in the same way, none of you can be my disciple unless he gives up all his possessions.'

This is the Gospel of the Lord.

Prayer over the Gifts
God of peace and love,
may our offering bring you true worship
and make us one with you.

Preface of Sundays in Ordinary Time I-VIII, P29-P36

Communion Antiphon: Like a deer that longs for running streams, my soul longs for you, my God. My soul is thirsting for the living God.

or

I am the light of the world, says the Lord; the man who follows me will have the light of life.

Prayer after Communion
Lord,
your word and your sacrament
give us food and life.
May this gift of your Son
lead us to share his life for ever.

TWENTY-FOURTH SUNDAY
IN ORDINARY TIME

C

Christ Who Welcomes Sinners

The Christ we celebrate in this Mass is the second Moses who interceded for sinners, who came into the world to save them, and who loves them and welcomes them.

Entrance Antiphon: Give peace, Lord, to those who wait for you and your prophets will proclaim you as you deserve. Hear the prayers of your servant and of your people Israel.

Opening Prayer
Let us pray
   [that God will keep us faithful in his service]

Almighty God,
our creator and guide,
may we serve you with all our heart
and know your forgiveness in our lives.

or

Let us pray
   [for the peace which is born of faith and hope]

Father in heaven, Creator of all,
look down upon your people in their moments of need,
for you alone are the source of our peace.
Bring us to the dignity which distinguishes the poor in spirit
and show us how great is the call to serve,
that we may share in the peace of Christ
who offered his life in the service of all.

FIRST READING

A reading from the book of Exodus   32:7-11. 13-14
The Lord relented and did not bring on his people the disaster he had threatened.

The Lord spoke to Moses, 'Go down now, because your people whom you brought out of Egypt have apostasised. They have been quick to leave the way I marked out for them; they have made themselves a calf of molten metal and have worshipped it and offered it sacrifice. "Here is your God, Israel," they have cried "who brought you up from the land of Egypt!" I can see how headstrong these people are! Leave me, now, my wrath shall blaze out against them and devour them; of you, however, I will make a great nation.'

But Moses pleaded with the Lord his God. 'Lord,' he said, 'why should your wrath blaze out against this people of yours whom you brought out of the land of Egypt with arm outstretched and mighty hand? Remember Abraham, Isaac and Jacob, your servants to whom by your own self you swore and made this promise: I will make your offspring as many as the stars of heaven, and all this land which I promised I will give to your descendants, and it shall be their heritage for ever.' So the Lord relented and did not bring on his people the disaster he had threatened.

This is the word of the Lord.

Responsorial Psalm   Ps 50:3-4. 12-13. 17. 19. ℟ Lk 15:18

℟ **I will leave this place and go to my father.**

1 Have mercy on me, God, in your kindness.
   In your compassion blot out my offence.
   O wash me more and more from my guilt
   and cleanse me from my sin.   ℟

2 A pure heart create for me, O God,
   put a steadfast spirit within me.
   Do not cast me away from your presence,
   nor deprive me of your holy spirit.   ℟

3 O Lord, open my lips
   and my mouth shall declare your praise.
   My sacrifice is a contrite spirit;
   a humbled, contrite heart you will not spurn.   ℟

SECOND READING

A reading from the first letter of St Paul to Timothy   1:12-17
Christ Jesus came into the world to save sinners.

I thank Christ Jesus our Lord, who has given me strength, and who judged me faithful enough to call me into his service even though I used to be a blasphemer and did all I could to injure and discredit the faith. Mercy, however, was shown me, because until I became a believer I had been acting in ignorance; and the grace of our Lord filled me with faith and with the love that is in Christ Jesus. Here is a saying that you can rely on and nobody should doubt: that Christ Jesus came into the world to save sinners. I myself am the greatest of them; and if mercy has been shown to me, it is because Jesus Christ meant to make me the greatest evidence of his inexhaustible patience for all the other people who would later have to trust in him to come to eternal life. To the eternal King, the undying, invisible and only God, be honour and glory for ever and ever. Amen.

This is the word of the Lord.

Gospel Acclamation cf. Eph 1:17. 18
Alleluia, alleluia!
May the Father of our Lord Jesus Christ
enlighten the eyes of our mind,
so that we can see what hope his call holds for us.
Alleluia!

or 2 Cor 5:19
Alleluia, alleluia!
God in Christ was reconciling the world to himself,
and he has entrusted to us the news that they are reconciled.
Alleluia!

GOSPEL

A reading from the holy Gospel according to Luke 15:1-32
There will be rejoicing in heaven over one repentant sinner.

*The tax collectors and the sinners were all seeking the company of Jesus to hear what he had to say, and the Pharisees and the scribes complained. 'This man' they said 'welcomes sinners and eats with them.' So he spoke this parable to them:

'What man among you with a hundred sheep, losing one, would not leave the ninety-nine in the wilderness and go after the missing one till he found it? And when he found it, would he not joyfully take it on his shoulders and then, when he got home, call together his friends, and neighbours? "Rejoice with me," he would say "I have found my sheep that was lost." In the same way, I tell you, there will be more rejoicing in heaven over one repentant sinner than over ninety-nine virtuous men who have no need of repentance.

'Or again, what woman with ten drachmas would not, if she lost one, light a lamp and sweep out the house and search thoroughly till she found it? And then, when she had found it, call together her friends and neighbours? "Rejoice with me," she would say "I have found the drachma I lost." In the same way, I tell you, there is rejoicing among the angels of God over one repentant sinner.'*

He also said, 'A man had two sons. The younger said to his father, "Father, let me have the share of the estate that would come to me." So the father divided the property between them. A few days later, the younger son got together everything he had and left for a distant country where he squandered his money on a life of debauchery.

'When he had spent it all, that country experienced a severe famine, and now he began to feel the pinch, so he hired himself out to one of the local inhabitants who put him on his farm to feed the pigs. And he would willingly have filled his belly with the husks the pigs were eating but no one offered him anything. Then he came to his senses and said, "How many of my father's paid servants have more food than they want, and here am I dying of hunger! I will leave this place and go to my father and say: Father, I have sinned against heaven and against you; I no longer deserve to be called your son; treat me as one of your paid servants.' So he left the place and went back to his father.

'While he was still a long way off, his father saw him and was moved with pity. He ran to the boy, clasped him in his arms and kissed him tenderly. Then his son said, "Father, I have sinned against heaven and against you. I no longer deserve to be called your son." But the father said to his servants, "Quick! Bring out the best robe and put it on him; put a ring on his finger and sandals on his feet. Bring the calf we have been fattening, and kill it; we are going to have a feast, a celebration, because this son of mine was dead and has come back to life; he was lost and is found." And they began to celebrate.

'Now the elder son was out in the fields, and on his way back, as he drew near the house, he could hear music and dancing. Calling one of the servants he asked what it was all about. "Your brother has come" replied the servant "and your father has killed the calf we had fattened because he has got him back safe and sound." He was angry then and refused to go in, and his father came out to plead with him; but he answered his father, "Look, all these years I have slaved for you and never once disobeyed your orders, yet you never offered me so much as a kid for me to celebrate with my friends. But, for this son of yours, when he comes back after swallowing up your property – he and his women – you kill the calf we had been fattening."

'The father said, "My son, you are with me always and all I have is yours. But it was only right we should celebrate and rejoice, because your brother here was dead and has come to life; he was lost and is found."'

This is the Gospel of the Lord.

*Shorter Form, verses 1-10. Read between *

Prayer over the Gifts
Lord,
hear the prayers of your people
and receive our gifts.
May the worship of each one here
bring salvation to all.

Preface of Sundays in Ordinary Time I-VIII, P29-P36

Communion Antiphon: O God, how much we value your mercy!
All mankind can gather under your protection.

or

The cup that we bless is a communion with the blood of Christ;
and the bread that we break is a communion with the body of the
Lord.

Prayer after Communion
Lord,
may the eucharist you have give us
influence our thoughts and actions.
May your Spirit guide and direct us in your way.

TWENTY-FIFTH SUNDAY IN ORDINARY TIME   C

Lord Of The Oppressed

*Christ is the defender of all who are sacrificed to the god of money, who
are manipulated for economic gain. He sacrificed himself as a ransom for
them all.*

Entrance Antiphon: I am the Saviour of all people, says the Lord.
Whatever their troubles, I will answer their cry, and I will always
be their Lord.

Opening Prayer
Let us pray
    [that we will grow in the love of God
    and of one another]

Father,
guide us, as you guide creation
according to your law of love.
May we love one another
and come to perfection

in the eternal life prepared for us.

or

Let us pray
    [to the Lord who is a God of love to all peoples]

Father in heaven,
the perfection of justice is found in your love
and all mankind is in need of your law.
Help us to find this love in each other
that justice may be attained
through obedience to your law.

FIRST READING

A reading from the prophet Amos   8:4-7
Against those who 'buy up the poor for money'.

Listen to this, you who trample on the needy
and try to suppress the poor people of the country,
you who say, 'When will New Moon be over
so that we can sell our corn,
and sabbath, so that we can market our wheat?
Then by lowering the bushel, raising the shekel,
by swindling and tampering with the scales,
we can buy up the poor for money,
and the needy for a pair of sandals,
and get a price even for the sweepings of the wheat.'
The Lord swears it by the pride of Jacob,
'Never will I forget a single thing you have done.'

   This is the word of the Lord.

Responsorial Psalm   Ps 112:1-2. 4-8. R̺ cf. vv.1. 7
     R̺ **Praise the Lord, who raises the poor.**

or

     R̺ **Alleluia!**

1   Praise, O servants of the Lord,
    praise the name of the Lord!
    May the name of the Lord be blessed
    both now and for evermore!   R̺

2   High above all nations is the Lord,
    above the heavens his glory.
    Who is like the Lord, our God,

who has risen on high to his throne
yet stoops from the heights to look down,
to look down upon heaven and earth? ℟

3 From the dust he lifts up the lowly,
from the dungheap he raises the poor
to set him in the company of princes,
yes, with the princes of his people.   ℟

SECOND READING

A reading from the first letter of St Paul to Timothy   2:1-8

There should be prayers offered for everyone to God, who wants everyone to be saved.

My advice is that, first of all, there should be prayers offered for everyone – petitions, intercessions and thanksgiving – and especially for kings and others in authority, so that we may be able to live religious and reverent lives in peace and quiet. To do this is right, and will please God our saviour: he wants everyone to be saved and reach full knowledge of the truth. For there is only one God, and there is only one mediator between God and mankind, himself a man, Christ Jesus, who sacrificed himself as a ransom for them all. He is the evidence of this, sent at the appointed time, and I have been named a herald and apostle of it and – I am telling the truth and no lie – a teacher of the faith and the truth to the pagans.

In every place, then, I want the men to lift their hands up reverently in prayer, with no anger or argument.

This is the word of the Lord.

Gospel Acclamation   cf. Acts 16:14
     Alleluia, alleluia!
     Open our heart, O Lord,
     to accept the words of your Son,
     Alleluia!

or   2 Cor 8:9

     Alleluia, alleluia!
     Jesus Christ was rich,
     but he became poor for your sake,
     to make you rich out of his poverty.
     Alleluia!

GOSPEL

A reading from the holy Gospel according to Luke 16:1-13
You cannot be the slave both of God and of money.

Jesus said to his disciples, 'There was a rich man and he had a steward who was denounced to him for being wasteful with his property. He called for the man and said, "What is this I hear about you? Draw me up an account of your stewardship because you are not to be my steward any longer." Then the steward said to himself, "Now that my master is taking the stewardship from me, what am I to do? Dig? I am not strong enough. Go begging? I should be too ashamed. Ah, I know what I will do to make sure that when I am dismissed from office there will be some to welcome me into their homes."

'Then he called his master's debtors one by one. To the first he said, "How much do you owe my master?" "One hundred measures of oil" was the reply. The steward said, "Here, take your bond; sit down straight away and write fifty." To another he said, "And you, sir, how much do you owe?" "One hundred measures of wheat" was the reply. The steward said, "Here, take your bond and write eighty."

'The master praised the dishonest steward for his astuteness. For the children of this world are more astute in dealing with their own kind than are the children of light.

'And so I tell you this: use money, tainted as it is, to win you friends, and thus make sure that when it fails you, they will welcome you into the tents of eternity. *The man who can be trusted in little things can be trusted in great; the man who is dishonest in little things will be dishonest in great. If then you cannot be trusted with money, that tainted thing, who will trust you with genuine riches? And if you cannot be trusted with what is not yours, who will give you what is your very own?

'No servant can be the slave of two masters: he will either hate the first and love the second, or treat the first with respect and the second with scorn. You cannot be the slave both of God and of money.'

This is the Gospel of the Lord.*

*Shorter Form, verses 10-13. Read between *

Prayer over the Gifts
Lord,
may these gifts which we now offer

to show our belief and our love
be pleasing to you.
May they become for us
the eucharist of Jesus Christ your Son,
who is Lord for ever and ever.

Preface of Sundays in Ordinary Time I-VIII, P29-P36

Communion Antiphon: You have laid down your precepts to be
faithfully kept. May my footsteps be firm in keeping your
commands.

or

I am the Good Shepherd, says the Lord; I know my sheep, and
mine know me.

Prayer after Communion
Lord,
help us with your kindness
Make us strong through the eucharist.
May we put into action
the saving mystery we celebrate.

TWENTY-SIXTH SUNDAY IN ORDINARY TIME C

Behold The Man!

*It is our purple and fine linen, our life of ease and our love of wealth, that
is mocked today by Christ, the centre of our celebration, who in the
presence of Pilate stood like a Lazarus covered with sores and wounds
and spoke up as a witness for the truth.*

Entrance Antiphon: O Lord, you had just cause to judge men as
you did: because we sinned against you and disobeyed your will.
But now show us your greatness of heart, and treat us with your
unbounded kindness.

Opening Prayer
Let us pray
     [for God's forgiveness
     and for the happiness it brings]

Father,
you show your almighty power
in your mercy and forgiveness.

Continue to fill us with your gifts of love.
Help us to hurry toward the eternal life you promise
and come to share in the joys of your kingdom.

or

Let us pray
[for the peace of the kingdom
which we have been promised]

Father of our Lord Jesus Christ,
in your unbounded mercy
you have revealed the beauty of your power
through your constant forgiveness of our sins.
May the power of this love be in our hearts
to bring your pardon and your kingdom to all we meet.

FIRST READING

A reading from the prophet Amos   6:1. 4-7
Those who sprawl and those who bawl will be exiled.

The almighty Lord says this:

Woe to those ensconced so snugly in Zion
and to those who feel so safe on the mountain of Samaria.
Lying on ivory beds
and sprawling on their divans,
they dine on lambs from the flock,
and stall-fattened veal;
they bawl to the sound of the harp,
they invent new instruments of music like David,
they drink wine by the bowlful,
and use the finest oil for anointing themselves,
but about the ruin of Joseph they do not care at all.
That is why they will be the first to be exiled;
the sprawlers' revelry is over.

This is the word of the Lord.

Responsorial Psalm   Ps 145:6-10. ℟ v.2
    ℟ **My soul, give praise to the Lord.**

or

    ℟ **Alleluia!**

1 It is the Lord who keeps faith for ever,
   who is just to those who are oppressed.

It is he who gives bread to the hungry,
the Lord, who sets prisoners free. ℟

2   It is the Lord who gives sight to the blind,
who raises up those who are bowed down.
It is the Lord who loves the just,
the Lord, who protects the stranger. ℟

3   He upholds the widow and orphan
but thwarts the path of the wicked.
The Lord will reign for ever,
Zion's God, from age to age. ℟

SECOND READING

A reading from the first letter of St Paul to Timothy   6:11-16
Do all that you have been told until the Appearing of the Lord.

As a man dedicated to God, you must aim to be saintly and
religious, filled with faith and love, patient and gentle. Fight the
good fight of the faith and win for yourself the eternal life to
which you were called when you made your profession and
spoke up for the truth in front of many witnesses. Now, before
God the source of all life and before Jesus Christ, who spoke up
as a witness for the truth in front of Pontius Pilate, I put to you
the duty of doing all that you have been told, with no faults or
failures, until the Appearing of our Lord Jesus Christ,

who at the due time will be revealed
by God, the blessed and only Ruler of all,
the King of kings and the Lord of lords,
who alone is immortal,
whose home is in inaccessible light,
whom no man has seen and no man is able to see:
to him be honour and everlasting power. Amen.

This is the word of the Lord.

Gospel Acclamation   Jn 10:27
Alleluia, alleluia!
The sheep that belong to me listen to my voice,
says the Lord,
I know them and they follow me.
Alleluia!

or   2 Cor 8:9

Alleluia, alleluia!
Jesus Christ was rich,
but he became poor for your sake,
to make you rich out of his poverty.
Alleluia!

GOSPEL

A reading from the holy Gospel according to Luke   16:19-31
Good things came your way, just as bad things came the way of Lazarus.
Now he is being comforted here while you are in agony.

Jesus said to the Pharisees: 'There was a rich man who used to
dress in purple and fine linen and feast magnificently every day.
And at his gate there lay a poor man called Lazarus, covered with
sores, who longed to fill himself with the scraps that fell from the
rich man's table. Dogs even came and licked his sores. Now the
poor man died and was carried away by the angels to the bosom
of Abraham. The rich man also died and was buried.

'In his torment in Hades he looked up and saw Abraham a
long way off with Lazarus in his bosom. So he cried out, "Father
Abraham, pity me and send Lazarus to dip the tip of his finger in
water and cool my tongue, for I am in agony in these flames."
"My son," Abraham replied "remember that during your life
good things came your way, just as bad things came the way of
Lazarus. Now he is being comforted here while you are in agony.
But that is not all: between us and you a great gulf has been fixed,
to stop anyone, if he wanted to, crossing from our side to yours,
and to stop any crossing from your side to ours."

'The rich man replied, "Father, I beg you then to send
Lazarus to my father's house, since I have five brothers, to give
them warning so that they do not come to this place of torment
too." "They have Moses and the prophets," said Abraham "let
them listen to them." "Ah no, father Abraham," said the rich
man "but if someone comes to them from the dead, they will
repent." Then Abraham said to him, "If they will not listen either
to Moses or to the prophets, they will not be convinced even if
someone should rise from the dead." '

This is the Gospel of the Lord.

Prayer over the Gifts
God of mercy,
accept our offering
and make it a source of blessing for us.

Preface of Sundays in Ordinary Time I-VIII, P29-P36

Communion Antiphon: O Lord, remember the words you spoke to me, your servant, which made me live in hope and consoled me when I was downcast.

or

This is how we know what love is: Christ gave up his life for us; and we too must give up our lives for our brothers.

Prayer after Communion
Lord,
may this eucharist
in which we proclaim the death of Christ
bring us salvation
and make us one with him in glory,
for he is Lord for ever and ever.

TWENTY-SEVENTH SUNDAY   C
IN ORDINARY TIME

Our Faith

Faith gives us a new vision of the world. Without it we see only the darker side of life. We are still slaves. It is faith which liberates us and makes us see the Spirit of power and love at work in our lives.

Entrance Antiphon: O Lord, you have given everything its place in the world, and no one can make it otherwise. For it is your creation, the heavens and the earth and the stars: you are the Lord of all.

Opening Prayer
Let us pray
    [that God will forgive our failings
    and bring us peace]

Father,
your love for us
surpasses all our hopes and desires.
Forgive our failings,
keep us in your peace
and lead us in the way of salvation.
or

or

Let us pray
    [before the face of God, in trusting faith]

Almighty and eternal God,
Father of the world to come,
your goodness is beyond what our spirit can touch
and your strength is more than the mind can bear.
Lead us to seek beyond our reach
and give us the courage to stand before your truth.

FIRST READING

A reading from the prophet Habakkuk   1:2-3; 2:2-4
The upright man will live by his faithfulness.

How long, Lord, am I to cry for help
while you will not listen;
to cry 'Oppression!' in your ear
and you will not save?
Why do you set injustice before me,
why do you look on where there is tyranny?
Outrage and violence, this is all I see,
all is contention, and discord flourishes.
Then the Lord answered and said,

> 'Write the vision down,
> inscribe it on tablets
> to be easily read,
> since this vision is for its own time only:
> eager for its own fulfilment, it does not deceive;
> if it comes slowly, wait,
> for come it will, without fail.
> See how he flags, he whose soul is not at rights,
> but the upright man will live by his faithfulness.'

This is the word of the Lord.

Responsorial Psalm   Ps 94:1-2. 6-9. ℞ v.8
    ℞ **O that today you would listen to his voice!**
      Harden not your hearts.

1 Come, ring out our joy to the Lord;
    hail the rock who saves us.
    Let us come before him, giving thanks,
    with songs let us hail the Lord.   ℞

2   Come in; let us bow and bend low;
    let us kneel before the God who made us
    for he is our God and we
    the people who belong to his pasture,
    the flock that is led by his hand.   ℟

3   O that today you would listen to his voice!
    'Harden not your hearts as at Meribah,
    as on that day at Massah in the desert
    when your fathers put me to the test;
    when they tried me, though they saw my work.'   ℟

SECOND READING

A reading from the second letter of St Paul   1:6-8. 13-14
to Timothy
Never be ashamed of witnessing to our Lord.

I am reminding you to fan into a flame the gift that God gave you
when I laid my hands on you. God's gift was not a spirit of
timidity, but the Spirit of power, and love, and self-control. So
you are never to be ashamed of witnessing to the Lord, or
ashamed of me for being his prisoner; but with me, bear the
hardships for the sake of the Good News, relying on the power of
God.

Keep as your pattern the sound teaching you have heard from
me, in the faith and love that are in Christ Jesus. You have been
trusted to look after something precious; guard it with the help of
the Holy Spirit who lives in us.

This is the word of the Lord.

Gospel Acclamation   1 Sam 3:9; Jn 6:68
    Alleluia, alleluia!
    Speak, Lord, your servant is listening:
    you have the message of eternal life.
    Alleluia!

or   1 Peter 1:25

    Alleluia, alleluia!
    The word of the Lord remains for ever:
    What is this word?
    It is the Good News that has been brought to you.
    Alleluia!

GOSPEL

A reading from the holy Gospel according to Luke 17:5-10

If only you had faith!

The apostles said to the Lord, 'Increase our faith.' The Lord replied, 'Were your faith the size of a mustard seed you could say to this mulberry tree, "Be uprooted and planted in the sea," and it would obey you.

'Which of you, with a servant ploughing or minding sheep, would say to him when he returned from the fields, "Come and have your meal immediately?" Would he not be more likely to say, "Get my supper laid; make yourself tidy and wait on me while I eat and drink. You can eat and drink yourself afterwards?" Must he be grateful to the servant for doing what he was told? So with you: when you have done all you have been told to do, say, "We are merely servants: we have done no more than our duty." '

 This is the Gospel of the Lord.

Prayer over the Gifts
Father,
receive these gifts
which our Lord Jesus Christ
has asked us to offer in his memory.
May our obedient service
bring us to the fullness of your redemption.

Preface of Sundays in Ordinary Time I-VIII, P29-P36

Communion Antiphon: The Lord is good to those who hope in him,
to those who are searching for his love.

or

Because there is one bread, we, though many, are one body, for
we all share in the one loaf and in the one cup.

Prayer after Communion
Almighty God,
let the eucharist we share
fill us with your life.
May the love of Christ
which we celebrate here
touch our lives and lead us to you.

TWENTY-EIGHTH SUNDAY
IN ORDINARY TIME

C

Thanksgiving

Today we come to give thanks to God and to offer sacrifice to him for having made known to us his salvation and cleansed us from our sins.

Entrance Antiphon: If you, O Lord, laid bare our guilt, who could endure it? But you are forgiving, God of Israel.

Opening Prayer
Let us pray
    [that God will help us to love one another]

Lord,
our help and guide,
make your love the foundation of our lives.
May our love for you express itself
in our eagerness to do good for others.

or

Let us pray
    [in quiet for the grace of sincerity]

Father in heaven,
the hand of your loving kindness
powerfully yet gently guides all the moments of our day.

Go before us in our pilgrimage of life,
anticipate our needs and prevent our falling.
Send your Spirit to unite us in faith,
that sharing in your service,
we may rejoice in your presence.

FIRST READING
A reading from the second book of the Kings   5:14-17
Naaman returned to Elisha and acknowledged the Lord.

Naaman the leper went down and immersed himself seven times in the Jordan, as Elisha had told him to do. And his flesh became clean once more like the flesh of a little child.

    Returning to Elisha with his whole escort, he went in and stood before him. 'Now I know' he said 'that there is no God in all the earth except in Israel. Now, please, accept a present from your servant.' But Elisha replied, 'As the Lord lives, whom I serve, I will accept nothing.' Naaman pressed him to accept, but he refused. Then Naaman said, 'Since your answer is "No," allow your servant to be given as much earth as two mules may carry, because your servant will no longer offer holocaust or sacrifice to any god except the Lord.'

This is the word of the Lord.

Responsorial Psalm   Ps 97:1-4. ℟ cf. v.2
℟   **The Lord has shown his salvation to the nations.**

1   Sing a new song to the Lord
    for he has worked wonders.
    His right hand and his holy arm
    have brought salvation.   ℟

2   The Lord has made known his salvation;
    has shown his justice to the nations.
    He has remembered his truth and love
    for the house of Israel.   ℟

3   All the ends of the earth have seen
    the salvation of our God.
    Shout to the Lord all the earth,
    ring out your joy.   ℟

SECOND READING

A reading from the second letter of St Paul to Timothy   2:8-13
If we hold firm, then we shall reign with Christ.

Remember the Good News that I carry, 'Jesus Christ risen from the dead, sprung from the race of David'; it is on account of this that I have my own hardships to bear, even to being chained like a criminal – but they cannot chain up God's news. So I bear it all for the sake of those who are chosen, so that in the end they may have the salvation that is in Christ Jesus and the eternal glory that comes with it.

Here is a saying that you can rely on:

If we have died with him, then we shall live with him.
If we hold firm, then we shall reign with him.
If we disown him, then he will disown us.
We may be unfaithful, but he is always faithful,
for he cannot disown his own self.

This is the word of the Lord.

Gospel Acclamation   cf. Jn 6:63. 68

> Alleluia, alleluia!
> Your words are spirit, Lord,
> and they are life:
> you have the message of eternal life.
> Alleluia!

or   1 Thess 5:18

> Alleluia, alleluia!
> For all things give thanks,
> because this is what God expects you to do in Christ Jesus.
> Alleluia!

GOSPEL

A reading from the holy Gospel according to Luke   17:11-19

No one has come back to give praise to God, except this foreigner.

On the way to Jerusalem Jesus travelled along the border between Samaria and Galilee. As he entered one of the villages, ten lepers came to meet him. They stood some way off and called to him, 'Jesus! Master! Take pity on us.' When he saw them he said 'Go and show yourselves to the priests.' Now as they were going away they were cleansed. Finding himself cured, one of them turned back praising God at the top of his voice and threw himself at the feet of Jesus and thanked him. The man was a Samaritan. This made Jesus say, 'Were not all ten made clean? The other nine, where are they? It seems that no one has come back to give praise to God, except this foreigner.' And he said to the man, 'Stand up and go on your way. Your faith has saved you.'

This is the Gospel of the Lord.

Prayer over the Gifts

Lord,
accept the prayers and gifts
we offer in faith and love.
May this eucharist bring us to your glory.

Preface of Sundays in Ordinary Time I-VIII, P29-P36

Communion Antiphon: The rich suffer want and go hungry, but nothing shall be lacking to those who fear the Lord.

or

When the Lord is revealed we shall be like him, for we shall see him as he is.

Prayer after Communion
Almighty Father,
may the body and blood of your Son
give us a share in his life,
for he is Lord for ever and ever.

TWENTY-NINTH SUNDAY IN ORDINARY TIME C

Christ Always Interceding For Us

Christ who 'opened his arms on the cross' is like Moses whose arms were raised in prayer for his people. Today Christ asks us to join him in continual prayer and never to lose heart.

Entrance Antiphon: I call upon you, God, for you will answer me; bend your ear and hear my prayer. Guard me as the pupil of your eye; hide me in the shade of your wings.

Opening Prayer
Let us pray
    [for the gift of simplicity and joy
    in our service of God and man]

Almighty and ever-living God,
our source of power and inspiration,
give us strength and joy
in serving you as followers of Christ,
who lives and reigns with you and the Holy Spirit,
one God, for ever and ever.
or
Let us pray
    [to the Lord who bends close to hear our prayer]

Lord our God, Father of all,
you guard us under the shadow of your wings
and search into the depths of our hearts.

Remove the blindness that cannot know you
and relieve the fear that would hide us from your sight.

FIRST READING
A reading from the book of Exodus   17:8-13
As long as Moses kept his arms raised, Israel had the advantage.

The Amalekites came and attacked Israel at Rephidim. Moses

said to Joshua, 'Pick out men for yourself, and tomorrow morning march out to engage Amalek. I, meanwhile, will stand on the hilltop, the staff of God in my hand.' Joshua did as Moses told him and marched out to engage Amalek, while Moses and Aaron and Hur went up to the top of the hill. As long as Moses kept his arms raised, Israel had the advantage; when he let his arms fall, the advantage went to Amalek. But Moses' arms grew heavy, so they took a stone and put it under him and on this he sat, Aaron and Hur supporting his arms, one on one side, one on the other; and his arms remained firm till sunset. With the edge of the sword Joshua cut down Amalek and his people.

This is the word of the Lord.

Responsorial Psalm   Ps 120. ℟ cf. v.2

℟ **Our help is in the name of the Lord**
   who made heaven and earth.

1   I lift up my eyes to the mountains:
    from where shall come my help?
    My help shall come from the Lord
    who made heaven and earth. ℟

2   May he never allow you to stumble!
    Let him sleep not, your guard.
    No, he sleeps not nor slumbers,
    Israel's guard. ℟

3   The Lord is your guard and your shade;
    at your right side he stands.
    By day the sun shall not smite you
    nor the moon in the night. ℟

4   The Lord will guard you from evil,
    he will guard your soul.
    The Lord will guard your going and coming
    both now and for ever. ℟

SECOND READING

A reading from the second letter of St Paul   3:14 – 4:2
to Timothy

The man who is dedicated to God becomes fully equipped and ready for any good work.

You must keep to what you have been taught and know to be

true; remember who your teachers were, and how, ever since you were a child, you have known the holy scriptures – from these you can learn the wisdom that leads to salvation through faith in Christ Jesus. All scripture is inspired by God and can profitably be used for teaching, for refuting error, for guiding people's lives and teaching them to be holy. This is how the man who is dedicated to God becomes fully equipped and ready for any good work.

Before God and before Christ Jesus who is to be judge of the living and the dead, I put this duty to you, in the name of his Appearing and of his kingdom: proclaim the message and, welcome or unwelcome, insist on it. Refute falsehood, correct error, call to obedience – but do all with patience and with the intention of teaching.

This is the word of the Lord.

Gospel Acclamation   cf. Eph 1:17. 18
Alleluia, alleluia!
May the Father of our Lord Jesus Christ
enlighten the eyes of our mind,
so that we can see what hope his call holds for us.
Alleluia!

or   Heb 4:12

Alleluia, alleluia!
The word of God is something alive and active;
it can judge secret emotions and thoughts.
Alleluia!

GOSPEL

A reading from the holy Gospel according to Luke   18:1-8
God will see justice done to his chosen who cry to him.

Jesus told his disciples a parable about the need to pray continually and never lose heart. 'There was a judge in a certain town' he said 'who had neither fear of God nor respect for man. In the same town there was a widow who kept on coming to him and saying, "I want justice from you against my enemy!" For a long time he refused, but at last he said to himself, "Maybe I have neither fear of God nor respect for man, but since she keeps pestering me I must give this widow her just rights, or she will persist in coming and worry me to death."'

And the Lord said, 'You notice what the unjust judge has

to say? Now will not God see justice done to his chosen who cry to him day and night even when he delays to help them? I promise you, he will see justice done to them, and done speedily. But when the Son of Man comes, will he find any faith on earth?'

This is the Gospel of the Lord.

Prayer over the Gifts
Lord God,
may the gifts we offer
bring us your love and forgiveness
and give us freedom to serve you with our lives.

Preface of Sundays in Ordinary Time I-VIII, P29-P36

Communion Antiphon: See how the eyes of the Lord are on those who fear him, on those who hope in his love, that he may rescue them from death and feed them in time of famine.

or

The Son of Man came to give his life as a ransom for many.

Prayer after Communion
Lord,
may this eucharist help us to remain faithful.
May it teach us the way to eternal life.

THIRTIETH SUNDAY IN ORDINARY TIME   C

The Lord, The Righteous Judge

The Lord is our judge. The one thing we know for certain about his judgement is that it favours the humble, and he who humbles himself will be exalted.

Entrance Antiphon: Let hearts rejoice who search for the Lord. Seek the Lord and his strength, seek always the face of the Lord.

Opening Prayer
Let us pray
[for the strength to do God's will]

Almighty and ever-living God,
strengthen our faith, hope, and love.
May we do with loving hearts
what you ask of us
and come to share the life you promise.

or

Let us pray
    [in humble hope for salvation]

Praised be you, God and Father of our Lord Jesus Christ.
There is no power for good
which does not come from your covenant,
and no promise to hope in
that your love has not offered.
Strengthen our faith to accept your covenant
and give us the love to carry out your command.

FIRST READING

A reading from the book of Ecclesiasticus   35:12-14. 16-19
The humble man's prayer pierces the clouds.

The Lord is a judge
who is no respecter of personages.
He shows no respect of personages to the detriment of a poor
    man,
he listens to the plea of the injured party.
He does not ignore the orphan's supplication,
nor the widow's as she pours out her story.
The man who with his whole heart serves God will be accepted,
his petitions will carry to the clouds.
The humble man's prayer pierces the clouds,
until it arrives he is inconsolable,
nor will he desist until the Most High takes notice of him,
acquits the virtuous and delivers judgement.
And the Lord will not be slow,
nor will he be dilatory on their behalf.

    This is the word of the Lord.

Responsorial Psalm   Ps 32:2-3. 17-19. 23. R℣ v.7
    R℣ **This poor man called; the Lord heard him.**

1 I will bless the Lord at all times,
    his praise always on my lips;
    in the Lord my soul shall make its boast.
    The humble shall hear and be glad.   R℣

2 The Lord turns his face against the wicked
    to destroy their remembrance from the earth.
    The just call and the Lord hears

and rescues them in all their distress. ℟

3 The Lord is close to the broken-hearted;
   those whose spirit is crushed he will save.
   The Lord ransoms the souls of his servants.
   Those who hide in him shall not be condemned. ℟

SECOND READING

A reading from the second letter of St Paul
to Timothy   4:6-8. 16-18

All there is to come now is the crown of righteousness reserved for me.

My life is already being poured away as a libation, and the time
has come for me to be gone. I have fought the good fight to the
end; I have run the race to the finish; I have kept the faith; all
there is to come now is the crown of righteousness reserved for
me, which the Lord, the righteous judge, will give to me on that
Day; and not only to me but to all those who have longed for his
Appearing.

   The first time I had to present my defence, there was not a
single witness to support me. Every one of them deserted me –
may they not be held accountable for it. But the Lord stood by me
and gave me power, so that through me the whole message
might be proclaimed for all the pagans to hear; and so I was
rescued from the lion's mouth. The Lord will rescue me from all
evil attempts on me, and bring me safely to his heavenly
kingdom. To him be glory for ever and ever. Amen.

   This is the word of the Lord.

Gospel Acclamation   cf. Mt 11:25
   Alleluia, alleluia!
   Blessed are you, Father,
   Lord of heaven and earth,
   for revealing the mysteries of the kingdom
   to mere children.
   Alleluia!

or   2 Cor 5:19

   Alleluia, alleluia!
   God in Christ was reconciling the world to himself,
   and he has entrusted to us the news that they are reconciled.
   Alleluia!

GOSPEL

A reading from the holy Gospel according to Luke   18:9-14
The publican went home at rights with God; the Pharisee did not.

Jesus spoke the following parable to some people who prided themselves on being virtuous and despised everyone else. 'Two men went up to the Temple to pray, one a Pharisee, the other a tax collector. The Pharisee stood there and said this prayer to himself, "I thank you, God, that I am not grasping, unjust, adulterous like the rest of mankind, and particularly that I am not like this tax collector here. I fast twice a week; I pay tithes on all I get." The tax collector stood some distance away, not daring even to raise his eyes to heaven; but he beat his breast and said, "God, be merciful to me, a sinner." This man, I tell you, went home again at rights with God; the other did not. For everyone who exalts himself will be humbled, but the man who humbles himself will be exalted.'

This is the Gospel of the Lord.

Prayer over the Gifts
Lord God of power and might,
receive the gifts we offer
and let our service give you glory.

Preface of Sundays in Ordinary Time I-VIII, P29-P36

Communion Antiphon: We will rejoice at the victory of God and make our boast in his great name.

or

Christ loved us and gave himself up for us a fragrant offering to God.

Prayer after Communion
Lord,
bring to perfection within us
the communion we share in this sacrament.
May our celebration have an effect in our lives.

THIRTY-FIRST SUNDAY IN ORDINARY TIME C

Jesus In Our Midst

To him the whole world is like a grain of dust. Yet he loves all that exists, and comes to dwell with sinners.

Entrance Antiphon: Do not abandon me, Lord. My God, do not go away from me! Hurry to help me, Lord, my Saviour.

Opening Prayer
Let us pray
    [that our lives will reflect our faith]

God of power and mercy,
only with your help
can we offer you fitting service and praise.
May we live the faith we profess
and trust your promise of eternal life.

or

Let us pray
    [in the presence of God, the source of every good]

Father in heaven, God of power and Lord of mercy,
from whose fullness we have received,
direct our steps in our everyday efforts.
May the changing moods of the human heart
and the limits which our failings impose on hope
never blind us to you, source of every good.

Faith gives us the promise of peace
and makes known the demands of love.
Remove the selfishness that blurs the vision of faith.

FIRST READING

A reading from the book of Wisdom   11:22 – 12:2
You are merciful to all because you love all that exists.

In your sight, Lord, the whole world is like a grain of dust that
    tips the scales,
like a drop of morning dew falling on the ground.
Yet you are merciful to all, because you can do all things
and overlook men's sins so that they can repent.
Yes, you love all that exists, you hold nothing of what you have
    made in abhorrence,

for had you hated anything, you would not have formed it.
And how, had you not willed it, could a thing persist,
how be conserved if not called forth by you?
You spare all things because all things are yours, Lord, lover of
    life,
you whose imperishable spirit is in all.
Little by little, therefore, you correct those who offend,
you admonish and remind them of how they have sinned,
so that they may abstain from evil and trust in you, Lord.

This is the word of the Lord.

Responsorial Psalm   Ps 144:1-2. 8-11. 13-14. R/ cf. v.1
    R/ **I will bless your name for ever,**
        O God my King.

1   I will give you glory, O God my King,
    I will bless your name for ever.
    I will bless you day after day
    and praise your name for ever.   R/

2   The Lord is kind and full of compassion,
    slow to anger, abounding in love.
    How good is the Lord to all,
    compassionate to all his creatures.   R/

3   All your creatures shall thank you, O Lord,
    and your friends shall repeat their blessing.
    They shall speak of the glory of your reign
    and declare your might, O God.   R/

4   The Lord is faithful in all his words
    and loving in all his deeds.
    The Lord supports all who fall
    and raises all who are bowed down.   R/

SECOND READING

A reading from the second letter of St Paul   1:11 – 2:2
to the Thessalonians
The name of Christ will be glorified in you and you in him.

We pray continually that our God will make you worthy of his
call, and by his power fulfil all your desires for goodness and
complete all that you have been doing through faith; because in
this way the name of our Lord Jesus Christ will be glorified in you

and you in him, by the grace of our God and the Lord Jesus Christ.

To turn now, brothers, to the coming of our Lord Jesus Christ and how we shall all be gathered round him: please do not get excited too soon or alarmed by any prediction or rumour or any letter claiming to come from us, implying that the Day of the Lord has already arrived.

This is the word of the Lord.

Gospel Acclamation   Lk 19:38; 2:14
  Alleluia, alleluia!
  Blessings on the King who comes,
  in the name of the Lord!
  Peace in heaven
  and glory in the highest heavens!
  Alleluia!

or
                                                     Jn 3:16
  Alleluia, alleluia!
  God loved the world so much
  that he gave his only Son,
  so that everyone who believes in him
  may have eternal life.
  Alleluia!

GOSPEL
A reading from the holy Gospel according to Luke   19:1-10
The Son of Man has come to seek out and save what was lost.

Jesus entered Jericho and was going through the town when a man whose name was Zacchaeus made his appearance; he was one of the senior tax collectors and a wealthy man. He was anxious to see what kind of man Jesus was, but he was too short and could not see him for the crowd; so he ran ahead and climbed a sycamore tree to catch a glimpse of Jesus who was to pass that way. When Jesus reached the spot he looked up and spoke to him: 'Zacchaeus, come down. Hurry, because I must stay at your house today.' And he hurried down and welcomed him joyfully. They all complained when they saw what was happening. 'He has gone to stay at a sinner's house' they said. But Zacchaeus stood his ground and said to the Lord, 'Look, sir, I am going to give half my property to the poor, and if I have cheated anybody I will pay him back four times the amount.'

And Jesus said to him, 'Today salvation has come to this house, because this man too is a son of Abraham; for the Son of Man has come to seek out and save what was lost.'

This is the Gospel of the Lord.

Prayer over the Gifts
God of mercy,
may we offer a pure sacrifice
for the forgiveness of our sins.

Preface of Sundays in Ordinary Time I-VIII, P29-P36

Communion Antiphon: Lord, you will show me the path of life and fill me with joy in your presence.

or

As the living Father sent me, and I live because of the Father, so he who eats my flesh and drinks my blood will live because of me.

Prayer after Communion
Lord,
you give us new hope in this eucharist.
May the power of your love
continue its saving work among us
and bring us to the joy you promise.

THIRTY-SECOND SUNDAY IN ORDINARY TIME C

Such Sure Hope

However cruelly the world may treat us, we can always rejoice in the glorious future promised us by Christ, when we will be filled with the vision of God's glory.

Entrance Antiphon: Let my prayer come before you, Lord; listen, and answer me.

Opening Prayer
Let us pray
　　[for health of mind and body]

God of power and mercy,
protect us from all harm.

Give us freedom of spirit
and health in mind and body
to do your work on earth.

or

Let us pray
[that our prayer rise like incense
in the presence of the Lord]

Almighty Father,
strong is your justice and great is your mercy.
Protect us in the burdens and challenges of life.
Shield our minds from the distortion of pride
and enfold our desire with the beauty of truth.

Help us to become more aware of your loving design
so that we may more willingly give our lives in service to all.

FIRST READING

A reading from the second book of Maccabees   7:1-2. 9-14

The King of the world will raise us up to live again for ever.

There were seven brothers who were arrested with their mother.
The king tried to force them to taste pig's flesh, which the Law
forbids, by torturing them with whips and scourges. One of
them, acting as spokesman for the others, said, 'What are you
trying to find out from us? We are prepared to die rather than
break the Law of our ancestors.'

With his last breath the second brother exclaimed, 'Inhuman
fiend, you may discharge us from this present life, but the King
of the world will raise us up, since it is for his laws that we die, to
live again for ever.'

After him, they amused themselves with the third, who on
being asked for his tongue promptly thrust it out and boldly held
out his hands, with these honourable words, 'It was heaven that
gave me these limbs; for the sake of his laws I disdain them; from
him I hope to receive them again.' The king and his attendants
were astounded at the young man's courage and his utter
indifference to suffering.

When this one was dead they subjected the fourth to the same
savage torture. When he neared his end he cried, 'Ours is the
better choice, to meet death at men's hands, yet relying on God's
promise that we shall be raised up by him; whereas for you there
can be no resurrection, no new life.'

This is the word of the Lord.

Responsorial Psalm   Ps 16:1. 5-6. 8. 15. ℟ v.15
   ℟ **I shall be filled, when I awake,**
        with the sight of your glory, O Lord.

1   Lord, hear a cause that is just,
       pay heed to my cry.
    Turn your ear to my prayer:
       no deceit is on my lips.   ℟

2   I kept my feet firmly in your paths;
       there was no faltering in my steps.
    I am here and I call, you will hear me, O God.
    Turn your ear to me; hear my words.   ℟

3   Guard me as the apple of your eye.
    Hide me in the shadow of your wings.
    As for me, in my justice I shall see your face
    and be filled, when I awake, with the sight of your glory.   ℟

SECOND READING

A reading from the second letter of St Paul   2:16 – 3:5
to the Thessalonians
May the Lord strengthen you in everything good that you do or say.

May our Lord Jesus Christ himself, and God our Father who has
given us his love and, through his grace, such inexhaustible com
fort and such sure hope, comfort you and strengthen you in
everything good that you do or say.

   Finally, brothers, pray for us; pray that the Lord's message
may spread quickly, and be received with honour as it was
among you; and pray that we may be preserved from the
interference of bigoted and evil people, for faith is not given to
everyone. But the Lord is faithful, and he will give you strength
and guard you from the evil one, and we, in the Lord, have every
confidence that you are doing and will go on doing all that we tell
you. May the Lord turn your hearts towards the love of God and
the fortitude of Christ.

   This is the word of the Lord.

Gospel Acclamation   Lk 21:36
   Alleluia, alleluia!
   Stay awake, praying at all times
   for the strength to stand with confidence before the Son of
      Man.
   Alleluia!

or   Apoc 1:5. 6

Alleluia, alleluia!
Jesus Christ is the First-born from the dead;
to him be glory and power for ever and ever.
Alleluia!

GOSPEL

A reading from the holy Gospel according to Luke   20:27-38
He is God, not of the dead, but of the living.

*Some Sadducees – those who say that there is no resurrection –
approached Jesus and they put this question to him,* 'Master, we
have it from Moses in writing, that if a man's married brother
dies childless, the man must marry the widow to raise up
children for his brother. Well, then, there were seven brothers.
The first, having married a wife, died childless. The second and
then the third married the widow. And the same with all seven,
they died leaving no children. Finally the woman herself died.
Now, at the resurrection, to which of them will she be wife since
she had been married to all seven?'

*Jesus replied, 'The children of this world take wives and
husbands, but those who are judged worthy of a place in the
other world and in the resurrection from the dead do not marry
because they can no longer die, for they are the same as the
angels, and being children of the resurrection they are sons of
God. And Moses himself implies that the dead rise again, in the
passage about the bush where he calls the Lord the God of
Abraham, the God of Isaac and the God of Jacob. Now he is God,
not of the dead, but of the living; for to him all men are in fact
alive.'

This is the Gospel of the Lord.*

*Shorter Form, verses 27, 34-38. Read between *

Prayer over the Gifts
God of mercy,
in this eucharist we proclaim the death of the Lord.
Accept the gifts we present
and help us follow him with love,
for he is Lord for ever and ever.

Preface of Sundays in Ordinary Time I-VIII, P29-P36

Communion Antiphon: The Lord is my shepherd; there is nothing I shall want. In green pastures he gives me rest, he leads me beside the waters of peace.

or

The disciples recognised the Lord Jesus in the breaking of bread.

Prayer after Communion
Lord,
we thank you for the nourishment you give us
through your holy gift.
Pour out your Spirit upon us
and in the strength of this food from heaven
keep us single-minded in your service.

THIRTY-THIRD SUNDAY IN ORDINARY TIME C

The Triumph Of God

The day is coming when all that is evil will be brought to nothing. Already Christ has given us the strength to overcome evil: we receive it in the Eucharist.

Entrance Antiphon: The Lord says: my plans for you are peace and not disaster; when you call to me, I will listen to you, and I will bring you back to the place from which I exiled you.

Opening Prayer
Let us pray
    [that God will help us to be faithful]

Father of all that is good,
keep us faithful in serving you,
for to serve you is our lasting joy.

or

Let us pray
    [with hearts that long for peace]

Father in heaven,
ever-living source of all that is good,
from the beginning of time you promised man salvation
through the future coming of your Son, our Lord Jesus Christ.

Help us to drink of his truth
and expand our hearts with the joy of his promises,
so that we may serve you in faith and in love
and know for ever the joy of your presence.

FIRST READING

A reading from the prophet Malachi   3:19-20
For you the sun of righteousness will shine out.

The day is coming now, burning like a furnace; and all the
arrogant and the evil-doers will be like stubble. The day that is
coming is going to burn them up, says the Lord of hosts, leaving
them neither root nor stalk. But for you who fear my name, the
sun of righteousness will shine out with healing in its rays.

This is the word of the Lord.

Responsorial Psalm   Ps 97:5-9. ℟ cf. v.9
    ℟   **The Lord comes to rule the peoples with fairness.**

1 Sing psalms to the Lord with the harp
   with the sound of music.
   With trumpets and the sound of the horn
   acclaim the King, the Lord.   ℟

2 Let the sea and all within it, thunder;
   the world, and all its peoples.
   Let the rivers clap their hands
   and the hills ring out their joy
   at the presence of the Lord.   ℟

3 For the Lord comes,
   he comes to rule the earth.
   He will rule the world with justice
   and the peoples with fairness.   ℟

SECOND READING

A reading from the second letter of St Paul   3:7-12
to the Thessalonians
Do not let anyone have food if he refuses to work.

You know how you are supposed to imitate us: now we were not
idle when we were with you, nor did we ever have our meals at
anyone's table without paying for them; no, we worked night
and day, slaving and straining, so as not to be a burden on any of
you. This was not because we had no right to be, but in order to
make ourselves an example for you to follow.

We gave you a rule when we were with you: not to let anyone
have any food if he refused to do any work. Now we hear that
there are some of you who are living in idleness, doing no work

themselves but interfering with everyone else's. In the Lord Jesus Christ, we order and call on people of this kind to go on quietly working and earning the food that they eat.

This is the word of the Lord.

Gospel Acclamation Lk 21:36
Alleluia, alleluia!
Stay awake, praying at all times
for the strength to stand with confidence
before the Son of Man.
Alleluia!

or Lk 21:28

Alleluia, alleluia!
Stand erect, hold your heads high,
because your liberation is near at hand.
Alleluia!

GOSPEL

A reading from the holy Gospel according to Luke 21:5-19
Your endurance will win you your lives.

When some were talking about the Temple, remarking how it was adorned with fine stonework and votive offerings, Jesus said, 'All these things you are staring at now – the time will come when not a single stone will be left on another: everything will be destroyed.' And they put to him this question: 'Master,' they said 'when will this happen, then, and what sign will there be that this is about to take place?'

'Take care not to be deceived,' he said 'because many will come using my name and saying, "I am he" and, "The time is near at hand." Refuse to join them. And when you hear of wars and revolu tions, do not be frightened, for this is something that must happen but the end is not so soon.' Then he said to them, 'Nation will fight against nation, and kingdom against kingdom. There will be great earthquakes and plagues and famines here and there; there will be fearful sights and great signs from heaven.

'But before all this happens, men will seize you and persecute you; they will hand you over to the synagogues and to imprison- ment, and bring you before kings and governors because of my name – and that will be your opportunity to bear witness. Keep this carefully in mind: you are not to prepare your defence, because I myself shall give you an eloquence and a wisdom that none of your opponents will be able to resist or contradict. You will be betrayed even by parents and brothers, relations and friends; and some of you will be put to death. You will be hated by all men on account of my name, but not a hair of your head will be lost. Your endurance will win you your lives.'

This is the Gospel of the Lord.

Prayer over the Gifts
Lord God,
may the gifts we offer
increase our love for you
and bring us to eternal life.

Preface of Sundays in Ordinary Time I-VIII, P29-P36

Communion Antiphon: It is good for me to be with the Lord and to put my hope in him.

or

I tell you solemnly, whatever you ask for in prayer, believe that you have received it, and it will be yours, says the Lord.

Prayer after Communion
Father,
may we grow in love
by the eucharist we have celebrated
in memory of the Lord Jesus,
who is Lord for ever and ever.

Last Sunday in Ordinary Time
OUR LORD JESUS CHRIST, UNIVERSAL KING   C
Solemnity

Christ The King

We celebrate Christ our anointed King who overcame suffering and death and so brought us out of darkness into his kingdom of light.

Entrance Antiphon: The Lamb who was slain is worthy to receive strength and divinity, wisdom and power and honour: to him be glory and power for ever.

Opening Prayer
Let us pray
    [that all men will acclaim Jesus as Lord]

Almighty and merciful God,
you break the power of evil
and make all things new
in your Son Jesus Christ, the King of the universe.
May all in heaven and earth acclaim your glory
and never cease to praise you.

or

Let us pray
    [that the kingdom of Christ
    may live in our hearts and come to our world]

Father all-powerful, God of love,
you have raised our Lord Jesus Christ from death to life,
resplendent in glory as King of creation.

Open our hearts,
free all the world to rejoice in his peace,
to glory in his justice, to live in his love.
Bring all mankind together in Jesus Christ your Son,
whose kingdom is with you and the Holy Spirit,
one God, for ever and ever.

FIRST READING

A reading from the second book of Samuel   5:1-3
They anointed David king of Israel.

All the tribes of Israel came to David at Hebron. 'Look' they said
'we are your own flesh and blood. In days past when Saul was
our king, it was you who led Israel in all their exploits; and the
Lord said to you, "You are the man who shall be shepherd of my
people Israel, you shall be the leader of Israel." ' So all the elders
of Israel came to the king at Hebron, and King David made a pact
with them at Hebron in the presence of the Lord, and they
anointed David king of Israel.

This is the word of the Lord.

Responsorial Psalm   Ps 121:1-5. ℟ cf. v.2
  ℟ **I rejoiced when I heard them say:**
      'Let us go to God's house.'

1 I rejoiced when I heard them say:
   'Let us go to God's house.'
   And now our feet are standing
   within your gates, O Jerusalem.   ℟

2 Jerusalem is built as a city
   strongly compact.
   It is there that the tribes go up,
   the tribes of the Lord.   ℟

3 For Israel's law it is,
   there to praise the Lord's name.
   There were set the thrones of judgement
   of the house of David.   ℟

SECOND READING
A reading from the letter of St Paul to the Colossians   1:12-20
He has created a place for us in the kingdom of the Son that he loves.

We give thanks to the Father who has made it possible for you to
join the saints and with them to inherit the light.

   Because that is what he has done: he has taken us out of the
power of darkness and created a place for us in the kingdom of
the Son that he loves, and in him, we gain our freedom, the
forgiveness of our sins.

   He is the image of the unseen God
   and the first-born of all creation,
   for in him were created
   all things in heaven and on earth:
   everything visible and everything invisible,
   Thrones, Dominations, Sovereignties, Powers –
   all things were created through him and for him.
   Before anything was created, he existed,
   and he holds all things in unity.
   Now the Church is his body,
   he is its head.
   As he is the Beginning,
   he was first to be born from the dead,
   so that he should be first in every way;
   because God wanted all perfection

to be found in him
and all things to be reconciled through him and for him,
everything in heaven and everything on earth,
when he made peace
by his death on the cross.

This is the word of the Lord.

Gospel Acclamation   Mk 11:9. 10
Alleluia, alleluia!
Blessings on him who comes in the name of the Lord!
Blessings on the coming kingdom of our father David!
Alleluia!

GOSPEL

A reading from the holy Gospel according to Luke   23:35-43
Lord, remember me when you come into your kingdom.

The people stayed there before the cross watching Jesus. As for
the leaders, they jeered at him. 'He saved others,' they said 'let
him save himself if he is the Christ of God, the Chosen One.' The
soldiers mocked him too, and when they approached to offer him
vinegar they said, 'If you are the king of the Jews, save yourself.'
Above him there was an inscription: 'This is the King of the
Jews.'

One of the criminals hanging there abused him. 'Are you not
the Christ?' he said. 'Save yourself and us as well.' But the other
spoke up and rebuked him. 'Have you no fear of God at all?' he
said, 'You got the same sentence as he did, but in our case we
deserved it: we are paying for what we did. But this man has
done nothing wrong. Jesus,' he said 'remember me when you
come into your kingdom.' 'Indeed, I promise you,' he replied
'today you will be with me in paradise.'

This is the Gospel of the Lord.

Prayer over the Gifts
Lord,
we offer you the sacrifice
by which your Son reconciles mankind.
May it bring unity and peace to the world.

Preface of Christ the King, P51

Communion Antiphon: The Lord will reign for ever and will give
his people the gift of peace.

Prayer after Communion
Lord,
you give us Christ, the King of all creation,
as food for everlasting life.
Help us to live by his gospel
and bring us to the joy of his kingdom,
where he lives and reigns for ever and ever.

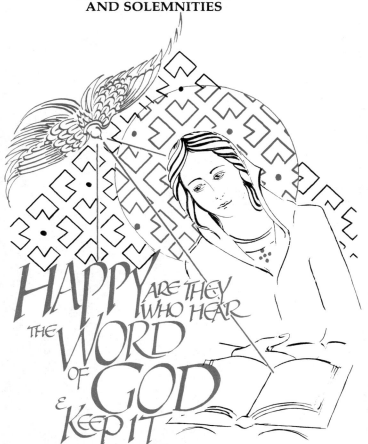

HAPPY ARE THEY WHO HEAR THE WORD OF GOD & KEEP IT

2 February

THE PRESENTATION OF THE LORD
Feast

Today we celebrate the close of the Christmas festival of light. Candles are blessed and we carry them in procession to welcome Christ, the light to enlighten the Gentiles and the glory of his people.

BLESSING OF CANDLES AND PROCESSION

First Form: Procession

The people gather in a chapel or other suitable place outside the church where the Mass will be celebrated. They carry unlighted candles. While the candles are being lighted, this canticle or another hymn is sung:

The Lord will come with mighty power,
and give light to the eyes of all who serve him, alleluia.

The priest greets the people in these or similar words:

Forty days ago we celebrated the joyful feast of the birth of our Lord Jesus Christ. Today we recall the holy day on which he was presented in the temple, fulfilling the law of Moses and at the same time going to meet his faithful people. Led by the Spirit, Simeon and Anna came to the temple, recognised Christ as their Lord, and proclaimed him with joy.

United by the Spirit, may we now go to the house of God to welcome Christ the Lord. There we shall recognise him in the breaking of bread until he comes again in glory.

The priest blesses the candles:

Let us pray.
God our Father, source of all light,
today you revealed to Simeon
your Light of revelation to the nations.
Bless ✠ these candles and make them holy.
May we who carry them to praise your glory
walk in the path of goodness
and come to the light that shines for ever.
or
God our Father, source of eternal light,
fill the hearts of all believers
with the light of faith.

May we who carry these candles in your church
come with joy to the light of glory.

The priest then takes the candle prepared for him, and the
procession begins with the acclamation:

Let us go in peace to meet the Lord.

During the procession, the canticle of Simeon, or another hymn,
is sung:

Antiphon: Christ is the light of the nations
and the glory of Israel his people.

Now, Lord, you have kept your word:
let your servant go in peace. (*Ant.*)

With my own eyes I have seen the salvation
which you have prepared in the sight of every people. (*Ant.*)

A light to reveal you to the nations
and the glory of your people Israel. (*Ant.*)

As the procession enters the church, the entrance chant of the
Mass is sung. The Mass continues as usual.

Second Form: Solemn Entrance

The people, carrying unlighted candles, assemble in the church.
The priest, accompanied by his ministers and by a representative
group of the faithful, goes to a suitable place where most of the
congregation can easily take part.

The candles are lighted while the antiphon, *Christ is the Light*
(see above) or another hymn is sung.

After the greeting and introduction, the priest blesses the
candles, as above, and goes in procession to the altar, while all
are singing. The Mass continues as usual.

THE MASS

Entrance Antiphon: Within your temple, we ponder your loving
kindness, O God. As your name, so also your praise reaches to
the ends of the earth; your right hand is filled with justice.

Opening Prayer
All-powerful Father,
Christ your Son became man for us
and was presented in the temple.
May he free our hearts from sin
and bring us into your presence.

FIRST READING

A reading from the prophet Malachi   3:1-4
The Lord you are seeking will suddenly enter his Temple.

The Lord God says this: Look, I am going to send my messenger
to prepare a way before me. And the Lord you are seeking will
suddenly enter his Temple; and the angel of the covenant whom
you are longing for, yes, he is coming, says the Lord of hosts.
Who will be able to resist the day of his coming? Who will remain
standing when he appears? For he is like the refiner's fire and the
fullers' alkali. He will take his seat as refiner and purifier; he will
purify the sons of Levi and refine them like gold and silver, and
then they will make the offering to the Lord as it should be made.
The offering of Judah and Jerusalem will then be welcomed by
the Lord as in former days, as in the years of old.

This is the word of the Lord.

Responsorial Psalm   Ps 23:7-10. ℟ v.8
    ℟ **Who is the king of glory?**
       It is the Lord.

1 O gates, lift up your heads;
    grow higher, ancient doors.
    Let him enter, the king of glory!   ℟

2 Who is the king of glory?
    The Lord, the mighty, the valiant,
    the Lord, the valiant in war.   ℟

3 O gates, lift high your heads;
    grow higher, ancient doors.
    Let him enter, the king of glory!   ℟

4 Who is he, the king of glory?
    He, the Lord of armies,
    he is the king of glory.   ℟

SECOND READING

A reading from the letter to the Hebrews   2:14-18
*It was essential that he should in this way become completely like his
brothers.*

Since all the children share the same blood and flesh, Jesus too
shared equally in it, so that by his death he could take away all
the power of the devil, who had power over death, and set free

all those who had been held in slavery all their lives by the fear of death. For it was not the angels that he took to himself; he took to himself descent from Abraham. It was essential that he should in this way become completely like his brothers so that he could be a compassionate and trustworthy high priest of God's religion, able to atone for human sins. That is, because he has himself been through temptation he is able to help others who are tempted.

This is the word of the Lord.

Gospel Acclamation   Lk 2:32
    Alleluia, alleluia!
    The light to enlighten the Gentiles
    and give glory to Israel, your people.
    Alleluia!

GOSPEL

A reading from the holy Gospel according to Luke   2:22-40
My eyes have seen your salvation.

*When the day came for them to be purified as laid down by the Law of Moses, the parents of Jesus took him up to Jerusalem to present him to the Lord – observing what stands written in the Law of the Lord: Every first-born male must be consecrated to the Lord – and also to offer in sacrifice, in accordance with what is said in the Law of the Lord, a pair of turtledoves or two young pigeons. Now in Jerusalem there was a man named Simeon. He was an upright and devout man; he looked forward to Israel's comforting and the Holy Spirit rested on him. It had been revealed to him by the Holy Spirit that he would not see death until he had set eyes on the Christ of the Lord. Prompted by the Spirit he came to the Temple; and when the parents brought in the child Jesus to do for him what the law required, he took him into his arms and blessed God; and he said:

    'Now, Master, you can let your servant go in peace,
    just as you promised;
    because my eyes have seen the salvation
    which you have prepared for all the nations to see,
    a light to enlighten the pagans
    and the glory of your people Israel.'*

As the child's father and mother stood there wondering at

the things that were being said about him, Simeon blessed them and said to Mary his mother, 'You see this child: he is destined for the fall and for the rising of many in Israel, destined to be a sign that is rejected – and a sword will pierce your own soul too – so that the secret thoughts of many may be laid bare.'

There was a prophetess also, Anna the daughter of Phanuel, of the tribe of Asher. She was well on in years. Her days of girlhood over, she had been married for seven years before becoming a widow. She was now eighty-four years old and never left the Temple, serving God night and day with fasting and prayer. She came by just at that moment and began to praise God; and she spoke of the child to all who looked forward to the deliverance of Jerusalem.

When they had done everything the Law of the Lord required, they went back to Galilee, to their own town of Nazareth. Meanwhile the child grew to maturity, and he was filled with wisdom; and God's favour was with him.

This is the Gospel of the Lord.

*Shorter Form, Luke 2:22-32. Read between *

Prayer over the Gifts
Lord,
accept the gifts your Church offers you with joy,
since in fulfilment of your will
your Son offered himself as a lamb without blemish
for the life of the world.

Preface of the Presentation of the Lord, P49

Communion Antiphon: With my own eyes I have seen the salvation which you have prepared in the sight of all the nations.

Prayer after Communion
Lord,
you fulfilled the hope of Simeon,
who did not die
until he had been privileged to welcome the Messiah.
May this communion perfect your grace in us
and prepare us to meet Christ
when he comes to bring us into everlasting life,
for he is Lord for ever and ever.

19 March

ST JOSEPH
HUSBAND OF THE BLESSED VIRGIN MARY
Solemnity

A simple village carpenter, Joseph, the husband of Mary and guardian of the child Jesus, has become the guardian and patron of Christ's universal Church.

Entrance Antiphon: The Lord has put his faithful servant in charge of his household.

Opening Prayer

Let us pray
  [that the Church will continue
  the saving work of Christ]

Father,
you entrusted our Saviour to the care of Saint Joseph.
By the help of his prayers
may your Church continue to serve its Lord, Jesus Christ,
who lives and reigns with you and the Holy Spirit,
one God, for ever and ever.

FIRST READING

A reading from the second book of Samuel   7:4-5. 12-14. 16
The Lord will give him the throne of his ancestor David.

The word of the Lord came to Nathan:
  'Go and tell my servant David, "Thus the Lord speaks: When your days are ended and you are laid to rest with your ancestors, I will preserve the offspring of your body after you and make his sovereignty secure. (It is he who shall build a house for my name, and I will make his royal throne secure for ever.) I will be a father to him and he a son to me. Your House and your sovereignty will always stand secure before me and your throne be established for ever." '

  This is the word of the Lord.

Responsorial Psalm   Ps 88:2-5. 27. 29. ℟ v.37
  ℟ **His dynasty shall last for ever.**

1   I will sing for ever of your love, O Lord;
      through all ages my mouth will proclaim your truth.
      Of this I am sure, that your love lasts for ever,
      that your truth is firmly established as the heavens.   ℟

2   'I have made a covenant with my chosen one;
I have sworn to David my servant:
I will establish your dynasty for ever
and set up your throne through all ages.'   ℟

3   He will say to me: 'You are my father,
my God, the rock who saves me.'
I will keep my love for him always;
for him my covenant shall endure.   ℟

SECOND READING

A reading from the letter of St Paul
to the Romans   4:13. 16-18. 22

Though it seemed Abraham's hope could not be fulfilled, he hoped and he
believed.

The promise of inheriting the world was not made to Abraham
and his descendants on account of any law but on account of the
righteousness which consists in faith. That is why what fulfils the
promise depends on faith, so that it may be a free gift and be
available to all of Abraham's descendants, not only those who
belong to the Law but also those who belong to the faith of
Abraham who is the Father of all of us. As scripture says: I have
made you the ancestor of many nations – Abraham is our father
in the eyes of God, in whom he put his faith, and who brings the
dead to life and calls into being what does not exist.

Though it seemed Abraham's hope could not be fullfilled, he
hoped and he believed, and through doing so he did become the
father of many nations exactly as he had been promised: Your
descendants will be as many as the stars. This is the faith that
was 'considered as justifying him'.

This is the word of the Lord.

Gospel Acclamation   Ps 83:5
Glory and praise to you, O Christ.
They are happy who dwell in your house, O Lord,
for ever singing your praise.
Glory and praise to you, O Christ.

GOSPEL

A reading from the holy Gospel   1:16. 18-21. 24
according to Matthew

Joseph did what the angel of the Lord had told him to do.

Jacob was the father of Joseph the husband of Mary; of her was born Jesus who is called Christ.

This is how Jesus Christ came to be born. His mother Mary was betrothed to Joseph; but before they came to live together she was found to be with child through the Holy Spirit. Her husband Joseph, being a man of honour and wanting to spare her publicity, decided to divorce her informally. He had made up his mind to do this when the angel of the Lord appeared to him in a dream and said, 'Joseph son of David, do not be afraid to take Mary home as your wife, because she has conceived what is in her by the Holy Spirit. She will give birth to a son and you must name him Jesus, because he is the one who is to save his people from their sins.' When Joseph woke up he did what the angel of the Lord had told him to do.

This is the Gospel of the Lord.

Alternative Gospel

A reading from the holy Gospel according to Luke   2:41-51

See how worried your father and I have been, looking for you.

Every year the parents of Jesus used to go to Jerusalem to the feast of the Passover. When he was twelve years old, they went up for the feast as usual. When they were on their way home after the feast, the boy Jesus stayed behind in Jerusalem without his parents knowing it. They assumed he was with the caravan, and it was only after a day's journey that they went to look for him among their relations and acquaintances. When they failed to find him they went back to Jerusalem looking for him everywhere.

Three days later, they found him in the Temple, sitting among the doctors, listening to them, and asking them questions; and all those who heard him were astounded at his intelligence and his replies. They were overcome when they saw him, and his mother said to him, 'My child, why have you done this to us? See how worried your father and I have been, looking for you.' 'Why were you looking for me?' he replied 'Did you not know that I must be busy with my Father's affairs?' But they did not understand what he meant.

He then went down with them and came to Nazareth and lived under their authority.

This is the Gospel of the Lord.

The profession of faith is made.

Prayer over the Gifts
Father,
with unselfish love Saint Joseph cared for your Son,
born of the Virgin Mary.
May we also serve you at your altar with pure hearts.
Preface of St Joseph, P62

Communion Antiphon: Come, good and faithful servant! Share the joy of your Lord!

Prayer after Communion
Lord,
today you nourish us at this altar
as we celebrate the feast of Saint Joseph.
Protect your Church always
and in your love watch over the gifts you have given us.

25 March
THE ANNUNCIATION OF THE LORD
Solemnity

We celebrate that great day of decision: Mary's acceptance of the role that God had chosen for her in his plan of redemption.

Entrance Antiphon: As Christ came into the world, he said: Behold! I have come to do your will, O God.

Opening Prayer
Let us pray
    [that Christ, the Word made flesh,
    will make us more like him]

God our Father,
your Word became man and was born of the Virgin Mary.
May we become more like Jesus Christ,
whom we acknowledge as our redeemer, God and man.

or
Let us pray
    [that we may become more like Christ
    who chose to become one of us]

Almighty Father of our Lord Jesus Christ,
you have revealed the beauty of your power
by exalting the lowly virgin of Nazareth
and making her the mother of our Saviour.
May the prayers of this woman
bring Jesus to the waiting world
and fill the void of incompletion
with the presence of her child,
who lives and reigns with you and the Holy Spirit,
one God, for ever and ever.

FIRST READING

A reading from the prophet Isaiah   7:10-14. 8:10
The maiden is with child.

The Lord spoke to Ahaz and said, 'Ask the Lord your God for a
sign for yourself coming either from the depths of Sheol or from
the heights above.' 'No,' Ahaz answered, 'I will not put the Lord
to the test.'
    Then Isaiah said:

Listen now, House of David:
are you not satisfied with trying the patience of men
without trying the patience of my God, too?
The Lord himself, therefore,
will give you a sign.
It is this: the maiden is with child
and will soon give birth to a son
whom she will call Emmanuel,
a name which means, 'God-is-with-us'.

This is the word of the Lord.

Responsorial Psalm   Ps 39:7-11. ℟ vv.8. 9.
    ℟   **Here I am, Lord!**
        I come to do your will.

1   You do not ask for sacrifice and offerings,
    but an open ear.
    You do not ask for holocaust and victim.
    Instead, here am I.   ℟

2 In the scroll of the book it stands written
  that I should do your will.
  My God, I delight in your law
  in the depth of my heart.   ℟

3 Your justice I have proclaimed
  in the great assembly.
  My lips I have not sealed;
  you know it, O Lord.   ℟

4 I have not hidden your justice in my heart
  but declared your faithful help.
  I have not hidden your love and your truth
  from the great assembly.   ℟

SECOND READING

A reading from the letter to the Hebrews   10:4-10

*I was commanded in the scroll of the book, 'God, here I am! I am coming
to obey your will.'*

Bulls' blood and goats' blood are useless for taking away sins,
and this is what Christ said, on coming into the world:

> You who wanted no sacrifice or oblation,
> prepared a body for me.
> You took no pleasure in holocausts or sacrifices for sin;
> then I said,
> just as I was commanded in the scroll of the book,
> 'God, here I am! I am coming to obey your will.'

Notice that he says first: You did not want what the Law lays
down as the things to be offered, that is: the sacrifices, the
oblations, the holocausts and the sacrifices for sin, and you took
no pleasure in them; and then he says: Here I am! I am coming to
obey your will. He is abolishing the first sort to replace it with the
second. And this will was for us to be made holy by the offering
of his body made once and for all by Jesus Christ.

This is the word of the Lord.

Gospel Acclamation   Jn 1:14. 12
> Praise to you, O Christ, king of eternal glory!
> The Word was made flesh,
> he lived among us,
> and we saw his glory.
> Praise to you, O Christ, king of eternal glory!

GOSPEL

A reading from the holy Gospel according to Luke   1:26-38
Listen! You are to conceive and bear a son.

The angel Gabriel was sent by God to a town in Galilee called
Nazareth, to a virgin betrothed to a man named Joseph, of the
House of David; and the virgin's name was Mary. He went in
and said to her, 'Rejoice, so highly favoured! The Lord is with
you.' She was deeply disturbed by these words and asked herself
what this greeting could mean, but the angel said to her, 'Mary,
do not be afraid; you have won God's favour. Listen! You are to
conceive and bear a son, and you must name him Jesus. He will
be great and will be called Son of the Most High. The Lord God
will give him the throne of his ancestor David; he will rule over
the House of Jacob for ever and his reign will have no end.' Mary
said to the angel, 'But how can this come about, since I am a
virgin?' 'The Holy Spirit will come upon you,' the angel
answered, 'and the power of the Most High will cover you with
its shadow. And so the child will be holy and will be called Son of
God. Know this too: your kinswoman Elizabeth has, in her old
age, herself conceived a son, and she whom people called barren
is now in her sixth month, for nothing is impossible to God.' 'I
am the handmaid of the Lord,' said Mary, 'let what you have said
be done to me.' And the angel left her.

This is the Gospel of the Lord.

In the profession of faith, all genuflect at the words, and was made
man.

Prayer over the Gifts
Almighty Father,
as we recall the beginning of the Church
when your Son became man,
may we celebrate with joy today
this sacrament of your love.

Preface of the Annunciation, P44

Communion Antiphon: The Virgin is with child and shall bear a
son, and she will call him Emmanuel.

Prayer after Communion
Lord,
may the sacrament we share
strengthen our faith and hope in Jesus, born of a virgin

and truly God and Man.
By the power of his resurrection
may we come to eternal joy.

24 June
THE BIRTH OF JOHN THE BAPTIST
Solemnity

We celebrate the birthday of John the Baptist, the man specially chosen by God to be the herald of the Saviour and to prepare the people for his coming.

Vigil Mass

Entrance Antiphon: From his mother's womb, he will be filled with the Holy Spirit, he will be great in the sight of the Lord, and many will rejoice at his birth.

The Gloria is sung or said.

Opening Prayer
Let us pray
[that we will follow the way of salvation]

All-powerful God,
help your people to walk the path to salvation.
By following the teaching of John the Baptist,
may we come to your Son, our Lord Jesus Christ,
who lives and reigns with you and the Holy Spirit,
one God, for ever and ever.

FIRST READING

A reading from the prophet Jeremiah   1:4-10
Before I formed you in the womb I knew you.

The word of the Lord was addressed to me, saying,

'Before I formed you in the womb I knew you;
before you came to birth I consecrated you;
I have appointed you as prophet to the nations.'

I said, 'Ah, Lord; look, I do not know how to speak: I am a child!'

But the Lord replied:

'Do not say, "I am a child."
Go now to those to whom I send you
and say whatever I command you.
Do not be afraid of them,
for I am with you to protect you –
it is the Lord who speaks!'

Then the Lord put out his hand and touched my mouth and said to me:

'There! I am putting my words into your mouth.
Look, today I am setting you
over nations and over kingdoms,
to tear up and to knock down,
to destroy and to overthrow,
to build and to plant.'

This is the word of the Lord.

Responsorial Psalm   Ps 70:1-6. 15. 17. ℟ v.6

℟   **From my mother's womb you have been my help.**

1   In you, O Lord, I take refuge;
     let me never be put to shame.
     In your justice rescue me, free me:
     pay heed to me and save me.   ℟

2   Be a rock where I can take refuge,
     a mighty stronghold to save me;
     for you are my rock, my stronghold.
     Free me from the hand of the wicked.   ℟

3   It is you, O Lord, who are my hope,
     my trust, O Lord, since my youth.
     On you I have leaned from my birth,
     from my mother's womb you have been my help.   ℟

4   My lips will tell of your justice
     and day by day of your help.
     O God, you have taught me from my youth
     and I proclaim your wonders still.   ℟

SECOND READING

A reading from the first letter of St Peter 1:8-12

It was this salvation that the prophets were looking and searching so hard for.

You did not see Jesus Christ, yet you love him; and still without seeing him, you are already filled with a joy so glorious that it cannot be described, because you believe; and you are sure of the end to which your faith looks forward, that is, the salvation of your souls.

It was this salvation that the prophets were looking and searching so hard for; their prophecies were about the grace which was to come to you. The Spirit of Christ which was in them foretold the sufferings of Christ and the glories that would come after them, and they tried to find out at what time and in what circumstances all this was to be expected. It was revealed to them that the news they brought of all the things which have now been announced to you, by those who preached to you the Good News through the Holy Spirit sent from heaven, was for you and not for themselves. Even the angels long to catch a glimpse of these things.

This is the word of the Lord.

Gospel Acclamation Jn 1:7; Lk 1:17
Alleluia, alleluia!
He came as a witness,
as a witness to speak for the light,
preparing for the Lord a people fit for him.
Alleluia!

GOSPEL

A reading from the holy Gospel according to Luke 1:5-17

She is to bear you a son and you must name him John.

In the days of King Herod of Judaea there lived a priest called Zechariah who belonged to the Abijah section of the priesthood, and he had a wife, Elizabeth by name, who was a descendant of Aaron. Both were worthy in the sight of God, and scrupulously observed all the commandments and observances of the Lord. But they were childless: Elizabeth was barren and they were both getting on in years.

Now it was the turn of Zechariah's section to serve, and he was exercising his priestly office before God when it fell to him by lot, as the ritual custom was, to enter the Lord's sanctuary and burn incense there. And at the hour of incense the whole congregation was outside, praying.

Then there appeared to him the angel of the Lord, standing on the right of the altar of incense. The sight disturbed Zechariah and he was overcome with fear. But the angel said to him, 'Zechariah, do not be afraid, your prayer has been heard. Your wife Elizabeth is to bear you a son and you must name him John. He will be your joy and delight and many will rejoice at his birth, for he will be great in the sight of the Lord; he must drink no wine, no strong drink. Even from his mother's womb he will be filled with the Holy Spirit, and he will bring back many of the sons of Israel to the Lord their God. With the spirit and power of Elijah, he will go before him to turn the hearts of fathers towards their children and the disobedient back to the wisdom that the virtuous have, preparing for the Lord a people fit for him.'

This is the Gospel of the Lord.

The profession of faith is made.

Prayer over the Gifts
Lord,
look with favour on the gifts we bring
on this feast of John the Baptist.
Help us put into action
the mystery we celebrate in this sacrament.

Preface of St John the Baptist, P61

Communion Antiphon: Blessed be the Lord God of Israel, for he has visited and redeemed his people.

Prayer after Communion

Father,
may the prayers of John the Baptist
lead us to the Lamb of God.
May this eucharist bring us the mercy of Christ,
who is Lord for ever and ever.

Mass During the Day

Entrance Antiphon: There was a man sent from God whose name was John. He came to bear witness to the light, to prepare an upright people for the Lord.

Opening Prayer
Let us pray
> [that God will give us joy and peace]

God our Father,
you raised up John the Baptist
to prepare a perfect people for Christ the Lord.
Give your Church joy in spirit
and guide those who believe in you
into the way of salvation and peace.

or

Let us pray
> [as we honour John the Baptist
> for the faith to recognise Christ in our midst]

God our Father,
the voice of John the Baptist challenges us to repentance
and points the way to Christ the Lord.

Open our ears to his message, and free our hearts
to turn from our sins and receive the life of the gospel.

FIRST READING
A reading from the prophet Isaiah   49:1-6
I will make you the light of the nations.

Islands, listen to me,
pay attention, remotest peoples.
The Lord called me before I was born,
from my mother's womb he pronounced my name.

He made my mouth a sharp sword,
and hid me in the shadow of his hand.
He made me into a sharpened arrow,
and concealed me in his quiver.

He said to me, 'You are my servant (Israel)
in whom I shall be glorified';
while I was thinking 'I have toiled in vain,
I have exhausted myself for nothing';

and all the while my cause was with the Lord,
my reward with my God.
I was honoured in the eyes of the Lord,
my God was my strength.

And now the Lord has spoken,
he who formed me in the womb to be his servant,
to bring Jacob back to him,
to gather Israel to him:
'It is not enough for you to be my servant,
to restore the tribes of Jacob and bring back the survivors of
    Israel;
I will make you the light of the nations
so that my salvation may reach to the ends of the earth.'

    This is the word of the Lord.

Responsorial Psalm   Ps 138:1-3. 13-15. R̦ v.14
    R̦   **I thank you for the wonder of my being.**

1   O Lord, you search me and you know me,
     you know my resting and my rising,
     you discern my purpose from afar.
     You mark when I walk or lie down,
     all my ways lie open to you.   R̦

2   For it was you who created my being,
     knit me together in my mother's womb.
     I thank you for the wonder of my being,
     for the wonders of all your creation.   R̦

3   Already you knew my soul,
     my body held no secret from you
     when I was being fashioned in secret
     and moulded in the depths of the earth.   R̦

SECOND READING

A reading from the Acts of the Apostles   13:22-26
Jesus, whose coming was heralded by John.

Paul said: 'God made David the king of our ancestors, of whom
he approved in these words, "I have selected David son of Jesse,
a man after my own heart, who will carry out my whole
purpose." To keep his promise, God has raised up for Israel one
of David's descendants, Jesus, as Saviour, whose coming was
heralded by John when he proclaimed a baptism of repentance

for the whole people of Israel. Before John ended his career he
said, "I am not the one you imagine me to be; that one is coming
after me and I am not fit to undo his sandal."

'My brothers, sons of Abraham's race, and all you who fear
God, this message of salvation is meant for you.'

This is the word of the Lord.

Gospel Acclamation   cf. Lk 1:76
Alleluia, alleluia!
As for you, little child, you shall be called
a prophet of God, the Most High.
You shall go ahead of the Lord
to prepare his ways before him.
Alleluia!

GOSPEL

A reading from the holy Gospel according to Luke   1:57-66. 80
His name is John.

The time came for Elizabeth to have her child, and she gave birth
to a son; and when her neighbours and relations heard that the
Lord had shown her so great a kindness, they shared her joy.

Now on the eighth day they came to circumcise the child; they
were going to call him Zechariah after his father, but his mother
spoke up. 'No,' she said 'he is to be called John.' They said to her,
'But no one in your family has that name', and made signs to his
father to find out what he wanted him called. The father asked
for a writing tablet and wrote, 'His name is John.' And they were
all astonished. At that instant his power of speech returned and
he spoke and praised God. All their neighbours were filled with
awe and the whole affair was talked about throughout the hill
country of Judaea. All those who heard of it treasured it in their
hearts. 'What will this child turn out to be?' they wondered. And
indeed the hand of the Lord was with him. The child grew up
and his spirit matured. And he lived out in the wilderness until
the day he appeared openly to Israel.

This is the Gospel of the Lord.

The profession of faith is made.

Prayer over the Gifts
Father,
accept the gifts we bring to your altar

to celebrate the birth of John the Baptist,
who foretold the coming of our Saviour
and made him known when he came.

Preface of St John the Baptist, P61

Communion Antiphon: Through the tender compassion of our
God, the dawn from on high shall break upon us.

Prayer after Communion
Lord,
you have renewed us with this eucharist,
as we celebrate the feast of John the Baptist,
who foretold the coming of the Lamb of God.
May we welcome your Son as our Saviour,
for he gives us new life,
and is Lord for ever and ever.

29 June

SAINTS PETER AND PAUL, APOSTLES
Solemnity

*We celebrate the feast of the princes of the apostles, from whom we derive
our Christian faith. The Lord stood by them and gave them power, so
that through them the whole message might be proclaimed for all the
world to hear.*

Vigil Mass

Entrance Antiphon: Peter the apostle and Paul the teacher of the
Gentiles have brought us to know the law of the Lord.

The Gloria is sung or said.

Opening Prayer
Let us pray
　　[that the prayers of the apostles
　　will lead us to salvation.]

Lord our God,
encourage us through the prayers of Saints Peter and Paul.
May the apostles who strengthened the faith of the infant Church
help us on our way of salvation.

or

Let us pray
[to be true to the faith
which has come to us through the apostles Peter and Paul]

Father in heaven,
the light of your revelation brought Peter and Paul
the gift of faith in Jesus your Son.

Through their prayers
may we always give thanks for your life
given us in Christ Jesus,
and for having been enriched by him
in all knowledge and love.

FIRST READING

A reading from the Acts of the Apostles

3:1-10

I will give you what I have: in the name of Jesus stand up and walk!

Once, when Peter and John were going up to the Temple for the prayers at the ninth hour, it happened that there was a man being carried past. He was a cripple from birth; and they used to put him down every day near the Temple entrance called the Beautiful Gate so that he could beg from the people going in. When this man saw Peter and John on their way into the Temple he begged from them. Both Peter and John looked straight at him and said, 'Look at us.' He turned to them expectantly, hoping to get something from them, but Peter said, 'I have neither silver nor gold, but I will give you what I have: in the name of Jesus Christ the Nazarene, walk!' Peter then took him by the hand and helped him to stand up. Instantly his feet and ankles became firm, he jumped up, stood, and began to walk, and he went with them into the Temple, walking and jumping and praising God. Everyone could see him walking and praising God, and they recognised him as the man who used to sit begging at the Beautiful Gate of the Temple. They were all astonished and unable to explain what had happened to him.

This is the word of the Lord.

Responsorial Psalm   Ps 18:2-5. ℟ v.5

℟   **Their word goes forth through all the earth.**

1   The heavens proclaim the glory of God
    and the firmament shows forth the work of his hands.
    Day unto day takes up the story
    and night unto night makes known the message.   ℟

2   No speech, no word, no voice is heard
    yet their span extends through all the earth,
    their words to the utmost bounds of the world.   ℟

SECOND READING

A reading from the letter of St Paul to the Galatians   1:11-20

God specially chose me while I was still in my mother's womb.

The Good News I preached is not a human message that I was
given by men, it is something I learnt only through a revelation of
Jesus Christ. You must have heard of my career as a practising
Jew, how merciless I was in persecuting the Church of God, how
much damage I did to it, how I stood out among other Jews of my
generation, and how enthusiastic I was for the traditions of my
ancestors.

Then God, who had specially chosen me while I was still in
my mother's womb, called me through his grace and chose to
reveal his Son to me, so that I might preach the Good News about
him to the pagans. I did not stop to discuss this with any human
being, nor did I go up to Jerusalem to see those who were already
apostles before me, but I went off to Arabia at once and later
went straight back from there to Damascus. Even when after
three years I went up to Jerusalem to visit Cephas and stayed
with him for fifteen days, I did not see any of the other apostles; I
only saw James, the brother of the Lord, and I swear before God
that what I have just written is the literal truth.

This is the word of the Lord.

Gospel Acclamation   Jn 21:17
    Alleluia, alleluia!
    Lord, you know everything;
    you know I love you.
    Alleluia!

GOSPEL

A reading from the holy Gospel according to John   21:15-19
Feed my lambs, feed my sheep.

After Jesus had shown himself to his disciples and eaten with them, he said to Simon Peter, 'Simon son of John, do you love me more than these others do?' He answered, 'Yes, Lord, you know I love you.' Jesus said to him, 'Feed my lambs.' A second time he said to him, 'Simon son of John, do you love me?' He replied, 'Yes, Lord, you know I love you.' Jesus said to him, 'Look after my sheep.' Then he said to him a third time, 'Simon son of John, do you love me?' Peter was upset that he asked him the third time, 'Do you love me?' and said, 'Lord, you know everything; you know I love you.' Jesus said to him, 'Feed my sheep.

> 'I tell you most solemnly,
> when you were young
> you put on your own belt
> and walked where you liked;
> but when you grow old
> you will stretch out your hands,
> and somebody else will put a belt round you
> and take you where you would rather not go.'

In these words he indicated the kind of death by which Peter would give glory to God. After this he said, 'Follow me.'

This is the Gospel of the Lord.

The profession of faith is made.

Prayer over the Gifts
Lord,
we present these gifts
on this feast of the apostles Peter and Paul.
Help us to know our own weakness
and to rejoice in your saving power.

Preface of Peter and Paul, P63

Communion Antiphon: Simon, son of John, do you love me more than these? Lord, you know all things; you know that I love you.

Prayer after Communion
Father,
you give us light by the teaching of your apostles.
In this sacrament we have received
fill us with your strength.

Mass during the Day

Entrance Antiphon: These men, conquering all human frailty, shed their blood and helped the Church to grow. By sharing the cup of the Lord's suffering, they became the friends of God.

Opening Prayer
Let us pray
[that we will remain true to the faith of the apostles]

God our Father,
today you give us the joy
of celebrating the feast of the apostles Peter and Paul.
Through them your Church first received the faith.
Keep us true to their teaching.

or

Let us pray
[One with Peter and Paul in our faith in Christ the Son of the living God]

Praise to you, the God and Father of our Lord Jesus Christ,
who in your great mercy
have given us new birth and hope
through the power of Christ's resurrection.

Through the prayers of the apostles Peter and Paul
may we who receive this faith through their preaching
share their joy in following the Lord
to the unfading inheritance
reserved for us in heaven.

FIRST READING

A reading from the Acts of the Apostles   12:1-11
Now I know the Lord really did save me from Herod.

King Herod started persecuting certain members of the Church. He beheaded James the brother of John, and when he saw that this pleased the Jews he decided to arrest Peter as well. This was during the days of Unleavened Bread, and he put Peter in prison, assigning four squads of four soldiers each to guard him in turns. Herod meant to try Peter in public after the end of Passover week. All the time Peter was under guard the Church prayed to God for him unremittingly.

On the night before Herod was to try him, Peter was sleeping between two soldiers, fastened with double chains, while guards kept watch at the main entrance to the prison. Then suddenly the angel of the Lord stood there, and the cell was filled with light. He tapped Peter on the side and woke him. 'Get up!' he said 'Hurry!' – and the chains fell from his hands. The angel then said, 'Put on your belt and sandals.' After he had done this, the angel next said, 'Wrap your cloak round you and follow me.' Peter followed him, but had no idea that what the angel did was all happening in reality; he thought he was seeing a vision. They passed through two guard posts one after the other, and reached the iron gate leading to the city. This opened of its own accord; they went through it and had walked the whole length of one street when suddenly the angel left him. It was only then that Peter came to himself. 'Now I know it is all true,' he said. 'The Lord really did send his angel and has saved me from Herod and from all that the Jewish people were so certain would happen to me.'

This is the word of the Lord.

Responsorial Psalm   Ps 33:2-9. ℟ v.5. Alt. ℟ v.8

℟ **From all my terrors the Lord set me free.**

or

℟ **The angel of the Lord rescues those who revere him.**

1   I will bless the Lord at all times,
     his praise always on my lips;
     in the Lord my soul shall make its boast.
     The humble shall hear and be glad.   ℟

2   Glorify the Lord with me.
     Together let us praise his name.
     I sought the Lord and he answered me;
     from all my terrors he set me free.   ℟

3   Look towards him and be radiant;
     let your faces not be abashed.
     This poor man called; the Lord heard him
     and rescued him from all his distress.   ℟

4   The angel of the Lord is encamped
     around those who revere him, to rescue them.
     Taste and see that the Lord is good.
     He is happy who seeks refuge in him.   ℟

SECOND READING

A reading from the second letter of St Paul   4:6-8. 17-18
to Timothy
All there is to come now is the crown of righteousness reserved for me.

My life is already being poured away as a libation, and the time
has come for me to be gone. I have fought the good fight to the
end; I have run the race to the finish; I have kept the faith; all
there is to come now is the crown of righteousness reserved for
me, which the Lord, the righteous judge, will give to me on that
Day; and not only to me but to all those who have longed for his
Appearing.

The Lord stood by me and gave me power, so that through
me the whole message might be proclaimed for all the pagans to
hear; and so I was rescued from the lion's mouth. The Lord will
rescue me from all evil attempts on me, and bring me safely to his
heavenly kingdom. To him be glory for ever and ever. Amen

This is the word of the Lord.

Gospel Acclamation   Mt 16:18
Alleluia, alleluia!
You are Peter and on this rock I will build my Church.
And the gates of the underworld can never hold out against it.
Alleluia!

GOSPEL

A reading from the holy Gospel according to Matthew   16:13-19
You are Peter, and I will give you the keys of the kingdom of heaven.

When Jesus came to the region of Caesarea Philippi he put this
question to his disciples, 'Who do people say the Son of Man is?'
And they said, 'Some say he is John the Baptist, some Elijah, and
others Jeremiah or one of the prophets.' 'But you,' he said 'who
do you say I am?' Then Simon Peter spoke up, 'You are the
Christ,' he said 'the Son of the living God.' Jesus replied, 'Simon
son of Jonah, you are a happy man! Because it was not flesh and
blood that revealed this to you but my Father in heaven. So I now
say to you: You are Peter and on this rock I will build my Church.
And the gates of the underworld can never hold out against it. I
will give you the keys of the kingdom of heaven: whatever you
bind on earth shall be considered bound in heaven; whatever you
loose on earth shall be considered loosed in heaven.'

This is the Gospel of the Lord.

Prayer over the Gifts
Lord,
may your apostles join their prayers to our offering
and help us to celebrate this sacrifice in love and unity.

Preface of Peter and Paul, Apostles, P63

Communion Antiphon: Peter said: You are the Christ, the Son of
the living God. Jesus answered: You are Peter, the rock on which
I will build my Church.

Prayer after Communion
Lord,
renew the life of your Church
with the power of this sacrament.
May the breaking of bread
and the teaching of the apostles
keep us united in your love.

Solemn Blessing
Bow your heads and pray for God's blessing.

The Lord has set you firm within his Church,
which he built upon the rock of Peter's faith.
May he bless you with a faith that never falters.   ℟   **Amen.**

The Lord has given you knowledge of the faith
through the labours and preaching of Saint Paul.
May his example inspire you to lead others to Christ
by the manner of your life.   ℟   **Amen.**

May the keys of Peter, and the words of Paul,
their undying witness and their prayers,
lead you to the joy of that eternal home
which Peter gained by his cross, and Paul by the sword.
    ℟   **Amen.**

May almighty God bless you,
the Father, and the Son ✠ and the Holy Spirit.   ℟   **Amen.**

6 August

THE TRANSFIGURATION OF THE LORD
Feast

It is wonderful for us to be here today as we celebrate the transfigured Christ, the Christ of prophecy, in whom we have believed.

Entrance Antiphon: In the shining cloud the Spirit is seen; from it the voice of the Father is heard: This is my Son, my beloved, in whom is all my delight. Listen to him.

Opening Prayer
Let us pray
    [that we may hear the Lord Jesus
    and share his everlasting life]

God our Father,
in the transfigured glory of Christ your Son,
you strengthen our faith
by confirming the witness of your prophets,
and show us the splendour of your beloved sons and daughters.
As we listen to the voice of your Son,
help us to become heirs to eternal life with him
for he lives and reigns with you and the Holy Spirit,
one God, for ever and ever.

FIRST READING

A reading from the book of Daniel   7:9-10. 13-14
His robe was white as snow.

As I watched:
Thrones were set in place
and one of great age took his seat.
His robe was white as snow,
the hair of his head as pure as wool.
His throne was a blaze of flames,
its wheels were a burning fire.
A stream of fire poured out,
issuing from his presence.
A thousand thousand waited on him,
ten thousand times ten thousand stood before him.
A court was held and the books were opened.
I gazed into the visions of the night.
And I saw, coming on the clouds of heaven,

one like a son of man.
He came to the one of great age
and was led into his presence
On him was conferred sovereignty,
glory and kingship,
and men of all peoples, nations and languages became his
  servants.
His sovereignty is an eternal sovereignty
which shall never pass away,
nor will his empire ever be destroyed.

This is the word of the Lord.

Responsorial Psalm Ps 96:1-2. 5-6. 9. ℟ vv.1.9
  ℟ **The Lord is king,**
      most high above all the earth.

1 The Lord is king, let earth rejoice,
    let all the coastlands be glad.
    Cloud and darkness are his raiment;
    his throne, justice and right. ℟

2 The mountains melt like wax
    before the Lord of all the earth.
    The skies proclaim his justice;
    all peoples see his glory. ℟

3 For you indeed are the Lord
    most high above all the earth
    exalted far above all spirits. ℟

SECOND READING
A reading from the second letter of St Peter 1:16-19
We heard this ourselves, spoken from heaven.

It was not any cleverly invented myths that we were repeating
when we brought you the knowledge of the power and the
coming of our Lord Jesus Christ; we had seen his majesty for
ourselves. He was honoured and glorified by God the Father,
when the Sublime Glory itself spoke to him and said, 'This is my
Son, the Beloved; he enjoys my favour.' We heard this ourselves,
spoken from heaven, when we were with him on the holy
mountain.

So we have confirmation of what was said in prophecies; and
you will be right to depend on prophecy and take it as a lamp

for lighting a way through the dark until the dawn comes and the morning star rises in your minds.

This is the word of the Lord.

Gospel Acclamation   Mt 17:5
Alleluia, alleluia!
This is my Son, the Beloved,
he enjoys my favour;
listen to him.
Alleluia!

GOSPEL

Year A

A reading from the holy Gospel according to Matthew   17:1-9
We heard this ourselves, spoken from heaven.

Jesus took with him Peter and James and his brother John and led them up a high mountain where they could be alone. There in their presence he was transfigured: his face shone like the sun and his clothes became as white as the light. Suddenly Moses and Elijah appeared to them; they were talking with him. Then Peter spoke to Jesus. 'Lord,' he said 'it is wonderful for us to be here; if you wish, I will make three tents here, one for you, one for Moses and one for Elijah.' He was still speaking when suddenly a bright cloud covered them with shadow, and from the cloud there came a voice which said, 'This is my Son; the Beloved; he enjoys my favour. Listen to him.' When they heard this, the disciples fell on their faces, overcome with fear. But Jesus came up and touched them. 'Stand up,' he said 'do not be afraid.' And when they raised their eyes they saw no one but only Jesus.

As they came down from the mountain Jesus gave them this order, 'Tell no one about the vision until the Son of Man has risen from the dead.'

This is the Gospel of the Lord.

Year B

A reading from the holy Gospel according to Mark   9:2-10
This is my Son the Beloved.

Jesus took with him Peter and James and John and led them up a high mountain where they could be alone by themselves. There in their presence he was transfigured: his clothes became dazzlingly white, whiter than any earthly bleacher could make them. Elijah appeared to them with Moses; and they were talking with Jesus. Then Peter spoke to Jesus: 'Rabbi,' he said 'it is wonderful for us to be here; so let us make three tents, one for you, one for Moses and one for Elijah.' He did not know what to say; they were so frightened. And a cloud came, covering them in shadow; and there came a voice from the cloud, 'This is my Son, the Beloved. Listen to him.' Then suddenly, when they looked round, they saw no one with them any more but only Jesus.

As they came down from the mountain he warned them to tell no one what they had seen, until after the Son of Man had risen from the dead. They observed the warning faithfully, though among themselves they discussed what 'rising from the dead' could mean.

This is the Gospel of the Lord.

Year C

A reading from the holy Gospel according to Luke   9:28-36

Moses and Elijah were talking about his death.

Jesus took with him Peter and John and James and went up the mountain to pray. As he prayed, the aspect of his face was changed and his clothing became brilliant as lightning. Suddenly there were two men there talking to him; they were Moses and Elijah appearing in glory, and they were speaking of his passing which he was to accomplish in Jerusalem. Peter and his companions were heavy with sleep, but they kept awake and saw his glory and the two men standing with him. As these were leaving him, Peter said to Jesus, 'Master, it is wonderful for us to be here; so let us make three tents, one for you, one for Moses and one for Elijah.' – He did not know what he was saying. As he spoke, a cloud came and covered them with shadow; and when they went into the cloud the disciples were afraid. And a voice came from the cloud, saying, 'This is my Son, the Chosen One. Listen to him.' And after the voice had spoken, Jesus was found alone. The disciples kept silence and, at that time, told no one what they had seen.

This is the Gospel of the Lord.

Prayer over the Gifts
Lord,
by the transfiguration of your Son

make our gifts holy,
and by his radiant glory free us from our sins.

Preface of the Transfiguration, P50

Communion Antiphon: When Christ is revealed we shall be like him, for we shall see him as he is.

Prayer after Communion
Lord,
you revealed the true radiance of Christ
in the glory of his transfiguration.
May the food we receive from heaven
change us into his image.

15 August

THE ASSUMPTION
OF THE BLESSED VIRGIN MARY
Solemnity

*In Mary's glorious assumption we celebrate the fulfilment of our
Christian destiny, and with her we proclaim the greatness of the Lord.*

Vigil Mass

Entrance Antiphon: All honour to you, Mary! Today you were raised above the choirs of angels to lasting glory with Christ.

The Gloria is sung or said.

Opening Prayer
Let us pray
    [that the Virgin Mary will help us
    with her prayers]

Almighty God,
you gave a humble virgin
the privilege of being the mother of your Son,
and crowned her with the glory of heaven.
May the prayers of the Virgin Mary
bring us to the salvation of Christ
and raise us up to eternal life.

or

Let us pray
  [with Mary to the Father,
  in whose presence she now dwells]

Almighty Father of our Lord Jesus Christ,
you have revealed the beauty of your power
by exalting the lowly virgin of Nazareth
and making her the mother of our Saviour.
May the prayers of this woman clothed with the sun
bring Jesus to the waiting world
and fill the void of incompletion
with the presence of her child
who lives and reigns . . .

FIRST READING

A reading from the first book of Chronicles   15:3-4. 15-16; 16:1-2

They brought in the ark of God and set it inside the tent which David had pitched for it.

David gathered all Israel together in Jerusalem to bring the ark of God up to the place he had prepared for it. David called together the sons of Aaron and the sons of Levi. And the Levites carried the ark of God with the shafts on their shoulders, as Moses had ordered in accordance with the word of the Lord.

David then told the heads of the Levites to assign duties for their kinsmen as cantors, with their various instruments of music, harps and lyres and cymbals, to play joyful tunes. They brought the ark of God in and put it inside the tent that David had pitched for it; and they offered holocausts before God, and communion sacrifices. And when David had finished offering holocausts and communion sacrifices, he blessed the people in the name of the Lord.

This is the word of the Lord.

Responsorial Psalm   Ps 131:6-7. 9-10. 13-14. ℞ v.8

  ℞ **Go up, Lord, to the place of your rest,
      you and the ark of your strength.**

1   At Ephrata we heard of the ark;
    we found it in the plains of Yearim.
    'Let us go to the place of his dwelling;
    let us go to kneel at his footstool.'   ℞

2 Your priests shall be clothed with holiness:
   your faithful shall ring out their joy.
   For the sake of David your servant
   do not reject your anointed.

   ℟ **Go up, Lord, to the place of your rest,**
      you and the ark of your strength.

3 For the Lord has chosen Zion;
   he has desired it for his dwelling:
   'This is my resting-place for ever,
   here have I chosen to live.' ℟

SECOND READING

A reading from the first letter of St Paul   15:54-57
to the Corinthians
He gave us victory through our Lord Jesus Christ.

When this perishable nature has put on imperishability, and
when this mortal nature has put on immortality, then the words
of scripture will come true: Death is swallowed up in victory.
Death, where is your victory? Death, where is your sting? Now
the sting of death is sin, and sin gets its power from the Law. So
let us thank God for giving us the victory through our Lord Jesus
Christ.

   This is the word of the Lord.

Gospel Acclamation   Lk 11:28
   Alleluia, alleluia!
   Happy are those
   who hear the word of God,
   and keep it.
   Alleluia!

GOSPEL

A reading from the holy Gospel according to Luke   11:27-28
Happy the womb that bore you!

As Jesus was speaking, a woman in the crowd raised her voice
and said, 'Happy the womb that bore you and the breasts you
sucked!' But he replied, 'Still happier those who hear the word of
God and keep it!'

   This is the Gospel of the Lord.

The profession of faith is made.

Prayer over the Gifts
Lord,
receive this sacrifice of praise and peace
in honour of the assumption of the Mother of God.
May our offering bring us pardon
and make our lives a thanksgiving to you.

Preface of the Assumption, P59

Communion Antiphon: Blessed is the womb of the Virgin Mary; she
carried the Son of the eternal Father.

Prayer after Communion
God of mercy,
we rejoice because Mary, the mother of our Lord,
was taken into the glory of heaven.
May the holy food we receive at this table
free us from evil.

Mass during the Day

Entrance Antiphon: A great sign appeared in heaven: a woman
clothed with the sun, the moon beneath her feet, and a crown of
twelve stars on her head.

or

Let us rejoice in the Lord and celebrate this feast in honour of the
Virgin Mary, at whose assumption the angels rejoice, giving
praise to the Son of God.

Opening Prayer
Let us pray
[that we will join Mary, the mother of the Lord, in the glory of
heaven]
All-powerful and ever-living God,
you raised the sinless Virgin Mary, mother of your Son,
body and soul to the glory of heaven.
May we see heaven as our final goal
and come to share her glory.

or

Let us pray
[that with the help of Mary's prayers
we too may reach our heavenly home]

Father in heaven,
all creation rightly gives you praise,
for all life and all holiness come from you.

In the plan of your wisdom
she who bore the Christ in her womb
was raised body and soul in glory to be with him in heaven.
May we follow her example in reflecting your holiness
and join in her hymn of endless life and praise.

FIRST READING

A reading from the book of the Apocalypse   11:19; 12:1-6. 10
A woman adorned with the sun standing on the moon.

The sanctuary of God in heaven opened, and the ark of the covenant could be seen inside it.

Now a great sign appeared in heaven: a woman, adorned with the sun, standing on the moon, and with the twelve stars on her head for a crown. She was pregnant, and in labour, crying aloud in the pangs of childbirth. Then a second sign appeared in the sky, a huge red dragon which had seven heads and ten horns, and each of the seven heads crowned with a coronet. Its tail dragged a third of the stars from the sky and dropped them to the earth, and the dragon stopped in front of the woman as she was having the child, so that he could eat it as soon as it was born from its mother. The woman brought a male child into the world, the son who was to rule all the nations with an iron sceptre, and the child was taken straight up to God and to his throne, while the woman escaped into the desert, where God had made a place of safety ready. Then I heard a voice shout from heaven, 'Victory and power and empire for ever have been won by our God, and all authority for his Christ.'

This is the word of the Lord.

Responsorial Psalm   Ps 44:10-12. 16. ℟ v.10

℟ **On your right stands the queen,
   in garments of gold.**

1 The daughters of kings are among your loved ones.
   On your right stands the queen in gold of Ophir.
   Listen, O daughter, give ear to my words:
   forget your own people and your father's house.   ℟

2 So will the king desire your beauty:
   He is your lord, pay homage to him.

They are escorted amid gladness and joy;
they pass within the palace of the king. ℟

SECOND READING

A reading from the first letter of St Paul
to the Corinthians

15:20-26

Christ as the first-fruits and then those who belong to him.

Christ has been raised from the dead, the first-fruits of all who
have fallen asleep. Death came through one man and in the same
way the resurrection of the dead has come through one man. Just
as all men die in Adam, so all men will be brought to life in
Christ; but all of them in their proper order: Christ as the
first-fruits and then, after the coming of Christ, those who belong
to him. After that will come the end, when he hands over the
kingdom to God the Father, having done away with every
sovereignty, authority and power. For he must be king until he
has put all his enemies under his feet and the last of the enemies
to be destroyed is death, for everything is to be put under his
feet.

This is the word of the Lord.

Gospel Acclamation
Alleluia, alleluia!
Mary has been taken up into heaven;
all the choirs of angels are rejoicing.
Alleluia!

GOSPEL

A reading from the holy Gospel according to Luke

1:39-56

The Almighty has done great things for me, he has exalted the lowly.

Mary set out and went as quickly as she could to a town in the hill
country of Judah. She went into Zechariah's house and greeted
Elizabeth. Now as soon as Elizabeth heard Mary's greeting, the
child leapt in her womb and Elizabeth was filled with the Holy
Spirit. She gave a loud cry and said, 'Of all women you are the
most blessed, and blessed is the fruit of your womb. Why should
I be honoured with a visit from the mother of my Lord? From the
moment your greeting reached my ears, the child in my womb
leapt for joy. Yes, blessed is she who believed that the promise
made her by the Lord would be fulfilled.'
And Mary said:

'My soul proclaims the greatness of the Lord
and my spirit exults in God my saviour;
because he has looked upon his lowly handmaid.
Yes, from this day forward all generations will call me
     blessed,
for the Almighty has done great things for me.
Holy is his name,
and his mercy reaches from age to age for those who fear him.
He has shown the power of his arm,
he has routed the proud of heart.
He has pulled down princes from their thrones and exalted
     the lowly.
The hungry he has filled with good things, the rich sent
     empty away.
He has come to the help of Israel his servant, mindful of his
     mercy
– according to the promise he made to our ancestors –
of his mercy to Abraham and to his descendants for ever.'

Mary stayed with Elizabeth about three months and then went
back home.

   This is the Gospel of the Lord.

The profession of faith is made.

Prayer over the Gifts
Lord,
receive this offering of our service.
You raised the Virgin Mary to the glory of heaven.
By her prayers, help us to seek you
and to live in your love.

Preface of the Assumption, P59

Communion Antiphon: All generations will call me blessed, for the
Almighty has done great things for me.

Prayer after Communion
Lord,
may we who receive this sacrament of salvation
be led to the glory of heaven
by the prayers of the Virgin Mary.

14 September
THE TRIUMPH OF THE CROSS
Feast

The cross on which Jesus, the Son of Man, was lifted up has become the symbol of his victory over the power of evil. He made the instrument of humiliation, torture and death the instrument of our redemption.

Entrance Antiphon: We should glory in the cross of our Lord Jesus Christ, for he is our salvation, our life and our resurrection; through him we are saved and made free.

Opening Prayer
Let us pray
    [that the death of Christ on the cross
    will bring us to the glory of the resurrection]

God our Father,
in obedience to you
your only Son accepted death on the cross
for the salvation of mankind.
We acknowledge the mystery of the cross on earth.
May we receive the gift of redemption in heaven.

FIRST READING
A reading from the book of Numbers   21:4-9
If anyone was bitten by a serpent, he looked at the bronze serpent and lived.

On the way through the wilderness, the Israelites lost patience. They spoke against God and against Moses, 'Why did you bring us out of Egypt to die in this wilderness? For there is neither bread nor water here; we are sick of this unsatisfying food.'

At this God sent fiery serpents among the people; their bite brought death to many in Israel. The people came and said to Moses, 'We have sinned by speaking against the Lord and against you. Intercede for us with the Lord to save us from these serpents.' Moses interceded for the people, and the Lord answered him, 'Make a fiery serpent and put it on a standard. If anyone is bitten and looks at it, he shall live.' So Moses fashioned a bronze serpent which he put on a standard, and if anyone was bitten by a serpent, he looked at the bronze serpent and lived.

This is the word of the Lord.

Responsorial Psalm   Ps 77:1-2. 34-38. ℞ v.7
  ℞ **Never forget the deeds of the Lord.**

1 Give heed, my people, to my teaching;
   turn your ear to the words of my mouth.
   I will open my mouth in a parable
   and reveal hidden lessons of the past.   ℞

2 When he slew them then they would seek him,
   return and seek him in earnest.
   They would remember that God was their rock,
   God the Most High their redeemer.   ℞

3 But the words they spoke were mere flattery;
   they lied to him with their lips.
   For their hearts were not truly with him;
   they were not faithful to his covenant.   ℞

4 Yet he who is full of compassion
   forgave their sin and spared them.
   So often he held back his anger
   when he might have stirred up his rage.   ℞

SECOND READING

A reading from the letter of St Paul to the Philippians   2:6-11
He humbled himself, therefore God raised him high.

The state of Jesus Christ was divine,
yet he did not cling
to his equality with God
but emptied himself
to assume the condition of a slave,
and became as men are;
and being as all men are,
he was humbler yet,
even to accepting death,
death on a cross.
But God raised him high
and gave him the name
which is above all other names
so that all beings
in the heavens, on earth and in the underworld,
should bend the knee at the name of Jesus
and that every tongue should acclaim
Jesus Christ as Lord,

to the glory of God the Father.

This is the word of the Lord.

Gospel Acclamation
Alleluia, alleluia!
We adore you, O Christ,
and we bless you;
because by your cross
you have redeemed the world.
Alleluia!

GOSPEL

A reading from the holy Gospel according to John　　　3:13-17
The Son of Man must be lifted up.

Jesus said to Nicodemus:

'No one has gone up to heaven
except the one who came down from heaven,
the Son of Man who is in heaven;
and the Son of Man must be lifted up
as Moses lifted up the serpent in the desert,
so that everyone who believes may have eternal life in him.
Yes, God loved the world so much
that he gave his only Son,
so that everyone who believes in him may not be lost
but may have eternal life.
For God sent his Son into the world
not to condemn the world,
but so that through him the world might be saved.'

This is the Gospel of the Lord.

Prayer over the Gifts
Lord,
may this sacrifice once offered on the cross
to take away the sins of the world
now free us from our sins.

Preface of the Triumph of the Cross, P46 or of the Passion of the
Lord I, P17

Communion Antiphon: When I am lifted up from the earth, I will
draw all men to myself, says the Lord.

Prayer after Communion
Lord Jesus Christ,
you are the holy bread of life.
Bring to the glory of the resurrection.
the people you have redeemed by the wood of the cross.

1 November

ALL SAINTS
Solemnity

*Today we offer the Lamb and celebrate the victory of our God in the
company of all the redeemed in the heavenly kingdom.*

Entrance Antiphon: Let us all rejoice in the Lord and keep a festival
in honour of all the saints. Let us join with the angels in joyful
praise to the Son of God.

Opening Prayer
Let us pray
    [that the prayers of all the saints
    will bring us forgiveness for our sins]

Father, all-powerful and ever-living God,
today we rejoice in the holy men and women
of every time and place.
May their prayers bring us your forgiveness and love.

or

Let us pray
    [as we rejoice and keep festival
    in honour of all the saints]

God our Father,
source of all holiness,
the work of your hands is manifest in your saints,
the beauty of your truth is reflected in their faith.

May we who aspire to have part in their joy
be filled with the Spirit that blessed their lives,
so that having shared their faith on earth
we may also know their peace in your kingdom.

FIRST READING

A reading from the book of the Apocalypse   7:2-4. 9-14

I saw a huge Number, impossible to count, of people from every nation, race, tribe and language.

I, John, saw another angel rising where the sun rises, carrying the seal of the living God; he called in a powerful voice to the four angels whose duty was to devastate land and sea, 'Wait before you do any damage on land or at sea or to the trees, until we have put the seal on the foreheads of the servants of our God.' Then I heard how many were sealed: a hundred and forty-four thousand, out of all the tribes of Israel.

After that I saw a huge number, impossible to count, of people from every nation, race, tribe and language; they were standing in front of the throne and in front of the Lamb, dressed in white robes and holding palms in their hands. They shouted aloud, 'Victory to our God, who sits on the throne, and to the Lamb!' And all the angels who were standing in a circle round the throne, surrounding the elders and the four animals, prostrated themselves before the throne, and touched the ground with their foreheads, worshipping God with these words: 'Amen. Praise and glory and wisdom and thanksgiving and honour and power and strength to our God for ever and ever. Amen.'

One of the elders then spoke, and asked me, 'Do you know who these people are, dressed in white robes, and where they have come from?' I answered him, 'You can tell me, my Lord.' Then he said, 'These are the people who have been through the great persecution, and they have washed their robes white again in the blood of the Lamb.'

This is the word of the Lord.

Responsorial Psalm   Ps 23:1-6. ℟ cf. v.6

    ℟ **Such are the men who seek your face, O Lord.**

1   The Lord's is the earth and its fullness,
     the world and all its peoples.
     It is he who set it on the seas;
     on the waters he made it firm.   ℟

2   Who shall climb the mountain of the Lord?
     Who shall stand in his holy place?
     The man with clean hands and pure heart,
     who desires not worthless things.   ℟

(continued)

3   He shall receive blessings from the Lord
and reward from the God who saves him.
Such are the men who seek him,
seek the face of the God of Jacob.

℟   **Such are the men who seek your face, O Lord.**

SECOND READING

A reading from the first letter of St John   3:1-3
We shall see God as he really is.

Think of the love that the Father has lavished on us,
by letting us be called God's children;
and that is what we are.
Because the world refused to acknowledge him,
therefore it does not acknowledge us.
My dear people, we are already the children of God
but what we are to be in the future has not yet been revealed;
all we know is, that when it is revealed
we shall be like him
because we shall see him as he really is.
Surely everyone who entertains this hope
must purify himself, must try to be as pure as Christ.

This is the word of the Lord.

Gospel Acclamation   Mt 11:28
Alleluia, alleluia!
Come to me, all you who labour and are overburdened,
and I will give you rest, says the Lord.
Alleluia!

GOSPEL

A reading from the holy Gospel according to Matthew   5:1-12
Rejoice and be glad, for your reward will be great in heaven.

Seeing the crowds, Jesus went up the hill. There he sat down and
was joined by his disciples. Then he began to speak. This is what
he taught them:

'How happy are the poor in spirit;
theirs is the kingdom of heaven.
Happy the gentle:
they shall have the earth for their heritage.
Happy those who mourn:

they shall be comforted.
Happy those who hunger and thirst for what is right:
they shall be satisfied.
Happy the merciful:
they shall have mercy shown them.
Happy the pure in heart:
they shall see God.
Happy the peacemakers:
they shall be called sons of God
Happy those who are persecuted in the cause of right:
theirs is the kingdom of heaven.

'Happy are you when people abuse you and persecute you and speak all kinds of calumny against you on my account. Rejoice and be glad, for your reward will be great in heaven.'

This is the Gospel of the Lord.

The profession of faith is made.

Prayer over the Gifts
Lord,
receive our gifts in honour of the holy men and women
who live with you in glory.
May we always be aware
of their concern to help and save us.
Preface of All Saints, P71

Communion Antiphon: Happy are the pure of heart for they shall see God. Happy the peacemakers; they shall be called sons of God. Happy are they who suffer persecution for justice' sake; the kingdom of heaven is theirs.

Prayer after Communion
Father, holy one,
we praise your glory reflected in the saints.
May we who share at this table
be filled with your love
and prepared for the joy of your kingdom,
where Jesus is Lord for ever and ever.

Solemn Blessing
Bow your heads and pray for God's blessing.

God is the glory and joy of all his saints,
whose memory we celebrate today.

May his blessing be with you always.   ℞   **Amen.**

May the prayers of the saints deliver you from present evil;
may their example of holy living
turn your thoughts to the service of God and neighbour.
℞   **Amen.**

God's holy Church rejoices that her children
are one with the saints in lasting peace.
May you come to share with them
in all the joys of our Father's house.   ℞   **Amen.**

May almighty God bless you,
the Father, and the Son, ✠ and the Holy Spirit.   ℞   **Amen.**

2 November

THE COMMEMORATION OF ALL THE FAITHFUL DEPARTED

Three Masses are given below. They are followed by one series of
readings. Other readings, given in the full Lectionary, may be
used.

FIRST MASS

Entrance Antiphon: Just as Jesus died and rose again, so will the
Father bring with him those who have died in Jesus. Just as in
Adam all men die, so in Christ all will be made alive.

Opening Prayer

Let us pray
[for all our departed brothers and sisters]

Merciful Father,
hear our prayers and console us.
As we renew our faith in your Son,
whom you raised from the dead,
strengthen our hope that all our departed brothers and sisters
will share in his resurrection,
who lives and reigns with you and the Holy Spirit,
one God, for ever and ever.

Readings: see below, pp.969ff.

Prayer over the Gifts

Lord,
we are united in this sacrament
by the love of Jesus Christ.
Accept these gifts
and receive our brothers and sisters
into the glory of your Son,
who is Lord for ever and ever.

Preface of Christian Death I-V, P77-81

Communion Antiphon: I am the resurrection and the life, says the
Lord. If anyone believes in me, even though he dies, he will live.
Any one who lives and believes in me, will not die.

Prayer after Communion

Lord God,
may the death and resurrection of Christ
which we celebrate in this eucharist
bring the departed faithful to the peace of your eternal home.

An appropriate Solemn Blessing or Prayer over the People may
be used, see above, pp.90ff.

SECOND MASS

Entrance Antiphon: Give them eternal rest, O Lord, and may your
light shine on them for ever.

Opening Prayer

Let us pray
    [for all our departed brothers and sisters]

Lord God,
you are the glory of believers
and the life of the just.
Your Son redeemed us
by dying and rising to life again.
Since our departed brothers and sisters believed in the mystery of
    our resurrection,
let them share the joys and blessings of the life to come.

Readings: see below, pp.969ff.

Prayer over the Gifts

All-powerful Father,
may this sacrifice wash away

the sins of our departed brothers and sisters in the blood of
    Christ.
You cleansed them in the waters of baptism.
In your loving mercy grant them pardon and peace.

Preface of Christian Death I-V, P77-P81

Communion Antiphon: May eternal life shine on them, O Lord,
with all your saints for ever, for you are rich in mercy. Give them
eternal rest, O Lord, and may perpetual light shine on them for
ever, for you are rich in mercy.

Prayer after Communion

Lord,
in this sacrament you give us your crucified and risen Son.
Bring to the glory of the resurrection our departed brothers and
    sisters
who have been purified by this holy mystery.

An appropriate Solemn Blessing or Prayer over the People may
be used, see above, pp.90ff.

THIRD MASS

Entrance Antiphon: God, who raised Jesus from the dead, will give
new life to our own mortal bodies through his Spirit living in us.

Opening Prayer

Let us pray
    [for all our departed brothers and sisters]

God, our creator and redeemer,
by your power Christ conquered death
and returned to you in glory.
May all your people who have gone before us in faith
share his victory
and enjoy the vision of your glory for ever.

Readings: see below, pp.969ff.

Prayer over the Gifts

Lord,
in your kindness accept these gifts for our departed brothers and
    sisters
and for all who sleep in Christ.
May his perfect sacrifice
free them from the power of death
and give them eternal life.

Preface of Christian Death I-V, P77-P81

Communion Antiphon: We are waiting for our Saviour, the Lord Jesus Christ; he will transfigure our lowly bodies into copies of his own glorious body.

Prayer after Communion
Lord,
may our sacrifice bring peace and forgiveness
to our brothers and sisters who have died.
Bring the new life given to them in baptism
to the fullness of eternal joy.

An appropriate Solemn Blessing or Prayer over the People may be used, see above, pp.90ff.

FIRST READING

A reading from the prophet Isaiah   25:6-9

The Lord will destroy death for ever.

On this mountain,
the Lord of hosts will prepare for all peoples
a banquet of rich food.
On this mountain he will remove
the mourning veil covering all peoples,
and the shroud enwrapping all nations,
he will destroy Death for ever.
The Lord will wipe away
the tears from every cheek;
he will take away his people's shame
everywhere on earth,
for the Lord has said so.
That day, it will be said: See, this is our God
in whom we hoped for salvation;
the Lord is the one in whom we hoped.
We exult and we rejoice
that he has saved us.

This is the word of the Lord.

Responsorial Psalm   Ps 26:1. 4. 7-9. 13-14.. ℟ v.1. Alt. ℟ v.13

℟ **The Lord is my light and my help.**

or

℟ **I am sure I shall see the Lord's goodness
in the land of the living.**

1 The Lord is my light and my help;
   whom shall I fear?
   The Lord is the stronghold of my life;
   before whom shall I shrink?

2 There is one thing I ask of the Lord,
   for this I long,
   to live in the house of the Lord,
   all the days of my life,
   to savour the sweetness of the Lord,
   to behold his temple.   ℟

3 O Lord, hear my voice when I call;
   have mercy and answer.
   It is your face, O Lord, that I seek;
   hide not your face.   ℟

4 I am sure I shall see the Lord's goodness
   in the land of the living.
   Hope in him, hold firm and take heart.
   Hope in the Lord!   ℟

SECOND READING

A reading from the letter of St Paul to the Romans   5:5-11

*Having died to make us righteous, is it likely that he would now fail to
save us from God's anger?*

Hope is not deceptive, because the love of God has been poured
into our hearts by the Holy Spirit which has been given us. We
were still helpless when at his appointed moment Christ died for
sinful men. It is not easy to die even for a good man – though of
course for someone really worthy, a man might be prepared to
die – but what proves that God loves us is that Christ died for us
while we were still sinners. Having died to make us righteous, is
it likely that he would now fail to save us from God's anger?
When we were reconciled to God by the death of his Son, we
were still enemies; now that we have been reconciled, surely we
may count on being saved by the life of his Son? Not merely

because we have been reconciled but because we are filled with joyful trust in God, through our Lord Jesus Christ, through whom we have already gained our reconciliation.

This is the word of the Lord.

Gospel Acclamation   Jn 6:39
Alleluia, alleluia!
It is my Father's will, says the Lord,
that I should lose nothing of all that he has given to me,
and that I should raise it up on the last day.
Alleluia!

GOSPEL

Year A: Matthew 11:25-30, see Fourteenth Sunday of Year A, p.418 above.

Year B

A reading from the holy Gospel according to Mark 15:33-39;16: 1-6
Jesus gave a loud cry and breathed his last.

When the sixth hour came there was darkness over the whole land until the ninth hour. And at the ninth hour Jesus cried out in a loud voice, 'Eloi, Eloi, lama sabachthani?' which means, 'My God, my God, why have you deserted me?' When some of those who stood by heard this, they said, 'Listen, he is calling on Elijah.' Someone ran and soaked a sponge in vinegar and, putting it on a reed, gave it him to drink saying, 'Wait and see if Elijah will come to take him down.' But Jesus gave a loud cry and breathed his last. And the veil of the Temple was torn in two from top to bottom. The centurion, who was standing in front of him, had seen how he had died and he said, 'In truth this man was a son of God.'

When the sabbath was over, Mary of Magdala, Mary the mother of James, and Salome, bought spices with which to go and anoint him. And very early in the morning on the first day of the week they went to the tomb, just as the sun was rising.

They had been saying to one another, 'Who will roll away the stone for us from the entrance to the tomb?' But when they looked they could see that the stone – which was very big – had already been rolled back. On entering the tomb they saw a young man in a white robe seated on the right-hand side, and they were struck with amazement. But he said to them, 'There is no need for alarm. You are looking for Jesus of Nazareth, who was crucified: he has risen, he is not here. See, here is the place where they laid him.'

    This is the Gospel of the Lord.

*Shorter Form, verses 33-39. Read between *

Year C: Luke 7:11-17, see Tenth Sunday of Year C, p.827 above.

9 November

THE DEDICATION OF THE LATERAN BASILICA
Feast

The basilica of St John Lateran is the cathedral of the bishop of Rome.

Entrance Antiphon: I saw the holy city, new Jerusalem, coming down from God out of heaven, like a bride adorned in readiness for her husband.

Opening Prayer
God our Father,
from living stones, your chosen people,
you built an eternal temple to your glory.
Increase the spiritual gifts you have given to your Church,
so that your faithful people may continue to grow
into the new and eternal Jerusalem.

or

Father,
you called your people to be your Church.
As we gather together in your name,
may we love, honour, and follow you
to eternal life in the kingdom you promise.

FIRST READING

A reading from the prophet Ezekiel   47:1-2. 8-9. 12
I saw a stream of water coming from the Temple, bringing life to all wherever it flowed.

The angel brought me to the entrance of the Temple, where a stream came out from under the Temple threshold and flowed eastwards, since the Temple faced east. The water flowed from under the right side of the Temple, south of the altar. He took me out by the north gate and led me right round outside as far as the outer east gate where the water flowed out on the right-hand side. The man went to the east holding his measuring line and measured off a thousand cubits; he then made me wade across the stream; the water reached my ankles. He measured off another thousand and made me wade across the stream again; the water reached my knees. He measured off another thousand and made me wade across again; the water reached my waist. He measured off another thousand; it was now a river which I could not cross; the stream had swollen and was now deep water, a river impossible to cross. He then said, 'Do you see, son of man?' He took me further, then brought me back to the bank of the river. When I got back, there were many trees on each bank of the river. He said, 'This water flows east down to the Arabah and to the sea; and flowing into the sea it makes its waters wholesome. Wherever the river flows, all living creatures teeming in it will live. Fish will be very plentiful, for wherever the water goes it brings health, and life teems wherever the river flows. Along the river, on either bank, will grow every kind of fruit tree with leaves that never wither and fruit that never fails; they will bear new fruit every month, because this water comes from the sanctuary. And their fruit will be good to eat and the leaves medicinal.'

This is the word of the Lord.

Responsorial Psalm   Ps 45:2-3. 5-6. 8-9. ℟ v.5
   ℟   **The waters of a river give joy to God's city,
        the holy place where the Most High dwells.**

1   God is for us a refuge and strength,
      a helper close at hand, in time of distress:
      so we shall not fear though the earth should rock,
      though the mountains fall into the depths of the sea.   ℟

2   The waters of a river give joy to God's city,
      the holy place where the Most High dwells.
      God is within, it cannot be shaken;
      God will help it at the dawning of the day.   ℟

3   The Lord of hosts is with us:
      the God of Jacob is our stronghold.
      Come, consider the works of the Lord
      the redoubtable deeds he has done on the earth.   ℟

SECOND READING

A reading from the first letter of St Paul
to the Corinthians   3:9-11. 16-17

You are the temple of God.

You are God's building. By the grace God gave me, I succeeded
as an architect and laid the foundations, on which someone else
is doing the building. Everyone doing the building must work
carefully. For the foundation, nobody can lay any other than the
one which has already been laid, that is Jesus Christ.

Didn't you realise that you were God's temple and that the
Spirit of God was living among you? If anybody should destroy
the temple of God, God will destroy him, because the temple of
God is sacred; and you are that temple.

This is the word of the Lord.

Gospel Acclamation   2 Chron 7:16
  Alleluia, alleluia!
  I have chosen and consecrated this house, says the Lord,
  for my name to be there for ever.
  Alleluia!

GOSPEL

A reading from the holy Gospel according to John   2:13-22

He was speaking of the sanctuary that was his body.

Just before the Jewish Passover Jesus went up to Jerusalem, and
in the Temple he found people selling cattle and sheep and
pigeons, and the money changers sitting at their counters there.
Making a whip out of some cord, he drove them all out of the
Temple, cattle and sheep as well, scattered the money changers'
coins, knocked their tables over and said to the pigeon-sellers,
'Take all this out of here and stop turning my Father's house into
a market.' Then his disciples remembered the words of scripture:
Zeal for your house will devour me. The Jews intervened and
said, 'What sign can you show us to justify what you have done?'
Jesus answered, 'Destroy this sanctuary, and in three days I will
raise it up.' The Jews replied, 'It has taken forty-six years to build
this sanctuary: are you going to raise it up in three days?' But he
was speaking of the sanctuary that was his body, and when Jesus
rose from the dead, his disciples remembered that he had said
this, and they believed the scripture and the words he had said.

This is the Gospel of the Lord.

Prayer over the Gifts
Lord, receive our gifts
May we who share this sacrament
experience the life and power it promises,
and hear the answer to our prayers.

Preface of the Dedication of a Church II, P53

Communion Antiphon: Like living stones let your selves be built on
Christ as a spiritual house, a holy priesthood.

Prayer after Communion
Father,
you make your Church on earth
a sign of the new and eternal Jerusalem.
By sharing in this sacrament
may we become the temple of your presence
and the home of your glory.

8 December

THE IMMACULATE CONCEPTION OF THE BLESSED VIRGIN MARY
Solemnity

*We celebrate the conception of her whom God chose to be the mother of
Christ and the new Eve, the mother of all the living. He chose her to be
the first of the redeemed, holy and spotless, to live through love in his
presence.*

Entrance Antiphon: I exult for joy in the Lord, my soul rejoices in
my God; for he has clothed me in the garment of salvation and
robed me in the cloak of justice, like a bride adorned with her
jewels.

Opening Prayer
Let us pray
　　[that through the prayers of the sinless Virgin Mary,
　　God will free us from our sins]

Father,
you prepared the Virgin Mary
to be the worthy mother of your Son.
You let her share beforehand

in the salvation Christ would bring by his death,
and kept her sinless from the first moment of her conception.
Help us by her prayers
to live in your presence without sin.

or

Let us pray
    [on this feast of Mary
        who experienced the perfection of God's saving power]

Father,
the image of the Virgin is found in the Church.
Mary had a faith that your Spirit prepared
and a love that never knew sin,
for you kept her sinless from the first moment of her conception.

Trace in our actions the lines of her love,
in our hearts her readiness of faith.
Prepare once again a world for your Son
who lives and reigns with you and the Holy Spirit,
one God, for ever and ever.

FIRST READING

A reading from the book of Genesis   3:9-15. 20
I will make you enemies of each other; your offspring and her offspring.

After Adam had eaten of the tree, the Lord God called to him.
'Where are you?' he asked. 'I heard the sound of you in the
garden,' he replied. 'I was afraid because I was naked, so I hid.'
'Who told you that you were naked?' he asked. 'Have you been
eating of the tree I forbade you to eat?' The man replied, 'It was
the woman you put with me; she gave me the fruit, and I ate it.'
Then the Lord God asked the woman, 'What is this you have
done?' The woman replied, 'The serpent tempted me and I ate.'

   Then the Lord God said to the serpent, 'Because you have
done this,

   'Be accursed beyond all cattle,
   all wild beasts.
   You shall crawl on your belly and eat dust
   every day of your life.
   I will make you enemies of each other:
   you and the woman,
   your offspring and her offspring.
   It will crush your head
   and you will strike its heel.'

The man named his wife 'Eve' because she was the mother of all those who live.

This is the word of the Lord.

Responsorial Psalm   Ps 97:1-4. ℟ v.1
  ℟ **Sing a new song to the Lord**
      for he has worked wonders.

1   Sing a new song to the Lord
    for he has worked wonders.
    His right hand and his holy arm
    have brought salvation.   ℟

2   The Lord has made known his salvation;
    has shown his justice to the nations.
    He has remembered his truth and love
    for the house of Israel.   ℟

3   All the ends of the earth have seen
    the salvation of our God.
    Shout to the Lord all the earth,
    ring out your joy.   ℟

SECOND READING

A reading from the letter of St Paul to the Ephesians   1:3-6. 11-12
Before the world was made, God chose us in Christ.

Blessed be God the Father of our Lord Jesus Christ,
who has blessed us with all the spiritual blessings of heaven in
    Christ.
Before the world was made, he chose us, chose us in Christ,
to be holy and spotless, and to live through love in his presence,
determining that we should become his adopted sons, through
    Jesus Christ
for his own kind purposes,
to make us praise the glory of his grace,
his free gift to us in the Beloved.
And it is in him that we were claimed as God's own,
chosen from the beginning,
under the predetermined plan of the one who guides all things
as he decides by his own will;
chosen to be,
for his greater glory,
the people who would put their hopes in Christ before he came.

This is the word of the Lord.

Gospel Acclamation   cf. Lk 1:28
Alleluia, alleluia!
Hail, Mary, full of grace; the Lord is with thee!
Blessed art thou among women.
Alleluia!

GOSPEL

A reading from the holy Gospel according to Luke   1:26-38
You are to conceive and bear a Son.

The angel Gabriel was sent by God to a town in Galilee called
Nazareth, to a virgin betrothed to a man named Joseph, of the
House of David; and the virgin's name was Mary. He went in
and said to her, 'Rejoice, so highly favoured! The Lord is with
you.' She was deeply disturbed by these words and asked herself
what this greeting could mean, but the angel said to her, 'Mary,
do not be afraid; you have won God's favour. Listen! You are to
conceive and bear a son, and you must name him Jesus. He will
be great and will be called Son of the Most High. The Lord God
will give him the throne of his ancestor David; he will rule over
the House of Jacob for ever and his reign will have no end.' Mary
said to the angel, 'But how can this come about, since I am a
virgin?' 'The Holy Spirit will come upon you,' the angel
answered, 'and the power of the Most High will cover you with
its shadow. And so the child will be holy and will be called Son of
God. Know this too: your kinswoman Elizabeth has, in her old
age, herself conceived a son, and she whom people called barren
is now in her sixth month, for nothing is impossible to God.' 'I
am the handmaid of the Lord,' said Mary, 'let what you have said
be done to me.' And the angel left her.

This is the Gospel of the Lord.

Prayer over the Gifts
Lord,
accept this sacrifice
on the feast of the sinless Virgin Mary.
You kept her free from sin
from the first moment of her life.
Help us by her prayers,
and free us from our sins.

Preface of the Immaculate Conception, P58

Communion Antiphon: All honour to you, Mary! From you arose
the sun of justice, Christ our God.

Prayer after Communion
Lord our God,
in your love, you chose the Virgin Mary
and kept her free from sin.
May this sacrament of your love
free us from our sins.

An appropriate Solemn Blessing or Prayer over the People may be used, see above, pp.90ff.

FROM THE NATIONAL CALENDARS OF SAINTS

FOR ENGLAND, IRELAND, SCOTLAND AND WALES

1 March

SAINT DAVID, BISHOP

Patron of Wales

In Wales: Solemnity   In England: Feast

Entrance Antiphon: My teaching, which I have put in your mouth, will never fail, says the Lord; the gifts which you offered on my altar will be accepted.

or

You, Lord, are my portion and cup, you restore my inheritance to me; the way of life you marked out for me has made my heritage glorious.

Opening Prayer
God our Father,
you gave the bishop David to the Welsh Church
to uphold the faith
and to be an example of Christian perfection.
In this changing world
may he help us to hold fast to the values
which bring eternal life.

FIRST READING

A reading from the letter of St Paul to the Philippians   3:8-14
I am racing for the finish, for the prize to which God calls us upward to receive in Christ Jesus.

I believe nothing can happen that will outweigh the supreme advantage of knowing Christ Jesus my Lord. For him I have accepted the loss of everything, and I look on everything as so much rubbish if only I can have Christ and be given a place in him. I am no longer trying for perfection by my own efforts, the perfection that comes from the Law, but I want only the perfection that comes through faith in Christ, and is from God and based on faith. All I want is to know Christ and the power of his resurrection and to share his sufferings by reproducing the pattern of his death. That is the way I can hope to take my place in the resurrection of the dead. Not that I have become perfect yet: I have not yet won, but I am still running, trying to capture the prize for which Christ Jesus captured me. I can assure you my brothers, I am far from thinking that I have already won. All I can say is that I forget the past and I strain ahead for what is still to come; I am racing for the finish, for the prize to which God calls us upwards to receive in Christ Jesus.

This is the word of the Lord.

Responsorial Psalm Ps 1. ℟ Ps 39:5

℟ **Happy the man who has placed
his trust in the Lord.**

1 Happy indeed is the man
who follows not the counsel of the wicked;
nor lingers in the way of sinners
nor sits in the company of scorners,
but whose delight is the law of the Lord
and who ponders his law day and night. ℟

2 He is like a tree that is planted
beside the flowing waters,
that yields its fruit in due season
and whose leaves shall never fade;
and all that he does shall prosper. ℟

3 Not so are the wicked, not so!
For they like winnowed chaff
shall be driven away by the wind;
for the Lord guards the way of the just
but the way of the wicked leads to doom. ℟

Gospel Acclamation Jn 8:31-32

Outside Lent

Alleluia, alleluia!
If you make my word your home
you will indeed be my disciples,
and you will learn the truth, says the Lord.
Alleluia!

In Lent

Glory to you, O Christ, you are the Word of God.
If you make my word your home
you will indeed be my disciples,
and you will learn the truth, says the Lord.
Glory to you, O Christ, you are the Word of God.

GOSPEL

A reading from the holy Gospel according to Matthew   5:13-16
You are the light of the world.

Jesus said to his disciples: 'You are the salt of the earth. But if salt becomes tasteless, what can make it salty again? It is good for nothing, and can only be thrown out to be trampled underfoot by men.

'You are the light of the world. A city built on a hill-top cannot be hidden. No one lights a lamp to put it under a tub; they put it on the lamp-stand where it shines for everyone in the house. In the same way your light must shine in the sight of men, so that, seeing your good works, they may give the praise to your Father in heaven.'

This is the Gospel of the Lord.

Prayer over the Gifts
Lord, accept the gifts we bring
on the feast of Saint David.
We offer them to win your forgiveness
and to give honour to your name.

Preface of Holy Men and Women I or II, P69 or P70.

Communion Antiphon: The Son of Man came to give his life as a ransom for all.
or
I assure you who left all and followed me: you will receive a hundredfold in return and inherit eternal life.

Prayer after Communion
All-powerful God,
you have strengthened us with this sacrament.
May we learn from Saint David's example
to seek you above all things,
and to live always as new men in Christ,
who lives and reigns for ever and ever.

17 March

SAINT PATRICK, BISHOP

Patron of Ireland
In Ireland: Solemnity
In England, Wales and Scotland: Feast

Entrance Antiphon: Go from your country and your kindred and your father's house to the land that I will show you; and I will make you the father of a great people.

Opening Prayer
Let us pray
    [that like Saint Patrick the missionary
    we will be fearless witnesses
    to the gospel of Jesus Christ]

God our Father,
you sent Saint Patrick
to preach your glory to the people of Ireland.
By the help of his prayers,
may all Christians proclaim your love to all men.

or

Let us pray
    [that, like Saint Patrick,
    we may be loyal to our faith in Christ]

Father in heaven,
you sent the great bishop Patrick
to the people of Ireland to share his faith
and to spend his life in loving service.
May our lives bear witness
to the faith we profess,
and our love bring others
to the peace and joy of your gospel.

FIRST READING

A reading from the prophet Jeremiah   1:4-9
Go now to those to whom I send you.

The word of the Lord was addressed to me, saying,

   'Before I formed you in the womb I knew you;
   before you came to birth I consecrated you;
   I have appointed you as prophet to the nations.'

I said, 'Ah, Lord God; look, I do not know how to speak: I am a child!'
But the Lord replied,

'Do not say, "I am a child".
Go now to those to whom I send you
and say whatever I command you.
Do not be afraid of them,
for I am with you to protect you –
it is the Lord who speaks!'

Then the Lord put out his hand and touched my mouth and said to me:

'There! I am putting my words into your mouth.'

This is the word of the Lord.

Responsorial Psalm   Ps 116. ℞ Mk 16:15

℞   **Go out to all the world,**
     and tell the Good News.

or (outside Lent only)

℞   **Alleluia!**

1   O praise the Lord, all you nations,
    acclaim him all you peoples!   ℞

2   Strong is his love for us;
    he is faithful for ever.   ℞

SECOND READING

A reading from the Acts of the Apostles   13:46-49
We must turn to the pagans.

Paul and Barnabas spoke out boldly to the Jews, 'We had to proclaim the word of God to you first, but since you have rejected it, since you do not think yourselves worthy of eternal life, we must turn to the pagans. For this is what the Lord commanded us to do when he said:

'I have made you a light for the nations,
so that my salvation may reach the ends of the earth.'

It made the pagans very happy to hear this and they thanked the Lord for his message; all who were destined for eternal life became believers. Thus the word of the Lord spread through the whole countryside.

This is the word of the Lord.

Gospel Acclamation Lk 4:18

Outside Lent

Alleluia, alleluia!
The Lord sent me to bring Good News to the poor,
and freedom to prisoners.
Alleluia!

In Lent

Praise and honour to you, Lord Jesus!
The Lord sent me to bring Good News to the poor,
and freedom to prisoners.
Praise and honour to you, Lord Jesus!

GOSPEL

A reading from the holy Gospel according to Luke 10:1-12. 17-20
Your peace will rest on that man.

The Lord appointed seventy-two others and sent them out ahead of him, in pairs, to all the towns and places he himself was to visit. He said to them, 'The harvest is rich but the labourers are few, so ask the Lord of the harvest to send labourers to his harvest. Start off now, but remember, I am sending you out like lambs among wolves. Carry no purse, no haversack, no sandals. Salute no one on the road. Whatever house you go into, let your first words be, "Peace to this house!" And if a man of peace lives there, your peace will go and rest on him; if not, it will come back to you. Stay in the same house, taking what food and drink they have to offer, for the labourer deserves his wages; do not move from house to house. Whenever you go into a town where they make you welcome, eat what is set before you. Cure those in it who are sick, and say, "The kingdom of God is very near to you." But whenever you enter a town and they do not make you welcome, go out into its streets and say, "We wipe off the very dust of your town that clings to our feet, and leave it with you. Yet be sure of this: the kingdom of God is very near." I tell you, on that day it will not go as hard with Sodom as with that town.'

The seventy-two came back rejoicing. 'Lord,' they said 'even the devils submit to us when we use your name.' He said to them, 'I watched Satan fall like lightning from heaven. Yes, I have given you power to tread underfoot serpents and scorpions and the whole strength of the enemy; nothing shall ever hurt you. Yet do not rejoice that the spirits submit to you; rejoice rather that your names are written in heaven.'

This is the Gospel of the Lord.

Prayer over the Gifts
Lord our God,
by the power of this sacrament
deepen our love
and strengthen our faith:
as we celebrate the feast of Saint Patrick
bind us more and more to each other
in unity and peace.

Preface of Holy Men and Women I or II, P69 or P79.

Communion Antiphon: The Lord sent disciples to proclaim to the people: the Kingdom of God is very near to you.

Prayer after Communion
Lord,
by the power of this sacrament
strengthen our faith;
may all we do or say
proclaim your truth
in imitation of Saint Patrick,
who did not spare himself
but gave his whole life
to the preaching of your Word.

23 April

SAINT GEORGE, MARTYR
Patron of England
In England and Wales: Feast

Entrance Antiphon: Light for ever will shine on your saints, O Lord, alleluia.

Opening Prayer
Lord, hear the prayers of those who praise your mighty power.
As Saint George was ready to follow Christ in suffering and
    death,
so may he be ready to help us in our weakness.

FIRST READING

A reading from the book of the Apocalypse 12:10-12

In the face of death they would not cling to life.

I, John, heard a voice shout from heaven, 'Victory and power and empire for ever have been won by our God, and all authority for his Christ, now that the persecutor, who accused our brothers day and night before our God, has been brought down. They have triumphed over him by the blood of the Lamb and by the witness of their martyrdom, because even in the face of death they would not cling to life. Let the heavens rejoice and all who live there.'

This is the word of the Lord.

Responsorial Psalm Ps 125. ℟ v.5

℟ **Those who are sowing in tears**
   will sing when they reap.

1 When the Lord delivered Zion from bondage,
   it seemed like a dream.
   Then was our mouth filled with laughter,
   on our lips there were songs. ℟

2 The heathens themselves said: 'What marvels
   the Lord worked for them!'
   What marvels the Lord worked for us!
   Indeed we were glad. ℟

3 Deliver us, O Lord, from our bondage
   as streams in dry land.
   Those who are sowing in tears
   will sing when they reap. ℟

4 They go out, they go out, full of tears,
   carrying seed for the sowing;
   they come back, they come back, full of song,
   carrying their sheaves. ℟

Gospel Acclamation James 1:12
   Alleluia, alleluia!
   Happy the man who stands firm.
   for he has proved himself,
   and will win the crown of life.
   Alleluia!

GOSPEL

A reading from the holy Gospel according to John   15:18-21

If they persecuted me, they will persecute you.

Jesus said to his disciples:

'If the world hates you,
remember that it hated me before you.
If you belonged to the world,
the world would love you as its own;
but because you do not belong to the world,
because my choice withdrew you from the world,
therefore the world hates you.
Remember the words I said to you:
A servant is not greater than his master.
If they persecuted me,
they will persecute you too;
if they kept my word,
they will keep yours as well.
But it will be on my account that they will do this,
because they do not know the one who sent me.'

This is the Gospel of the Lord.

Alternative Gospel

A reading from the holy Gospel according to John   15:1-8

Whoever remains in me, with me in him, bears fruit in plenty.

Jesus said to his disciples:

'I am the true vine,
and my Father is the vinedresser.
Every branch in me that bears no fruit
he cuts away,
and every branch that does bear fruit he prunes
to make it bear even more.
You are pruned already,
by means of the word that I have spoken to you.
Make your home in me, as I make mine in you.
As a branch cannot bear fruit all by itself,
but must remain part of the vine,
neither can you unless you remain in me.
I am the vine,
you are the branches.

Whoever remains in me, with me in him,
bears fruit in plenty;
for cut off from me you can do nothing.
Anyone who does not remain in me
is like a branch that has been thrown away
– he withers;
these branches are collected and thrown on the fire,
and they are burnt.
If you remain in me
and my words remain in you,
you may ask what you will
and you shall get it.
It is to the glory of my Father that you should bear much fruit,
and then you will be my disciples.'

This is the Gospel of the Lord.

Prayer over the Gifts
Lord, bless our offerings and make them holy.
May these gifts fill our hearts
with the love which gave Saint George victory
over all his suffering.

Preface of Martyrs, P66.

Communion Antiphon: I tell you solemnly: Unless a grain of wheat
falls on the ground and dies, it remains a single grain; but if it
dies, it yields a rich harvest, alleluia.

Prayer after Communion
Lord,
we receive your gifts from heaven
at this joyful feast.
May we who proclaim at this holy table
the death and resurrection of your Son
come to share his glory with Saint George
and all your holy martyrs.

25 October

THE FORTY MARTYRS OF ENGLAND AND WALES
In England: Feast

THE SIX WELSH MARTYRS AND COMPANIONS, MARTYRS
In Wales: Feast

Entrance Antiphon: The saints are happy in heaven because they followed Christ. They rejoice with him for ever because they shed their blood for love of him.

Opening Prayer
God our Father,
you raised up martyrs – saints among our countrymen
from every walk of life.
They vindicated the authority of your Church
in teaching and worship.
Through their prayers
may all our people be gathered once again
to celebrate the same sacraments
under one Shepherd, Jesus Christ, your Son,
who lives and reigns . . .

FIRST READING

A reading from the letter to the Hebrews   11:33-40

Through faith they conquered kingdoms. God will make provision for us to have something better.

Gideon, Barak, Samson, Jephthah, David, Samuel and the prophets – these were men who through faith conquered kingdoms, did what is right and earned the promises. They could keep a lion's mouth shut, put out blazing fires and emerge unscathed from battle. They were weak people who were given strength, to be brave in war and drive back foreign invaders. Some came back to their wives from the dead, by resurrection; and others submitted to torture, refusing release so that they would rise again to a better life. Some had to bear being pilloried and flogged, or even chained up in prison. They were stoned or sawn in half, or beheaded; they were homeless, and dressed in the skins of sheep and goats; they were penniless and were given nothing but ill-treatment. They were too good for the world and they went out to live in deserts and mountains and in caves and ravines. These are all heroes of faith, but they did not receive what was promised, since God had made provision for us to have something better, and they were not to reach perfection except with us.

This is the word of the Lord.

Responsorial Psalm Ps 15:1-2. 5. 7. 8-11 ℟ v.5
℟ **You are my inheritance, O Lord.**

1 Preserve me, God, I take refuge in you.
I say to the Lord: 'You are my God.'
O Lord, it is you who are my portion and cup;
it is you yourself who are my prize. ℟

2 I will bless the Lord who gives me counsel,
who even at night directs my heart.
I keep the Lord ever in my sight:
since he is at my right hand, I shall stand firm. ℟

3 You will show me the path of life,
the fullness of joy in your presence,
at your right hand happiness for ever. ℟

Gospel Acclamation
Alleluia, alleluia!
We praise you, O God,
we acknowledge you to be the Lord;
the noble army of martyrs praise you, O Lord.
Alleluia!

GOSPEL

A reading from the holy Gospel according to John 12:24-26
If a grain of wheat dies, it yields a rich harvest.

Jesus said to his disciples:

'I tell you, most solemnly,
unless a wheat grain falls on the ground and dies,
it remains only a single grain;
but if it dies,
it yields a rich harvest.
Anyone who loves his life loses it;
anyone who hates his life in this world
will keep it for the eternal life.
If a man serves me, he must follow me,

wherever I am, my servant will be there too.
If anyone serves me, my Father will honour him.'

This is the Gospel of the Lord.

Alternative Gospel 1
A reading from the holy Gospel according to John   15:18-21
If they persecuted me, they will persecute you too.

Jesus said to his disciples:

'If the world hates you,
remember that it hated me before you.
If you belonged to the world,
the world would love you as its own;
but because you do not belong to the world,
because my choice withdrew you from the world,
therefore the world hates you.
Remember the words I said to you:
A servant is not greater than his master.
If they persecuted me,
they will persecute you too;
if they kept my word,
they will keep yours as well.
But it will be on my account that they will do all this,
because they do not know the one who sent me.'

This is the Gospel of the Lord.

Alternative Gospel 2
A reading from the holy Gospel according to John   17:11-19
The world hated them.

Jesus raised his eyes to heaven and said,

'Holy Father,
keep those you have given me true to your name,
so that they may be one like us.
While I was with them,
I kept those you had given me true to your name.
I have watched over them and not one is lost
except the one who chose to be lost
and this was to fulfil the scriptures.
But now I am coming to you
and while still in the world I say these things

to share my joy with them to the full.
I passed your word on to them,
and the world hated them,
because they belong to the world
no more than I belong to the world.
I am not asking you to remove them from the world,
but to protect them from the evil one.
They do not belong to the world
any more than I belong to the world.
Consecrate them in the truth;
your word is truth.
As you sent me into the world,
I have sent them into the world,
and for their sake I consecrate myself
so that they too may be consecrated in truth.'

This is the Gospel of the Lord.

Prayer over the Gifts
Lord,
accept the gifts of your people
who honour the suffering and death
of these forty martyrs.
As the eucharist gave them strength in persecution
may it keep us faithful in every difficulty.

Preface of Martyrs, P66.

Communion Antiphon: Neither death nor life nor anything in all
creation can come between us and Christ's love for us.

Prayer after Communion
Lord,
we eat the bread from heaven
and become one body in Christ.
Never let us be separated from his love
and, through the example of your martyrs,
may all who glory in the name of Christian
come to serve you in the unity of faith.

30 November

SAINT ANDREW, APOSTLE AND MARTYR
Patron of Scotland
In Scotland: Solemnity

Entrance Antiphon: By the Sea of Galilee the Lord saw two brothers, Peter and Andrew. He called them: come and follow me, and I will make you fishers of men.

Opening Prayer
Lord,
in your kindness hear our petitions.
You called Andrew the apostle
to preach the gospel and guide your Church in faith.
May he always be our friend in your presence
to help us with his prayers.

FIRST READING

A reading from the book of Wisdom   3:1-9

He accepted them as a holocaust.

The souls of the virtuous are in the hands of God,
no torment shall ever touch them.
In the eyes of the unwise, they did appear to die,
their going looked like a disaster,
their leaving us, like annihilation;
but they are in peace.
If they experienced punishment as men see it,
their hope was rich with immortality;
slight was their affliction, great will their blessings be.
God has put them to the test
and proved them worthy to be with him;
he has tested them like gold in a furnace,
and accepted them as a holocaust.
When the time comes for his visitation they will shine out;
as sparks run through the stubble, so will they.
They shall judge nations, rule over peoples,
and the Lord will be their king for ever.
They who trust in him will understand the truth,
those who are faithful will live with him in love;
for grace and mercy await those he has chosen.

This is the word of the Lord.

Responsorial Psalm   Ps 30:3-4. 6. 8. 17. 21. ℟ v.6

   ℟   **Into your hands, O Lord,**
        I commend my spirit.

1   Be a rock of refuge for me,
    a mighty stronghold to save me,
    for you are my rock, my stronghold.
    For your name's sake, lead me and guide me.   ℟

2   Into your hands I commend my spirit.
    It is you who will redeem me, Lord.
    As for me, I trust in the Lord:
    let me be glad and rejoice in your love.   ℟

3   Let your face shine on your servant.
    Save me in your love.
    You hide them in the shelter of your presence
    from the plotting of men.   ℟

SECOND READING

A reading from the letter of St Paul to the Romans   10:9-18

Faith comes from what is preached, and what is preached comes from the word of Christ.

If your lips confess that Jesus is Lord and if you believe in your heart that God raised him from the dead, then you will be saved. By believing from the heart you are made righteous; by confessing with your lips you are saved. When scripture says: those who believe in him will have no cause for shame, it makes no distinction between Jew and Greek: all belong to the same Lord who is rich enough, however many ask his help, for everyone who calls on the name of the Lord will be saved.

But they will not ask his help unless they believe in him, and they will not believe in him unless they have heard of him, and they will not hear of him unless they get a preacher, and they will never have a preacher unless one is sent, but as scripture says: The footsteps of those who bring good news are a welcome sound. Not everyone, of course, listens to the Good News. As Isaiah says: Lord, how many believed what we proclaimed? So faith comes from what is preached, and what is preached comes from the word of Christ.

Let me put the question: is it possible that they did not hear? Indeed they did; in the words of the psalm, their voice has gone out through all the earth, and their message to the ends of the world.

This is the word of the Lord.

Gospel Acclamation   Mt 4:19
Alleluia, alleluia!
Follow me, says the Lord,
and I will make you into fishers of men.
Alleluia!

GOSPEL
A reading from the holy Gospel according to Matthew   4:18-22
And they left their nets at once and followed him.

As Jesus was walking by the Sea of Galilee he saw two brothers, Simon, who was called Peter, and his brother Andrew; they were making a cast in the lake with their net, for they were fishermen. And he said to them, 'Follow me and I will make you fishers of men.' And they left their nets at once and followed him.

Going on from there he saw another pair of brothers, James son of Zebedee and his brother John; they were in their boat with their father Zebedee, mending their nets, and he called them. At once, leaving the boat and their father, they followed him.

This is the Gospel of the Lord.

Prayer over the Gifts
All-powerful God,
may these gifts we bring on the feast of Saint Andrew
be pleasing to you
and give life to all who receive them.

Preface of the Apostles I or II, P64 or P65

Communion Antiphon: Andrew told his brother Simon: we have found the Messiah, the Christ; and he brought him to Jesus.

Prayer after Communion
Lord,
may the sacrament we have received give us courage
to follow the example of Andrew the apostle.
By sharing in Christ's suffering
may we live with him for ever in glory,
for he is Lord for ever and ever.

ANNIVERSARY OF THE
DEDICATION OF A CHURCH

This Mass is for use in the Dedicated Church. For Mass outside the Dedicated Church, the prayers and antiphons given for the Dedication of the Lateran Basilica, pp.972 ff above, are used, with readings as below, or as in the full Lectionary.

Mass in the Dedicated Church

This building in which we assemble to celebrate the divine mysteries is a symbol of the universal Church, a people dedicated to God.

Entrance Antiphon: Greatly to be feared is God in his sanctuary; he, the God of Israel, gives power and strength to his people. Blessed be God!

Opening Prayer
Father,
each year we recall the dedication of this church to your service.
Let our worship always be sincere
and help us to find your saving love in this church.

FIRST READING

A reading from the second book of Chronicles   5:6-11. 13–6:2
I have built you a dwelling, a place for you to live in for ever.

King Solomon, and all the community of Israel gathering with him in front of the ark, sacrificed sheep and oxen, countless, innumerable. The priests brought the ark of the covenant of the Lord to its place, in the Debir of the Temple, that is, in the Holy of Holies, under the cherubs' wings. For there where the ark was placed the cherubs spread out their wings and sheltered the ark and its shafts. These were long enough for their ends to be seen from the Holy Place in front of the Debir, but not from outside. There was nothing in the ark except the two tablets that Moses had placed in it at Horeb, where the Lord had made a covenant with the Israelites when they came out of Egypt.

Now when the priests came out of the sanctuary, a cloud filled the sanctuary, the Temple of the Lord.

All those who played the trumpet, or who sang, united in giving praise and glory to the Lord. Lifting their voices to the sound of the trumpet and cymbal and instruments of music, they gave praise to the Lord, 'for he is good, for his love is everlasting'.

Because of the cloud the priests could no longer perform their duties; the glory of the Lord filled the Temple of God. Then Solomon said:

'The Lord has chosen to dwell in the thick cloud.
Yes, I have built you a dwelling,
a place for you to live in for ever.'

This is the word of the Lord.

In the Easter Season

A reading from the Acts of the Apostles   7:44-50
The Most High does not live in a house that human hands have built.

Stephen said to the people, the elders and scribes, 'While they were in the desert our ancestors possessed the Tent of Testimony that had been constructed according to the instructions God gave Moses, telling him to make an exact copy of the pattern he had been shown. It was handed down from one ancestor of ours to another until Joshua brought it into the country we had conquered from the nations which were driven out by God as we advanced. Here it stayed until the time of David. He won God's favour and asked permission to have a temple built for the House of Jacob, though it was Solomon who actually built God's house for him. Even so the Most High does not live in a house that human hands have built: for as the prophet says:

"With heaven my throne
and earth my footstool,
what house could you build me,
what place could you make for my rest?
Was not all this made by my hand?" '

This is the word of the Lord.

Responsial Psalm   Ps 83:3-5. 10-11. ℟ v.2. Alt. ℟ Apoc 21:3
     ℟   **How lovely is your dwelling place,**
          Lord, God of hosts.

or

     ℟   **Here God lives among men.**

1   My soul is longing and yearning,
     is yearning for the courts of the Lord.
     My heart and my soul ring out their joy
     to God, the living God.   ℟

2   The sparrow herself finds a home
     and the swallow a nest for her brood;
     she lays her young by your altars,
     Lord of hosts, my king and my God. ℟

3   They are happy, who dwell in your house
     for ever singing your praise.
     Turn your eyes, O God, our shield,
     look on the face of your anointed. ℟

4   One day within your courts
     is better than a thousand elsewhere.
     The threshold of the house of God
     I prefer to the dwelling of the wicked. ℟

SECOND READING

A reading from the first letter of St Paul to the Corinthians

3:9-13. 16-17

You are the temple of God.

You are God's building. By the grace God gave me, I succeeded as an architect and laid the foundations, on which someone else is doing the building. Everyone doing the building must work carefully. For the foundation, nobody can lay any other than the one which has already been laid, that is Jesus Christ. On this foundation you can build in gold, silver and jewels, or in wood, grass and straw, but whatever the material, the work of each building is going to be clearly revealed when the day comes. That day will begin with fire, and the fire will test the quality of each man's work.

Didn't you realise that you were God's temple and that the Spirit of God was living among you? If anybody should destroy the temple of God, God will destroy him, because the temple of God is sacred; and you are the temple.

This is the word of the Lord.

Gospel Acclamation   Ez 37:27
     Alleluia, alleluia!
     I shall make my home among them, says the Lord;
     I will be their God,
     they shall be my people.
     Alleluia!

GOSPEL

A reading from the holy Gospel according to John   4:19-24
True worshippers will worship the Father in spirit and truth.

The Samaritan woman said to Jesus, 'I see you are a prophet, sir.
Our fathers worshipped on this mountain, while you say that
Jerusalem is the place where one ought to worship.' Jesus said:

> 'Believe me, woman, the hour is coming
> when you will worship the Father
> neither on this mountain nor in Jerusalem.
> You worship what you do not know;
> we worship what we do know;
> for salvation comes from the Jews.
> But the hour will come – in fact it is here already –
> when true worshippers will worship the Father in spirit and
>   truth:
> that is the kind of worshipper
> the Father wants.
> God is spirit,
> and those who worship
> must worship in spirit and truth.'

> This is the Gospel of the Lord.

Prayer over the Gifts
Lord,
as we recall the day you filled this church
with your glory and holiness,
may our lives also become an acceptable offering to you.

Preface of the Dedication of a Church I, P52

Communion Antiphon: You are the temple of God, and God's Spirit
dwells in you. The temple of God is holy; you are that temple.

Prayer after Communion
Lord,
we know the joy and power of your blessing in our lives.
As we celebrate the dedication of this church,
may we give ourselves once more to your service.

MASS FOR THE DEAD

Two Masses for Christian Death are given here to be used at the Funeral, and two to be used on the Anniversary of Death. The Roman Missal contains many other texts. Readings are not given here.

A great variety of readings, to suit particular occasions and circumstances, are given in the full Lectionary, in the readings for Masses of the Dead.

FUNERAL MASS

Today, with this bread and wine which human hands have made, we offer the greatest gift we have to offer: the life of a human person who is flesh of our flesh, whom we have known and loved, and in whose life we have been involved. And we pray to our Father that he will accept our offering and raise up our brother/sister with his Son in glory.

Outside the Easter Season

Entrance Antiphon: Give them eternal rest, O Lord, and may perpetual light shine on them for ever.

Opening Prayer
Almighty God, our Father,
we firmly believe that your Son died and rose to life.
We pray for our brother (sister) N.,
who has died in Christ.
Raise him (her) at the last day
to share the glory of the risen Christ,
who lives and reigns with you and the Holy Spirit,
one God, for ever and ever.

Prayer over the Gifts
Lord,
receive the gifts we offer
for the salvation of N.
May Christ be merciful in judging our brother (sister) N.
for he (she) believed in Christ
as his (her) Lord and Saviour.

Preface of Christian Death I-V, P77-P81

Communion Antiphon: May eternal light shine on them, O Lord, with all your saints for ever, for you are rich in mercy. Give them eternal rest, O Lord, and may perpetual light shine on them for ever, for you are rich in mercy.

Prayer after Communion

Lord God,
your Son Jesus Christ gave us
the sacrament of his body and blood
to guide us on our pilgrim way to your kingdom.
May our brother (sister) N., who shared in the eucharist,
come to the banquet of life Christ has prepared for us.

In the Easter Season

Entrance Antiphon: Just as Jesus died and rose again, so will the Father bring with him those who have died in Jesus. Just as in Adam all men die, so in Christ all will be made alive, alleluia.

Opening Prayer

Lord, hear our prayers.
By raising your Son from the dead, you have given us faith.
Strengthen our hope that N., our brother (sister),
will share in his resurrection.

Prayer over the Gifts

Lord,
we are united in this sacrament
by the love of Jesus Christ.
Accept these gifts
and receive our brother (sister) N.
in the glory of your Son,
who is Lord for ever and ever.

Preface of Christian Death I-V, P77-81

Communion Antiphon: I am the resurrection and the life, says the Lord. If any one believes in me, even though he dies, he will live. Anyone who lives and believes in me, will not die, alleluia.

Prayer after Communion

Lord God,
may the death and resurrection of Christ
which we celebrate in this eucharist
bring our brother (sister) N. the peace of your eternal home.

ANNIVERSARY MASS

Outside the Easter Season

Entrance Antiphon: God will wipe every tear from their eyes; there will be no more death, no more weeping or pain, for the old order has passed away.

Opening Prayer
Lord God,
you are the glory of believers
and the life of the just.
Your Son redeemed us
by dying and rising to life again.
Our brother (sister) N. was faithful
and believed in our own resurrection.
Give to him (her) the joys and blessings
of the life to come.

Prayer over the Gifts
Lord,
accept these gifts we offer
for N. our brother (sister).
May they free him (her) from sin
and bring him (her) to the happiness of life in your presence.

Preface of Christian Death I-V, P77-P81

Communion Antiphon: I am the resurrection and the life, says the Lord. Anyone who believes in me will have eternal life; he will not be condemned but pass from death to life.

Prayer after Communion
Lord,
you renew our lives by this holy eucharist;
free N. our brother (sister) from sin
and raise him (her) to eternal life.

In the Easter Season

Entrance Antiphon: God, who raised Jesus from the dead, will give new life to our own mortal bodies through his Spirit living in us, alleluia.

Opening Prayer

Almighty and merciful God,
may our brother (sister) N. share the victory of Christ
who loved us so much that he died and rose again
to bring us new life.

Prayer over the Gifts

God of love,
by this sacrifice
wash away the sins of our brother (sister) N.
in the blood of Jesus Christ.
In your love complete what you began
in the waters of baptism.

Preface to Christian Death I-V, P77-P81

Communion Antiphon: I am the living bread from heaven, says the Lord. If anyone eats this bread he will live for ever; the bread I shall give is my flesh for the life of the world, alleluia.

Prayer after Communion

Lord, we celebrate your Son's death for us
and his rising to eternal glory.
May these Easter mysteries free our brother (sister) N.
and bring him (her) to share in the joyful resurrection to come.

THE SACRAMENTS

THE VINE YOU THE BRANCHES HE WHO LIVES IN ME & I IN HIM BEARS FRUIT

Stages in the **Christian Initiation of Adults** are given during the Sundays of Lent Year A as follows:

The **Rite of Baptism** (p.308) and the **Rite of Confirmation** (p.309) are given during the Easter Vigil celebration.

Extracts from the **Rite of Pardon and Reconciliation** (p.1007), the **Wedding Mass** (p.1014), and the **Rites of the Sick and Dying** (p.1017) are given in the pages that follow.

A selection of the texts provided for the celebration of the Rite is given in each case. Alternative texts are to be found in the full edition of each Rite.

This section is reprinted from the *Glenstal Bible Missal*, where commentary and catechesis on the Sacraments will also be found.

THE RITE OF PARDON AND RECONCILIATION
INDIVIDUAL PENITENTS

Greeting, Sign of the Cross and Invitation to Trust in God

The priest welcomes and greets the penitent with kindness.

The penitent makes the sign of the cross which the priest may also make. The priest invites the penitent to trust in God. The following or similar words may be used:

May God, who has enlightened every heart,
help you to know your sins
and trust in his mercy.
Penitent   **Amen.**

LITURGY OF THE WORD (OPTIONAL)

Then the priest may read or say from memory a text of scripture which proclaims God's mercy and calls man to conversion. This text may be read or said by the penitent. If this part of the rite is omitted, it is fitting that the penitent read one of these texts as part of the preparation for reception of the sacrament.

The following texts are suitable:

After John had been arrested, Jesus went into Galilee. There he proclaimed the Good News from God. 'The time has come' he said 'and the kingdom of God is close at hand. Repent, and believe the Good News.' (*Mark 1:14-15*)

We give thanks to the Father who has made it possible for you to join the saints and with them to inherit the light.
  Because that is what he has done: he has taken us out of the power of darkness and created a place for us in the kingdom of the Son he loves, and in him, we gain our freedom, the forgiveness of our sins. (*Col 1:12-14*)

LITURGY OF RECONCILIATION

Confession of Sins and Acceptance of Satisfaction

Where it is the custom, the penitent says a general formula for confession (such as the '*I confess*') before the confession of sins.

The penitent then confesses his or her sins. If necessary the priest helps the penitent to make a full confession and gives suitable counsel. Urging the penitent to be sorry for his or her faults, the priest recalls that through the sacrament of reconciliation, the christian dies and rises with Christ and is renewed in the Easter mystery.

The priest proposes an act of penance which the penitent accepts to make satisfaction for sin and to amend his or her life.

Penitent's Prayer of Sorrow

The priest then asks the penitent to express sorrow for sins committed. This may be done by using an Act of Contrition familiar to the penitent or a prayer taken from or based on the scriptures, such as the following:

Lord Jesus,
you opened the eyes of the blind,
healed the sick,
forgave the sinful woman,
and after Peter's denial confirmed him in your love.
Listen to my prayer:
forgive all my sins,
renew your love in my heart,
help me to live in perfect unity with my fellow christians
that I may proclaim your saving power to all the world.

Absolution

Then the priest extends his hands over the penitent's head (or at least extends his right hand) and says:

God, the Father of mercies,
through the death and resurrection of his Son
has reconciled the world to himself
and sent the Holy Spirit among us
for the forgiveness of sins;
through the ministry of the Church
may God give you pardon and peace,
and I absolve you from your sins
in the name of the Father, and of the Son ✠
and of the Holy Spirit.
Penitent   **Amen.**

Praise of God and Dismissal
After the absolution the priest continues:
Give thanks to the Lord, for he is good.
Penitent　　**His mercy endures for ever.**

Then the priest dismisses the penitent, saying:
The Lord has freed you from your sins. Go in peace.

In place of the proclamation of God's praise and the dismissal, the priest may say the following, or similar, words:
The Lord has freed you from sin.
May he bring you safely to his kingdom in heaven.
Glory to him for ever.
Penitent　　**Amen.**

THE RITE OF PARDON AND RECONCILIATION

SEVERAL PENITENTS WITH INDIVIDUAL CONFESSION AND ABSOLUTION

INTRODUCTORY RITES

When the faithful have assembled, they may sing a psalm, antiphon, or other appropriate song while the priest is entering the church. After the song, all make the sign of the cross together:
In the name of the Father, and of the Son, and of the Holy Spirit. Amen.

The priest greets the congregation in these or similar words:
May God open your hearts to his law
and give you peace:
may he answer your prayers
and restore you to friendship.
All　　**Amen.**

The greetings from the introductory rites of Mass may also be used. Then the priest or another minister speaks briefly about the importance and purpose of the celebration and the order of the service.

Opening Prayer
The priest invites all to pray. All pray in silence for a brief period.
Then the priest sings or says the opening prayer, for example:
Father of mercies
and God of all consolation,
you do not wish the sinner to die
but to be converted and live.
Come to the aid of your people,
that they may turn from their sins
and live for you alone.
May we be attentive to your word,
confess our sins, receive your forgiveness,
and be always grateful for your loving kindness.
Help us to live the truth in love
and grow into the fullness of Christ, your Son,
who lives and reigns for ever and ever.
All   **Amen.**

LITURGY OF THE WORD

The celebration of the Word follows. A psalm, an appropriate
song or a period of silence should punctuate the readings. If
there is only one reading, it is preferable that it be from the
gospel. The readings are chosen from those given in the Lectionary.

Homily

Examination of Conscience
A period of time may be spent in making an examination of
conscience and in arousing true sorrow for sins. The priest,
deacon, or another minister may help the faithful by brief
statements or a kind of litany, taking into consideration their
circumstances, age, etc.

LITURGY OF RECONCILIATION

General Confession of Sins
The deacon or another minister invites all to kneel or bow, and to
join in saying a general formula of confession (e.g. *I confess*).

Deacon or minister   **Brothers and sisters, let us call to mind the**
goodness of God our Father, and acknowledge our sins, so that
we may receive his merciful forgiveness.

All   **I confess to almighty God,**
and to you, my brothers and sisters,
that I have sinned through my own fault
   They strike their breast:
in my thoughts and in my words,
in what I have done,
and in what I have failed to do;
and I ask blessed Mary, ever virgin,
all the angels and saints,
and you, my brothers and sisters,
to pray for me to the Lord our God.

All stand and say or sing a litany or an appropriate song, for
example:
Deacon or minister   Christ our Saviour is our advocate with the
   Father:
with humble hearts let us ask him to forgive us our sins
and cleanse us from every stain.

You were sent with good news for the poor and healing for the
   contrite.
All   **Lord, be merciful to me, a sinner.**
or
   Lord, have mercy.

You came to call sinners, not the just.
All   **Lord, be merciful to me, a sinner.**
or
   Lord, have mercy.

You forgave the many sins of the woman who showed you great
   love.
All   **Lord, be merciful to me, a sinner.**
or
   Lord, have mercy.

You did not shun the company of outcasts and sinners.
All   **Lord, be merciful to me, a sinner.**
or
   Lord, have mercy.

You carried back to the fold the sheep that had strayed.
All   **Lord, be merciful to me, a sinner.**
or
   Lord, have mercy.

You did not condemn the woman taken in adultery, but sent her
   away in peace.

All   **Lord, be merciful to me, a sinner.**
or
        Lord, have mercy.

You called Zacchaeus to repentance and a new life.
All   **Lord, be merciful to me, a sinner.**
or
        Lord, have mercy.

You promised Paradise to the repentant thief.
All   **Lord, be merciful to me, a sinner.**
or
        Lord, have mercy.

You are always interceding for us at the right hand of the Father.
All   **Lord, be merciful to me, a sinner.**
or
        Lord, have mercy.

Deacon or minister   Now, in obedience to Christ himself, let us join in prayer to the Father, asking him to forgive us as we forgive others.
All   **Our Father . . .**

The priest concludes:
Father, our source of life,
you know our weakness.
May we reach out with joy to grasp your hand
and walk more readily in your ways.
We ask this through Christ our Lord.
All   **Amen.**

Individual Confession and Absolution

Then the penitents go to the priest or priests designated for individual confession, and confess their sins. Each one receives and accepts an appropriate act of satisfaction. The priest may offer suitable counsel. The penitent is then absolved with the formula used for the reconciliation of individual penitents. Everything else which is customary in individual confession is omitted.

Proclamation of God's Mercy

When the individual confessions have been completed, the priest or priests return to the sanctuary. The presiding priest invites all to offer thanks and encourage them to do good works which will proclaim the grace of repentance in the life of the community and in each of its members. It is fitting for all to sing a psalm or hymn or to say a litany in acknowledgement of God's power and mercy.

Concluding Prayer of Thanksgiving

After the song of praise or the litany, the priest concludes with the following or a similar prayer:

Father,
in your love you have brought us
from evil to good and from misery to happiness.
Through your blessings
give the courage of perseverance
to those you have called and justified in faith.
Grant this through Christ our Lord.
All **Amen.**

Blessing and Dismissal

Then the priest blesses all present in these or similar words:

May the Lord guide your hearts in the way of his love
and fill you with Christ-like patience. *All* **Amen.**

May he give you strength
to walk in newness of life
and to please him in all things. *All* **Amen.**

May almighty God bless you,
the Father, and the Son, ✠ and the Holy Spirit. *All* **Amen.**

The deacon or other minister or the priest himself dismisses the assembly:

The Lord has freed you from your sins. Go in peace. *All* **Amen.**

Any other appropriate form may be used.

WEDDING MASS

A variety of Masses for the celebration of marriage is given in the *Roman Missal*. Formula A is given here.

Entrance Antiphon: **May the Lord send you help from his holy place and from Zion may he watch over you. May he grant you your heart's desire and lend his aid to all your plans.**

The Greeting and Penitential Rite follow.

Opening Prayer

Father,
you have made the bond of marriage
a holy mystery,
a symbol of Christ's love for his Church.
Hear our prayers for N. and N.
With faith in you and in each other
they pledge their love today.
May their lives always bear witness
to the reality of that love.

Liturgy of the Word

A great variety of readings is offered in the full Lectionary. It is recommended that the couple choose readings to suit the occasion, in consultation with the celebrant.

Prayer over the Gifts

Lord,
accept our offering
for this newly-married couple, N. and N.
By your love and providence
    you have brought them together;
now bless them all the days of their married life.

Preface of Christian Marriage, P72–P74.

When Eucharistic Prayer I is used, the special form of *Father, accept this offering*, is said. The words in brackets may be omitted:

Father, accept this offering
from your whole family
and from N. and N., for whom we now pray.
You have brought them to their wedding day:
grant them [the gift and joy of children and]
a long and happy life together.
[Through Christ our Lord. Amen.]

Nuptial Blessing

After the Lord's Prayer, the prayer *Deliver us* is omitted. The priest facing the bride and bridegroom says, with hands joined:

My dear friends, let us turn to the Lord and pray
that he will bless with his grace this woman (or N.)
now married in Christ to this man (or N.)
and that (through the sacrament of the body and blood of Christ),
he will unite in love the couple he has joined in this holy bond.

All pray silently for a short while. Then the priest extends his hands and continues:

Father,
by your power you have made everything out of nothing.
In the beginning you created the universe
and made mankind in your own likeness.

You gave man the constant help of woman
so that man and woman should no longer be two, but one flesh,
and you teach us that what you have united
may never be divided.

Father,
by your plan man and woman are united,
and married life has been established
as the one blessing that was not forfeited by original sin
or washed away in the flood.

Look with love upon this woman, your daughter,
now joined to her husband in marriage.
She asks your blessing.
Give her the grace of love and peace.
May she always follow the example of the holy women
whose praises are sung in the scriptures.

May her husband put his trust in her
and recognise that she is his equal
and the heir with him to the life of grace.

May he always honour her and love her
as Christ loves his bride, the Church.

Father,
keep them always true to your commandments.
Keep them faithful in marriage
and let them be living examples of Christian life.
Give them the strength which comes from the gospel
so that they may be witnesses of Christ to others.
[Bless them with children

and help them to be good parents.
May they live to see their children's children.]
And, after a happy old age,
grant them fullness of life with the saints
in the kingdom of heaven.
We ask this through Christ our Lord.

The priest continues

Lord Jesus Christ, you said to your apostles . . .

Communion Antiphon: Christ loves his Church, and he sacrificed himself for her so that she could become like a holy and untouched bride.

The bride and bridegroom may receive communion under both kinds.

Prayer after Communion

Lord,
in your love
you have given us this eucharist
to unite us with one another and with you.
As you have made N. and N.
one in this sacrament of marriage
[and in the sharing of the one bread and the one cup],
so now make them one in love for each other.

Solemn Blessing and Dismissal

Priest   God the eternal Father keep you in
    love with each other,
so that the peace of Christ may stay with you
and be always in your home.

Couple   **Amen.**

Priest   May [your children bless you,]
your friends console you
and all men live in peace with you.

Couple   **Amen.**

Priest   May you always bear witness to the love of God in this world
so that the afflicted and the needy
will find in you generous friends
and welcome you into the joys of heaven.

Couple   **Amen.**

Priest   May almighty God bless you,
the Father, and the Son, ✠ and the Holy Spirit.

All   **Amen.**

The dismissal follows as usual.

THE RITE OF
COMMUNION OF THE SICK

Greeting
The minister greets the sick person and the others present in these or similar words:

The grace of our Lord Jesus Christ
and the love of God
and the fellowship of the Holy Spirit
be with you all.
All   **And also with you.**

[Sprinkling with Holy Water
A priest or deacon may sprinkle the sick person and those present with holy water with these or similar words:

Let this water call to mind our baptism into Christ,
who by his death and resurrection has redeemed us.]

If the sacrament of penance is now celebrated, the penitential rite is omitted.

Penitential Rite
The minister invites the sick person and those present to recall their sins and to repent of them in these or similar words:

My brothers and sisters,
to prepare ourselves for this celebration,
let us call to mind our sins.

The minister may continue with one of the penitential rites from the Missal, or all may say: **I confess . . .**

The minister concludes:

May almighty God have mercy on us,
forgive us our sins,
and bring us to everlasting life.   *All*   **Amen.**

Liturgy of the Word
Several readings may follow, as at Mass. There should be at least one reading, read by one of those present or by the minister.

A brief period of silence may follow the reading. The minister may give a brief explanation of the reading.

[Prayer of the Faithful
The prayer of the faithful may follow. The minister introduces the prayer and says the concluding prayer. It is desirable that someone other than the minister announce the intentions.]

LITURGY OF HOLY COMMUNION

The Lord's Prayer
The minister introduces the Lord's Prayer in these or similar words:
Now let us pray together to the Father
in the words given us by our Lord Jesus Christ.

All say together:
Our Father . . .

Communion
Then the minister shows the eucharist, saying:
This is the Lamb of God
who takes away the sins of the world.
Happy are those who are called to his supper.

The sick person and other communicants reply:
**Lord, I am not worthy to receive you,
but only say the word and I shall be healed.**

The minister goes to the sick person and, showing the sacrament says:
The body of Christ (or: The blood of Christ)

The sick person replies:
Amen.

Others present then receive communion in the usual manner.

Silent Prayer
A period of silence may be observed.

Prayer after Communion
The minister says the concluding prayer, for example:
Let us pray

God our Father,
you have called us to share the one bread and one cup
and so become one in Christ.

Help us to live in him
that we may bear fruit,
rejoicing that he has redeemed the world.
We ask this through Christ our Lord.
All   **Amen.**

Blessing

A priest or deacon gives the blessing in these or similar words:

May God the Father bless you.

All **Amen.**

Priest/Deacon May God the Son heal you.

All **Amen.**

Priest/Deacon May God the Holy Spirit enlighten you.

All **Amen.**

Priest/Deacon May almighty God bless you
the Father, and the Son, ✛ and the Holy Spirit.

All **Amen.**

A minister who is not a priest or deacon, invokes God's blessing
and makes the sign of the cross on himself or herself, saying:

May the Lord bless us,
protect us from all evil,
and bring us to everlasting life.

All **Amen.**

or

May the almighty and merciful God bless and protect us,
the Father, and the Son, and the Holy Spirit.

All **Amen.**

THE RITE OF ANOINTING OF THE SICK
WITHIN MASS

Entrance Antiphon: **The Lord has truly borne our sufferings; he has carried all our sorrows.**   (from the Mass of the Sick)

Greeting and Reception of the Sick
After the greeting the priest welcomes the sick in these or similar words:
We have come together to celebrate the sacraments of anointing and the eucharist. Christ is always present when we gather in his name; today we welcome him especially as physician and healer. We pray that the sick may be restored to health by the gift of his mercy and made whole in his fullness.

Opening Prayer
Father,
you raised your Son's cross
as the sign of victory and life.
May all who share in his suffering
find in these sacraments
a source of fresh courage and healing.

Liturgy of the Word
Readings are taken from the Lectionary. A homily normally follows the readings, and may be followed by a period of silence.

LITURGY OF ANOINTING

Litany
The litany which follows replaces the prayer of the faithful. It may be adapted or shortened according to the condition of the sick.

Priest   Let us pray to God for our brothers and sisters and for all those who devote themselves to caring for them.

Bless N. and N. and fill them with new hope and strength:
℟   **Lord, have mercy.**
Relieve their pain: Lord, have mercy.   ℟ **Lord, have mercy.**

Free them from sin and do not let them give way to temptation:
Lord, have mercy.   ℟ **Lord, have mercy.**

Sustain all the sick with your power: Lord, have mercy. ℟ **Lord, have mercy.**

Assist all who care for the sick: Lord, have mercy. ℟ **Lord, have mercy.**

Give life and health to our brothers and sisters on whom we lay our hands in your name: Lord, have mercy. ℟ **Lord, have mercy.**

Laying on of Hands

All priests present lay hands in silence on the sick. If numbers are large, the assistant priests lay hands on some of the sick only.

Prayer over the Oil

If the oil is blessed already, the priest says a prayer of thanksgiving over it as, for example, the following:
Praise to you, God, the almighty Father.
You sent your Son to live among us
and bring us salvation.
℟ **Blessed be God who heals us in Christ.**

Praise to you, God the only-begotten Son.
You humbled yourself to share in our humanity
and you heal our infirmities.
℟ **Blessed be God who heals us in Christ.**

Praise to you, God, the Holy Spirit, the Consoler.
Your unfailing power gives us strength
in our bodily weakness.
℟ **Blessed be God who heals us in Christ.**

God of mercy,
ease the sufferings and comfort the weakness of your servants
whom the Church anoints with this holy oil.
We ask this through Christ our Lord.
℟ **Amen.**

When the oil is blessed during the rite, the priest uses one of two blessings. One blessing is as follows:

God of all consolation,
you chose and sent your Son to heal the world.
Graciously listen to our prayer of faith:
send the power of your Holy Spirit, the Consoler,
into this precious oil, this soothing ointment,
this rich gift, this fruit of the earth.

Bless this oil ✠ and sanctify it for our use.

Make this oil a remedy for all who are anointed with it;
heal them in body, in soul, and in spirit,
and deliver them from every affliction.

We ask this through our Lord Jesus Christ, your Son,
who lives and reigns with you and the Holy Spirit,
one God, for ever and ever.
℞ **Amen.**

Anointing

The priest or priests anoint the sick. The head and hands of each sick person are anointed, the sacramental formula being said for each individual.

Priest (anointing the forehead):
Through this holy anointing
may the Lord in his love and mercy help you
with the grace of the Holy Spirit. ℞ **Amen.**

Priest (anointing the hands):
May the Lord who frees you from sin
save you and raise you up. ℞ **Amen.**

When the anointings are completed, the presiding priest says a prayer, for example:
Father in heaven,
through this holy anointing
grant our brothers and sisters comfort in their suffering.

When they are afraid, give them courage,
when afflicted, give them patience,
when dejected, afford them hope,
and when alone, assure them of the support
of your holy people.
We ask this through Christ our Lord. ℞ **Amen.**

LITURGY OF THE EUCHARIST

Prayer over the Gifts
Merciful God,
as these simple gifts of bread and wine
will be transformed into the risen Lord,
so may he unite our sufferings with his
and cause us to rise to new life.

When Eucharistic Prayer II is used, after the words, 'and all the clergy', the following is added:
Remember also those who ask for healing
in the name of your Son,
that they may never cease to praise you
for the wonders of your power.

When Eucharistic Prayer III is used, after the words 'the family you have gathered here', the following is added:
Hear especially the prayers of those who ask for healing
in the name of your Son,
that they may never cease to praise you
for the wonders of your power.

Communion Antiphon: I will make up in my own body what is lacking in the suffering of Christ, for the sake of his body, the Church.

Prayer after Communion
Merciful God,
in celebrating these mysteries
your people have received the gifts of unity and peace.
Heal the afflicted
and make them whole
in the name of your only Son,
who lives and reigns for ever and ever.

Blessing and Dismissal
The priest blesses the sick and all present with a special formula such as:
May the God of all consolation
bless you in every way
and grant you hope all the days of your life.   ℟   **Amen.**

May God restore you to health
and grant you salvation. ℞ **Amen.**

May God fill your heart with peace
and lead you to eternal life. ℞ **Amen.**

May almighty God bless you,
the Father, and the Son, ✠ and the Holy Spirit. ℞ **Amen.**

The deacon, or the priest himself, dismisses the people, commending the sick to their care.

THE RITE OF VIATICUM OUTSIDE MASS

Viaticum, food for the journey, is the proper sacrament of the dying. Whenever possible, it should be received within Mass, in the company of family and friends.

Greeting
The minister greets the sick person and all present in these or similar words:
The peace of the Lord be with you always.
And also with you.

[Sprinkling with Holy Water
A priest or deacon may sprinkle those present with holy water, saying these or similar words:
Let this water call to mind our baptism into Christ,
who by his death and resurrection has redeemed us.]

Instruction
The minister addressses those present in these or similar words:
My brothers and sisters, before our Lord Jesus Christ passed from this world to return to the Father, he left us the sacrament of his body and blood. When the hour comes for us to pass from this life and join him, he strengthens us with this food for our journey and comforts us by this pledge of our resurrection.

[If necessary, the sacrament of penance is now celebrated. When the sacrament is celebrated, the penitential rite is omitted.]

Penitential Rite
This may take one of the forms from the Missal or the following may be used:
By your paschal mystery you have won for us salvation:
Lord, have mercy.

All   **Lord, have mercy.**
You renew among us now the wonders of your passion:
Christ, have mercy.
All   **Lord, have mercy.**
When we receive your body,
you share with us your paschal sacrifice:
Lord, have mercy.
All   **Lord, have mercy.**
May almighty God have mercy on us
forgive us our sins,
and bring us to everlasting life.   *All*   **Amen.**

[Apostolic Pardon
At the conclusion of the sacrament of penance or of the penitential rite, a priest may give the Apostolic Pardon for the dying.
Either of the following formulae may be used:
Through the holy mysteries of our redemption,
may almighty God release you from all punishments
in this life and in the life to come.

May he open to you the gates of paradise
and welcome you to everlasting joy.   ℟   **Amen.**

or

By the authority which the Apostolic See has given me,
I grant you a full pardon and the remission of all your sins
in the name of the Father, and of the Son,   and of the Holy
   Spirit.   ℟   **Amen.]**

LITURGY OF THE WORD

One of the following texts is read by one of those present or by
the minister. The texts given in the Lectionary for the rite of
anointing may also be used:
Jn 6:54-55; Jn 14:23; Jn 15:4; 1 Cor 11:26.

Homily
If the time allows, the minister may give a short explanation of
the reading.

Baptismal Profession of Faith
The minister gives a brief introduction and then asks the
following questions:

N., do you believe in God, the Father almighty,
creator of heaven and earth?
℟   **I do.**

Do you believe in Jesus Christ, his only Son, our Lord,
who was born of the Virgin Mary,
was crucified, died, and was buried,
rose from the dead,
and is now seated at the right hand of the Father?
℟   **I do.**
Do you believe in the Holy Spirit,
the holy catholic Church, the communion of saints,
the forgiveness of sins, the resurrection of the body,
and life everlasting?
℟   **I do.**

Litany
This litany may be adapted or shortened according to the
condition of the sick person. If the profession of faith has been
made and if the sick person seems to be tiring, the litany may be
omitted.

Minister   My brothers and sisters, with one heart let us call on
our Saviour Jesus Christ.
    You loved us to the very end and gave yourself over to death
in order to give us life. For our brother/sister, Lord, we pray:
℟ **Lord, hear our prayer.**
    You said to us, 'All who eat my flesh and drink my blood will
live for ever'. For our brother/sister, Lord, we pray:
℟ **Lord, hear our prayer.**
    You invite us to join in the banquet where pain and sorrow,
sadness and separation will be no more. For our brother/sister,
Lord, we pray:
℟ **Lord, hear our prayer.**

The Lord's Prayer
The minister invites all to recite the Lord's prayer.

Communion as Viaticum
The sick person and all present may receive communion under
both kinds. When the minister gives communion to the sick
person, the formula for viaticum is used.

The minister shows the bread to those present and says in these or similar words:

Jesus Christ is the food for our journey;
he calls us to the heavenly table.

The sick person and all who are to receive communion reply:

Lord, I am not worthy to receive you,
but only say the word and I shall be healed.

The minister goes to the sick person and, showing the sacrament says:
The body of Christ.
The sick person answers:
Amen.

Then the minister says:
The blood of Christ.

The sick person answers:
Amen.

Immediately, or after giving communion to the sick person, the minister says:

May the Lord Jesus Christ protect you .
and lead you to eternal life.

The sick person answers:

Amen.

Others present receive communion in the usual manner.

Prayer after Communion
After a period of silence, the minister recites this or a similar prayer:

Father,
your Son, Jesus Christ, is our way, our truth, and our life.
Look with compassion on your servant N.
who has trusted in your promises.
You have refreshed him/her with the body
**   and blood of your Son;**
may he/she enter your kingdom in peace.

Blessing and Dismissal

A priest or deacon blesses the sick person and all present using this or a similar formula:

May the Lord be with you to protect you.

All **Amen.**

May the Lord guide you and give you strength.

All **Amen.**

May the Lord watch over you, keep you in his care,
and bless you with his peace.

All **Amen.**

May almighty God bless you,
the Father, and the Son, ✠ and the Holy Spirit.

All **Amen.**

A minister who is not a priest or deacon invokes God's blessing and makes the sign of the cross on himself or herself, saying:

May the Lord bless us,
protect us from all evil,
and bring us to everlasting life. ℞ **Amen.**

or

May the almighty and merciful God bless and protect us,
the Father, and the Son, and the Holy Spirit. ℞ **Amen.**

Sign of Peace

The minister and all present may give the sick person a sign of peace.

FROM THE MASSES FOR VARIOUS NEEDS AND OCCASIONS[1]

FOR THE UNITY OF CHRISTIANS

One Mass on the Sunday between 18 and 25 January may be a Mass for the Unity of Christians.
Other texts may be chosen from *The Roman Missal*.

Entrance Antiphon: I am the Good Shepherd. I know my sheep, and mine know me, says the Lord, just as the Father knows me and I know the Father. I give my life for my sheep.

Opening Prayer
Almighty and eternal God,
you keep together those you have united.
Look kindly on all who follow Jesus your Son.
We are all consecrated to you by our common baptism;
make us one in the fullness of faith
and keep us one in the fellowship of love.

or

Lord,
lover of mankind,
fill us with the love your Spirit gives.
May we live in a manner worthy of our calling;
make us witnesses of your truth to all men
and help us work to bring all believers together
in the unity of faith and the fellowship of peace.

Other readings may be chosen from the Lectionary.

OLD TESTAMENT READING
A reading from the prophet Ezekiel   36:24-28
I am going to gather you from all the foreign countries; and I shall give you a new heart.

The Lord God says this:
    I am going to take you from among the nations and gather you together from all the foreign countries, and bring you home to your own land. I shall pour clean water over you and you will be cleansed; I shall cleanse you of all your defilement and all your idols. I shall give you a new heart, and put a new spirit in you; I

---

[1] Dates suggested in the rubrics apply to England and Wales.

shall remove the heart of stone from your bodies and give you a heart of flesh instead. I shall put my spirit in you, and make you keep my laws and sincerely respect my observances. You will live in the land which I gave your ancestors. You shall be my people and I will be your God.

This is the word of the Lord.

Responsorial Psalm   Ps 22. ℞ v.1
     ℞   **The Lord is my shepherd;**
          there is nothing I shall want.

1   The Lord is my shepherd;
     there is nothing I shall want.
     Fresh and green are the pastures
     where he gives me repose.
     Near restful waters he leads me.
     to revive my drooping spirit.   ℞

2   He guides me along the right path;
     he is true to his name.
     If I should walk in the valley of darkness
     no evil would I fear.
     You are there with your crook and your staff;
     with these you give me comfort.   ℞

3   You have prepared a banquet for me
     in the sight of my foes.
     My head you have anointed with oil;
     my cup is overflowing.   ℞

4   Surely goodness and kindness shall follow me
     all the days of my life.
     In the Lord's own house shall I dwell
     for ever and ever.   ℞

NEW TESTAMENT READING

A reading from the letter of St Paul to the Ephesians   4:30 – 5:2
Forgive each other as readily as God forgave you in Christ.

Do not grieve the Holy Spirit of God who has marked you with his seal for you to be set free when the day comes. Never have grudges against others, or lose your temper, or raise your voice to anybody, or call each other names, or allow any sort of spitefulness. Be friends with one another, and kind, forgiving each other as readily as God forgave you in Christ.

Try, then, to imitate God, as children of his that he loves, and follow Christ by loving as he loved you, giving himself up in our place as a fragrant offering and a sacrifice to God.

This is the word of the Lord.

Gospel Acclamation   Jn 17:21
Alleluia, alleluia!
May they all be one,
Father, may they be one in us,
as you are in me and I am in you,
so that the world may believe it was you who sent me,
says the Lord.
Alleluia!

GOSPEL

A reading from the holy Gospel according to John   17:20-26
May they be so completely one.

Jesus raised his eyes to heaven and said:

'Holy Father,
I pray not only for these,
but for those also
who through their words will believe in me.
May they all be one.
Father, may they be one in us,
as you are in me and I am in you
so that the world may believe it was you who sent me.
I have given them the glory you gave to me,
that they may be one as we are one.
With me in them and you in me,
may they be so completely one
that the world will realise that it was you who sent me
and that I have loved them as much as you loved me.
Father,
I want those you have given me
to be with me where I am,
so that they may always see the glory
you have given me
because you loved me
before the foundation of the world.
Father, Righteous One,
the world has not known you,
but I have known you,
and these have known

that you have sent me.
I have made your name known to them
and will continue to make it known,
so that the love with which you loved me may be in them,
and so that I may be in them.'

This is the Gospel of the Lord.

Prayer over the Gifts
Lord,
by one perfect sacrifice
you gained us as your people.
Bless us and all your Church
with gifts of unity and peace.

Preface   P76

Father, all-powerful and ever-living God,
we do well always and everywhere to give you thanks
through Jesus Christ our Lord.

Through Christ you bring us to the knowledge of your truth,
that we may be united by one faith and one baptism
to become his body.
Through Christ you have given the Holy Spirit to all peoples.
How wonderful are the works of the Spirit,
revealed in so many gifts!
Yet how marvellous is the unity
the Spirit creates from their diversity,
as he dwells in the hearts of your children,
filling the whole Church with his presence
and guiding it with his wisdom!

In our joy we sing to your glory
with all the choirs of angels: **Holy, holy, holy . . .**

Communion Antiphon: Because there is one bread, we, though
many, are one body, for we all share in the one loaf and in the
one cup.

Prayer after Communion
Lord,
may this holy communion,
the sign and promise of our unity in you,
make that unity a reality in your Church.

FOR PEACE AND JUSTICE

This may be used on the Fourth Sunday of Ordinary Time.

Entrance Antiphon: Give peace, Lord, to those who wait for you; listen to the prayers of your servants, and guide us in the way of justice.

Opening Prayer
God our Father,
you reveal that those who work for peace
will be called your sons.
Help us to work without ceasing
for that justice
which brings true and lasting peace.

or

Lord,
you guide all creation with fatherly care.
As you have given all men one common origin,
bring them together peacefully into one family
and keep them united in brotherly love.

OLD TESTAMENT READING

A reading from the prophet Isaiah   9:1-6
Wide is his dominion in a peace that has no end.

The people that walked in darkness
has seen a great light;
on those who live in a land of deep shadow
a light has shone.
You have made their gladness greater,
you have made their joy increase;
they rejoice in your presence
as men rejoice at harvest time,
as men are happy when they are dividing the spoils.
For the yoke that was weighing on him,
the bar across his shoulders,
the rod of his oppressor,
these you break as on the day of Midian.
For all the footgear of battle,
every cloak rolled in blood,
is burnt,
and consumed by fire.

For there is a child born for us,
a son given to us
and dominion is laid on his shoulders;
and this is the name they give him:
Wonder-Counsellor, Mighty-God,
Eternal-Father, Prince-of-Peace.
Wide is his dominion
in a peace that has no end,
for the throne of David
and for his royal power,
which he establishes and makes secure
in justice and integrity.
From this time onwards and for ever,
the jealous love of the Lord of Hosts will do this.

This is the word of the Lord.

Responsorial Psalm   Ps 71:2-4. 7-8. 12-13. 17. ℟ v.7

℟   **In his days justice shall flourish
    and peace till the moon fails.**

1   O God, give your judgement to the King,
    to a king's son your justice,
    that he may judge your people in justice
    and your poor in right judgement.   ℟

2   May the mountains bring forth peace for the people
    and the hills, justice.
    May he defend the poor of the people
    and save the children of the needy.   ℟

3   In his days justice shall flourish
    and peace till the moon fails.
    He shall rule from sea to sea,
    from the Great River to earth's bounds.   ℟

4   For he shall save the poor when they cry
    and the needy who are helpless.
    He will have pity on the weak
    and save the lives of the poor.   ℟

5   May his name be blessed for ever
    and endure like the sun.
    Every tribe shall be blessed in him,
    all nations bless his name.   ℟

NEW TESTAMENT READING

A reading from the letter of St James   3:13-18

Peacemakers, when they work for peace, sow the seeds which will bear fruit in holiness.

If there are any wise or learned men among you, let them show it by their good lives, with humility and wisdom in their actions. But if at heart you have the bitterness of jealousy, or a self-seeking ambition, never make any claims for yourself or cover up the truth with lies – principles of this kind are not the wisdom that comes down from above: they are only earthly, animal and devilish. Wherever you find jealousy and ambition, you find disharmony, and wicked things of every kind being done; whereas the wisdom that comes down from above is essentially something pure; it also makes for peace, and is kindly and considerate; it is full of compassion and shows itself by doing good; nor is there any trace of partiality or hypocrisy in it. Peacemakers, when they work for peace, sow the seeds which will bear fruit in holiness.

This is the word of the Lord.

Gospel Acclamation   Mt 5:9
    Alleluia, alleluia!
    Happy the peacemakers:
    they shall be called sons of God.
    Alleluia!

GOSPEL

A reading from the holy Gospel according to Matthew   5:38-48

I say this to you: offer the wicked man no resistance.

Jesus said to his disciples: 'You have learnt how it was said: Eye for eye and tooth for tooth. But I say this to you: offer the wicked man no resistance. On the contrary, if anyone hits you on the right cheek, offer him the other as well; if a man takes you to law and would have your tunic, let him have your cloak as well. And if anyone orders you to go one mile, go two miles with him. Give to anyone who asks, and if anyone wants to borrow, do not turn away.

'You have learnt how it was said: You must love your neighbour and hate your enemy. But I say this to you: love your enemies and pray for those who persecute you; in this way you will be sons of your Father in heaven, for he causes his sun to rise on bad men as well as good, and his rain to fall on honest and dishonest men alike. For if you love those who love you, what right have you to claim any credit? Even the tax collectors do as much, do they not? And if you save your greetings for your brothers, are you doing anything exceptional? Even the pagans do as much, do they not? You must therefore be perfect just as your heavenly Father is perfect.'

This is the Gospel of the Lord.

Prayer over the Gifts
Lord,
may the saving sacrifice of your Son, our King and peacemaker,
which we offer through these sacramental signs of unity and
     peace,
bring harmony and concord to all your children.

Communion Antiphon: Happy the peacemakers; they shall be called sons of God.

or

Peace I leave with you, my own peace I give you, says the Lord.

Prayer after Communion
Lord,
you give us the body and blood of your Son
and renew our strength.
Fill us with the spirit of love
that we may work effectively to establish among men
Christ's farewell gift of peace.

AFTER THE HARVEST

This Mass may be celebrated on a Sunday in September, to suit local custom.

Entrance Antiphon: The earth has yielded its fruit, the Lord our God has blessed us.

Opening Prayer
Father, God of goodness,
you give man the land to provide him with food.
May the produce we harvest sustain our lives,
and may we always use it for your glory and the good of all.

or

Lord,
we thank you for the harvest earth has produced
for the good of man.
These gifts witness to your infinite love;
may the seeds of charity and justice also bear fruit in our hearts.

OLD TESTAMENT READING

A reading from the prophet Joel   2:21-24. 26-27
The threshing floors will be full of grain.

O soil, do not be afraid;
be glad, rejoice,
for the Lord has done great things.

Beasts of the field, do not be afraid;
the pastures on the heath are green again,
the trees bear fruit,
vine and fig tree yield abundantly.

Sons of Zion, be glad,
rejoice in the Lord your God;
for he has given you
the autumn rain, since he is just,
and has poured the rains down for you,
the autumn and spring rain as before.
The threshing-floors will be full of grain,
the vats overflow with wine and oil.

You will eat to your heart's content, will eat your fill,
and praise the name of the Lord your God
who has treated you so wonderfully.
(My people will not be disappointed any more.)
And you will know that I am in the midst of Israel,
that I am the Lord your God, with none to equal me.
My people will not be disappointed any more.

This is the word of the Lord.

Responsorial Psalm   Ps 66:2-3. 5. 7-8. ℟ v.7. Alt. ℟ v.4

> ℟ **The earth has yielded its fruit**
> **for God, our God, has blessed us.**

or

> ℟ **Let the peoples praise you, O God;**
> **let all the peoples praise you.**

1 O God, be gracious and bless us
   and let your face shed its light upon us.
   So will your ways be known upon earth
   and all nations learn your saving help.   ℟

2 Let the nations be glad and exult
   for you rule the world with justice.
   With fairness you rule the peoples,
   you guide the nations on earth.   ℟

3 The earth has yielded its fruit
   for God, our God, has blessed us.
   May God still give us his blessing
   till the ends of the earth revere him.   ℟

NEW TESTAMENT READING

A reading from the first letter of St Paul to Timothy   6:6-11. 17-19

Warn those who are rich not to set their hopes on money.

Religion brings large profits, but only to those who are content
with what they have. We brought nothing into the world, and we
can take nothing out of it; but as long as we have food and
clothing, let us be content with that. People who long to be rich
are a prey to temptation; they get trapped into all sorts of foolish
and dangerous ambitions which eventually plunge them into
ruin and destruction. 'The love of money is the root of all evils'
and there are some who, pursuing it, have wandered away from
the faith, and so given their souls any number of fatal wounds.
But, as a man dedicated to God, you must avoid all that. You
must aim to be saintly and religious, filled with faith and love,
patient and gentle.

   Warn those who are rich in this world's goods that they are
not to look down on other people; and not to set their hopes on
money, which is untrustworthy, but on God who, out of his
riches, gives us all that we need for our happiness. Tell them that
they are to do good, and be rich in good works, to be generous
and willing to share – this is the way they can save up a good

capital sum for the future if they want to make sure of the only life that is real.

This is the word of the Lord.

Gospel Acclamation Ps 125:5
Alleluia, alleluia!
Those who are sowing in tears
will sing when they reap.
Alleluia!

GOSPEL

A reading from the holy Gospel according to Luke 12:15-21
A man's life is not made secure by what he owns.

Jesus said to the crowd: 'Watch, and be on your guard against avarice of any kind, for a man's life is not made secure by what he owns, even when he has more than he needs'.

Then he told them a parable: 'There was once a rich man who, having had a good harvest from his land, thought to himself, "What am I to do? I have not enough room to store my crops." Then he said, "This is what I will do: I will pull down my barns and build bigger ones, and store all my grain and my goods in them, and I will say to my soul: My soul, you have plenty of good things laid by for many years to come; take things easy, eat, drink, have a good time". But God said to him, "Fool! This very night the demand will be made for your soul; and this hoard of yours, whose will it be then?" So it is when a man stores up treasure for himself in place of making himself rich in the sight of God.'

This is the Gospel of the Lord.

Prayer over the Gifts
Lord,
make holy the gifts we offer with gratitude
from the produce of the earth.
As you have made our land bear a rich harvest,
make our hearts fruitful with your life and love.

Communion Antiphon: Lord, the earth is filled with your gift from heaven; man grows bread from earth, and wine to cheer his heart.

Prayer after Communion
Lord,
we thank you for the fruits of the earth.
May the power of this saving mystery
bring us even greater gifts.

FOR THE BLESSING OF
MAN'S LABOUR

This Mass may be celebrated on 1 May or the Monday before Ascension Day.

Entrance Antiphon: May the goodness of the Lord be upon us, and give success to the work of our hands.

Opening Prayer
God our Creator,
it is your will that man accept the duty of work.
In your kindness may the work we begin
bring us growth in this life
and help to extend the kingdom of Christ.

or

God our Father,
by the labour of man you govern and guide to perfection
the work of creation.
Hear the prayers of your people
and give all men work that enhances their human dignity
and draws them closer to each other
in the service of their brothers.

Other readings may be chosen from the Lectionary.

FIRST READING

A reading from the book of Genesis   2:4-9. 15
The Lord God settled man in the garden of Eden to cultivate it.

At the time when the Lord God made earth and heaven there was as yet no wild bush on the earth nor had any wild plant yet sprung up, for the Lord God had not sent rain on the earth, nor was there any man to till the soil. However, a flood was rising from the earth and watering all the surface of the soil. The Lord God fashioned man of dust from the soil. Then he breathed into his nostrils a breath of life, and thus man became a living being.

The Lord God planted a garden in Eden which is in the east, and there he put the man he had fashioned. The Lord God caused to spring up from the soil every kind of tree, enticing to look at and good to eat, with the tree of life and the tree of the knowledge of good and evil in the middle of the garden. The Lord God took the man and settled him in the garden of Eden to cultivate and take care of it.

This is the word of the Lord.

Responsorial Psalm   Psalm 126:1-2. ℟ cf. v.1

℟ **May the Lord build us a house,**
   and watch over the city.

1   If the Lord does not build the house,
    in vain do its builders labour;
    if the Lord does not watch over the city,
    in vain does the watchman keep vigil.   ℟

2   In vain is your earlier rising,
    your going later to rest,
    you who toil for the bread you eat:
    when he pours gifts on his beloved while they slumber.   ℟

SECOND READING

A reading from the second letter of St Paul
to the Thessalonians   3:6-12. 16
Do not let anyone have any food if he refuses to do any work.

In the name of the Lord Jesus Christ, we urge you, brothers, to keep away from any of the brothers who refuses to work or to live according to the tradition we passed on to you.

You know how you are supposed to imitate us: now we were not idle when we were with you, nor did we ever have our meals at anyone's table without paying for them; no, we worked night and day, slaving and straining, so as not to be a burden on any of you. This was not because we had no right to be, but in order to make ourselves an example for you to follow.

We gave you a rule when we were with you: not to let anyone have any food if he refused to do any work. Now we hear that there are some of you who are living in idleness, doing no work themselves but interfering with everyone else's. In the Lord Jesus Christ, we order and call on people of this kind to go on quietly working and earning the food that they eat.

May the Lord of peace himself give you peace all the time and in every way. The Lord be with you all.

This is the word of the Lord.

Gospel Acclamation   Ps 67:20
Alleluia, alleluia!
May the Lord be blessed day after day;
he bears our burdens, God our saviour.
Alleluia!

GOSPEL

A reading from the holy Gospel according to Matthew   6:31-34
Do not worry about tomorrow.

Jesus said to his disciples: 'Do not worry; do not say, "What are we to eat? What are we to drink? How are we to be clothed?" It is the pagans who set their hearts on all these things. Your heavenly Father knows you need them all. Set your hearts on his kingdom first, and on his righteousness, and all these other things will be given you as well. So do not worry about tomorrow: tomorrow will take care of itself. Each day has enough trouble of its own.'

This is the Gospel of the Lord.

Prayer over the Gifts
God our Father,
you provide the human race with food for strength
and with the eucharist for its renewal;
may these gifts which we offer
always bring us health of mind and body.

Communion Antiphon: Let everything you do or say be in the name of the Lord with thanksgiving to God.

Prayer after Communion
Lord,
hear the prayers
of those who gather at your table of unity and love.
By doing the work you have entrusted to us
may we sustain our life on earth
and build up your kingdom in faith.

FOR THE SPREAD OF THE GOSPEL

This Mass may be celebrated on Mission Sunday, whose date is announced each year, on a Sunday in October.
Other texts may be chosen from *The Roman Missal*.

Entrance Antiphon: May God bless us in his mercy; may he make his face shine on us, that we might know his ways on earth and his saving power among all the nations.

Opening Prayer
God our Father,
you will all men to be saved
and come to the knowledge of your truth.
Send workers into your great harvest
that the gospel may be preached to every creature
and your people, gathered together by the word of life
and strengthened by the power of the sacraments,
may advance in the way of salvation and love.

or

God our Father,
you sent your Son into the world to be its true light.
Pour out the Spirit he promised us
to sow the truth in men's hearts
and awaken in them obedience to the faith.
May all men be born again to new life in baptism
and enter the fellowship of your one holy people.

Other readings may be chosen from the Lectionary.

FIRST READING

A reading from the prophet Isaiah   2:1-5

All the nations will stream to the mountain of the Lord.

The vision of Isaiah son of Amoz, concerning Judah and Jerusalem.

In the days to come
the mountain of the Temple of the Lord
shall tower above the mountains
and be lifted higher than the hills.
All the nations will stream to it,
peoples without number will come to it; and they will say:
'Come, let us go up to the mountain of the Lord,

to the Temple of the God of Jacob
that he may teach us his ways
so that we may walk in his paths;
since the Law will go out from Zion,
and the oracle of the Lord from Jerusalem.'

He will wield authority over the nations
and adjudicate between many peoples;
these will hammer their swords into ploughshares,
their spears into sickles.
Nation will not lift sword against nation,
there will be no more training for war.

O House of Jacob, come,
let us walk in the light of the Lord.

This is the word of the Lord.

Responsorial Psalm   Ps 97:1-6. ℟ v.2. Alt. ℟ v.3

℟ **The Lord has shown his salvation to the nations.**

or

℟ **All the ends of the earth have seen
     the salvation of our God.**

1 Sing a new song to the Lord
   for he has worked wonders.
   His right hand and his holy arm
   have brought salvation. ℟

2 The Lord has made known his salvation;
   has shown his justice to the nations.
   He has remembered his truth and love
   for the house of Israel. ℟

3 All the ends of the earth have seen
   the salvation of our God.
   Shout to the Lord all the earth,
   ring out your joy. ℟

4 Sing psalms to the Lord with the harp
   with the sound of music.
   With trumpets and the sound of the horn
   acclaim the King, the Lord. ℟

SECOND READING
A reading from the letter of St Paul to the Ephesians 3:2-12

The mystery that has now been revealed means that pagans now share the same inheritance.

You have probably heard how I have been entrusted by God with the grace he meant for you, and that it was by a revelation that I was given the knowledge of the mystery, as I have just described it very shortly. If you read my words, you will have some idea of the depths that I see in the mystery of Christ. This mystery that has now been revealed through the Spirit to his holy apostles and prophets was unknown to any men in past generations; it means that pagans now share the same inheritance, that they are parts of the same body, and that the same promise has been made to them in Christ Jesus, through the gospel. I have been made the servant of that gospel by a gift of grace from God who gave it to me by his own power. I, who am less than the least of all the saints, have been entrusted with this special grace, not only of proclaiming to the pagans the infinite treasure of Christ but also of explaining how the mystery is to be dispensed. Through all the ages, this has been kept hidden in God, the creator of everything. Why? So that the Sovereignties and Powers should learn only now, through the Church, how comprehensive God's wisdom really is, exactly according to the plan which he had had from all eternity in Christ Jesus our Lord. This is why we are bold enough to approach God in complete confidence, through our faith in him.

This is the word of the Lord.

Gospel Acclamation Mk 16:5
Alleluia, alleluia!
Go out to the whole world,
says the Lord,
proclaim the Good News
to all creation.
Alleluia!

GOSPEL
A reading from the holy Gospel according to Mark 16:15-20

Go out to the whole world; proclaim the Good News.

Jesus said to the Eleven, 'Go out to the whole world, proclaim the Good News to all creation. He who believes and is baptised will be saved; he who does not believe will be condemned. These are the signs that will be associated with believers; in my name they will cast out devils; they will have the gift of tongues; they will pick up snakes in their hands, and be unharmed should they drink deadly poison; they will lay their hands on the sick, who will recover.'

And so the Lord Jesus, after he had spoken to them, was taken up into heaven; there at the right hand of God he took his place, while they, going out, preached everywhere, the Lord working with them and confirming the word by the signs that accompanied it.

This is the Gospel of the Lord.

Prayer over the Gifts
Lord,
look upon the face of Christ your Son
who gave up his life to set all men free.
Through him may your name be praised
among all peoples from East to West,
and everywhere may one sacrifice be offered to give you glory.

Communion Antiphon: Teach all nations to carry out everything I have commanded you. I am with you always, until the end of the world.

Prayer after Communion
Lord,
you renew our life with this gift of redemption.
Through this help to eternal salvation
may the true faith continue to grow throughout the world.

EVENING PRAYER FOR SUNDAYS

from
The Divine Office

To facilitate the saying of Evening Prayer on Sundays, either with a group or privately, a simple order of service is given here. The changing parts of the Proper of Seasons are not given.

The psalms may be sung or said in one of three ways:

directly: ie, all sing the entire psalm

antiphonally: ie, two sections of the congregation sing alternate verses

responsorially: ie, the congregation sings verses alternately with a cantor or leader

Week 1
SUNDAY EVENING PRAYER II

STAND

℣   O God, come to our aid.
℟ O Lord, make haste to help us.
Glory be to the Father and to the Son and to the Holy Spirit, as it was in the beginning, is now, and ever shall be, world without end.
Amen. Alleluia.

A hymn suitable to the day and the season is said or sung.

PSALMODY

SIT
Antiphon 1
Advent: Rejoice greatly, daughter of Sion, shout with gladness, daughter of Jerusalem, alleluia.
Lent, Sunday 1: You must worship the Lord, your God, and serve him alone.
Lent, Sunday 5: As Moses lifted up the serpent in the desert, so the Son of Man must be lifted up.
Eastertide: The Lord has risen and sits at the right hand of God, alleluia.

Through the Year: The Lord will send his mighty sceptre from Sion, and he will rule for ever, alleluia.

THE MESSIAH IS KING AND PRIEST PSALM 109(110):1–5,7
He must be king so that he may put all his enemies under his feet
(1 Cor 15:25)

The Lórd's revelátion to my Máster:†
'Sít on my ríght:*
your fóes I will pút beneath your féet.'

The Lórd will wíeld from Síon†
your scéptre of pówer:*
rúle in the mídst of all your fóes.

A prínce from the dáy of your bírth†
on the hóly móuntains;*
from the wómb before the dáwn I begót you.

Lórd has sworn an óath he will not chánge.†
'You are a príest for éver,*
a príest like Melchízedek of óld.'

The Máster stánding at your right hand*
will shatter kíngs in the dáy of his wráth.

He shall drínk from the stréam by the wáyside*
and thérefore he shall líft up his héad.   Glory be.

Repeat Antiphon 1.

Antiphon 2

Advent: Christ our King will come. He is the Lamb that John announced.

Lent, Sunday 1: Now is the favourable time; this is the day of salvation.

Lent, Sunday 5: The Lord of hosts protects and rescues; he spares and he saves.

Eastertide: He has freed us from the power of darkness and has given us a place in the kingdom of his Son, alleluia.

Through the Year: The earth trembled before the Lord, alleluia.

ISRAEL IS FREED FROM EGYPT   PSALM 113a(114):1–8
You, who have renounced this world, have also been led forth from Egypt
(St Augustine)

When Ísrael came fórth from Égypt,*
Jacob's sóns from an álien péople,
Júdah becáme the Lord's témple,*
Ísrael becáme his kingdom.

The séa fléd at the síght:*
the Jórdan turned báck on its cóurse,
the móuntains léapt like ráms*
and the hílls like yéarling shéep.

Whý was it, séa, that you fléd,*
that you túrned back, Jórdan, on your cóurse?

Móuntains, that you léapt like ráms,*
hílls, like yéarling shéep?

Trémble, O éarth, before the Lórd,*
in the présence of the Gód of Jácob,
who túrns the róck into a póol*
and flínt into a spríng of wáter.   Glory be.

Repeat Antiphon 2.

Outside Lent

Antiphon 3
Advent: Behold I am coming soon to reward every man according to his deeds, says the Lord.
Eastertide: Alleluia, the Lord, our God, is King; let us rejoice and give glory to him, alleluia.

Through the Year: The Lord is King, our God, the Almighty! alleluia.

When chanted, this canticle is sung with Alleluia *as set out below. When recited, it suffices to say* Alleluia *at the beginning and end of each strophe.*

THE MARRIAGE FEAST OF THE LAMB   CANTICLE: cf REV 19:1–2, 5–7

Alleluia.
Salvation and glory and power belong to our God,*
(℟ Alleluia.)
His judgments are true and just.
℟ Alleluia (alleluia).

Alleluia.
Praise our God, all you his servants,
(℟ Alleluia.)
You who fear him, small and great.
℟ Alleluia (alleluia).

Alleluia.
The Lord our God, the Almighty, reigns,*
(℟ Alleluia.)
Let us rejoice and exult and give him the glory.
℟ Alleluia (alleluia).

Alleluia.
The marriage of the Lamb has come,*
(℟ Alleluia)
And his bride has made herself ready.
℟ Alleluia (alleluia).   Glory be.

Repeat Antiphon 3.

Lent

Antiphon 3

Lent, Sunday 1: Now we are going up to Jerusalem, and everything that is written about the Son of Man will come true.
Lent, Sunday 5: He was wounded for our faults, he was bruised for our sins. Through his wounds we are healed.

CHRIST, THE SERVANT OF GOD,   CANTICLE
   FREELY ACCEPTS HIS PASSION   1 PET 2:21–24

Christ suffered for you,†
leaving you an example*
that you should follow in his steps.

He committed no sin;*
no guile was found on his lips.
When he was reviled,*
he did not revile in return.

When he suffered,*
he did not threaten;
but he trusted to him*
who judges justly.

He himself bore our sins*
in his body on the tree,
that we might die to sin*
and live to righteousness.

By his wounds you have been healed.   Glory be.

Repeat Antiphon 3.

Through the Year

Scripture Reading

2 Cor 1:3–4

Let us give thanks to the God and Father of our Lord Jesus Christ, the merciful Father, the God from whom all help comes! He helps us in all our troubles, so that we are able to help those who have all kinds of troubles, using the same help that we ourselves have received from God.

STAND

Short Responsory
Cantor: Blessed are you in the vault of heaven.
All: Blessed are you in the vault of heaven.
Cantor: You are exalted and glorified above all else for ever.
All: Blessed are you in the vault of heaven.
Cantor: Glory be to the Father and to the Son and to the Holy Spirit.
All: Blessed are you in the vault of heaven.

The Magnificat: The Canticle of Mary Lk 1:46–55
The Magnificat antiphon is recited before and after the canticle. It varies each day.

My soul rejoices in the Lord

My soul glorifies the Lord,*
my spirit rejoices in God, my Saviour.
He looks on his servant in her lowliness;*
henceforth all ages will call me blessed.

The Almighty works marvels for me.*
Holy his name!
His mercy is from age to age,*
on those who fear him.

He puts forth his arm in strength*
and scatters the proud-hearted.
He casts the mighty from their thrones*
and raises the lowly.

He fills the starving with good things,*
sends the rich away empty.

He protects Israel, his servant,*
remembering his mercy,
the mercy promised to our fathers,*
to Abraham and his sons for ever.   Glory be.

Intercessions

Christ is the Head of his body, the Church, and we are the members of that body; gathered this evening to pray in his name, we say:

℟ **Your kingdom come!**

May your Church be a light to the nations, the sign and source of your power to unite all men: – may she lead mankind to the mystery of your love. ℟

Guide the Pope and all the bishops of your church: – grant them the gifts of unity, of love, and of peace. ℟

Lord, give peace to our troubled world – and give to your children security of mind and freedom from anxiety. ℟

Help us to bring your compassion to the poor, the sick, the lonely, the unloved; – lead us to find you in the coming week. ℟

Awaken the dead to a glorious resurrection: – may we be united with them at the end of time. ℟

Our Father

The concluding prayer of the day.

Conclusion

When a priest or deacon presides over the Office, and no other Hour follows:

The Lord be with you.
℟ **And also with you.**
May almighty God bless you, the Father, and the Son, and the Holy Spirit. ℟ **Amen.**

Another form of blessing may be used as in the Missal. The people are then invited to leave:

Go in the peace of Christ.
℟ **Thanks be to God.**

When no priest or deacon is present, or in recitation on one's own, the conclusion is as follows:

The Lord bless us, and keep us from all evil, and bring us to everlasting life. ℟ **Amen.**

Week 2
SUNDAY EVENING PRAYER II

STAND

℣ O God, come to our aid.
℟ O Lord, make haste to help us.
Glory be . . . . .

A hymn suitable to the day and the season is said or sung.

PSALMODY

SIT

Antiphon 1
Advent: Behold, the Lord will come on the clouds of heaven with great strength, alleluia.
Lent, Sunday 2: The Lord will send forth your sceptre of power with the splendour of the saints.
Lent, Palm Sunday: He was wounded and humbled, but God has raised him up with his own right hand.
Eastertide: He raised Christ from the dead and placed him at his own right hand, in heaven, alleluia.

———————————————

Through the Year: Christ the Lord is a priest for ever according to the order of Melchizedek, alleluia.

Psalm 109(110): 1,5–7. See above, p.1048.

Repeat Antiphon 1.

Antiphon 2
Advent: The Lord will come and will not disappoint us. Wait for him if he seems to delay, for he will surely come, alleluia.
Lent, Sunday 2: We worship the one God, who made heaven and earth.
Palm Sunday: The blood of Christ purifies us to serve the living God.
Eastertide: You have been converted from idolatry to the living God, alleluia.

———————————————

Through the Year: Our God is in heaven: he has power to do whatever he will, alleluia.

PRAISE OF THE GOD OF TRUTH PSALM 113b(115)
Turn away from idols and worship the living and true God (1 Thess 1:9)

Not to ús, Lórd, not to ús,*
but to yóur náme give the glóry
for the sáke of your lóve and your trúth,*
lest the héathen say: 'Whére is their Gód?'

But our Gód is ín the héavens;*
he dóes whatéver he wílls.
Their ídols are silver and góld,*
the wórk of húman hánds.

They have móuths but they cánnot spéak;*
they have éyes but they cánnot sée;
they have éars but they cánnot héar;*
they have nóstrils but they cánnot sméll.

With their hánds they cánnot féel;†
with their féet they cánnot wálk.*
No sóund cómes from their thróats.
Their mákers will cóme to be líke them*
and so will áll who trúst in thém.

Sons of Ísrael, trúst in the Lórd;*
hé is their hélp and their shíeld.
He remémbers us, and hé will bléss us:†
he will bléss the sóns of Ísrael.*
He will bléss the sóns of Áaron.

The Lord will bléss thóse who féar him,*
the líttle no léss than the gréat:
to yóu may the Lórd grant íncrease,*
to yóu and áll your chíldren.

May yóu be bléssed by the Lórd,*
the máker of héaven and éarth.
The héavens belóng to the Lórd*
but the éarth he has gíven to mén.

The déad shall not práise the Lórd,*
nor thóse who go dówn into the sílence.
But wé who líve bless the Lórd*
nów and for éver. Amén.   Glory be.

Repeat Antiphon 2.

Outside Lent

Antiphon 3
Advent: The Lord is our judge, the Lord is our King. He will come and make us whole.
Eastertide: Alleluia, victory and glory and power belong to our God, alleluia.

Through the year: Praise God, all you his servants, both great and small, alleluia.

Canticle: cf Rev 19:1–2,5–7. See above, p.1050.

Repeat Antiphon 3.

Lent

Antiphon 3
Lent, Sunday 2: God did not spare his own Son but gave him up for us all.
Palm Sunday: He carried our sins in his own body on the cross, so that we might die to sin and live for holiness.

Canticle: 1 Peter 2:21–24. See above, p.1051.

Repeat Antiphon 3.

Through the Year

Scripture Reading   2 Thess 2:13–14
We feel that we must be continually thanking God for you, brothers whom the Lord loves, because God chose you as first fruits to be saved by the sanctifying Spirit and by faith in the truth. Through the Good News that we brought he called you to this so that you should share the glory of our Lord Jesus Christ.

STAND

Short Responsory
℟ Great is our Lord; great is his might. *Repeat* ℟
℣ His wisdom can never be measured.   ℟ Glory be. ℟

Magnificat. See above, p.1052.

Intercessions

Through the gospel, the Lord Jesus calls us to share in his glory. Let us make our prayer with him to our heavenly Father.

℟ **Lord, in your mercy hear our prayer.**

We pray for all nations: – that they may seek the way that leads to peace; that human rights and freedom may be everywhere respected, and that the world's resources may be generously shared. ℟

We pray for the Church: – that her leaders may be faithful ministers of your word, that all her members may be strong in faith and hope and that you may be recognized in the love she bears to all. ℟

We pray for our families, and the community in which we live: – that we may find you in them. ℟

We pray for ourselves: – that in the coming week we may serve others in our work, and find peace when we rest. ℟

We pray for the faithful departed: – that through your mercy they may rest in peace. ℟

Our Father

The concluding prayer of the day.

Week 3
SUNDAY EVENING PRAYER II

STAND

℣ O God, come to our aid.
℟ O Lord, make haste to help us.
Glory be . . .

A hymn suitable to the day and the season is said or sung.

PSALMODY

SIT

Antiphon 1
Advent: See, the Lord will come. He will sit with princes and he will mount the glorious throne.
Lent: Lord, almighty king, deliver us for the sake of your name. Give us the grace to return to you.
Eastertide: When he had made purification for sin, he sat at the right hand of the Majesty on high, alleluia.

Through the Year: The Lord's revelation to my Master: 'Sit on my right', alleluia.†

Psalm 109(110):1,5–7. See above, p.1048.

Repeat Antiphon 1.

Antiphon 2
Advent: The mountains will bring forth joy and the hills justice; for the Lord, the light of the world, comes in strength.
Lent: We were ransomed with the precious blood of Christ, the Lamb who is without blemish.
Eastertide: The Lord has delivered his people, alleluia.

Through the Year: The Lord is full of merciful love, he makes us remember his wonders, alleluia.

GREAT ARE THE WORKS OF THE LORD   PSALM 110(111)
How great and wonderful are all your works, Lord God Almighty (Rev 15:3)

> I will thánk the Lórd with all my héart*
> in the méeting of the júst and their assémbly.
> Gréat are the wórks of the Lórd;*
> to be póndered by áll who lóve them.

Majéstic and glórious his wórk,*
his jústice stands fírm for éver.
He mákes us remémber his wónders.*
The Lórd is compássion and lóve.

He gives fóod to thóse who féar him;*
keeps his cóvenant éver in mind.
He has shówn his míght to his péople*
by gíving them the lánds of the nátions.

His wórks are jústice and trúth:*
his précepts are áll of them súre,
standing fírm for éver and éver:*
they are máde in úprightness and trúth.

He has sént delíverance to his péople†
and estáblished his cóvenant for éver.*
Hóly his náme, to be féared.
To fear the Lórd is the fírst stage of wísdom;†
all who dó so próve themselves wíse.*
His práise shall lást for éver!   Glory be.

Repeat Antiphon 2.

Outside Lent

Antiphon 3
Advent: Let us live justly and honestly while we are awaiting, in
hope, the coming of the Lord.
Eastertide: Alleluia, the Lord our God is king; let us rejoice and
give glory to him alleluia.

Through the Year: The Lord our God almighty is king, alleluia.

Canticle: cf Rev 19:1–2,5–7. See above, p.1050.

Repeat Antiphon 3.

Lent

Antiphon 3
Ours were the sufferings he bore, ours the sorrows he carried.

Canticle: 1 Peter 2:21–24. See above, p.1051.
Repeat Antiphon 3.

Through the Year

Scripture Reading   *1 Pet 1:3–5*

Blessed be God the Father of our Lord Jesus Christ, who in his great mercy has given us a new birth as his sons, by raising Jesus Christ from the dead, so that we have a sure hope and the promise of an inheritance that can never be spoilt or soiled and never fade away, because it is being kept for you in the heavens. Through your faith, God's power will guard you until the salvation which has been prepared is revealed at the end of time.

STAND

Short Responsory

℟ Blessed are you, O Lord, in the vault of heaven. *Repeat* ℟

℣ You are exalted and glorified above all else for ever. ℟
   Glory be. ℟

Magnificat. See above, p.1052.

Intercessions

God is ever creative. His love renews all things and is the source of our hope. Let us turn to him in confidence:

℟ **Lord, accept our thanks and our prayers.**

We give thanks for the order of created things: – you have blessed us with the resources of the earth and the gift of human life. ℟

We give thanks for man's share in your continuing work of creation: – we praise you for your gifts to him of inventive skill and creative vision.

We pray for all the nations of the world: – may those in authority work for peace and goodwill among men. ℟

We pray for all who are homeless today: – we pray for families searching for a place to live, and for refugees driven from their homeland. ℟

Life was your first gift to us: – may those who have died come to its fulness in you. ℟

Our Father

The concluding prayer of the day.

Week 4
SUNDAY EVENING PRAYER II

STAND

℣ O God, come to our aid.
℟ O Lord, make haste to help us.
Glory be . . .

A hymn suitable to the day and the season is said or sung.

PSALMODY

SIT

Antiphon 1
Advent: See, how splendid is he who comes to save the peoples.
Lent: God has appointed him to judge everyone, living and dead.
Eastertide: You must look for the things of heaven, where Christ is, sitting at God's right hand, alleluia.

Through the Year: In holy splendour I begot you before the dawn, alleluia.

Psalm 109:1–5,7. See above, p.1048.

Antiphon 2
Advent: The rugged places shall be made smooth and the mountain-ranges shall become plains. Come, Lord, and do not delay, alleluia.
Lent: Happy is the man to whom the Lord shows mercy; he will never waver.
Eastertide: He has risen as a light in the darkness, for the upright of heart, alleluia.

Through the Year: Blessed are those who hunger and thirst for justice, for they shall have their fill.

THE HAPPINESS OF A JUST MAN   PSALM 111(112)
Be like children of the light; for the fruits of the light are seen in complete goodness and right living and truth (Eph 5:8–9)

Happy the mán who féars the Lórd,*
who tákes delíght in all his commánds.
His sóns will be pówerful on éarth;*
the chíldren of the úpright are bléssed.

Ríches and wéalth are in his hóuse;*
his jústice stands fírm for éver.
He is a líght in the dárkness for the úpright:*
he is génerous, mérciful and júst.

The góod man takes píty and lénds,*
he condúcts his affáirs with hónour.
The júst man will néver wáver:*
hé will be remémbered for éver.

He has no féar of évil néws;*
with a fírm heart he trústs in the Lórd.
With a stéadfast héart he will not féar;*
he will sée the dównfall of his fóes.

Open-hánded, he gíves to the póor;†
his jústice stands fírm for éver.*
His héad will be ráised in glóry.

The wícked man sées and is ángry,†
grinds his téeth and fádes awáy;*
the desíre of the wícked leads to dóom.   Glory be.

Repeat Antiphon 2.

Outside Lent

Antiphon 3
Advent: Great will be his reign and peace will be everlasting,
alleluia.
Eastertide: Alleluia, victory and glory and power to our God,
alleluia.

Through the Year: Praise God, all you his servants, both great and
small, alleluia.

Canticle: cf Rev 19:1–2,5–7. See above, p.1050.

Repeat Antiphon 3.

Lent

Antiphon 3
God fulfilled what he had foretold in the words of all the
prophets: that Christ would suffer.

Canticle: 1 Peter 2:21–24. See above, p.1051.

Repeat Antiphon 3.

Through the Year

Scripture Reading   Heb 12:22–24

What you have come to is Mount Zion and the city of the living
God, the heavenly Jerusalem where the millions of angels have
gathered for the festival, with the whole Church in which
everyone is a 'first-born son' and a citizen of heaven. You have
come to God himself, the supreme judge, and been placed with
spirits of the saints who have been made perfect; and to Jesus,
the mediator who brings a new covenant and a blood for
purification which pleads more insistently than Abel's.

STAND

Short Responsory

℟ Great is our Lord; great is his might. *Repeat*   ℟
℣   His wisdom can never be measured.   ℟ Glory be.   ℟

Magnificat. See above, p.1052.

Intercessions

In the Church, God has made known to us his hidden purpose:
to make all things one in Christ. Let us pray that his will may be
done.   ℟ **Father, unite all things in Christ.**
We give you thanks for the presence and power of your Spirit in
the Church: – give us the will to search for unity, and inspire us
to pray and work together.   ℟
We give you thanks for all whose work proclaims your love: –
help us to serve the communities in whose life we share.   ℟
Father, care for all who serve in the Church as ministers of your
word and sacraments: – may they bring your whole family to the
unity for which Christ prayed.   ℟
Your people have known the ravages of war and hatred: – grant
that they may know the peace left by your Son.   ℟
Fulfil the hopes of those who sleep in your peace: – bring them to
that final resurrection when you will be all in all.   ℟
Our Father

The concluding prayer of the day

NIGHT PRAYER
(Compline)

Either of these two forms of Night Prayer may be used on any day of the week.

AFTER EVENING PRAYER I OF SUNDAYS AND SOLEMNITIES

STAND

℣ O God, come to our aid . . .

Here an examination of conscience is commended. In a common celebration this may be inserted in a penitential act using the formulas given in the Missal.

Hymn
A hymn suitable to the Hour is said or sung.

PSALMODY

SIT

Ant. 1: Lord, have mercy and hear me.
Eastertide: Alleluia, alleluia, alleluia.

THANKSGIVING   PSALM 4
The Lord raised him from the dead and made him worthy of all admiration (St Augustine)

When I cáll, ánswer me, O Gód of jústice;*
from ánguish you reléased me, have mércy and héar me!

O mén, how lóng will your héarts be clósed,*
will you lóve what is fútile and séek what is fálse?

It is the Lórd who grants fávours to thóse whom he lóves;*
the Lórd héars me whenéver I cáll him.

Fear him; do not sín: pónder on your béd and be stíll.*
Make jústice your sácrifice and trúst in the Lórd.

'What can bríng us háppiness?' mány sáy.*

You have pút into my héart a gréater jóy*
than théy have from abúndance of córn and new wíne.

I will líe down in péace and sléep comes at ónce*
for yóu alone, Lórd, make me dwéll in sáfety.   Glory be.

Ant. Lord, have mercy and hear me.

Ant. 2: **Bless the Lord through the night.**

EVENING PRAYER IN THE TEMPLE PSALM 133(134)
Praise our God, all you his servants, and all who revere him, both great and small (Rev 19:5)

O cóme, bléss the Lórd,*
all yóu who sérve the Lórd,*
in the cóurts of the hóuse of our Gód.

Lift up your hánds to the hóly pláce*
and bléss the Lórd through the night.

May the Lórd bléss you from Síon,*
he who máde both héaven and éarth.   Glory be.

Ant. **Bless the Lord through the night.**
Eastertide: **Alleluia, alleluia, alleluia.**

Scripture Reading Deut 6:4–7
Hear, O Israel: the Lord our God is one Lord; and you shall love the Lord your God with all your heart, and with all your soul, and with all your might. And these words which I command you this day shall be upon your heart; and you shall teach them diligently to your children, and shall talk of them when you sit in your house, and when you walk by the way, and when you lie down, and when you rise.

STAND

Short Responsory

Outside Eastertide
℟ Into your hands, Lord, I commend my spirit. *Repeat* ℟
℣   You have redeemed us, Lord God of truth. ℟ Glory be.
       ℟

Easter Octave
This is the day which was made by the Lord: let us rejoice and be glad, alleluia.

Eastertide
℟ Into your hands, Lord, I commend my spirit, alleluia, alleluia.
Repeat ℟
℣   You have redeemed us, Lord God of truth. ℟ Glory be.
       ℟

Ant. Save us, Lord, while we are awake; protect us while we sleep; that we may keep watch with Christ and rest with him in peace (alleluia).

NUNC DIMITTIS   CANTICLE: LK 2:29–32
Christ is the light of the nations and the glory of Israel

> At last, all-powerful Master,†
> you give leave to your servant*
> to go in peace, according to your promise.
>
> For my eyes have seen your salvation*
> which you have prepared for all nations,
> the light to enlighten the Gentiles*
> and give glory to Israel, your people.   Glory be.

Ant. Save us, Lord, while we are awake; protect us while we sleep; that we may keep watch with Christ and rest with him in peace (alleluia).

Concluding Prayer

Sundays and Easter Octave
Come to visit us, Lord, this night,
so that by your strength we may rise at daybreak
to rejoice in the resurrection of Christ, your Son,
who lives and reigns for ever and ever.

Solemnities which do not occur on a Sunday
Visit this house, we pray you, Lord:
drive far away from it all the snares of the enemy.
May your holy angels stay here and guard us in peace,
and let your blessing be always upon us.
Through Christ our Lord.

Blessing
The Lord grant us a quiet night and a perfect end. ℟ Amen.

Anthem to the Blessed Virgin, see p.1075.

AFTER EVENING PRAYER II OF SUNDAYS AND SOLEMNITIES

All as above except the following.

PSALMODY

Ant. He will conceal you with his wings; you will not fear the terror of the night.
Eastertide: Alleluia, alleluia, alleluia.

IN THE SHELTER OF THE MOST HIGH   PSALM 90(91)
Behold, I have given you power to tread underfoot serpents and scorpions
(Lk 10:19)

He who dwélls in the shélter of the Most High*
and abídes in the sháde of the Almíghty
sáys to the Lórd: 'My réfuge,*
my stróng hold, my Gód in whom I trúst!'

It is hé who will frée you from the snáre*
of the fówler who séeks to destróy you;
hé will concéal you with his pínions*
and únder his wíngs you will find réfuge.

You will not féar the térror of the níght*
nor the árrow that flíes by dáy,
nor the plágue that prówls in the dárkness*
nor the scóurge that lays wáste at nóon.

A thóusand may fáll at your síde,*
tén thousand fáll at your ríght,
yóu, it will néver appróach;*
his fáithfulness is búckler and shíeld.

Your éyes have ónly to lóok*
to sée how the wícked are repáid,
yóu who have said: 'Lórd, my réfuge!'*
and have máde the Most Hígh your dwélling.

Upon yóu no évil shall fáll,*
no plágue appróach where you dwéll.
For yóu has he commánded his ángels,*
to kéep you in áll your wáys.

They shall béar you upón their hánds*
lest you stríke your fóot against a stóne.

On the líon and the víper you will tréad*
and trámple the young líon and the drágon.

Since he clíngs to me in lóve, I will frée him;*
protéct him for he knóws my náme.
When he cálls I shall ánswer: 'I am wíth you.'*
I will sáve him in distréss and give him glóry.

With léngth of lífe I will contént him;*
I shall lét him see my sáving pówer.   Glory be.

Ant. He will conceal you with his wings; you will not fear the terror of the night.
Eastertide: Alleluia, alleluia, alleluia.

Scripture Reading   Rev 22:4–5
They will see the Lord face to face, and his name will be written on their foreheads. It will never be night again and they will not need lamplight or sunlight, because the Lord God will be shining on them. They will reign for ever and ever.

Concluding Prayer

Sundays and Easter Octave
God our Father,
as we have celebrated today the mystery of the Lord's
   resurrection,
grant our humble prayer:
free us from all harm
that we may sleep in peace
and rise in joy to sing your praise.
Through Christ our Lord.

Easter Triduum and Solemnities which do not fall on Sundays
Visit this house, we pray you, Lord:
drive far away from it all the snares of the enemy.
May your holy angels stay here and guard us in peace,
and let your blessing be always upon us.
Through Christ our Lord.

Blessing
The Lord grant us a quiet night and a perfect end. ℟ Amen.

Anthem to the Blessed Virgin, see pp.1075ff.

PRAYERS
FOR VARIOUS OCCASIONS

Prayer to the Holy Spirit
Come, Holy Spirit, fill the hearts of your faithful.
Enkindle in them the fire of your love.

Father,
you taught the hearts of your faithful people
by sending them the light of your Holy Spirit.
In that Spirit give us right judgement
and the joy of his comfort and guidance.
We ask this through our Lord Jesus Christ, your Son,
who lives and reigns with you and the Holy Spirit,
one God, for ever and ever.

Prayer of Self-Dedication to Jesus Christ
Lord Jesus Christ,
take all my freedom,
my memory, my understanding, and my will.
All that I have and cherish
you have given me.
I surrender it all to be guided by your will.
Your grace and your love are wealth enough for me.
Give me these, Lord Jesus,
and I ask for nothing more.

Tr. *ICEL*

Prayer to Christ Crucified
O kind and loving Jesus,
I kneel here before you,
asking you most fervently
to put into my heart
the virtues of faith, hope and charity,
with true contrition for my sins
and a firm purpose of amendment.
Help me to contemplate with sorrow
your five precious wounds,
while I remember David's prophecy:
They have pierced my hands and my feet;
they have counted all my bones.

Tr. *Stanbrook*

For the Pope
God our Father, shepherd and guide,
look with love on N. your servant,
the pastor of your Church.
May his word and example inspire and guide the Church,
and may he, and all those entrusted to his care,
come to the joy of everlasting life.   *Tr. ICEL*

For Priestly Vocations
Father,
in your plan for our salvation you provide shepherds for your
people.
Fill your Church with the spirit of courage and love.
Raise up worthy ministers for your altars
and ardent but gentle servants of the gospel.   *Tr. ICEL*

For Peace
God our Father,
creator of the world,
you establish the order which governs all the ages.
Hear our prayer and give us peace in our time
that we may rejoice in your mercy
and praise you without end.   *Tr. ICEL*

In Time of War or Civil Disturbance
God our Father,
maker and lover of peace,
to know you is to live, and to serve you is to reign.
All our faith is in your saving help;
protect us from men of violence
and keep us safe from weapons of hate.   *Tr. ICEL*

Prayer of Saint Francis
Lord, make me an instrument of your peace.
Where there is hatred, let me sow love;
where there is injury, pardon;
where there is discord, union;
where there is doubt, faith;
where there is despair, hope;
where there is darkness, light;
where there is sadness, joy,
for your mercy and truth's sake.

O Divine Master, grant that I may not so much seek
to be consoled as to console,
to be understood as to understand,
to be loved as to love,
for it is in giving that we receive,
it is pardoning that we are pardoned,
it is in dying that we are born to eternal life.

A Prayer of Saint Richard

Thanks be to thee, Lord Jesus Christ,
for all the benefits and blessings which thou hast given me,
for the pain and insults which thou hast borne for me.
O most merciful Friend, Brother and Redeemer,
may I know thee more clearly,
love thee more dearly,
and follow the more nearly.

Prayer of Saint Thomas More for His Opponents

Almighty God,
have mercy on N. and N.,
and on all that bear me evil will and would me harm,
and their faults and mine together,
by such easy, tender, merciful means as thine infinite wisdom
    best can devise;
vouchsafe to amend and redress and make us saved souls in
    heaven together,
where we may ever live and love
together with thee and thy blessed saints,
O glorious Trinity,
for the bitter passion of our sweet Saviour. Amen.

Prayers for our Daily Work

Whatever your work is, put your heart into it as if it were for the
Lord and not for men, knowing that the Lord will repay you by
making you his heirs. It is Christ the Lord that you are serving.
Colossians 3:23–24

Our gifts differ according to the grace given us. Use your gift as
faith suggests.
Romans 12:6

Whatever you do, do it for the glory of God.
1 Corinthians 11:31

The 'Jesus Prayer'
Lord Jesus, Son of the living God,
be merciful to me, a sinner.

For a Happy Death
Father,
you made us in your image
and your Son accepted death for our salvation.
Help us to keep watch in prayer at all times.
May we be free from sin when we leave this world
and rejoice in peace with you for ever.   Tr. *ICEL*

An Evening Prayer
May the Lord support us all the day long,
till the shades lengthen and the evening comes,
and the busy world is hushed,
and the fever of life is over,
and our work is done.
Then in his mercy
may he give us a safe lodging,
and a holy rest,
and peace at the last. Amen.   *J.H. Newman*

The world, life and death, the present and the future,
are all your servants;
but you belong to Christ
and Christ belongs to God.   *1 Corinthians 3:22*

For the Sick
See above, pp.1017ff.

Father,
your Son accepted our sufferings
to teach us the virtue of patience in human illness.
Hear the prayers we offer for our sick brothers and sisters.
May all who suffer pain, illness or disease
realise that they are chosen to be saints,
and know that they are joined to Christ
in his sufferings for the salvation of the world,
for he lives and reigns with you and the Holy Spirit,
one God, for ever and ever.   Tr. *ICEL*

FOR THE DYING

See above, p.1024.
When the moment of death seems near, some of the following may be said:

Go forth, Christian soul, from this world
in the name of God the almighty Father,
who created you,
in the name of Jesus Christ, Son of the living God,
who suffered for you,
in the name of the Holy Spirit,
who was poured out upon you,
go forth, faithful Christian.

May you live in peace this day,
may your home be with God in Zion,
with Mary, the virgin Mother of God,
with Joseph, and all the angels and saints.

I commend you, my dear brother/sister, to almighty God,
and entrust you to your Creator.
May you return to him
who formed you from the dust of the earth.
May holy Mary, the angels, and all the saints
come to meet you as you go forth from this life.
May Christ who was crucified for you bring you freedom and
    peace.
May Christ who died for you
admit you into his garden of paradise.
May Christ, the true Shepherd,
acknowledge you as one of his flock.
May he forgive all your sins,
and set you among those he has chosen.
May you see your Redeemer face to face,
and enjoy the vision of God for ever. Amen.   Tr. *ICEL*

The Hail, holy Queen, p.1076, may be said.

Immediately after death, the following may be said:
Saints of God, come to his (her) aid!
Come to meet him (her), angels of the Lord!

℟ Receive his (her) soul and present him (her) to God the Most
    High.

May Christ, who called you, take you to himself;
may angels lead you to Abraham's side. ℟ . . .

Give him (her) eternal rest, O Lord,
and may your light shine on him (her) for ever. ℟ . . .
Let us pray:
All-powerful and merciful God,
we commend to you N., your servant.
In your mercy and love,
blot out the sins he/she has committed
through human weakness.
In this world he/she has died:
let him/her live for ever.
We ask this through Christ our Lord. Amen.

TO OUR LADY

The Angelus

The angel of the Lord declared unto Mary,
and she conceived by the Holy Spirit.

Hail Mary, full of grace,
the Lord is with thee.
Blessed art thou among women,
and blessed is the fruit of thy womb, Jesus.
Holy Mary, Mother of God,
pray for us sinners, now, and at the hour of our death. Amen.

Behold the handmaid of the Lord:
be it done unto me according to thy word. Hail Mary . . .

The Word was made flesh,
and dwelt among us. Hail Mary . . .

Pray for us, O holy Mother of God,
that we may be made worthy of the promises of Christ.

Let us pray: Pour forth, we beseech you, O Lord, your grace into
our hearts, that we to whom the incarnation of Christ, your Son,
was made known by the message of an angel, may by his passion
and cross, be brought to the glory of his resurrection, through
Christ our Lord. Amen.

Magnificat

My soul proclaims the greatness of the Lord,
my spirit rejoices in God my Saviour;
for he has looked with favour on his lowly servant,
and from this day all generations will call me blessed.
The Almighty has done great things for me:
holy is his Name.
He has mercy on those who fear him
in every generation.
He has shown the strength of his arm,
he has scattered the proud in their conceit.
He has cast down the mighty from their thrones,
and has lifted up the lowly.
He has filled the hungry with good things,
and has sent the rich away empty.
He has come to the help of his servant Israel
for he has remembered his promise of mercy,
the promise he made to our fathers,
to Abraham and his children for ever.

Tr. *ICET*

Memorare

Remember, O most blessed Virgin Mary, that never was it
known that anyone who fled to your protection, implored your
aid or sought your intercession, was left unaided. Filled, therefore, with confidence in your goodness, I fly to you, Virgin of
virgins, my mother. To you I come, before you I stand, sinful and
sorrowful. O Mother of the Word Incarnate, despise not my
petition, but in your mercy hear and answer me. Amen.

Alma Redemptoris Mater

Loving Mother of the world's Redeemer,
Star of the sea, and heaven's open door;
Answer the cry of all your sinful children,
Help us who fall, yet strive to rise once more.

Truly Mother of your own Creator,
Wonder of nature, Virgin you remained.
We who are sinners plead with you for pity,
Who by the angel Full of Grace were named.   Tr. *Stanbrook*

Ave Regina Caelorum

Hail, Queen of Heav'n, beyond compare,
To whom the angels homage pay,
Hail, Root of Jesse, Gate of light
That opened for the world's new Day.

Rejoice, O Virgin unsurpassed,
In whom our ransom was begun,
For all your loving children pray
To Christ our Saviour, and your Son.   Tr. *Stanbrook*

Regina Caeli (Eastertide)

Joy fill your heart, O Queen most high, alleluia!
Your Son who in the tomb did lie, alleluia!
Has risen as he did prophesy, alleluia!
Pray for us, Mother, when we die, alleluia!
Alleluia, alleluia, alleluia!   *James Quinn SJ*

Salve Regina

Hail, holy Queen, mother of mercy,
our life, our sweetness, and our hope.
To you do we cry,
poor banished children of Eve.
To you do we send up our sighs,

mourning and weeping in this vale of tears.
Turn then, most gracious advocate,
your eyes of mercy towards us,
and after this our exile
show to us the blessed fruit of your womb, Jesus.
O clement, O loving,
O sweet Virgin Mary.

Hail, our Queen and Mother blest!
Joy when all was sadness,
Life and hope you gave mankind,
Mother of our gladness!
Children of the sinful Eve,
Sinless-Eve, befriend us,
Exiled in this vale of tears:
Strength and comfort send us!

Pray for us, O Patroness,
Be our consolation!
Lead us home to see your Son,
Jesus, our salvation!
Gracious are you, full of grace,
Loving as none other,
Joy of heaven and joy of earth,
Mary, God's own Mother!

O most holy one, O most pitiful, O sweet Virgin Mary!
Mother best beloved, Mother undefiled, pray for us!

Thou art our comfort, and our refuge, Virgin Mother Mary!
All that we long for, through thee we hope for; Pray for us!

See how weak we are, lost in tears; save us, O Mary!
Lighten our anguish; soothe our sorrows; pray for us!

Virgin, turn and look; Mother behold us; hear us, O Mary!
Thou art the bearer of health divine; pray for us!

May thy joys and thy sorrows be our help, O Mary!
In thee we hope; to thee we cry; pray for us!

mourning and weeping in this vale of tears.
Turn then, most gracious advocate,
thine eyes of mercy towards us;
and after this our exile
show unto us the blessed fruit of your womb, Jesus.
O clement, O loving,
O sweet virgin Mary.

Hail, holy Queen and Mother blest!
Joy when all was sadness;
Life and hope you gave mankind,
Mother of our gladness!
Children of the sinful Eve,
Sinless Eve, befriend us,
Exiled in this vale of tears:
Strength and comfort send us.

Pray for us, O Patroness,
Be our consolation!
Lead us home to see your Son,
Jesus, our salvation!
Gracious are you, full of grace,
Loving as none other,
Joy of heaven and joy of earth,
Mary, God's own Mother!

O dear beloved, O most pitiful, O sweet Virgin Mary!
World's best beloved, Mother undefiled, pray for us!

Draw out our comfort and our refuge, Virgin Mother Mary,
all that we long for through thee we hope for. Pray for us!

Sad how weak we are, lost in emptiness, O Mary!
Lighten our anguish, soothe our sorrows, pray for us!

Virgin, turn and look, Mother, behold us; hear us, O Mary!
Thou art the bearer of the rich divine, pray for us!

Mary, by love and thy sorrows be our help, O Mary!
Safe in thee we hope: to thee we cry, pray for us!